Accountancy

Class XII

Authors
Richa Makkar
Parul Jain

ARIHANT PRAKASHAN (School Division Series)

arihant

ARIHANT PRAKASHAN (School Division Series)

卐 ADMINISTRATIVE & PRODUCTION OFFICES

Regd. Office

'Ramchhaya' 4577/15, Agarwal Road, Darya Ganj, New Delhi -110002
Tele: 011- 47630600, 43518550

Head Office

Kalindi, TP Nagar, Meerut (UP) - 250002, Tel: 0121-7156203, 7156204

卐 SALES & SUPPORT OFFICES

Agra, Ahmedabad, Bengaluru, Bareilly, Chennai, Delhi, Guwahati, Hyderabad, Jaipur, Jhansi, Kolkata, Lucknow, Nagpur & Pune.

PO No : TXT-XX-XXXXXXX-X-XX

Published By Arihant Publications (India) Ltd.

For further information about the books published by Arihant, log on to www.arihantbooks.com or e-mail at info@arihantbooks.com

Follow us on   

卐 ISBN

PREFACE

The school examinations play the most important role in the life of any student. Also in today's scenario, the importance of school examination is maximum as ever, government has fixed the weightage of these examinations in the process of admission to any higher level education programme.

Now, the question rises what should be the way of study to get higher percentage of marks. The answer is simple that we should plan our way of studies in such a way that along with the school studies, we should also keep an eye on what type of questions are being asked in the real examinations and what can be better than that if we practise the real examination questions in a chapterwise manner which are further divided into topics, it is the same way in which we study in our classroom.

To serve this purpose, here we are presenting CBSE Chapterwise Solutions Accountancy containing Previous Years' Question-Answers (2022-2010) asked in CBSE Class 12th Examination. The previous years' questions in each topic have been arranged as per their marks i.e. 1 Mark Questions, 3 Marks Questions, 4 Marks Questions, 6 Marks Questions and 8 Marks Questions. The next important feature of the book is that the solutions to all the questions have been given according to CBSE Marking Scheme. This book for sure will prove to be the most important tool in getting a high end success in CBSE Class 12th Examination.

We have put our best efforts in preparing this book, but if any error or what so ever has been skipped out, then that is purely incidental, apology for the same, please write to us so that it can be corrected in the further edition of the book. Apart from those who helped in completing the book, a special note of thanks goes to Mr. Saurabh Gupta.

At the end, We wish Best of Luck to our readers!

Authors

CONTENTS

PART A

PART B

LATEST SYLLABUS

Class XII

PART A Accounting for Partnership Firms and Companies

UNIT 1 Accounting for Partnership Firms — 105 Periods/36 Marks

Units/Topics

- Partnership: features, Partnership Deed.
- Provisions of the Indian Partnership Act 1932 in the absence of partnership deed.
- Fixed v/s fluctuating capital accounts. Preparation of Profit & Loss Appropriation account- division of profit among partners, guarantee of profits.
- Past adjustments (relating to interest on capital, interest on drawing, salary and profit sharing ratio).
- Goodwill: Meaning, nature, factors affecting and methods of valuation - average profit, super profit and capitalization.

Note: Interest on partner's loan is to be treated as a charge against profits.

Goodwill to be adjusted through partners capital/current account or by raising and writing off goodwill (AS 26) .

Accounting for Partnership Firms : Reconstitution and Dissolution

- **Change in the Profit Sharing Ratio** among the existing partners - sacrificing ratio, gaining ratio, accounting for revaluation of assets and reassessment of liabilities and treatment of reserves, accumulated profits and losses. Preparation of revaluation account and balance sheet.
- **Admission of a Partner** effect of admission of a partner on change in the profit sharing ratio, treatment of goodwill (as per AS 26), treatment for revaluation of assets and reassessment of liabilities, treatment of reserves, accumulated profits and losses, adjustment of capital accounts and preparation of capital, current account and balance sheet.
- **Retirement and Death of a Partner** effect of retirement / death of a partner on change in profit sharing ratio, treatment of goodwill (as per AS 26), treatment for revaluation of assets and reassessment of liabilities, adjustment of accumulated profits, losses and reserves, adjustment of capital accounts and preparation of capital, current account and balance sheet. Preparation of loan account of the retiring partner.
- Calculation of deceased partner's share of profit till the date of death. Preparation of deceased partner's capital account and his executor's account.
- **Dissolution of a partnership firm:** Meaning of dissolution of partnership and partnership firm, types of dissolution of a firm. Settlement of accounts - preparation of realization account, and other related accounts: capital accounts of partners and cash/bank a/c (excluding piecemeal distribution, sale to a company and insolvency of partner(s)).

Note

(i) If the realized value of tangible assets is not given it should be considered as realized at book value itself.

(ii) If the realized value of intangible assets is not given it should be considered as nil (zero value).

(iii) In case, the realization expenses are borne by a partner, clear indication should be given regarding the payment thereof.

UNIT 2 Accounting for Companies
45 Periods /24 Marks

Units/Topics

Accounting for Share Capital

- Features and types of companies
- Share and share capital: nature and types.
- Accounting for share capital: issue and allotment of equity and preference shares, Public subscription of shares - over subscription and under subscription of shares; issue at par and at premium, calls in advance and arrears (excluding interest), issue of shares for consideration other than cash.
- Concept of Private Placement and Employee Stock Option Plan (ESOP), sweat equity.
- Accounting treatment of forfeiture and re-issue of shares.
- Disclosure of share capital in company's Balance Sheet.

Accounting for Debentures

- Debentures: Meaning types, Issue of debentures at par, at a premium and at a discount. Issue of debentures for consideration other than cash; Issue of debentures with terms of redemption; debentures as collateral security-concept, interest on debentures. Writing off discount/loss on issue of debentures.

Note : Discount or loss on issue of debentures to be written off in the year debentures are allotted from Security Premium Reserve (if it exists) and then from Statement of Profit and Loss as Financial Cost (AS 16).

PART B Financial Statement Analysis

UNIT 3 Analysis of Financial Statements
30 Periods/12 Marks

Units/Topics

- **Financial Statements of a Company:** Meaning, nature, uses and importance of financial statement. Statement of Profit and Loss and Balance Sheet in the prescribed form with major headings and sub headings (as per Schedule III to the Companies Act, 2013).

Note: Exceptional items, extraordinary items and profit (loss) from discontinued operations are excluded.

- **Financial Statement Analysis :** Meaning, objectives, importance and limitations.
- **Tools for Financial Statement Analysis:** Cash flow analysis, ratio analysis.
- **Accounting Ratios:** Meaning, objectives, advantages, classification and computation.
- **Liquidity Ratios:** Current ratio and Quick ratio.
- **Solvency Ratios**: Debt to Equity Ratio, Total Asset to Debt Ratio, Proprietary Ratio and Interest Coverage Ratio. Debt to Capital Employed Ratio.
- **Activity Ratios:** Inventory Turnover Ratio, Trade Receivables Turnover Ratio, Trade Payables Turnover Ratio, Fixed Asset Turnover Ratio, Net Asset Turnover Ratio & Working Capital Turnover Ratio
- **Profitability Ratios:** Gross Profit Ratio, Operating Ratio, Operating Profit Ratio, Net Profit Ratio and Return on Investment.

Note: *Net Profit ratio is to be calculated on the basis of profit before and after tax.*

UNIT 4 Cash Flow Statement

20 Periods/8 Marks

Units/Topics

- Meaning, Objectives, Benefits, Cash and Cash Equivalents, Classification of Activities and Preparation [as per AS 3 (Revised) (Indirect Method only]

Scope:

(i) Adjustments relating to depreciation and amortization, profit or loss on sale of assets including investments, dividend (both final and interim) and tax.

(ii) Bank overdraft and cash credit to be treated as short term borrowings.

(iii) Current Investments to be taken as Marketable securities unless otherwise specified.

Note: *Previous years' proposed dividend to be given effect, as prescribed in AS-4, events occurring after the balance sheet date. Current years' proposed dividend will be accounted for in the next year after it is declared by the shareholders.*

PART C Project Work

20 Periods/20 Marks

Please refer to the guidelines published by CBSE.

Accountancy-1	Class XII	NCERT Publication	Accountancy-II	Class XII	NCERT Publication

List of Topics Added/Deleted in 2022-23 Syllabus

Unit	Topic Added/Deleted
Financial Statements of Not-for-Profit Organisations	• Complete Unit Deleted
Accounting for Partnership Firms	**Added/Update** • Goodwill adjustment through raising and writing-off goodwill. • **In dissolution** If realised value of **tangible assets** not given, it should be considered as realised at book value itself.
Accounting for Companies	**Added** • Concept of Sweat Equity **Deleted** • Redemption of Debentures : Lumpsum, draw of lots. • Creation of debenture redemption reserve.
Analysis of Financial Statements	**Added** • Solvency Ratios - Debt to Capital Employed Ratio. • Activity Ratios - Fixed Asset Turnover Ratio, Net Asset Turnover Ratio **Deleted** • Tools for Financial Statement Analysis - Comparative Statements, Common Size Statements.

PART A

Accounting for Partnership Firms and Companies

CHAPTER 01

Accounting for Partnership Firm : Basic Concepts

TOPIC 1

Concepts of Partnership and Partnership Deed

Partnership

According to Section 4 of the Indian Partnership Act, 1932, Partnership is defined as, "the relation between persons who have agreed to share the profits of a business carried on by all or any of them acting for all".

Partnership is a separate business entity from accounting point of view, but from a legal view point, partnership firm is not a separate legal entity from its partners.

The essential **features of partnership** are

(*i*) Two or more persons
(*ii*) Agreement
(*iii*) Business
(*iv*) Mutual agency
(*v*) Sharing of profits
(*vi*) Liability of partnership
(*vii*) Management and control
(*viii*) Registration

Partnership Deed

It is a document which contains the terms and conditions of partnership agreement. A firm should have a partnership deed because

(*i*) It regulates the rights, duties and liabilities of the partners.
(*ii*) It avoids disputes in future by acting as a proof.
(*iii*) It serves as an evidence in the court of law.

Provisions in the Absence of Partnership Deed

The various provisions of the Indian Partnership Act, 1932 in the absence of partnership deed are as follows

(*i*) Sharing of profits and losses—Profits and losses are to be shared equally.
(*ii*) Interest on capital—No interest is to be allowed on capital.
(*iii*) Salary/Commission to the partners— No remuneration is to be paid to any partner.

(*iv*) Interest on advances/loans by a partner—Interest @ 6% per annum is to be allowed on loans and advances.

(*v*) Interest on drawings—No interest is to be charged on drawings.

Apart from the above, the Indian Partnership Act specifies, that subject to contract between the partners

(*i*) If a partner derives any profit for himself or herself from any transaction of the firm or form the use of the property or business connection of the firm or the firm name, he/she shall account for the profit and pay it to the firm.

(*ii*) If a partner carries on any business of the same nature and in competition with the firm, he/she shall account for and pay to the firm, all profits made by him/her in that business.

Previous Years' Examination Questions

1 Mark Questions

1. A new partner acquires two main rights in the partnership firm which he joins. State one of these rights. **All India 2019**

Ans. Right to share future profits of the firm.

2. Ritesh and Hitesh are childhood friends. Ritesh is a consultant whereas Hitesh is an architect. They contributed equal amounts and purchased a building for ₹ 2 crore. After a year, they sold it for ₹ 3 crore and shared the profits equally. Are they doing the business in partnership?
Give reason in support of your answer. **CBSE 2018**

Ans. No, they are not doing the business in partnership. They are mere co-owners of the property.

3. Does partnership firm has a separate legal entity? Give reason in support of your answer. **Delhi 2017**

Ans. No, partnership firm does not have a separate legal entity. In case a business firm is not able to meet its liabilities out of its business assets, then private assets of partners can be used to meet firm's liabilities.

4. A group of 40 people wants to form a partnership firm. They want your advice regarding the maximum number of persons that can be there in a partnership firm and the name of the Act under whose provisions it is given. **All India 2016**

Or What is the maximum number of partners that a partnership firm can have?

Name the act that provides for the maximum number of partners in a partnership firm. **Delhi 2016**

Ans. The maximum number of partners that a firm can have is 50. The limit has been given as per Rule 10 of Companies (Miscellaneous) Rules Act, 2014.

5. State the provisions of Indian Partnership Act, 1932 regarding interest on partners' capital and interest on partners' loan when there is no partnership deed. **All India 2015, 2010**

Ans. According to Indian Partnership Act, 1932, in the absence of partnership deed, no interest on partners' capital is allowed and interest on partners' loan is allowed @ 6% per annum.

6. The partnership deed is silent on payment of salary to partners. Anita, a partner, claimed that, since she managed the business, she should get a monthly salary of ₹10,000. Is she entitled for the salary? Give reason. **Delhi (C) 2014**

Ans. No, Anita is not entitled for the salary.
Since, the partnership deed is silent on the payment of salary to partners, in that case provisions of Partnership Act will be followed which prohibits payment of salary to the partners.

7. State the provisions of Indian Partnership Act, 1932 regarding the payment of remuneration to a partner for the services rendered. **Delhi 2012**

Ans. In the absence of partnership deed, a partner is not entitled to get any remuneration from the firm.

8. What share of profit would a 'sleeping partner', who has contributed 75% of the total capital, get in the absence of a deed? **Delhi 2011**

Ans. In the absence of partnership deed, sleeping partner will get equal share of profit, no matter how much share of total capital he has contributed.

9. Is a sleeping partner liable for the acts of other partners? **Delhi (C) 2011**

Ans. Yes, a sleeping partner is also liable for the acts of other partners.

10. Would a 'charitable dispensary' run by 8 members be deemed a partnership firm? Give reason in support of your answer. **All India 2011**

Ans. No, a 'charitable dispensary' run by 8 members cannot be deemed to be a partnership firm because

(*i*) For partnership, there must be a business.

(*ii*) There must be sharing of profits among the partners from such business.

In this case, there is no business and no sharing of profits.

11. What is meant by a partnership deed? **Delhi 2011, 2010; All India 2010**

Ans. Partnership deed is a document which contains the terms and conditions of partnership agreement.

12. Why should a firm have a partnership deed? **All India 2011**

Ans. A firm should have a partnership deed because

(*i*) It regulates the rights, duties and liabilities of the partners.

(*ii*) It avoids disputes in future by acting as a proof.

(*iii*) It serves as an evidence in the court of law.

13. What is meant by 'unlimited liability of a partner'? **Delhi 2010**

Ans. Unlimited liability of a partner means that each partner is liable jointly and also severally with all the other partners to the third party for all the acts of the firm done, while he is a partner. His private assets can also be used for paying off the firm's debts.

14. A, B and C decided that interest on capitals will be provided to each partner @ 5% per annum, but after one year C wants that no interest on capital is to be provided to any partner. State how 'C' can do this? **Delhi 2010**

Ans. C can do this only when all partners agree to it or if there is no partnership deed.

15. A, B and C are partners and decided that no interest on drawings is to be charged to any partner. But after one year, C wants that interest on drawings should be charged to every partner. State how C can do this. **Delhi 2010**

Ans. C can do this only when all the partners agree to it.

TOPIC 2

Computation of Appropriation Items and Charge Items

Interest on Capital

Interest on capital is generally allowed to compensate partners for contributing capital to the firm in excess of profit sharing ratio. Interest on capital is an appropriation out of profits and is provided only if there is a profit. It will be provided in case of loss also if it is to be treated as a charge against profits.

$$\text{Interest on Capital} = \text{Amount of Capital} \times \frac{\text{Rate}}{100} \times \text{Time}$$

NOTE (*i*) Interest on additional capital will be calculated for the period it remained with the firm, i.e. from the date of introduction of additional capital to the last day of accounting year.

(*ii*) Interest on capital is calculated on the opening balance of the capital for the full year.

If opening capital is not given, it can be calculated as

Opening Capital = Closing Capital + Drawings − Profits − Additional Capital

Different cases related to interest on capital are

(*i*) When partnership agreement is silent–Not allowed

(*ii*) When partnership agreement provides that interest on capital is to be allowed but is silent as to the treatment of interest as a charge or appropriation, then it is to be treated as appropriation of profit.

There are three possible conditions

(a) **In Case of Loss** Not allowed.

(b) **In Case of Sufficient Profits** Interest on capital is allowed in full.

(c) **In Case of Insufficient Profits** Interest on capital is allowed proportionately to the extent of profits. In this case profits are distributed in capital ratio.

(*iii*) When partnership agreement says interest on capital is to be provided as a charge– It is allowed in full, irrespective of profit or losses.

Interest on Partners' Drawings

The amount withdrawn by partners in cash or in kind for their personal use in anticipation of profits, is termed as drawings. When the partnership deed is silent, no interest on drawings is charged as it is an appropriation out of profit. Interest on drawings is calculated with reference to time period for which money was withdrawn. Interest on drawings in different cases is calculated as follows

(*i*) *When fixed amount is withdrawn at fixed intervals*

$$\text{Interest on Drawings} = \text{Annual Drawings} \times \frac{\text{Rate}}{100} \times \frac{\text{Average Period}}{12}$$

Value of time under different circumstances will be as under

	Monthly Drawings for 12 Months	Quarterly Drawings for 12 Months	Half Yearly Drawings for 12 Months	Monthly Drawings for 6 Months	Monthly Drawings for 9 Months
When drawings are made in the beginning of each period	6.5	7.5	9	3.5	5
When drawings are made in the middle of each period	6	6	6	3	4.5
When drawings are made at the end of each period	5.5	4.5	3	2.5	4

(*ii*) *When unequal amount is withdrawn at irregular intervals*

In this case, the interest on drawings is calculated with the help of

(a) Simple method

$$\text{Interest on Drawings} = \text{Amount of Drawings} \times \frac{\text{Rate}}{100} \times \frac{\text{Months Remaining}}{12}$$

(b) Product method

$$\text{Interest on Drawings} = \text{Total of Product} \times \frac{\text{Rate}}{100} \times \frac{1}{365} \text{ or } \frac{1}{12}$$

If the date of withdrawal is not given, then the interest on total drawings for the year is calculated for a six months period on an average basis.

Salary or Commission and Rent Paid to a Partner

Salary or Commission It is to be allowed to a partner only, if the partnership agreement provides for the same. Salary or commission to a partner is an appropriation out of profits and not a charge against the profits, *i.e.* they are to be allowed only if there are profits and hence, must be transferred to the debit of profit and loss appropriation account and not to the debit of profit and loss account. Commission may be allowed as a percentage of net profit before charging such commission or after charging such commission.

(*i*) Commission as percentage of net profit before charging such commission

$$= \text{Net Profit before Commission} \times \frac{\text{Rate of Commission}}{100}$$

(*ii*) Commission as percentage of net profit after charging such commission

$$= \text{Net Profit before Commission} \times \frac{\text{Rate of Commission}}{100 + \text{Rate of Commission}}$$

Rent Paid to a Partner It is a charge against the profit and not an appropriation out of profits. It is therefore, debited to profit and loss account and credited to partners' current account in case of fixed capitals or to partners' capital account, when capitals are fluctuating.

Interest on Partners' Loan to the Firm

Interest on partners' loan is a charge against the profits and not an appropriation out of profits. Hence, it must be transferred to the debit of profit and loss account and not to the debit of profit and loss appropriation account.

NOTE (*i*) If there is an agreement as to the rate of interest, partner is entitled to interest on loan at an agreed rate of interest. If there is no agreement as to the rate of interest, partner is entitled to interest on loan @ 6% per annum.

(*ii*) Interest on partners' loan is not recorded in the partners' capital/current account but it should be recorded to the credit side of partner's loan account, if it is outstanding.

Previous Years' Examination Questions

1 Mark Questions

1. Fill in the blanks for the transaction 'Interest on drawings' ₹ 4,000. **CBSE 2020**

JOURNAL

Date	Particulars	LF	Amt (Dr)	Amt (Cr)
	… … … … Dr		4,000	
	To … … … …			4,000
	(Being interest on drawings charged)			

Ans

JOURNAL

Date	Particulars	LF	Amt (Dr)	Amt (Cr)
	Partners' Capital A/c Dr		4,000	
	To Interest on Drawings A/c			4,000
	(Being interest on drawings charged)			

2. Dev withdrew ₹ 10,000 on 15th day of every month. Interest on drawings was to be charged @ 12% per annum. Calculate interest on Dev's drawings. **All India 2019**

Ans. Interest on Dev's Drawings $= 10{,}000 \times 12 \times \frac{12}{100} \times \frac{6}{12} =$ ₹ 7,200

3. Chhavi and Neha were partners in a firm sharing profits and losses equally. Chhavi withdrew a fixed amount at the beginning of each quarter. Interest on drawings is charged @ 6% p.a. At the end of the year, interest on Chhavi's drawings amounted to ₹ 900. Pass necessary journal entry for charging interest on drawings. **Delhi 2019**

Ans.

JOURNAL

Date	Particulars		LF	Amt (Dr)	Amt (Cr)
	Chhavi's Capital A/c	Dr		900	
	To Interest on Drawings A/c				900
	(Being interest on drawings charged)				
	Interest on Drawings A/c	Dr		900	
	To Profit and Loss Appropriation A/c				900
	(Being amount of interest on drawings is transferred to profit and loss appropriation account)				

4. Give two items which may appear on the debit side of a Partner's Current Account. **Compartment 2018**

Ans. Two items which may appear on the debit side of a Partners' Current Account are

(*i*) Drawings (*ii*) Interest on drawings

5. Tom and Harry were partners in a firm sharing profits in the ratio of 5 : 3. During the year ended 31st March, 2015 Tom had withdrawn ₹ 40,000. Interest on his drawings amounted to ₹ 2,000. Pass necessary journal entry for charging interest on drawings assuming that the capitals of the partners were fluctuating. **All India 2016**

Ans.

JOURNAL

Date	Particulars		LF	Amt (Dr)	Amt (Cr)
2015 Mar 31	Tom's Capital A/c	Dr		2,000	
	To Interest on Drawings A/c				2,000
	(Being interest on drawings charged on Tom's capital account)				

6. Nusrat and Sonu were partners in a firm sharing profits in the ratio of 3:2. During the year ended 31st March, 2015 Nusrat had withdrawn ₹ 15,000. Interest on her drawings amounted to ₹ 300.

Pass necessary journal entry for charging interest on drawings assuming that the capitals of the partners were fixed. **Delhi 2016**

Ans. Solve as Q. No. 5 on page 8.

Debit Nusrat's Current Account and Credit Interest on Drawings with ₹ 300.

7. Anna and Bobby were partners sharing profits and losses in the ratio of 5 : 3. On 1st April, 2014 their capital accounts showed balances of ₹ 3,00,000 and ₹ 2,00,000 respectively.

Calculate the amount of profit to be distributed between the partners if the partnership deed provided for interest on capital @ 10% per annum and the firm earned a profit of ₹ 45,000 for the year ended 31st March, 2015. **All India (C) 2016**

Ans. No profit will be distributed as the amount of profit (*i.e.* ₹ 45,000) is not sufficient to pay the interest on capital (₹ 50,000).

8. A partnership deed provides for the payment of interest on capital but there was a loss instead of profit during the year 2010-2011. At what rate will the interest on capital be allowed? **All India 2012**

Ans. No interest on capital will be allowed as there was loss in the firm.

9. Give the average period in months for charging interest on drawings for the same amount withdrawn at the beginning of each quarter. **All India 2011**

Ans. The average period for charging interest on drawings for the same amount withdrawn at the beginning of each quarter is $7\frac{1}{2}$ months which can be computed as follows $= \frac{12+3}{2} = \frac{15}{2} = 7.5$ months

$$\therefore \text{ Interest on Drawings} = \text{Total Drawings} \times \frac{\text{Rate}}{100} \times \frac{7\frac{1}{2}}{12}$$

10. Where would you record interest on drawings when capitals are fixed? **All India 2010**

Ans. When capitals are fixed, interest on drawings will be recorded on the debit side of partners current account.

11. Where would you record interest on drawings when capitals are fluctuating? **All India 2010**

Ans. When capital are fluctuating interest on drawings will be recorded on the debit side of partners' capital accounts.

6 Marks Question

12. On 1st April, 2013 Mohan and Sohan entered into partnership for doing business of dry fruits. Mohan introduced ₹ 1,00,000 as capital and Sohan introduced ₹ 50,000. Since Sohan could introduce only ₹ 50,000 it was further agreed that as and when there will be a need Sohan will introduce further capital. Sohan was also allowed to withdraw from his capital when the need for the capital was less. During the year ended 31st March, 2014, Sohan introduced and withdrew the following amounts of capital.

Date	Capital Introduced	Capital Withdrawn
1st May, 2013	10,000	—
30th June, 2013	—	5,000
30th September, 2013	97,000	—
1st February, 2014	—	87,000

The partnership deed provided for interest on capital @ 6% per annum. Calculate interest on capitals of the partners. **Foreign 2015**

Ans. **Calculation of Interest on Capital**

$$\text{Mohan} = 1,00,000 \times \frac{6}{100} = ₹\ 6,000$$

Sohan =

Particulars	Capital Balances	Months Remaining	Interest
From April 1 to April 30	50,000	1	$50,000 \times \frac{6}{100} \times \frac{1}{12} =$ ₹ 250
From May 1 to June 30	60,000	2	$60,000 \times \frac{6}{100} \times \frac{2}{12} =$ ₹ 600
From July 1 to September 30	55,000	3	$55,000 \times \frac{6}{100} \times \frac{3}{12} =$ ₹ 825
From October 1 to January 31	1,52,000	4	$1,52,000 \times \frac{6}{100} \times \frac{4}{12} =$ ₹ 3,040
From February 1 to March 31	65,000	2	$65,000 \times \frac{6}{100} \times \frac{2}{12} =$ ₹ 650
Interest on Capital			₹ 5,365

TOPIC 3

Partners' Capital Accounts and Profit & Loss Appropriation Account

Partners' Capital Accounts

The partners capital accounts may be maintained by following any of the two methods

1. **Fixed Capital Accounts Method** Under this method, the capital of the partners shall remain fixed, unless additional capital is introduced or a part of the capital is withdrawn, as per the agreement among the partners. Two accounts are maintained under this method, *i.e.* Capital accounts and current accounts.

   Transactions related to introduction and withdrawal of capital are recorded in capital account, rest are recorded in current account. Capital account will always have a credit balance and current account may have credit or debit balance.

   Format of Accounts Maintained under Fixed Capital Method

   Dr **Partners' Capital Account** Cr

Particulars	X (₹)	Y (₹)	Particulars	X (₹)	Y (₹)
To Cash/Bank A/c (Capital withdrawn)	...	...	By Balance b/d (Opening credit balance)	...	...
To Balance c/d (Closing balance)	...	...	By Cash/Bank A/c (Additional capital introduced)	...	...
	...	...		...	...

   Dr **Partners' Current Account** Cr

Particulars	X (₹)	Y (₹)	Particulars	X (₹)	Y (₹)
To Balance b/d * (Opening debit balance)	...	...	By Balance b/d * (Opening credit balance)	...	...
To Drawings A/c (Out of profits)	...	...	By Interest on Capital A/c	...	...
To Interest on Drawings A/c	...	...	By Partner's Salary or Commission A/c	...	...
To Profit and Loss Appropriation A/c (Share in losses) **	...	...	By Profit and Loss Appropriation A/c (Share in profits) **	...	...
To Balance c/d *** (Closing credit balance)	...	...	By Balance c/d *** (Closing debit balance)	...	...
	...	...		...	...

   *Any one, **Any one, ***Any one

2. **Fluctuating Capital Accounts Method** Under this method, only one account, *i.e.* capital account of each partner is maintained.

   All transactions are recorded in capital accounts. Generally, capital account has credit balance but in exceptional cases it may have debit balance due to heavy losses or withdrawals.

Format of Account Maintained under Fluctuating Capital Method

Dr **Partners' Capital Account** Cr

Particulars	X (₹)	Y (₹)	Particulars	X (₹)	Y (₹)
To Balance b/d * (Opening debit balance)	...	...	By Balance b/d * (Opening credit balance)	...	...
To Cash/Bank A/c (Capital withdrawn)	...	...	By Cash/Bank A/c (Additional capital introduced)	...	...
To Drawings A/c (Out of profits)	...	...	By Interest on Capital A/c	...	...
To Profit and Loss Appropriation A/c ** (Share in losses)	...	...	By Partners' Salary or Commission A/c	...	...
			By Profit and Loss Appropriation A/c (Share in profits) **	...	...
To Balance c/d *** (Closing credit balance)	...	...	By Balance c/d *** (Closing debit balance)	...	...
	...	...		...	...

*Any one, **Any one, ***Any one

Profit and Loss Appropriation Account

It is an extension of profit and loss account. It is prepared to show the appropriation or distribution of profits among the partners. After the profit and loss account has been prepared, the profit for the year is transferred to the profit and loss appropriation account. This account shows how the net profit or net loss of the firm is being appropriated among the partners. It is a nominal account in nature.

NOTE Students should note that profit and loss appropriation account will never show loss under any situation.

Format of Profit and Loss Appropriation Account

Profit and Loss Appropriation Account

Dr for the year ended... Cr

Particulars		Amt (₹)	Particulars		Amt (₹)
To Interest on Capitals A/c			By Profit and Loss A/c (Net profit subject to appropriations)		...
A	...		By Interest on Drawings A/c		
B	...	...	A	...	
To Partners' Salaries A/c		...	B	...	...
To Partners' Commission A/c		...			
To Reserve A/c		...			
To Profit Transferred to					
A's Capital A/c * (or A's Current A/c)**	...				
B's Capital A/c * (or B's Current A/c)**	...	...			
		...			...

*Under Fluctuating Capital Method **Under Fixed Capital Method

Treatment of Appropriations

Appropriations are more than Available Profit

Sometimes, it is possible that amount of appropriations is more than the available profit.

In such a situation, following procedure is followed

Firstly, the amount that should have been appropriated is determined for each partner.

Then, the determined amount for each partner becomes the ratio for distribution of available profits among the partners.

Appropriations are to be Treated as a Charge and the Firm Incurs Loss

Sometimes, it is possible that appropriations are to be treated as a charge and the firm incurs a loss. In such a case, temporary account named as profit and loss adjustment account is opened instead of profit and loss appropriation account.

Previous Years' Examination Questions

1 Mark Questions

1. Distinguish between 'fixed capital account' and 'fluctuating capital account, on the basis of credit balance. **All India 2017**

Ans. Difference between fixed and fluctuating capital account is stated below

Basis	Fixed capital account	Fluctuating capital account
Credit Balance	It always shows credit balance in capital account.	Fluctuating capital can also show credit balance, as well as, debit balance.

2. What is meant by fixed capital of a partner? **Delhi (C) 2016**

Ans. Under this system of maintaining capital account of partners, partners capital remains fixed unless an additional capital is introduced or a part of it is withdrawn.

3. What is meant by fluctuating capital of a partner? **All India (C) 2016**

Ans. Under this system of maintaining capital accounts of partners, partners capital fluctuates when all the adjustment regarding interest on capital, drawings, share of profit etc are recorded directly in the capital account.

4. Name the accounts which are maintained for the partners when capitals of the partners are fixed. **Compartment 2014**

Ans. When capitals of the partners are fixed, following accounts are required to be maintained

(*i*) Partners' fixed capital accounts

(*ii*) Partners' current capital accounts

5. Distinguish between fixed and fluctuating capital accounts.
Compartment 2014; Delhi; All India 2011

Ans. The differences between fixed and fluctuating capital accounts are

Basis	Fixed capital account	Fluctuating capital account
No. of Account(s)	Each partner has two accounts, i.e. capital account and current account.	Each partner has only one account, i.e. capital account.
Balance	Capital account always shows a credit balance.	Sometimes capital account may show a debit balance due to huge drawings or losses.

6. When the partners' capitals are fixed, where the drawings made by a partner will be recorded? **Delhi; All India 2013**

Ans. When the partners' capitals are fixed, the drawings made by a partner will be recorded in partners' current account (debit side).

7. The firm XYZ earned a profit of ₹ 2,75,000 during the year ending on 31st March, 2009. 10% of this profit was to be transferred to general reserve. Pass necessary journal entry for the same. **Delhi (C) 2010**

Ans. **JOURNAL**

Date	Particulars		LF	Amt (Dr)	Amt (Cr)
2009 Mar 31	Profit and Loss Appropriation A/c	Dr		27,500	
	To General Reserve A/c (2,75,000×10%)				27,500
	(Being 10% of profit transferred to general reserve account)				

3 Marks Questions

8. On 1st April, 2013, Brij and Nandan entered into partnership to construct toilets in government girls schools in the remote areas of Uttarakhand. They contributed capitals of ₹ 10,00,000 and ₹ 15,00,000 respectively.

Their profit sharing ratio was 2:3 and interest allowed on capital as provided in the partnership deed was 12% per annum. During the year ended 31st March, 2014, the firm earned a profit of ₹ 2,00,000.

Prepare profit and loss appropriation account of Brij and Nandan for the year ended 31st March, 2014. **All India 2015**

Ans. **Profit and Loss Appropriation Account**

Dr for the year ending 31st March, 2014 Cr

Particulars		Amt (₹)	Particulars	Amt (₹)
To Interest on Capital A/c			By Net Profit as per Profit and Loss A/c	2,00,000
Brij	80,000			
Nandan	1,20,000	2,00,000		
		2,00,000		2,00,000

Working Note

Calculation of Interest on Capital

$$\text{Brij} = 10,00,000 \times \frac{12}{100} = ₹\ 1,20,000$$

$$\text{Nandan} = 15,00,000 \times \frac{12}{100} = ₹\ 1,80,000$$

$$= ₹\ 3,00,000$$

$$\text{But profit earned} = ₹\ 2,00,000$$

$$\text{Brij will get} = \frac{1,20,000}{3,00,000} \times 2,00,000 = ₹\ 80,000$$

$$\text{Nandan will get} = \frac{1,80,000}{3,00,000} \times 2,00,000 = ₹\ 1,20,000$$

9. On 1st April, 2013, Jay and Vijay entered into partnership for supplying laboratory equipments to government schools situated in remote and backward areas. They contributed capitals of ₹ 80,000 and ₹ 50,000 respectively and agreed to share the profits in the ratio of 3 : 2. The partnership deed provided that interest on capital shall be allowed at 9% per annum. During the year the firm earned a profit of ₹ 7,800.

Showing your calculations clearly, prepare profit and loss appropriation account of Jay and Vijay for the year ended 31st March, 2014. **Delhi 2015**

Ans. Solve as Q. No. 8 on page 13.

[Interest on capital : Jay = ₹ 4,800, Vijay = ₹ 3,000]

4 Marks Questions

10. P and Q were partners in a firm sharing profits in 3 : 1 ratio. Their respective fixed capitals were ₹ 10,00,000 and ₹ 6,00,000. The partnership deed provided interest on capital @ 12% p.a. The partnership deed further provided that interest on capital will be allowed fully even if it will result into a loss to the firm. The net profit of the firm for the year ended 31st March, 2018 was ₹ 1,50,000.

Pass necessary journal entries in the books of the firm allowing interest on capital and division of profit/loss among the partners. **All India 2019**

Ans. **JOURNAL**

Date	Particulars	LF	Amt (Dr)	Amt (Cr)
	Profit and Loss A/c Dr		1,92,000	
	To P's Current A/c			1,20,000
	To Q's Current A/c			72,000
	(Being interest on capital charged)			
	Profit and Loss Appropriation A/c Dr		42,000	
	To Profit and Loss A/c			42,000
	(Being loss transferred to profit and loss appropriation account)			
	P's Current A/c Dr		31,500	
	Q's Current A/c Dr		10,500	
	To Profit and Loss Appropriation A/c			42,000
	(Being loss distributed among the partners)			

Working Note

Calculation of Interest on Capital

P = 10,00,000 × 12% = ₹ 20,000

Q = 6,00,000 × 12% = ₹ 72,000

11. E, F and G were partners in a firm sharing profits in the ratio of 3 : 3 : 4. Their respective fixed capitals were E ₹ 3,00,000; F ₹ 4,00,000 and G ₹ 5,00,000. The partnership deed provided for allowing interest on capital @ 2% p.a. even if it results into a loss to the firm. The net profit of the firm for the year ended 31st March, 2018 was ₹ 2,10,000.

Pass necessary journal entries for allowing interest on capital and distribution of profit/loss in the books of the firm. **All India 2019**

Ans.

JOURNAL

Date	Particulars		LF	Amt (Dr)	Amt (Cr)
	Profit and Loss A/c	Dr		1,44,000	
	To E's Current A/c (3,00,000 × 12%)				36,000
	To F's Current A/c (4,00,000 × 12%)				48,000
	To G's Current A/c (5,00,000 × 12%)				60,000
	(Being interest on capital charged)				
	Profit and Loss A/c (2,10,000 – 1,44,000)	Dr		66,000	
	To Profit and Loss Appropriation A/c				66,000
	(Being amount of profit transferred to profit and loss appropriation account)				
	Profit and Loss Appropriation A/c	Dr		66,000	
	To E's Current A/c				19,800
	To F's Current A/c				19,800
	To G's Current A/c				26,400
	(Being distribution of profit among the partners)				

12. A and B were partners in a firm sharing profits in the ratio of 5 : 3. Their fixed capitals on 31st March, 2017 were A ₹ 60,000 and B ₹ 80,000. They agreed to allow interest on capital @ 12% p.a. The profit of the firm for the year ended 31st March, 2018 before allowing interest on capitals was ₹ 12,600.

Pass necessary journal entries for the above transactions in the books of A and B. Also show your working notes clearly. **All India 2019**

Ans.

JOURNAL

Date	Particulars		LF	Amt (Dr)	Amt (Cr)
	Profit and Loss A/c	Dr		12,600	
	To A's Current A/c				5,400
	To B's Current A/c				7,200
	(Being interest on capital given)				

Working Note

Interest on A's Capital = 60,000 × 12% = ₹ 7,200

Interest on B's Capital = 80,000 × 12% = ₹ 9, 600

16,800

As interest on capital is more than profit available, *i.e.* ₹ 12,600

So, interest on capital will be provided to the maximum of profit available.

Hence,

$$\text{Interest on A's Capital} = 12{,}600 \times \frac{7{,}200}{16{,}800} = ₹\ 5{,}400$$

$$\text{Interest on B's Capital} = 12{,}600 \times \frac{9{,}600}{16{,}800} = ₹\ 7{,}200$$

13. Jain, Gupta and Singh were partners in a firm. Their fixed capitals were : Jain ₹ 4,00,000, Gupta ₹ 6,00,000 and Singh ₹ 10,00,000. They were sharing profits in the ratio of their capitals. The firm was engaged in the processing and distribution of flavoured milk. The partnership deed provided for interest on capital at 10% per annum. During the year ended 31st March, 2014 the firm earned a profit of ₹ 1,47,000.

Showing your working notes clearly, prepare profit and loss appropriation account of the firm. **Foreign 2015**

Ans. Solve as Q. No. 8 on page 13.

[Interest on Capital : Jain's Current Account = ₹ 29,400; Gupta's Current Account = ₹ 44,100 and Singh's Current Account = ₹ 73,500]

14. Lalan and Balan were partners in a firm sharing profits in the ratio of 3 : 2. Their fixed capitals on 1st April, 2010 were Lalan ₹ 1,00,000 and Balan ₹ 2,00,000. They agreed to allow interest on capital @ 12% per annum and charge on drawings @ 15% per annum. The firm earned a profit, before all above adjustments, of ₹ 30,000 for the year ended 31st March, 2011. The drawings of Lalan and Balan during the year were ₹ 3,000 and ₹ 5,000 respectively. Showing your calculation clearly, prepare profit and loss appropriation account of Lalan and Balan. The interest on capital will be allowed even if the firm incurs loss. **All India 2012**

Ans.

Profit and Loss Appropriation Account

Dr for the year ending 31st March, 2011 Cr

Particulars		Amt (₹)	Particulars		Amt (₹)
To Interest on Capital A/cs			By Net Profit as per Profit and Loss A/c		30,000
Lalan's Current A/c	12,000		By Interest on Drawings A/c		
Balan's Current A/c	24,000	36,000	Lalan's Current A/c	225	
			Balan's Current A/c	375	600
			By Net Loss Transferred to		
			Lalan's Current A/c	3,240	
			Balan's Current A/c	2,160	5,400
		36,000			36,000

Working Notes

1. Interest on drawings is to be calculated on an average basis for 6 months as the time period is not given, *i.e.*

$$\text{Interest on Lalan's drawings} = 3,000 \times \frac{15}{100} \times \frac{6}{12} = ₹\ 225$$

$$\text{Interest on Balan's drawings} = 5,000 \times \frac{15}{100} \times \frac{6}{12} = ₹\ 375$$

2. Interest on capital

$$\text{Lalan} = 1,00,000 \times \frac{12}{100} = ₹\ 12,000$$

$$\text{Balan} = 2,00,000 \times \frac{12}{100} = ₹\ 24,000$$

15. Arun and Arora were partners in a firm sharing profits in the ratio of 5 : 3. Their fixed capitals on 1st April, 2010 were Arun ₹ 60,000 and Arora ₹ 80,000. They agreed to allow interest on capital @ 12% per annum and to charge on drawings @ 15% per annum.
The profit of the firm for the year ended 31st March, 2011 before all the above adjustments were ₹ 12,600. The drawings made by Arun were ₹ 2,000 and by Arora ₹ 4,000 during the year.

Prepare profit and loss appropriation account of Arun and Arora. Show your calucaltions clearly. The interest on capital will be allowed even if the firm incurs loss. **Delhi 2012**

Ans. Solve as Q. No. 14 on page 16.
[Net loss transferred to Arun's current account = ₹ 2,344, Arora = ₹ 1,406]

6 Marks Question

16. Sonu and Rajat started a partnership firm on 1st April, 2017. They contributed ₹ 8,00,000 and ₹ 6,00,000 respectively as their capitals and decided to share profits and losses in the ratio of 3 : 2.

The partnership deed provided that Sonu was to be paid a salary of ₹ 20,000 per month and Rajat a commission of 5% on turnover. It also provided that interest on capital be allowed @ 8% p.a. Sonu withdrew ₹ 20,000 on 1st December, 2017 and Rajat withdrew ₹ 5,000 at the end of each month. Interest on drawings was charged @ 6% p.a. The net profit as per Profit and Loss Account for the year ended 31st March, 2018 was ₹ 4,89,950. The turnover of the firm for the year ended 31st March, 2018 amounted to ₹ 20,00,000. Pass necessary journal entries for the above transactions in the books of Sonu and Rajat. **Delhi 2019**

Ans. **JOURNAL**

Date	Particulars		LF	Amt (Dr)	Amt (Cr)
2018					
Mar 31	Profit and Loss Appropriation A/c	Dr		2,40,000	
	To Sonu's Capital A/c (20,000 × 12)				2,40,000
	(Being salary paid)				
	Profit and Loss Appropriation A/c	Dr		1,00,000	
	To Rajat's Capital A/c (20,00,000 × 5%)				1,00,000
	(Being commission paid)				
	Profit and Loss Appropriation A/c	Dr		1,12,000	
	To Sonu's Capital A/c (8,00,000 × 8%)				64,000
	To Rajat's Capital A/c (6,00,000 × 8%)				48,000
	(Being interest on capital @ 8% paid)				
	Sonu's Capital A/c (20,000 × 6% × 4 / 12)	Dr		400	
	Rajat's Capital A/c (5,000 × 12 × 6% × 5.5 / 12)	Dr		1,650	
	To Profit and Loss Appropriation A/c				2,050
	(Being interest on drawings charged)				
	Profit and Loss Appropriation A/c	Dr		40,000	
	To Sonu's Capital A/c				24,000
	To Rajat's Capital A/c				16,000
	(Being profit distributed among partner)				

Working Note

Particulars		Amt (₹)
Net Profit		4,89,950
(–) Salary paid	(2,40,000)	
Commission	(1,00,000)	
Interest on capital	(1,12,000)	(4,52,000)
		37,950
(+) Interest on drawings		2,050
Profit available to be distributed among partners		40,000

TOPIC 4

Past Adjustments and Guarantee of Minimum Profits to a Partner

Past Adjustments

Sometimes, after closing the accounts of a partnership firm, some errors or omissions are discovered in the accounts. Under such circumstances, the accounts once closed are not reopened. Such errors and omissions are rectified by recording an adjusting entry in the next accounting period.

Such adjustments are called past adjustments as they relate to past period.

Steps to pass adjusting journal entry

***Step* 1** Calculate the amount already recorded.

***Step* 2** Calculate the amount which should have been recorded.

***Step* 3** Calculate the difference between Step 1 and Step 2.

***Step* 4** Find out the partner who received excess and the partner who received less.

***Step* 5** Pass the adjusting journal entry by debiting the partner who received excess and by crediting the partner who received less.

Guarantee of Minimum Profits to a Partner

A partner may be admitted into the firm with a guarantee of minimum profits, which means that if his share of profit is less than that of guaranteed profit, then he would be paid the guaranteed share of profit. The deficiency (difference between guaranteed profit and actual profit) is borne by partner or partners who have guaranteed the profit in agreed ratio.

Different conditions regarding guarantee of profit are

(*i*) Guarantee by the firm to a partner.

(*ii*) Guarantee by one partner to another partner.

(*iii*) Guarantee given by the partner to the firm.

(*iv*) Simultaneous guarantee by the firm to the partner and by the partner to the firm.

Steps Involved in the Distribution of Profits under Guarantee Arrangement are

***Step* 1** Calculate the actual share of profit/loss of guaranteed partner.

***Step* 2** Calculate the guaranteed amount.

Step **3** Calculate the amount of deficiency

Deficiency = Guaranteed Amount – Actual Share of Profit

Step **4** Distribute the deficiency among the guaranteeing partners in their guaranteeing ratio.

Step **5** Distribute the actual profits/losses among all the partners in their profit sharing ratio as if there is no guarantee arrangement.

Step **6** Recover share of deficiency (as per Step 3) from the guaranteeing partners and give credit for the same to guaranteed partner.

Previous Years' Examination Questions

1 Mark Questions

1. P and Q were partners in a firm sharing profits and losses equally. Their fixed capitals were ₹ 2,00,000 and ₹ 3,00,000 respectively. The partnership deed provided for interest on capital @12% per annum. For the year ended 31st March, 2016, the profits of the firm were distributed without providing interest on capital.

Pass necessary adjustment entry to rectify the error. **All India 2017**

Ans.

JOURNAL

Date	Particulars		LF	Amt (Dr)	Amt (Cr)
	P's Current A/c	Dr		6,000	
	To Q's Current A/c				6,000
	(Being the adjustment entry passed)				

Statement Showing Adjustments

Particulars	P (₹)	Q (₹)	Total
I. **Amount to be Credited**			
Interest on Capital @ 12%	24,000	36,000	60,000
II. **Amount to be Debited**			
Share of Profit (60,000 in 1 : 1)	30,000	30,000	60,000
III. Net Effect (I – II)	6,000 (Dr)	6,000 (Cr)	Nil

2. P and Q were partners in a firm sharing profits equally. Their fixed capitals were ₹ 1,00,000 and ₹ 50,000 respectively. The partnership deed provided for interest on capital at the rate of 10% per annum. For the year ended 31st March, 2016 the profits of the firm were distributed without providing interest on capital. Pass necessary adjustment entry to rectify the error. **Delhi 2017**

Ans. Solve as Q. no. 1 on Page 19.

Debit Q's Current Account and Credits P's Current Account with ₹ 2,500.

3 Marks Questions

3. A and B are partners in a firm sharing profits in the ratio of 3 : 2. On 31st March, 2014, the balance sheet of the firm was as follows

Balance Sheet
as at 31st March, 2014

Liabilities		Amt (₹)	Assets	Amt (₹)
Capital A/cs			Sundry Assets	80,000
A	60,000			
B	20,000	80,000		
		80,000		80,000

The profit of ₹ 80,000 for the year ended 31st March, 2014 was divided between the partners without allowing interest on capital @12% per annum and a salary to A at ₹ 1,000 per month. During the year A withdrew ₹ 10,000 and B ₹ 20,000.
Pass a single journal entry to rectify the error. **Foreign 2015**

Ans. **JOURNAL**

Date	Particulars		LF	Amt (Dr)	Amt (Cr)
	B's Capital A/c	Dr		5,280	
	To A's Capital A/c				5,280
	(Being the adjustment entry passed)				

Working Notes

Calculation of Opening Capital and Interest on Capital

Particulars	A (₹)	B (₹)
Closing Capitals	60,000	20,000
(+) Drawings	10,000	20,000
(–) Share of Profit already Credited (80,000 in 3 : 2)	(48,000)	(32,000)
Opening Capitals	22,000	8,000
Interest @ 12%	2,640	960

Adjustment Table

Particulars	A (₹)	B (₹)	Total
I. Amount already Recorded	48,000	32,000	80,000
II. Amount which should have been Recorded			
Interest on Capital	2,640	960	3,600
Salary to A	12,000	—	12,000
Share of Profit (64,400 in 3 : 2)	38,640	25,760	64,400
	53,280	26,720	80,000
III. Net Effect (I – II)	5,280 (Cr)	5,280 (Dr)	Nil

Calculation of Adjusted Profits

Adjusted Profits = Given Profit – Salary – Interest on Capital = 80,000 – 12,000 – (2,640 + 960) = ₹ 64,400

4. Mukesh and Ramesh are partners sharing profits and losses in the ratio of 2 : 1 respectively. They admit Rupesh as a partner with 1/4 share in profits with a guarantee that his share of profit shall be atleast ₹ 55,000. The net profit of the firm for the year ending 31st March, 2013 was ₹ 1,60,000. Prepare profit and loss appropriation account. **All India (C) 2014**

Ans.

Profit and Loss Appropriation Account

Dr for the year ending 31st March, 2013 Cr

Particulars		Amt (₹)	Particulars	Amt (₹)
To Profit Transferred to			By Net Profit as per Profit and Loss A/c	1,60,000
Mukesh's Capital A/c	80,000			
(–) to Rupesh	(10,000)	70,000		
Ramesh's Capital A/c	40,000			
(–) to Rupesh	(5,000)	35,000		
Rupesh's Capital A/c	40,000			
(+) from Mukesh	10,000			
(+) from Ramesh	5,000	55,000		
		1,60,000		1,60,000

Working Note

Calculation of New Profit Sharing Ratio

Rupesh's share $= \frac{1}{4}$ Remaining share $= 1 - \frac{1}{4} = \frac{3}{4}$

Mukesh's share $= \frac{3}{4} \times \frac{2}{3} = \frac{2}{4}$ Ramesh's share $= \frac{3}{4} \times \frac{1}{3} = \frac{1}{4}$

$\therefore$ New ratio $= 2:1:1$

Distributable profits = ₹ 1,60,000 to be distributed between Mukesh, Ramesh and Rupesh in 2 : 1 : 1 ratio.

Mukesh's share $= 1{,}60{,}000 \times \frac{2}{4} =$ ₹ 80,000; Ramesh's share $= 1{,}60{,}000 \times \frac{1}{4} =$ ₹ 40,000;

Rupesh's share $= 1{,}60{,}000 \times \frac{1}{4} =$ ₹ 40,000;

Rupesh's share is less than the guaranteed amount of ₹ 55,000, therefore deficiency of ₹ 15,000 (55,000 – 40,000) shall be borne by Mukesh and Ramesh in 2 : 1 ratio,

i.e. Mukesh will give $= 15{,}000 \times \frac{2}{3} =$ ₹ 10,000 and Ramesh will give $= 15{,}000 \times \frac{1}{3} =$ ₹ 5,000.

4 Marks Questions

5. Neena and Sara were partners in a firm with fixed capitals of ₹ 5,00,000 and ₹ 4,00,000 respectively. It was discovered that interest on capital @ 6% p.a. was credited to the partners for the two years ending 31st March, 2018 and 31st March, 2019 whereas there was no such provision in the partnership deed. Their profit sharing ratio during the last two years was

2017-18 4 : 5

2018-19 5 : 1

Showing your working clearly, pass the necessary adjustment entry to rectify the error.
CBSE 2020

Ans. **Calculation of Amount to be Adjusted**

Particulars	Neena (₹)	Sara (₹)	Total (₹)
Interest on capital to be debited for 2 years	60,000	48,000	1,08,000
Profit to be credited			
(2017-18) 54,000 in the ratio 4 : 5	24,000	30,000	54,000
(2018-19) 54,000 in the ratio 5 : 1	45,000	9,000	54,000
	69,000	39,000	1,08,000
Amount to be adjusted	9,000 (Cr)	9,000 (Dr)	NIL

JOURNAL

Date	Particulars		LF	Amt (Dr)	Amt (Cr)
	Sara's Current A/c	Dr		9,000	
	To Neena's Current A/c				9,000
	(Being adjustment entry passed)				

6. Rajiv and Sanjeev were partners in a firm. Their partnership deed provided that the profits shall be divided as follows

First ₹ 20,000 to Rajeev and the balance in the ratio of 4 : 1. The profits for the year ended 31st March, 2017 were ₹ 60,000 which had been distributed among the partners.

On 1-4-2016 their capitals were Rajeev ₹ 90,000 and Sanjeev ₹ 80,000. Interest on capital was to be provided @ 6% p.a. While preparing the profit and loss appropriation interest on capital was omitted.

Pass necessary rectifying entry for the same. Show your workings clearly. **Compartment 2018**

Ans.

Date	Particulars		LF	Amt (Dr)	Amt (Cr)
2017 Apr 1	Rajiv's Capital A/c	Dr		2,762	
	To Sanjeev's Capital				2,760
	(Being an adjustment entry passed for interest on capital omitted previously)				

Working Note

Calculation of amount to be adjusted

Particulars	Rajiv	Sanjeev	Total
I. Amount to be Debited-Profit Credited Wrongly-First	20,000	—	20,000
Balance 40,000 in 4 :1	32,000	8,000	40,000
	52,000	8,000	60,000
II. Amount to be Credited-Interest on Capital	5,400	4,800	10,200
Share of Profit-First	20,000	—	20,000
Balance (49,800 – 20,000 = 29,800) in 4 : 1	23,840	5,960	29,800
	49,240	10,760	60,000
III. Amount to be Adjusted	2,760 Dr	2,760 Cr	

7. Praveen, Sahil and Riya are partners having fixed capitals of ₹ 2,00,000, ₹ 1,60,000 and ₹ 1,20,000 respectively. They share profits in the ratio of 3 : 1 : 1. The partnership deed provided for the following which were not recorded in the books.

(*i*) Interest on capital @ 5% per annum.

(*ii*) Salary to Praveen ₹ 1,500 per month and to Riya ₹ 1,000 per month.

(*iii*) Transfer of profit to general reserve ₹ 10,000. Net profit for the year ended 31st March, 2015 was ₹ 1,00,000.

Pass necessary rectifying entry for the above adjustments in the books of the firm. Also show your workings clearly. **All India (C) 2016**

Ans.

JOURNAL

Date	Particulars		LF	Amt (Dr)	Amt (Cr)
	Praveen's Current A/c	Dr		10,400	
	Sahil's Current A/c	Dr		4,800	
	To Riya's Current A/c				5,200
	To General Reserve A/c				10,000
	(Being the adjustment entry passed)				

Working Notes

Adjustment Table

Particulars	Praveen (₹)	Sahil (₹)	Riya (₹)	Total
I. Amount already Recorded				
Share of Profit i.e., ₹ 1,00,000 in 3 : 1 : 1	60,000	20,000	20,000	1,00,000
II. Amount which should have been Recorded				
Interest on Capital	10,000	8,000	6,000	24,000
Salary	18,000	—	12,000	30,000
Share of Profit i.e., 36,000 in 3 : 1 : 1	21,600	7,200	7,200	36,000
	49,600	15,200	25,200	90,000
III. Net Effect (I-II)	10,400 (Dr)	4,800 (Dr)	5,200 (Cr)	10,000 (Cr)

Interest on Capital

Praveen = $2,00,000 \times \frac{5}{100}$ = ₹10,000, Sahil = $1,60,000 \times \frac{5}{100}$ = ₹8,000, Riya = $1,20,000 \times \frac{5}{100}$ = ₹6,000

Salary: Praveen (1,500 × 12) = ₹ 18,000, Riya (1,000 × 12) = ₹ 12,000

Calculation of Adjusted Profits

Adjusted Profits = Given Profit – Transfer to Reserve – Interest on Capital – Salary

= 1,00,000 – 10,000 – 24,000 (10,000 + 8,000 + 6,000) – 30,000 (18,000 + 12,000) = ₹ 36,000

8. Ajay, Binay and Chetan were partners sharing profits in the ratio of 3 : 3 : 2. The partnership deed provided for the following

(i) Salary of ₹ 2,000 per quarter to Ajay and Binay.

(ii) Chetan was entitled to a commission of ₹ 8,000.

(iii) Binay was guaranteed a profit of ₹ 50,000 per annum.

The profit of the firm for the year ended 31st March, 2015 was ₹ 1,50,000 which was distributed among Ajay, Binay and Chetan in the ratio of 2 : 2 : 1, without taking into consideration the provisions of partnership deed. Pass necessary rectifying entry for the above adjustments in the books of the firm. Show your workings clearly. **Delhi (C) 2016**

Ans.

JOURNAL

Date	Particulars		LF	Amt (Dr)	Amt (Cr)
	Ajay's Capital A/c	Dr		6,400	
	Binay's Capital A/c	Dr		2,000	
	To Chetan's Capital A/c				8,400
	(Being adjustment entry passed)				

Working Notes

Adjustment Table

Particulars	Ajay (₹)	Binay (₹)	Chetan (₹)	Total
I. Amount already Recorded				
Share of Profit, i.e., ₹ 1,50,000 in 2 : 2 : 1	60,000	60,000	30,000	1,50,000
II. Amount which should have been Recorded				
Salary (2,000 × 4)	8,000	8,000	—	16,000
Commission	—	—	8,000	8,000
Guarantee to Binay	—	50,000	—	50,000
Share of Profit, i.e., ₹ 76,000 in 3 : 2	45,600	—	30,400	76,000
	53,600	58,000	38,400	1,50,000
III. Net Effect (I-II)	6,400 (Dr)	2,000 (Dr)	8,400 (Cr)	Nil

Calculation of Adjusted Profits

Adjusted Profit = Given Profit − Salary − Commission − Guarantee to Binay

= 1,50,000 − 16,000 (8,000 + 8,000) − 8,000 − 50,000 = ₹ 76,000

9. Vikas and Vivek were partners in a firm sharing profits in the ratio of 3 : 2. On 1st April, 2014, they admitted Vandana as a new partner for 1/8th share in the profits with a guaranteed profit of ₹ 1,50,000. The new profit sharing ratio between Vivek and Vikas will remain the same but they decided to bear any deficiency on account of guarantee to Vandana in the ratio 2 : 3. The profit of the firm for the year ended 31st March, 2015 was ₹ 9,00,000.

Prepare profit and loss appropriation account of Vikas, Vivek and Vandana for the year ended 31st March, 2015. **All India 2016**

Ans.

Profit and Loss Appropriation Account
for the year ended 31st March, 2015

Dr Particulars		Amt (₹)	Particulars	Cr Amt (₹)
To Profit Transferred to Capital A/cs			By Net Profit as per Profit and Loss A/c	9,00,000
Vikas [(9,00,000−1,12,500)×3/5]	4,72,500			
(−) To Vandana	(22,500)	4,50,000		
Vivek [(9,00,000−1,12,500)×2/5]	3,15,000			
(−) To Vandana	(15,000)	3,00,000		
Vandana (9,00,000 × 1/8)	1,12,500			
(+) From Vikas	22,500			
(+) From Vivek	15,000	1,50,000		
		9,00,000		9,00,000

Working Note

Vandana's share in profit $= 9,00,000 \times \frac{1}{8} =$ ₹ 1,12,500

Minimum profit guaranteed to Vandana = ₹ 1,50,000

Deficiency = 37,500 (1,50,000 − 1,12,500) is to be borne by Vivek and Vikas in 2 : 3 ratio.

Deficiency to be borne by Vivek $= 37,500 \times \frac{2}{5} =$ ₹ 15,000

Deficiency to be borne by Vikas $= 37,500 \times \frac{3}{5} =$ ₹ 22,500

10. P and Q were partners in a firm sharing profits in the ratio of 5:3. On 1st April, 2014 they admitted R as a new partner for 1/8th share in the profits with a guaranteed profit of ₹ 75,000. The new profit sharing ratio between P and Q will remain the same but they agreed to bear any deficiency on account of guarantee to R in the ratio of 3:2. The profit of the firm for the year ended 31st March, 2015 was ₹ 4,00,000.

Prepare profit and loss appropriation account of P, Q and R for the year ended 31st March, 2015. **Delhi 2016**

Ans. Solve as Q. no. 9 on Page 24 and 25.

Amount Transferred to Capital Accounts: P = ₹ 2,03,750; Q, = ₹ 1,21,250; R = ₹ 75,000

11. Prem, Param and Priya were partners in a firm. Their fixed capitals were Prem ₹ 2,00,000; Param ₹ 3,00,000 and Priya ₹ 5,00,000. They were sharing profits in the ratio of their capitals. The firm was engaged in the sale of ready-to-eat food packets at three different locations in the city, each being managed by Prem, Param and Priya. The outlet managed by Prem was doing more business than the outlets managed by Param and Priya.

Prem requested Param and Priya for a higher share in the profits of the firm which Param and Priya accepted. It was decided that the new profit sharing ratio will be 2:1:2 and its effect will be introduced retrospectively for the last four years. The profits of the last four years were ₹ 2,00,000, ₹ 3,50,000, ₹ 4,75,000 and ₹ 5,25,000 respectively.

Showing your calculations clearly, pass a necessary adjustment entry to give effect to the new agreement between Prem, Param and Priya. **All India 2015**

Ans.

JOURNAL

Date	Particulars		LF	Amt (Dr)	Amt (Cr)
	Param's Current A/c	Dr		1,55,000	
	Priya's Current A/c	Dr		1,55,000	
	To Prem's Current A/c				3,10,000
	(Being profit of last four years adjusted due to change in profit sharing ratio)				

Working Note

Adjustment Table

Particulars	Prem (₹)	Param (₹)	Priya (₹)	Total
I. **Amount already Recorded**				
Profits of Past Four Years i.e., (2,00,000 + 3,50,000 + 4,75,000 + 5,25,000) in the ratio 2 : 3 :5	3,10,000	4,65,000	7,75,000	15,50,000
II. **Amount which should have been Recorded**				
Profit of Past Four Years i.e. in the Ratio 2 : 1 : 2	6,20,000	3,10,000	6,20,000	15,50,000
III. **Net Effect** (I-II)	3,10,000 (Cr)	1,55,000 (Dr)	1,55,000 (Cr)	Nil

12. A and B are partners in a firm sharing profit and losses in the ratio of 3 : 2. The following was the balance sheet of the firm as at 31st March, 2010.

Balance Sheet
as at 31st March, 2010

Liabilities		Amt (₹)	Assets	Amt (₹)
Capital A/cs			Sundry Assets	80,000
A	60,000			
B	20,000	80,000		
		80,000		80,000

The profits ₹ 30,000 for the year ended 31st March, 2010 were divided between the partners without allowing interest on capital @ 12% per annum and salary to A @ ₹ 1,000 per month. During the year, A withdrew ₹ 10,000 and B ₹ 20,000.

Pass the necessary adjustment journal entry and show your working clearly. **Delhi 2011**

Ans. Solve as Q. no. 3 given on Page 20.
Debit B's Capital Account and Credit A's Capital Account with ₹ 5,280.

13. A, B and C were partners in a firm. On 1st April, 2008, their fixed capitals stood at ₹ 50,000, ₹ 25,000 and ₹ 25,000 respectively.

As per the provisions of the partnership deed

(*i*) B was entitled for a salary of ₹ 5,000 per annum.

(*ii*) All the partners were entitled to interest on capital at 5% per annum.

(*iii*) Profits were to be shared in the ratio of capitals.

The net profit for the year ending 31st March, 2009 of ₹ 33,000 and 31st March, 2010 of ₹ 45,000 was divided equally without providing for the above terms.

Pass an adjustment journal entry to rectify the above error. **All India 2011**

Ans.

Adjusting Journal Entry

Date	Particulars	LF	Amt (Dr)	Amt (Cr)
	C's Current A/c Dr		9,000	
	To A's Current A/c			8,000
	To B's Current A/c			1,000
	(Being interest on capital and salary not provided previously and profit distributed wrongly, now adjusted)			

Working Notes

1. **Adjustment Table**

Particulars		A (₹)	B (₹)	C (₹)	Total
I. **Amount already Recorded**					
Profit, i.e., 33,000 (1 : 1 : 1)	31st March, 2009	11,000	11,000	11,000	33,000
Profit, i.e., 45,000 in (1 : 1 : 1)	31st March, 2010	15,000	15,000	15,000	45,000
		26,000	26,000	26,000	78,000
II. **Amount which should have been Recorded**					
Salary	31st March, 2009	—	5,000	—	5,000
	31st March, 2010	—	5,000	—	5,000
Interest on Capital	31st March, 2009	2,500	1,250	1,250	5,000
	31st March, 2010	2,500	1,250	1,250	5,000
Profits, i.e. 23,000 in capital ratio, i.e. 2 : 1 : 1	31st March, 2009	11,500	5,750	5,750	23,000
Profits, i.e. 35,000 in 2 : 1 : 1	31st March, 2010	17,500	8,750	8,750	35,000
		34,000	27,000	17,000	78,000
III. Net Effect (I – II)		8,000 (Cr)	1,000 (Cr)	9,000 (Dr)	Nil

2. **Calculation of Adjusted Profit**

Adjusted Profit = Given Profit – Salary – Interest on Capital

31st March, 2009 $\Rightarrow$ 33,000 – 5,000 – 5,000 (2,500 + 1,250 + 1,250) $\Rightarrow$ ₹ 23,000

31st March, 2010 $\Rightarrow$ 45,000 – 5,000 – 5,000 (2,500 + 1,250 + 1,250) $\Rightarrow$ ₹ 35,000

Calculation of Interest on Capital

$$A = 50{,}000 \times \frac{5}{100} = ₹\,2{,}500;\ B = 25{,}000 \times \frac{5}{100} = ₹\,1{,}250;\ C = 25{,}000 \times \frac{5}{100} = ₹\,1{,}250$$

14. A, B and C were partners. Their capitals were ₹ 30,000, ₹ 20,000 and ₹ 10,000 respectively. According to the partnership deed, they were entitled to interest on capital @ 5% per annum. In addition, B was also entitled to draw a salary of ₹ 500 per month.

C was entitled to a commission of 5% on the profits after charging the interest on capitals but before charging the salary payable to B. The net profits for the year were ₹ 30,000 distributed in the ratio of their capitals without providing for any of the above adjustments. The profits were to be shared in the ratio of 2 : 2 : 1.
Pass the necessary adjustment entry showing the working clearly. **Delhi; All India 2010**

Ans.

JOURNAL

Date	Particulars		LF	Amt (Dr)	Amt (Cr)
	A's Capital A/c	Dr		5,640	
	To B's Capital A/c				4,860
	To C's Capital A/c				780
	(Being profit distributed wrongly, now adjusted)				

Working Notes

1. **Adjustment Table**

Particulars	A (₹)	B (₹)	C (₹)	Total
I. **Amount already Recorded**				
Profit, i.e., 30,000 (In capital ratio i.e. 3 : 2 : 1)	15,000	10,000	5,000	30,000
II. **Amount which should have been Recorded**				
Interest on Capital @ 5% per annum	1,500	1,000	500	3,000
Commission (30,000 – 3,000) × 5%	—	—	1,350	1,350
Salary (500 × 12)	—	6,000	—	6,000
Profit i.e., 19,650 in (2 : 2 : 1)	7,860	7,860	3,930	19,650
	9,360	14,860	5,780	30,000
III. **Net Effect** (I – II)	5,640 (Dr)	4,860 (Cr)	780 (Cr)	Nil

2. **Calculation of Adjusted Profit**

Adjusted Profit = Given Profit – Interest on Capital – Salary – Commission
= 30,000 – 3,000 (1,500 + 1,000 + 500) – 6,000 – 1,350 = ₹ 19,650

3. **Interest on Capital**

$A = 30{,}000 \times \frac{5}{100} = ₹1{,}500;\quad B = 20{,}000 \times \frac{5}{100} = ₹1{,}000;\quad C = 10{,}000 \times \frac{5}{100} = ₹\,500$

6 Marks Questions

15. On 31st March, 2018 the balance in the capital accounts of Abhir, Bobby and Vineet, after making adjustemnts for profits and drawings were ₹ 8,00,000, ₹ 6,00,000 and ₹ 4,00,000 respectively.

Subsequently, it was discovered that interest on capital and interest on drawings had been omitted. The partners were entitled to interest on capital @ 10% p.a. and were to be charged interest on drawings @ 6% p.a. The drawings during the year were Abhir ₹ 20,000 drawn at the end of each month, Bobby ₹ 50,000 drawn at the beginning of every half year and Vineet ₹ 1,00,000 withdrawn on 31st October, 2017. The net profit for the year ended 31st March, 2018 was ₹ 1,50,000. The profit sharing ratio was 2 : 2 : 1.

Pass necessary adjusting entry for the above adjustments in the books of the firm. Also, show your workings clearly. **All India 2019**

Ans. **JOURNAL**

Date	Particulars		LF	Amt (Dr)	Amt (Cr)
2018					
Apr 1	Bobby's Capital A/c	Dr		14,402	
	To Abhir's Capital A/c				10,112
	To Vineet's Capital A/c				4,290
	(Being an adjustment entry passed for past adjustment)				

Calculation of Opening Capital

Particulars	Abhir (₹)	Bobby (₹)	Vineet (₹)
Capital at the End	8,00,000	6,00,000	4,00,000
(+) Drawings	2,40,000	1,00,000	1,00,000
	10,40,000	7,00,000	5,00,000
(−) Profit	(60,000)	(60,000)	(30,000)
Capital at the Beginning	9,80,000	6,40,000	(4,70,000)

Calculation of Interest on Drawings

$$\text{Abhir} = 20{,}000 \times 12 \times \frac{6}{100} \times \frac{5.5}{12} = ₹\ 6{,}600$$

$$\text{Bobby} = 50{,}000 \times 2 \times \frac{6}{100} \times \frac{9}{12} = ₹\ 4{,}500$$

$$\text{Vineet} = 1{,}00{,}000 \times \frac{6}{100} \times \frac{5}{12} = ₹\ 2{,}500$$

Calculation of Amount to be Adjusted

Particulars	Abhir (₹)	Bobby (₹)	Vineet (₹)	Total (₹)
Amount to be Debited				
Profit	60,000	60,000	30,000	1,50,000
Interest on Drawings	6,600	4,500	2,500	13,600
	66,600	64,500	32,500	1,63,600
Amount to be Credited				
Interest on Capital @ 10% p.a.	76,712	50,098	36,790	1,63,600
Interest on Capital will be Allowed to the Extent of Maximum Profit Available	10,112 Cr	14,402 Dr	4,290 Cr	

16. Naveen, Qadir and Rajesh were partners doing an electronic goods business in Uttarakhand. After the accounts of partnership were drawn up and closed, it was discovered that interest on capital has been allowed to partners @ 6% p.a. for the years ending 31st March, 2017 and 2018, although there is no provision for interest on capital in the partnership deed. On the other hand, Naveen and Qadir were entitled to a salary of ₹ 3,500 and ₹ 4,000 per quarter respectively, which has not been taken into consideration.

Their fixed capitals were ₹ 4,00,000, ₹ 3,60,000 and ₹ 2,40,000 respectively. During the last two years they had shared the profits and losses as follows

Year Ended	Ratio
31st March, 2017	3 : 2 : 1
31st March, 2018	5 : 3 : 2

Pass necessary adjusting entry for the above adjustments in the books of the firm. Also, show your workings clearly. **All India 2019**

Ans. **JOURNAL**

Date	Particulars		LF	Amt (Dr)	Amt (Cr)
2018					
Apr 1	Rajesh's Current A/c	Dr		17,800	
	To Naveen's Current A/c				10,000
	To Qadir's Current A/c				7,800
	(Being an adjustment entry passed for past adjustment)				

Calculation of Amount to be Adjusted

Particulars		Naveen (₹)	Qadir (₹)	Rajesh (₹)	Total (₹)
Amount to be Debited					
Interest on Capital	2017	24,000	21,600	14,400	60,000
	2018	24,000	21,600	14,400	60,000
		48,000	43,200	28,800	1,20,000
Amount to be Credited					
Salary	2017	14,000	16,000	—	30,000
	2018	14,000	16,000	—	30,000
Share of Profit 2017 (60,000 – 30,000) in Ratio 3 : 2 : 1		15,000	10,000	5,000	30,000
2018 (60,000 – 30,000) in 5 : 3 : 2		15,000	9,000	6,000	30,000
		58,000	51,000	11,000	1,20,000
		10,000 Cr	7,800 Cr	17,800 Dr	

17. Pass necessary rectifying journal entries for the following omissions committed while preparing profit and loss appropriation Account. You are also required to show your workings clearly.

(*i*) A, B and C were partners sharing profits and losses equally. Their fixed capitals were A ₹ 4,00,000; B ₹ 5,00,000 and C ₹ 6,00,000. The partnership deed provided that interest on partners' capital will be allowed @10% per annum. The same was omitted.

(*ii*) P, Q and R were partners in a firm sharing profits and losses in the ratio of 2 : 2 : 1. Their partnership deed provided that interest on partners' drawings will be charged @ 18% p.a. Interest on the partners' drawings was ₹ 1,000, ₹ 500 and ₹ 2,000 respectively. The same was omitted. **All India 2019**

Ans. (*i*)

Rectifying Journal

Date	Particulars		LF	Amt (Dr)	Amt (Cr)
	A's Current A/c	Dr		10,000	
	To C's Current A/c				10,000
	(Being interest on capital previously omitted, now adjusted)				

Particulars	A (₹)	B (₹)	C (₹)	Total (₹)
Amount to be Credited				
Interest on Capital	40,000	50,000	60,000	1,50,000
Amount to be Debited	50,000	50,000	50,000	1,50,000
	10,000 Cr	NIL	10,000 Dr	NIL

(*ii*)

Rectifying Journal

Date	Particulars		LF	Amt (Dr)	Amt (Cr)
	R's Capital A/c	Dr		1,300	
	To P's Capital A/c				400
	To Q's Capital A/c				900
	(Being interest on drawings previously omitted, now adjusted)				

Particulars	P (₹)	Q (₹)	R (₹)	Total (₹)
Amount to be Debited				
Interest on Drawings	1,000	500	2,000	3,500
Amount to be Credited	1,400	1,400	700	3,500
	400 Cr	900 Cr	1,300 Dr	Nill —

18. Jay, Vijay and Karan were partners of an architect firm sharing profits in the ratio of 2 : 2 : 1. Their partnership deed provided the following:

(*i*) A monthly salary of ₹ 15,000 each to Jay and Vijay.

(*ii*) Karan was guaranteed a profit of ₹ 5,00,000 and Jay guaranteed that he will earn an annual fee of ₹ 2,00,000. Any deficiency arising because of guarantee to Karan will be borne by Jay and Vijay in the ratio of 3 : 2.

During the year ended 31st March, 2018 Jay earned fee of ₹ 1,75,000 and the profits of the firm amounted to ₹ 15,00,000.

Showing your workings clearly prepare Profit and Loss Appropriation Account and the Capital Account of Jay, Vijay and Karan for the year ended 31st March, 2018. **Delhi 2019**

Ans.

Profit and Loss Appropriation Account

Dr — for the year ended 31st March, 2018 — Cr

Particulars	Amt (₹)	Particulars	Amt (₹)
To Salary Jay's Capital A/c (15,000 × 12)	1,80,000	By Profit	15,00,000
To Vijay's Capital A/c (15,000 × 12)	1,80,000	By Jay's Capital A/c (Shortfall of guaranteed fee)	25,000

Particulars		Amt (₹)	Particulars	Amt (₹)
To Profit transferred to Partners Capital A/c				
Jay	4,66,000			
(−) Transfer to Karan (2,67,000 × 3/ 5)	(1,60,200)	3,05,800		
Vijay	4,66,000			
(−) Transfer to Karan(2,67,000 × 2/ 5)	(1,06,800)	3,59,200		
Karan	2,33,000			
(+) Shortage	2,67,000	5,00,000		
		15,25,000		15,25,000

Dr **Partners' Capital Account** Cr

Particulars	Jay (₹)	Vijay (₹)	Karan (₹)	Particulars	Jay (₹)	Vijay (₹)	Karan (₹)
To Profit and Loss Appropriation A/c (Shortage of guaranteed fee)	25,000	—	—	By Balance b/d	—	—	—
				By Profit and Loss Appropriation A/c (Salary)	1,80,000	1,80,000	—
To Balance c/d	—	—	—	By Profit and Loss Appropriation A/c (Profit)	3,05,800	3,59,200	5,00,000

NOTE In the absence of any information of capital at the beginning, it is not possible to close capital account and calculate capital at the end. Alternatively, we can calculate the balance also.

19. Moli, Bhola and Raj were partners in a firm sharing profits and losses in the ratio of 3 : 3: 4. Their partnership deed provided for the following

(*i*) Interest on capital @ 5% per annum.

(*ii*) Interest on drawing @ 12% per annum.

(*iii*) Interest on partners' loan @ 6% per annum.

(*iv*) Moli was allowed an annual salary of ₹ 4,000, Bhola was allowed a commission of 10% of net profit as shown by profit and loss account and Raj was guaranteed a profit of ₹ 1,50,000 after making all the adjustments as provided in the partnership agreement.

Their fixed capitals were Moli ₹ 5,00,000; Bhola ₹ 8,00,000 and Raj ₹ 4,00,000. On 1st April, 2016 Bhola extended a loan of ₹ 1,00,000 to the firm. The net profit of the firm for the year ended 31st March, 2017 before interest on Bhola's loan was ₹ 3,06,000.

Prepare profit and loss oppropriation account of Moli, Bhola and Raj for the year ended 31st March, 2017 and their current accounts assuming that Bhola withdrew ₹ 5,000 at the end of each month, Moli withdrew ₹ 10,000 at the end of each quarter and Raj withdrew ₹ 40,000 at the end of each half year. **CBSE 2018**

Ans.

Profit and Loss Appropriation Account
for the year ended 31st March, 2017

Dr Particulars		Amt (₹)	Particulars		Cr Amt (₹)
To Interest on Capital A/c			By Net Profit from Profit and Loss A/c		3,00,000
Moli's Current A/c	25,000		By Interest on Drawings A/c		
Bhola's Current A/c	40,000		Moli's Current A/c	1,800	
Raj's Current A/c	20,000	85,000	Bhola's Current A/c	3,300	
To Moli's Current A/c (Salary)		4,000	Raj's Current A/c	2,400	7,500
To Bhola's Current A/c (Commission)		30,000			
To Profit Transferred to Current A/c					
Moli's (56,550 – 37,300)	19,250				
Bhola's (56,550 – 37,300)	19,250				
Raj's (75,400 + 37,300 + 37,300)	1,50,000	1,88,500			
		3,07,500			3,07,500

Partners' Current Account

Dr Particulars	Moli (₹)	Bhola (₹)	Raj (₹)	Particulars	Moli (₹)	Bhola (₹)	Cr Raj (₹)
To Drawings A/c	60,000	40,000	80,000	By Interest on Capital A/c	25,000	40,000	20,000
To Interest on Drawing A/c	1,800	3,300	2,400	By Salary A/c	4,000	—	—
To Balance c/d	—	45,950	87,600	By Commission A/c	—	30,000	—
				By Profit and Loss Appropriation A/c (Profit)	19,250	19,250	1,50,000
				By Balance c/d	13,550	—	—
	61,800	89,250	1,70,000		61,800	89,250	1,70,000

Working Notes

1. **Profit and Loss Account**
for the year ended ...

Dr Particulars	Amt (₹)	Particulars	Cr Amt (₹)
To Interest on Loan A/c (1,00,000 ×6%)	6,000	By Net Profit	3,06,000
To Profit Transferred to Profit and Loss Appropriation A/c	3,00,000		
	3,06,000		3,06,000

2. Calculation of Interest on Drawings

$$\text{Moli} = (10{,}000 \times 4) \times \frac{12}{100} \times \frac{4.5}{12} = ₹\,1{,}800$$

$$\text{Bhola} = (5{,}000 \times 12) \times \frac{12}{100} \times \frac{5.5}{12} = ₹\,3{,}300$$

$$\text{Raj} = 40{,}000 \times \frac{12}{100} \times \frac{6}{12} = ₹\,2{,}400$$

3. Calculation of Commission Payable to Bhola

$$3,00,000 \times \frac{10}{100} = ₹\ 30,000$$

4. Distributable profits = 3,00,000 + 7,500 − 85,000 − 4,000 − 30,000 = ₹ 1,88,500

Moli's share $= 1,88,500 \times \frac{3}{10} =$ ₹ 56,550; Bhola's share $= 1,88,500 \times \frac{3}{10} =$ ₹ 56,500

Raj's share $= 1,88,500 \times \frac{4}{10} =$ ₹ 75,400; Amount guaranteed to Raj = ₹ 1,50,000

Deficiency = Guaranteed amount − Actual amount

= 1,50,000 − 75,400 = ₹ 74,600 to be borne by Moli and Bhola equally, *i.e.* 37,300 each.

20. On 31st March, 2014, the balances in the capital accounts of Eleen, Monu and Ahmad after making adjustments for profits and drawings were ₹ 1,60,000, ₹ 1,20,000 and ₹ 80,000 respectively. Subsequently, it was discovered that the interest on capital and drawings had been omitted.

(*i*) The profit for the year ended 31st March, 2014 was ₹ 40,000.

(*ii*) During the year Eleen and Monu each withdrew a total sum of ₹ 24,000 in equal instalments in the beginning of each month and Ahmad withdrew a total sum of ₹ 48,000 in equal instalments at the end of each month.

(*iii*) The interest on drawings was to be charged @ 5% per annum and interest on capital was to be allowed @ 10% per annum.

(*iv*) The profit sharing ratio among the partners was 2 : 1 : 1.

Showing your working notes clearly, pass the necessary rectifying entry. **Delhi (C) 2015**

Ans.

Adjusting Journal Entry

Date	Particulars		LF	Amt (Dr)	Amt (Cr)
2014					
Mar 31	Eleen's Capital A/c	Dr		3,850	
	To Monu's Capital A/c				2,950
	To Ahmad's Capital A/c				900
	(Being the adjustment entry passed)				

Adjustment Table

Particulars	Eleen (₹)	Monu (₹)	Ahmad (₹)	Total
I. **Amount already Recorded**				
Profit i.e., 40,000 (in 2 : 1 : 1)	20,000	10,000	10,000	40,000
II. **Amount which should have been Recorded**				
Interest on Capital	16,400	13,400	11,800	41,600
Interest on Drawings	(650)	(650)	(1,100)	(2,400)
Profit i.e. 800 in (2 : 1 : 1)	400	200	200	800
	16,150	12,950	10,900	40,000
III. **Net Effect** (I-II)	3,850 (Dr)	2,950 (Cr)	900 (Cr)	Nil

Calculation of Opening Capital and Interest on Capitals

Particulars	Eleen (₹)	Monu (₹)	Ahmad (₹)
Closing Capitals	1,60,000	1,20,000	80,000
(–) Profit i.e. 40,000 in 2 : 1 : 1	(20,000)	(10,000)	(10,000)
(+) Drawings	24,000	24,000	48,000
Opening Capitals	1,64,000	1,34,000	1,18,000
Interest on Capital @ 10%	16,400	13,400	11,800

Interest on Drawings

$$\text{Eleen} = 24{,}000 \times \frac{5}{100} \times \frac{6.5}{12} = ₹650$$

$$\text{Monu} = 24{,}000 \times \frac{5}{100} \times \frac{6.5}{12} = ₹650$$

$$\text{Ahmad} = 48{,}000 \times \frac{5}{100} \times \frac{5.5}{12} = ₹1{,}100$$

Calculation of Adjusted Profit

Adjusted Profit = Given Profit – Interest on Capital + Interest on Drawings

= 40,000 – 41,600 (16,400 + 13,400 + 11,800) + 2,400 (650 + 650 + 1,100) = ₹ 800

21. A, B and C were partners in a firm. On 1st April, 2012 their capitals stood as ₹ 5,00,000; ₹ 2,50,000 and ₹ 2,50,000 respectively.

As per provisions of the partnership deed

(*i*) C was entitled for a salary of ₹ 5,000 per month.

(*ii*) A was entitled for a commission of ₹ 80,000 per annum.

(*iii*) Partners were entitled to interest on capital @ 6% per annum.

(*iv*) Partners will share profits in the ratio of capitals.

Net profit for the year ended 31st March, 2013 was ₹ 3,00,000 which was distributed equally, without taking into consideration the above provisions. Showing your working clearly, pass necessary adjustment entry for the above. **Delhi (C) 2014**

Ans. Solve as Q. no. 13 on page 26 and 27.

Debit B's Capital Account and Credit A's Capital Accounts with ₹ 60,000

22. Ali, Bimal and Deepak are partners in a firm. On 1st April, 2011 their capital accounts stood at ₹ 4,00,000, ₹ 3,00,000 and ₹ 2,00,000 respectively. They shared profits and losses in the ratio of 5 : 3 : 2 respectively. Partners are entitled to interest on capital @ 10% per annum and salary to Bimal and Deepak @ ₹ 2,000 per month and ₹ 3,000 per quarter respectively as per the provisions of the partnership deed.

Bimal's share of profit (excluding interest on capital but including salary) is guaranteed at a minimum of ₹ 50,000 per annum. Any deficiency arising on that account shall be met by Deepak. The profits of the firm for the year ended 31st March, 2012 amount to ₹ 2,00,000.

Prepare profit and loss appropriation account for the year ended on 31st March, 2012.

Delhi 2013

Ans.

Profit and Loss Appropriation Account

Dr — for the year ending 31st March, 2012 — Cr

Particulars		Amt (₹)	Particulars	Amt (₹)
To Interest on Capital A/cs			By Net Profit as per Profit and Loss A/c	2,00,000
Ali (1,00,000 × 10/ 100)	40,000			
Bimal (3,00,000 × 10/ 100)	30,000			
Deepak (2,00,000 × 10/ 100)	20,000	90,000		
To Salary A/c				
Bimal's Capital A/c (2,000×12)	24,000			
Deepak's Capital A/c (3,000×4)	12,000	36,000		
To Profit Distributed to				
Ali's Capital A/c		37,000		
Bimal's Capital A/c	22,200			
(+) from Deepak	3,800	26,000		
Deepak's Capital A/c	14,800			
(−) to Bimal	(3,800)	11,000		
		2,00,000		2,00,000

Working Note

Distributable profits = 2,00,000 − 90,000 − 36,000 = ₹ 74,000 to be distributed in 5 : 3 : 2

Ali's share $= 74,000 \times \frac{5}{10} =$ ₹ 37,000; Deepak's share $= 74,000 \times \frac{2}{10} =$ ₹ 14,800

Bimal's share (excluding interest on capital and salary) $= 74,000 \times \frac{3}{10} =$ ₹ 22,200

Bimal's share (excluding interest on capital and including salary) = 22,200 + 24,000 (Salary)
= ₹ 46, 200

Guarantee by Deepak = ₹ 50,000

Deficiency to be borne by Deepak = 50,000 − 46, 200 = ₹ 3,800

23. Anwar, Biswas and Divya are partners in a firm. Their capital accounts stood at ₹ 8,00,000, ₹ 6,00,000 and ₹ 4,00,000 respectively on 1st April, 2011. They shared profits and losses in the ratio of 3 : 2 : 1 respectively. Partners are entitled to interest on capital @ 6% per annum and salary to Biswas and Divya @ ₹ 4,000 per month and ₹ 6,000 per quarter respectively as per the provisions of partnership deed.

Biswas's share of profit (including interest on capital but excluding salary) is guaranteed at a minimum of ₹ 82,000 per annum. Any deficiency arising on that account shall be met by Divya. The profits for the year ended 31st March, 2012 amounted to ₹ 3,12,000. Prepare profit and loss appropriation account for the year ended 31st March,2012. **Delhi 2013**

Ans.

Profit and Loss Appropriation Account

Dr for the year ending 31st March, 2012 Cr

Particulars		Amt (₹)	Particulars	Amt (₹)
To Interest on Capital A/cs			By Net Profit as per Profit and Loss A/c	3,12,000
Anwar (8,00,000×6 / 100)	48,000			
Biswas (6,00,000×6 / 100)	36,000			
Divya (4,00,000×6 / 100)	24,000	1,08, 000		
To Salary A/c				
Biswas's Capital A/c (4,000×12)	48,000			
Divya's Capital A/c (6,000×4)	24,000	72,000		
To Profit Transferred to				
Anwar's Capital A/c		66,000		
Biswas's Capital A/c	44,000			
(+) from Divya	2,000	46,000		
Divya's Capital A/c	22,000			
(−) to Biswas	(2,000)	20,000		
		3,12,000		3,12,000

Working Note

Distributable profits $= 3{,}12{,}000 - 1{,}08{,}000 - 72{,}000 =$ ₹ 1,32,000 to be distributed in 3 : 2 : 1

Anwar's share $= 1{,}32{,}000 \times \frac{3}{6} =$ ₹ 66,000; Divya's share $= 1{,}32{,}000 \times \frac{1}{6} =$ ₹ 22,000

Biswas's share of profit (excluding interest on capital an salary) $= 1{,}32{,}000 \times \frac{2}{6} =$ ₹ 44,000

Biswas's share (excluding salary and including interest on capital)

$= 44{,}000 + 36{,}000$ (Interest on Capital) = ₹ 80,000

Guarantee by Divya = ₹ 82,000.

Therefore, deficiency of ₹ 2,000 (82,000 − 80,000) should be contributed by Divya.

24. Ahmad, Bheem and Daniel are partners in a firm. On 1st April, 2011, the balance in their capital accounts stood at ₹ 8,00,000, ₹ 6,00,000 and ₹ 4,00,000 respectively. They shared profits in the proportion of 5 : 3 : 2 respectively. Partners are entitled to interest on capital @ 5% per annum and salary to Bheem @ ₹ 3,000 per month and a commission of ₹ 12,000 to Daniel as per the provisions of the partnership deed.

Ahmad's share of profit (excluding interest on capital) is guaranteed at not less than ₹ 25,000 per annum. Bheem's share of profit (including interest on capital but excluding salary) is guaranteed at not less than ₹ 55,000 per annum. Any deficiency arising on that account shall be met by Daniel. The profits of the firm for the year ended 31st March, 2012 amounted to ₹ 2,16,000. Prepare 'profit and loss appropriation account' for the year ended 31st March, 2012. **All India 2013**

Ans.

Profit and Loss Appropriation Account
for the year ending 31st March, 2012

Dr | Cr

Particulars		Amt (₹)	Particulars	Amt (₹)
To Interest on Capital A/cs			By Net Profit as per Profit and Loss A/c	2,16,000
Ahmad (8,00,000 × 5 / 100)	40,000			
Bheem (6,00,000 × 5 / 100)	30,000			
Daniel (4,00,000 × 5 / 100)	20,000	90,000		
To Salary A/c (Bheem) (3,000×12)		36,000		
To Commission A/c (Daniel)		12,000		
To Profit Transferred to				
Ahmad's Capital A/c		39,000		
Bheem's Capital A/c	23,400			
(+) From Daniel	1,600	25,000		
Daniel's Capital A/c	15,600			
(−) To Bheem	(1,600)	14,000		
		2,16,000		2,16,000

Working Note

Distributable profits = 2,16,000 − 90,000 − 36,000 − 12,000 = ₹ 78,000 to be distributed in 5 : 3 : 2.

Ahmad's share of profit $= 78{,}000 \times \frac{5}{10} =$ ₹ 39,000

Ahmad's share of profit is already above the guaranteed amount, therefore no adjustment is required.

Bheem's share of profit (excluding interest on capital and salary) $= 78{,}000 \times \frac{3}{10} =$ ₹ 23,400

Bheem's share (excluding salary and including interest on capital) = 23,400 + 30,000 = ₹ 53,400

Guarantee by Daniel = ₹ 55,000

Therefore, deficiency of ₹ 1,600 (55,000 − 53,400) should be contributed by Daniel.

Daniel's share $= 78{,}000 \times \frac{2}{10} =$ ₹15,600

TOPIC 5

Valuation and Treatment of Goodwill

Goodwill

Goodwill means the good name or reputation of a business earned by a businessman through his hard work and honesty. This helps the business to earn more profit.

Nature of Goodwill

Goodwill is an intangible asset (an asset not having physical existence) and not a fictitious asset, because it has a realisable value and fictitious assets don't have a realisable value.

Factors Affecting the Value of Goodwill

The various factors affecting goodwill are

(*i*) Nature of business
(*ii*) Efficiency of management
(*iii*) Location
(*iv*) Market situation
(*v*) Special advantages

Need for Valuation of Goodwill

Need for valuation of goodwill arises in the following circumstances

(*i*) At the time of change in profit sharing ratio.
(*ii*) At the time of admission of a new partner.
(*iii*) At the time of retirement or death of a partner.
(*iv*) When the partnership firm is sold.
(*v*) Amalgamation of partnership firm.

Classification of Goodwill

Goodwill can be classified into two categories

(*i*) **Purchased** (Acquired) **Goodwill** It is the goodwill that is acquired by a business after paying consideration in cash or in kind.

NOTE Purchased goodwill is recorded in the books of accounts.

(*ii*) **Self-generated Goodwill** It is the internally generated or hard earned goodwill which arises due to continued hard work of the organisation, its better quality products, better customer service etc.

NOTE Self-generated goodwill is not recorded in the books because no consideration in money or money's worth is paid for it.

Methods of Valuation of Goodwill

(i) Average Profit Method

Under this method, goodwill is valued on the basis of simple average or weighted average of profits of the firm multiplied by the number of years' of purchase.

(a) **Simple Average Profit Method**
Value of Goodwill = Average Profit × Number of Year's Purchase

NOTE Any abnormal gain or abnormal loss should not be taken into consideration while calculating the average profit.

(b) **Weighted Average Profit Method**
Goodwill = Weighted Average Profit × Number of Years' Purchase

(ii) Super Profit Method

In any business, a certain amount or percentage of profits is normally expected. But in practice, we may earn more than normal profit or we may earn less than that normal profit. Excess of actual profits over the normal profit is called super profit.

Super Profit = Average Profit − Normal Profit

Value of Goodwill = Super Profit × Number of Years' Purchase

(iii) Capitalisation Method

Under this method, goodwill can be calculated in two ways

(a) **Capitalisation of Average Profit** In this method, goodwill of the firm is calculated by deducting actual capital employed (net assets) in the business from the capitalised value of average (actual) profits on the basis of normal rate of return.

Capitalised value of the business is ascertained by capitalising profits earned at the normal rate of profit.

Capitalised Value of Average Profit

$$= \text{Average Profit} \times \frac{100}{\text{Normal Rate of Return}}$$

Value of Goodwill = Capitalised Value of Average Profit – Actual Capital Employed

(b) **Capitalisation of Super Profit Method**

In this method, goodwill is calculated by the capitalisation of super profit on the basis of normal rate of return.

Value of Goodwill

$$= \text{Super Profit} \times \frac{100}{\text{Normal Rate of Return}}$$

Previous Years' Examination Questions

1 Mark Questions

1. How does nature of business affect the value of goodwill of a firm? **All India 2019; 2011**

Ans. If the nature of the products, in which the firm deals, are in high demand, the profit of the firm will be higher and therefore the value of goodwill will increase.

2. How does the market situation affect the value of goodwill of a firm? **Delhi 2011**

Ans. The monopoly condition or limited competition enables the concern to earn high profits which leads to higher value of goodwill.

3. How does the factor 'quality of product' affect the goodwill of a firm? **Delhi; All India 2010**

Ans. If the firm enjoys good reputation for its product quality, there will be higher sales and the value of its goodwill will increase.

4. How does the factor 'efficiency of management' affect the goodwill of a firm? **Delhi; All India 2010**

Ans. When the management of a firm is capable and competent, the firm will earn higher profits therefore the 'efficiency of management' surely will affect or increase the goodwill.

5. How does the factor location affect the goodwill of a firm? **Delhi 2010**

Ans. The value of business will be more, if it is located in a convenient or prominent locality.

3 Marks Questions

6. The firm of P, Q and R earned ₹ 4,00,000 average profits during the last three years. The capital employed in the business was ₹ 6,00,000. Normal rate of return of the industry is 8%.

Calculate the goodwill of the firm by capitalising the super profits. **All India 2019**

Ans. Average Profit = ₹ 4,00,000

Capital Employed = ₹ 6,00,000

Normal Rate of Return = 8%

$$\text{Normal Profit} = 6,00,000 \times \frac{8}{100} = ₹\ 48,000$$

Super Profit = Average Profit – Normal Profit

= 4,00,000 – 48,000 = ₹ 3,52,000

$$\text{Goodwill} = \text{Super Profit} \times \frac{100}{\text{Normal Rate of Return}}$$

$$= 3,52,000 \times \frac{100}{8} = ₹\ 44,00,000$$

7. Average profits of a firm during the last few years are ₹ 80,000 and the normal rate of return in a similar business is 10%. If the goodwill of the firm is ₹ 1,00,000 at 4 years' purchase of super profit, find the capital employed by the firm. **All India 2019**

Ans. $$\text{Super Profit} = \frac{\text{Goodwill}}{\text{Number of Years's Purchase}}$$

$$= \frac{1,00,000}{4} = ₹\ 25,000$$

Normal Profit = Average Profit – Super Profit

= 80,000 – 25,000 = ₹ 55,000

$$\text{Capital Employed} = \frac{\text{Normal Profit}}{\text{Normal Rate of Return}}$$

$$= \frac{55,000}{10\%} = ₹\ 5,50,000$$

8. A firm earned average profit of ₹ 3,00,000 during the last few years. The normal rate of return of the industry is 15%. The assets of the business were ₹ 17,00,000 and its liabilities were ₹ 2,00,000. Calculate the goodwill of the firm by capitalisation of average profits. **Dehli 2019**

Ans. Average Profit = ₹ 3,00,000

Normal Rate of Return = 15%

Capitalised Value of Average Profits

$$= \frac{\text{Average Profit}}{\text{Normal Rate of Return}} \times 100 = \frac{3,00,000}{15} \times 100$$

$$= ₹\ 20,00,000 \qquad \ldots(1)$$

Capital Employed = Total Assets − Liabilities

$$= 17,00,000 - 2,00,000 = ₹\ 15,00,000 \qquad \ldots(2)$$

Goodwill = Capitalised Value of verage Profit − Capital employed

$$= 20,00,000 - 15,00,000 = ₹\ 5,00,000$$

9. The capital of the firm of Anuj and Benu is ₹ 10,00,000 and the market rate of interest were is 15%. Annual salary to the partner is ₹ 60,000 each. The profit for the last three years ₹ 3,00,000, ₹ 3,60,000 and ₹ 4,20,000. Goodwill of the firm is to be valued on the basis of two years purchase of last three years average super profits. Calculate the goodwill of the firm. **Delhi 2019**

Ans. Capital Employed = ₹ 10,00,000

Normal Rate of Return = 15%

Normal Profit = 10,00,000 × 15% = ₹ 1,50,000

3 Year's Average Profit

$$= \frac{3,00,000 + 3,60,000 + 4,20,000}{3}$$

$$= ₹\ 3,60,000$$

Average profit after partners salary

$$= 3,60,000 - 60,000 \times 2 = ₹\ 2,40,000$$

Super Profit = Average Profit − Normal Profit

$$= 2,40,000 - 1,50,000 = ₹\ 90,000$$

Goodwill = Super Profit × No. of Year's Purchase

$$= 90,000 \times 2 = ₹\ 1,80,000$$

10. State any three circumstances other than (*i*) death of a partner (*ii*) admission of a partner and (*iii*) retirement of a partner when need for valuation of goodwill of a firm may arise. **Delhi; All India 2016**

Ans. The need for valuation of goodwill may arise

(*i*) **When there is a Change in Profit Sharing Ratio** In case the existing partners in the firm decide to mutually change the profit sharing ratio between them, there is a need to value the goodwill.

(*ii*) **When the Partnership Firm is Sold as Going Concern** The need for valuation of goodwill arises, in case the partnership firm is sold to some other concern on going basis.

(*iii*) **When Two Firms Amalgamate** The need for valuing also arises in case of amalgamation of two firms that is merger or acquisition of two business.

11. On 1st April, 2014 a firm had assets of ₹ 1,00,000 excluding stock of ₹ 20,000. Partners' capital accounts showed a balance of ₹ 60,000. The current liabilities were ₹ 10,000 and the balance constituted the reserve. If the normal rate of return is 8% the 'Goodwill' of the firm is valued at ₹ 60,000 at four years' purchase of super profit, find the average profit of the firm. **All India (C) 2015**

Ans. Goodwill = Super Profit × Number of Years' Purchase

$$60,000 = \text{Super profit} \times 4$$

$$\text{Super profit} = \frac{60,000}{4} = ₹\ 15,000$$

Capital Employed

⇒ Total Assets − Current Liabilities

⇒ (1,00,000 + 20,000) −10,000

⇒ ₹ 1,10,000

Normal Profit = Capital Employed × Normal Rate of Return

$$= 1,10,000 \times \frac{8}{100} = ₹\ 8,800$$

Super Profit = Average Profit − Normal Profit

15,000 = Average profit − 8,800

Average profit = 15,000 + 8,800 = ₹ 23,800

12. The average profit earned by a firm is ₹ 75,000 which includes undervaluation of stock of ₹ 5,000 on an average basis. The capital invested in the business is ₹ 7,00,000 and the normal rate of return is 7%.

Calculate goodwill of the firm on the basis of 5 times the super profit.

Delhi (C) 2015

Ans. Average profit = 75,000 + 5,000 = ₹ 80,000

Normal Profit = Capital Employed × Normal Rate of Return

$= 7,00,000 \times \frac{7}{100} =$ ₹ 49,000

Super Profit = Average Profit – Normal Profit

= 80,000 – 49,000 = ₹ 31,000

Goodwill = Super Profit × Number of Years' Purchase

= 31,000 × 5 = ₹ 1,55,000

4 Marks Questions

13. A business has earned average profits of ₹ 1,00,000 during the last few years and the normal rate of return in similar business is 10%. Find out the value of goodwill by

(*i*) Capitalisation of super profit method.

(*ii*) Super profit method, if the goodwill is valued at 3 years' purchase of super profit.

The assets of the business were ₹ 10,00,000 and its external liabilities ₹ 1,80,000.

Delhi 2011

Ans. Actual average profit = ₹ 1,00,000

Normal rate of return = 10%

Total assets = ₹ 10,00,000

External liabilities = ₹ 1,80,000

Capital Employed = Total Assets – External Liabilities

= 10,00,000 – 1,80,000

= ₹ 8,20,000

Normal Profit = Capital Employed $\times \frac{\text{Normal Rate of Return}}{100}$

$= 8,20,000 \times \frac{10}{100} =$ ₹ 82,000

Super Profit = Average Profit – Normal Profit

= 1,00,000 – 82,000 = ₹ 18,000

(*i*) **Calculation of Goodwill by Capitalisation of Super Profit Method**

Goodwill

$= \text{Super Profit} \times \frac{100}{\text{Normal Rate of Return}}$

$= 18,000 \times \frac{100}{10} =$ ₹ 1,80,000

(*ii*) **Calculation of Goodwill by Super Profit Method**

Goodwill = Super Profit × Number of Years' Purchase

= 18,000 × 3 = ₹ 54,000

14. A partnership firm earned net profits during the last 3 years as follows

Year	Net Profit
2007-2008	1,90,000
2008-2009	2,20,000
2010-2011	2,50,000

The capital employed in the firm throughout the above mentioned period has been ₹ 4,00,000. Having regard to the risk involved, 15% is considered to be a fair return on the capital. The remuneration of all the partners during this period is estimated to be ₹ 1,00,000 per annum.

Calculate the value of goodwill on the basis of

(*i*) 2 years' purchase of super profits earned on average basis during the above mentioned 3 years and

(*ii*) By capitalisation method. **All India 2011**

Ans. 3 years' total profit

= 1,90,000 + 2,20,000 + 2,50,000

= ₹ 6,60,000

Average profit $= \frac{6,60,000}{3} =$ ₹ 2,20,000

(–) Remuneration to partners = ₹ 1,00,000

Actual average profit = ₹ 1,20,000

Capital employed = ₹ 4,00,000

Normal rate of return = 15%

Normal profit $= 4,00,000 \times \frac{15}{100} =$ ₹ 60,000

Super Profit = Actual Average Profit – Normal Profit

$= 1{,}20{,}000 - 60{,}000 = ₹\ 60{,}000$

(*i*) Goodwill = Super Profit × Number of Years' Purchase

$= 60{,}000 \times 2 = ₹\ 1{,}20{,}000$

(*ii*) Capitalised Value of Goodwill

$= \text{Super Profit} \times \dfrac{100}{\text{Normal Rate of Return}}$

$= 60{,}000 \times \dfrac{100}{15} = ₹\ 4{,}00{,}000$

Multiple Choice Questions

For Complete Chapter (1 Mark)

1. The partnership deed should be properly drafted and prepared as per the provisions of the .... and preferably registered with the ....
CBSE Term I 2021

(a) Indian Partnership Act, 1932, Registrar of Companies.
(b) Indian Partnership Act, 1932, Registrar of Firms.
(c) Stamp Act, Registrar of Companies.
(d) Stamp Act, Registrar of Firms.

2. The difference between the fixed capital method and fluctuating capital method of maintaining partner's capitals is whether or not the transactions other than .... are recorded in the capital accounts of the partners. **CBSE Term I 2021**

(a) additional capital introduced
(b) withdrawal of capital
(c) partner's loan (d) Both (a) and (b)

3. R, S and T were partners sharing profits and losses in the ratio of 5 : 3 : 2. On 31st March, 2021, their books reflected a net profit of ₹ 3,10,000. As per the terms of the partnership deed they were entitled for interest on capital which amounted to ₹ 90,000, ₹ 60,000 and ₹ 30,000 respectively for R, S and T. Besides this an annual salary of ₹ 60,000 each was payable to R and S. The ratio in which the profits would be appropriated is
CBSE Term I 2021

(a) 1 : 1 : 1 (b) 5 : 3 : 2
(c) 5 : 4 : 1 (d) 4 : 3 : 2

4 Amit and Sumit were partners in a firm with capitals of ₹ 3,00,000 and ₹ 2,00,000 respectively. The normal rate of return was 20% and the capitalised value of average profits was ₹ 8,50,000. The goodwill of the firm by capitalisation of average profit method will be ....
CBSE Term I 2021

(a) ₹ 10,00,000
(b) ₹ 1,50,000
(c) ₹ 3,50,000
(d) ₹ 5,00,000

Hint: Goodwill = Capitalised value of profits – Actual capital employed

$= 8{,}50{,}000 - (3{,}00{,}000 + 2{,}00{,}000) = ₹\ 3{,}50{,}000$

5. A and B are partners in a firm sharing profit in the ratio of 3 : 2. Their balance sheet as on 31st March, 2021 was as follow **CBSE Term I 2021**

Liabilities	Amt (₹)	Assets		Amt (₹)
A's Capital	30,000	Drawings:		
		A	4,000	
B's Capital	10,000	B	2,000	6,000
		Other Assets		34,000
	40,000			40,000

Net profit of the year ended 31st March, 2021, ₹ 5,000 was divided without providing for interest on capital @ 10% p.a. What will be the amount of interest on A's Capital?

(a) ₹ 3,000 (b) Nil
(c) ₹ 3,100 (d) ₹ 2,700

Hint: Interest on A's Capital

$= (30{,}000 + 4{,}000 - 3{,}000) \times 10\% = ₹\ 3{,}100$

6. Devi withdrew ₹ 12,000 at the middle of every month. Interest on drawings was to be charged @ 12% per annum. Amount of interest on Devi's drawings will be
CBSE Term I 2021

(a) ₹ 14,400 (b) ₹ 8,640
(c) ₹ 7,200 (d) ₹ 1,200

Hint: Interest on Drawings

$= 12{,}000 \times 12 \times \dfrac{12}{100} \times \dfrac{6}{12} = ₹\ 8{,}640$

7. **Assertion** (A) The fixed capital account balance of a partner may change due to additional capital introduced or capital withdrawn or both, during the year.

Reason (R) Under fixed capital method, the partner's capital accounts balance always remains same. **CBSE Term I 2021**

Alternatives

(a) Both Assertion (A) and Reason (R) are correct
(b) Assertion (A) is correct, but Reason (R) is wrong
(c) Assertion (A) is wrong, but Reason (R) is correct
(d) Both Assertion (A) and Reason (R) are wrong

8. If partnership deed is silent or has not been formulated, then partners are entitled for

(a) salary
(b) commission
(c) interest on loan
(d) profit share in capital ratio

9. In partnership business, partner's liability is

(a) in proportion to profit/loss
(b) in proportion to capital
(c) limited
(d) unlimited

Hint: Generally, in partnership business, partners have unlimited liability. It means that in case of dissolution of a partnership firm, if the assets of the business are not adequate to discharge the liabilities of the firm, then the partners will be required to pay the deficiency from their personal assets.

10. If a partner individually carries on any business of the same nature as competing with that of firm, he shall account for

(a) retire from partnership
(b) all profits made by him
(c) dissolve the firm
(d) None of the above

Hint: If a partner individually carries on any business of the same nature as competing with that of the firm, he shall account for and pay to the firm, all profits made by him in that business. He is required to share the profits of such a business with all other partners.

11. In a partnership, manager's commission is shown in

(a) profit and loss account
(b) profit and loss appropriation account
(c) balance sheet
(d) None of the above

Hint: Manager commission is a charge against profit and not an appropriation of profit, so it will be shown in profit and loss account.

12. In a partnesship, interest on partner's capital is

(a) debited to profit and loss appropriation account
(b) credited to profit and loss appropriation acoount
(c) debited to profit and loss account
(d) credited to profit and loss account

Hint: Interest on partner's capital is an appropriation of profit, so it is debited to profit and loss appropriation account.

13. If a partner draws a fixed amount on the first day of every month, then for what period the interest on total drawings is calculated?

(a) 5.5 months
(b) 6.5 months
(c) 6 months
(d) None of the above

Hint: 6.5 months is the average period for drawings of a partner, if he withdraws same amount at the beginning of each month.

14. 'A' and 'B' were partners in a firm. They share their profits in the ratio of 2:1. 'A' withdraws an amount of ₹ 2,000 on 1st July, 2017. Journalise it.

(a) Profit and Loss App. A/c	Dr	2,000	
To A's Capital A/c			2,000
(b) A's Capital A/c	Dr	2,000	
To Profit and Loss A/c			2,000
(c) A's Drawings A/c	Dr	2,000	
To Cash/Bank A/c			2,000
(d) A's Capital A/c	Dr	2,000	
To A's Drawings A/c			2,000

Hint: Drawings does not affect profits, so profit and loss appropriation has no consideration. The drawings are made in cash, so cash/bank account are credited and drawings account is debited.

15. Gupta and Bansal are partners in a firm, Gupta withdraw ₹ 800 per month at the beginning of every month for 6 months ending on 31st December, 2017.

Bansal withdraw ₹ 800 per month at the end of every month for 6 months ending on 31st December, 2017. Calculate interest on drawings @ 15% per annum on 31st December, 2017.

(a) Gupta = ₹ 320, Bansal = ₹ 280
(b) Gupta = ₹ 180, Bansal = ₹ 220
(c) Gupta = ₹ 720, Bansal = ₹ 720
(d) Gupta = ₹ 210, Bansal = ₹ 150

Hint: Interest on Drawings = Amount × Months of Withdrawal $\times \frac{\text{Rate}}{100} \times \frac{\text{Average Months}}{12}$, where

Interest on Drawings for Gupta

$$= 800 \times 6 \times \frac{15}{100} \times \frac{3.5}{12} = ₹\ 210$$

Interest on Drawings for Bansal

$$= 800 \times 6 \times \frac{15}{100} \times \frac{2.5}{12} = ₹\ 150$$

Average Months

$$= \frac{\text{Time Left after First Drawings + Time Left after Last Drawings}}{2}$$

Average Months for Gupta $= \frac{6+1}{2} = 3.5$ months

Average Months for Bansal $= \frac{5+0}{2} = 2.5$ months

16. 'A' and 'B' were partners in a firm. They share profits in the ratio of 2:3. Their capital account balance as on 1st April, 2017 was ₹ 10,00,000 and ₹ 20,00,000. Additional capital introduced by them, A = ₹ 3,00,000, B = ₹ 2,00,000. Journalise it.

(a) Bank A/c	Dr	5,00,000	
To A's Capital A/c			3,00,000
To B's Capital A/c			2,00,000
(b) A's Capital A/c	Dr	3,00,000.	
B's Capital A/c	Dr	2,00,000	
To Bank A/c			5,00,000
(c) A's Capital A/c	Dr	3,00,000	
To Bank A/c			3,00,000
(d) B's Capital A/c	Dr	2,00,000	
To Bank A/c			2,00,000

Hint: Since, they introduced additional amount of capital, so bank balance of firm will increase, that's why bank account will be debited. Partners' capital will also increase, so their capital accounts will be credited.

17. Asha and Bipasha are partners in a firm. They share profits in the ratio of 1:1. In this year, they suffered a loss. They maintain capital accounts under fluctuating account method. Pass journal entry to transfer the loss to the capital accounts of Asha and Bipasha.

(a) Profit and Loss Appropriation A/c Dr
  To Asha's Capital A/c
  To Bipasha's Capital A/c
(b) Asha's Capital A/c Dr
  To Bipasha's Capital A/c
(c) Asha's Capital A/c Dr
 Bipasha's Capital A/c Dr
  To Pofit and Loss A/c
(d) None of the above

Hint: In case of loss, profit and loss account is credited and partner's capital account is debited. Because of loss, partners' capital will be reduced, so capital accounts will be debited. Also, loss is directly transferred from profit and loss account, so it will be credited.

18. 'R' and 'S' were partners in a firm. They share their profits and losses in 1:2 ratio. 'R' is hard working and dedicated to the affairs of the firm. As per contract or deed he is to receive ₹ 500 per month as salary. Journalise it if capital account is maintained under fixed capital method.

(a) Profit and Loss A/c	Dr	6,000	
To R's Capital A/c			6,000
(b) Profit and Loss App. A/c	Dr	6,000	
To R's Current A/c			6,000
(c) Salary A/c	Dr	6,000	
To Profit and Loss A/c			6,000
(d) Salary A/c	Dr	6,000	
To R's Current A/c			6,000

Hint: Since, salary to any partner is an appropriation of profit, so under fixed capital method, it will be credited to R's current account and debited to profit and loss appropriation account.

19. Pass the journal entry to record salary of partner

(a) Profit and Loss Appropriation A/c Dr
  To Partners' Capital A/c
(b) Profit and Loss A/c Dr
  To Salary A/c
(c) Partner's Capital A/c Dr
  To Salary A/c
(d) Salary A/c Dr
  To Profit and Loss Appropriation A/c

20. 'X' and 'Y' are partners in a firm sharing profits in the ratio of 3:2. As per their agreement, 'X' will receive 5% per annum interest on his loan of ₹ 1,00,000 and 'Y' will receive 2% commission on sales affected by him, which were ₹ 1,00,000. Calculate X's share of profit when net profit as per profit and loss account is ₹ 1,00,000.

(a) ₹ 58,800 (b) ₹ 58,000
(c) ₹ 60,000 (d) ₹ 48,200

Hint: Net profit as per profit and loss account (after interest on loan) = 1,00,000

(–) Y's Commission @2% = (2,000)

Distributable profit = 98,000

X's share = 98,000 × 3/5 = ₹58,800

NOTE Interest on loan is debited to profit and loss account and net profit is ascertained after charging it.

21. 'A' and 'B' are partners sharing profits in the ratio of 3:2. Calculate interess on A/s capital if profits for the year are ₹ 15,000 and interest on capital to all partners is ₹ 20,000 each.

(a) ₹ 20,000
(b) ₹ 12,500
(c) ₹ (7,500) (loss)
(d) ₹ 7,500

Hint: The interest on A's capital and B's capital is ₹ 20,000 each. Thus, total interest comes to ₹ 40,000, while profit for the year is ₹ 15 ,000. If profit is less than the interest on capital, then interest is allowed only to the extent of profit in the ratio of interest on capital of each partner.

In this case, the ratio will be 1:1 (i.e. 20,000 : 20,000)

∴ Interest on A's capital $=15{,}000\times\frac{1}{2}=$ ₹7,500

ANSWERS

1. *(d)*	2. *(d)*	3. *(b)*	4. *(c)*	5. *(c)*	6. *(b)*	7. *(b)*	8. *(c)*	9. *(d)*	10. *(b)*
11. *(a)*	12. *(a)*	13. *(b)*	14. *(c)*	15. *(d)*	16. *(a)*	17. *(c)*	18. *(b)*	19. *(a)*	20. *(a)*
21. *(d)*									

CHAPTER 02

Reconstitution of a Partnership Firm:

Change in Profit Sharing Ratio Among the Existing Partners

Any change in the existing agreement of partnership amounts to reconstitution of a firm. As a result of reconstitution, the existing agreement comes to an end and a new agreement comes into existence and the firm continues.

Reconstitution of a firm can take place in any of the following ways

(*i*) Change in the profit sharing ratio of existing partners.

(*ii*) Admission of a new partner.

(*iii*) Retirement of an existing partner.

(*iv*) Death of a partner.

(*v*) Amalgamation of two partnership firms.

This chapter discusses, the reconstitution of a firm due to change in profit sharing ratio among the existing partners.

Change in Profit Sharing Ratio Among the Existing Partners

When one or more partners acquire an interest in the business from another partner(s), it is said to be a change in the profit sharing ratio in a partnership firm. A change in the profit sharing ratio among the existing partners means it is a reconstitution of the firm without admission, retirement, death or amalgamation. The sacrifice made or gain received by a partner is calculated by deducting the new share from the old share of a partner.

Sacrificing/(Gaining) Share = Old Share – New Share

Adjustments Required at the Time of Change in Profit Sharing Ratio

(*i*) **Determination of Sacrificing Ratio and Gaining Ratio**

New Profit Sharing Ratio It is the ratio in which the partners are to share profits/losses in future.

Sacrificing Ratio It is the ratio in which the partner(s) has/have agreed to sacrifice their share of profit in favour of other partner or partners.

This ratio is calculated by taking out the difference between old profit share and new profit share.

Sacrificing Ratio = Old Share – New Share

Gaining Ratio It is the ratio in which the partner(s) has/have agreed to gain their share of profit from other partner(s). This ratio is calculated by taking out the difference between new profit share and old profit share.

Gaining Ratio = New Share – Old Share

(*ii*) **Accounting Treatment of Goodwill**

If the partners decide to change their profit sharing ratio, the gaining partner must compensate the sacrificing partner by way of payment to him as goodwill in the gaining ratio.

The accounting treatment for adjustment of goodwill, in case of change in profit sharing ratio, is as follows

(a) **When Goodwill is Adjusted through Partners' Capital Account**

The entry to be passed for adjustment of goodwill in this case is

Gaining Partners' Capital*/Current** A/c	Dr	[In gaining ratio]
To Sacrificing Partners' Capital*/Current** A/c		[In sacrificing ratio]

*When capitals are fluctuating **When capitals are fixed

(b) **When Goodwill is Raised and Written-off**

When goodwill is raised and credited to old partners' capital account

Goodwill A/c	Dr	[Full value of goodwill]
To Partners' Capital/Current A/c		[In old profit sharing ratio]

When goodwill is debited to partners' capital account to write-off

Partners' Capital/Current A/c	Dr	[In new profit sharing ratio]
To Goodwill A/c		

(*iii*) **Revaluation of Assets and Reassessment of Liabilities**

(a) **When Revised Values are to be Recorded in the Books of Accounts**

In this case, an account titled 'Revaluation account' or 'Profit and loss adjustment account' is opened for revaluation of assets and reassessment of liabilities.

Format of Revaluation Account

Dr **Revaluation Account** Cr

Particulars	Amt (₹)	Particulars	Amt (₹)
To Decrease in Value of Assets (Loss)	...	By Increase in Value of Assets (Profit)	...
To Increase in Value of Liabilities (Loss)	...	By Decrease in Value of Liabilities (Profit)	...
To Unrecorded Liabilities (At an agreed value)	...	By Unrecorded Assets (At an agreed value)	...
To Profit Transferred to Old Partners' Capital/Current A/c (In old ratio)	...	By Loss Transferred to Old Partners' Capital/Current A/c (In old ratio)	...

(b) **When Revised Values are not to be Recorded in the Books of Accounts**

If partners decide to record the net effect of revaluation of assets and reassessment of liabilities without affecting the old amount of assets and liabilities, then a single adjusting entry involving the capital accounts of gaining partners and sacrificing partners is passed.

The journal entries passed are

For Profit on Revaluation	Gaining Partners' Capital A/c To Sacrificing Partners' Capital A/c	Dr
For Net Loss on Revaluation	Sacrificing Partners' Capital A/c To Gaining Partners' Capital A/c	Dr

(*iv*) **Accounting Treatment of Reserves, Accumulated Profits or Losses**

(a) **When These are not Required to be Shown in the Books of the New Firm**

At the time of change in profit sharing ratio, if any reserves or accumulated profits/losses exist in the books of the firm, they are transferred to partners' capital/current accounts in their old profit sharing ratio.

The journal entries passed are

For Transfer of Reserves and Accumulated Profits	Reserve/Profit and Loss A/c	Dr	
	Workmen's Compensation Reserve A/c	Dr	[Excess of reserve over actual liability]
	Investments Fluctuation Reserve A/c	Dr	[Excess of reserve over the difference between book value and market value]
	To All Partners' Capital/Current A/c (Individually)		[In old ratio]
For Transfer of Accumulated Losses	All Partners' Capital/Current A/c (Individually)	Dr	[In old ratio]
	To Profit and Loss A/c		
	To Deferred Revenue Expenditure A/c		

(b) **When These are Required to be Shown in the Books of the New Firm**

A single adjusting entry involving the capital accounts of sacrificing and gaining partner is passed, when the partners decide to record net effect of reserves and accumulated profits/losses without affecting the old figures.

The journal entries passed are

In Case of Profit	Gaining Partner's Capital A/c To Sacrificing Partner's Capital A/c	Dr
In Case of Loss	Sacrificing Partner's Capital A/c To Gaining Partner's Capital A/c	Dr

Previous Years'
Examination Questions

1 Mark Questions

1. Anant, Gulab and Khushbu were partners in a firm sharing profits in the ratio of 5 : 3 : 2. From 1st April, 2014, they decided to share the profits equally. For this purpose, the goodwill of the firm was valued at ₹ 2,40,000.

Pass necessary journal entry for the treatment of goodwill on change in the profit sharing ratio of Anant, Gulab and Khushbu. **All India 2015**

Ans. JOURNAL

Date	Particulars		LF	Amt (Dr)	Amt (Cr)
2014 Apr 1	Gulab's Capital A/c	Dr		8,000	
	Khushbu's Capital A/c	Dr		32,000	
	To Anant's Capital A/c				40,000
	(Being share of goodwill adjusted on change in profit sharing ratio)				

Working Note

(*i*) **Calculation of Change in Profit Share of Partners**

Sacrificing/(Gaining) Share = Old Share – New Share

$$\text{Anant's Sacrifice/(Gain)} = \frac{5}{10} - \frac{1}{3} = \frac{15-10}{30} = \frac{5}{30}\ \text{Sacrifice}$$

$$\text{Gulab's Sacrifice/(Gain)} = \frac{3}{10} - \frac{1}{3} = \frac{9-10}{30} = \left(\frac{1}{30}\right)\ \text{Gain}$$

$$\text{Khushbu's Sacrifice/(Gain)} = \frac{2}{10} - \frac{1}{3} = \frac{6-10}{30} = \left(\frac{4}{30}\right)\ \text{Gain}$$

(*ii*) **Calculation of Share of Goodwill**

$$\text{Anant} = 2{,}40{,}000 \times \frac{5}{30} = ₹\ 40{,}000; \quad \text{Gulab} = 2{,}40{,}000 \times \frac{1}{30} = ₹\ 8{,}000$$

$$\text{Khushbu} = 2{,}40{,}000 \times \frac{4}{30} = ₹\ 32{,}000$$

2. Give the meaning of 'reconstitution of a partnership firm'. **All India; Delhi 2014**

Ans. Change in the existing agreement of partnership is considered as reconstitution of a partnership firm. Due to this, existing agreement comes to an end and the new agreement comes into existence and the firm continues.

3. State the ratio in which the partners share the accumulated profits when there is a change in the profit sharing ratio amongst the existing partners. **All India 2013**

Ans. Accumulated profits are distributed in old profit sharing ratio, at the time of change in profit sharing ratio amongst the existing partners.

4. State the ratio in which the partners share profits or losses on revaluation of assets and liabilities, when there is a change in profit sharing ratio amongst the existing partners. **Delhi 2013**

Ans. Revaluation profits or losses are distributed in old profit sharing ratio, at the time of change in profit sharing ratio amongst the existing partners.

5. State any two occasions on which a firm can be reconstituted. **Delhi 2012**

Or List any two situations which may result in the reconstitution of a partnership firm. **All India 2011**

Ans. A firm can be reconstituted on the following occasions (any two)

(*i*) When there is a change in the profit sharing ratio of existing partners.
(*ii*) When a new partner is admitted.
(*iii*) When an existing partner retires.
(*iv*) When an existing partner dies.

6. Why are 'reserves and surplus' distributed at the time of reconstitution of the firm? **Delhi 2010**

Ans. At the time of reconstitution of the firm, reserves and surplus should be transferred to old partners' capital/current accounts in their old profit sharing ratio because the new partner is not entitled to any share in such undistributed profits or losses as these are earned/accrued by the old partners.

4 Marks Questions

7. Asha, Rina and Chahat were partners in a firm sharing profits and losses in the ratio of 2 : 2 : 1. Their Balance Sheet as at 31st March, 2019 was as follows **CBSE 2020**

Balance Sheet of Asha, Rina and Chahat
as at 31st March, 2019

Liabilities		Amt (₹)	Assets		Amt (₹)
Creditors		12,00,000	Plant and Machinery		14,80,000
General Reserve		2,00,000	Stock		2,20,000
			Sundry Debtors	2,60,000	
Capitals			(–) Provision for		
Asha	3,00,000		Doubtful Debts	(20,000)	2,40,000
Rina	2,00,000		Bank		60,000
Chahat	1,00,000	6,00,000			
		20,00,000			20,00,000

Asha, Rina and Chahat decided to share future profits equally with effect from 1st April, 2019. For this, it was agreed that

(*i*) Goodwill of the firm be valued at ₹ 1,50,000.
(*ii*) Bad debts amounted to ₹ 40,000. A provision for doubtful debts was to be made @ 5% on debtors.

Pass the necessary journal entries to record the above transactions in the books of the firm.

Ans. **Calculation of Sacrificing/Gaining ratio**

Sacrificing Ratio = Old Ratio – New Ratio

Asha $= \frac{2}{5} - \frac{1}{3} = \frac{6-5}{15} = \frac{1}{15}$; Rina $= \frac{2}{5} - \frac{1}{3} = \frac{6-5}{15} = \frac{1}{15}$; Chahat $= \frac{1}{5} - \frac{1}{3} = \frac{3-5}{15} = \left(\frac{2}{15}\right)$

JOURNAL

Date	Particulars		LF	Amt (Dr)	Amt (Cr)
	Chahat's Capital A/c	Dr		20,000	
	To Asha's Capital A/c				10,000
	To Rina's Capital A/c				10,000
	(Being amount of goodwill adjusted)				
	Provision for Doubtful Debts A/c	Dr		20,000	
	Revaluation A/c	Dr		20,000	
	To Debtors A/c				40,000
	(Being bad debts written-off)				
	Revaluation A/c	Dr		11,000	
	To Provision for Doubtful Debts				11,000
	(Being 5% PFDD created)				

8. Hari, Kunal and Uma are partners in a firm sharing profits and losses in the ratio of 5 : 3 : 2. From 1st April, 2018 they decided to share future profits and losses in the ratio of 2 : 5 : 3. Their Balance Sheet showed a balance of ₹ 75,000 in the Profit and Loss Account and a balance of ₹ 15,000 in Investment Fluctuation Fund. For this purpose, it was agreed that

(*i*) Goodwill of the firm was valued at ₹ 3,00,000.

(*ii*) Investments (having a book value of ₹ 50,000) were valued at ₹ 35,000.

(*iii*) Stock having a book value of ₹ 50,000 be depreciated by 10%.

Pass the necessary journal entries for the above in the books of the firm. **All India 2019**

Ans. **JOURNAL**

Date	Particulars		LF	Amt (Dr)	Amt (Cr)
	Profit and Loss A/c	Dr		75,000	
	To Hari's Capital A/c				37,500
	To Kunal's Capital A/c				22,500
	To Uma's Capital A/c				15,000
	(Being balance of profit and loss distributed among partners in old ratio)				
	Kunal's Capital A/c $\left(3{,}00{,}000 \times \frac{2}{10}\right)$	Dr		60,000	
	Uma's Capital A/c $\left(3{,}00{,}000 \times \frac{1}{10}\right)$	Dr		30,000	
	To Hari's Capital A/c $\left(3{,}00{,}000 \times \frac{3}{10}\right)$				90,000
	(Being amount of goodwill adjusted)				

Date	Particulars		LF	Amt (Dr)	Amt (Cr)
	Investment Fluctuation Fund A/c	Dr		15,000	
	To Investment A/c				15,000
	(Being investment loss adjusted through investment fluctuation fund)				
	Revaluation A/c	Dr		5,000	
	To Stock A/c				5,000
	(Being value of stock depreciated)				
	Hari's Capital A/c	Dr		2,500	
	Kunal's Capital A/c	Dr		1,500	
	Uma's Capital A/c	Dr		1,000	
	To Revaluation A/c				5,000
	(Being loss on revaluation transferred to old partners' capital account in old ratio)				

Working Note

Calculation of Gaining or Sacrificing Ratio

Sacrificing Ratio = Old Ratio – New Ratio

$$\text{Hari} = \frac{5}{10} - \frac{2}{10} = \frac{3}{10};\ \text{Kunal} = \frac{3}{10} - \frac{5}{10} = \left(\frac{2}{10}\right);\ \text{Uma} = \frac{2}{10} - \frac{3}{10} = \left(\frac{1}{10}\right)$$

9. Satish and Taruna were partners in a firm sharing profits and losses in the ratio of 3 : 2. From 1st April, 2018 they decided to share profits equally. On that date, their Balance Sheet showed a credit balance of ₹ 35,000 in workmen compensation fund and ₹ 40,000 in general reserve. The goodwill of the firm on that date was valued at ₹ 50,000. The firm accepted a claim of ₹ 40,000 for workmen compensation.

Pass necessary journal entries for the above transactions on the reconstitution of the firm.
All India 2019

Ans. **Calculation of Sacrificing or Gaining Ratio**

Sacrificing Ratio = Old Share – New Share

$$\text{Satish} = \frac{3}{5} - \frac{1}{2} = \frac{6-5}{10} = \frac{1}{10}; \qquad \text{Taruna} = \frac{2}{5} - \frac{1}{2} = \frac{4-5}{10} = \left(\frac{1}{10}\right)$$

JOURNAL

Date	Particulars		LF	Amt (Dr)	Amt (Cr)
	Workmen Compensation Reserve A/c	Dr		35,000	
	Revaluation A/c	Dr		5,000	
	To Provision for Claim for Workmen Compensation Reserve A/c				40,000
	(Being the amount of estimated claim debited to workmen compensation reserve and revaluation account)				
	Satish's Capital A/c	Dr		3,000	
	Taruna's Capital A/c	Dr		2,000	
	To Revaluation A/c				5,000
	(Being loss on revaluation transferred to partner capital account in old ratio)				

Date	Particulars		LF	Amt (Dr)	Amt (Cr)
	General Reserve A/c	Dr		40,000	
	To Satish's Capital A/c				24,000
	To Taruna's Capital A/c				16,000
	(Being amount of general reserve distributed among partners in old ratio)				
	Taruna's Capital A/c	Dr		5,000	
	To Satish's Capital A/c				5,000
	(Being adjustment for goodwill made)				

10. L, M and N were partners in a firm sharing profits in the ratio of 2 : 3 : 5. From 1st April, 2018 they decided to share the profits in the ratio of 1 : 2 : 2. On this date, the Balance Sheet showed a credit balance of ₹ 1,17,000 in General Reserve and a debit balance of ₹ 35,000 in profit and loss account. The goodwill of the firm was valued at ₹ 5,00,000. The revaluation of assets and reassessment of liabilities resulted into a gain of ₹ 30,000.

Pass necessary journal entries for the above transactions on the reconstitution of the firm.
All India 2019

Ans. **JOURNAL**

Date	Particulars		LF	Amt (Dr)	Amt (Cr)
2018					
Apr 1	General Reserve A/c	Dr		1,17,000	
	To L's Capital A/c				23,400
	To M'S Capital A/c				35,100
	To N's Capital A/c				58,500
	(Being general reserve distributed)				
	L's Capital A/c	Dr		7,000	
	M's Capital A/c	Dr		10,500	
	N's Capital A/c	Dr		17,500	
	To Profit and Loss A/c				
	(Being debit balance of profit and loss transferred to partners capital account)				35,000
Apr 1	M's Capital A/c $\left(5,00,000 \times \frac{1}{10}\right)$	Dr		50,000	
	To N's Capital A/c				50,000
	(Being amount of goodwill adjusted)				
Apr 1	Revaluation A/c	Dr		30,000	
	To L's Capital A/c				6,000
	To M's Capital A/c				9,000
	To N's Capital A/c				15,000
	(Being revaluation profit distributed among partners)				

Working Note

Calculation of Sacrificing and Gaining Ratio

Sacrificing Ratio = Old Share – New Share

$$L = \frac{2}{10} - \frac{1}{5} = \frac{2-2}{10} = \text{Nil};\ M = \frac{3}{10} - \frac{2}{5} = \frac{3-4}{10} = \left(\frac{1}{10}\right);\ N = \frac{5}{10} - \frac{2}{5} = \frac{5-4}{10} = \frac{1}{10}$$

11. P, Q and R were partners in a firm sharing profits in the ratio of 1 : 1 : 2. On 31st March, 2018, their balance sheet showed a credit balance of ₹ 9,000 in the profit and loss account and a Workmen Compensation Fund of ₹ 64,000. From 1st April, 2018 they decided to share profits in the ratio of 2 : 2 : 1. For this purpose it was agreed that

(a) Goodwill of the firm was valued at ₹ 4,00,000.

(b) A claim on account of workmen compensation of ₹ 30,000 was admitted.

Pass necessary journal entries on reconstitution of the firm. **Delhi 2019**

Ans.

JOURNAL

Date	Particulars		LF	Amt (Dr)	Amt (Cr)
2018					
Mar 31	Profit and Loss A/c	Dr		9,000	
	To P's Capital A/c				2,250
	To Q's Capital A/c				2,250
	To R's Capital A/c				4,500
	(Being profit distributed among the partners)				
	Workmen Compensation Fund A/c	Dr		64,000	
	To Workmen Compensation Claim A/c				30,000
	To P's Capital A/c				8,500
	To Q's Capital A/c				8,500
	To R's Capital A/c				17,000
	(Being WCF settled and distributed)				
	P's Capital A/c	Dr		60,000	
	Q's Capital A/c	Dr		60,000	
	To R's Capital A/c				1,20,000
	(Being goodwill adjusted)				

Working Note

Calculation of Sacrificing or Gaining Ratio

Sacrificing ratio = Old share – New share

$$P = \frac{1}{4} - \frac{2}{5} = \frac{5-8}{20} = \left(\frac{3}{20}\right)$$

$$Q = \frac{1}{4} - \frac{2}{5} = \frac{5-8}{20} = \left(\frac{3}{20}\right)$$

$$R = \frac{2}{4} - \frac{1}{5} = \frac{10-4}{20} = \frac{6}{20}$$

12. Aman, Bobby and Chandani were partners in a firm sharing profit and losses in the ratio of 5 : 4 : 1. From 1st April, 2018 they decided to share profit equally. The revaluation of assets and re-assessment of liabilities resulted in a loss ₹ 5,000. The goodwill of the firm on its reconstitution was valued at ₹ 1,20,000. The firm had a balance ₹ 20,000 in general reserve.

Showing your workings clearly pass necessary journal entries on the reconstitution of the firm. **Delhi 2019**

Ans. **JOUNRAL**

Date	Particulars		LF	Amt (Dr)	Amt (Cr)
2018					
Apr 1	Aman's Capital A/c	Dr		2,500	
	Bobby's Capital A/c	Dr		2,000	
	Chandani's Capital A/c	Dr		500	
	To Revaluation A/c				5,000
	(Being loss on revaluation transferred to partners capital account in old ratio)				
	Chandani's Capital A/c	Dr		28,000	
	To Aman's Capital A/c				20,000
	To Bobby's Capital A/c				8,000
	(Being goodwill adjusted)				
	General Reserve A/c	Dr		20,000	
	To Aman's Capital A/c				10,000
	To Bobby's Capital A/c				8,000
	To Chandani's Capital A/c				2,000
	(Being general reserve distributed among old partners in old ratio)				

Working Note

Calculation of Sacrificing or Gaining Ratio

Sacrificing Ratio = Old Share – New Share

$$\text{Aman} = \frac{5}{10} - \frac{1}{3} = \frac{15-10}{30} = \frac{5}{30}; \ \text{Bobby} = \frac{4}{10} - \frac{1}{3} = \frac{12-10}{30} = \frac{2}{30}$$

$$\text{Chandani} = \frac{1}{10} - \frac{1}{3} = \frac{3-10}{30} = \left(\frac{7}{30}\right)$$

13. Radhika, Bani and Chitra were partners in a firm sharing profits and losses in the ratio of 2 : 3 : 1. With effect from 1st April, 2018 they decided to share future profits and losses in the ratio of 3 : 2 : 1. On that date their Balance Sheet showed a debit balance of ₹ 24,000 in Profit and Loss Account and a balance of ₹ 1,44,000 in general reserve. It was also agreed that:

(a) The goodwill of the firm be valued at ₹ 1,80,000.

(b) The land (having book value of ₹ 3,00,000) will be valued at ₹ 4,80,000.

Pass the necessary journal entries for the above changes. **Delhi 2019**

Ans. **JOURNAL**

Date	Particulars		LF	Amt (Dr)	Amt (Cr)
2018					
Apr 1	Radhika's Capital A/c	Dr		8,000	
	Bani's Capital A/c	Dr		12,000	
	Chitra's Capital A/c	Dr		4,000	
	To Profit and Loss A/c				24,000
	(Being amount of profit and loss debit balance distributed among old partners)				

Date	Particulars		LF	Amt (Dr)	Amt (Cr)
	General Reserve A/c	Dr		1,44,000	
	To Radhika's Capital A/c				48,000
	To Bani's Capital A/c				72,000
	To Chitra's Capital A/c				24,000
	(Being general reserve distributed)				
	Radhika's Capital A/c	Dr		30,000	
	To Bani's Capital A/c				30,000
	(Being amount of goodwill adjusted)				
	Land and Building A/c	Dr		1,80,000	
	To Revaluation A/c				1,80,000
	(Being an asset revalued)				
	Revaluation A/c	Dr		1,80,000	
	To Radhika's Capital A/c				60,000
	To Bani's Capital A/c				90,000
	To Chitra's Capital A/c				30,000
	(Being profit on revaluation distributed among partner)				

Working Notes

1. **Calculation of Sacrificing or Gaining Ratio**

Sacrificing Ratio = Old Share – New Share

$$\text{Radhika} = \frac{2}{6} - \frac{3}{6} = \left(\frac{1}{6}\right);\ \text{Bani} = \frac{3}{6} - \frac{2}{6} = \frac{1}{6};\ \text{Chitra} = \frac{1}{6} - \frac{1}{6} = \text{Nil}$$

2. Firms Goodwill = ₹ 1,80,000

$$\text{Radhika gains and Bani sacrifice} = 1,80,000 \times \frac{1}{6} = ₹\ 30,000$$

14. Kumar, Gupta and Kavita were partners in a firm sharing profits and losses equally. The firm was engaged in the storage and distribution of canned juice and its godowns were located at three different places in the city. Each godown was being managed individually by Kumar, Gupta and Kavita. Because of increase in business activities at the godown managed by Gupta, he had to devote more time.

Gupta demanded that his share in the profits of the firm be increased, to which Kumar and Kavita agreed. The new profit sharing ratio was agreed to be 1 : 2 : 1.

For this purpose the goodwill of the firm was valued at two years' purchase of the average profits of last five years. The profits of the last five years were as follows

Year	Profit (₹)
I	4,00,000
II	4,80,000
III	7,33,000
IV (Loss)	33,000
V	2,20,000

You are required to

(*i*) Calculate the goodwill of the firm.

(*ii*) Pass necessary journal entry for the treatment of goodwill on change in profit sharing ratio of Kumar, Gupta and Kavita. **Delhi 2015**

Ans. (*i*) **Calculation of Goodwill of the Firm**

$$\text{Average profits} = \frac{4{,}00{,}000 + 4{,}80{,}000 + 7{,}33{,}000 - 33{,}000 + 2{,}20{,}000}{5} = \frac{18{,}00{,}000}{5} = ₹3{,}60{,}000$$

$$\text{Goodwill} = \text{Average Profits} \times \text{Number of Years' Purchase} = 3{,}60{,}000 \times 2 = ₹7{,}20{,}000$$

(*ii*) **JOURNAL**

Date	Particulars		LF	Amt (Dr)	Amt (Cr)
	Gupta's Capital A/c	Dr		1,20,000	
	To Kumar's Capital A/c				60,000
	To Kavita's Capital A/c				60,000
	(Being recording of Gupta's share of goodwill on change in profit sharing ratio)				

Working Note

Calculation of Sacrifice or Gain of Each Partner

Sacrificing/(Gaining) Share = Old Share – New Share

$$\text{Kumar's} = \frac{1}{3} - \frac{1}{4} = \frac{4-3}{12} = \frac{1}{12} \text{ Sacrifice;} \qquad \text{Gupta's} = \frac{1}{3} - \frac{2}{4} = \frac{4-6}{12} = \left(\frac{2}{12}\right) \text{Gain}$$

$$\text{Kavita's} = \frac{1}{3} - \frac{1}{4} = \frac{4-3}{12} = \frac{1}{12} \text{ Sacrifice}$$

Calculation of Share of Goodwill

$$\text{Kumar} = 7{,}20{,}000 \times \frac{1}{12} = ₹60{,}000, \qquad \text{Gupta} = 7{,}20{,}000 \times \frac{2}{12} = ₹1{,}20{,}000$$

$$\text{Kavita} = 7{,}20{,}000 \times \frac{1}{12} = ₹60{,}000$$

15. Anita, Asha and Amrit are partners sharing profits in the ratio of 3 : 2 : 1 respectively. From 1st January, 2010, they decided to share profits in the ratio of 1 : 1 : 1. The partnership deed provided that in the event of any change in profit sharing ratio, the goodwill should be valued at three years' purchase of the average of five years' profits. The profits and losses of the preceding five years are

Year	Profit (₹)
2005	1,20,000
2006	3,00,000
2007	3,40,000
2008	3,80,000
2009	1,40,000 (Loss)

Showing the working clearly, give the necessary journal entry to record the above change. **Delhi (C) 2010**

Ans Solve as Q no. 14 on page 57 and 58.

Debit Amrit's Capital Account with ₹ 1,00,000 and Credit Anita's Capital Account with ₹ 1,00,000.

6 Marks Questions

16. P, Q and R were partners in a firm sharing profits and losses in the ratio of 3 : 2 : 1. On 31st March, 2018 their Balance Sheet was as follows

Balance Sheet of P, Q and R
as at 31st March, 2018

Liabilities		Amt (₹)	Assets	Amt (₹)
Creditors		50,000	Cash in Hand	40,000
General Reserve		60,000	Cash at Bank	2,00,000
Capital:			Stock	50,000
P	2,00,000		Debtors	60,000
Q	3,00,000		Fixed Assets	5,60,000
R	3,00,000	8,00,000		
		9,10,000		9,10,000

On the above date the firm was reconstituted and it was decided that

(*i*) The new profit sharing ratio will be 2 : 2 : 1.

(*ii*) Bad debts ₹ 6,000 were to be written-off and a provision of ₹ 3,000 was to be made for bad and doubtful debts.

(*iii*) The capital of the partners will be adjusted in the new firms in their profit sharing ratio. For this, partners' current accounts will be opened.

Pass the necessary journal entries on the reconstitution of the firm. **All India 2019**

Ans. **JOURNAL**

Date	Particulars		LF	Amt (Dr)	Amt (Cr)
	General Reserve A/c	Dr		60,000	
	To P's Capital A/c				30,000
	To Q's Capital A/c				20,000
	To R's Capital A/c				10,000
	(Being general reserve distributed among old partners in old ratio)				
	Revaluation A/c	Dr		9,000	
	To Debtors				6,000
	To Provision for Bad and Doubtful Debts				3,000
	(Being bad debts written-off and provision created)				
	P's Capital A/c	Dr		4,500	
	Q's Capital A/c	Dr		3,000	
	R's Capital A/c	Dr		1,500	
	To Revaluation A/c				9,000
	(Being loss on revaluation transferred to partners capital account)				
	R's Current A/c	Dr		1,38,300	
	To P's Current A/c				1,14,900
	To Q's Current A/c				23,400
	(Being capital adjusted in new ratio)				

Particulars	P (₹)	Q (₹)	R (₹)	Total (₹)
Opening Balance	2,00,000	3,00,000	3,00,000	8,00,000
(+) General Reserve	30,000	20,000	10,000	60,000
(–) Revalued Loss	(4,500)	(3,000)	(1,500)	(9,000)
	2,25,500	3,17,000	3,08,500	8,51,000
To be adjusted in new ratio i.e., 2 : 2 : 1	3,40,400	3,40,400	1,70,200	8,51,000
	1,14,900	23,400	1,38,300	
	Cr	Cr	Dr	

17. Parth, Raman and Zaisha are partners in a firm manufacturing furniture. They have been sharing profits and losses in the ratio of 5 : 3 : 2. From 1st April, 2017 they decided to share future profits and losses in the ratio of 2 : 5 : 3. Their Balance Sheet showed a debit balance of ₹ 4,000 in Profit and Loss Account; balance of ₹ 36,000 in General Reserve and a balance of ₹ 12,000 in Workmen's Compensation Reserve. It was agreed that

(*i*) The goodwill of the firm be valued at ₹ 76,000.

(*ii*) The stock (book value of ₹ 40,000) was to be depreciated by 8%.

(*iii*) Creditors amounting to ₹ 900 were not likely to be claimed.

(*iv*) Claim on account of Workmen's Compensation amounted to ₹ 20,000.

(*v*) Investments (bool value ₹ 38,000) were revalued at ₹ 40,000.

Pass necessary journal entries for the above. **Compartment 2018 Modified**

Ans.

JOURNAL

Date	Particulars	LF	Amt (Dr)	Amt (Cr)
2017				
Apr 1	Parth's Capital A/c Dr		2,000	
	Raman's Capital A/c Dr		1,200	
	Zaisha's Capital A/c Dr		800	
	To Profit and Loss A/c			4,000
	(Being debit balance of P and L account distributed among partners in old ratio)			
Apr 1	General Reserve A/c Dr		36,000	
	To Parth's Capital A/c			18,000
	To Raman's Capital A/c			10,800
	To Zaisha's Capital A/c			7,200
	(Being general reserve distributed in old ratio)			
	Revaluation A/c Dr		8,000	
	Workmen Compensation Reserve A/c Dr		12,000	
	To Workmen Compensation Claim A/c			20,000
	(Being claim for workmen compensation provided)			
	Raman's Capital A/c Dr		15,200	
	Zaisha's Capital A/c Dr		7,600	
	To Parth's Capital A/c			22,800
	(Being adjustment made for goodwill due to change in profit sharing ratio)			

Date	Particulars		LF	Amt (Dr)	Amt (Cr)
	Revaluation A/c	Dr		3,200	
	To Stock A/c				3,200
	(Being decrease in the value of assets)				
	Creditors A/c	Dr		900	
	Investment A/c	Dr		2,000	
	To Revaluation A/c				2,900
	(Being creditors not likely to be claimed and increase in the value of investment recorded)				
	Parth's Capital A/c	Dr		4,150	
	Raman's Capital A/c	Dr		2,490	
	Zaisha's Capital A/c	Dr		1,660	
	To Revaluation A/c				8,300
	(Being loss on revaluation transferred to partners capital account)				

Working Note

Calculation of Gaining/Sacrificing Ratio

Sacrificing Ratio = Old Ratio – New Ratio

$$\text{Parth} = \frac{5}{10} - \frac{2}{10} = \frac{3}{10}; \ \text{Raman} = \frac{3}{10} - \frac{5}{10} = \left(\frac{2}{10}\right) \text{Gaining} ; \ \text{Zaisha} = \frac{2}{10} - \frac{3}{10} = \left(\frac{1}{10}\right) \text{Gaining}$$

18. A, B, C and D were partners in a firm sharing profits in the ratio of 3 : 2 : 3 : 2. On 1st April, 2016 their balance sheet was as follows

Balance Sheet

as at 1st April, 2016

Liabilities		Amt (₹)	Assets	Amt (₹)
Sundry Creditors		90,000	Fixed Assets	8,25,000
Workmen Compensation Reserve		25,000	Current Assets	3,00,000
Capital A/cs				
A	2,00,000			
B	2,50,000			
C	2,50,000			
D	3,10,000	10,10,000		
		11,25,000		11,25,000

From the above date the partners decided to share the future profits in the ratio of 4 : 3 : 2 : 1. For this purpose the goodwill of the firm was valued at ₹ 2,70,000.

It was also considered that

(*i*) Claim against workmen compensation reserve will be estimated at ₹ 30,000 and fixed assets will be depreciated by 25,000.

(*ii*) The capitals of the partners will be adjusted according to the new profit sharing ratio by opening current accounts of the partners.

Prepare revaluation account, partners' capital accounts and the balance sheet of the reconstituted firm. **All India 2017**

Ans. Dr **Revaluation Account** Cr

Particulars	Amt (₹)	Particulars		Amt (₹)
To Depreciation on Fixed Assets A/c	25,000	By Loss on Revaluation Transferred to Capital A/cs		
To Provision for Workmen Compensation Fund	5,000	A	9,000	
		B	6,000	
		C	9,000	
		D	6,000	30,000
	30,000			30,000

Dr **Partners' Capital Account** Cr

Particulars	A (₹)	B (₹)	C (₹)	D (₹)	Particulars	A (₹)	B (₹)	C (₹)	D (₹)
To Revl. A/c	9,000	6,000	9,000	6,000	By Balance b/d	2,00,000	2,50,000	2,50,000	3,10,000
To C's Cap. A/c	27,000	—	—	—	By A's Cap. A/c	—	—	27,000	—
To D's Cap. A/c	—	27,000	—	—	By B's Cap. A/c	—	—	—	27,000
To Current A/cs (Balancing Figure)	—	—	72,000	2,33,000	By Current A/c (Balancing Figure)	2,28,000	77,000	—	—
To Balance c/d	3,92,000	2,94,000	1,96,000	98,000					
	4,28,000	3,27,000	2,77,000	3,37,000		4,28,000	3,27,000	2,77,000	3,37,000

Balance Sheet
as at 1st April, 2016

Liabilities		Amt (₹)	Assets		Amt (₹)
Capital A/cs			Fixed Assets	8,25,000	
A	3,92,000		(−) Depreciation	(25,000)	8,00,000
B	2,94,000		Current Assets		3,00,000
C	1,96,000		Current A/cs		
D	98,000	9,80,000	C	72,000	
Current A/cs			D	2,33,000	3,05,000
A	2,28,000				
B	77,000	3,05,000			
Workmen Compensation Reserve		30,000			
Sundry Creditors		90,000			
		14,05,000			14,05,000

Working Notes

1. **Calculation of Sacrificing/(Gaining) Share**

Sacrificing/(Gaining) Share = Old Share − New Share

$A = \frac{3}{10} - \frac{4}{10} = \frac{3-4}{10} = \left(\frac{1}{10}\right)$ Gain; $B = \frac{2}{10} - \frac{3}{10} = \frac{2-3}{10} = \left(\frac{1}{10}\right)$ Gain

$C = \frac{3}{10} - \frac{2}{10} = \frac{3-2}{10} = \frac{1}{10}$ Sacrifice; $D = \frac{2}{10} - \frac{1}{10} = \frac{2-1}{10} = \frac{1}{10}$ Sacrifice

2. **Calculation of Goodwill**

A's share of goodwill $= 2{,}70{,}000 \times \frac{1}{10} =$ ₹ 27,000 ; B's share of goodwill $= 2{,}70{,}000 \times \frac{1}{10} =$ ₹ 27,000

C's share of goodwill $= 2{,}70{,}000 \times \frac{1}{10} =$ ₹ 27,000 ; D's share of goodwill $= 2{,}70{,}000 \times \frac{1}{10} =$ ₹ 27,000

3. **Journal Entry Showing Adjustment for Goodwill**

A's Capital A/c	Dr	27,000	
B's Capital A/c	Dr	27,000	
To C's Capital A/c			27,000
To D's Capital A/c			27,000

While posting in ledger, it has been assumed that A pays to C and B pays to D.

4. **Calculation of Adjusted Capitals**

Adjusted capital of A = ₹ 1,64,000
Adjusted capital of B = ₹ 2,17,000
Adjusted capital of C = ₹ 2,68,000
Adjusted capital of D = ₹ 3,31,000
Total combined capital = ₹ 9,80,000

New capital of A $= 9{,}80{,}000 \times \frac{4}{10} =$ ₹ 3,92,000 ; New capital of B $= 9{,}80{,}000 \times \frac{3}{10} =$ ₹ 2,94,000

New capital of C $= 9{,}80{,}000 \times \frac{2}{10} =$ ₹ 1,96,000 ; New capital of D $= 9{,}80{,}000 \times \frac{1}{10} =$ ₹ 98,000

19. S, T, U and V were partners in a firm sharing profits in the ratio of 4 : 3 : 2 : 1. On 1st April, 2016 their balance sheet was as follows

Balance Sheet
as at 1st April, 2016

Liabilities		Amt (₹)	Assets	Amt (₹)
Sundry Creditors		80,000	Fixed Assets	4,40,000
Workmen Compensation Reserve		60,000	Current Assets	2,00,000
Capital A/cs				
S	2,00,000			
T	1,50,000			
U	1,00,000			
V	50,000	5,00,000		
		6,40,000		6,40,000

From the above date the partners decided to share the future profits in 3 : 1 : 2 : 4 ratio. For this purpose the goodwill of the firm was valued at ₹ 90,000.

The partners also agreed for the following

(*i*) The claim for workmen compensation has been estimated at ₹ 70,000.

(*ii*) To adjust the capitals of the partners according to new profit sharing ratio by opening partners' current accounts.

Prepare revaluation account, partners' capital accounts and the balance sheet of the reconstituted firm. **Delhi 2017**

Ans. Solve as Q no. 18 on page 61-63.

Loss on Revaluation : S = ₹ 4,000, T = ₹ 3,000, U = ₹ 2,000, V = ₹ 1,000

Balance in Partners' Capital Account : S = ₹ 1,47,000, T = ₹ 49,000, U = ₹ 98,000, V = ₹ 1,96,000.

Balance in Partners' Current Account : S = ₹ 58,000 (Cr), T = ₹ 1,16,000 (Cr), V = ₹ 1,74,000 (Dr)

Total of Balance Sheet = ₹ 8,14,000

20. R, S and T were partners in a firm sharing profits in 1 : 2 : 3 ratio. Their balance sheet as at 31st March, 2015 was as follows

Balance Sheet
as at 31st March, 2015

Liabilities		Amt (₹)	Assets	Amt (₹)
Creditors		50,000	Land	50,000
Bills Payable		20,000	Building	50,000
General Reserve		30,000	Plant	1,00,000
Capital A/cs			Stock	40,000
R	1,00,000		Debtors	30,000
S	50,000		Bank	5,000
T	25,000	1,75,000		
		2,75,000		2,75,000

From 1st April, 2015 R, S and T decided to share the future profits equally. For this purpose it was decided that

(*i*) Goodwill of the firm be valued at ₹ 1,50,000.

(*ii*) Land be revalued at ₹ 80,000 and building be depreciated by 6%.

(*iii*) Creditors of ₹ 6,000 were not likely to be claimed and hence be written-off.

Prepare revaluation account, partners' capital accounts and the balance sheet of the reconstituted firm. **All India 2016**

Ans. Dr **Revaluation Account** Cr

Particulars		Amt (₹)	Particulars	Amt (₹)
To Building A/c		3,000	By Land A/c	30,000
To Profit Transferred to Capital A/cs			By Creditors A/c	6,000
R	5,500			
S	11,000			
T	16,500	33,000		
		36,000		36,000

Dr **Partners' Capital Account** Cr

Particulars	R (₹)	S (₹)	T (₹)	Particulars	R (₹)	S (₹)	T (₹)
To T's Capital A/c (Goodwill)	25,000	—	—	By Balance b/d	1,00,000	50,000	25,000
To Balance c/d	85,500	71,000	81,500	By Revaluation A/c (Profit)	5,500	11,000	16,500
				By R's Capital A/c	—	—	25,000
				By General Reserve A/c	5,000	10,000	15,000
	1,10,500	71,000	81,500		1,10,500	71,000	81,500

Balance Sheet
as at 1st April, 2015

Liabilities		Amt (₹)	Assets		Amt (₹)
Creditors	50,000		Land	50,000	
(–) Written-off	(6,000)	44,000	(+) Appreciation	30,000	80,000
Bills Payable		20,000	Building	50,000	
Capital A/cs			(–) Depreciation	(3,000)	47,000
R	85,500		Plant		1,00,000
S	71,000		Stock		40,000
T	81,500	2,38,000	Debtors		30,000
			Bank		5,000
		3,02,000			3,02,000

Working Note

Calculation of Sacrifice or Gain of Each Partner

Sacrificing/(Gaining) Share = Old Share – New Share

$R = \frac{1}{6} - \frac{1}{3} = \frac{1-2}{6} = \left(\frac{1}{6}\right)$ Gain ; $S = \frac{2}{6} - \frac{1}{3} = \frac{2-2}{6} =$ Nil ; $T = \frac{3}{6} - \frac{1}{3} = \frac{3-2}{6} = \frac{1}{6}$ Sacrifice

Firm's goodwill = ₹ 1,50,000

R will pay for goodwill $= 1,50,000 \times \frac{1}{6} =$ ₹ 25,000

R's Capital A/c	Dr	25,000	
To T's Capital A/c			25,000

21. Ashok, Bhim and Chetan were partners in a firm sharing profits in the ratio of 3 : 2 : 1. Their balance sheet as at 31st March, 2015 was as follows

Balance Sheet
as at 31st March, 2015

Liabilities	Amt (₹)	Assets	Amt (₹)
Creditors	1,00,000	Land	1,00,000
Bills Payable	40,000	Building	1,00,000
General Reserve	60,000	Plant	2,00,000

Liabilities		Amt (₹)	Assets	Amt (₹)
Capital A/cs			Stock	80,000
Ashok	2,00,000		Debtors	60,000
Bhim	1,00,000		Bank	10,000
Chetan	50,000	3,50,000		
		5,50,000		5,50,000

Ashok, Bhim and Chetan decided to share the future profits equally, with effect from 1st April, 2015. For this it was agreed that

(*i*) Goodwill of the firm be valued at ₹ 3,00,000.

(*ii*) Land be revalued at ₹ 1,60,000 and building be depreciated by 6%.

(*iii*) Creditors of ₹ 12,000 were not likely to be claimed and hence be written off.

Prepare revaluation account, partners' capital accounts and balance sheet of the reconstituted firm. **Delhi 2016**

Ans. Solve as Q no. 20 on page 64 and 65.
Profit on Revaluation: Ashok = ₹ 33,000, Bhim = ₹ 22,000, Chetan = ₹ 11,000;
Balance in Partners' Capital Account: Ashok = ₹ 3,13,000, Bhim = ₹ 1,42,000, Chetan = ₹ 21,000;
Total of Balance Sheet = ₹ 6,04,000.

Multiple Choice Questions

(1 Mark)

1. Any change in the relationship of existing partners which results in an end of the existing agreement and entering into a new agreement is called **CBSE Term I 2021**

(a) Revaluation of partnership firm
(b) Reconstitution of partnership firm
(c) Dissolution of partnership firm
(d) Amalgamation of partnership firms

2. Malika , Meera and Madhu were partners sharing profits in the ratio of 2 : 2 : 1. They decided to share future profits in the ratio of 7 : 5 : 3 with effect from 1st April, 2021. Their balance sheet as on that date showed a balance of ₹ 30,000 in advertisement suspense account. Amount, that will be debited/credited to the capital accounts of Malika, Meera and Madhu if they decide to carry forward the amount of advertisement suspense account. **CBSE Term I 2021**

(a) ₹ 12,000 (Dr); ₹ 12,000 (Dr) and ₹ 6,000 (Dr) respectively to the capital accounts of Malika, Meera and Madhu.
(b) Debit ₹ 10,000 each to all partner's capital accounts.
(c) Debit Meera's Capital A/c and credit Malika's Capital A/c by ₹ 2,000.
(d) Debit Malika's Capital A/c and credit Meera's Capital A/c by ₹ 2,000 each.

Hint: Gaining ratio

Malika $= \frac{7}{15} - \frac{2}{5} = \frac{1}{15}$

Meera $= \frac{5}{15} - \frac{2}{5} = \left(\frac{1}{15}\right)$; Madhu $= \frac{3}{15} - \frac{1}{5} =$ Nil

Amount to be compensated by Malika

$= 30{,}000 \times \frac{1}{15} =$ ₹ 2,000

3. Arun, Babita and Charu are partners in a firm sharing profits in the ratio of 3 : 3 : 2. They decided to share future profits and losses in the ratio of 1 : 1 : 1 with effect from 1st April, 2021. They decided to record the effect of the following without affecting their book values.

(*i*) Profit and Loss A/c (Cr) ₹ 8,000
(*ii*) General Reserve ₹ 4,000.

The necessary adjusting entry for the same will be **CBSE Term I 2021**

(a)	Charu's Capital A/c	Dr	1,000	
	To Arun's Capital A/c			500
	To Babita's Capital A/c			500
(b)	Arun's Capital A/c	Dr	500	
	Babita's Capital A/c	Dr	500	
	To Charu's Capital A/c			1,000

(c) Charu's Capital A/c Dr 1,000
  To Babita's Capital A/c 1,000

(d) Charu's Capital A/c Dr 3,000
  To Arun's Capital A/c 1,500
  To Babita's Capital A/c 1,500

Hint: Sacrificing /(Gaining) Ratio

Arun $= \frac{3}{8} - \frac{1}{3} = \frac{1}{24}$; Babita $= \frac{3}{8} - \frac{1}{3} = \frac{1}{24}$

Charu $= \frac{2}{8} - \frac{1}{3} = (2/24)$

Amount to be compensated by Charu

$= (8{,}000 + 4{,}000) \times \frac{2}{24} =$ ₹ 1,000

4. Which of the following is used to find out sacrificing ratio?

(a) Old Share – New Share
(b) New Share – Old Share
(c) Old Share – Gain Share
(d) None of the above

5. X, Y and Z are partners sharing profits and losses in the ratio of 5: 4 : 1. Calculate sacrificing or gaining share for each if Z acquires $\frac{1}{10}$th share of X and $\frac{1}{2}$ share of Y.

(a) X Sacrifice $= \frac{5}{100}$, Y Sacrifice $= \frac{20}{100}$, Z Sacrifice $= \frac{25}{100}$

(b) X Sacrifice $= \frac{5}{100}$, Y Sacrifice $= \frac{20}{100}$, Z Gains $= \frac{25}{100}$

(c) X Gains $= \frac{5}{100}$, Y Gains $= \frac{20}{100}$, Z Sacrifice $= \frac{25}{100}$

(d) None of the above

Hint: X Sacrifice $= \frac{1}{10} \times \frac{5}{10} = \frac{5}{100}$;

Y Sacrifice $= \frac{1}{2} \times \frac{4}{10} = \frac{4}{20} \times \frac{5}{5} = \frac{20}{100}$

Z gains $= \frac{5}{100} + \frac{20}{100} = \frac{25}{100}$

6. 'P', 'Q' and 'R' are partners sharing profits and losses in the ratio of 5 : 3 : 2. Their new profit sharing ratio will be equal. Which partner has sacrificed and by how much?

(a) $Q = \frac{4}{30}$ (b) $R = \frac{1}{30}$

(c) $P = \frac{5}{30}$ (d) $Q = \frac{1}{30}$ and $R = \frac{4}{30}$

Hint: Sacrificing Ratio = Old Share – New Share

$P = \frac{5}{10} - \frac{1}{3} = \frac{15-10}{30} = \frac{5}{30}$; $Q = \frac{3}{10} - \frac{1}{3} = \frac{9-10}{30}$

$= \left(\frac{1}{30}\right)$; $R = \frac{2}{10} - \frac{1}{3} = \frac{6-10}{30} = \left(\frac{4}{30}\right)$

After the change in profit sharing ratio, only P has sacrificed 5/30 of his share. Q and R have gained.

7. Reserves are distributed in old partners in .... ratio.

(a) old (b) gain (c) new (d) sacrifice

Hint: At the time of reconstitution of firm, all reserves/profits are distributed in old partners in their old ratio. This is because it represents undistributed profits earned by old partners.

8. The entry to be passed for adjustment of goodwill when there is a change in profit (loss) sharing ratio of partners, without opening goodwill account is

(a) Sacrificing Partners' Capital A/c Dr
  To Gaining Partners' Capital A/c

(b) Gaining Partners' Capital A/c Dr
  To Sacrificing Partners' Capital A/c

(c) Gaining Partners' Current A/c Dr
  To Sacrificing Partners' Current A/c

(d) Either (b) or (c)

Hint: If partners decide to change their profit sharing ratio, the gaining partner must compensate the sacrificing partner on the basis of goodwill. So, gaining partner's capital or current account is debited in gaining ratio and sacrificing partner's capital or current account is credited.

9. When a firm is reconstituted, reserves and accumulated profits are distributed among partners by passing the following journal entry.

(a) Reserves/Profit and Loss A/c Dr
Workmen's Compensation Reserve A/c Dr
Investment Fluctuation Reserve A/c Dr
To All Partner's Capital A/c

(b) Reserves/Profit and Loss A/c Dr
Workmen's Compensation Reserve A/c Dr
Investment Fluctuation Reserve A/c Dr
To All Partner's Current A/c

(c) Either (a) or (b)

(d) None of the above

Hint: Whenever partners share reserves or profits or any other incomes then their capital is increased, so it will be credited and the reserves or profits or incomes account is closed, so it is debited. When partners use fluctuating capital method, then their capital accounts and when they follow fixed capital method, their current accounts will be credited.

10. If their is a change in profit sharing ratio of existing partners and the question is silent about investment fluctuation reserve, then it is distributed among partners in

(a) old ratio (b) new ratio
(c) sacrificing ratio (d) gaining ratio

11. Revaluation account is .... account in nature.

(a) real
(b) personal
(c) nominal
(d) None of the above

Hint: Since, revaluation account is only for revaluation of assets or liabilities, therefore it results in profit or loss to partners of firm. So, it is not personal or real account. It is a nominal account.

12. Whenever revaluation account is prepared, the journal entry for unrecorded assets is

(a) Unrecorded Assets A/c Dr
To Revaluation A/c

(b) Revaluation A/c Dr
To Unrecorded Assets A/c

(c) Revaluation A/c Dr
To Partner's Capital A/c

(d) None of the above

Hint: Unrecorded assets are debited as they are not recorded in books as it will cause assets of the firm to increase and revaluation account is credited.

ANSWERS

1. *(b)*	2. *(d)*	3. *(a)*	4. *(a)*	5. *(b)*	6. *(c)*	7. *(a)*	8. *(d)*	9. *(c)*	10. *(a)*
11. *(c)*	12. *(a)*								

CHAPTER 03

Reconstitution of a Partnership Firm: Admission of a Partner

TOPIC 1

Introduction

Admission of a partner is one of the modes of reconstituting the firm under which old partnership comes to an end and a new one between all partners (including incoming partner) comes into existence. According to Section 31(1) of Indian Partnership Act, 1932, "A new partner can be admitted only with the consent of all the existing partners".

A new partner is admitted for the following purposes

(*i*) For procuring additional capital.

(*ii*) For acquiring additional managerial skills.

(*iii*) To benefit from the goodwill of the admitted partner.

(*iv*) To benefit from the efficiency of an experienced person.

A newly admitted partner acquires following two main rights in the firm

(*i*) Share in the future profits of the firm-goodwill brought in for this right.

(*ii*) Share in the assets of the firm-capital brought in for this right.

In addition to the above two main rights, a newly admitted partner also acquires the following rights

(*i*) Right to participate in the affairs of the business.

(*ii*) Right to inspect the books of accounts.

(*iii*) Right to be consulted before taking a decision which affects the business.

Effects of Admission of a New Partner

On admission of a new partner

(*i*) Old partnership comes to an end and new partnership comes into existence and the firm continues.

(*ii*) The combined share of the old partners gets reduced as the incoming partner becomes entitled to share future profits of the firm.

(*iii*) Incoming partner contributes an agreed amount of capital to the firm.

(*iv*) Incoming partner becomes liable for the liabilities of the firm and also acquires right on the assets.

(*v*) Adjustment is made in regard to accumulated profits and losses.

(*vi*) Assets are revalued and liabilities are reassessed. The net change is adjusted in existing or old partners' capital accounts.

(*vii*) Goodwill of the firm is valued. It is to be paid to sacrificing partners by the gaining partners through their capital accounts.

Adjustments Required at the Time of Admission of a New Partner

(*i*) Calculation of new profit sharing ratio and sacrificing ratio.

(*ii*) Adjustment for goodwill.

(*iii*) Adjustment for profit/loss arising from revaluation of assets and reassessment of liabilities.

(*iv*) Adjustment for accumulated profits, reserves and losses.

(*v*) Adjustment for capital. (if agreed)

New Profit Sharing Ratio

It is the ratio in which all the partners (including incoming partner) share the future profits and losses of the firm.

New Profit Sharing Ratio
= Old Share – Sacrificing Share

Sacrificing Ratio

It is the ratio in which the old partners have agreed to sacrifice their share of profits in favour of new or incoming partner.

Sacrificing Ratio = Old Share – New Share

NOTE Rest of the adjustments have been discussed in the subsequent topics.

Previous Years' Examination Questions

1 Mark Questions

1. Puneet and Deepak were in partnership sharing profits and losses in the ratio of 2 : 1. They admitted Manya as a new partner. Manya brought ₹ 1,00,000 as her share of goodwill premium, which was entirely credited to Puneet's capital account. On the date of admission, goodwill of the firm was valued at ₹ 3,00,000. Calculate the new profit sharing ratio of Puneet, Deepak and Manya. **CBSE 2020**

Ans Manya's Share $= \dfrac{\text{Share of Goodwill She Brought}}{\text{Firm's Total Goodwill}}$

$= \dfrac{1,00,000}{3,00,000} = \dfrac{1}{3}$

Puneet and Deepak's old share = 2:1

Puneet's New Share

$= \text{Old share} - \text{Sacrificing share} = \dfrac{2}{3} - \dfrac{1}{3} = \dfrac{1}{3}$

New Ratio of Puneet, Deepak and Manya

$\Rightarrow \dfrac{1}{3} : \dfrac{1}{3} : \dfrac{1}{3}$; i.e. 1 : 1 : 1

2. A and B were partners in a firm sharing profits in the ratio of 3 : 2. C and D were admitted as new partners. A sacrificed $\frac{1}{4}$th of his share in favour of C and B sacrificed 50% of his share in favour of D. Calculate the new profit sharing ratio of A, B, C and D. **All India 2019**

Ans. A sacrifice in favour of C $= \dfrac{1}{4} \times \dfrac{3}{5} = \dfrac{3}{20}$

B sacrifice in favour of D $= 50\% \times \dfrac{2}{5} = \dfrac{2}{10}$

A's new share $= \dfrac{3}{5} - \dfrac{3}{20} = \dfrac{12-3}{20} = \dfrac{9}{20}$

B's new share $= \dfrac{2}{5} - \dfrac{2}{10} = \dfrac{4-2}{10} = \dfrac{2}{10} \times \dfrac{2}{2} = \dfrac{4}{20}$

C's new share $= \dfrac{3}{20}$; D's new share $= \dfrac{2}{10} \times \dfrac{2}{2} = \dfrac{4}{20}$

New ratio = 9 : 4 : 3 : 4

3. Kiya and Leela are partners sharing profits in the ratio of 3 : 2. Kiran was admitted as a new partner with $\frac{1}{5}$ th share in the profits and brought in ₹ 24,000 as her share of goodwill premium that was credited to the capital accounts of Kiya and Leela respectively with ₹ 18,000 and ₹ 6,000. Calculate the new profit sharing ratio of Kiya, Leela and Kiran. **All India 2019**

Ans. Premium for goodwill ₹ 24,000 brought in by new partner Kiran was distributed among old partners was ₹ 18,000 and ₹ 6,000, *i.e.* in the sacrificing ratio of 3 : 1.

$$\text{Now, Kiya sacrifice} = \frac{3}{4} \times \frac{1}{5} = \frac{3}{20}$$

$$\text{Leela sacrifice} = \frac{1}{4} \times \frac{1}{5} = \frac{1}{20}$$

$$\text{Kiya's new share} = \frac{3}{5} - \frac{3}{20} = \frac{12-3}{20} = \frac{9}{20}$$

$$= \frac{12-3}{20} = \frac{9}{20}$$

$$\text{Leela's new share} = \frac{2}{5} - \frac{1}{20} = \frac{8-1}{20} = \frac{7}{20}$$

$$\text{Kiran's new share} = \frac{3}{20} + \frac{1}{20} = \frac{3+1}{20} = \frac{4}{20}$$

$$= \frac{3+1}{20} = \frac{4}{20}$$

$\therefore$ New ratio = 9 : 7 : 4

4. Atul and Neera were partners in a firm sharing profits in the ratio of 3 : 2. They admitted Mitali as a new partner. Goodwill of the firm was valued at ₹ 2,00,000. Mitali brings her share of goodwill premium of ₹ 20,000 in cash, which is entirely credited to Atul's capital account. Calculate the new profit sharing ratio. **Delhi 2019**

Ans. Firms goodwill = ₹ 2,00,000

Premium for goodwill brought in by new partner Mitali = ₹ 20,000

$$\text{So, Mitali's share} = \frac{20,000}{2,00,000} = \frac{1}{10}\text{ th}$$

Premium for goodwill is entirely credited to Atul's capital account means only Atul sacrifice.

$$\text{So, Atul's sacrificing ratio} = \frac{1}{10}$$

$$\therefore \text{Atul's new share} = \frac{3}{5} - \frac{1}{10} = \frac{6-1}{10} = \frac{5}{10}$$

$$\text{Neera's new share} = \frac{2}{5} \times \frac{2}{2} = \frac{4}{10}$$

$$\text{Mitali's new share} = \frac{1}{10} = \frac{1}{10}$$

New ratio = 5 : 4 : 1

5. Amit and Beena were partners in a firm sharing profits and losses in the ratio of 3 : 1. Chaman was admitted as a new partner for $\frac{1}{6}$ th share in the period.

Chaman acquired $\frac{2}{5}$ th of his share from Amit. How much share did Chaman acquire from Beena? **CBSE 2018**

Ans. $\text{Chaman's share} = \frac{1}{6}$

$$\text{Share acquired from Amit} = \frac{2}{5} \times \frac{1}{6} = \frac{2}{30}$$

Share acquired from Beena = Chaman's share − Share acquired from Amit

$$\text{Share acquired from Beena} = \frac{1}{6} - \frac{2}{30} = \frac{5-2}{30} = \frac{3}{30}$$

6. A and B were partners in a firm sharing profits and losses in the ratio of 5 : 3. They admitted C as a new partner. The new profit sharing ratio between A, B and C was 3 : 2 : 3. A surrendered 1/5th of his share in favour of C. Calculate B's sacrifice. **All India 2017**

Ans. **Calculation of B's Sacrifice**

B's Sacrifice = Old Share − New Share

$$= \frac{3}{8} - \frac{2}{8} = \frac{3-2}{8} = \frac{1}{8}$$

7. Durga and Naresh were partners in a firm. They wanted to admit five more members in the firm. List any two categories of individuals other than minors who cannot be admitted by them. **All India 2017**

Or Gupta and Sharma were partners in a firm. They wanted to admit two more members in the firm. List the categories of individuals other than minors who cannot be admitted by them. **Delhi 2017**

Ans. The individuals other than minors who cannot be admitted by the them are

(*i*) Person of unsound mind

(*ii*) Person disqualified by law

8. A and B were partners in a firm sharing profits and losses in the ratio of 4 : 3. They admitted C as a new partner. The new profit sharing ratio between A, B and C was 3 : 2 : 2. A surrendered 1/4 of his share in favour of C. Calculate B's sacrifice. **Delhi 2017**

Ans. Solve as Q no. 6 on page 71, B's sacrifice $= \frac{1}{7}$

9. P, Q and R were partners in a firm sharing profits in the ratio of 3 : 2 : 1. They admitted S as a new partner for $\frac{1}{8}$th share in the profits which he acquired $\frac{1}{16}$th from P and $\frac{1}{16}$th from Q. Calculate new profit sharing ratio of P, Q, R and S. **Delhi; All India 2016**

Ans. Profit sharing ratio of P : Q : R = 3 : 2 : 1

S is admitted for $\frac{1}{8}$th share which he acquires $\frac{1}{16}$th from P and $\frac{1}{16}$th from Q.

$$\text{P's new share} = \frac{3}{6} - \frac{1}{16} = \frac{24-3}{48} = \frac{21}{48}$$

$$\text{Q's new share} = \frac{2}{6} - \frac{1}{16} = \frac{16-3}{48} = \frac{13}{48}$$

$$\text{R's share} = \frac{1}{6} \times \frac{8}{8} = \frac{8}{48}$$

$$\text{S's share} = \frac{1}{8} \times \frac{6}{6} = \frac{6}{48}$$

New profit sharing ratio of

P : Q : R : S is

21 : 13 : 8 : 6

10. Nishtha and Anshu were partners sharing profits in the ratio of 3 : 2. They admitted Jyoti as a new partner for 3/10th share which she acquired 2/10th from Nishtha and 1/10th from Anshu.

Calculate the new profit sharing ratio of Nishtha, Anshu and Jyoti. **All India (C) 2016**

Ans. Solve as Q no. 9 on page 97.
New profit sharing ratio of
Nishtha : Anshu : Jyoti = 4 : 3 : 3

11. Anurag and Bhawana entered into partnership on 1st April, 2014. On 1st January, 2015 they admitted Monika as a new partner for 3/10th share in the profits which she acquired equally from Anurag and Bhawana. The new profit sharing ratio of Anurag, Bhawana and Monika was 4 : 3 : 3. Calculate the profit sharing ratio of Anurag and Bhawana at the time of forming the partnership. **Foreign 2015**

Ans. New ratio = 4 : 3 : 3

Old Share = New Share + Share Sacrificed

$$\text{Anurag} = \frac{4}{10} + \left(\frac{3}{10} \times \frac{1}{2}\right) = \frac{4}{10} + \frac{3}{20} = \frac{8+3}{20} = \frac{11}{20}$$

$$\text{Bhawana} = \frac{3}{10} + \left(\frac{3}{10} \times \frac{1}{2}\right)$$

$$= \frac{3}{10} + \frac{3}{20} = \frac{6+3}{20} = \frac{9}{20}$$

Old share of Anurag and Bhawana is 11 : 9.

12. State the rights acquired by a newly admitted partner. **All India 2014; Delhi 2011**

Ans. (*i*) Share in the future profits of the firm.

(*ii*) Share in the assets of the firm.

13. What is meant by sacrificing ratio? **All India (C) 2014**

Or State the meaning of sacrificing ratio. **All India 2011**

Ans. It is the ratio in which the old partners have agreed to sacrifice their share of profits in favour of new or incoming partner.

Sacrificing Ratio = Old Share − New Share

14. List any two items that need adjustments in the books of accounts of a firm at the time of admission of a partner. **All India (C) 2014**

Ans. Two items that need adjustment at the time of admission are

(*i*) Goodwill of the firm.

(*ii*) Reserves and accumulated profits/losses.

15. X and Y are partners. Y wants to admit his son K into business. Can K become the partner of the firm? Give reason. **Delhi (C) 2014**

Ans. K can be admitted as a partner with the consent of X, and that to if he is a major.

16. State any one purpose for admitting a new partner in a firm. **All India 2012**

Ans. A new partner may be admitted for the following purpose: For procuring additional capital.

2 Marks Questions

17. A and B are partners sharing profits in the ratio of 5 : 4. They admit C for 1/10th share of profit which he acquires in equal proportion from both. Find the new profit sharing ratio. **Delhi (C) 2011**

Ans. Old ratio = 5 : 4; C's share $=\frac{1}{10}$th

Which he acquires in equal proportion from both,

$\therefore$ A's sacrifice $=\frac{1}{10}\times\frac{1}{2}=\frac{1}{20}$

B's sacrifice $=\frac{1}{10}\times\frac{1}{2}=\frac{1}{20}$

A's new share $=\frac{5}{9}-\frac{1}{20}=\frac{100-9}{180}=\frac{91}{180}$

B's new share $=\frac{4}{9}-\frac{1}{20}=\frac{80-9}{180}=\frac{71}{180}$

C's new share $=\frac{1}{10}\times\frac{18}{18}=\frac{18}{180}$

$\therefore$ New ratio among A, B and C

$= 91:71:18$

18. A and B are partners sharing profits in the ratio of 5 : 4. They admit C for 1/3rd share, which he acquires in equal proportion from both. Find the new profit sharing ratio. **All India 2011**

Ans. Solve as Q no. 17 on page 73.

New Profit Sharing Ratio of A, B and C = 7:5:6

4 Marks Questions

19. (*i*) Rajeev and Sanjeev are partners in a firm sharing profits in the ratio of 3 : 2 respectively. They admit Vijay as a new partner.

Rajeev surrenders $\frac{1}{4}$ of his share and Sanjeev $\frac{1}{3}$ of his share in favour of Vijay. Calculate new profit sharing ratio of Rajeev, Sanjeev and Vijay.

(*ii*) Anita and Sunita are partners in a firm sharing profits in the ratio of 3 : 2 respectively. They admitted Vinita as a new partner for $\frac{1}{4}$th share. The new profit sharing ratio between Anita and Sunita will be 2 : 1. Calculate their sacrificing ratio. **Delhi (C) 2014**

Ans. (*i*) Old ratio between Rajeev and Sanjeev = 3 : 2

Share given by Rajeev to Vijay $=\frac{3}{5}\times\frac{1}{4}=\frac{3}{20}$

Share given by Sanjeev to Vijay $=\frac{2}{5}\times\frac{1}{3}=\frac{2}{15}$

$\therefore$ New share of Rajeev $=\frac{3}{5}-\frac{3}{20}=\frac{12-3}{20}=\frac{9}{20}$

New share of Sanjeev $=\frac{2}{5}-\frac{2}{15}=\frac{6-2}{15}=\frac{4}{15}$

Share of Vijay $=\frac{3}{20}+\frac{2}{15}=\frac{9+8}{60}=\frac{17}{60}$

New ratio $=\frac{9}{20}:\frac{4}{15}:\frac{17}{60}=27:16:17$

(*ii*) Old ratio between Anita and Sunita = 3 : 2

Vinita is admitted for $\frac{1}{4}$th share.

Remaining share $=1-\frac{1}{4}=\frac{3}{4}$ which will be shared among Anita and Sunita in the ratio of 2 : 1. Accordingly,

Anita's new share $=\frac{3}{4}\times\frac{2}{3}=\frac{2}{4}$

Sunita's new share $=\frac{3}{4}\times\frac{1}{3}=\frac{1}{4}$

$\therefore$ New profit sharing ratio = 2:1:1

Sacrificing Ratio = Old Share − New Share

Anita $=\frac{3}{5}-\frac{2}{4}=\frac{12-10}{20}=\frac{2}{20}$

Sunita $=\frac{2}{5}-\frac{1}{4}=\frac{8-5}{20}=\frac{3}{20}$

$\therefore$ Sacrificing ratio = 2 : 3

20. (*i*) Rohan and Mohan are partners in a firm sharing profits in the ratio of 5 : 3 respectively. They admit Bhim as a partner for 1/7th share in the profit. The new profit sharing ratio will be 4 : 2 : 1. Calculate the sacrificing ratio of Rohan and Mohan.

(*ii*) Amla and Kamla are partners in a firm sharing profits in the ratio of 4 : 1 respectively. They admitted Bimla as a new partner for $\frac{1}{4}$th share in the profits, which she acquired wholly from Amla. Determine the new profit sharing ratio of the partners. **Delhi (C) 2014**

Ans. (*i*) Old ratio between Rohan and Mohan = 5 : 3

New ratio after Bhim's admission = 4 : 2 : 1

Sacrificing Ratio = Old Share – New Share

$$\text{Rohan} = \frac{5}{8} - \frac{4}{7} = \frac{35-32}{56} = \frac{3}{56}$$

$$\text{Mohan} = \frac{3}{8} - \frac{2}{7} = \frac{21-16}{56} = \frac{5}{56}$$

∴ Sacrificing ratio = 3 : 5

(*ii*) Old ratio between Amla and Kamla = 4 : 1.

Bimla is admitted for $\frac{1}{4}$th share, which she gets wholly from Amla. Accordingly,

$$\text{New share of Amla} = \frac{4}{5} - \frac{1}{4} = \frac{16-5}{20} = \frac{11}{20}$$

Share of Kamla = $\frac{1}{5}$; Share of Bimla = $\frac{1}{4}$

$$\therefore \quad \text{New ratio} = \frac{11}{20} : \frac{1}{5} : \frac{1}{4} = 11 : 4 : 5$$

6 Marks Question

21. On 1st April, 2010 Sahil and Charu entered into partnership for sharing profits in the ratio of 4 : 3. They admitted Tanu as a new partner on 1st April, 2012 for $\frac{1}{5}$th share which she acquired equally from Sahil and Charu. Sahil, Charu and Tanu earned profits at a higher rate than the normal rate of return for the year ended 31st March, 2013. Therefore, they decided to expand their business. To meet the requirements of additional capital they admitted Puneet as a new partner on 1st April, 2013 for $\frac{1}{7}$th share in profits which he acquired from Sahil and Charu in 7 : 3 ratio. Calculate

(*i*) New profit sharing ratio of Sahil, Charu and Tanu for the year 2012-13.

(*ii*) New profit sharing ratio of Sahil, Charu, Tanu and Puneet on Puneet's admission. **Delhi 2015**

Ans. (*i*) **Calculation of New Profit Sharing Ratio of Sahil, Charu and Tanu for the year 2012-13**

Tanu is admitted for $\frac{1}{5}$ th share

Tanu acquired profit share from Sahil

$$= \frac{1}{5} \times \frac{1}{2} = \frac{1}{10}$$

Tanu acquired profit share form Charu

$$= \frac{1}{5} \times \frac{1}{2} = \frac{1}{10}$$

Sahil's New Share = Old Share – Sacrifice

$$\text{Share} = \frac{4}{7} - \frac{1}{10} = \frac{40-7}{70} = \frac{33}{70}$$

Charu's New Share = Old Share – Sacrifice

$$\text{Share} = \frac{3}{7} - \frac{1}{10} = \frac{30-7}{70} = \frac{23}{70}$$

$$\text{New profit sharing ratio will be} = \frac{33}{70} : \frac{23}{70} : \frac{1}{5}$$

$$= \frac{33:23:14}{70} \quad Or \quad 33:23:14$$

(*ii*) **Calculation of New Profit Sharing Ratio**

Old ratio = 33 : 23 : 14

Puneet is admitted for $\frac{1}{7}$ th share

Which he acquired from Sahil and Charu in 7 : 3 ratio

$$\text{Puneet acquired share from Sahil} = \frac{1}{7} \times \frac{7}{10} = \frac{7}{70}$$

$$\text{Puneet acquired share from Charu} = \frac{1}{7} \times \frac{3}{10} = \frac{3}{70}$$

$$\text{Sahil's new share} = \frac{33}{70} - \frac{7}{70} = \frac{26}{70}$$

$$\text{Charu's new share} = \frac{23}{70} - \frac{3}{70} = \frac{20}{70}$$

$$\text{New ratio} = \frac{26}{70} : \frac{20}{70} : \frac{14}{70} : \frac{1}{7}$$

$$\Rightarrow \quad \frac{26}{70} : \frac{20}{70} : \frac{14}{70} : \frac{10}{70}$$

Or 13 : 10 : 7 : 5

TOPIC 2

Treatment of Goodwill

When a new partner is admitted, his share in future profits of the firm is equal to the sacrifice of profit by an existing partner or partners of the firm, the amount the new partner pays to compensate for this sacrifice is called goodwill.

Cases Related to the Treatment of Goodwill

The various cases related to the treatment of goodwill are as follows

***Case* I When Premium for Goodwill is Paid Privately by New Partner**

In case, a new partner pays premium to the old partners privately or directly or outside the business, it will not be recorded because it is an out of business transaction. However, following entry will be passed for capital brought in by new partner

Cash/Bank A/c	Dr
To New Partner's Capital A/c	

Also, if existing goodwill appears in the books, then it will be written-off in old ratio by passing the following entry

Old Partner's Capital A/c	Dr
To Goodwill A/c	

***Case* II When Premium for Goodwill is Brought in Business by New Partner in Cash and Retained in the Business**

(a)	Write-off the existing goodwill (if any) appearing in the books of the firms	Old Partners' Capital/Current A/c To Goodwill A/c	Dr	[In old ratio]
(b)	For bringing premium for goodwill and capital in cash by a new partner	Cash/Bank A/c To Premium for Goodwill A/c To New Partner's CapitalA/c	Dr	[With share of capital and goodwill] [With share of goodwill] [With share of capital]
(c)	For sharing of premium for goodwill by sacrificing partners	Premium for Goodwill A/c To Sacrificing Partners' Capital/Currrent A/c	Dr	[With share of goodwill] [In sacrificing ratio]

***Case* III When Premium for Goodwill is Brought in Kind**

(a)	For assets brought in by new partner	Assets A/c To Premium for Goodwill A/c To New Partner's Capital A/c	Dr	[Individually] [With share of goodwill brought in] [With amount of capital]
(b)	For distributing premium for goodwill to sacrificing (old) partners in their sacrificing ratio	Premium for Goodwill A/c To Sacrificing Partners' Capital A/c	Dr	

Case IV When Premium for Goodwill is Brought in by New Partner and is Withdrawn by Old (Sacrificing) Partners Fully or Partly

First three entries will be same as discussed in case II.

For withdrawal of premium money by sacrificing partners fully/partly	Sacrificing Partner's Capital/Current A/c To Cash/Bank A/c	Dr	[Amount withdrawn]

Case V When a New Partner Brings only a Part of Premium for Goodwill in Cash

First two entries will be same as discussed in case II.

For credit given to sacrificing partners by incoming partner's full share of goodwill	Premium for Goodwill A/c New Partner's Capital/ Current A/c To Sacrificing Partners' Capital/Current A/c	Dr Dr	[With share of goodwill brought in] [With unpaid share of goodwill] [In sacrificing ratio]

Case VI When the New or Incoming Partner is Unable to Bring his Share of Premium for Goodwill in Cash

First entry will be same as discussed in case II.

New Partner's Capital/Current A/c To Sacrificing (Old) Partners' Capital/Current A/c	Dr	[For his share of goodwill] [In sacrificing ratio]

Beside the above treatment, following alternative treatment is also available where goodwill account is **raised** and thereafter **written-off**

(i) When the new partner does not bring in his share of goodwill in cash

When goodwill is raised	Goodwill A/c To Sacrificing Partners' Capitals/Current A/c	Dr	[With unpaid part of goodwill]
When goodwill account is written-off	New Partners' Capital/Current A/c To Goodwill A/c	Dr	

(ii) If a partner brings a part of his share of goodwill

In this case, after distributing the amount brought in for goodwill among the old partners in their sacrificing ratio, the goodwill account is raised with the amount of premium not brought by the new partner and written-off immediately by debiting new partners' capital account and crediting goodwill account.

Case VII When the Goodwill is Inferred on the Basis of Capital of Partners (Hidden Goodwill)

Hidden or inferred goodwill is the excess of desired total capital of the firm over the actual combined capital of all the partners. In case, the value of goodwill is not given at the time of admission of a new partner, it is to be inferred on the basis of net worth (capital) of the firm.

Calculation of Hidden Goodwill

A.	Net Worth (Including goodwill) on the Basis of Capital brought in by Incoming Partner (Incoming partner's capital × Reciprocal of share of incoming partner)	...
B.	(–) Net Worth (Excluding goodwill of the reconstituted firm including incoming partner's capital)	(...)
C.	Value of Goodwill (A – B)	...

Net Worth = Total Assets – Total Outside Liabilities

Or Net Worth = Total of Adjusted Capitals of all the Partners.

Previous Years' Examination Questions

1 Mark Questions

1. Vinay and Naman are partners sharing profit in the ratio of 4:1. Their capitals were ₹ 90,000 and ₹ 70,000 respectively. They admitted Prateek for 1/3 share in the profits. Prateek brought ₹ 1,00,000 as his capital. Calculate the value of firm's goodwill. **Compartment 2018**

Ans. Prateek's Capital for $\frac{1}{3}$ share = ₹ 1,00,000

Firm's Total Capital = 1,00,000 × 3 = ₹ 3,00,000

On the basis of Prateek's Capital,

Firm Actual Capital = 90,000 + 70,000 + 1,00,000
= ₹ 2,60,000

Firm's goodwill = 3,00,000 − 2,60,000 = ₹ 40,000

2. A, B, C and D were partners in a firm sharing profits in the ratio of 4 : 3 : 2 : 1. On 1st January, 2015, they admitted E as a new partner for $\frac{1}{10}$th share in the profits. E brought ₹ 10,000 for his share of goodwill premium which was correctly recorded in the books by the accountant. The accountant showed goodwill at ₹ 1,00,000 in the books. Was the accountant correct in doing so? Give reason in support of your answer. **Delhi 2015**

Ans. No, the accountant is not correct because according to AS-26, internally generated goodwill shall not be recognised as an asset because it is not an identifiable resource controlled by the entity that can be measured reliably at cost.

3. When the new partner brings cash for goodwill, the amount is credited to which account? **Delhi (C) 2015; Modified**

Ans. When the new partner brings cash for goodwill, the amount is credited to premium for goodwill account.

4. Under what circumstances will the premium for goodwill paid by the incoming partner not be recorded in the books of accounts? **Delhi (C) 2014**

Ans. When the incoming partner pays his share of goodwill privately to the sacrificing partners, outside the business, then no entry is passed in the books of the firm.

5. State the need for treatment of goodwill on admission of a partner. **Delhi 2010**

Ans. When a new partner is admitted, his share in future profits of the firm is equal to the sacrifice of profit by an existing partner or partners of the firm. The amount he pays to compensate this sacrifice, is in the form of goodwill. Therefore, it is important to treat goodwill at the time of admission of a partner.

3 Marks Questions

6. A, B, C and D were partners in a firm sharing profits and losses equally. E was admitted as a new partner for $\frac{1}{3}$rd share in the profits of the firm which he acquires equally from C and D. On E's admission the goodwill of the firm was valued at ₹ 3,00,000.

Calculate the new profit sharing ratio on E's admission. Also pass necessary journal entry on E's admission, assuming that he failed to bring his share of goodwill in cash. **All India 2019**

Ans. (*i*) E's Share = $\frac{1}{3}$rd which he acquires equally from C and D.

C sacrifice = $\frac{1}{3} \times \frac{1}{2} = \frac{1}{6}$

D sacrifice = $\frac{1}{3} \times \frac{1}{2} = \frac{1}{6}$

A's new share = $\frac{1}{4} \times \frac{3}{3} = \frac{3}{12}$

B's new share = $\frac{1}{4} \times \frac{3}{3} = \frac{3}{12}$

C's new share = $\frac{1}{4} - \frac{1}{6} = \frac{3-2}{12} = \frac{1}{12}$

D's new share = $\frac{1}{4} - \frac{1}{6} = \frac{3-2}{12} = \frac{1}{12}$

E's new share = $\frac{1}{3} \times \frac{4}{4} = \frac{4}{12}$

New Ratio = 3 : 3 : 1 : 1 : 4

(*ii*) Firms goodwill = ₹ 3,00,000; E's share of goodwill = $3{,}00{,}000 \times \frac{1}{3}$ = ₹ 1,00,000 to be distributed among sacrificing partners i.e. C and D in sacrificing ratio of 1 : 1.

JOURNAL

Date	Particulars		LF	Amt (Dr)	Amt (Cr)
	E's Capital A/c	Dr		1,00,000	
	To C's Capital A/c				50,000
	To D's Capital A/c				50,000
	(Being premium for goodwill adjusted)				

7. A, B and C were partners in a firm sharing profits in the ratio of 2 : 1 : 1. On 1st April, 2018 they admitted D as a new partner. D brought ₹ 2,00,000 for his capital and ₹ 24,000 for his share of goodwill premium. The new profit sharing ratio between A, B, C and D will be 1 : 2 : 1 : 1.

Pass necessary journal entries for the above transactions in the books of the firm on D's admission. **All India 2019**

Ans. JOURNAL

Data	Particulars		LF	Amt (Dr)	Amt (Cr)
2018 Apr 1	Cash A/c	Dr		2,24,000	
	To D's Capital A/c				2,00,000
	To Premium for Goodwill A/c				24,000
	(Being amount of capital and premium brought in by D)				
	Premium for Goodwill A/c	Dr		24,000	
	B's Capital A/c	Dr		18,000	
	To A's Capital A/c				36,000
	To C's Capital A/c				6,000
	(Being premium adjusted through sacrificing partner's capital account)				

Working Notes

1. **Calculation of Sacrificing Ratio**

Sacrificing Ratio = Old Share – New Share

$$A = \frac{2}{4} - \frac{1}{5} = \frac{10-4}{20} = \frac{6}{20};\ B = \frac{1}{4} - \frac{2}{5} = \frac{5-8}{20} = \left(\frac{3}{20}\right);\ C = \frac{1}{4} - \frac{1}{5} = \frac{5-4}{20} = \frac{1}{20}$$

2. $\frac{1}{5}$th share of goodwill = ₹ 24,000

Firms goodwill = 24,000 × 5 = ₹ 1,20,000; B would compensate = $1{,}20{,}000 \times \frac{3}{20}$ = ₹ 18,000

A would sacrifice = $1{,}20{,}000 \times \frac{6}{20}$ = ₹ 36,000; C would sacrifice = $1{,}20{,}000 \times \frac{1}{20}$ = ₹ 6,000

8. Devi, Dayal and Daya were partners in a firm sharing profits in the ratio of 2 : 1 : 2. On 31st March, 2018, they admitted Divya as a new partner for $\frac{1}{5}$th share in the profits. Their new profit sharing ratio was 1 : 2 : 1 : 1. Divya bought ₹ 5,00,000 as her capital and ₹ 50,000 for her share of goodwill premium.

Pass necessary journal entries for the above transactions in the books of the firm on Divya's admission. **All India 2019**

Ans. Solve as Q. No. 7 on page 78; Sacrificing or Gaining Ratio = Devi $\frac{1}{5}$, Dayal $\left(\frac{1}{5}\right)$ and Daya = $\frac{1}{5}$

Debit premium for goodwill account and Dayal's capital account with ₹ 50,000 each and credit Devi's and Daya's capital accounts with ₹ 50,000 each.

9. L, M and N were partner in a firm sharing profits and losses in the ratio of 5 : 3 : 2. On 1st April, 2018 they admitted S as a new partner in the firm for 1/5th share in the profits. On S' admission the goodwill of the firm was valued at 3 years purchase of last five average profits. The profits during the last five year were

Year ended 31st March	Profit (₹)
2014	4,00,000
2015	3,00,000
2016	2,00,000
2017	50,000
2018	(50,000)

Calculate the value of the goodwill of the firm. Pass necessary journal entry for the treatment of goodwill on S's admission. **Delhi 2019**

Ans. 5 Years Average Profit $= \frac{4{,}00{,}000 + 3{,}00{,}000 + 2{,}00{,}000 + 50{,}000 + (50{,}000)}{5} =$ ₹ 1,80,000

Firm's Goodwill = 5 Years Average Profit × No. of Years Purchase = 1,80,000 × 3 = ₹ 5,40,000

S's share of goodwill $= 5{,}40{,}000 \times \frac{1}{5} =$ ₹ 1,08,000

JOURNAL

Date	Particulars		LF	Amt (Dr)	Amt (Cr)
2018 Apr 1	Cash A/c	Dr		1,08,000	
	To Premium for Goodwill A/c				1,08,000
	(Being goodwill brought in by new partner)				
	Premium for Goodwill A/c	Dr		1,08,000	
	To L's Capital A/c				54,000
	To M's Capital A/c				32,400
	To N's Capital A/c				21,600
	(Being premium for goodwill distributed among old partners in sacrificing ratio)				

NOTE It is not clearly mentioned in the question that new partner S bring his share of goodwill in cash or not. So, it is assumed that goodwill premium is brought in cash.

Alternatively, entry for not bringing goodwill premium in cash can be passed.

10. Amit and Kartik are partners sharing profits and losses equally. They decided to admit Saurabh for an equal share in the profits. For this purpose, the goodwill of the firm was to be valued for four years' purchase of super profits.

The Balance Sheet of the firm of Saurabh's admission was as follows

Liabilities		Amt (₹)	Assets	Amt (₹)
Capitals :			Machinery	75,000
Amit	90,000		Furniture	15,000
Kartik	50,000	1,40,000	Stock	30,000
Reserve		20,000	Sundry Debtors	20,000
Loan		25,000	Cash	50,000
Sundry Creditors		5,000		
		1,90,000		1,90,000

The normal rate of return is 12% per annum. Average profit of the firm for the last four years was ₹ 30,000. Calculate Saurabh's share of goodwill. **Compartment 2018**

Ans. Capital Employed = Amit's Capital + Kartik's Capital + Reserve

= 90,000 + 50,000 + 20,000 = ₹ 1,60,000

Normal Profit = Capital Employed × Normal Rate of Return = $1,60,000 \times \frac{12}{100}$ = ₹ 19,200

Average Profit = ₹ 30,000

Super Profit = Average Profit − Normal Profit = 30,000 − 19,200 = ₹ 10,800

Firms Goodwill = Super Profit × Number of Years Purchase = 10,800 × 4 = ₹ 43,200

Saurabh's Share of Goodwill = $43,200 \times \frac{1}{3}$ = ₹ 14,400

4 Marks Questions

11 Veena and Somesh were partners in a firm with capitals of ₹ 1,00,000 and ₹ 80,000 respectively. They admitted Nisha on 1st April, 2019 as a new partner for $\frac{1}{4}$th share in the future profits of the firm. Nisha brought ₹ 90,000 as her capital. Nisha acquired her share as $\frac{1}{12}$th from Veena and the remaining from Somesh. Calculate the value of goodwill of the firm and pass the necessary journal entries on Nisha's admission. **CBSE 2020**

Ans Veena sacrifice = $\frac{1}{12}$th

Somesh sacrifice = $\frac{1}{4} - \frac{1}{12} = \frac{3-1}{12} = \frac{2}{12} = \frac{1}{6}$

Sacrificing ratio = 1 : 2

$\frac{1}{4}$th share capital = ₹ 90,000

Total capital = 90,000 × 4	= ₹ 3,60,000
(−) Actual capital employed (1,00,000 + 80,000 + 90,000)	= ₹ (2,70,000)
Value of firm's goodwill	= ₹ 90,000

Nisha's share of goodwill = $90,000 \times \frac{1}{4}$ = ₹ 22,500

JOURNAL

Date	Particulars		LF	Amt (Dr)	Amt (Cr)
	Bank A/c	Dr		90,000	
	To Nisha's Capital A/c				90,000
	(Being cash for capital brought-in)				
	Nisha's Current A/c	Dr		22,500	
	To Veena's Capital A/c				7,500
	To Somesh's Capital A/c				15,000
	(Being adjustment for goodwill)				

12. Asha and Aditi are partners in a firm sharing profits and losses in the ratio of 3 : 2. They admit Raghav as a partner for $\frac{1}{4}$th share in the profits of the firm Raghav brings ₹ 6,00,000 as his capital and his share of goodwill in cash. Goodwill of the firm is to be valued at two years' purchase of average profits of the last four years.

The profits of the firm during the last four years are given below

Year	Profit (₹)
2013-14	3,50,000
2014-15	4,75,000
2015-16	6,70,000
2016-17	7,45,000

The following additional information is given

(*i*) To cover management cost an annual charge of ₹ 56,250 should be made for the purpose of valuation of goodwill.

(*ii*) The closing stock for the year ended 31st March, 2017 was overvalued by ₹ 15,000.

Pass necessary journal entries on Raghav's admission showing the working notes clearly.
CBSE 2018

Ans.

JOURNAL

Date	Particulars		LF	Amt (Dr)	Amt (Cr)
2017 Apr 1	Cash A/c	Dr		8,50,000	
	To Raghav's Capital A/c				6,00,000
	To Premium for Goodwill A/c				2,50,000
	(Being Raghav brought his share of capital and goodwill premium in cash)				
Apr 1	Premium for Goodwill A/c	Dr		2,50,000	
	To Asha's Capital A/c				1,50,000
	To Aditi's Capital A/c				1,00,000
	(Being premium distributed among the partners)				

Working Note

Calculation of Adjusted Profit

2013-14 $3,50,000 - 56,250 = 2,93,750$

2014-15 $4,75,000 - 56,250 = 4,18,750$

2015-16 $6,70,000 - 56,250 = 6,13,750$

2016-17 $7,45,000 - 56,250 - 15,000 = 6,73,750$

$$\text{Total profit} = 2{,}93{,}750 + 4{,}18{,}750 + 6{,}13{,}750 + 6{,}73{,}750 = ₹\ 20{,}00{,}000$$

$$\text{Average profit} = \frac{20{,}00{,}000}{4} = ₹\ 5{,}00{,}000$$

$$\text{Goodwill} = \text{Average Profit} \times \text{Number of Years' Purchase}$$

$$= 5{,}00{,}000 \times 2 = ₹\ 10{,}00{,}000$$

Raghav's share of goodwill $= 10{,}00{,}000 \times \frac{1}{4} = ₹\ 2{,}50{,}000$ to be shared by Asha and Aditi in 3 : 2 ratio.

13. Madhu and Neha were partners in a firm sharing profits and losses in the ratio of 3 : 5. Their fixed capitals were ₹ 4,00,000 and ₹ 6,00,000 respectively. On 1st January, 2016. Tina was admitted as a new partner for $\frac{1}{4}$th share in the profits. Tina acquired her share of profit from Neha. Tina brought ₹ 4,00,000 as her capital which was to be kept fixed like the capitals of Madhu and Neha. Calculate the goodwill of the firm on Tina's admission and the new profit sharing ratio of Madhu, Neha and Tina. Also, pass necessary journal entry for the treatment of goodwill on Tina's admission considering that Tina did not bring her share of goodwill premium in cash. **All India 2017**

Ans.

JOURNAL

Date	Particulars		LF	Amt (Dr)	Amt (Cr)
2016 Jan 1	Cash A/c	Dr		4,00,000	
	To Tina's Capital A/c				4,00,000
	(Being capital brought in by Tina)				
	Tina's Current A/c	Dr		50,000	
	To Neha's Current A/c				50,000
	(Being adjustment entry passed for goodwill)				

Calculation of New Profit Sharing Ratio

Madhu's share $= \frac{3}{8}$ (same as before)

Neha's share $= \frac{5}{8} - \frac{1}{4} = \frac{5-2}{8} = \frac{3}{8}$; Tina's share $= \frac{1}{4} \times \frac{2}{2} = \frac{2}{8}$

New profit sharing ratio of Madhu : Neha : Tina = 3 : 3 : 2

Calculation of Goodwill of the Firm on Tina's Admission

Net worth of new firm on the basis of capital brought in by Tina $\left(4{,}00{,}000 \times \frac{4}{1}\right)$ = 16,00,000

(–) Net worth (excluding goodwill) of new firm [Adjusted capital of old partners + Incoming partners' capital]

[(4,00,000 + 6,00,000) + 4,00,000] = (14,00,000)

Hidden goodwill ₹ 2,00,000

Working Notes

1. **Calculation of Sacrificing Ratio**

   Sacrificing Ratio = Old Share – New Share

   Madhu $= \frac{3}{8} - \frac{3}{8} = \frac{3-3}{8} =$ Nil; Neha $= \frac{5}{8} - \frac{3}{8} = \frac{5-3}{8} = \frac{2}{8}$

2. Tina's share of goodwill $= 2{,}00{,}000 \times \frac{1}{4} =$ ₹ 50,000

14. Karan and Varun were partners in a firm sharing profits and losses in the ratio of 1 : 2. Their fixed capitals were ₹ 2,00,000 and ₹ 3,00,000 respectively. On 1st April, 2016, Kishore was admitted as a new partner for $\frac{1}{4}$ th share in the profits. Kishore brought ₹ 2,00,000 for his capital which was to be kept fixed like the capitals of Karan and Varun. Kishore acquired his share of profit from Varun.

Calculate goodwill of the firm on Kishore's admission and the new profit sharing ratio of Karan, Varun and Kishore. Also, pass necessary journal entry for the treatment of goodwill on Kishore's admission considering that Kishore did not bring his share of goodwill premium in cash. **Delhi 2017**

Ans. Solve as Q no. 13 on page 82.

Hidden goodwill = ₹ 1,00,000

New profit sharing ratio of Karan : Varun : Kishore = 4 : 5 : 3

Debit Kishore's current account with ₹ 25,000 and credit Varun's current account with ₹ 25,000.

15. Anu and Bhagwan were partners in a firm sharing profits in the ratio of 3 : 1. Goodwill appeared in the books at ₹ 4,40,000. Raja was admitted to the partnership. The new profit sharing ratio among Anu, Bhagwan and Raja was 2 : 2 : 1. Raja brought ₹ 1,00,000 for his capital and necessary cash for his goodwill premium. The goodwill of the firm was valued at ₹ 2,50,000. Record the necessary journal entries in the books of the firm for the above transactions. **All India (C) 2015**

Ans.

JOURNAL

Date	Particulars		LF	Amt (Dr)	Amt (Cr)
	Anu's Capital A/c (4,40,000 × 3/4)	Dr		3,30,000	
	Bhagwan's Capital A/c (4,40,000 × 1/4)	Dr		1,10,000	
	To Goodwill A/c				4,40,000
	(Being the existing goodwill written-off)				
	Cash A/c	Dr		1,50,000	
	To Raja's Capital A/c				1,00,000
	To Premium for Goodwill A/c (2,50,000 × 1/5)				50,000
	(Being the capital and premium for goodwill brought in by Raja)				
	Premium for Goodwill A/c	Dr		50,000	
	Bhagwan's Capital A/c	Dr		37,500	
	To Anu's Capital A/c				87,500
	(Being the premium for goodwill adjusted through sacrificing partners' capital account)				

Working Note

Calculation of Sacrificing Ratio

Sacrificing Ratio = Old Share − New Share

$$\text{Anu} = \frac{3}{4} - \frac{2}{5} = \frac{15-8}{20} = \frac{7}{20}; \ \text{Bhagwan} = \frac{1}{4} - \frac{2}{5} = \frac{5-8}{20} = \left(\frac{3}{20}\right) \text{Gain}$$

Since Bhagwan is gaining, he will also compensate Anu proportionately.

$$\text{Bhagwan will compensate} = 2,50,000 \times \frac{3}{20} = ₹\ 37,500$$

16. Hemant and Nishant were partners in a firm sharing profits in the ratio of 3 : 2. Their capitals were ₹ 1,60,000 and ₹ 1,00,000 respectively. They admitted Somesh on 1st April, 2013 as a new partner for $\frac{1}{5}$th share in the future profits. Somesh brought ₹ 1,20,000 as his capital. Calculate the value of goodwill of the firm and record necessary journal entries for the above transactions on Somesh's admission. **All India 2014**

Ans. Solve as Q no. 13 on page 82.

Debit Somesh's capital account with ₹ 44,000 and credit Hemant's and Nishant's capital accounts with ₹ 26,400 and ₹ 17,600 respectively; Hidden goodwill = ₹ 2,20,000

17. Saloni and Shrishti were partners in a firm sharing profits in the ratio of 7 : 3. Their capitals were ₹ 2,00,000 and ₹ 1,50,000 respectively. They admitted Aditi on 1st April, 2013 as a new partner for 1/6th share in future profits. Aditi brought ₹ 1,00,000 as her capital. Calculate the value of goodwill of the firm and record necessary journal entries for the above transaction on Aditi's admission. **Delhi 2014**

Ans. Solve as Q no. 13 on page 82.

Hidden goodwill = ₹ 1,50,000

Debit Aditi's capital account with ₹ 25,000 and credit Saloni's capital account and Shrishti's capital account with ₹ 17,500 and ₹ 7,500 respectively.

18. Asin and Shreya are partners in a firm. They admit Ajay as a new partner with 1/5th share in the profits of the firm. Ajay brings ₹ 5,00,000 as his share of capital. The value of the total assets of the firm was ₹ 15,00,000 and outside liabilities were valued at ₹ 5,00,000 on that date. Give the necessary journal entry to record goodwill at the time of Ajay's admission. Also, show your workings. **All India 2013**

Ans.

JOURNAL

Date	Particulars		LF	Amt (Dr)	Amt (Cr)
	Ajay's Capital A/c	Dr		2,00,000	
	To Asin's Capital A/c (2,00,000 × 1/2)				1,00,000
	To Shreya's Capital A/c (2,00,000 × 1/2)				1,00,000
	(Being adjustment entry passed for goodwill)				

Working Note

1. **Calculation of Ajay's Share of Goodwill**

(a) New firm's capital on the basis of Ajay's capital and his profit share $= 5,00,000 \times \frac{5}{1} =$ ₹ 25,00,000

(b) Adjusted Capital of Old Partners = Assets – Liabilities

= 15,00,000 – 5,00,000 = 10,00,000

(+) New partner's capital = 5,00,000

₹ 15,00,000

Value of hidden goodwill (a – b) = 25,00,000 – 15,00,000 = ₹ 10,00,000

Ajay's share = $10,00,000 \times \frac{1}{5} =$ ₹ 2,00,000

2. Sacrificing ratio has been taken as equal as old partners' profit sharing ratio is not given.

19. Abhay and Beena are partners in a firm. They admit Chetan as a partner with 1/4th share in the profits of the firm. Chetan brings ₹ 2,00,000 as his share of capital. The value of the total assets of the firm is ₹ 5,40,000 and outside liabilities are valued at ₹ 1,00,000 on that date. Give the necessary entry to record goodwill at the time of Chetan's admission. Also show your working notes. **Delhi 2013**

Ans. Solve as Q no. 18 on page 84.

Hidden goodwill = ₹ 1,60,000

Debit Chetan's capital account with ₹ 40,000 and credit Abhay and Beena's capital account with ₹ 20,000 respectively.

TOPIC 3

Revaluation of Assets and Reassessment of Liabilities

The account which is prepared to record changes in the value of assets and liabilities at the time of admission, retirement, death and change in profit sharing ratio is called revaluation account. It is also known as Profit and Loss Adjustment Account.

The accounting treatment of revaluation of assets and reassessment of liabilities

JOURNAL

Particulars	Entry		Amount
For increase in the value of asset	Assets A/c To Revaluation A/c	Dr	Revised value – Book value
For reduction in the value of asset	Revaluation A/c To Asset A/c	Dr	Book value – Revised value
For appreciation in the amount of liabilities	Revaluation A/c To Liabilities A/c	Dr	Revised amount – Amount as per books
For reduction in the amount of liabilities	Liabilities A/c To Revaluation A/c	Dr	Amount as per books – Revised amount
For an unrecorded asset	Asset A/c To Revaluation A/c	Dr	Agreed amount
For an unrecorded liability	Revaluation A/c To Liabilities A/c	Dr	Agreed amount
For increase in workmen compensation reserve	Revaluation A/c To Workmen Compensation Reserve A/c	Dr	Revised value – Book value
For increase in investment fluctuation fund	Revaluation A/c To Investment Fluctuation Fund A/c	Dr	Revised value – Book value
If there is profit on revaluation	Revaluation A/c To Old Partners' Capital/Current A/c	Dr	In old ratio
If there is loss on revaluation	Old Partners' Capital/Current A/c To Revaluation A/c	Dr	In old ratio

Format of Revaluation Account

Dr **Revaluation Account** Cr

Particulars	Amt (₹)	Particulars	Amt (₹)
To Decrease in Value of Assets	...	By Increase in Value of Assets	...
To Increase in Value of Liabilities	...	By Decrease in Value of Liabilities	...
To Unrecorded Liability	...	By Unrecorded Assets	...
To Profit Transferred to Old Partners'* Capital/Current A/c (Old ratio)	...	By Loss Transferred to Old Partners'* Capital/Current A/c (Old ratio)	...
	...		...

* Any one will appear

Accounting Treatment of Reserves, Undistributed Profits or Losses

If at the time of admission of a partner, any reserves and accumulated profits or losses exist in the books of the firm, then these should be transferred to old partners capital/current accounts in their old profit sharing ratio. The new partner is not entitled to any share in undistributed profits or losses as these are earned by the old partners.

Journal entries passed will be

(a) **For Transfer of Reserves and Accumulated Profits**	General Reserve A/c Profit and Loss A/c Workmen Compensation Fund A/c Investment Fluctuation Fund A/c To Old Partners' Capital/Current A/c	Dr Dr Dr Dr	 [Excess of reserve over actual liability] [Excess of reserve over the difference between book value and market value] [Old ratio]
(b) **For Undistributed** Losses	Old Partners' Capital/Current A/c To Profit and Loss A/c To Deferred Revenue Expenditure A/c	Dr	[Old ratio]

Previous Years' Examination Questions

1 Mark Questions

1. Geeta, Sunita and Anita were partners in a firm sharing profits in the ratio of 5:3:2. On 1st January, 2015 they admitted Yogita as a new partner for 1/10th share in the profits. On Yogita's admission, the profit and loss account of the firm was showing a debit balance of ₹ 20,000 which was credited by the accountant of the firm to the capital accounts of Geeta, Sunita and Anita in their profit sharing ratio. Did the accountant give correct treatment? Give reason in support of your answer. **All India 2015**

Ans. No, the accountant has done wrong treatment. The correct treatment would be as under

JOURNAL

Date	Particulars		LF	Amt (Dr)	Amt (Cr)
2015 Jan 1	Geeta's Capital A/c (20,000 × 5/10)	Dr		10,000	
	Sunita's Capital A/c (20,000 × 3/10)	Dr		6,000	
	Anita's Capital A/c (20,000 × 2/10)	Dr		4,000	
	To Profit and Loss A/c				20,000
	(Being debit balance in profit and loss account divided in 5 : 3 : 2)				

2. When a new partner is admitted, the balance of general reserve appearing in the balance sheet at the time of admission is credited to which account? **All India (C) 2015; Modified**

Ans. The balance of general reserve appearing in the balance sheet at the time of admission is credited to capital accounts of old partners.

3. Why are assets and liabilities revalued at the time of admission of a partner? **Delhi (C) 2014**

Ans. Assets and liabilities are revalued at the time of admission of a partner, so that profit or loss arising on account of revaluation, may be adjusted among old partners in their old profit sharing ratio, since it belongs to them.

6 Marks Questions

4. Chander and Damini were partners in a firm sharing profits and losses equally. On 31st March, 2017 their balance sheet was as follows

Balance Sheet
as on 31st March, 2017

Liabilities		Amt (₹)	Assets	Amt (₹)
Sundry Creditors		1,04,000	Cash at Bank	30,000
Capitals A/cs			Bills Receivable	45,000
Chander	2,50,000		Debtors	75,000
Damini	2,16,000	4,66,000	Furniture	1,10,000
			Land and Building	3,10,000
		5,70,000		5,70,000

On 1st April, 2017, they admitted Elina as a new partner for $\frac{1}{3}$rd share in the profits on the following conditions

(*i*) Elina will bring ₹ 3,00,000 as her capital and ₹ 50,000 as her share of goodwill premium, half of which will be withdrawn by Chander and Damini.

(*ii*) Debtors to the extent of ₹ 5,000 were unrecorded.

(*iii*) Furniture will be reduced by 10% and 5% provision for bad and doubtful debts will be created on bills receivables and debtors.

(*iv*) Value of land and building will be appreciated by 20%.

(*v*) There being a claim against the firm for damages, a liability to the extent of ₹ 8,000 will be created for the same.

Prepare revaluation account and partners' capital accounts. **CBSE 2018**

Ans. Dr **Revaluation Account** Cr

Particulars		Amt (₹)	Particulars	Amt (₹)
To Furniture A/c		11,000	By Debtors A/c	5,000
To Provision for Doubtful Debts A/c		6,250	By Land and Building A/c	62,000
To Claim for Damages A/c		8,000		
To Profit Transferred to Capital A/c				
Chander	20,875			
Damini	20,875	41,750		
		67,000		67,000

Dr **Partners' Capital Account** Cr

Particulars	Chander (₹)	Damini (₹)	Elina (₹)	Particulars	Chander (₹)	Damini (₹)	Elina (₹)
To Bank A/c	12,500	12,500	—	By Balance b/d	2,50,000	2,16,000	—
To Balance c/d	2,83,375	2,49,375	3,00,000	By Bank A/c	—	—	3,00,000
				By Premium for Goodwill A/c	25,000	25,000	—
				By Revaluation A/c	20,875	20,875	—
	2,95,875	2,61,875	3,00,000		2,95,875	2,61,875	3,00,000

Working Notes

1. Provision for Doubtful Debts $= (45{,}000 + 80{,}000) \times \frac{5}{100} = ₹ 6,250$

2. **JOURNAL**

Date	Particulars		LF	Amt (Dr)	Amt (Cr)
	Bank A/c	Dr		3,50,000	
	To Elina's Capital A/c				3,00,000
	To Premium for Goodwill A/c				50,000
	Premium for Goodwill A/c	Dr		50,000	
	To Chander's Capital A/c				25,000
	To Damini's Capital A/c				25,000
	Chander's Capital A/c	Dr		12,500	
	Damini's Capital A/c	Dr		12,500	
	To Bank A/c				25,000

5. Krishna and Suresh were partners in a firm sharing profits in the ratio of 3 : 1. On 1st April, 2015 they admitted Rahul as a new partner for 1/5th share in profits of the firm. On the date of Rahul's admission, the balance sheet of Krishna and Suresh showed a general reserve of ₹ 1,20,000, a debit balance of ₹ 60,000 in profit and loss account and workmen compensation fund of ₹ 1,50,000.

The following was agreed upon on Rahul's admission

(*i*) Rahul will bring ₹ 1,50,000 as his capital and his share of goodwill premium in cash.
(*ii*) Goodwill of the firm be valued at ₹ 2,40,000.
(*iii*) There was a claim of workmen compensation for ₹ 1,70,000.
(*iv*) The partners decided to share future profits in the ratio of 3:1:1.

Pass the necessary journal entries for the above on Rahul's admission. **All India (C) 2016**

Ans. **JOURNAL**

Date	Particulars		LF	Amt (Dr)	Amt (Cr)
2015					
Apr 1	General Reserve A/c	Dr		1,20,000	
	To Krishna's Capital A/c (1,20,000 × 3/4)				90,000
	To Suresh's Capital A/c (1,20,000 × 1/4)				30,000
	(Being general reserve distributed between old partners in old ratio)				
	Krishna's Capital A/c (60,000 × 3/4)	Dr		45,000	
	Suresh's Capital A/c (60,000 × 1/4)	Dr		15,000	
	To Profit and Loss A/c				60,000
	(Being debit balance of profit and loss distributed between old partners in old ratio)				
	Workmen Compensation Fund A/c	Dr		1,50,000	
	Revaluation A/c	Dr		20,000	
	To Claim for Workmen Compensation Fund A/c				1,70,000
	(Being claim against workmen compensation fund adjusted)				
	Krishna's Capital A/c (20,000 × 3/4)	Dr		15,000	
	Suresh's Capital A/c (20,000 × 1/4)	Dr		5,000	
	To Revaluation A/c				20,000
	(Being loss on revaluation distributed among old partners in old ratio)				
	Cash A/c	Dr		1,98,000	
	To Rahul's Capital A/c				1,50,000
	To Premium for Goodwill A/c (2,40,000 × 1/5)				48,000
	(Being cash brought in by Rahul for capital and premium for goodwill)				
	Premium for Goodwill A/c	Dr		48,000	
	To Krishna's Capital A/c (48,000 × 3/4)				36,000
	To Suresh's Capital A/c (48,000 × 1/4)				12,000
	(Being the premium for goodwill adjusted through sacrificing partners capital account)				

Working Note

Calculation of Sacrificing Ratio

Sacrificing Ratio = Old Share − New Share

$$\text{Krishna} = \frac{3}{4} - \frac{3}{5} = \frac{15-12}{20} = \frac{3}{20};\ \text{Suresh} = \frac{1}{4} - \frac{1}{5} = \frac{5-4}{20} = \frac{1}{20};\ \text{Sacrificing ratio} = 3:1$$

6. Anil and Beena were partners in a firm sharing profits in the ratio of 4 : 3.

On 1st April, 2015 they admitted Chahat as a new partner for 1/4th share in the profits of the firm. On the date of Chahat's admission, the balance sheet of Anil and Beena showed a general reserve of ₹ 70,000, a debit balance of ₹ 7,000 in the profit and loss account and an investment fluctuation fund of ₹ 10,000.

The following was agreed upon, on Chahat's admission

(*i*) Chahat will bring ₹ 80,000 as her capital and her share of goodwill premium of ₹ 21,000 in cash.

(ii) The market value of investments was ₹ 17,000 less than the book value.

(iii) New profit sharing ratio was agreed at 2 : 1 : 1.

Pass the necessary journal entries for the above on Chahat's admission. **Delhi (C) 2016**

Ans. Solve as Q no. 5 on page 88 and 89.

Hint: Treatment of investment fluctuation fund will be same as treatment of workmen compensation fund in Q no. 5.

8 Marks Questions

7. C and D are partners in a firm sharing profits in the ratio of 4 : 1. On 31st March, 2016, their balance sheet was as follows

Balance Sheet
as at 31st March, 2016

Liabilities		Amt (₹)	Assets	Amt (₹)
Sundry Creditors		40,000	Cash	24,000
Provision for Bad Debts		4,000	Debtors	36,000
Outstanding Salary		6,000	Stock	40,000
General Reserve		10,000	Furniture	80,000
Capital A/cs			Plant and Machinery	80,000
C	1,20,000			
D	80,000	2,00,000		
		2,60,000		2,60,000

On the above date, E was admitted for $\frac{1}{4}$th share in the profits on the following terms

(i) E will bring ₹ 1,00,000 as his capital and ₹ 20,000 for his share of goodwill premium, half of which will be withdrawn by C and D.

(ii) Debtors ₹ 2,000 will be written off as bad debts and a provision of 4% will be created on debtors for bad and doubtful debts.

(iii) Stock will be reduced by ₹ 2,000, furniture will be depreciated by ₹ 4,000 and 10%, depreciation will be charged on plant and machinery.

(iv) Investments ₹ 7,000 not shown in the balance sheet will be taken into account.

(v) There was an outstanding repairs bill of ₹ 2,300 which will be recorded in the books.

Pass necessary journal entries for the above transactions in the books of the firm on E's admission. **All India 2017**

Ans.

JOURNAL

Date	Particulars		LF	Amt (Dr)	Amt (Cr)
2016					
Mar 31	Cash A/c	Dr		1,20,000	
	To E's Capital A/c				1,00,000
	To Premium for Goodwill A/c				20,000
	(Being cash and premium for goodwill brought in by E)				
	Premium for Goodwill A/c	Dr		20,000	
	To C's Capital A/c				16,000
	To D's Capital A/c				4,000
	(Being premium for goodwill shared by old partners in sacrificing ratio, i.e. 4 : 1)				

Date	Particulars		LF	Amt (Dr)	Amt (Cr)
	C's Capital A/c	Dr		8,000	
	D's Capital A/c	Dr		2,000	
	To Cash A/c				10,000
	(Being half the goodwill withdrawn by C and D)				
	General Reserve A/c	Dr		10,000	
	To C's Capital A/c				8,000
	To D's Capital A/c				2,000
	(Being general reserve distributed among old partners in old ratio)				
	Revaluation A/c	Dr		16,300	
	To Outstanding Repair Bill A/c				2,300
	To Stock A/c				2,000
	To Furniture A/c				4,000
	To Plant and Machinery A/c (80,000 × 10%)				8,000
	(Being the decrease in the value of assets and increase in the value of liabilities recorded)				
	Bad Debts A/c	Dr		2,000	
	To Debtors A/c				2,000
	(Being bad debts charged)				
	Provision for Doubtful Debts A/c	Dr		2,000	
	To Bad debts A/c				2,000
	(Being Bad debts written-off)				
	Investment A/c	Dr		7,000	
	Provision for Doubtful Debts A/c (WN)	Dr		640	
	To Revaluation A/c				7,640
	(Being decrease in the value of liabilities and increase in the value of assets recorded)				
	C's Capital A/c	Dr		6,928	
	D's Capital A/c	Dr		1,732	
	To Revaluation A/c				8,660
	(Being loss on revaluation transferred to old partners in old ratio)				

Working Notes

1. **Distribution of Goodwill in Sacrificing Ratio**

   C's share $= 20{,}000 \times \frac{4}{5} =$ ₹16,000 D's share $= 20{,}000 \times \frac{1}{5} =$ ₹ 4,000

NOTE It has been assumed that *C* and *D* sacrifice in ratio of 4 : 1 [equal to old profit sharing ratio].

2. **Provision for Bad Debts**

   Debtors = 36,000
   (–) Bad debts = (2,000), which will be adjusted against provision for bad debts
   ₹ 34,000

New provision for doubtful debts @ 4% $= 34,000 \times \frac{4}{100} =$ ₹ 1,360

Existing provision after adjusting bad debts (4,000 – 2,000) = 2,000

(–) New provision = (1,360)

Excess Provision ₹ 640

3. **Loss on Revaluation**

It can be ascertained by preparing revaluation account in the following manner

Dr **Revaluation Account** Cr

Particulars	Amt (₹)	Particulars		Amt (₹)
To Outstanding Repair Bill A/c	2,300	By Investment A/c		7,000
To Stock A/c	2,000	By Provision for Doubtful Debts A/c		640
To Furniture A/c	4,000	By Loss on Revaluation Transferred to		
To Plant and Machinery A/c	8,000	C's Capital A/c	6,928	
		D's Capital A/c	1,732	8,660
	16,300			16,300

8. W and R are partners in a firm sharing profits in the ratio of 3 : 2. Their balance sheet as at 31st March, 2016 was as follows

Balance Sheet
as at 31st March, 2016

Liabilities		Amt (₹)	Assets	Amt (₹)
Sundry Creditors		20,000	Cash	12,000
Provision for Bad Debts		2,000	Debtors	18,000
Outstanding Salary		3,000	Stock	20,000
General Reserve		5,000	Furniture	40,000
Capital A/cs			Plant and Machinery	40,000
W	60,000			
R	40,000	1,00,000		
		1,30,000		1,30,000

On the above date, C was admitted for $\frac{1}{6}$th share in the profits on the following terms

(*i*) C will bring ₹ 30,000 as his capital and ₹ 10,000 for his share of goodwill premium, half of which will be withdrawn by W and R.

(*ii*) Debtors ₹ 1,500 will be written off as bad debts and a provision of 5% will be created for bad and doubtful debts.

(*iii*) Outstanding salary will be paid-off.

(*iv*) Stock will be depreciated by 10%, furniture by ₹ 500 and plant and machinery by 8%.

(*v*) Investments ₹ 2,500 not mentioned in the balance sheet were to be taken into account.

(*vi*) A creditor of ₹ 2,100 not recorded in the books was to be taken into account.

Pass necessary journal entries for the above transactions in the books of the firm on C's admission. **Delhi 2017**

Ans. **JOURNAL**

Date	Particulars		LF	Amt (Dr)	Amt (Cr)
2016 Mar 31	Cash A/c	Dr		40,000	
	To C's Capital A/c				30,000
	To Premium for Goodwill A/c				10,000
	(Being cash and premium for goodwill brought in by C)				
	Premium for Goodwill A/c	Dr		10,000	
	To W's Capital A/c				6,000
	To R's Capital A/c				4,000
	(Being premium for goodwill shared by old partners in sacrificing ratio)				
	W's Capital A/c	Dr		3,000	
	R's Capital A/c	Dr		2,000	
	To Cash A/c				5,000
	(Being half goodwill withdrawn by W and R in old ratio)				
	General Reserve A/c	Dr		5,000	
	To W's Capital A/c				3,000
	To R's Capital A/c				2,000
	(Being general reserve distributed among old partners in old ratio)				
	Outstanding Salary A/c	Dr		3,000	
	To Cash A/c				3,000
	(Being outstanding salary paid)				
	Revaluation A/c	Dr		8,125	
	To Provision for Doubtful Debts A/c				325
	To Stock A/c				2,000
	To Furniture A/c				500
	To Plant and Machinery A/c				3,200
	To Creditors A/c				2,100
	(Being the decrease in the value of assets and increase in value of liabilities and unrecorded liability recorded)				
	Investment A/c	Dr		2,500	
	To Revaluation A/c				2,500
	(Being increase in the value of asset recorded)				
	W's Capital A/c $(5{,}625 \times 3/5)$	Dr		3,375	
	R's Capital A/c $(5{,}625 \times 2/5)$	Dr		2,250	
	To Revaluation A/c				5,625
	(Being loss on revaluation transferred to partners' capital accounts)				

Working Notes

1. **Distribution of Goodwill in Sacrificing Ratio**

$$\text{W's share} = 10{,}000 \times \frac{3}{5} = ₹\,6{,}000; \quad \text{R's share} = 10{,}000 \times \frac{2}{5} = ₹\,4{,}000$$

NOTE It has been assumed that *W* and *R* sacrifice in ratio 3 : 2 [equal to old profit sharing ratio].

2. **Provision for Bad and Doubtful Debts**

	Amt (₹)
Debtors	18,000
(–) Bad debts, to be adjusted against provision for bad debts	(1,500)
	16,500
Provision for doubtful debts @ 5% on 16,500	825
(–) Existing provision after adjusting bad debts (2,000 – 1,500)	(500)
Amount to be debited to revaluation account	325

3. **Loss on Revaluation**

Loss on revaluation can be ascertained by preparing revaluation account in the following manner

Dr **Revaluation Account** Cr

Particulars	Amt (₹)	Particulars		Amt (₹)
To Provision for Doubtful Debts A/c	325	By Investment A/c		2,500
To Stock A/c	2,000	By Loss on Revaluation		
To Furniture A/c	500	Transfered to		
To Plant and Machinery A/c	3,200	W	3,375	
To Creditors A/c	2,100	R	2,250	5,625
	8,125			8,125

9. W and R were partners in a firm sharing profits in the ratio of 3 : 2 respectively. On 31st March, 2013, their balance sheet was as follows

Balance Sheet
as at 31st March, 2013

Liabilities		Amt (₹)	Assets		Amt (₹)
Creditors		17,500	Cash		2,500
Investment Fluctuation Fund		4,000	Debtors	10,000	
Bank Loan		10,000	(–) Provision for Doubtful Debts	(350)	9,650
Capital A/cs			Stock		12,500
W	20,000		Plant		17,500
R	15,000	35,000	Patents		10,350
			Investments		10,000
			Goodwill		4,000
		66,500			66,500

B was admitted as a new partner on the following conditions

(*i*) B will get $\frac{4}{15}$th share of profits. (*ii*) B had to bring ₹ 15,000 as his capital.

(*iii*) B would pay cash for his share of goodwill based on 2.5 years purchase of average profit of last 4 years.

(*iv*) The profits of the firm for the years ending 31st March, 2010, 2011, 2012 and 2013 were ₹ 10,000, ₹ 7,000 , ₹ 8,500 and ₹ 7,500 respectively.

(*v*) Stock was valued at ₹ 10,000 and provision for doubtful debts was raised up to ₹ 500.

(*vi*) Plant was revalued at ₹ 20,000.

Prepare revaluation account, partners' capital account and the balance sheet of the new firm. **All India (C) 2014**

Ans. Dr **Revaluation Account** Cr

Particulars	Amt (₹)	Particulars		Amt (₹)
To Stock A/c	2,500	By Plant A/c		2,500
To Provision for Doubtful Debts A/c	150	By Loss in Revaluation Transferred to		
		W's Capital A/c	90	
		R's Capital A/c	60	150
	2,650			2,650

Dr **Partners' Capital Account** Cr

Particulars	W (₹)	R (₹)	B (₹)	Particulars	W (₹)	R (₹)	B (₹)
To Revaluation A/c	90	60	—	By Balance b/d	20,000	15,000	—
To Goodwill A/c	2,400	1,600	—	By Cash A/c	—	—	15,000
To Balance c/d	23,210	17,140	15,000	By Investment Fluctuation Fund A/c	2,400	1,600	—
				By Premium for Goodwill A/c	3,300	2,200	—
	25,700	18,800	15,000		25,700	18,800	15,000

Balance Sheet
as at...

Liabilities		Amt (₹)	Assets		Amt (₹)
Creditors		17,500	Cash		23,000
Bank Loan		10,000	Debtors	10,000	
Capital A/cs			(–) Provision for Doubtful Debts	(500)	9,500
W	23,210		Stock (12,500 – 2,500)		10,000
R	17,140		Patents		10,350
B	15,000	55,350	Plant (17,500 + 2,500)		20,000
			Investments		10,000
		82,850			82,850

Working Note

$$\text{Average profit} = \frac{10,000 + 7,000 + 8,500 + 7,500}{4} = ₹\,8,250$$

$$\text{Goodwill} = \text{Average Profit} \times \text{Number of Years' Purchase}$$
$$= 8,250 \times 2.5 = ₹\,20,625$$

B's share $= 20,625 \times \frac{4}{15} =$ ₹ 5,500 which will be distributed among W and R in their sacrificing ratio, i.e. 3 : 2.

10. Murari and Vohra were partners in a firm with capitals of ₹ 1,20,000 and ₹ 1,60,000 respectively. On 1st April, 2010 they admitted Yadav as a partner for 1/4th share in profits on his payment of ₹ 2,00,000 as his capital and ₹ 90,000 for his 1/4th share of goodwill. On that date, the creditors of Murari and Vohra were ₹ 60,000 and bank overdraft was ₹ 15,000. Their assets apart from cash included stock ₹ 10,000; debtors ₹ 40,000; plant and machinery ₹ 80,000; land and building ₹ 2,00,000. It was agreed that stock should be depreciated by ₹ 2,000; plant and machinery by 20%, ₹ 5,000 should be written-off as bad debts and land and building should be appreciated by 25%.

Prepare revaluation account, capital accounts of Murari, Vohra and Yadav and the balance sheet of the new firm. **All India 2011**

Ans. Dr **Revaluation Account** Cr

Particulars		Amt (₹)	Particulars	Amt (₹)
To Stock A/c		2,000	By Land and Building A/c	50,000
To Plant and Machinery A/c		16,000		
To Provision for Doubtful Debts A/c		5,000		
To Profit Transferred to				
Murari's Capital A/c	13,500			
Vohra's Capital A/c	13,500	27,000		
		50,000		50,000

Dr **Partners' Capital Account** Cr

Particulars	Murari (₹)	Vohra (₹)	Yadav (₹)	Particulars	Murari (₹)	Vohra (₹)	Yadav (₹)
To Balance c/d	1,78,500	2,18,500	2,00,000	By Balance b/d	1,20,000	1,60,000	—
				By Cash A/c	—	—	2,00,000
				By Premium for Goodwill A/c	45,000	45,000	—
				By Revaluation A/c (Profit)	13,500	13,500	—
	1,78,500	2,18,500	2,00,000		1,78,500	2,18,500	2,00,000

Balance Sheet
as at 1st April, 2010

Liabilities		Amt (₹)	Assets		Amt (₹)
Creditors		60,000	Stock (10,000 – 2,000)		8,000
Bank Overdraft		15,000	Plant and Machinery (80,000 – 16,000)		64,000
Capital A/cs			Debtors	40,000	
Murari	1,78,500		(–) Provision for Doubtful Debts	(5,000)	35,000
Vohra	2,18,500		Land and Building (2,00,000 + 50,000)		2,50,000
Yadav	2,00,000	5,97,000	Cash		3,15,000
		6,72,000			6,72,000

Working Notes

1. **Memorandum Balance Sheet**

Liabilities		Amt (₹)	Assets	Amt (₹)
Creditors		60,000	Stock	10,000
Bank Overdraft		15,000	Debtors	40,000
Capital A/cs			Plant and Machinery	80,000
Murari	1,20,000		Land and Building	2,00,000
Vohra	1,60,000	2,80,000	Cash (Balancing figure)	25,000
		3,55,000		3,55,000

2. Dr **Cash Account** Cr

Particulars	Amt (₹)	Particulars	Amt (₹)
To Balance b/d	25,000	By Balance c/d	3,15,000
To Yadav's Capital A/c	2,00,000		
To Premium for Goodwill A/c	90,000		
	3,15,000		3,15,000

TOPIC 4

Adjustment of Capital

At the time of admission of a new partner, the partners may agree that their capitals should also be adjusted so as to be proportionate to their profit sharing ratio.

Cases Related to Adjustment of Capital

The capitals of partners may be adjusted in any of the following ways

Case **I** **Adjusting the Capitals of Old Partners on the Basis of the Capital of Incoming Partner** (When the total capital of the new firm is not given)

Practical steps involved in this case are

Step **1** Calculate the new profit sharing ratio.

Step **2** Calculate total capital of the new firm

Total Capital = New Partner's Capital × Reciprocal of Proportion of Share of New Partner

Step **3** Calculate the new capitals of old partners by dividing the total capital in their new profit sharing ratio.

Step **4** Calculate the adjusted old capitals of old partners by preparing their capital accounts.

Step **5** Calculate the surplus/deficiency in each of the old partner's capital account by comparing Step 3 and Step 4.

Step **6** Adjust the surplus by paying-off or by transfer to credit of his current account and adjust the deficiency by asking the concerned partner to bring in required amount or by transfer to debit of his current account. If question is silent, then adjustments should be made through cash.

Case **II** **Determining the New Partner's Capital on the Basis of Total Capital of the Firm**

Practical steps involved in this case are

Step **1** Calculate the new profit sharing ratio.

Step **2** Calculate the adjusted old capitals of old partners (after all adjustments have been made).

Step **3** Calculate the total capital of new firm.

Total Capital = Combined Adjusted Old Capital of Old Partners × Reciprocal of Proportion of Share of Old Partners

Step **4** Calculate the proportionate capital of new partners as follows

New Partner's Capital = Total Capital (*Step* 3) × Proportion of Share of New Partner

NOTE Students should read the question carefully whether new partner's capital is to be computed on the basis of total capital (as discussed above) or on the basis of adjusted combined capitals of old partners.

In case of latter, new partner's share will be computed with the help of the following formula

New Partner's Capital = Combined Adjusted Capitals of Old Partners × Share of New Partner

Case **III** **Determining the New Partner's Capital on the Basis of the Total Capital of Firm and also Adjusting the Capitals of the Old Partners in New Profit Sharing Ratio**

Practical steps involved in this case are

Steps 1, 2, 3 and 4 are the same as discussed in case II.

Step **5** Calculate the new capitals of old partners with the help of the given formula = Total Capital × New Share of Old Partner

Step **6** Calculate the actual cash to be paid off or brought in by old partners by comparing their new capitals with adjusted old capitals.

Case **IV** **When Total Capital of the New Firm is Given**

Practical steps involved in this case are

Step **1** Calculate the new profit sharing ratio.

Step **2** Find out the adjusted capitals of the old partners after necessary adjustments.

Step **3** Calculate the capital of all the partners with the help of the given formula = Capital given × Partners share

Step **4** Calculate surplus/deficiency of old partners by comparing their adjusted capitals with computed capitals.

Step **5** Adjust the surplus/deficiency through cash or current accounts (as given in the question). If the question is silent then adjustments should be made through cash.

NOTE Another case of adjustment of capital can arise when total capital of the firm is computed by adding up the capitals (adjusted) of all the partners (including the new partner) and the total capital is then distributed in new ratio to compute the capital of each partner.

Previous Years' Examination Questions

6 Marks Questions

1. Abha and Bimal are partners in a firm sharing profits and losses in the ratio of 3 : 2. On 31st March, 2015 they admitted Chintu into partnership for 1/5th share in the profits of the firm. On that date their balance sheet stood as under

Balance Sheet

as at 31st March, 2015

Liabilities		Amt (₹)	Assets	Amt (₹)
General Reserve		20,000	Plant and Machinery	1,30,000
Sundry Creditors		1,00,000	Furniture	25,000
Capital A/c			Investments	1,00,000
Abha	1,20,000		Sundry Debtors	50,000
Bimal	1,00,000	2,20,000	Bank	35,000
		3,40,000		3,40,000

Chintu was admitted on the following terms

(*i*) He will bring ₹ 80,000 as capital and ₹ 30,000 for his share of goodwill premium.

(*ii*) Partners will share future profits in the ratio of 5 : 3 : 2.

(*iii*) Profit on revaluation of assets and reassessment of liabilities was ₹ 7,000.

(*iv*) After making adjustments, the capital accounts of the partners will be in proportion to Chintu's capital. Balance to be paid off or brought in by the old partners by cheque as the case may be.

Prepare the capital accounts of the partners and bank account. **All India (C) 2016**

Ans. Dr **Partners' Capital Account** Cr

Particulars	Abha (₹)	Bimal (₹)	Chintu (₹)	Particulars	Abha (₹)	Bimal (₹)	Chintu (₹)
To Bank A/c (Balancing figure)	—	5,800	—	By Balance b/d	1,20,000	1,00,000	—
To Balance c/d	2,00,000	1,20,000	80,000	By Revaluation A/c (Profit)	4,200	2,800	—
				By General Reserve A/c	12,000	8,000	—
				By Bank A/c	—	—	80,000
				By Premium for Goodwill A/c	15,000	15,000	—
				By Bank A/c (Balancing figure)	48,800	—	—
	2,00,000	1,25,800	80,000		2,00,000	1,25,800	80,000

Dr **Bank Account** Cr

Particulars	Amt (₹)	Particulars	Amt (₹)
To Balance b/d	35,000	By Bimal's Capital A/c	5,800
To Chintu's Capital A/c	80,000	By Balance c/d	1,88,000
To Premium for Goodwill A/c	30,000		
To Abha's Capital A/c	48,800		
	1,93,800		1,93,800

Working Notes

1. **Calculation of Sacrificing Ratio**

Sacrificing Ratio = Old Share – New Share

$$\text{Abha} = \frac{3}{5} - \frac{5}{10} = \frac{6-5}{10} = \frac{1}{10}, \quad \text{Bimal} = \frac{2}{5} - \frac{3}{10} = \frac{4-3}{10} = \frac{1}{10}$$

Sacrificing ratio $= 1:1$

2. **Calculation of New Capitals**

$$\text{Chintu's share} = \frac{1}{5}$$

Capital brought in by Chintu for $\frac{1}{5}$th share = ₹80,000

$$\text{Firm's capital} = 80{,}000 \times \frac{5}{1} = ₹\ 4{,}00{,}000; \quad \text{Abha's capital} = 4{,}00{,}000 \times \frac{5}{10} = ₹\ 2{,}00{,}000$$

$$\text{Bimal's capital} = 4{,}00{,}000 \times \frac{3}{10} = ₹\,1{,}20{,}000; \quad \text{Chintu's capital} = 4{,}00{,}000 \times \frac{2}{10} = ₹\,80{,}000$$

2. Angad, Baloo and Chitra were partners in a firm sharing profits and losses in the ratio of 6 : 5 : 3. Their balance sheet as at 31st March, 2015 was as follows

Balance Sheet
as at 31st March, 2015

Liabilities		Amt (₹)	Assets	Amt (₹)
Creditors		2,52,000	Bank	18,900
General Reserve		1,05,000	Stock	5,58,600
Capitals A/cs			Machinery	52,500
Angad	3,54,000		Land and Building	5,25,000
Baloo	2,98,500			
Chitra	1,45,500	7,98,000		
		11,55,000		11,55,000

They agreed to admit Dinesh into partnership and give him 1/8th share in the profits on the following terms

(*i*) Dinesh will bring ₹ 1,47,000 as his capital and ₹ 1,40,700 as his share of goodwill premium.

(*ii*) That after making adjustments, the capital accounts of the old partners will be in proportion of Dinesh's capital to his share in the business i.e., actual cash to be paid-off or brought in by the old partners by cheque as the case may be.

Prepare partners' capital account and bank account considering that gain on revaluation was ₹ 95,200. **Delhi (C) 2016**

Ans. Solve as Q no. 1 on page 98 and 99.

Balance in Partners' Capital A/c : Angad = ₹ 4,41,000; Baloo = ₹ 3,67,500; Chitra = ₹ 2,20,500 and Dinesh = ₹ 1,47,000

Chitra brings ₹ 1,950, Angad and Baloo withdraw ₹ 59,100 and ₹ 52,750 respectively.

Balance of Bank Account = ₹ 1,96,700

8 Marks Questions

3. Ashish and Nimish were partners in a firm sharing profits and losses in the ratio of 3 : 2. On 31st March, 2019 their Balance Sheet was as follows

Balance Sheet of Ashish and Nimish
as at 31st March, 2019

Liabilities		Amt (₹)	Assets		Amt (₹)
Capitals			Plant and Machinery		2,90,000
Ashish	3,10,000		Furniture		2,20,000
Nimish	2,90,000	6,00,000	Debtors	90,000	
			(–) Provision for doubtful debts	(1,000)	89,000
General Reserve		50,000			
Workmen's Compensation Fund		20,000	Stock		1,40,000
Creditors		1,10,000	Cash		41,000
		7,80,000			7,80,000

On 1st April, 2019, Geeta was admitted into the partnership for 1/4th share in the profits on the following terms

(*i*) Goodwill of the firm was valued at ₹ 2,00,000.

(*ii*) Geeta brought ₹ 3,00,000 as her capital and her share of goodwill premium in cash.

(*iii*) Bad debts amounted to ₹ 2,000. Create a provision for doubtful debts @ 5% on debtors.

(*iv*) Furniture was found undervalued by ₹ 65,400.

(*v*) Stock was taken over by Nimish for ₹ 1,30,000.

(*vi*) The liability against workmen's compensation fund was determined at ₹ 30,000.

(*vii*) After the above adjustments, the capitals of Ashish and Nimish were to be adjusted taking Geeta's capital as the base. Excess or shortage was to be adjusted by opening current accounts.

Prepare Revalution Account, Partners'Capital Accounts and the Balance Sheet of the firm after Geeta's admission. **CBSE 2020**

Sol. Dr **Revaluation Account** Cr

Particulars		Amt (₹)	Particulars	Amt (₹)
To Bad debts		1,000	By Furniture	65,400
To Provision for Doubtful Debts		4,400		
To Stock		10,000		
To Workmen Compensation Fund		10,000		
To Profit transferred to Capital A/c				
Ashish	24,000			
Nimish	16,000	40,000		
		65,400		65,400

Dr **Partners' Capital Account** Cr

Particulars	Ashish (₹)	Nimish (₹)	Geeta (₹)	Particulars	Ashish (₹)	Nimish (₹)	Geeta (₹)
To Stock	—	1,30,000	—	By Balance b/d	3,10,000	2,90,000	—
To Balance c/d	5,40,000	3,60,000	3,00,000	By Cash	—	—	3,00,000
				By Premium for Goodwill	30,000	20,000	—
				By General Reserve	30,000	20,000	—
				By Revaluation	24,000	16,000	—
				By Current A/c	1,46,000	1,44,000	—
	5,40,000	4,90,000	3,00,000		5,40,000	4,90,000	3,00,000

Balance Sheet
as at 1st April, 2019

Liabilities		Amt (₹)	Assets		Amt (₹)
Workmen's Compensation Fund		30,000	Debtors	90,000	
Creditors		1,10,000	(−) Bad debts	(2,000)	
Capital A/cs				88,000	
Ashish	5,40,000		(−) Provision for doubtful debts	(4,400)	83,600
Nimish	3,60,000		Furniture		2,85,400
Geeta	3,00,000	12,00,000	Plant and Machinery		2,90,000

Liabilities	Amt (₹)	Assets	Amt (₹)
		Cash	3,91,000
		Ashish's Current A/c	1,46,000
		Nimish's Current A/c	1,44,000
	13,40,000		13,40,000

Working Notes

1. 1/4th share capital = ₹ 3,00,000; Total capital = 3,00,000 × 4 = ₹ 12,00,000

   Ashish capital $= 12{,}00{,}000 \times 9/20 =$ ₹ 5,40,000 ; Nimish capital $= 12{,}00{,}000 \times 6/20 =$ ₹ 3,60,000

2. Geeta's share = 1/4th; Remaining share $= 1 - 1/4 = 3/4$

   Ashish's share $= 3/4 \times 3/5 = 9/20$; Nimish's share $= 3/4 \times 2/5 = 6/20$;

   Geeta's share $= 1/4 \times 5/5 = 5/20$; New Ratio $= 9:6:5$

4. Sanjana and Alok were partners in a firm sharing profits and losses in the ratio 3:2. On 31st March, 2018, their balance sheet was as follows

Balance Sheet of Sanjana and Alok
as on 31-3-2018

Liabilities		Amt (₹)	Assets		Amt (₹)
Creditors		60,000	Cash		1,66,000
Workmen's Compensation Fund		60,000	Debtors	1,46,000	
			(–) Provision		
			for Doubtful Debts	(2,000)	1,44,000
Capitals A/c			Stock		1,50,000
Sanjana	5,00,000		Investments		2,00,000
Alok	4,00,000	9,00,000	Furniture		3,00,000
		10,20,000			10,20,000

On 1st April, 2018, they admitted Nidhi as a new partner for 1/ 4th share in the profits on the following terms

(*i*) Goodwill of the firm was valued at ₹ 4,00,000 and Nidhi brought the necessary amount in cash for her share of goodwill premium, half of which was withdrawn by the old partners.

(*ii*) Stock was to be increased by 20% and furniture was to be reduced to 90%.

(*iii*) Investments were to be value at ₹ 3,00,000. Alok took over investment at this value.

(*iv*) Nidhi brought ₹ 3,00,000 a her capital and the capitals of Sanjana and Alok were adjusted in the new profit sharing ratio.

Prepare revaluation account, partners' capital accounts and the balance sheet of the reconstituted firm on Nidhi's admission. **Delhi 2019**

Ans. Dr **Revaluation Account** Cr

Particulars		Amt (₹)	Particulars	Amt (₹)
To Furniture		30,000	By Stock	30,000
To Profit Transferred to			By Investment	40,000
Sanjana's Capital A/c	24,000			
Alok's Capital A/c	16,000	40,000		
		70,000		70,000

Dr **Partners' Capital Account** Cr

Particulars	Sanjana (₹)	Alok (₹)	Nidhi (₹)	Particulars	Sanjana (₹)	Alok (₹)	Nidhi (₹)
To Cash	30,000	20,000	—	By Balance b/d	5,00,000	4,00,000	—
To Investment	—	3,00,000	—	By Premium for Goodwill	60,000	40,000	—
To Cash A/c	1,40,000	—	—	By Cash A/c	—	—	3,00,000
To Balance c/d	4,50,000	3,00,000	3,00,000	By Revaluation (Profit)	24,000	16,000	—
				By Workmens' Compensation Fund	36,000	24,000	—
				By Cash A/c	—	1,40,000	—
	6,20,000	6,20,000	3,00,000		6,20,000	6,20,000	3,00,000

Dr **Cash Account** Cr

Particulars	Amt (₹)	Particulars	Amt (₹)
To Balance b/d	1,66,000	By Sanjana's Capital A/c	30,000
To Premium for Goodwill	1,00,000	By Alok's Capital A/c	20,000
To Nidhi's Capital A/c	3,00,000	By Sanjana's Capital A/c	1,40,000
To Alok's Capital A/c	1,40,000	By Balance c/d	5,16,000
	7,06,000		7,06,000

Balance Sheet
as at .....

Liabilities		Amt (₹)	Assets		Amt (₹)
Creditors		60,000	Stock		1,80,000
Capital A/c			Furniture		2,70,000
Sanjana	4,50,000		Debtors	1,46,000	
Alok	3,00,000		(–) Provision for Doubtful Debts	(2,000)	1,44,000
Nidhi	3,00,000	10,50,000	Cash		5,16,000
		11,10,000			11,10,000

Working Notes

1. Firm's goodwill = ₹ 4,00,000

   Nidhi's share of goodwill $= 4,00,000 \times \frac{1}{4} =$ ₹ 1,00,000 to be distributed among Sanjana and Alok in sacrificing ratio.

2. Sanjana's capital after adjustment = ₹ 5,90,000

   Alok's capital after adjustment = ₹ 1,60,000

   ₹ 7,50,000

   to be in profit sharing ratio

   Sanjana $= 7,50,000 \times \frac{3}{5} = 4,50,000 - 5,90,000 =$ ₹ 1,40,000 cash withdrew

   Alok $= 7,50,000 \times \frac{2}{5} = 3,00,000 - 1,60,000 =$ ₹ 1,40,000 cash brought in

5. A and B were partners sharing profits and losses in the ratio of 3 : 2. Their Balance Sheet as at 31st March, 2018, was as follows

Balance Sheet of A and B
as at 31st March, 2018

Liabilities		Amt (₹)	Assets		Amt (₹)
Capital			Cash		8,000
A	1,04,000		Sundry Debtors	37,600	
B	52,000	1,56,000	(–) Provision for Doubtful Debts	(1,600)	36,000
Creditors		1,54,000	Stock		60,000
Employees' Provident Fund		16,000	Prepaid Insurance		6,000
Workmen's Compensation Fund		10,000	Plant and Machinery		76,000
Contingency Reserve		10,000	Building		1,40,000
			Furniture		20,000
		3,46,000			3,46,000

C was admitted as a new partner and brought ₹ 64,000 as capital and ₹ 15,000 for his share of goodwill premium. The new profit sharing ratio was 5 : 3 : 2.

On C's admission, the following was agreed upon

(*i*) Stock was to be depreciated by 5%.

(*ii*) Provision for doubtful debts was to be made at ₹ 2,000.

(*iii*) Furniture was to be depreciated by 10%.

(*iv*) Building was valued at ₹ 1,60,000.

(*v*) Capitals of A and B were to be adjusted on the basis of C's capital by bringing or paying of cash as the case may be.

Prepare revaluation account, partners' capital accounts and the balance sheet of reconstituted firm. **All India 2019**

Ans. Dr **Revaluation Account** Cr

Particulars		Amt (₹)	Particulars	Amt (₹)
To Stock		3,000	By Building	20,000
To Provision for Doubtful Debts		400		
To Furniture		2,000		
To Profit Transferred to				
A's Capital A/c	8,760			
B's Capital A/c	5,840	14,600		
		20,000		20,000

Dr **Partners' Capital Account** Cr

Particulars	A (₹)	B (₹)	C (₹)	Particulars	A (₹)	B (₹)	C (₹)
To Balance c/d	1,60,000	96,000	64,000	By Balance b/d	1,04,000	52,000	—
				By Workmen' Compensation Fund	6,000	4,000	—
				By Contingency Reserve	6,000	4,000	—
				By Cash	—	—	64,000
				By Premium for Goodwill	7,500	7,500	—
				By Revaluation (Profit)	8,760	5,840	—
				By Cash A/c (Balancing figure)	27,740	22,660	—
	1,60,000	96,000	64,000		1,60,000	96,000	64,000

Dr **Cash Account** Cr

Particulars	Amt (₹)	Particulars	Amt (₹)
To Balance b/d	8,000	By Balance c/d	1,37,400
To C's Capital	64,000		
To Premium for Goodwill	15,000		
To A's Capital A/c	27,740		
To B's Capital A/c	22,660		
	1,37,400		1,37,400

Balance Sheet
as at 31st March, 2018

Liabilities		Amt (₹)	Assets		Amt (₹)
Creditors		1,54,000	Stock		57,000
Employees' Provident Fund		16,000	Debtors	37,600	
Capital A/Cs A	1,60,000		(–) Provision for Doubtful Debts	(2,000)	35,600
B	96,000		Furniture		18,000
C	64,000	3,20,000	Building		1,60,000
			Prepaid Insurance		6,000
			Plant and Machinery		76,000
			Cash		1,37,400
		4,90,000			4,90,000

Working Notes

1. **Calculation of Sacrificing Ratio**

   A sacrifice $= \frac{3}{5} - \frac{5}{10} = \frac{6-5}{10} = \frac{1}{10}$; B sacrifice $= \frac{2}{5} - \frac{3}{10} = \frac{4-3}{10} = \frac{1}{10}$

   Sacrificing ratio = 1 : 1

2. $\frac{2}{10}$th share capital = ₹ 64,000

   Firm's capital $= 64{,}000 \times \frac{10}{2} =$ ₹ 3,20,000; A's new capital $= 3{,}20{,}000 \times \frac{5}{10} =$ ₹ 1,60,000

   B's new capital $= 3{,}20{,}000 \times \frac{3}{10} =$ ₹ 96,000

6. Leena and Rohit are partners in a firm sharing profits in the ratio of 3 : 2. On 31st March, 2018, their balance sheet was as follows

Balance Sheet of Leena and Rohit
as at 31st March, 2018

Liabilities		Amt (₹)	Assets		Amt (₹)
Sundry Creditors		80,000	Cash		42,000
Bills Payable		38,000	Debtors	1,32,000	
General Reserve		50,000	(–) Provision for Doubtful Debts	(2,000)	1,30,000
Capital A/c			Stock		1,46,000
Leena	1,60,000		Plant and Machinery		1,50,000
Rohit	1,40,000	3,00,000			
		4,68,000			4,68,000

On the above date, Manoj was admitted as a new partner for $\frac{1}{5}$th share in the profits of the firm on the following terms

(*i*) Manoj brought proportionate capital. He also brought his share of goodwill premium of ₹ 80,000 in cash.

(*ii*) 10% of the general reserve was to be transferred to provision for doubtful debts.

(*iii*) Claim on account of workmen's compensation amounted to ₹ 40,000.

(*iv*) Stock was overvalued by ₹ 16,000.

(*v*) Leena, Rohit and Manoj will share future profits in the ratio of 5 : 3 : 2.

Prepare revaluation account, partners' capital accounts and the balance sheet of the reconstituted firm. **All India 2019**

Ans. Dr **Revaluation Account** Cr

Particulars	Amt (₹)	Particulars		Amt (₹)
To Claim for Workmen's Compensation	40,000	By Loss Transferred to		
To Stock	16,000	Leena's Capital A/c	33,600	
		Rohit's Capital A/c	22,400	56,000
	56,000			56,000

Dr **Partners' Capital Account** Cr

Particulars	Leena (₹)	Rohit (₹)	Manoj (₹)	Particulars	Leena (₹)	Rohit (₹)	Manoj (₹)
To Revaluation (Loss)	33,600	22,400	—	By Balance b/d	1,60,000	1,40,000	—
To Balance c/d	1,93,400	1,75,600	92,250	By General Reserve	27,000	18,000	—
				By Premium for Goodwill	40,000	40,000	—
				By Cash	—	—	92,250
	2,27,000	1,98,000	92,250		2,27,000	1,98,000	92,250

Dr **Cash Account** Cr

Particulars	Amt (₹)	Particulars	Amt (₹)
To Balance b/d	42,000	By Balance c/d	2,14,250
To Premium for Goodwill	80,000		
To Manoj's Capital	92,250		
	2,14,250		2,14,250

Balance Sheet
as at...

Liabilities		Amt (₹)	Assets		Amt (₹)
Claim for Workmen's Compensation		40,000	Debtors	1,32,000	
Sundry Creditors		80,000	(–) Provision for Doubtful Debts	(7,000)	1,25,000
Bills Payable		38,000	Stock		1,30,000
Capital Leena	1,93,400		Plant and Machinery		1,50,000
Rohit	1,75,600		Cash		2,14,250
Manoj	92,250	4,61,250			
		6,19,250			6,19,250

Working Notes

1. **Calculation of Sacrifice Ratio**

   Leena sacrifice $= \frac{3}{5} - \frac{5}{10} = \frac{6-5}{10} = \frac{1}{10}$; Rohit sacrifice $= \frac{2}{5} - \frac{3}{10} = \frac{4-3}{10} = \frac{1}{10}$

   Sacrificing ratio = 1 : 1

		Amt (₹)
2. General Reserve	=	50,000
Transferred to Provision for Doubtful Debts	=	(5,000)
To be distributed among old partners in old ratio	=	45,000

3. Leena's Capital $= 1{,}93{,}400$

   Rohit's Capital $= 1{,}75{,}600$

   $= 3{,}69{,}000$

   Manoj's share $= \frac{1}{5}$; Remaining Share $= 1 - \frac{1}{5} = \frac{4}{5}$

   $\frac{4}{5}$ th share capital = ₹ 3,69,000; $\frac{1}{5}$ th share capital = ₹ $3{,}69{,}000 \times \frac{5}{4} \times \frac{1}{5}$ = ₹ 92,250

7. On 31st March 2017, the balance sheet of Abhir and Divya, who were sharing profits in the ratio of 3 : 1 was as follows

Liabilities		Amt (₹)	Assets		Amt (₹)
Creditors		2,20,000	Cash at Bank		1,40,000
Employee's Provident Fund		1,00,000	Debtors	6,50,000	
Investment Fluctuation Fund		1,00,000	(–) Provision		
General Reserve		1,20,000	for bad debts	50,000	6,00,000
Capitals :			Stock		3,00,000
Abhir	6,00,000		Investments (market value ₹ 4,40,000)		5,00,000
Divya	4,00,000	10,00,000			
		15,40,000			15,40,000

They decided to admit Vibhor on 1st April, 2017 for 1/5th share

(*i*) Vibhor shall bring ₹ 80,000 as his share of goodwill premium.

(*ii*) Stock was overvalued by ₹ 20,000.

(*iii*) A debtors whose dues of ₹ 5,000 were written-off as bad debts, paid ₹ 4,000 in full settlement.

(*iv*) Two months salary @ ₹ 6,000 per month was outstanding.

(*v*) Vibhor was to bring in capital to the extent of 1/5th of the total capital of the new firm.

Prepare revaluation account, partners' capital account and the balance sheet of the reconstituted firm. **Compartment 2018**

Ans.

Revaluation Account

Dr | | | | Cr

Particulars	Amt (₹)	Particulars		Amt (₹)
To Stock	20,000	By Bad Debts Recovered		4,000
To Outstanding Salary	12,000	By Loss Transferred to		
		Abhir's Capital A/c	21,000	
		Divya's Capital A/c	7,000	28,000
	32,000			32,000

Partners' Capital Account

Dr | | Cr

Particulars	Abhir (₹)	Divya (₹)	Vibhor (₹)	Particulars	Abhir (₹)	Divya (₹)	Vibhor (₹)
To Revaluation (Loss)	21,000	7,000	—	By Balance b/d	6,00,000	4,00,000	—
To Balance c/d	7,59,000	4,53,000	3,03,000	By Premium for Goodwill A/c	60,000	20,000	—
				By Investment Fluctuation Fund A/c	30,000	10,000	—
				By General Reserve A/c	90,000	30,000	—
				By Bank	—	—	3,03,000
	7,80,000	4,60,000	3,03,000		7,80,000	4,60,000	3,03,000

Balance Sheet
as on 1st April, 2017

Liabilities		Amt (₹)	Assets		Amt (₹)
Outstanding Salary		12,000	Stock		
Creditors		2,20,000	Debtors	6,50,000	
Employees' Provident Fund		1,00,000	(–) Provision for bad debts	(50,000)	6,00,000
Partners Capital A/c			Investment		4,40,000
Abhir	7,59,000		Cash at Bank		5,27,000
Divya	4,53,000				
Vibhor	3,03,000	15,15,000			
		18,47,000			18,47,000

Working Notes

1. Abhir's capital = ₹ 7,59,000

   Divya's capital = ₹ 4,53,000

   ₹ 12,12,000

   Vibhor's share = $\frac{1}{5}$; Remaining Share $= 1 - \frac{1}{5} = \frac{4}{5}$

   $\frac{4}{5}$th share capital = 12,12,000 ; $\frac{1}{5}$th share capital $= 12{,}12{,}000 \times \frac{5}{4} \times \frac{1}{5}$

   Vibhor's capital = ₹ 3,03,000

2. Dr **Bank Account** Cr

Particular	Amt (₹)	Particulars	Amt (₹)
To Balance b/d	1,40,000	By Balance c/d	5,27,000
To Premium for Goodwill	80,000		
To Bad Debts Recovered	4,000		
To Vibhor's Capital	3,03,000		
	5,27,000		5,27,000

8. L, M and N were partners in a firm sharing profits in the ratio of 3 : 2 : 1. Their balance sheet as at 31st March, 2015 was as follows

Balance Sheet
as at 31st March, 2015

Liabilities		Amt (₹)	Assets	Amt (₹)
Creditors		1,68,000	Bank	34,000
General Reserve		42,000	Debtors	46,000
Capital A/cs			Stock	2,20,000
L	1,20,000		Investments	60,000
M	80,000		Furniture	20,000
N	40,000	2,40,000	Machinery	70,000
		4,50,000		4,50,000

On the above date, O was admitted as a new partner and it was decided that

(*i*) The new profit sharing ratio between L, M, N and O will be 2 : 2 : 1 : 1.

(*ii*) Goodwill of the firm was valued at ₹ 1,80,000 and O brought his share of goodwill premium in cash.

(*iii*) The market value of investments was ₹ 36,000.

(*iv*) Machinery will be reduced to ₹ 58,000.

(*v*) A creditor of ₹ 6,000 was not likely to claim the amount and hence was to be written-off.

(*vi*) O will bring proportionate capital so as to give him 1/6th share in the profits of the firm.

Prepare revaluation account, partners' capital accounts and the balance sheet of the new firm. **All India 2016**

Ans.

Revaluation Account

Dr Particulars	Amt (₹)	Particulars		Amt (₹) Cr
To Investment A/c	24,000	By Creditors A/c		6,000
To Machinery A/c	12,000	By Loss Transferred to Capital A/cs		
		L	15,000	
		M	10,000	
		N	5,000	30,000
	36,000			36,000

Partners' Capital Account

Dr Particulars	L (₹)	M (₹)	N (₹)	O (₹)	Particulars	L (₹)	M (₹)	N (₹)	O (₹) Cr
To Revaluation A/c (Loss)	15,000	10,000	5,000	—	By Balance b/d	1,20,000	80,000	40,000	—
To Balance c/d	1,56,000	84,000	42,000	56,400	By General Reserve A/c	21,000	14,000	7,000	—
					By Premium for Goodwill A/c	30,000	—	—	—
					By Cash A/c	—	—	—	56,400
	1,71,000	94,000	47,000	56,400		1,71,000	94,000	47,000	56,400

Balance Sheet
as at 31st March, 2015

Liabilities		Amt (₹)	Assets		Amt (₹)
Creditors (1,68,000 – 6,000)		1,62,000	Debtors		46,000
Capital A/cs			Stock		2,20,000
L	1,56,000		Investments (60,000 – 24,000)		36,000
M	84,000		Furniture and Fittings		20,000
N	42,000		Machinery	70,000	
O	56,400	3,38,400	(–) Depreciation	(12,000)	58,000
			Bank		1,20,400
		5,00,400			5,00,400

Working Notes

1. **Calculation of Sacrificing Ratio**

Sacrificing Ratio = Old Share – New Share

$$L = \frac{3}{6} - \frac{2}{6} = \frac{3-2}{6} = \frac{1}{6};\ M = \frac{2}{6} - \frac{2}{6} = \frac{2-2}{6} = \text{Nil};\ N = \frac{1}{6} - \frac{1}{6} = \frac{1-1}{6} = \text{Nil}$$

2. **Adjustment for Goodwill**

$$\text{Firm's goodwill} = ₹\,1,80,000$$

$$\text{O's share of goodwill} = 1,80,000 \times \frac{1}{6} = ₹\,30,000$$

O's share of goodwill will be credited to L's capital account as he is the only sacrificing partner.

3. **Calculation of Adjustment of Capital**

Adjusted capital of L	=	1,56,000
Adjusted capital of M	=	84,000
Adjusted capital of N	=	42,000
Total adjusted capital	=	₹ 2,82,000

For 5/6th share, combined capital of L, M and N after adjustment is ₹ 2,82,000

$\therefore$ Total capital of the firm is $2{,}82{,}000 \times \frac{6}{5} =$ ₹ $3{,}38{,}400$

$\therefore$ O's share in capital $= 3{,}38{,}400 \times \frac{1}{6} =$ ₹ $56{,}400$

Dr **Bank Account** Cr

Particulars	Amt (₹)	Particulars	Amt (₹)
To Balance b/d	34,000	By Balance c/d	1,20,400
To Premium for Goodwill A/c	30,000		
To O's Capital A/c	56,400		
	1,20,400		1,20,400

9. A, B and C were partners in a firm sharing profits in the ratio of 3:2:1. On 31st March, 2015 their balance sheet was as follows

Balance Sheet
as at 31st March, 2015

Liabilities		Amt (₹)	Assets	Amt (₹)
Creditors		84,000	Bank	17,000
General Reserve		21,000	Debtors	23,000
Capital A/cs			Stock	1,10,000
A	60,000		Investments	30,000
B	40,000		Furniture and Fittings	10,000
C	20,000	1,20,000	Machinery	35,000
		2,25,000		2,25,000

On the above date, D was admitted as a new partner and it was decided that

(*i*) The new profit sharing ratio between A, B, C and D will be 2 : 2 : 1 : 1.

(*ii*) Goodwill of the firm was valued at ₹ 90,000 and D brought his share of goodwill premium in cash.

(*iii*) The market value of investments was ₹ 24,000.

(*iv*) Machinery will be reduced to ₹ 29,000.

(*v*) A creditor of ₹ 3,000 was not likely to claim the amount and hence to be written-off.

(*vi*) D will bring proportionate capital so as to give him 1/6th share in the profits of the firm.

Prepare revaluation account, partners' capital accounts and the balance sheet of the reconstituted firm. **Delhi 2016**

Ans. Solve as Q no. 8 on page 109-111.

Loss on Revaluation Account: A = ₹ 4,500, B = ₹ 3,000, C = ₹ 1,500; Balance in Partners' Capital Accounts A = ₹ 81,000, B = ₹ 44,000, C = ₹ 22,000, D = ₹ 29,400; Total of Balance Sheet = ₹ 2,57,400.

10. Charu and Harsha were partners in a firm sharing profits in the ratio of 3 : 2. On 1st April, 2014 their balance sheet was as follows

Balance Sheet
as at 1st April, 2014

Liabilities		Amt (₹)	Assets	Amt (₹)
Creditors		17,000	Cash	6,000
General Reserve		4,000	Debtors	15,000
Workmen's Compensation Fund		9,000	Investments	20,000
Investment Fluctuation Fund		11,000	Plant	14,000
Provision for Doubtful Debts		2,000	Land and Building	38,000
Capital A/cs				
Charu	30,000			
Harsha	20,000	50,000		
		93,000		93,000

On the above date, Vaishali was admitted for 1/4th share in the profits of the firm on the following terms

(*i*) Vaishali will bring ₹ 20,000 for her capital and ₹ 4,000 for her share of goodwill premium.

(*ii*) All debtors were considered good.

(*iii*) The market value of investments was ₹ 15,000.

(*iv*) There was a liability of ₹ 6,000 for workmen compensation.

(*v*) Capital accounts of Charu and Harsha are to be adjusted on the basis of Vaishali's capital by opening current accounts.

Prepare revaluation account and partners' capital accounts. **Delhi 2015**

Ans. Dr **Revaluation Account** Cr

Particulars		Amt (₹)	Particulars	Amt (₹)
To Profit Transferred to Capital A/c			By Provision for Doubtful Debts A/c	2,000
Charu	1,200			
Harsha	800	2,000		
		2,000		2,000

Dr **Partners' Capital Account** Cr

Particulars	Charu (₹)	Harsha (₹)	Vaishali (₹)	Particulars	Charu (₹)	Harsha (₹)	Vaishali (₹)
To Current A/c	5,400	3,600	—	By Balance b/d	30,000	20,000	—
(Balancing figure)				By General Reserve A/c	2,400	1,600	—
To Balance c/d	36,000	24,000	20,000	By Workmen Compensation Fund A/c	1,800	1,200	—

Particulars	Charu (₹)	Harsha (₹)	Vaishali (₹)	Particulars	Charu (₹)	Harsha (₹)	Vaishali (₹)
				By Investment Fluctuation Fund A/c	3,600	2,400	—
				By Revaluation A/c (Profit)	1,200	800	—
				By Cash A/c	—	—	20,000
				By Premium for Goodwill A/c	2,400	1,600	—
	41,400	27,600	20,000		41,400	27,600	20,000

Working Notes

1. **Calculation of New Profit Sharing Ratio**

Old ratio $= 3:2$

Let the total profit of the firm $= 1$

Remaining profit share of the firm $= 1 - \frac{1}{4} = \frac{3}{4}$

So, Charu's new share $= \frac{3}{5} \times \frac{3}{4} = \frac{9}{20}$; Harsha's new share $= \frac{2}{5} \times \frac{3}{4} = \frac{6}{20}$

$\therefore$ New profit sharing ratio $= \frac{9}{20} : \frac{6}{20} : \frac{1}{4} = 9:6:5$

2. **Calculation of Sacrificing Ratio**

Old ratio $= 3:2$; New ratio $= 9:6:5$

Sacrificing Ratio = Old Share − New Share

Charu $= \frac{3}{5} - \frac{9}{20} = \frac{12-9}{20} = \frac{3}{20}$; Harsha $= \frac{2}{5} - \frac{6}{20} = \frac{8-6}{20} = \frac{2}{20}$

$\therefore$ Sacrificing ratio $= 3:2$

3. **Distribution of Goodwill**

Charu will get $= 4{,}000 \times \frac{3}{5} =$ ₹ 2,400; Harsha will get $= 4{,}000 \times \frac{2}{5} =$ ₹ 1,600

4. **Adjustment of Capital**

Vaishali's capital for $\frac{1}{4}$th share = 20,000

Total capital of firm $= 20{,}000 \times \frac{4}{1} =$ ₹ 80,000

New profit sharing ratio $= 9:6:5$

Charu's new capital $= 80{,}000 \times \frac{9}{20} =$ ₹ 36,000

Harsha's new capital $= 80{,}000 \times \frac{6}{20} =$ ₹ 24,000; Vaishali's new capital $= 80{,}000 \times \frac{5}{20} =$ ₹ 20,000

11. O, R and S were partners in a firm sharing profits in the ratio of 3 : 2 : 1. On 1st April, 2014 their balance sheet was as follows

Balance Sheet
as at 1st April, 2014

Liabilities		Amt (₹)	Assets	Amt (₹)
General Reserve		15,000	R's Current A/c	7,000
Profit and Loss A/c		7,000	Land and Building	1,75,000
Creditors		80,000	Plant and Machinery	67,500
Bills Payable		45,000	Furniture	80,000
Capital A/cs			Investments	36,500
O	1,75,000		Bills Receivable	17,000
R	1,50,000		Sundry Debtors	43,500
S	1,25,000	4,50,000	Stock	1,37,000
Current A/cs			Bank	43,500
O	4,000			
S	6,000	10,000		
		6,07,000		6,07,000

On the above date, H was admitted on the following terms

(*i*) H will bring ₹ 50,000 as his capital and will get 1/6th share in the profits.

(*ii*) He will bring necessary cash for his share of goodwill premium. The goodwill of the firm was valued at ₹ 90,000.

(*iii*) The new profit sharing ratio will be 2 : 2 : 1 : 1.

(*iv*) A liability of ₹ 7,004 will be created against bills receivables discounted.

(*v*) The value of stock, furniture and investments is reduced by 20%, whereas the value of land and building and plant and machinery will be appreciated by 20% and 10% respectively.

(*vi*) The capital accounts of the partners will be adjusted on the basis of H's capital through their current accounts.

Prepare revaluation account and partners' current accounts and capital accounts. **Foreign 2015**

Ans. Dr **Revaluation Account** Cr

Particulars	Amt (₹)	Particulars		Amt (₹)
To Stock A/c	27,400	By Land and Building A/c		35,000
To Furniture A/c	16,000	By Plant and Machinery A/c		6,750
To Investments A/c	7,300	By Loss Transferred to Capital A/cs		
To Liability against Bills Receivable Discounted	7,004	O	7,977	
		R	5,318	
		S	2,659	15,954
	57,704			57,704

Dr **Partners' Capital Account** Cr

Particulars	O (₹)	R (₹)	S (₹)	H (₹)	Particulars	O (₹)	R (₹)	S (₹)	H (₹)
To Current A/c	75,000	50,000	75,000	—	By Balance b/d	1,75,000	1,50,000	1,25,000	—
To Balance c/d	1,00,000	1,00,000	50,000	50,000	By Cash A/c	—	—	—	50,000
	1,75,000	1,50,000	1,25,000	50,000		1,75,000	1,50,000	1,25,000	50,000

Dr **Partners' Current Account** Cr

Particulars	O (₹)	R (₹)	S (₹)	Particulars	O (₹)	R (₹)	S (₹)
To Balance b/d	—	7,000	—	By Balance b/d	4,000	—	6,000
To Revaluation A/c (Loss)	7,977	5,318	2,659	By General Reserve A/c	7,500	5,000	2,500
To Balance c/d	97,023	45,015	82,008	By Profit and Loss A/c	3,500	2,333	1,167
				By Premium for Goodwill A/c	15,000	—	—
				By Capital A/c	75,000	50,000	75,000
	1,05,000	57,333	84,667		1,05,000	57,333	84,667

Working Notes

1. **Calculation of Sacrificing Ratio**

Old ratio = 3 : 2 : 1 ; New ratio = 2 : 2 : 1 : 1

Sacrificing Ratio = Old Share – New Share

$$O = \frac{3}{6} - \frac{2}{6} = \frac{1}{6}; R = \frac{2}{6} - \frac{2}{6} = \text{Nil}; S = \frac{1}{6} - \frac{1}{6} = \text{Nil}$$

Here, only O has sacrificed his $\frac{1}{6}$ th share.

2. **Adjustment of Goodwill**

H's share of goodwill $= 90,000 \times \frac{1}{6} =$ ₹ 15,000

As only O has sacrificed his share, therefore, he will get = ₹ 15,000

3. **Adjustment of Capital**

Total Capital of the Firm = H's Capital × Reciprocal of his Share

$= 50,000 \times \frac{6}{1} =$ ₹ 3,00,000

New profit sharing ratio = 2 : 2 : 1 : 1

O's new capital $= 3,00,000 \times \frac{2}{6} =$ ₹ 1,00,000; R's new capital $= 3,00,000 \times \frac{2}{6} =$ ₹ 1,00,000

S's new capital $= 3,00,000 \times \frac{1}{6} =$ ₹ 50,000; H's new capital $= 3,00,000 \times \frac{1}{6} =$ ₹ 50,000

12. Om, Ram and Shanti were partners in a firm sharing profits in the ratio of 3:2:1. On 1st April, 2014 their balance sheet was as follows

Balance Sheet
as at 1st April, 2014

Liabilities		Amt (₹)	Assets	Amt (₹)
General Reserve		48,000	Land and Building	3,64,000
Creditors		1,60,000	Plant and Machinery	2,95,000
Bills Payable		90,000	Furniture	2,33,000
Capital A/cs			Bills Receivable	38,000
Om	3,58,000		Sundry Debtors	90,000
Ram	3,00,000		Stock	1,11,000
Shanti	2,62,000	9,20,000	Bank	87,000
		12,18,000		12,18,000

On the above date, Hanuman was admitted on the following terms

(i) He will bring ₹ 1,00,000 for his capital and will get 1/10th share in the profits.

(ii) He will bring necessary cash for his share of goodwill premium. The goodwill of the firm was valued at ₹ 3,00,000.

(iii) A liability of ₹ 18,000 will be created against bills receivables discounted.

(iv) The value of stock and furniture will be reduced by 20%.

(v) The value of land and building will be increased by 10%.

(vi) Capital accounts of the partners will be adjusted on the basis of Hanuman's capital in their profit sharing ratio by opening current accounts.

Prepare revaluation account and partners' capital accounts. **All India 2015**

Ans. Solve as Q no. 11 on page 114-115.

Loss on Revaluation = ₹ 50,400; Balance in Partners' Capital Account : Om = ₹ 4,50,000, Ram = ₹ 3,00,000, Shanti = ₹ 1,50,000, Hanuman = ₹ 1,00,000; New Profit Sharing Ratio = 9 : 6 : 3 : 2

13. Following is the balance sheet of Amit and Vidya as on 31st March, 2014.

Balance Sheet
as at 31st March, 2014

Liabilities		Amt (₹)	Assets		Amt (₹)
Creditors		26,000	Bank		20,000
Employees Provident Fund		16,000	Stock		30,000
Workmen's Compensation Fund		30,000	Debtors	44,000	
Capital A/cs			(−) Provision for Bad Debts	(2,000)	42,000
Amit	1,10,000		Plant and Machinery		1,20,000
Vidya	60,000	1,70,000	Goodwill		20,000
			Profit and Loss Account		10,000
		2,42,000			2,42,000

On the above date, Chintan was admitted as a partner for 1/4th share in the profits of the firm with the following terms

(i) ₹ 2,900 will be written off as bad debts.

(ii) Stock was taken over by Vidya at ₹ 35,000.

(iii) Goodwill of the firm was valued at ₹ 40,000. Chintan brought his share of goodwill premium in cash.

(iv) Chintan brought proportionate capital and the capitals of the other partners were adjusted on the basis of Chintan's capital. For this necessary cash was to be brought in or paid off to the partners as the case may be.

Prepare revaluation account and partners' capital accounts. **All India (C) 2015**

Ans. Dr **Revaluation Account** Cr

Particulars		Amt (₹)	Particulars	Amt (₹)
To Bad Debts		900	By Stock A/c	5,000
To Profit Transferred to Capital A/cs				
Amit	2,050			
Vidya	2,050	4,100		
		5,000		5,000

Dr **Partners' Capital Account** Cr

Particulars	Amit (₹)	Vidya (₹)	Chintan (₹)	Particulars	Amit (₹)	Vidya (₹)	Chintan (₹)
To Goodwill A/c	10,000	10,000	—	By Balance b/d	1,10,000	60,000	—
To Profit and Loss A/c	5,000	5,000	—	By Revaluation A/c (Profit)	2,050	2,050	—
To Stock A/c	—	35,000	—	By Workmen's Compensation Fund A/c	15,000	15,000	—
To Cash A/c (Balancing figure)	42,500	—	—	By Premium for Goodwill A/c	5,000	5,000	—
To Balance c/d	74,550	74,550	49,700	By Cash A/c	—	42,500	—
				By Cash A/c (Balancing figure)	—	—	49,700
	1,32,050	1,24,550	49,700		1,32,050	1,24,550	49,700

Working Notes

1. **Calculation of New Profit Sharing Ratio**

Let total profit be $=1$

Chintan gets $=\frac{1}{4}$th share

Remaining share $=1-\frac{1}{4}=\frac{3}{4}$ will be shared by Amit and Vidya in their old profit sharing ratio

Amit's share $=\frac{3}{4}\times\frac{1}{2}=\frac{3}{8}$; Vidya's share $=\frac{3}{4}\times\frac{1}{2}=\frac{3}{8}$; Chintan's share $=\frac{1}{4}\times\frac{1}{2}=\frac{2}{8}$

New profit sharing ratio $=3:3:2$

2. **Calculation of Chintan's Share of Goodwill**

Firm's goodwill = ₹ 40,000

Chintan's share $=40{,}000\times\frac{1}{4}=10{,}000$ to be credited to Amit and Vidya in sacrificing ratio.

3. **Adjustment of Capital** **Amt (₹)**

		Amt (₹)
Amit's capital after adjustment	=	1,17,050
Vidya's capital after adjustment	=	32,050
Combined capital for 3/4 share	=	1,49,100

Total capital of new firm $=1{,}49{,}100\times\frac{4}{3}=1{,}98{,}800$

Amit's capital $=1{,}98{,}800\times\frac{3}{8}=$ ₹ 74,550; Vidya's capital $=1{,}98{,}800\times\frac{3}{8}=$ ₹74,550

Chintan's capital $=1{,}98{,}800\times\frac{1}{4}=$ ₹ 49,700

14. Shikhar and Rohit were partners in a firm sharing profits in the ratio of 7 : 3. On 1st April, 2013 they admitted Kavi as a new partner for 1/4 share in profits of the firm. Kavi brought ₹ 4,30,000 as his capital and ₹ 25,000 for his share of goodwill premium. The balance sheet of Shikhar and Rohit as on 1st April, 2013 was as follows

Balance Sheet
as at 1st April, 2013

Liabilities		Amt (₹)	Assets		Amt (₹)
General Reserve		1,50,000	Land and Building		3,50,000
Workmen's Compensation Fund		1,00,000	Machinery		4,50,000
Creditors		1,00,000	Debtors	2,20,000	
Capital A/cs			(−) Provision for Doubtful Debts	(20,000)	2,00,000
Shikhar	8,00,000		Stock		3,50,000
Rohit	3,50,000	11,50,000	Cash		1,50,000
		15,00,000			15,00,000

It was agreed that

(*i*) The value of land and building will be appreciated by 20%.
(*ii*) The value of machinery will be depreciated by 10%.
(*iii*) The liabilities of workmen's compensation fund was determined at ₹ 50,000.
(*iv*) Capitals of Shikhar and Rohit will be adjusted on the basis of Kavi's capital and actual cash to be brought in or to be paid off as the case may be.

Prepare revaluation account, partners' capital accounts and the balance sheet of the new firm. **All India 2014**

Ans. Dr **Revaluation Account** Cr

Particulars		Amt (₹)	Particulars	Amt (₹)
To Machinery A/c		45,000	By Land and Building A/c	70,000
To Profit Transferred to Capital A/cs				
Shikhar	17,500			
Rohit	7,500	25,000		
		70,000		70,000

Dr **Partners' Capital Account** Cr

Particulars	Shikhar (₹)	Rohit (₹)	Kavi (₹)	Particulars	Shikhar (₹)	Rohit (₹)	Kavi (₹)
To Cash A/c (Balancing figure)	37,000	23,000	—	By Balance b/d	8,00,000	3,50,000	—
				By General Reserve A/c	70,000	30,000	—
To Balance c/d	9,03,000	3,87,000	4,30,000	By Workmen's Compensation Fund A/c	35,000	15,000	—
				By Cash A/c	—	—	4,30,000
				By Premium for Goodwill A/c	17,500	7,500	—
				By Revaluation A/c (Profit)	17,500	7,500	—
	9,40,000	4,10,000	4,30,000		9,40,000	4,10,000	4,30,000

Balance Sheet
as at 1st April, 2013

Liabilities		Amt (₹)	Assets		Amt (₹)
Creditors		1,50,000	Land and Building	3,50,000	
Liability for Workmen's Compensation Fund		50,000	(+) Appreciation	70,000	4,20,000
Capital A/cs			Machinery	4,50,000	
Shikar	9,03,000		(−) Depreciation	(45,000)	4,05,000
Rohit	3,87,000		Stock		3,50,000
Kavi	4,30,000	17,20,000	Debtors	2,20,000	
			(−) Provision for Doubtful Debts	(20,000)	2,00,000
			Cash		5,45,000
		19,20,000			19,20,000

Working Note

1. **Calculation of New Profit Sharing Ratio**

   Let total profit be = 1, Kavi gets $= \frac{1}{4}$th share

   Remaining share $= 1 - \frac{1}{4} = \frac{4-1}{4} = \frac{3}{4}$

   Shikhar's share $= \frac{7}{10} \times \frac{3}{4} = \frac{21}{40}$; Rohit's share $= \frac{3}{10} \times \frac{3}{4} = \frac{9}{40}$; Kavi' share $= \frac{1}{4} \times \frac{10}{10} = \frac{10}{40}$

   New profit sharing ratio = 21 : 9 : 10

2. **Determination of the Combined Capital of New Firm**

   Taking Kavi's capital as base,

   The combined capital of new firm is $4,30,000 \times \frac{4}{1} =$ ₹ 17,20,000

   This capital will be shared by the partners in new profit sharing ratio, *i.e.* 21: 9: 10.

   Therefore, new capitals of partners will be

   Shikhar $= 17,20,000 \times \frac{21}{40} =$ ₹ 9,03,000; Rohit $= 17,20,000 \times \frac{9}{40} =$ ₹ 3,87,000

   Kavi's $= 17,20,000 \times \frac{10}{40} =$ ₹ 4,30,000

Dr **Cash Account** Cr

Particulars	Amt (₹)	Particulars	Amt (₹)
To Balance b/d	1,50,000	By Shikhar's Capital A/c	37,000
To Kavi's Capital A/c	4,30,000	By Rohit's Capital A/c	23,000
To Premium for Goodwill A/c	25,000	By Balance c/d	5,45,000
	6,05,000		6,05,000

15. Mohan and Mahesh were partners in a firm sharing profits in the ratio of 3 : 2. On 1st April, 2012, they admitted Nusrat as a partner in the firm. The balance sheet of Mohan and Mahesh on that date was as under

Balance Sheet
as at 1st April, 2012

Liabilities		Amt (₹)	Assets	Amt (₹)
Creditors		2,10,000	Cash in Hand	1,40,000
Workmen's Compensation Fund		2,50,000	Debtors	1,60,000
General Reserve		1,60,000	Stock	1,20,000
Capital A/cs			Machinery	1,00,000
Mohan	1,00,000		Building	2,80,000
Mahesh	80,000	1,80,000		
		8,00,000		8,00,000

It was agreed that

(*i*) The value of building and stock be appreciated to ₹ 3,80,000 and ₹ 1,60,000 respectively.

(*ii*) The liabilities of workmen's compensation fund was determined at ₹ 2,30,000.

(*iii*) Nusrat brought in her share of goodwill ₹ 1,00,000 in cash.

(*iv*) Nusrat was to bring further cash as would make her capital equal to 20% of the combined capital of Mohan and Mahesh after above revaluation and adjustments are carried out.

(*v*) The future profit sharing ratio will be Mohan 2/5th, Mahesh 2/5th, Nusrat 1/5th.

Prepare revaluation account, partners' capital accounts and balance sheet of the new firm. Also, show clearly the calculation of capital brought by Nusrat. **Delhi 2014**

Ans. Dr **Revaluation Account** Cr

Particulars		Amt (₹)	Particulars	Amt (₹)
To Profit Transferred to Capital A/cs			By Building A/c	1,00,000
Mohan	84,000		By Stock A/c	40,000
Mahesh	56,000	1,40,000		
		1,40,000		1,40,000

Dr **Partners' Capital Account** Cr

Particulars	Mohan (₹)	Mahesh (₹)	Nusrat (₹)	Particulars	Mohan (₹)	Mahesh (₹)	Nusrat (₹)
To Balance c/d	3,92,000	2,08,000	1,20,000	By Balance b/d	1,00,000	80,000	—
				By Revaluation A/c (Profit)	84,000	56,000	—
				By General Reserve A/c	96,000	64,000	—
				By Workmen's Compensation Fund A/c	12,000	8,000	—
				By Premium for Goodwill A/c	1,00,000	—	—
				By Cash A/c	—	—	1,20,000
	3,92,000	2,08,000	1,20,000		3,92,000	2,08,000	1,20,000

Balance Sheet
as at 1st April, 2012

Liabilities		Amt (₹)	Assets		Amt (₹)
Creditors		2,10,000	Building	2,80,000	
Liabilities for Workmen's Compensation Fund		2,30,000	(+) Appreciation	1,00,000	3,80,000
Capital A/cs			Stock	1,20,000	
			(+) Appreciation	40,000	1,60,000
Mohan	3,92,000		Machinery		1,00,000
Mahesh	2,08,000		Debtors		1,60,000
Nusrat	1,20,000	7,20,000	Cash in Hand		3,60,000
		11,60,000			11,60,000

Working Notes

1. **Calculation of Sacrificing Ratio**

Sacrificing Ratio = Old Share – New Share

$$\text{Mohan} = \frac{3}{5} - \frac{2}{5} = \frac{3-2}{5} = \frac{1}{5};\ \text{Mahesh} = \frac{2}{5} - \frac{2}{5} = \frac{2-2}{5} = \text{Nil}$$

Here, the entire sacrifice has been made by Mohan.

2. **Calculation of Cash Brought in by Nusrat as her Capital**

Adjusted capital of Mohan	= 3,92,000
Adjusted capital of Mahesh	= 2,08,000
Total adjusted capital	₹ 6,00,000

Nursrat's capital should be equal to 20% of the combined adjusted capital of Mohan and Mahesh, *i.e.* 6,00,000 × 20% = ₹ 1,20,000

Dr **Cash Account** Cr

Particulars	Amt (₹)	Particulars	Amt (₹)
To Balance b/d	1,40,000	By Balance c/d	3,60,000
To Premium for Goodwill A/c	1,00,000		
To Nusrat's Capital A/c	1,20,000		
	3,60,000		3,60,000

16. Atal and Madan were partners in a firm sharing profits in the ratio of 5 : 3. On 31st March, 2011, they admitted Mehra as a new partner for 1/5th share in the profit. The new profit sharing ratio was 5 : 3 : 2. On Mehra's admission, the balance sheet of the firm was as follows

Balance Sheet
as at 31st March, 2011

Liabilities		Amt (₹)	Assets	Amt (₹)
Provision for Bad Debt		1,200	Land and Building	1,50,000
Creditors		20,000	Machinery	40,000
Workmen's Compensation Fund		32,000	Patents	5,000
Capital A/cs			Stock	27,000
Atal	1,50,000		Debtors	47,000
Madan	90,000	2,40,000	Cash	4,200
			Profit and Loss A/c	20,000
		2,93,200		2,93,200

On Mehra's admission, it was agreed that

(*i*) Mehra will bring ₹ 40,000 as his capital and ₹ 16,000 for his share of goodwill premium, half of which was withdrawn by Atal and Madan.

(*ii*) A provision of 2.5% for bad and doubtful debt was to be created.

(*iii*) Included in the sundry creditors was an item of ₹ 2,500 which was not to be paid.

(*iv*) A provision was to be made for an outstanding bill for electricity ₹ 3,000.

(*v*) A claim of ₹ 325 for damages against the firm was likely to be admitted. Provision for the same was to be made.

After the above adjustment, the capitals of Atal and Madan were to be adjusted on the basis of Mehra's capital. Actual cash was to be brought in or to be paid off to Atal and Madan, as the case may be.

Prepare revaluation account, capital accounts of the partners and the balance sheet of the new firm. **All India 2012**

Ans. Dr **Revaluation Account** Cr

Particulars	Amt (₹)	Particulars		Amt (₹)
To Provision for Outstanding Electricity Bill A/c	3,000	By Creditors A/c		2,500
To Provision for Claim for Damages A/c	325	By Provision for Bad and Doubtful Debts A/c		25
		By Loss Transferred to		
		Atal's Capital A/c	500	
		Madan's Capital A/c	300	800
	3,325			3,325

Dr **Partners' Capital Account** Cr

Particulars	Atal (₹)	Madan (₹)	Mehra (₹)	Particulars	Atal (₹)	Madan (₹)	Mehra (₹)
To Cash A/c (Goodwill withdrawn)	5,000	3,000	—	By Balance b/d	1,50,000	90,000	—
				By Cash A/c	—	—	40,000
To Profit and Loss A/c	12,500	7,500	—	By Premium for Goodwill A/c	10,000	6,000	—
To Revaluation A/c (Loss)	500	300	—	By Workmen's Compensation Fund A/c	20,000	12,000	—
To Cash A/c (Balancing figure)	62,000	37,200	—				
To Balance c/d	1,00,000	60,000	40,000				
	1,80,000	1,08,000	40,000		1,80,000	1,08,000	40,000

Balance Sheet
as at 31st March, 2011

Liabilities	Amt (₹)	Assets		Amt (₹)
Outstanding Electricity Bill	3,000	Debtors	47,000	
Creditors (20,000 − 2,500)	17,500	(−) Provision for Doubtful Debts	(1,175)	45,825
Bank Overdraft	47,000	Land and Building		1,50,000
Provision for Claim for Damages	325	Machinery		40,000

Liabilities		Amt (₹)	Assets	Amt (₹)
Capital A/cs			Patents	5,000
Atal	1,00,000		Stock	27,000
Madan	60,000			
Mehra	40,000	2,00,000		
		2,67,825		2,67,825

Working Notes

1. **Calculation of Sacrificing Ratio**

   Sacrificing Ratio = Old Share – New Share

   Atal's sacrifice $= \frac{5}{8} - \frac{5}{10} = \frac{25-20}{40} = \frac{5}{40}$; Madan's sacrifice $= \frac{3}{8} - \frac{3}{10} = \frac{15-12}{40} = \frac{3}{40}$

   Sacrificing ratio = 5 : 3

2. **Calculation of Adjustment of Capital**

   Mehra's share = 2/10 ; Mehra's capital = ₹ 40,000

   For 2/10th share, capital = ₹ 40,000

   $$\text{Total capital} = 40,000 \times \frac{10}{2} = ₹\,2,00,000$$

   Atal's new capital $= 2,00,000 \times \frac{5}{10} =$ ₹ 1,00,000; Madan's new capital $= 2,00,000 \times \frac{3}{10} =$ ₹ 60,000

   Mehra's new capital $= 2,00,000 \times \frac{2}{10} =$ ₹ 40,000

Dr **Cash Account** Cr

Particulars	Amt (₹)	Particulars	Amt (₹)
To Balance b/d	4,200	By Atal's Capital A/c	5,000
To Mehra's Capital A/c	40,000	By Madan's Capital A/c	3,000
To Premium for Goodwill A/c	16,000	By Atal's Capital A/c	62,000
To Bank Overdraft A/c (Balancing figure)	47,000	By Madan's Capital A/c	37,200
	1,07,200		1,07,200

17. B and C were partners sharing profits in the ratio of 3 : 2. Their balance sheet as on 31st March, 2011 was as follows

Balance Sheet
as at 31st March, 2011

Liabilities		Amt (₹)	Assets	Amt (₹)
Provision for Bad Debts		1,000	Land and Building	80,000
Creditors		60,000	Machinery	20,000
Capital A/cs			Furniture	10,000
B	60,000		Debtors	25,000
C	40,000	1,00,000	Cash	16,000
			Profit and Loss A/c	10,000
		1,61,000		1,61,000

D was admitted to the partnership for 1/5th share in the profits on the following terms

(*i*) The new profit sharing ratio was decided as 2 : 2 : 1.

(*ii*) D will bring ₹ 30,000 as his capital and ₹ 15,000 for his share of goodwill.

(*iii*) Half of goodwill amount was withdrawn by the partner who sacrificed his share of profit in favour of D.

(*iv*) A provision of 5% for bad and doubtful debt was to be maintained.

(*v*) An item of ₹ 500 included in sundry creditors was not likely to be paid.

(*vi*) A provision of ₹ 800 was to be made for claims for damages against the firm.

After making the above adjustments, the capital accounts of B and C were to be adjusted on the basis of D's capital. Actual cash was to be brought in or to be paid off as the case may be.

Prepare revaluation account, capital accounts of the partners and the balance sheet of the new firm. **Delhi 2012**

Ans. Solve as Q no. 16 on page 121-123.

Loss on Revaluation = ₹ 550; Balance in Partners' Capital Account : B = ₹ 60,000, C = ₹ 60,000, D = ₹ 30,000; Total of Balance Sheet = ₹ 2,10,300; C will bring 24,220, B will withdraw = ₹ 1,170

18. The balance sheet of Madan and Mohan, who share profits and losses in the ratio of 3 : 2. On 31st March, 2010 was as follows

Balance Sheet

as at 31st March, 2010

Liabilities		Amt (₹)	Assets		Amt (₹)
Creditors		28,000	Cash at Bank		10,000
Workmen's Compensation Fund		12,000	Debtors	65,000	
General Reserve		20,000	(−) Provision for Doubtful Debts	(5,000)	60,000
Capital A/cs			Stock		30,000
Madan	60,000		Investment		50,000
Mohan	40,000	1,00,000	Patents		10,000
		1,60,000			1,60,000

They decided to admit Gopal on 1st April, 2010 for 1/4th share on the following terms

(*i*) Gopal shall bring ₹ 20,000 as his share of premium for goodwill.

(*ii*) That unaccounted accrued income of ₹ 1,000 be provided for.

(*iii*) The market value of investments was ₹ 45,000.

(*iv*) A debtor whose dues of ₹ 5,000 were written-off as bad debts paid ₹ 4,000 in full settlement.

(*v*) A claim of ₹ 3,000 on account of workmen's compensation to be provided for.

(*vi*) Patents are overvalued by ₹ 2,000.

(*vii*) Gopal to bring in capital equal to 1/4th of the total capital of the firm after all adjustments.

Prepare the revaluation account, capital accounts of the partners and the balance sheet of the new firm. **All India (C) 2011**

Ans. Dr **Revaluation Account** Cr

Particulars	Amt (₹)	Particulars		Amt (₹)
To Investment A/c	5,000	By Accrued Income A/c		1,000
To Patents A/c	2,000	By Bad Debts Recovered A/c		4,000
		By Loss Transferred to		
		Madan's Capital A/c	1,200	
		Mohan's Capital A/c	800	2,000
	7,000			7,000

Dr **Partners' Capital Account** Cr

Particulars	Madan (₹)	Mohan (₹)	Gopal (₹)	Particulars	Madan (₹)	Mohan (₹)	Gopal (₹)
To Revaluation A/c (Loss)	1,200	800	—	By Balance b/d	60,000	40,000	—
To Balance c/d	88,200	58,800	49,000	By Premium for Goodwill A/c	12,000	8,000	—
				By Workmen's Compensation Fund A/c	5,400	3,600	—
				By General Reserve A/c	12,000	8,000	—
				By Bank A/c	—	—	49,000
	89,400	59,600	49,000		89,400	59,600	49,000

Balance Sheet
as at 31st March, 2010

Liabilities		Amt (₹)	Assets		Amt (₹)
Workmen's Compensation Fund		3,000	Accrued Income		1,000
Creditors		28,000	Investment (50,000 − 5,000)		45,000
Capital A/cs			Patents (10,000 − 2,000)		8,000
Madan	88,200		Debtors	65,000	
Mohan	58,800		(−) Provision for Doubtful Debts	(5,000)	60,000
Gopal	49,000	1,96,000	Stock		30,000
			Bank		83,000
		2,27,000			2,27,000

Working Note

Calculation of Gopal's Capital

Madan's capital after all adjustment $= 88,200$

Mohan's capital after all adjustment $= 58,800$

₹ 1,47,000

Gopal's share in new firm $= \frac{1}{4}$th

Remaining share to be shared between Madan and Mohan $= 1 - \frac{1}{4} = \frac{3}{4}$th

For $\frac{3}{4}$th share, capital = ₹ 1,47,000 ; Total capital $= 1,47,000 \times \frac{4}{3} =$ ₹ 1,96,000

Gopal's capital $= 1,96,000 \times \frac{1}{4} =$ ₹ 49,000

Dr **Bank Account** Cr

Particulars	Amt (₹)	Particulars	Amt (₹)
To Balance b/d	10,000	By Balance c/d	83,000
To Premium for Goodwill A/c	20,000		
To Bad Debts Recovered A/c	4,000		
To Gopal's Capital A/c	49,000		
	83,000		83,000

19. The balance sheet of Ram and Shyam, who were sharing profits in the ratio of 3 : 1 on 31st March, 2009 was as follows

Liabilities		Amt (₹)	Assets		Amt (₹)
Creditors		2,800	Cash at Bank		2,000
Employees' Provident Fund		1,200	Debtors	6,500	
General Reserve		2,000	(−) Reserve for Doubtful Debts	(500)	6,000
Capital A/cs			Stock		3,000
Ram	6,000		Investments		5,000
Shyam	4,000	10,000			
		16,000			16,000

They decided to admit Mohan on 1st April, 2009 for 1/5th share on the following terms

(*i*) Mohan shall bring ₹ 6,000 as his share of premium.

(*ii*) That unaccounted accrued income of ₹ 100 be provided for.

(*iii*) The market value of investments was ₹ 4,500.

(*iv*) A debtor whose dues of ₹ 500 was written off as bad debts paid ₹ 400 in full settlement.

(*v*) Mohan to bring in capital to the extent of 1/5th of the total capital of the new firm.

Prepare revaluation account, partners' capital account and the balance sheet of the new firm. **Delhi 2010; All India 2010**

Ans. Solve as Q no. 18 on page 124–126.

Profit/Loss on Revaluation = Nil

Balance in Partners' Capital Account : Ram = ₹ 12,000; Shyam = ₹ 6,000; Mohan = ₹ 4,500

Total of Balance Sheet = ₹ 26,500

20. Ishu and Vishnu are partners sharing profits in the ratio of 3 : 2. Their balance sheet on 31st March, 2009 was as follows

Balance Sheet
as at 31st March, 2009

Liabilities		Amt (₹)	Assets		Amt (₹)
Creditors		66,000	Cash at Bank		87,000
General Reserves		10,000	Debtors	42,000	
Investment Fluctuation Fund		4,000	(−) Provision for Doubtful Debts	(7,000)	35,000
Capital A/cs			Investment (Market price 19,000)		21,000
Ishu	1,19,000		Buildings		98,000
Vishnu	1,12,000	2,31,000	Plant and Machinery		70,000
		3,11,000			3,11,000

Nishu was admitted on that date for 1/6th share on the following terms

(*i*) Nishu will bring ₹ 56,000 as his share of capital.

(*ii*) Goodwill of the firm is valued at ₹ 84,000 and Nishu will bring his share of goodwill in cash.

(*iii*) Plant and machinery to be appreciated by 20%.

(*iv*) All debtors are good.

(*v*) There is a liability of ₹ 9,800 included in sundry creditors that is not likely to arise.

(*vi*) Capital of Ishu and Vishnu will be adjusted on the basis of Nishu's capital and any excess or deficiency will be made by withdrawing or bringing in cash by the concerned partner.

Prepare the revaluation account, the partners' capital accounts and the balance sheet of the firm after the above adjustments. **All India (C) 2010**

Ans. Dr **Revaluation Account** Cr

Particulars		Amt (₹)	Particulars	Amt (₹)
To Profit Transferred to			By Plant and Machinery A/c	14,000
Ishu's Capital A/c	18,480		By Provision for Doubtful Debts A/c	7,000
Vishnu's Capital A/c	12,320	30,800	By Creditors A/c	9,800
		30,800		30,800

Dr **Partners' Capital Account** Cr

Particulars	Ishu (₹)	Vishnu (₹)	Nishu (₹)	Particulars	Ishu (₹)	Vishnu (₹)	Nishu (₹)
To Bank A/c (Balancing figure)	—	22,720	—	By Balance b/d	1,19,000	1,12,000	—
				By Bank A/c	—	—	56,000
To Balance c/d	1,68,000	1,12,000	56,000	By Premium for Goodwill A/c	8,400	5,600	—
				By General Reserve A/c	6,000	4,000	—
				By Investment Fluctuation Fund A/c	1,200	800	—
				By Revaluation A/c (Profit)	18,480	12,320	—
				By Bank A/c (Balancing figure)	14,920	—	—
	1,68,000	1,34,720	56,000		1,68,000	1,34,720	56,000

Balance Sheet
as at 31st March, 2009

Liabilities		Amt (₹)	Assets	Amt (₹)
Creditors (66,000 − 9,800)		56,200	Plant and Machinery (70,000 + 14,000)	84,000
Capital A/cs			Debtors	42,000
Ishu	1,68,000		Investment	19,000
Vishnu	1,12,000		Building	98,000
Nishu	56,000	3,36,000	Bank	1,49,200
		3,92,200		3,92,200

Bank Account

Dr Particulars	Amt (₹)	Particulars	Cr Amt (₹)
To Balance b/d	87,000	By Vishnu's Capital A/c	22,720
To Nishu's Capital A/c	56,000	By Balance c/d	1,49,200
To Premium for Goodwill A/c	14,000		
To Ishu's Capital A/c	14,920		
	1,71,920		1,71,920

Working Notes

1. **Calculation of Nishu's Share of Goodwill**

$$\text{Firm's goodwill} = ₹\ 84{,}000;\ \text{Nishu's share of goodwill} = 84{,}000 \times \frac{1}{6} = ₹\ 14{,}000$$

To be credited to Ishu and Vishnu in sacrificing ratio i.e., 3 : 2.

2. **Calculation of New Ratio**

$$\text{Nishu's share} = \frac{1}{6}\text{th; Remaining share} = 1 - \frac{1}{6} = \frac{5}{6}\text{th}$$

$$\text{Ishu's new share} = \frac{5}{6} \times \frac{3}{5} = \frac{15}{30}$$

$$\text{Vishnu's new share} = \frac{5}{6} \times \frac{2}{5} = \frac{10}{30}$$

$$\text{Nishu's new share} = \frac{1}{6} \times \frac{5}{5} = \frac{5}{30}$$

∴ New ratio = 15 : 10 : 5, i.e. 3 : 2 : 1

3. **Calculation of Adjustment of Capital**

For $\frac{1}{6}$th share, capital = ₹ 56,000

$$\text{Total capital} = 56{,}000 \times \frac{6}{1} = ₹\ 3{,}36{,}000;\ \text{Ishu's capital} = 3{,}36{,}000 \times \frac{3}{6} = ₹\ 1{,}68{,}000$$

$$\text{Vishnu's capital} = 3{,}36{,}000 \times \frac{2}{6} = ₹1{,}12{,}000;\ \text{Nishu's capital} = 3{,}36{,}000 \times \frac{1}{6} = ₹\ 56{,}000$$

Entry for Investment Fluctuation Fund

Particulars		Amt (Dr)	Amt (Cr)
Investment Fluctuation Fund A/c	Dr	4,000	
To Investment A/c			2,000
To Ishu's Capital A/c			1,200
To Vishu's Capital A/c			800
(Being investment fluctuation fund written-off)			

Multiple Choice Questions

For Complete Chapter **(1 Mark)**

1. X and Y were partners sharing profits in the ratio of 3 : 2. Z was admitted as a new partner for 1/5th share. X sacrificed 3/20 from his share and Y sacrificed 1/20 from his share in favour of Z, the new profit sharing ratio would be **CBSE Term I 2021**

(a) 9 : 7 : 4
(b) 8 : 8 : 4
(c) 6 : 10 : 4
(d) 10 : 6 : 5

Hint: Z's share $= \frac{1}{5}$; X sacrifice $= \frac{3}{20}$; Y sacrifice $= \frac{1}{20}$; X's new share $= \frac{3}{5} - \frac{3}{20} = \frac{12-3}{20} = \frac{9}{20}$

Y's new share $= \frac{2}{5} - \frac{1}{20} = \frac{8-1}{20} = \frac{7}{20}$; Z's new share $= \frac{3}{20} + \frac{1}{20} = \frac{4}{20}$

$\therefore$ New profit sharing ratio = 9 : 7 : 4

2. At the time of admission of a new partner, general reserve appearing in the old balance sheet is transferred to **CBSE Term I 2021**

(a) all partners' capital account
(b) new partners' capital account
(c) old partners' capital account
(d) revaluation account

3. Assertion (A) It is necessary to revalue assets and liabilities of a firm in case of admission of a partner.

Reason (R) It is because the incoming partner is neither put to an advantage nor to a disadvantage due to change in the value of assets and liabilities. **CBSE Term I 2021**

Alternatives

(a) Both Assertion (A) and Reason (R) are correct and Reason (R) is the correct reason of Assertion (A)
(b) Both Assertion (A) and Reason (R) Reason are correct, but Reason (R) is not the correct reason of Assertion (A)
(c) Only Reason (R) is correct
(d) Both Assertion (A) and Reason (R) are wrong

4. Gopal and Govind are partners in a firm sharing profits equally. They admitted Chetan for 1/3rd share in profits. On admission debtor whose dues of ₹ 5,000 were earlier written-off as bad-debts, paid ₹ 4,000 in full, settlement. Bad debts recovered ₹ 4,000 will be debited to .... and credited to .... **CBSE Term I 2021**

(a) Cash/Bank A/c, Revaluation A/c
(b) Bad Debts recovered A/c, Bad Debts A/c
(c) Cash/Bank A/c, Bad Debts A/c
(d) Revaluation A/c, Bad Debts Recovered A/c

5. Ram and Krishna were partners sharing profits and losses in the ratio of 2 : 1. They admitted Shanker as a partner for 1/5th share in the profits. For this purpose the goodwill of the firm was to be valued on the basis of three times of last five years average profits. The profits for the last five years were **CBSE Term I 2021**

Year	2016-17	2017-18	2018-19	2019-20	2020-21
Profit (₹)	50,000	40,000	75,000	(25,000)	50,000

Profit of 2017-18 was calculated after charging ₹ 10,000 for abnormal loss of goods by fire. The value of goodwill of the firm is

(a) ₹ 1,28,000
(b) ₹ 2,00,000
(c) ₹ 1,90,000
(d) ₹ 1,20,000

Hint: Goodwill $= 3 \times$ Last five years' average profit*

$= 3 \times 40{,}000 = ₹\ 1{,}20{,}000$

*Average profit (last 5 years) $= \dfrac{50{,}000 + (40{,}000 + 10{,}000) + 75{,}000 - 25{,}000 + 50{,}000}{5} = \dfrac{2{,}00{,}000}{5} = ₹\ 40{,}000$

6. Santa and Banta are partners in a firm sharing profits in the ratio of 3 : 2. Kanta was admitted as a new partner for 1/5th share of profits. On Kanta's admission it was decided that machinery would be appreciated by 10% (Book value ₹ 80,000) and Building would be depreciated 20% (Book value ₹ 2,00,000). Unrecorded debtors of ₹ 1,250 would be brought to books. There was a liability of ₹ 2,750 included in sundry creditors that is not to be paid. What will be the gain/loss on revaluation? **CBSE Term I 2021**

(a) Loss ₹ 28,000
(b) Loss ₹ 40,000
(c) Profit ₹ 28,000
(d) Profit ₹ 40,000

Hint: Gain/Loss on Revaluation $= 8{,}000 - 4{,}000 + 1{,}250 + 2{,}750 = ₹\ (28{,}000)$

7. Mani and Neeru are partners in a firm sharing profits in the ratio of 5 : 3. On 1st April, 2021 they admitted Lily as a new partner on the following terms **CBSE Term I 2021**

(*i*) The new profit sharing ratio will be 2 : 3 : 3.

(*ii*) Lily will bring ₹ 1,00,000 for her capital and the necessary amount of goodwill premium in cash.

(*iii*) Goodwill of the firm was valued at ₹ 1,40,000.

The journal entry for treatment or goodwill premium brought by Lily will be

			Dr	Cr
(a)	Premium for Goodwill A/c	Dr	52,500	
	To Mani's Capital A/c			37,500
	To Neeru's Capital A/c			15,000
(b)	Premium for Goodwill A/c	Dr	52,500	
	To Mani's Capital A/c			52,500
(c)	Premium for Goodwill A/c	Dr	52,500	
	Neeru's Capital A/c	Dr	12,500	
	To Mani's Capital A/c			65,000
(d)	Lily's Current A/c	Dr	1,40,000	
	To Mani's Capital A/c			1,00,000
	To Neeru's Capital A/c			40,000

8. Seema and Teena are partners in a firm sharing profits and losses in the ratio of 3 : 2. They agreed to admit Reena into partnership for 1/5th share of profits on 1st April, 2021. On that date, workmen's compensation fund stood in the balance sheet at ₹ 50,000. The liability against workmen's compensation fund is determined at ₹ 20,000 which is to be paid later in the year.

What will be the journal entry for the treatment of workmen compensation fund on the admission of new partner Reena? **CBSE Term I 2021**

			Dr	Cr
(a)	Workmen Compensation Fund A/c	Dr	30,000	
	To Seema's Capital A/c			18,000
	To Teena's Capital A/c			12,000
(b)	Workmen Compensation Fund A/c	Dr	50,000	
	To Revaluation A/c			20,000
	To Seema's Capital A/c			18,000
	To Teena's Capital A/c			12,000

(c) Workmen Compensation Fund A/c	Dr	50,000	
To Workmen Compensation Claim A/c			20,000
To Seema's Capital A/c			18,000
To Teena's Capital A/c			12,000
(d) Workmen Compensation Fund A/c	Dr	50,000	
To Seema's Capital A/c			30,000
To Teena's Capital A/c			20,000

9. Ashok and Sudha were partners in a firm sharing profits and losses in the ratio of 3 : 1. They admitted Bani as a new partner. Ashok sacrificed $\frac{1}{4}$ th of his share and Sudha sacrificed $\frac{1}{4}$th of her share in favour of Bani. Bani's share in the profits of the firm will be **CBSE 2020**

(a) $\frac{5}{8}$ (b) $\frac{1}{8}$ (c) $\frac{1}{4}$ (d) $\frac{7}{16}$

Hint: Ashok sacrificed $= \frac{1}{4} \times \frac{3}{4} = \frac{3}{16}$; Sudha sacrificed $= \frac{1}{4} \times \frac{1}{4} = \frac{1}{16}$;

Bani's new share $= \frac{3}{16} + \frac{1}{16} = \frac{4}{16} = \frac{1}{4}$

10. 'X' and 'Y' are partners in a firm which develops software for industries. X's minor son 'Z' is a computer wizard. Can he be admitted in the partnership firm?

(a) Yes, if X agrees (b) Yes, if Y agrees

(c) Yes, if 'X' and 'Y' both agree (d) No, he cannot be admitted

Hint: According to Section 30 of the Indian Partnership Act, 1932, a minor can be admitted in the firm only with the consent of all the partners.

11. When share of new or incoming partner is given without giving the details of sacrifice made by old or existing partners, then

(*i*) it is assumed that old partners make sacrifice in their old profit sharing ratio.

(*ii*) there is no change in profit sharing ratio of the old partners.

(a) Only (i) is correct (b) Only (ii) is correct

(c) Both (i) and (ii) are correct (d) Both (i) and (ii) are incorrect

12. The amount of goodwill brought in by new partner is credited to .... partners' capital account.

(a) old (b) sacrificing

(c) gaining (d) All of these

Hint: The amount of goodwill brought in by the new partner is credited to the capital accounts of sacrificing partners to compensate them for their sacrifice.

13. 'X' and 'Y' are partners sharing profits in the ratio of 3 : 1. They admit 'Z' as a partner who pays ₹ 4,000 as goodwill, the new profit sharing ratio being 2 : 1 : 1 among 'X', 'Y' and 'Z'. The amount of goodwill will be credited to

(a) 'X' and 'Y' as ₹ 3,000 and ₹ 1,000 (b) 2,000 each

(c) only 'Y' (d) only 'X'

Hint: Goodwill will be credited in that partners' capital account who sacrifices.

Sacrificing Ratio = Old Share – New Share

'X's' sacrifice $= \frac{3}{4} - \frac{2}{4} = \frac{1}{4}$; 'Y's' sacrifice $= \frac{1}{4} - \frac{1}{4} =$ Nil

Here, only 'X' sacrifices. So, goodwill will be credited in 'X's' capital account only.

14. Workmen Compensation Reserve (WCR) appears in the balance sheet of Rashmi and Suman, who share profits in the ratio of 2 : 3, at ₹ 80,000. Deepa is admitted and the new profit sharing ratio is 1 : 1 : 1. If the claim on account of WCR is estimated at ₹ 1,00,000, then

(a) the difference of ₹ 20,000 will be debited to revaluation account

(b) the difference of ₹ 20,000 will be debited to Rashmi's capital account

(c) the difference of ₹ 20,000 will be debited to Suman's capital account

(d) None of the above

Hint: In this case, the difference amount is debited to revaluation account as it results in increase in the amount of liability.

15. Can employee provident fund be distributed among old partners in old ratio at the time of admission?

(a) It can be distributed
(b) It can't be distributed
(c) Can be distributed if tax is paid
(d) None of these

Hint: Employee provident fund is neither a free reserve nor is an accumulation of profit. Therefore, it is not distributed amongst old partners.

16. If the market value of investments is ₹ 1,47,000, then the share of Kim, Mansi and Poorvi in the Investment Fluctuation Fund (IFF) will be

(a) ₹ 5,250 ; ₹ 3,150; ₹ 2,100
(b) ₹ 6,750; ₹ 4,050; ₹ 2,700
(c) ₹ 5,000; ₹ 5,000; ₹ 3,500
(d) None of these

Hint: The appearance of investment fluctuation fund at ₹ 13,500 indicates that the market value of investments at the time of creation of fund was ₹ 1,36,500 (1,50,000 – 13,500). The market value is now ₹ 1,47,000. So, IFF will be shown in the books at ₹ 3,000 and ₹ 10,500 will be distributed among old partners in the old ratio of 5 : 3 : 2.

17. 'A' and 'B' carry on business and share profits and losses in the ratio of 3 : 2. Their respective capitals are ₹ 1,20,000 and ₹ 54,000. 'C' is admitted for 1/3rd share in profit and brings ₹ 1,50,000 as his share of capital. Capitals of 'A' and 'B' to be adjusted according to 'C's' share. Calculate the amount brought in by 'A'.

(a) ₹ 30,000
(b) ₹ 32,000
(c) ₹ 60,000
(d) Nil

Hint: Capital contributed by 'C' for 1/3 rd share = ₹ 1,50,000

Capital of firm based on 'C's' share $= 1,50,000 \times \frac{3}{1} =$ ₹ 4,50,000

Remaining share $= 1 - \frac{1}{3} = \frac{2}{3}$; 'A's' new share $= \frac{2}{3} \times \frac{3}{5} = \frac{6}{15}$ and 'B's' new share $= \frac{2}{3} \times \frac{2}{5} = \frac{4}{15}$

New profit sharing ratio = 6 : 4 : 5

A's capital based on new share $= 4,50,000 \times \frac{6}{15} =$ ₹ 1,80,000

Deficient capital to be brought in by 'A' = 1,80,000 – 1,20,000 = ₹ 60,000

18. 'A' and 'B' are partners sharing profits and losses in the ratio of 3 : 2. 'A's' capital is ₹ 1,60,000 and 'B's' capital is ₹ 1,30,000. They admit 'C' for 1/5th share of profits. How much 'C' should bring in towards his capital?

(a) ₹ 38,000 (b) ₹ 24,000
(c) ₹ 72,500 (d) ₹ 22,000

Hint:

Particulars	Amt (₹)
'A's' Capital	1,60,000
'B's' Capital	1,30,000
Capital of 'A' and 'B' for $\frac{4}{5}$ share $\left(\text{i.e. } 1-\frac{1}{5}\right)$	2,90,000
Total Capital of Firm $\left(2{,}90{,}000 \times \frac{5}{4}\right)$	3,62,500
C's Share in Capital $\left(3{,}62{,}500 \times \frac{1}{5}\right)$	72,500

Direction *Read the following hypothetical text and answer the questions 19 to 22.*

Amit and Mahesh were partners in a fast food corner sharing profits and losses in ratio 3:2. They sold fast food items across the counter and did home delivery too. Their initial fixed capital contribution was ₹ 1,20,000 and ₹ 80,000 respectively.

At the end of first year their profit was ₹ 1,20,000 before allowing the remuneration of ₹ 3,000 per quarter to Amit and ₹ 2,000 per half year to Mahesh. Such a promising performance for first year was encouraging, therefore, they decided to expand the area of operations.

For this purpose, they needed a delivery van, a few Scotties and an additional person to support. Six months into the accounting year they decided to admit Sundaram as a new partner and offered him 20% as a share of profits along with monthly remuneration of ₹ 2,500. Sundaram was asked to introduce ₹ 1,30,000 for capital and ₹ 70,000 for premium for goodwill. Besides this Sundaram was required to provide ₹ 1,00,000 as loan for two years. Sundaram readily accepted the offer. The terms of the offer were duly executed and he was admitted as a partner. **CBSE QB**

19. Remuneration will be transferred to .... of Amit and Mahesh at the end of the accounting period.

(a) Capital account (b) Loan account
(c) Current account (d) None of these

20. Upon the admission of Sundaram the sacrifice for providing his share of profits would be done

(a) by Amit only (b) by Mahesh only
(c) by Amit and Mahesh equally (d) by Amit and Mahesh in the ratio of 3:2

21. Sundaram will be entitled to a remuneration of .... at the end of the year.

22. While taking up the accounting procedure for this reconstitution the accountant of the firm Mr. Suraj Marwaha faced a difficulty. Solve it be answering the following

For the amount of loan that Sundaram has agreed to provide, he is entitled to interest thereon at the rate of ....

Direction *Read the following hypothetical text and answer the questions 23 to 26.*

Sterling Enterprises is a partnership business with Ryan, Williams and Sania as partners engaged in production and sales of electrical items and equipment.

Their capital contributions were ₹ 50,00,000, ₹ 50,00,000 and ₹ 80,00,000 respectively with the profit sharing ratio of 5:5:8. As they are now looking forward to expanding their business, it was decided that they would bring in sufficient cash to double their respective capitals.

This was duly followed by Ryan and Williams but due to unavoidable reasons Sania could not do so and ultimately it was agreed that to bridge the shortfall in the required capital a new partner should be admitted who would bring in the amount that Sania could not bring and that the new partner would get share of profits equal to half of Sania's share which would be sacrificed by Sania only.

Consequent to this agreement Ejaz was admitted and he brought in the required capital and ₹ 30,00,000 as premium for goodwill. Based on the above information you are required to answer the following questions. **CBSE QB**

23. What will be the new profit sharing ratio of Ryan, Williams, Sania and Ejaz?

(a) 1:1:1:1 (b) 5:5:8:8 (c) 5:5:4:4 (d) None of these

Hint: 5:5:4:4

Sania sacrificed $\frac{8}{18} \times \frac{1}{2} = \frac{2}{9}$ in favour of Ejaz

Ryan $= \frac{5}{18}$; Williams $= \frac{5}{18}$; Sania $= \frac{8}{18} - \frac{2}{9} = \frac{8-4}{18} = \frac{4}{18}$; Ejaz $= \frac{2}{9}$

New profit sharing ratio = Ryan : Williams : Sania : Ejaz

$= \frac{5}{18} : \frac{5}{18} : \frac{4}{18} : \frac{2}{9}$ or $= 5 : 5 : 4 : 4$

24. What is the amount of capital brought in by the new partner Ejaz?

(a) ₹ 50,00,000 (b) ₹ 80,00,000
(c) ₹ 40,00,000 (d) ₹ 30,00,000

Hint: Sania to bring ₹ 80,00,000 to double her capital. Thus Ejaz would bring ₹ 80,00,000 as his share of capital.

25. What is the value of the goodwill of the firm?

(a) ₹ 1,35,00,000 (b) ₹ 30,00,000
(c) ₹ 1,50,00,000 (d) Cannot be determined from the given data

Hint: Goodwill of firm = ₹ 30,00,000

Ejaz's share = $\frac{4}{18}$ for which he bought ₹ 30,00,000 as his share of goodwill

Firm's Goodwill = $30,00,000 \times \frac{18}{4}$ = ₹ 1,35,00,000

26. What will be correct journal entry for distribution of Premium for Goodwill brought in by Ejaz?

(a)	Ejaz Capital A/c	Dr 30,00,000	
	To Sania's Capital A/c		30,00,000
	(Being...............................)		
(b)	Premium for Goodwill A/c......	Dr 30,00,000	
	To Sania's Capital A/c		30,00,000
	(Being...............................)		

(c)	Premium for Goodwill A/c......	Dr	30,00,000	
	To Ryan's Capital A/c			8,33,333
	To William's Capital A/c			8,33,333
	To Ejaz's Capital A/c			13,33,333
	(Being................................)			
(d)	Premium for Goodwill A/c......	Dr	30,00,000	
	To Ryan's Capital A/c			10,00,000
	To William's Capital A/c			10,00,000
	To Ejaz's Capital A/c			10,00,000
	(Being................................)			

ANSWERS

1. *(a)*	2. *(c)*	3. *(a)*	4. *(a)*	5. *(d)*	6. *(a)*	7. *(b)*	8. *(c)*	9. *(c)*	10. *(c)*
11. *(c)*	12. *(b)*	13. *(d)*	14. *(a)*	15. *(b)*	16. *(a)*	17. *(c)*	18. *(c)*	19. *(c)*	20. *(d)*
21. *₹ 15,000 (2,500 × 6)*			22. *6% p.a.*		23. *(c)*	24. *(b)*	25. *(a)*	26. *(b)*	

CHAPTER 04

Reconstitution of a Partnership Firm:

Retirement/Death of a Partner

TOPIC 1

Introduction

Retirement of a partner means ceasing to be a partner of the firm. Retirement of a partner is one of the modes of reconstituting the firm under which an old partnership comes to an end and a new one between the continuing partners comes into existence, however the firm continues its business.

The different ways by which a partner can retire from the firm are

(*i*) With the consent of all the partners.

(*ii*) By giving notice in writing to all other partners of his intention to retire, in case of partnership at will.

(*iii*) In accordance with the terms of agreement between the partners.

Liability of a Retiring Partner

The liability of the retiring partner can be studied under the following two heads

Liability of the Retiring Partner for the Acts before Retirement

[Section 32(2)] A retiring partner remains liable for all the acts of the firm up to the date of his retirement. However, a retiring partner may be discharged from his liability by an agreement between himself, third party and the continuing partners.

Liability of the Retiring Partner for the Acts after Retirement

[Section 32 (3)] A retiring partner also continues to be liable to third parties for the acts of the firm even after his retirement until a public notice of his retirement is given.

Adjustments Required at the Time of Retirement of a Partner

Various matters that need accounting adjustment at the time of retirement are

(*i*) Determination of new profit sharing ratio and gaining ratio.

(*ii*) Adjustment for goodwill.

(*iii*) Adjustment for profit/loss arising on revaluation of assets and reassessment of liabilities.

(*iv*) Adjustment for accumulated profits, reserves and losses.

(*v*) Adjustment for capital (if agreed).

New Profit Sharing Ratio

The ratio in which the continuing partners decide to share future profits and losses is called new profit sharing ratio.

New Ratio = Old Share + Acquired Gaining Share

Gaining Ratio

The ratio in which the remaining, *i.e.* continuing partners acquire the outgoing (retiring) partner's share is called gaining ratio.

Gaining Ratio = New Share – Old Share

NOTE The rest of the adjustments have been discussed in the subsequent topics.

Previous Years' Examination Questions

1 Mark Questions

1. What is meant by 'gaining ratio' on retirement of a partner? **Delhi 2019**

Ans. The ratio in which the continuing partners acquire the outgoing partner's share is called as gaining ratio.

2. Aman, Yatin and Uma were partners and were sharing profits and losses in the ratio of 5 : 3 : 2. Uma retired and her share was taken over by Aman and Yatin 5 : 3 in ratio. Calculate gaining ratio of Aman and Yatin. **Compartment 2018**

Ans. **Calculation of Gaining Ratio**

Uma's share $= \frac{2}{10}$; Aman gains $= \frac{5}{8} \times \frac{2}{10} = \frac{10}{80}$; Yatin gains $= \frac{3}{8} \times \frac{2}{10} = \frac{6}{80}$

Gaining ratio of Aman and Yatin = 10 : 6 or 5 : 3

3. X, Y and Z are partners sharing profits in the ratio of $\frac{1}{2}, \frac{2}{5}$ and $\frac{1}{10}$. Find the new ratio of remaining partners, if Z retires. **Delhi 2014**

Ans. Old ratio of X : Y : Z $= \frac{1}{2} : \frac{2}{5} : \frac{1}{10} = \frac{5}{10} : \frac{4}{10} : \frac{1}{10} = 5 : 4 : 1$

Z retires, after striking of the retiring partner's ratio, remaining ratio will be new profit sharing ratio, *i.e.* 5 : 4.

4. X, Y and Z were partners sharing profits in the ratio of 1/2, 3/10 and 1/5. X retired from the firm. Calculate the gaining ratio of the remaining partners. **All India 2014**

Ans. Old ratio of X : Y : Z $= \frac{1}{2} : \frac{3}{10} : \frac{1}{5} = \frac{5}{10} : \frac{3}{10} : \frac{2}{10}$

$= 5 : 3 : 2$

X retired, after striking of the retiring partner's ratio, remaining ratio will be new profit sharing ratio, i.e. 3 : 2.

New profit sharing ratio = Y : Z = 3 : 2

Gaining Ratio = New Share – Old Share

$Y = \frac{3}{5} - \frac{3}{10} = \frac{6-3}{10} = \frac{3}{10}$; $Z = \frac{2}{5} - \frac{2}{10} = \frac{4-2}{10} = \frac{2}{10}$

Gaining ratio = 3 : 2

5. Give any one distinction between sacrificing ratio and gaining ratio. **All India 2012**

Ans. The difference between sacrificing ratio and gaining ratio is stated below

Basis	Sacrificing ratio	Gaining ratio
Meaning	It is the ratio in which old partners agree to sacrifice their share of profit in favour of new partner(s).	It is the ratio in which continuing partners acquire the share of profit from outgoing partner(s).

2 Mark Question

6. A, B, C and D were partners in a firm sharing profits and losses in the ratio of 1 : 2 : 3 : 4. On 31st March, 2022, C retired from the firm and his share was acquired by A and B in the ratio of 3 : 2. Calculate the new profit sharing ratio of A, B and D. **CBSE Term II 2022**

Ans. Old ratio between A, B, C and D = 1 : 2 : 3 : 4

C's share acquired by A and B in the ratio = 3 : 2

A acquires C's share $= \frac{3}{10} \times \frac{3}{5} = \frac{9}{50}$

B acquires C's share $= \frac{3}{10} \times \frac{2}{5} = \frac{6}{50}$

Calculation of New ratio

$A = \frac{1}{10} + \frac{9}{50} = \frac{5+9}{50} = \frac{14}{50}$

$B = \frac{2}{10} + \frac{6}{50} = \frac{10+6}{50} = \frac{16}{50}$; $D = \frac{4}{10} \times \frac{5}{5} = \frac{20}{50}$

∴ New ratio = 14 : 16 : 20 or 7 : 8 : 10

4 Marks Question

7. (*i*) K, L and Z are partners sharing profits in the ratio of 4 : 3 : 2 respectively. L retired and surrendered $\frac{1}{9}$th of his share of profit to K and remaining in favour of Z. Calculate the new profit sharing ratio of K and Z.

(*ii*) Arun, Varun and Charan are partners sharing profits in the ratio of $\frac{1}{2}, \frac{3}{10}$ and $\frac{1}{5}$ respectively. Varun retired from the firm and Arun and Charan decided to share future profits in 3 : 2 ratio. Calculate gaining ratio of Arun and Charan. **All India (C) 2014**

Ans. (*i*) Old ratio between K, L and Z

$= 4 : 3 : 2.$

Share surrendered in favour of K by L

$= \frac{3}{9} \times \frac{1}{9} = \frac{3}{81}$

Share surrendered in favour of Z by L

$= \frac{3}{9} - \frac{3}{81}$

$= \frac{27-3}{81} = \frac{24}{81}$

New share of K $= \frac{4}{9} + \frac{3}{81}$

$= \frac{36+3}{81} = \frac{39}{81}$

New share of Z $= \frac{2}{9} + \frac{24}{81}$

$= \frac{18+24}{81} = \frac{42}{81}$

∴ New ratio = 39 : 42 *or* 13 : 14

(*ii*) Old ratio between Arun, Varun and Charan

$= \frac{1}{2} : \frac{3}{10} : \frac{1}{5}$ *or* 5 : 3 : 2

New ratio between Arun and Charan = 3 : 2

Gaining Ratio = New Share – Old Share

Arun $= \frac{3}{5} - \frac{5}{10} = \frac{6-5}{10} = \frac{1}{10}$

Charan $= \frac{2}{5} - \frac{2}{10} = \frac{4-2}{10} = \frac{2}{10}$

∴ Gaining ratio = 1 : 2

TOPIC 2

Treatment of Goodwill

The retiring or deceased partner is entitled to his share of goodwill at the time of retirement/death because the goodwill has been earned by the firm with the efforts of all the existing partners.

Adjustment for retiring partner's share of goodwill will be made through the following journal entry

Continuing/Gaining Partners' Capital/Current A/c To Outgoing/Sacrificing/Retiring Partner's Capital/Current A/c	Dr	[In gaining ratio] [With share of goodwill]

If goodwill already appears in the old balance sheet, then it is to be written-off in old ratio.

All Partners' Capital/Current A/c To Goodwill A/c	Dr

Beside the above method of adjusting goodwill, following alternative methods are also available where **goodwill account is raised** and **thereafter written-off**

(i) Goodwill is raised at its full value and written-off immediately

When goodwill account is raised	Goodwill A/c Dr To All Partners' Capital / Current A/c	[Full value of goodwill] [In old profit sharing ratio]
When goodwill account is written-off	Continuing Partners' Capital / Current A/c Dr To Goodwill A/c	[In new profit sharing ratio]

(ii) Goodwill is raised to the extent of retired /deceased partner's share and written-off immediately

When goodwill account is raised	Goodwill A/c Dr To Retiring Partner's Capital/Current A/c	[Retiring Partner's share]
When goodwill account is written-off	Gaining Partners' Capital / Current A/c Dr To Goodwill A/c	

Hidden Goodwill

Sometimes, the firm agrees to settle the retiring or deceased partners' account by payment of a lumpsum amount. If such amount is in excess of his capital and share in reserves/revaluation of assets and reassessment of liabilities, etc, the excess will be treated as his share of goodwill. It will be recorded by debiting the continuing partners' capital accounts in gaining ratio and crediting retiring partners' capital account.

Previous Years'
Examination Questions

1 Mark Questions

1. Aman, Bimal and Deepak are partners sharing profits in the ratio of 2 : 3 : 5 . The goodwill of the firm has been valued at ₹ 37,500. Aman retired, Bimal and Deepak decided to share profits equally in future. Calculate gain/sacrifice of Bimal and Deepak on Aman's retirement and also pass necessary journal entry for the treatment of goodwill. **All India 2019**

Ans. **Calculation of Sacrificing or Gaining Ratio**

Sacrificing Ratio = Old share – New share

Bimal $= \frac{3}{10} - \frac{1}{2} = \frac{3-5}{10} = \left(\frac{2}{10}\right)$; Deepak $= \frac{5}{10} - \frac{1}{2} = \frac{5-5}{10} =$ Nil

Aman's Share of Goodwill $= 37{,}500 \times \frac{2}{10} =$ ₹ 7,500

JOURNAL

Date	Particulars		LF	Amt (Dr)	Amt (Cr)
	Bimal's Capital A/c	Dr		7,500	
	To Aman's Capital A/c				7,500
	(Being amount of goodwill adjusted)				

2. Neetu, Meetu and Teetu were partners in a firm. On 1st January, 2018, Meetu retired. On Meetu's retirement, the goodwill of the firm was valued at ₹ 4,20,000. Pass necessary journal entry for the treatment of goodwill on Meetu's retirement. **CBSE 2018**

Ans.

JOURNAL

Date	Particulars		LF	Amt (Dr)	Amt (Cr)
	Neetu's Capital A/c	Dr		70,000	
	Teetu's Capital A/c	Dr		70,000	
	To Meetu's Capital A/c				1,40,000
	(Being the adjustment made for goodwill on retirement)				

Working Note

Meetu's share of goodwill $= 4{,}20{,}000 \times \frac{1}{3} =$ ₹ 1,40,000

3. Why are heirs of a retiring/deceased partner entitled to the share of goodwill of the firm? **Delhi 2014**

Ans. The retiring or deceased partner is entitled to his share of goodwill at the time of retirement/death because the goodwill has been earned by the firm at the time when he was a partner.

4. P, Q and R were partners in a firm sharing profits in the ratio of 5 : 4 : 3 respectively. Their capitals were ₹ 50,000, ₹ 40,000 and ₹ 30,000 respectively. State the ratio in which the goodwill of the firm, amounting to ₹ 6,00,000, will be adjusted in the capital accounts of the remaining partners on the retirement of Q. **Delhi (C) 2014**

Ans. The goodwill will be adjusted in the gaining ratio of the continuing partners.

5. For which share of goodwill, a partner is entitled at the time of his retirement? **Delhi 2012**

Ans. At the time of retirement, a partner is entitled to get an amount equal to his share out of firm's goodwill.

6. P, Q and R were partners in a firm sharing profits in the ratio of 5 : 4 : 3. Their capitals were ₹ 40,000, ₹ 50,000 and ₹ 1,00,000 respectively. State the ratio in which the goodwill of the firm amounting to ₹ 1,20,000 will be adjusted on the retirement of R. **All India (C) 2010**

Ans. R's share of goodwill, i.e. ₹30,000 (1,20,000 × 3/12) will be contributed by P and Q in their gaining ratio, i.e. 5 : 4.

7. State the need for treatment of goodwill on the retirement of a partner. **All India 2010**

Ans. At the time of retirement, retiring partner sacrifices his share of profit in favour of continuing partners, so the remaining partners compensate the retiring partner a share of the firm's goodwill.

3 Marks Questions

8. Kavi, Ravi, Kumar and Guru were partners in a firm sharing profits in the ratio of 3 : 2 : 2 : 1. On 1st February, 2017, Guru retired and the new profit sharing ratio decided between Kavi, Ravi and Kumar was 3 : 1 : 1. On Guru's retirement, the goodwill of the firm was valued at ₹ 3,60,000. Showing your working notes clearly, pass necessary journal entry in the books of the firm for the treatment of goodwill on Guru's retirement. **All India 2017**

Ans.

JOURNAL

Date	Particulars		LF	Amt (Dr)	Amt (Cr)
2017					
Feb 1	Kavi's Capital A/c	Dr		81,000	
	To Ravi's Capital A/c				18,000
	To Kumar's Capital A/c				18,000
	To Guru's Capital A/c				45,000
	(Being amount of goodwill adjusted)				

Working Notes

1. **Calculation of Gaining Ratio**

Gaining Ratio = New Share − Old Share

$$\text{Kavi} = \frac{3}{5} - \frac{3}{8} = \frac{24-15}{40} = \frac{9}{40};\ \text{Ravi} = \frac{1}{5} - \frac{2}{8} = \frac{8-10}{40} = \left(\frac{2}{40}\right) \text{Sacrifice}$$

$$\text{Kumar} = \frac{1}{5} - \frac{2}{8} = \frac{8-10}{40} = \left(\frac{2}{40}\right) \text{Sacrifice}$$

2. **Calculation of Share of Goodwill**

$$\text{Guru's share of goodwill} = 3{,}60{,}000 \times \frac{1}{8} = ₹\,45{,}000\ ;\ \text{Kavi gains} = 3{,}60{,}000 \times \frac{9}{40} = ₹\,81{,}000$$

$$\text{Ravi sacrifices} = 3{,}60{,}000 \times \frac{2}{40} = ₹\,18{,}000\ ;\ \text{Kumar sacrifices} = 3{,}60{,}000 \times \frac{2}{40} = ₹\,18{,}000$$

9. Amar, Ram, Mohan and Sohan were partners in a firm sharing profits in the ratio of 2 : 2 : 2 : 1, on 31st January, 2017 Sohan retired. On Sohan's retirement the goodwill of the firm was valued at ₹ 70,000. The new profit sharing ratio between Amar, Ram and Mohan was agreed as 5 : 1 : 1. Showing your working notes clearly, pass necessary journal entry for the treatment of goodwill in the books of the firm on Sohan's retirement. **Delhi 2017**

Ans. Solve as Q no. 8 on page 161 and 162.

Debit Amar's Capital Account with ₹ 30,000 and Credit Ram's, Mohan's and Sohan's Capital account with ₹ 10,000 each.

4 Marks Questions

10. Arjun, Bheem and Nakul are partners sharing profits and losses in the ratio of 14 : 5 : 6 respectively. Bheem retires and surrenders his 5/25th share in favour of Arjun. The goodwill of the firm is valued at 2 years' purchase of super profits based on average profits of last 3 years. The profits of the last three years are ₹ 50,000, ₹ 55,000 and ₹ 60,000 respectively. The normal profits of the similar firms are ₹ 30,000. Goodwill already appears in the books of the firm at ₹ 75,000. The profit for the first year after the Bheem's retirement was ₹ 1,00,000. Give necessary journal entries to adjust goodwill and distribute profits showing your workings. **Delhi 2012**

Ans. **JOURNAL**

Date	Particulars		LF	Amt (Dr)	Amt (Cr)
	Arjun's Capital A/c (75,000 × 14/25)	Dr		42,000	
	Bheem's Capital A/c (75,000 × 5/25)	Dr		15,000	
	Nakul's Capital A/c (75,000 × 6/25)	Dr		18,000	
	To Goodwill A/c				75,000
	(Being amount of goodwill written-off in old ratio)				
	Arjun's Capital A/c	Dr		10,000	
	To Bheem's Capital A/c				10,000
	(Being amount of goodwill adjusted in gaining ratio)				
	Profit and Loss Appropriation A/c	Dr		1,00,000	
	To Arjun's Capital A/c (1,00,000 × 19/25)				76,000
	To Nakul's Capital A/c (1,00,000 × 6/25)				24,000
	(Being profit distributed among partners)				

Working Notes

1. **Calculation of New Profit Sharing Ratio and Gaining Ratio**

Old ratio of Arjun, Bheem and Nakul = 14 : 5 : 6

Bheem surrenders in favour of Arjun = $\frac{5}{25}$th share, Arjun's new share = $\frac{14}{25}+\frac{5}{25}=\frac{19}{25}$

New ratio of Arjun and Nakul = 19 : 6

Gaining Ratio = New Share − Old Share

Arjun = $\frac{19}{25}-\frac{14}{25}=\frac{19-14}{25}=\frac{5}{25}$; Nakul = $\frac{6}{25}-\frac{6}{25}=\frac{6-6}{25}$ = Nil

2. **Calculation of Bheem's Share of Goodwill**

Actual average profit = $\frac{50,000+55,000+60,000}{3}$ = ₹ 55,000; Normal profit = ₹ 30,000

Super Profit = Average Profit − Normal Profit = 55,000 − 30,000 = ₹ 25,000

Firm's goodwill = 25,000 × 2 = ₹ 50,000

Bheem's share of goodwill = $50,000\times\frac{5}{25}$ = ₹ 10,000 (to be contributed by Arjun alone)

11. A, B, C and D are partners sharing profits in the ratio of 3 : 3 : 2 : 2 respectively. D retires and A, B and C decide to share the future profits in the ratio of 3 : 2 : 1. Goodwill of the firm is valued at ₹ 6,00,000. Goodwill already appears in the books at ₹ 4,50,000. The profit for the 1st year after D's retirement amount to ₹ 12,00,000. Give the necessary journal entries to record goodwill and to distribute the profits. Show your calculations clearly. **All India 2012**

Ans. Solve as Q no. 10 on page 142.

A gains $\frac{6}{30}$th share, B gains $\frac{1}{30}$th share and C sacrifices $\frac{1}{30}$th share.

12. A, B and C were partners in a firm sharing profits in the ratio of 6 : 5 : 4. Their capitals were A ₹ 1,00,000, B ₹ 80,000 and C ₹ 60,000 respectively. On 1st April, 2009, C retired from the firm and the new profit sharing ratio between A and B was decided as 11 : 4. On C's retirement, the goodwill of the firm was valued at ₹ 90,000. Showing your calculations clearly, pass necessary journal entry for the treatment of goodwill on C's retirement. **All India 2010**

Ans. Solve as Q no. 8 on page 141.

Debit A's capital account with ₹ 30,000, Credit B's capital account and C's capital account with ₹ 6,000 and ₹ 24,000 respectively.

13. A, B and C were partners sharing profits in the ratio of 6 : 4 : 5. Their capitals were A ₹ 1,00,000, B ₹ 80,000 and C ₹ 60,000. On 1st April, 2009, B retired from the firm and the new profit sharing ratio between A and C was decided as 11 : 4. On B's retirement, the goodwill of the firm was valued at ₹ 1,80,000. Showing your calculations clearly, pass necessary journal entry for the treatment of goodwill on B's retirement. **Delhi 2010**

Ans. Solve as Q. no. 8 on page 141.

Debit A's capital account with ₹ 60,000, Credit B's capital account and C's capital account with ₹ 48,000 and ₹ 12,000 respectively.

TOPIC 3

Computation of Amount Due to Retiring Partner

Accounting treatment of revaluation of assets and re-assessment of liabilities and adjustment for reserves and accumulated profits/losses is to be done in the same way as in the case of admission of a partner.

Calculation of Amount Payable to Retiring Partner

The amount due to a retiring partner is ascertained by preparing retiring partner's capital account.

Format of Retiring Partner's Capital Account

Dr **Retiring Partner's Capital Account** Cr

Particulars	Amt (₹)	Particulars	Amt (₹)
To Revaluation A/c (Share in loss)	...	By Balance b/d	...
To Share in Accumulated Losses	...	By Profit and Loss Suspense A/c (Share in profit for current year till the date of retirement)	...
To Cash A/c (Drawings till retirement)	...		
To Interest on Drawings A/c	...	By Revaluation A/c (Share in gain)	...
To Goodwill A/c (Share in existing goodwill written-off)	...	By Share of Goodwill A/c	...
To Retiring Partner's Loan A/c (Transfer) (Balancing figure)	...	By Share in Accumulated Profits	
		General Reserve A/c	...
		Profit and Loss A/c	...
		By Interest on Capital A/c (Due till the date of his retirement)	...
		By Salary/Commission A/c (Due till the date of his retirement)	...
	...		...

In case, the question is silent on the settlement of retiring partner's capital account, the amount due to him is transferred to his loan account.

The journal entry passed is

Retiring Partner's Capital A/c	Dr
To Retiring Partner's Loan A/c	

The retiring partner's loan account will appear as a liability in the balance sheet.

Interest on Amount Due

Unless otherwise agreed, the retiring partner at his option is entitled to receive interest @ 6% per annum till the amount due to him is not paid. At his option, he may take, instead of the interest, share of profits that have been earned by the use of the amount due to him.

Methods of Payment of Amount Due to the Retiring Partner

The amount due to retiring partner is either paid off immediately or is transferred to his loan account. The retiring partner's loan account will appear in the books of the new firm as a liability until it is paid off finally.

Journal Entries

The following journal entries are passed in this regard

(*i*) **If the Amount is Paid in Lumpsum**

Retiring Partner's Capital A/c	Dr
To Cash/ Bank A/c	

(*ii*) **In Case the Amount is Paid in Instalments**

(a) For amount due, transferred to retiring partner's loan account	Retiring Partner's Capital A/c To Retiring Partner's Loan A/c	Dr
(b) On interest being provided	Interest on Loan A/c To Retiring Partner's Loan A/c	Dr
(c) On payment of instalment with interest	Retiring Partner's Loan A/c To Cash/Bank A/c	Dr

(*iii*) **If Payment is Partly Paid in Cash and the Remaining Amount is to be Treated as Loan**

Retiring Partner's Capital A/c	Dr
To Cash/ Bank A/c	
To Retiring Partners' Loan A/c	

Examination Questions

1 Mark Questions

1. P, Q and R were partners in a firm. On 31st March, 2018 R retired. The amount payable to R ₹ 2,17,000 was transferred to his loan account. R agreed to receive interest on this amount as per the provisions of Partnership Act, 1932. State the rate at which interest will be paid to R. **Delhi 2019**

Ans. As per the provisions of Partnership Act, 1932, the rate of interest payable to R will be 6% per annum.

2. Give the journal entry to distribute 'workmen compensation reserve of ₹ 60,000 at the time of retirement of Sajjan, when there is no claim against it. The firm has three partners Rajat, Sajjan and Kavita. **Delhi 2013**

Ans. JOURNAL

Date	Particulars		LF	Amt (Dr)	Amt (Cr)
	Workmen Compensation Reserve A/c	Dr		60,000	
	To Rajat's Capital A/c				20,000
	To Sajjan's Capital A/c				20,000
	To Kavita's Capital A/c				20,000
	(Being workmen compensation reserve distributed to old partners in old ratio)				

NOTE Since, the profit sharing ratio is not given, it is distributed equally.

3. Give the journal entry to distribute workmen compensation reserve of ₹ 70,000 at the time of retirement of Neeti, when there is a claim of ₹ 25,000 against it. The firm has three partners Raveena, Neeti and Rajat. **All India 2013**

Ans. JOURNAL

Date	Particulars		LF	Amt (Dr)	Amt (Cr)
	Workmen Compensation Reserve A/c	Dr		70,000	
	To Liability for Workmen Compensation A/c				25,000
	To Raveena's Capital A/c $[(70,000-25,000)\times 1/3]$				15,000
	To Neeti's Capital A/c $[(70,000-25,000)\times \frac{1}{3}]$				15,000
	To Rajat's Capital A/c $[(70,000-25,000)\times \frac{1}{3}]$				15,000
	(Being workmen compensation reserve distributed to old partners in old ratio)				

NOTE Since, the profit sharing ratio is not given, it is distributed equally.

4. Ram, Mohan and Sohan were partners in a firm sharing profits in the ratio of 4 : 3 : 2. Mohan retired and his share was taken over equally by Ram and Sohan. In which ratio will the profit or loss on revaluation of assets and liabilities on the retirement of Mohan be transferred to the capital accounts of the partners? **Delhi (C) 2010**

Ans. The profit or loss on revaluation of assets and liabilities on the retirement of Mohan will be transferred to the capital accounts of the partners in their old ratio, i.e. 4 : 3 : 2.

2 Marks Question

5. P, Q and R were partners in a firm sharing profits and losses in the ratio of 4 : 3 : 3. On 31st March, 2022, R retired from the firm. On R's retirement the balance sheet of the firm showed sundry debtors at ₹ 3,75,000. It was decided to write off ₹ 5,000 as bad debts and create a provision of $2\frac{1}{2}$% on debtors for bad and doubtful debts.

Pass necessary journal entries for the above transactions in the books of the firm on R's retirement. **CBSE Term II 2022**

Ans. JOURNAL

Date	Particulars		LF	Amt (Dr)	Amt (Cr)
2022					
Mar 31	Revaluation A/c	Dr		5,000	
	To Bad Debts A/c				5,000
	(Being bad debts written-off at the time of retirement)				
Mar 31	Revaluation A/c (WN)	Dr		9,250	
	To Provision for Doubtful Debts A/c				9,250
	(Being provision for doubtful debts created @ $2\frac{1}{2}$% on debtors)				

Working Note

Provision for Doubtful Debts

Debtors	= 3,75,000
(–) Bad Debts	= (5,000)
	3,70,000

$\therefore$ Provision = $2\frac{1}{2}$% of ₹ 3,70,000 = ₹ 9,250

4/5 Marks Questions

6. D, E and F were partners in a firm sharing profits in the ratio of 5 : 2 : 3. On 31st March, 2022 their balance sheet was as folows

Liabilities		Amt (₹)	Assets	Amt (₹)
Creditors		53,000	Cash	16,000
Bills Payable		62,000	Bank	17,000
General Reserve		2,00,000	Stock	18,000
Capitals			Debtors	1,99,000
D	7,00,000		Investments	1,15,000
E	5,00,000		Machinery	7,50,000
F	6,00,000	18,00,000	Land and Building	10,00,000
		21,15,000		21,15,000

On the above date D retired from the firm and the following was agreed upon

(*i*) Goodwill of the firm was valued at ₹ 1,00,000. D's share of goodwill was adjusted through the capital accounts of remaining partners.

(*ii*) Investments were to be brought to their market value which was ₹ 85,000.

(*iii*) Machinery was to be depreciated to ₹ 7,00,000.

(*iv*) Land and Building was to be appreciated to ₹ 12,00,000.

(*v*) The balance in D's capital account was transferred to his loan account.

Prepare Revaluation Account and D's Capital Account on his retirement. **CBSE Term II 2022**

Ans. Dr **Revaluation Account** Cr

Particulars		Amt (₹)	Particulars	Amt (₹)
To Investments A/c		30,000	By Land and Building A/c	2,00,000
To Machinery A/c		50,000		
To Profit on Revaluation Transferred to Capital A/cs				
D	60,000			
E	24,000			
F	36,000	1,20,000		
		2,00,000		2,00,000

Dr **D's Capital Account** Cr

Date	Particulars	Amt (₹)	Date	Particulars	Amt (₹)
2022			2022		
Mar 31	To D's Loan A/c	9,10,000	Mar 31	By Balance b/d	7,00,000
			Mar 31	By General Reserve A/c	1,00,000
			Mar 31	By Revaluation A/c	60,000
			Mar 31	By E's Capital A/c	20,000
			Mar 31	By F's Capital A/c	30,000
		9,10,000			9,10,000

7. Banwari, Girdhari and Murari are partners in a firm sharing profits and losses in the ratio of 4 : 5 : 6. On 31st March, 2014, Girdhari retired. On that date the capitals of Banwari, Girdhari and Murari before the necessary adjustments stood at ₹ 2,00,000, ₹ 1,00,000 and ₹ 50,000, respectively. On Girdhari's retirement, goodwill of the firm was valued at ₹ 1,14,000. Revaluation of assets and re-assessment of liabilities resulted in a profit of ₹ 6,000. General reserve stood in the books of the firm at ₹ 30,000.

The amount payable to Girdhari was transferred to his loan account. Banwari and Murari agreed to pay Girdhari two yearly instalments of ₹ 75,000 each including interest @ 10% per annum on the outstanding balance during the first two years and the balance including interest in the third year. The firm closes its books on 31st March every year.

Prepare Girdhari's loan account till it is finally paid showing the working notes clearly.
CBSE 2018

Ans.

Dr **Girdhari's Loan Account** Cr

Date	Particulars	Amt (₹)	Date	Particulars	Amt (₹)
2015			2014		
Mar 31	To Bank A/c	75,000	Apr 1	By Girdhari's Capital A/c	1,50,000
Mar 31	To Balance c/d	90,000	2015 Mar 31	By Interest A/c	15,000
		1,65,000			1,65,000
2016			2015		
Mar 31	To Bank A/c	75,000	Apr 1	By Balance c/d	90,000
Mar 31	To Balance c/d	24,000	2016 Mar 31	By Interest A/c	9,000
		99,000			99,000
2016			2016		
Mar 31	To Bank A/c	26,400	Apr 1	By Balance b/d	24,000
			2016 Mar 31	By Interest A/c	2,400
		26,400			26,400

Working Note

Dr **Girdhari's Capital Account** Cr

Particulars	Amt (₹)	Particulars	Amt (₹)
To Girdhari's Loan A/c	1,50,000	By Balance b/d	1,00,000
		By Share in Goodwill A/c $\left(1,14,000 \times \frac{5}{15}\right)$	38,000
		By Revaluation Profit A/c $\left(6,000 \times \frac{5}{15}\right)$	2,000
		By General Reserve A/c $\left(30,000 \times \frac{5}{15}\right)$	10,000
	1,50,000		1,50,000

8. Alok, Narendra and Shiv were partners in a firm sharing profits in the ratio of 5 : 3 : 2. Goodwill appeared at ₹ 90,000 and general reserve at ₹ 50,000 in the books of the firm. Narendra decided to retire from the firm. On the date of his retirement, goodwill of the firm was valued at ₹ 2,40,000. The new profit sharing ratio of Alok and Shiv was 2 : 3. Record necessary journal entries on Narendra's retirement. **All India (C) 2015**

Ans.

JOURNAL

Date	Particulars		LF	Amt (Dr)	Amt (Cr)
	Alok's Capital A/c (90,000 × 5/10)	Dr		45,000	
	Narendra's Capital A/c (90,000 × 3/10)	Dr		27,000	
	Shiv's Capital A/c (90,000 × 2/10)	Dr		18,000	
	To Goodwill A/c				90,000
	(Being the existing goodwill written-off in old ratio)				

Date	Particulars		LF	Amt (Dr)	Amt (Cr)
	General Reserve A/c	Dr		50,000	
	To Alok's Capital A/c (50,000 × 5/10)				25,000
	To Narendra's Capital A/c (50,000 × 3/10)				15,000
	To Shiv's Capital A/c (50,000 × 2/10)				10,000
	(Being general reserve distributed among the old partners in old ratio)				
	Shiv's Capital A/c (2,40,000 × 4/10)	Dr		96,000	
	To Alok's Capital A/c (2,40,000 × 1/10)				24,000
	To Narendra's Capital A/c (2,40,000 × 3/10)				72,000
	(Being adjustment made for goodwill)				

Working Note

Calculation of Gaining Ratio

Gaining Ratio = New Share – Old Share

Alok $= \frac{2}{5} - \frac{5}{10} = \frac{4-5}{10} = \left(\frac{1}{10}\right)$ sacrifice ; Shiv $= \frac{3}{5} - \frac{2}{10} = \frac{6-2}{10} = \frac{4}{10}$ gain

9. Raman, Ratan and Rajan were partners sharing profits in the ratio of 4:2:1 respectively. Following was their balance sheet as at 31st March, 2013.

Balance Sheet

as at 31st March, 2013

Liabilities		Amt (₹)	Assets	Amt (₹)
Creditors		30,000	Cash	14,000
Bills Payable		4,000	Stock	30,000
General Reserve		21,000	Debtors	22,000
Capitals A/cs			Building	40,000
Raman	60,000		Plant	53,000
Ratan	40,000		Motor Van	26,000
Rajan	30,000	1,30,000		
		1,85,000		1,85,000

On the above date, Raman retired and following were agreed

(*i*) The assets and liabilities were valued as: stock ₹ 24,000; debtors ₹ 21,000; building ₹ 45,200; plant ₹ 50,000 and creditors ₹ 28,000.

(*ii*) Amount due to Raman will be transferred to Raman's loan account.

Prepare revaluation account and Raman's capital account. **Delhi (C) 2014**

Ans. Dr **Revaluation Account** Cr

Particulars	Amt (₹)	Particulars		Amt (₹)
To Stock A/c	6,000	By Building A/c		5,200
To Debtors A/c	1,000	By Creditors A/c		2,000
To Plant A/c	3,000	By Loss on Revaluation Transferred to Capital A/cs		
		Raman	1,600	
		Ratan	800	
		Rajan	400	2,800
	10,000			10,000

Dr **Raman's Capital Account** Cr

Date	Particulars	Amt (₹)	Date	Particulars	Amt (₹)
2013			2013		
Mar 31	To Revaluation A/c (Loss)	1,600	Mar 31	By Balance b/d	60,000
Mar 31	To Raman's Loan A/c	70,400	Mar 31	By General Reserve (21,000 × 4/7)	12,000
		72,000			72,000

8 Marks Questions

10. Sameer, Yasmin and Saloni were partners in a firm sharing profits and losses in the ratio of 4 : 3 : 3. On 31st March, 2016, their balance sheet was as follows **All India 2017**

Balance Sheet
as at 31st March, 2016

Liabilities		Amt (₹)	Assets		Amt (₹)
Creditors		1,10,000	Cash		80,000
General Reserve		60,000	Debtors	90,000	
Capital A/cs			(−) Provision for Doubtful Debts	(10,000)	80,000
Sameer	3,00,000		Stock		1,00,000
Yasmin	2,50,000		Machinery		3,00,000
Saloni	1,50,000	7,00,000	Building		2,00,000
			Patents		60,000
			Profit and Loss A/c		50,000
		8,70,000			8,70,000

On the above date, Sameer retired and it was agreed that

(*i*) Debtors of ₹ 4,000 will be written-off as bad debts and a provision of 5% on debtors for bad and doubtful debts will be maintained.

(*ii*) An unrecorded creditor of ₹ 20,000 will be recorded.

(*iii*) Patents will be completely written-off and 5% depreciation will be charged on stock, machinery and building.

(*iv*) Yasmin and Saloni will share the future profits in the ratio of 3 : 2.

(*v*) Goodwill of the firm on Sameer's retirement was valued at ₹ 5,40,000.

Pass necessary journal entries for the above transactions in the books of the firm on Sameer's retirement.

Ans. **JOURNAL**

Date	Particulars		LF	Amt (Dr)	Amt (Cr)
2016					
Mar 31	General Reserve A/c	Dr		60,000	
	To Sameer's Capital A/c				24,000
	To Yasmin's Capital A/c				18,000
	To Saloni's Capital A/c				18,000
	(Being general reserve distributed among old partners in old ratio)				

Date	Particulars		LF	Amt (Dr)	Amt (Cr)
	Sameer's Capital A/c	Dr		20,000	
	Yasmin's Capital A/c	Dr		15,000	
	Saloni's Capital A/c	Dr		15,000	
	To Profit and Loss A/c				50,000
	(Being balance of profit and loss account distributed among old partners in old ratio)				
	Yasmin's Capital A/c	Dr		1,62,000	
	Saloni's Capital A/c	Dr		54,000	
	To Sameer's Capital A/c				2,16,000
	(Being Sameer's share of goodwill adjusted)				
	Revaluation A/c	Dr		1,10,000	
	To Patents A/c				60,000
	To Stock A/c (1,00,000 × 5%)				5,000
	To Machinery A/c (3,00,000 × 5%)				15,000
	To Building A/c (2,00,000 × 5%)				10,000
	To Creditors A/c				20,000
	(Being decrease in the value of assets and increase in the value of liabilities recorded)				
	Bad Debts A/c	Dr		4,000	
	To Debtors A/c				4,000
	(Being bad debts charged)				
	Provision for Doubtful Debts A/c	Dr		4,000	
	To Bad Debts A/c				4,000
	(Being bad debts written-off from provision)				
	Provision for Doubtful Debts A/c	Dr		1,700	
	To Revaluation A/c				1,700
	(Being decrease in the value of provision recorded)				
	Sameer's Capital A/c	Dr		43,320	
	Yasmin's Capital A/c	Dr		32,490	
	Saloni's Capital A/c	Dr		32,490	
	To Revaluation A/c				1,08,300
	(Being loss on revaluation distributed among old partners)				
	Sameer's Capital A/c	Dr		4,76,680	
	To Sammer's Loan A/c				4,76,680
	(Being amount due to Sameer transferred to his loan account)				

Working Notes

1. **Calculation of Gaining Ratio**

   Gaining Ratio = New Share – Old Share

   $\text{Yasmin} = \frac{3}{5} - \frac{3}{10} = \frac{6-3}{10} = \frac{3}{10}$; $\quad \text{Saloni} = \frac{2}{5} - \frac{3}{10} = \frac{4-3}{10} = \frac{1}{10}$

   Gaining ratio = 3 : 1

2. **Provision for Bad Debts**

Debtors	90,000
(−) Bad debts	(4,000), which will be adjusted against provision for bad debts
	86,000

Provision for doubtful debts @ 5% $= \left(86,000 \times \frac{5}{100}\right) =$ ₹ 4,300

Existing provision after adjusting bad debts (10,000 − 4,000)	= 6,000
(−) New provision	= (4,300)
Excess provision	= ₹ 1,700

3. **Calculation of Sameer's Share of Goodwill**

Firm's goodwill = ₹ 5,40,000

Sameer's share $= 5,40,000 \times \frac{4}{10} =$ ₹ 2,16,000

To be contributed by Yasmin and Saloni in their gaining ratio, *i.e.* 3 : 1.

4. **Loss on Revaluation**

It can be ascertained by preparing revaluation account in the following manner

Dr **Revaluation Account** Cr

Particulars	Amt (₹)	Particulars		Amt (₹)
To Patents A/c	60,000	By Provision for Doubtful Debts A/c		1,700
To Stock A/c	5,000	By Loss on Revaluation Transferred to		
To Machinery A/c	15,000	Sameer	43,320	
To Building A/c	10,000	Yasmin	32,490	
To Creditors A/c	20,000	Saloni	32,490	1,08,300
	1,10,000			1,10,000

11. M, N and G were partners in a firm sharing profits and losses in the ratio of 5:3:2. On 31st March, 2016 their balance sheet was as under **Delhi 2017**

Balance Sheet
as at 31st March, 2016

Liabilities		Amt (₹)	Assets		Amt (₹)
Creditors		55,000	Cash		40,000
General Reserve		30,000	Debtors	45,000	
Capital A/cs			(−) Provision for Doubtful Debts	(5,000)	40,000
M	1,50,000		Stock		50,000
N	1,25,000		Machinery		1,50,000
G	75,000	3,50,000	Patents		30,000
			Building		1,00,000
			Profit and Loss A/c		25,000
		4,35,000			4,35,000

M retired on the above data and it was agreed that

(*i*) Debtors of ₹ 2,000 will be written-off as bad debts and a provision of 5% on debtors for bad and doubtful debts will be maintained.

(*ii*) Patents will be completely written-off and stock, machinery and building will be depreciated by 5%.

(*iii*) An unrecorded creditor of ₹ 10,000 will be taken into account.

(*iv*) N and G will share the future profits in the ratio of 2 : 3.

(*v*) Goodwill of the firm on M's retirement was valued at ₹ 3,00,000.

Pass necessary journal entries for the above transactions in the books of the firm on M's retirement.

Ans. Solve as Q no. 10 on page 150-152.

Loss on Revaluation M = ₹ 27,075, N = ₹ 16,245, G = ₹ 10,830; Amount Transferred to M's Loan Account = ₹ 2,75,425, M's Share of Goodwill = ₹1,50,000, Gaining Ratio = 1 : 4

12. Lalit, Madhur and Neena were partners sharing profits as 50%, 30% and 20% respectively. On 31st March, 2013 their balance sheet was as follows

Balance Sheet
as at 31st March, 2013

Liabilities		Amt (₹)	Assets		Amt (₹)
Creditors		28,000	Cash		34,000
Provident Fund		10,000	Debtors	47,000	
Investment Fluctuation Fund		10,000	(−) Provision for Doubtful Debts	(3,000)	44,000
Capital A/cs			Stock		15,000
Lalit	50,000		Investments		40,000
Madhur	40,000		Goodwill		20,000
Neena	25,000	1,15,000	Profit and Loss A/c		10,000
		1,63,000			1,63,000

On this date, Madhur retired and Lalit and Neena agreed to continue on the following terms

(*i*) The goodwill of the firm was valued at ₹ 51,000.

(*ii*) There was a claim for workmen's compensation to the extent of ₹ 6,000.

(*iii*) Investments were brought down to ₹ 15,000.

(*iv*) Provision for bad debts was reduced by ₹ 1,000.

(*v*) Madhur was paid ₹ 10,300 in cash and the balance was transferred to his loan account payable in two equal instalments together with interest @ 12% per annum.

Prepare revaluation account, partners' capital accounts and Madhur's loan account till the loan is finally paid off. **Delhi (C) 2015**

Ans. Dr **Revaluation Account** Cr

Particulars	Amt (₹)	Particulars		Amt (₹)
To Workmen's Compensation Claim A/c	6,000	By Provision for Doubtful Debts		1,000
To Investments A/c	15,000	By Loss Transferred to Partners' Capital A/c		
		Lalit	10,000	
		Madhur	6,000	
		Neena	4,000	20,000
	21,000			21,000

Dr **Partners' Capital Account** Cr

Particulars	Lalit (₹)	Madhur (₹)	Neena (₹)	Particulars	Lalit (₹)	Madhur (₹)	Neena (₹)
To Profit and Loss A/c	5,000	3,000	2,000	By Balance b/d	50,000	40,000	25,000
To Goodwill A/c	10,000	6,000	4,000	By Lalit's Capital A/c	—	10,929	—
To Revaluation A/c (Loss)	10,000	6,000	4,000	By Neena's Capital A/c	—	4,371	—
To Madhur's Capital A/c	10,929	—	4,371				
To Cash A/c	—	10,300	—				
To Madhur's Loan A/c	—	30,000	—				
To Balance c/d	14,071	—	10,629				
	50,000	55,300	25,000		50,000	55,300	25,000

Dr **Madhur's Loan Account** Cr

Date	Particulars	Amt (₹)	Date	Particulars	Amt (₹)
2014			2013		
Mar 31	To Bank A/c (15,000+ 3,600)	18,600	Apr 1	By Madhur's Capital A/c	30,000
			2014		
Mar 31	To Balance c/d	15,000	Mar 31	By Interest A/c	3,600
		33,600			33,600
2015			2014		
Mar 31	To Bank A/c (15,000+ 1,800)	16,800	Apr 1	By Balance b/d	15,000
			2015		
			Mar 31	By Interest A/c	1,800
		16,800			16,800

Working Note

Madhur's share in goodwill $= 51,000 \times \frac{3}{10} =$ ₹15,300, which is contributed by Lalit and Neena in the ratio of 5 : 2.

Lalit will pay $= 15,300 \times \frac{5}{7} =$ ₹10,929; Neena will pay $= 15,300 \times \frac{2}{7} =$ ₹ 4,371

Reduction in the value of investments have been adjusted through revaluation account

Investments	40,000
(–) Investment Fluctuation Fund	(10,000)
	30,000
(–) Present Value	(15,000)
	₹ 15,000

TOPIC 4

Adjustment of Capital

After the retirement of a partner, the remaining partners may decide to adjust their capital contributions in their profit sharing ratio.

Cases Related to the Adjustment of Capital

The capitals of the continuing partners may be required to be adjusted in the following three cases

Case **I When the Total Capital of the New Firm is Given**

The various steps involved in adjusting the capitals of the continuing partners are given below

Step **1** Calculate new profit sharing ratio and gaining ratio of continuing partners (if not given).

Step **2** Calculate the adjusted old capitals of continuing partners (*i.e.* after all other adjustments).

Step **3** Calculate the new capitals of continuing partners by dividing the total capital in their new profit sharing ratio.

Step **4** Calculate the surplus/deficit capital by comparing Step 2 and 3.

Step **5** Adjust the surplus by paying-off or by transfer to the credit of current account and adjust the deficiency by asking the concerned partner to bring in the necessary amount or by transfer to debit of his current account.

Case **II When the Total Capital of the New Firm is Not Given**

The various steps involved in adjusting the capitals of the partners are given below

Step **1** Calculate the adjusted old capitals of continuing partners (*i.e.* after all other adjustments.)

Step **2** Calculate total capital of the new firm.

Total capital of the new firm = Aggregate of adjusted old capitals of continuing partners.

Step **3** Calculate the new capitals of continuing partners by dividing the total capital in their new profit sharing ratio.

Step **4** Calculate the surplus/deficit capital by comparing step 1 and 3.

Step **5** Adjust the surplus by paying off or asking the concerned partner to bring in the necessary amount. Adjustment can be made by transfer to current account (credit/debit) as well.

NOTE Sometimes, there may be a situation when the total capital of the new firm is same as before the retirement of a partner.

Case **III When the Outgoing Partner is to be Paid through Cash brought in by the Continuing Partners in such a way as to make their Capitals Proportionate to their New Profit Sharing Ratio**

Steps involved in adjusting the capitals of partners are given below

Step **1** Calculate the adjusted old capitals of continuing partners (*i.e.* after all other adjustments.)

Step **2** Calculate total capital of the new firm.
Total capital of the new firm = Aggregate of adjusted old capitals of continuing partners + Shortage of cash to be brought in by continuing partners in order to make payment to outgoing partner.

Step **3** Calculate the new capitals of continuing partners by dividing the total capital in their new profit sharing ratio.

Step **4** Calculate the surplus/deficit by comparing Step 1 and 3 above.

Step **5** Adjust the surplus by paying off or asking the concerned partner to bring in the necessary amount. Adjustment can be made by transfer to current account (credit/debit) as well.

NOTE Sometimes, there may be a situation when partners are required to maintain a minimum cash/bank balance.

NOTE If, in any case, question is silent whether adjustment is to be made through cash or current account, any surplus or deficiency should be adjusted in cash and not by transferring it to current account.

Previous Years' Examination Questions

3 Marks Questions

1. X, Y and Z are partners in a firm sharing profits in the ratio of 3 : 2 : 1. On 1st April , 2009, X retires from the firm, Y and Z agrees that the capital of the new firm shall be fixed at ₹ 2,10,000 in the profit sharing ratio. The capital accounts of Y and Z after all adjustments on the date of retirement showed balances of ₹ 1,45,000 and ₹ 63,000 respectively. State the amount of actual cash to be brought in or to be paid to the partners. **Delhi 2010**

Ans. **Calculation of Cash to be Brought In or Paid Out**

Particulars	Y (₹)	Z (₹)
Capital After All Adjustments	1,45,000	63,000
(–) New Capital Share (2,10,000 in 2 : 1)	(1,40,000)	(70,000)
Amount of Cash Adjustment	5,000	(7,000)

It means Y will take ₹ 5,000 and Z will bring ₹ 7,000 to make their capital in new ratio.

2. X, Y and Z are partners in a firm sharing profits in the ratio of 3 : 2 : 1. On 1st April, 2009, Y retires form the firm. X and Z agree that the capital of the new firm shall be fixed at ₹ 2,10,000 in the profit sharing ratio. The capital accounts of X and Z after all adjustments on the date of retirement showed balances of ₹1,45,000 and ₹ 63,000 respectively. State the amount of actual cash to be brought in or to be paid to the partners. **All India 2010**

Ans. **Calculation of Cash to be Brought In or Paid Out**

Particulars	X (₹)	Z (₹)
Capital After All Adjustments	1,45,000	63,000
(–) New Capital Share (2,10,000 in 3 : 1)	(1,57,500)	(52,500)
Amount of Cash Adjustment	(12,500)	10,500

Therefore, X will bring ₹ 12,500 and Z will take away ₹ 10,500 to make their capital in new ratio.

4 Marks Questions

3. Nandan, John and Rosa are partners sharing profits in the ratio of 4 : 3 : 2. On 1st April, 2012, John gave a notice to retire from the firm. Nandan and Rosa decided to share future profits in the ratio of 1 : 1. The capital accounts of Nandan and Rosa after all adjustments showed a balance of ₹ 43,000 and ₹ 80,500 respectively. The total amount to be paid to John was ₹ 95,500. This amount was to be paid by Nandan and Rosa in such a way that their capitals become proportionate to their new profit sharing ratio. Pass necessary journal entries in the books of the firm for the above transactions. Show your workings clearly. **All India 2013**

Ans. **JOURNAL**

Date	Particulars		LF	Amt (Dr)	Amt (Cr)
2012					
Apr 1	Cash A/c	Dr		95,500	
	To Nandan's Capital A/c				66,500
	To Rosa's Capital A/c				29,000
	(Being cash to be paid to John brought in by Nandan and Rosa)				
Apr 1	John's Capital A/c	Dr		95,500	
	To Cash A/c				95,500
	(Being cash paid to John for his capital)				

Working Notes

Adjusted Capitals of Nandan and Rosa (43,000 + 80,500)	1,23,500
(+) Amount to be Paid to John	95,500
Total Capital of New Firm	2,19,000

Amount to be Brought in or Withdrawn

Particulars	Nandan (₹)	Rosa (₹)
New Firm's Capital (2,19,000) in New Ratio, *i.e.* 1:1	1,09,500	1,09,500
(–) Existing Capitals	(43,000)	(80,500)
Cash to be Brought in	66,500	29,000

4. Naresh, David and Aslam are partners sharing profits in the ratio of 5 : 3 : 7. On 1st April, 2012, Naresh gave a notice to retire from the firm. David and Aslam decided to share future profits in the ratio of 2 : 3. The adjusted capital accounts of David and Aslam show a balance of ₹ 33,000 and ₹ 70,500 respectively. The total amount to be paid to Naresh is ₹ 90,500.

This amount is to be paid by David and Aslam in such a way their capitals become proportionate to their new profit sharing ratio. Pass necessary journal entries for the above transactions in the books of the firm. Show your workings clearly. **Delhi 2013**

Ans. Solve as Q no. 3 on page no. 157.

Cash to be brought in by David = ₹ 44,600; Aslam = ₹ 45,900

8 Marks Questions

5. Radha, Manas and Arnav were partners in a firm sharing profits and losses in the ratio of 3 : 1 : 1. Their Balance Sheet as at 31st March, 2019 was as follows

Balance Sheet of Radha, Manas and Arnav
as at 31st March, 2019

Liabilities		Amt (₹)	Assets		Amt (₹)
Capitals			Furniture		4,60,000
Radha	4,00,000		Investments		2,00,000
Manas	3,00,000		Stock		2,40,000
Arnav	2,00,000	9,00,000	Debtors	2,20,000	
Investment Fluctuation Fund		1,10,000	(–) Provision for doubtful debts	(10,000)	2,10,000
Creditors		2,50,000	Cash		1,50,000
		12,60,000			12,60,000

Manas retired on 1st April, 2019. It was agreed that

(*i*) Stock was to be appreciated by 20%.
(*ii*) Provision for doubtful debts was to be increased to ₹ 15,000.
(*iii*) Value of furniture was to be reduced by ₹ 3,000.
(*iv*) Market value of investments was ₹ 1,90,000.
(*v*) Goodwill of the firm was valued at ₹ 2,00,000 and Manas's share was adjusted in the accounts of Radha and Arnav.
(*vi*) Manas was paid ₹ 68,000 in cash and the balance was transferred to his loan account.
(*vii*) Capitals of Radha and Arnav were to be in proportion to their new profit sharing ratio. Surplus/deficit, if any, in their capital accounts was to be adjusted through current accounts.

Prepare Revaluation Account, Partner's Capital Accounts and the Balance Sheet of the reconstituted firm. **CBSE 2020**

Ans Solve as Q.no 10 on page no. 165 and 166.

Profit on Revaluation = ₹ 40,000

Capital A/c Balances

Radha = ₹ 5,04,000 ; Arnav = ₹ 1,68,000

Balance Sheet = ₹ 12,72,000

6. Akul, Bakul and Chandan were partners in a firm sharing profits in the ratio of 2 : 2 : 1. On 31st March, 2018 their balance sheet was as follows

Balance Sheet of Akul, Bakul and Chandan
as on 31st March, 2018

Liabilities		Amt (₹)	Assets		Amt (₹)
Sundry Creditors		45,000	Cash at Bank		42,000
Employees Provident Fund		13,000	Debtors	60,000	
General Reserve		20,000	(–) Provision for Doubtful Debts	(2,000)	58,000
Capitals A/cs:					
Akul	1,60,000		Stock		80,000
Bakul	1,20,000		Furniture		90,000
Chandan	92,000	3,72,000	Plant and Machinery		1,80,000
		4,50,000			4,50,000

Bakul retired on the above date and it was agreed that

(*i*) Plant and Machinery was undervalued by 10%.

(*ii*) Provision for doubtful debts was to be increased to 15% on debtors.

(*iii*) Furniture was to be decreased to ₹ 87,000.

(*iv*) Goodwill of the firm was valued at ₹ 3,00,000 and Bakul's share was to be adjusted through the capital accounts of Akul and Chandan.

(*v*) Capital of the new firm was to be in the new profit sharing ratio of the continuing partners.

Prepare revaluation account, partners' capital accounts and balance sheet of the reconstituted firm. **Delhi 2019**

Ans. Dr **Revaluation Account** Cr

Particulars		Amt (₹)	Particulars	Amt (₹)
To Provision for Doubtful Debts		7,000	By Plant and Machinery	20,000
To Furniture		3,000		
To Profit Transferred to Capital A/c				
Akul	4,000			
Bakul	4,000			
Chandan	2,000	10,000		
		20,000		20,000

Dr **Partners' Capital Account** Cr

Particulars	Akul (₹)	Bakul (₹)	Chandan (₹)	Particulars	Akul (₹)	Bakul (₹)	Chandan (₹)
To Bakul's Capital A/c	80,000	—	40,000	By Balance b/d	1,60,000	1,20,000	92,000
To Bakul's Loan A/c	—	2,52,000	—	By General Reserve	8,000	8,000	4,000
To Cash A/c	—	—	8,000	By Akul's Capital A/c	—	80,000	—
To Balance c/d	1,00,000	—	50,000	By Chandan's Capital A/c	—	40,000	—
				By Revaluation (Profit)	4,000	4,000	2,000
				By Cash A/c	8,000	—	—
	1,80,000	2,52,000	98,000		1,80,000	2,52,000	98,000

Dr **Cash/Bank Account** Cr

Particulars	Amt (₹)	Particulars	Amt (₹)
To Balance b/d	42,000	By Chandan's Capital A/c	8,000
To Akul's Capital A/c	8,000	By Balance c/d	42,000
	50,000		50,000

Balance Sheet
as at......

Liabilities		Amt (₹)	Assets		Amt (₹)
Sundry Creditors		45,000	Plant and Machinery		2,00,000
Employees Provident Fund		13,000	Debtors	60,000	
Bakul's Loan A/c		2,52,000	(−) Provision for Doubtful Debts @ 15%	(9,000)	51,000
Capitals					
Akul	1,00,000		Furniture		87,000
Chandan	50,000	1,50,000	Stock		80,000
			Cash at Bank		42,000
		4,60,000			4,60,000

Working Notes

1. Plant and machinery (original value) $= 1,80,000 \times \frac{100}{90} =$ ₹ 2,00,000
2. Firm's goodwill = ₹ 3,00,000

   Bakul's share of goodwill $= 3,00,000 \times \frac{2}{5} =$ ₹ 1,20,000 to be contributed by Akul and Chandan in the ratio 2 : 1.
3. Akul's capital after adjustment = ₹ 92,000

   Chandan's capital after adjustment = ₹ 58,000

   ₹ 1,50,000

   Akul's new capital $= 1,50,000 \times \frac{2}{3} = 1,00,000 - 92,000 =$ ₹ 8,000 cash brought in

   Chandan's new capital $= 1,50,000 \times \frac{1}{3} = 50,000 - 58,000 =$ ₹ 8,000 cash withdrew

7. G, E and F were partners in a firm sharing profits in the ratio of 7 : 2 : 1. The balance sheet of the firm as at 31st March, 2018 was as follows

Balance Sheet of G, E and F
as at 31st March, 2018

Liabilities		Amt (₹)	Assets	Amt (₹)
Capital A/cs			Cash	90,000
G	1,40,000		Sundry Debtors	24,000
E	40,000		Stock	14,000
F	20,000	2,00,000	Machinery	80,000
Creditors		28,000	Land and Building	1,20,000

Liabilities	Amt (₹)	Assets	Amt (₹)
General Reserve	40,000		
Loan from E	60,000		
	3,28,000		3,28,000

E retired on the above date. On E's retirement the following was agreed upon

(*i*) Land and building were revalued at ₹ 1,88,000, machinery at ₹ 76,000 and stock at ₹ 10,000 and goodwill of the firm was valued at ₹ 90,000.

(*ii*) A provision of 2.5% was to be created on debtors for doubtful debts.

(*iii*) The net amount payable to E was transferred to his loan account to be paid later on.

(*iv*) Total capital of the new firm was fixed at ₹ 2,40,000 which will be adjusted according to their new profit sharing ratio by opening current accounts.

Prepare revaluation account, partners' capital accounts and balance sheet of reconstituted firm. **All India 2019**

Ans. Dr **Revaluation Account** Cr

Particulars		Amt (₹)	Particulars	Amt (₹)
To Machinery		4,000	By Land and Building	68,000
To Stock		4,000		
To Provision for Doubtful Debts		600		
To Profit Transferred to				
G's Capital	41,580			
E's Capital	11,880			
F's Capital	5,940	59,400		
		68,000		68,000

Dr **Partners' Capital Account** Cr

Particulars	G(₹)	E(₹)	F(₹)	Particulars	G(₹)	E(₹)	F(₹)
To E's Capital A/c	15,750	—	2,250	By Balance b/d	1,40,000	40,000	20,000
To E's Loan A/c	—	77,880	—	By General Reserve	28,000	8,000	4,000
To Balance c/d	2,10,000	—	30,000	By G's Capital	—	15,750	—
				By F's Capital	—	2,250	—
				By Revaluation (Profit)	41,580	11,880	5,940
				By G's Current A/c (Balancing figure)	16,170	—	—
				By F's Current A/c (Balancing figure)	—	—	2,310
	2,25,750	77,880	32,250		2,25,750	77,880	32,250

Balance Sheet
as at 31st March, 2018

Liabilities		Amt (₹)	Assets		Amt (₹)
Creditors		28,000	Land and Building		1,88,000
Loan from E (60,000 + 77,880)		1,37,880	Machinery		76,000
Capital A/cs			Stock		10,000
G	2,10,000				
F	30,000	2,40,000	Debtors	24,000	
			(–) Provision for Doubtful Debts	(600)	23,400
			Cash		90,000
			G's Current A/c		16,170
			F's Current A/c		2,310
		4,05,880			4,05,880

8. Mohan, Vinay and Nitya were partners in a firm sharing profits and losses in the proportion of $\frac{1}{2}, \frac{1}{3}$ and $\frac{1}{6}$ respectively. On 31st March, 2018 their balance sheet was as follows

Balance Sheet of Mohan, Vinay and Nitya
as at 31st March, 2018

Liabilities		Amt (₹)	Assets		Amt (₹)
Creditors		48,000	Cash at Bank		31,000
Emloyees Provident Fund		1,70,000	Bills Receivable		54,000
Contingency Reserve		30,000	Book Debts	63,000	
Capital A/cs			(–) Provision for Doubtful Debts	(2,000)	61,000
Mohan	1,20,000		Plant and Machinery		1,20,000
Vinay	1,00,000		Land and Building		2,92,000
Nitya	90,000	3,10,000			
		5,58,000			5,58,000

Mohan retired on the above date and it was agreed that

(*i*) Plant and machinery will be depreciated by 5%.

(*ii*) An old computer previously written off was sold for ₹ 4,000.

(*iii*) Bad debts amounting to ₹ 3,000 will be written off and a provision of 5% on debtors for bad and doubtful debts will be maintained.

(*iv*) Goodwill of the firm was valued at ₹ 1,80,000 and Mohan's share of the same was credited in his account by debiting Vinay's and Nitya's accounts.

(*v*) The capital of the new firm was to be fixed at ₹ 90,000 and necessary adjustments were to be made by bringing in or paying off cash as the case may be.

(*vi*) Vinay and Nitya will share future profits in the ratio of 3 : 2.

Prepare revaluation account, partners' capital accounts and balance sheet of the reconstituted firm. **All India 2019**

Ans. Dr **Revaluation Account** Cr

Particulars	Amt (₹)	Particulars		Amt (₹)
To Plant and Machinery A/c	6,000	By Bank (Sale of old computer)		4,000
To Books Debts A/c	1,000	By Loss Transferred to		
To Provision for Bad and Doubtful Debts A/c	3,000	Mohan's Capital A/c	3,000	
		Vinay's Capital A/c	2,000	
		Nitya's Capital A/c	1,000	6,000
	10,000			10,000

Dr **Partners' Capital Account** Cr

Particulars	Mohan (₹)	Vinay (₹)	Nitya (₹)	Particulars	Mohan (₹)	Vinay (₹)	Nitya (₹)
To Mohan's Capital A/c	—	48,000	42,000	By Balance b/d	1,20,000	1,00,000	90,000
To Revaluation Loss	3,000	2,000	1,000	By Contingency Reserve	15,000	10,000	5,000
To Mohan's Loan A/c	2,22,000	—	—	By Vinay's Capital A/c	48,000	—	—
To Bank (Balancing figure)	—	6,000	16,000	By Nitya's Capital A/c	42,000	—	—
To Balance c/d	—	54,000	36,000				
	2,25,000	1,10,000	95,000		2,25,000	1,10,000	95,000

Dr **Bank Account** Cr

Particulars	Amt (₹)	Particulars	Amt (₹)
To Balance b/d	31,000	By Vinay's Capital A/c	6,000
To Revaluation A/c	4,000	By Nitya's Capital A/c	16,000
		By Balance c/d	13,000
	35,000		35,000

Balance Sheet
as at ...

Liabilities		Amt (₹)	Assets		Amt (₹)
Creditors		48,000	Plant and Machinery		1,14,000
Employee's Provident Fund		1,70,000	Book Debts	63,000	
Mohan's Loan A/c		2,22,000	(−) Bad Debts	(3,000)	
Capital A/cs : Vinay	54,000			60,000	
Nitya	36,000	90,000	(−) Provision for Bad and Doubtful Debts	(3,000)	57,000
			Bills Receivable		54,000
			Land and Building		2,92,000
			Bank		13,000
		5,30,000			5,30,000

Working Notes

1. **Calculation of Gaining Ratio**

   Vinay gain $= \frac{3}{5} - \frac{2}{6} = \frac{18-10}{30} = \frac{8}{30}$; Nitya $= \frac{2}{5} - \frac{1}{6} = \frac{12-5}{30} = \frac{7}{30}$

   Gaining ratio = 8 : 7

2. Firm's goodwill = ₹ 1,80,000

   Mohan's share of goodwill $= 1{,}80{,}000 \times \frac{3}{6} =$ ₹ 90,000

   to be adjusted in gaining ratio, *i.e.* 8 : 7

9. Kavya, Manya and Navita were partners sharing profits as 50%, 30% and 20% respectively. On March 31, 2016, their balance sheet stood as follows

Balance Sheet of Kavya, Manya and Navita
as at 31st March, 2016

Liabilities		Amt (₹)	Assets		Amt (₹)
Creditors		1,40,000	Fixed Assets		8,90,000
General Reserve		1,00,000	Investments		2,00,000
Capitals A/cs			Stock		1,30,000
Kavya	6,00,000		Debtors	4,00,000	
Manya	5,00,000		(−) Provision for		
Navita	4,00,000	15,00,000	Bad Debts	(30,000)	3,70,000
			Bank		1,50,000
		17,40,000			17,40,000

On the above date, Kavya retired and Manya and Navita agreed to continue the business on the following terms

(*i*) Firm's goodwill was valued at ₹ 60,000 and it was decided to adjust Kavya's share to goodwill in the capital accounts of continuing partners.

(*ii*) There was claim for workmen's compensation to the extent of ₹ 4,000.

(*iii*) Investments were revalued at ₹ 2,13,000.

(*iv*) Fixed assets were to be depreciated by 10%.

(*v*) Kavya was to be paid ₹ 20,000 through a bank draft and the ablance was transferred to her loan account which will be paid in two equal annual instalments together with interest @ 10% p.a.

Prepare revaluation account, partners' capital accounts and Kavya's loan account till it is finally paid. **Compartment 2018**

Ans. Solve as Q.no. 7 on page 160-162.

Revaluation loss Kavya = ₹ 40,000
Manya = ₹ 24,000
Navita = ₹ 16,000
Capital balance Manya = ₹ 4,88,000
Navita = ₹ 3,92,000
Kavya's Loan A/c = ₹ 6,20,000
1st Year = ₹ 3,72,000
2nd Year = ₹ 3,41,000

10. J, H and K were partners in a firm sharing profits in the ratio of 5 : 3 : 2. On 31st March, 2015 their balance sheet was as follows

Balance Sheet
as at 31st March, 2015

Liabilities		Amt (₹)	Assets		Amt (₹)
Creditors		42,000	Land and Building		1,24,000
Investment Fluctuation Fund		20,000	Motor Vans		40,000
Profit and Loss A/c		80,000	Investments		38,000
Capital A/cs			Machinery		24,000
J	1,00,000		Stock		30,000
H	80,000		Debtors	80,000	
K	40,000	2,20,000	(–) Provision for Doubtful Debts	(6,000)	74,000
			Cash		32,000
		3,62,000			3,62,000

On the above date, H retired and J and K agreed to continue the business on the following terms

(*i*) Goodwill of the firm was valued at ₹ 1,02,000.
(*ii*) There was a claim of ₹ 8,000 for workmen's compensation.
(*iii*) Provision for bad debts was to be reduced by ₹ 2,000.
(*iv*) H will be paid ₹ 14,000 in cash and the balance will be transferred in his loan account which will be paid in four equal yearly instalments together with interest @ 10% per annum.
(*v*) The new profit sharing ratio between J and K will be 3 : 2 and their capitals will be in their new profit sharing ratio. The capital adjustments will be done by opening current accounts.

Prepare revaluation account, partners' capital accounts and balance sheet of the new firm.

All India 2016

Ans. Dr **Revaluation Account** Cr

Particulars	Amt (₹)	Particulars		Amt (₹)
To Claim for Workmen's Compensation Fund A/c	8,000	By Provision for Doubtful Debts A/c		2,000
		By Loss Transferred to Capital A/cs		
		J	3,000	
		H	1,800	
		K	1,200	6,000
	8,000			8,000

Dr **Partners' Capital Account** Cr

Particulars	J (₹)	H (₹)	K (₹)	Particulars	J (₹)	H (₹)	K (₹)
To Loss on Revaluation A/c	3,000	1,800	1,200	By Balance b/d	1,00,000	80,000	40,000
To H's Capital A/c	10,200	—	20,400	By Investment Fluctuation Fund A/c	10,000	6,000	4,000
To Cash A/c	—	14,000	—				
To H's Loan A/c	—	1,24,800	—	By Profit and Loss A/c	40,000	24,000	16,000
To Current A/c (Balancing figure)	31,680	—	—	By J's Capital A/c	—	10,200	—
				By K's Capital A/c	—	20,400	—
To Balance c/d	1,05,120	—	70,080	By Current A/c (Balancing figure)	—	—	31,680
	1,50,000	1,40,600	91,680		1,50,000	1,40,600	91,680

Balance Sheet
as at 31st March, 2015

Liabilities		Amt (₹)	Assets		Amt (₹)
Creditors		42,000	Land and Building		1,24,000
J's Current A/c		31,680	Motor Van		40,000
Claim for Workmen's Compensation		8,000	Investments		38,000
H's Loan A/c		1,24,800	Machinery		24,000
Capital A/cs			Stock		30,000
J	1,05,120		Debtors	80,000	
K	70,080	1,75,200	(−) Provision for Doubtful Debts	(4,000)	76,000
			Cash (32,000 − 14,000)		18,000
			K's Current A/c		31,680
		3,81,680			3,81,680

Working Notes

1. **Calculation of Gaining Ratio**

Gaining Ratio = New Share − Old Share

$$J = \frac{3}{5} - \frac{5}{10} = \frac{6-5}{10} = \frac{1}{10};\quad K = \frac{2}{5} - \frac{2}{10} = \frac{4-2}{10} = \frac{2}{10}$$

Gaining ratio = 1 : 2

2. **Adjustment for Goodwill**

Firm's goodwill = ₹ 1,02,000

H's share of goodwill $= 1{,}02{,}000 \times \frac{3}{10} =$ ₹ 30,600 will be debited to gaining partners, *i.e.* J and K in gaining ratio, *i.e.* 1 : 2

J's share $= 30{,}600 \times \frac{1}{3} =$ ₹ 10,200; K's share $= 30{,}600 \times \frac{2}{3} =$ ₹ 20,400

3. **Adjustment of Capital**

J's capital after adjustment	=	1,36,800
K's capital after adjustment	=	38,400
Total capital of new firm	=	₹ 1,75,200

J's adjusted capital $= 1{,}75{,}200 \times \frac{3}{5} =$ ₹ 1,05,120; K's adjusted capital $= 1{,}75{,}200 \times \frac{2}{5} =$ ₹ 70,080

11. X, Y and Z were partners in a firm sharing profits in the ratio of 5 : 3 : 2. On 31st March, 2015 their balance sheet was as follows

Balance Sheet
as at 31st March, 2015

Liabilities	Amt (₹)	Assets	Amt (₹)
Creditors	21,000	Land and Building	62,000
Investment Fluctuation Fund	10,000	Motor Vans	20,000
Profit and Loss A/c	40,000	Investments	19,000

Liabilities		Amt (₹)	Assets		Amt (₹)
Capital A/cs			Machinery		12,000
X	50,000		Stock		15,000
Y	40,000		Debtors	40,000	
Z	20,000	1,10,000	(−) Provision for Doubtful Debts	(3,000)	37,000
			Cash		16,000
		1,81,000			1,81,000

On the above date, Y retired and X and Z agreed to continue the business on the following terms

(*i*) Goodwill of the firm was valued at ₹ 51,000.

(*ii*) There was a claim of ₹ 4,000 for workmen's compensation.

(*iii*) Provision for bad debts was to be reduced by ₹ 1,000.

(*iv*) Y will be paid ₹ 8,200 in cash and the balance will be transferred in his loan account which will be paid in four equal yearly instalments together with interest @ 10% per annum.

(*v*) The new profit sharing ratio between X and Z will be 3 : 2 and their capitals will be in their new profit sharing ratio. The capital adjustments will be done by opening current accounts.

Prepare revaluation account, partners' capital accounts and the balance sheet of the reconstituted firm. **Delhi 2016**

Ans. Solve as Q no. 10 on page 165-166.

Loss on Revaluation Account: X = ₹1,500, Y = ₹900, Z = ₹600; Balance in Partners' Capital Accounts: X = ₹52,560, Z = ₹35,040; Balance in Current Accounts: X = ₹15,840 (Credit) , Z = ₹15,840 (Debit); Balance Sheet Total = ₹1,89,640; Y's Loan Account = ₹61,200.

12. Leena, Madan and Naresh were partners in a firm sharing profits and losses in the ratio of 2 : 2 : 3. On 31st March, 2015 their balance sheet was as follows

Balance Sheet

as at 31st March, 2015

Liabilities		Amt (₹)	Assets	Amt (₹)
Trade Creditors		1,60,000	Land and Building	10,00,000
Bank Overdraft		44,000	Machinery	5,00,000
Long-term Debts		4,00,000	Furniture	7,00,000
Employees Provident Fund		76,000	Investments	2,00,000
Capital A/cs			Closing Stock	8,00,000
Leena	12,50,000		Sundry Debtors	4,00,000
Madan	8,00,000		Bank	80,000
Naresh	10,50,000	31,00,000	Deferred Advertisement Expenditure	1,00,000
		37,80,000		37,80,000

On 31st March, 2015, Madan retired from the firm and the remaining partners decided to carry on the business. It was decided to revalue assets and liabilities as under

(*i*) Land and building be appreciated by ₹ 2,40,000 and machinery be depreciated by 10%.

(*ii*) 50% of investments were taken over by the retiring partner at book value.

(*iii*) An old customer Mohit whose account was written-off as bad debt had promised to pay ₹ 7,000 in settlement of his full debt of ₹ 10,000.

(*iv*) Provision for doubtful debts was to be made at 5% on debtors.

(*v*) Closing stock will be valued at market price which is ₹ 1,00,000 less than the book value.

(*vi*) Goodwill of the firm be valued at ₹ 5,60,000 and Madan's share of goodwill be adjusted in the accounts of Leena and Naresh. Leena and Naresh decided to share future profits and losses in the ratio of 3 : 2.

(*vii*) The total capital of the new firm will be ₹ 32,00,000 which will be in the proportion of the profit sharing ratio of Leena and Naresh.

(*viii*) Amount due to Madan was settled by accepting a bill of exchange in his favour payable after 4 months.

Prepare revaluation account, partners' capital accounts and balance sheet of the firm after Madan's retirement. **All India (C) 2016**

Ans.

Dr **Revaluation Account** Cr

Particulars		Amt (₹)	Particulars	Amt (₹)
To Machinery A/c		50,000	By Land and Building A/c	2,40,000
To Provision for Doubtful Debts A/c		20,000	By Debtors A/c	7,000
To Closing Stock A/c		1,00,000		
To Profit Transferred to Partners' Capital A/c				
Leena	22,000			
Madan	22,000			
Naresh	33,000	77,000		
		2,47,000		2,47,000

Dr **Partners' Capital Account** Cr

Particulars	Leena (₹)	Madan (₹)	Naresh (₹)	Particulars	Leela (₹)	Madan (₹)	Naresh (₹)
To Investment A/c	—	1,00,000	—	By Balance b/d	12,50,000	8,00,000	10,50,000
To Deferred Advertisement Expenditure A/c	28,571	28,571	42,858	By Revaluation A/c (Profit)	22,000	22,000	33,000
To Madan's Capital A/c	1,60,000	—	—	By Leena's Capital A/c	—	1,60,000	16,000
To Naresh's Capital A/c	16,000	—	—	By Bank A/c	8,52,571	—	2,23,858
To Bills Payable A/c	—	8,53,429	—				
To Balance c/d	19,20,000	—	12,80,000				
	21,24,571	9,82,000	13,22,858		21,24,571	9,82,000	13,22,858

Balance Sheet
as at 31st March, 2015

Liabilities	Amt (₹)	Assets	Amt (₹)
Creditors	1,60,000	Land and Building (10,00,000 + 2,40,000)	12,40,000
Bank Overdraft	44,000	Machinery (5,00,000 − 50,000)	4,50,000
Long-term Debts	4,00,000	Furniture	7,00,000
Employees Provident Fund	76,000	Investments	1,00,000
Bills Payable	8,53,429	Closing Stock (8,00,000 − 1,00,000)	7,00,000

Liabilities		Amt (₹)	Assets		Amt (₹)
Capital A/cs			Debtors	4,07,000	
Leena	19,20,000		(–) Provision for Doubtful Debts	(20,000)	3,87,000
Naresh	12,80,000	32,00,000	Bank		11,56,429
		47,33,429			47,33,429

Working Notes

1. **Calculation of Gaining Ratio**

   Gaining Ratio = New Share – Old Share

   Leena $= \frac{3}{5} - \frac{2}{7} = \frac{21-10}{35} = \frac{11}{35}$; Naresh $= \frac{2}{5} - \frac{3}{7} = \frac{14-15}{35} = \left(\frac{1}{35}\right)$ sacrifice

2. **Calculation of Share of Goodwill**

   Madan's share of goodwill $= 5{,}60{,}000 \times \frac{2}{7} =$ ₹1,60,000 to be contributed by Leena alone. As she is the only gaining partner, she will compensate to Naresh also.

3. **Calculation of Capital of Partners in New Firm**

   New profit sharing ratio = 3 : 2

   Leena's capital $= 32{,}00{,}000 \times \frac{3}{5} =$ ₹19,20,000; Naresh's capital $= 32{,}00{,}000 \times \frac{2}{5} =$ ₹12,80,000

4. Dr **Bank Account** Cr

Particulars	Amt (₹)	Particulars	Amt (₹)
To Balance b/d	80,000	By Balance c/d	11,56,429
To Leela's Capital A/c	8,52,571		
To Naresh's Capital A/c	2,23,858		
	11,56,429		11,56,429

5. It is mentioned in the question that an old customer Mohit had promised to pay ₹ 7,000 in settlement of his debt, since it is an oral promise it is not considered as a transaction, therefore Mohit has been considered as the debtor of the firm.

13. On 31st March, 2015 the balance sheet of Saman, Harish and Meeta who were sharing profits and losses in the ratio of 2 : 3 : 2 stood as follows

Balance Sheet

as on 31st March, 2015

Liabilities		Amt (₹)	Assets	Amt (₹)
Workmen's Compensation Fund		8,40,000	Land and Buildings	19,00,000
Sundry Creditors		5,10,000	Machinery	5,00,000
Capital A/cs			Furniture	7,70,000
Saman	10,00,000		Closing Stock	5,00,000
Harish	15,00,000		Sundry Debtors	7,00,000
Meeta	10,00,000	35,00,000	Cash	4,80,000
		48,50,000		48,50,000

On 31st March, 2015 Harish retired from the firm and the remaining partners decided to carry on the business. It was agreed to revalue the assets and liabilities as follows

(*i*) Land and buildings be appreciated by 20%.

(*ii*) Machinery be depreciated by 20%.

(*iii*) Closing stock be valued at ₹ 4,50,000.

(*iv*) Provision for doubtful debts be made at 5% on debtors.

(*v*) Sundry creditors of ₹ 65,000 be written-off.

(*vi*) Goodwill of the firm be valued at ₹ 5,60,000 and Harish's share of the goodwill be adjusted in the accounts of Saman and Meeta who will share the future profits and losses in the ratio of 3 : 2.

(*vii*) The total capital of the newly constituted firm will be ₹ 35,00,000, which will be adjusted by opening current accounts.

(*viii*) Amount due to Harish was settled by accepting a bill of exchange in his favour payable after 4 months.

Prepare revaluation account, partners' capital accounts and balance sheet of the new firm on Harish's retirement. **Delhi (C) 2016**

Ans. Solve as Q no. 12 on page 167-169.

Profit on Revaluation Account: Saman = ₹ 74,286, Harish = ₹ 1,11,428, Meeta = ₹ 74,286; Balance in Partners' Capital Account :Saman = ₹ 21,00,000, Meena = ₹ 14,00,000; Total of Balance Sheet = ₹ 61,56,428, Gaining Ratio = 11 : 4; Partners' Current Account (Dr) Saman = ₹ 9,61,714, Meeta = ₹ 1,49,714

14. Xavier, Yusuf and Zaman were partners in a firm sharing profits in the ratio of 4 : 3 : 2. On 1st April, 2014 their balance sheet was as follows

Balance Sheet

as at 1st April, 2014

Liabilities		Amt (₹)	Assets		Amt (₹)
Sundry Creditors		41,400	Cash at Bank		33,000
Capital A/cs			Sundry Debtors	30,450	
Xavier	1,20,000		(–) Provision for Doubtful Debts	(1,050)	29,400
Yusuf	90,000		Stock		48,000
Zaman	60,000	2,70,000	Plant and Machinery		51,000
			Land and Building		1,50,000
		3,11,400			3,11,400

Yusuf had been suffering from ill health and thus gave notice of reitrement from the firm. An agreement was, therefore, enterd into as on 1st April, 2014, the terms of which were as follows

(*i*) That land and building be appreciated by 10%.

(*ii*) The provision for bad debts is no longer necessary.

(*iii*) That stock be appreciated by 20%.

(*iv*) That goodwill of the firm be fixed at ₹ 54,000. Yusuf's share of the same be adjusted into Xavier's and Zaman's capital accounts, who are going to share future profits in the ratio of 2 : 1.

(*v*) The entire capital of the newly constituted firm be readjusted by bringing in or paying necessary cash so that the future capitals of Xavier and Zaman will be in their profits sharing ratio.

Prepare revaluation account and partners' capital accounts. **All India 2015**

Ans. Dr **Revaluation Account** Cr

Particulars		Amt (₹)	Particulars	Amt (₹)
To Profit Transferred to Capital A/cs			By Land and Building A/c	15,000
Xavier	11,400		By Provision for Doubtful Debts A/c	1,050
Yusuf	8,550		By Stock A/c	9,600
Zaman	5,700	25,650		
		25,650		25,650

Dr **Partners' Capital Account** Cr

Particulars	Xavier (₹)	Yusuf (₹)	Zaman (₹)	Particulars	Xavier (₹)	Yusuf (₹)	Zaman (₹)
To Yusuf's Capital A/c	12,000	—	6,000	By Balance b/d	1,20,000	90,000	60,000
To Yusuf's Loan A/c	—	1,16,550	—	By Revaluation A/c (Profit)	11,400	8,550	5,700
To Balance c/d	1,97,100	—	98,550				
				By Xavier's Capital A/c	—	12,000	—
				By Zaman's Capital A/c	—	6,000	—
				By Cash A/c (Balancing figure)	77,700	—	38,850
	2,09,100	1,16,550	1,04,550		2,09,100	1,16,550	1,04,550

Working Notes

1. **Calculation of Gaining Ratio**

   Gaining Ratio = New Share – Old Share

   $\text{Xavier} = \frac{2}{3} - \frac{4}{9} = \frac{6-4}{9} = \frac{2}{9}$; $\text{Zaman} = \frac{1}{3} - \frac{2}{9} = \frac{3-2}{9} = \frac{1}{9}$

   Gaining ratio = 2 : 1

2. **Adjustment of Goodwill**

   Yusuf's share of goodwill = $54{,}000 \times \frac{3}{9}$ = ₹ 18,000 to be contributed in gaining ratio, *i.e.* 2 : 1

   Xavier will pay = $18{,}000 \times \frac{2}{3}$ = ₹ 12,000; Zaman will pay = $18{,}000 \times \frac{1}{3}$ = ₹ 6,000

3. **Calculation of New Capitals**

Particulars	Amt (₹)
Adjusted Capital of Xavier	1,19,400
Adjusted Capital of Zaman	59,700
Amount Due to Yusuf	1,16,550
Total Capital of New Firm	2,95,650

Xavier's new capital = $2{,}95{,}650 \times \frac{2}{3}$ = ₹ 1,97,100; Zaman's new capital = $2{,}95{,}650 \times \frac{1}{3}$ = ₹ 98,550

15. Amit, Balan and Chander were partners in a firm sharing profits in the proportion of $\frac{1}{2}, \frac{1}{3}$ and $\frac{1}{6}$ respectively. Chander retired on 1st April, 2014. The balance sheet of the firm on the date of Chander's retirement was as follows

Balance Sheet
as at 1st April, 2014

Liabilities		Amt (₹)	Assets		Amt (₹)
Sundry Creditors		12,600	Bank		4,100
Provident Fund		3,000	Debtors	30,000	
General Reserve		9,000	(–) Provision for Doubtful Debts	(1,000)	29,000
Capital A/cs			Stock		25,000
Amit	40,000		Investments		10,000
Balan	36,500		Patents		5,000
Chander	20,000	96,500	Machinery		48,000
		1,21,100			1,21,100

It was agreed that

(*i*) Goodwill will be valued at ₹ 27,000.
(*ii*) Depreciation of 10% was to be provided on machinery.
(*iii*) Patents were to be reduced by 20%.
(*iv*) Liability on account of provident fund was estimated at ₹ 2,400.
(*v*) Chander took over investments for ₹ 15,800.
(*vi*) Amit and Balan decided to adjust their capitals in proportion of their profit sharing ratio by opening current accounts.

Prepare revaluation account and partners' capital accounts on Chander's retirement.
Delhi 2015

Ans. Dr **Revaluation Account** Cr

Particulars		Amt (₹)	Particulars	Amt (₹)
To Machinery A/c		4,800	By Provident Fund A/c	600
To Patents A/c		1,000	By Investments A/c	5,800
To Profit Transferred to Capital A/cs				
Amit	300			
Balan	200			
Chander	100	600		
		6,400		6,400

Dr **Partners' Capital Accounts** Cr

Particulars	Amit (₹)	Balan (₹)	Chander (₹)	Particulars	Amit (₹)	Balan (₹)	Chander (₹)
To Investment A/c	—	—	15,800	By Balance b/d	40,000	36,500	20,000
To Chander's Capital A/c	2,700	1,800	—	By Revaluation A/c (Profit)	300	200	100
To Chander's Loan A/c	—	—	10,300	By General Reserve A/c	4,500	3,000	1,500

Particulars	Amit (₹)	Balan (₹)	Chander (₹)	Particulars	Amit (₹)	Balan (₹)	Chander (₹)
To Current A/c (Balancing figure)	—	5,900	—	By Amit's Capital A/c	—	—	2,700
				By Balan's Capital A/c	—	—	1,800
To Balance c/d	48,000	32,000	—	By Current A/c (Balancing figure)	5,900	—	—
	50,700	39,700	26,100		50,700	39,700	26,100

Working Notes

1. **Adjustment for Goodwill**

Chander's share in goodwill $= 27{,}000 \times \frac{1}{6} =$ ₹ 4,500; to be contributed in gaining ratio, *i.e.* 3 : 2

Amit will pay $= 4{,}500 \times \frac{3}{5} =$ ₹ 2,700 ; Balan will pay $= 4{,}500 \times \frac{2}{5} =$ ₹ 1,800

2. **Adjustment for Capital**

Combined capital ⇒ Amit's adjusted capital = 42,100
Balan's adjusted capital = 37,900
Total = 80,000

New profit sharing ratio = 3 : 2

Amit's new capital $= 80{,}000 \times \frac{3}{5} =$ ₹ 48,000 ; Chander's new capital $= 80{,}000 \times \frac{2}{5} =$ ₹ 32,000

16. Lokesh, Mansoor and Nihal were partners in a firm sharing profits as 50%, 30% and 20% respectively. On 31st March, 2014, their balance sheet was as follows

Balance Sheet
as at 31st March, 2014

Liabilities		Amt (₹)	Assets		Amt (₹)
Creditors		34,000	Cash		68,000
Provident Fund		10,000	Stock		38,000
Investment Fluctuation Fund		20,000	Debtors	94,000	
Capital A/cs			(−) Provision	(6,000)	88,000
Lokesh	1,40,000		Investments		80,000
Mansoor	80,000		Goodwill		40,000
Nihal	50,000	2,70,000	Profit and Loss		20,000
		3,34,000			3,34,000

On the above date, Mansoor retired and Lokesh and Nihal agreed to continue on the following terms

(*i*) Firm's goodwill was valued at ₹ 1,02,000 and it was decided to adjust Mansoor's share of goodwill into the capital accounts of the continuing partners.

(*ii*) There was a claim for workmen's compensation to the extent of ₹ 12,000 and investments were brought down to ₹ 30,000.

(*iii*) Provision for bad debts was to be reduced by ₹ 2,000.

(*iv*) Mansoor was to be paid ₹ 20,600 in cash and the balance will be transferred to his loan account which was paid in two equal instalments together with interest @ 10% per annum.

(v) Lokesh's and Nihal's capitals were to be adjusted in their new profit sharing ratio by bringing in or paying off cash as the case may be.

Prepare revaluation account and partners' capital accounts. **All India (C) 2015**

Ans. Dr **Revaluation Account** Cr

Particulars	Amt (₹)	Particulars		Amt (₹)
To Workmen's Compensation Claim A/c	12,000	By Provision for Bad Debts A/c		2,000
To Investment A/c	30,000	By Loss Transferred to Capital A/cs		
		Lokesh	20,000	
		Mansoor	12,000	
		Nihal	8,000	40,000
	42,000			42,000

Dr **Partners' Capital Account** Cr

Particulars	Lokesh (₹)	Mansoor (₹)	Nihal (₹)	Particulars	Lokesh (₹)	Mansoor (₹)	Nihal (₹)
To Profit and Loss A/c	10,000	6,000	4,000	By Balance b/d	1,40,000	80,000	50,000
To Goodwill A/c	20,000	12,000	8,000	By Lokesh's Capital A/c	—	21,857	—
To Revaluation A/c (Loss)	20,000	12,000	8,000	By Nihal's Capital A/c	—	8,743	—
To Mansoor's Capital A/c	21,857	—	8,743	By Cash A/c (Balancing figure)	—	—	4,286
To Cash A/c	—	20,600	—				
To Mansoor's Loan A/c	—	60,000	—				
To Cash A/c (Balancing Figure)	4,286	—	—				
To Balance c/d	63,857	—	25,543				
	1,40,000	1,10,600	54,286		1,40,000	1,10,600	54,286

Working Notes

1. **Calculation of Share of Goodwill**

Mansoor's share of goodwill $= 1,02,000 \times \frac{3}{10} =$ ₹ 30,600, to be contributed by Lokesh and Nihal in gaining ratio, *i.e.* 5 : 2

Lokesh will pay $= 30,600 \times \frac{5}{7} =$ ₹ 21,857; Nihal will pay $= 30,600 \times \frac{2}{7} =$ ₹ 8,743

2. **Calculation of Capital of New Firm after Mansoor's Retirement**

Lokesh's capital after adjustment =	68,143
Nihal's capital after adjustment =	21,257
	₹ 89,400

Lokesh's new capital $= 89,400 \times \frac{5}{7} =$ ₹ 63,857 ; Nihal's new capital $= 89,400 \times \frac{2}{7} =$ ₹ 25,543

17. L, M and N were partners in a firm sharing profits in the ratio of 2 : 1 : 1. On 1st April, 2013 their balance sheet was as follows

Balance Sheet
as at 1st April, 2013

Liabilities		Amt (₹)	Assets		Amt (₹)
General Reserve		4,40,000	Land		8,00,000
Workmen's Compensation Fund		3,60,000	Building		6,00,000
Creditors		2,40,000	Furniture		2,40,000
Capital A/cs			Debtors	4,00,000	
L	6,00,000		(–) Provision for Doubtful Debts	(20,000)	3,80,000
M	4,80,000		Stock		4,40,000
N	4,80,000	15,60,000	Cash		1,40,000
		26,00,000			26,00,000

On the above date, N retired. The following were agreed

(*i*) Goodwill of the firm was valued at ₹ 6,00,000.

(*ii*) Land was to be appreciated by 40% and building was to be depreciated by ₹ 1,00,000.

(*iii*) Furniture was to be depreciated by ₹ 30,000.

(*iv*) The liabilities for workmen's compensation fund was determined at ₹ 1,60,000.

(*v*) Amount payable to N was transferred to his loan account.

(*vi*) Capitals of L and M were to be adjusted in their new profit sharing ratio and for this purpose current accounts of the partners will be opened.

Prepare revaluation account, partner's capital accounts and the balance sheet of the new firm. **All India 2014**

Ans. Dr **Revaluation Account** Cr

Particulars		Amt (₹)	Particulars	Amt (₹)
To Building A/c		1,00,000	By Land A/c	3,20,000
To Furniture A/c		30,000		
To Profit Transferred to Capital A/cs				
L	95,000			
M	47,500			
N	47,500	1,90,000		
		3,20,000		3,20,000

Dr **Partners' Capital Account** Cr

Particulars	L (₹)	M (₹)	N (₹)	Particulars	L (₹)	M (₹)	N (₹)
To N's Capital A/c	1,00,000	50,000	—	By Balance b/d	6,00,000	4,80,000	4,80,000
To N's Loan A/c	—	—	8,37,500	By General Reserve	2,20,000	1,10,000	1,10,000
To M's Current A/c (Balancing figure)	—	1,20,000	—	By Revaluation A/c (Profit)	95,000	47,500	47,500
				By L's Capital A/c	—	—	1,00,000
To Balance c/d	10,35,000	5,17,500	—	By M's Capital A/c	—	—	50,000
				By Workmen's Compensation Fund A/c	1,00,000	50,000	50,000
				By L's Current A/c (Balancing figure)	1,20,000	—	—
	11,35,000	6,87,500	8,37,500		11,35,000	6,87,500	8,37,500

Balance Sheet
as at 1st April, 2013

Liabilities		Amt (₹)	Assets		Amt (₹)
Capital A/cs			Land	8,00,000	
L	10,35,000		(+) Appreciation	3,20,000	11,20,000
M	5,17,500	15,52,500	Buiding	6,00,000	
Liabilities for Workmen's Compensation Fund		1,60,000	(–) Depreciation	(1,00,000)	5,00,000
Creditors		2,40,000	Furniture	2,40,000	
L's Current Account		1,20,000	(–) Depreciation	(30,000)	2,10,000
N's Loan Account		8,37,500	Debtors	4,00,000	
			(–) Provision for Doubtful Debts	(20,000)	3,80,000
			Stock		4,40,000
			M's Current A/c		1,20,000
			Cash		1,40,000
		29,10,000			29,10,000

Working Notes

1. Firm's goodwill = ₹ 6,00,000

   N's share of goodwill $= 6,00,000 \times \frac{1}{4} = 1,50,000$ to be contributed by L and M in gaining ratio *i.e.*, 2 : 1;

   $L = 1,50,000 \times 2/3 =$ ₹1,00,000; $M = 1,50,000 \times 1/3 =$ ₹ 50,000

2. **Calculation of Proportionate's Capital**

   L's capital after all adjustment = 9,15,000
   M's capital after all adjustment = 6,37,500
   Total capital of new firm ₹ 15,52,500

   L's new capital $= 15,52,500 \times \frac{2}{3} =$ ₹10,35,000 ; M's new capital $= 15,52,500 \times \frac{1}{3} =$ ₹ 5,17,500

18. Kushal, Kumar and Kavita were partners in a firm sharing profits in the ratio of 3 : 1 : 1. On 1st April, 2012 their balance sheet was as follows

Balance Sheet
as on 1st April, 2012

Liabilities		Amt (₹)	Assets		Amt (₹)
Creditors		1,20,000	Cash		70,000
Bills Payable		1,80,000	Debtors	2,00,000	
General Reserve		1,20,000	(−) Provision	(10,000)	1,90,000
Capital A/cs			Stock		2,20,000
Kushal	3,00,000		Furniture		1,20,000
Kumar	2,80,000		Building		3,00,000
Kavita	3,00,000	8,80,000	Land		4,00,000
		13,00,000			13,00,000

On the above date, Kavita retired and the following was agreed

(*i*) Goodwill of the firm was valued at ₹ 40,000.

(ii) Land was to be appreciated by 30% and building was to be depreciated by ₹ 1,00,000.

(*iii*) Value of furniture was to be reduced by ₹ 20,000.

(*iv*) Bad debts reserve is to be increased to ₹ 15,000.

(*v*) 10% of the amount payable to Kavita was paid in cash and the balance was transferred to her loan account.

(*vi*) Capitals of Kushal and Kumar will be in proportion to their new profit sharing ratio. The surplus/deficit, if any in their capital accounts will be adjusted through current accounts.

Prepare revaluation account, partner's capital accounts and balance sheet of Kushal and Kumar after Kavita's retirement. **Delhi 2014**

Ans. Dr **Revaluation Account** Cr

Particulars	Amt (₹)	Particulars		Amt (₹)
To Building A/c	1,00,000	By Land A/c		1,20,000
To Furniture A/c	20,000	By Loss Transferred to Capital A/c		
To Provision for Bad Debts A/c	5,000	Kushal	3,000	
		Kumar	1,000	
		Kavita	1,000	5,000
	1,25,000			1,25,000

Dr **Partners' Capital Account** Cr

Particulars	Kushal (₹)	Kumar (₹)	Kavita (₹)	Particulars	Kushal (₹)	Kumar (₹)	Kavita (₹)
To Kavita's Capital A/c	6,000	2,000	—	By Balance b/d	3,00,000	2,80,000	3,00,000
To Revaluation A/c (Loss)	3,000	1,000	1,000	By General Reserve A/c	72,000	24,000	24,000
To Cash A/c	—	—	33,100	By Kushal's Capital A/c	—	—	6,000
To Kavita's Loan A/c	—	—	2,97,900	By Kumar's Capital A/c	—	—	2,000
To Kumar's Current A/c (Balancing figure)	—	1,35,000	—	By Kushal's Current A/c (Balancing figure)	1,35,000	—	—
To Balance c/d	4,98,000	1,66,000	—				
	5,07,000	3,04,000	3,32,000		5,07,000	3,04,000	3,32,000

Balance Sheet
as at ...

Liabilities		Amt (₹)	Assets		Amt (₹)
Bills Payable		1,80,000	Land (4,00,000 + 1,20,000)		5,20,000
Creditors		1,20,000	Building (3,00,000 − 1,00,000)		2,00,000
Kavita's Loan A/c		2,97,900	Furniture (1,20,000 − 20,000)		1,00,000
Kumar's Current A/c		1,35,000	Stock		2,20,000
Capital A/cs			Cash		36,900
Kushal	4,98,000		Debtors	2,00,000	
Kumar	1,66,000	6,64,000	(−) Provision for Doubtful Debts	(15,000)	1,85,000
			Kushal's Current A/c		1,35,000
		13,96,900			13,96,900

Working Notes

1. Firm's goodwill = ₹ 40,000

   Kavita's share of goodwill = $40,000 \times \frac{1}{5}$ = ₹ 8,000, to be contributed by Kushal and Kumar in gaining ratio, *i.e.* 3 : 1; Kushal = $8,000 \times \frac{3}{4}$ = ₹ 6,000; Kumar = $8,000 \times \frac{1}{4}$ = ₹ 2,000

2. **Adjustment of Capital**

   Adjusted capital of Kushal = 3,63,000
   Adjusted capital of Kumar = 3,01,000
   ₹ 6,64,000

   New profit sharing ratio = 3 : 1

   New capital of Kushal = $6,64,000 \times \frac{3}{4}$ = ₹ 4,98,000 ; New capital of Kumar = $6,64,000 \times \frac{1}{4}$ = ₹ 1,66,000

TOPIC 5

Death of a Partner

The partnership comes to an end immediately, whenever a partner dies although the firm may continue with the remaining partners. The deceased partner is entitled to get his share in the firm as per the provision of partnership agreement.

Computation of the Amount Due to the Deceased Partner

The deceased partner's share is also calculated in the same manner as in the case of retiring partner. Amount due to a deceased partner is ascertained by preparing **deceased partner's capital account** (It is prepared in the same manner as in the case of retirement of a partner) and the amount due to him is transferred to his executor's account by passing the following journal entry

Deceased Partner's Capital A/c	Dr
To Deceased Partner's Executors A/c	

Settlement of Deceased Partners' Executor Account

(*i*) If Payment is Made in Full/Lumpsum

Deceased Partner's Executor's A/c	Dr
To Cash/ Bank A/c	

(*ii*) If Payment is Made in Instalment

(a) When interest is due	Interest A/c To Deceased Partner's Executor's Loan A/c	Dr
(b) When instalment is paid	Deceased Partner's Executor's Loan A/c To Cash/Bank A/c	Dr

NOTE Interest is generally paid to deceased partner's executor's @ 6% per annum.

Accounting Treatment of Outgoing Partner's Share in Profits and Goodwill

(i) Outgoing Partner's Share in Profits

The calculation of outgoing partner's share in profits earned from the date of last balance sheet to date of death/retirement, involves the following two steps

***Step* 1** Determination of profits of the firm from the date of last balance sheet to the date of death/retirement.

Subject to agreement, such profits may be determined either on time basis or on sales basis using previous year's profits or average profits of the past years.

(a) **On Time Basis** Profit from the date of last balance sheet to the date of death

$$= \frac{\text{Number of Days or Months from the Date of Last Balance Sheet to the Date of Death}}{\text{365 Days or 12 Months}}$$

$\times$ Previous Year's Profits or Average Profits of a Given Number of Past Years

(b) **On Turnover or Sales Basis** Profit from the date of last balance sheet to the date of death

$$= \frac{\text{Sales from the Date of the Last Balance Sheet to the Date of Death}}{\text{Previous Year's Sales or Average Sales of a Given Number of Past Years}}$$

$\times$ Previous Year's Profits or Average Profits of a Given Number of Past Years

***Step* 2** Calculation of outgoing partner's share in profits

The share of an outgoing partner in profits may be calculated as under

Outgoing Partner's Share in Profits = Profits of the Firm for the Period Beginning with the Date of Accounting Year and ending with the Date of Death/ Retirement as Computed in Step 1 $\times$ Proportion of Share of Outgoing Partner

Accounting treatment of deceased partner's share in profits is done through the following

(a) **Through Profit and Loss Suspense Account** This method is used when the new profit sharing ratio of continuing partners does not differ from their old profit sharing ratio.

In Case of Profit	Profit and Loss Suspense A/c To Deceased Partner's Capital A/c	Dr

NOTE In this case, profit and loss suspense account will appear on the assets side of the balance sheet.

In Case of Loss	Deceased Partner's Capital A/c To Profit and Loss Suspense A/c	Dr

NOTE In this case, profit and loss suspense account will appear on the liabilities side of the balance sheet.

(b) **Through Capital Transfer** In case, the new profit sharing ratio of continuing partners differs from their old profit sharing ratio, outgoing partner's share of profit must be adjusted through capital accounts of gaining partners only.

(a) In Case of Profit	Gaining Partners' Capital A/c To Deceased Partner's Capital A/c	Dr	[Gaining ratio] [Share of profit]
(b) In Case of Loss	Deceased Partner's Capital A/c To Gaining Partners' Capital A/c	Dr	[Share of loss] [Gaining ratio]

(ii) Treatment of Goodwill

It is same as in the case of retirement of a partner. Following entry is passed for the treatment of goodwill

Gaining Partners' Capital A/c To Deceased Partner's Capital A/c	Dr	[In gaining ratio] [With his share of goodwill]

Previous Years' Examination Questions

1 Mark Questions

1. State the basis of calculating the amount of profit payable to the legal representative of a deceased partner in the year of death. **All India 2019**

Ans. Amount of profit can be calculated on time basis or sales basis.

2. Dinkar, Navita and Vani were partners sharing profits and losses in the ratio of 3 : 2 : 1. Navita died on 30th June, 2017. Her share of profit for the intervening period was based on the sales during that period, which were ₹ 6,00,000. The rate of profit during the past four years had been 10% on sales. The firm closes its books on 31st March every year.

Calculate Navita's share of profit. **All India 2019**

Ans. Total sales = ₹ 6,00,000 (1st April, 2017-30th June, 2017)

Firm's profit on sales = 6,00,000 × 10% = ₹ 60,000

Navita's share of profit = $60,000 \times \frac{2}{6}$ = ₹ 20,000

3. Jayant, Kartik and Leena were partners in a firm sharing profits and losses in the ratio of 5 : 2 : 3. Kartik died and Jayant and Leena decided to continue the business. Their gaining ratio was 2 : 3. Calculate the new profit sharing ratio of Jayant and Leena. **CBSE 2018**

Ans. Jayant's old share = $\frac{5}{10}$; Jayant's gaining share = $\frac{2}{5} \times \frac{2}{10} = \frac{4}{50}$

Jayant's New Share = Old Share + Gaining share = $\frac{5}{10} + \frac{4}{50} = \frac{25+4}{50} = \frac{29}{50}$

Leena's old share = $\frac{3}{10}$; Leena's gaining share = $\frac{3}{5} \times \frac{2}{10} = \frac{6}{50}$

Leena's new share = $\frac{3}{10} + \frac{6}{50} = \frac{15+6}{50} = \frac{21}{50}$

New profit sharing ratio = Jayant : Leena = 29 : 21

4. In which ratio do the remaining partners acquire the share of the deceased partner? **Compartment 2018**

Ans. The remaining partners will acquire the share of the deceased partner in gaining ratio.

5. Kumar, Verma and Naresh were partners in a firm sharing profit and loss in the ratio of 3 : 2 : 2. On 23rd January, 2015, Verma died. Verma's share of profit till the date of his death was calculated at ₹ 2,350.
Pass necessary journal entry for the same in the books of the firm. **Delhi 2015**

Ans.

JOURNAL

Date	Particulars		LF	Amt (Dr)	Amt (Cr)
2015					
Jan 23	Profit and Loss Suspense A/c	Dr		2,350	
	To Verma's Capital A/c				2,350
	(Being profit upto the date of death given to deceased partner)				

6. Differentiate between 'profit and loss appropriation account' and 'profit and loss suspense account'. **All India (C) 2015**

Ans.

Basis	Profit & Loss Appropriation Account	Profit & Loss Suspense Account
Objective	Profit and loss appropriation account is prepared to show the distribution of net profit among the partners.	Profit and loss suspense account is prepared to adjust the deceased partner's share of profit upto the date of his death.

7. Name the account which is opened to credit the share of profit of the deceased partner, till the time of his death to his capital account. **All India 2015; Modified; Delhi 2013**

Ans. 'Profit and loss suspense account' is opened, to credit the share of profit of the deceased partner.

8. A, T and R were partners in a firm sharing profits in the ratio of 5 : 6 : 7 respectively. Their capitals were ₹ 5,00,000; ₹ 6,00,000 and ₹ 7,00,000 respectively. State the ratio in which the goodwill of the firm amounting to ₹ 16,00,000 will be adjusted in the capital accounts of A and T in case of R's death. **Compartment 2014**

Ans. Goodwill of the firm, at the time of R's death, will be adjusted among A and T in gaining ratio, *i.e.* 5: 6.

9. At what rate is interest payable on the amount remaining unpaid to the executor of deceased partner? **All India 2013**

Ans. Interest is payable @ 6% per annum on the amount remaining unpaid to the executor of deceased partner.

3 Marks Questions

10. X, Y and Z were partners in a firm. The firm closes its books on 31st March every year. On 31st December 2021, X died. The partnership deed provided that the share of deceased partner in the profits of the firm till the date of his death will be calculated on the basis of last year's profit. The profit for the year ended 31st March, 2021 was ₹ 6,00,000.

Calculate X's share in the profits of the firm till the date of his death and pass the necessary journal entry for the same in the books of the firm. **CBSE Term II 2022**

Ans. Calculation of X's share in the profits till 31st December, 2021 $= 6,00,000 \times \frac{9}{12} \times \frac{1}{3}$

$= ₹1,50,000$

JOURNAL

Date	Particulars		LF	Amt (Dr)	Amt (Cr)
2021					
Dec 31	Profit and Loss Suspense A/c	Dr		1,50,000	
	To X's Capital A/c				1,50,000
	(Being X's share of profits till the date of death adjusted)				

11. Ajay, Bhawna and Shreya were partners sharing profits in the ratio 2 : 2 : 1. On 1st July, 2017, Shreya died. The books of accounts are closed on 31st March every year. Sales for the year 2016-17 amounted to ₹ 5,00,000 and that from 1st April to 30th June, 2017 were ₹ 1,40,000. The rate of profit during the past three years had been 10% on sales. It was decided that the profit for the purpose of settling Shreya's account is to be calculated as 20% on sales.

Calculate Shreya's share of profits till the date of her death and pass necessary a journal entry for the same. **Compartment 2018**

Ans. Shreya's share of profit $= 1,40,000 \times \frac{20}{100} \times \frac{1}{5} = ₹ 5,600$

JOURNAL

Date	Particulars		LF	Amt (Dr)	Amt (Cr)
2017					
July 1	Profit and Loss Suspense A/c	Dr		5,600	
	To Shreya's Capital A/c				5,600
	(Being Shreya's share of profit till the date of death transferred to her capital account)				

12. A, B and C are partners in a firm whose books are closed on 31st March each year. B died on 30th June, 2009 and according to the agreement, the share of profit of a deceased partner up to the date of the death is to be calculated on the basis of the average profits for the last five years.

The net profits for the last 5 years have been 2005 : ₹ 14,000; 2006 : ₹ 18,000; 2007 : ₹ 16,000; 2008 : ₹ 10,000 (loss) and 2009 : ₹ 16,000.

Calculate B's share of profits upto the date of death and pass necessary journal entry. **All India; Delhi 2010**

Ans. **Calculation of B's Share of Profit**

Last 5 years' total profit = 14,000 + 18,000 + 16,000 − 10,000 + 16,000 = ₹ 54,000

$$\text{Average profit} = \frac{54,000}{5} = ₹\ 10,800$$

$$\text{B's share of profit} = 10,800 \times \frac{1}{3} \times \frac{3}{12} = ₹\ 900$$

JOURNAL

Date	Particulars		LF	Amt (Dr)	Amt (Cr)
2009					
Jun 30	Profit and Loss Suspense A/c	Dr		900	
	To B's Capital A/c				900
	(Being share of profit transferred to deceased partner's capital account)				

4 Marks Questions

13. Aditi, Kartik and Tina were partners in a firm sharing profits and losses in the ratio of 5 : 3 : 2. On 31st March, 2019, their Balance Sheet was as follows

Balance Sheet of Aditi, Kartik and Tina
as at 31st March, 2019

Liabilities		Amt (₹)	Assets	Amt (₹)
Creditors		96,000	Furniture	4,30,000
Capitals			Stock	1,50,000
Aditi	3,00,000		Debtors	83,000
Kartik	2,00,000		Cash	33,000
Tina	1,00,000	6,00,000		
		6,96,000		6,96,000

Aditi died on 1st November, 2019. It was agreed that

(*i*) Goodwill of the firm be valued at ₹ 1,00,000.

(*ii*) Profit for the year 2019-20 be taken as having accured at the same rate as the previous year 2018-19. Profit for the year 2018-19 was ₹ 96,000.

(*iii*) Half the amount was paid to Aditi's executors immediately and the remaining half will be paid in two equal annual instalments with interest @6% p.a.

Pass the necessary journal entries to record the above transactions in the books of the firm on the date of her death. **CBSE 2020**

Ans. **JOURNAL**

Date	Particulars		LF	Amt (Dr)	Amt (Cr)
	Kartik's Capital A/c	Dr		30,000	
	Tina's Capital A/c	Dr		20,000	
	To Aditi's Capital A/c				50,000
	(Being amount of goodwill adjusted)				

Date	Particulars		LF	Amt (Dr)	Amt (Cr)
	Profit and Loss Suspense A/c	Dr		28,000	
	To Aditi's Capital A/c				28,000
	(Being share of profit due)				
	Aditi's Capital A/c	Dr		3,78,000	
	To Aditi's Executors A/c				3,78,000
	(Being share of deceased partner transferred to executors account)				
	Aditi's Executors A/c	Dr		1,89,000	
	To Bank A/c				1,89,000
	(Being half the amount paid to executor)				

Working Notes

(i) Aditi's share of goodwill $= 1,00,000 \times \frac{5}{10} = ₹\,50,000$

(ii) Aditi's share of profit $= 96,000 \times \frac{5}{10} \times \frac{7}{12} = ₹\,28,000$

14. Garima, Harish and Reena were partners in a firm sharing profits and losses equally. On 31st March, 2015, Harish died and the amount payable to his executors was ₹ 90,000. It was agreed between the remaining partners and Harish's executors that the executors will be paid in four equal yearly instalments alongwith interest @18% per annum starting from 31st March, 2018.

Prepare Harish's executor's account till it is finally closed. **All India 2019**

Ans. Dr **Harish's Executor's Account** Cr

Date	Particulars	Amt (₹)	Date	Particulars	Amt (₹)
2015			2015		
Mar 31	To Bank A/c	22,500	Mar 31	By Harish's Capital A/c	90,000
Mar 31	To Balance c/d	67,500			
		90,000			90,000
2016			2015		
Mar 31	To Bank A/c (22,500 + 12,150)	34,650	Apr 1	By Balance b/d	67,500
			2016		
Mar 31	To Balance c/d	45,000	Mar 31	By Interest A/c (67,500 × 18%)	12,150
		79,650			79,650
2017			2016		
Mar 31	To Bank A/c (22,500 + 8,100)	30,600	Apr 1	By Balance b/d	45,000
Mar 31	To Balance c/d	22,500	2017		
			Mar 31	By Interest A/c (45,000 × 18%)	8,100
		53,100			53,100
2018			2017		
Mar 31	To Bank A/c (22,500 + 4,050)	26,550	Apr 1	By Balance b/d	22,500
			2018		
			Mar 31	By Interest A/c (22,500 × 18%)	4,050
		26,550			26,550

15. Manika, Rekha and Mohit were partners sharing profits in the ratio of 5 : 4 : 1. On 31st March, 2018 their balance sheet was as follows

Balance Sheet of Manika, Rekha and Mohit
as at 31st March, 2018

Liabilities		Amt (₹)	Assets	Amt (₹)
Creditors		5,00,000	Fixed Assets	9,00,000
General Reserve		2,00,000	Stock	3,00,000
Capital A/cs			Debtors	3,00,000
Manika	6,00,000		Cash at Bank	4,50,000
Rekha	4,50,000			
Mohit	2,00,000	12,50,000		
		19,50,000		19,50,000

Rekha died on 1st July, 2018. According to the partnership deed, her executors were entitled to

(*i*) Balance in her capital account.

(*ii*) Her share of goodwill, which is calculated on the basis of average profits of last four years.

(*iii*) Her share of profit upto the date of death calculated on the basis of average profits of last two years. The time period for which she survived in the year of death will be calculated in months.

(*iv*) Interest on capital @ 10% p.a. upto the date of death.

The firm's profits for the last four years were

2014-15: ₹ 2,20,000, 2015-16: ₹ 3,00,000: 2016-17: ₹ 3,60,000 and 2017-18: ₹ 3,20,000.

Rekha's executors were paid the amount due immediately. Prepare Rekha's Capital Account to be presented to her executors. **All India 2019**

Ans. Dr **Rekha's Capital Account** Cr

Particulars	Amt (₹)	Particulars	Amt (₹)
To Rekha's Executors A/c	6,95,250	By Balance b/d	4,50,000
		By General Reserve $\left(2,00,000 \times \frac{4}{10}\right)$	80,000
		By Manika's Capital	1,00,000
		By Mohit's Capital	20,000
		By Profit and Loss Suspense A/c	34,000
		By Interest on Capital A/c	11,250
	6,95,250		6,95,250

Working Notes

1. 4 year's total profit = 2,20,000 + 3,00,000 + 3,60,000 + 3,20,000 = ₹ 12,00,000

Average profit or goodwill = $\frac{12,00,000}{4}$ = ₹ 3,00,000

Rekha's share of goodwill = 3,00,000 × $\frac{4}{10}$ = ₹ 120,000

to be contributed by Manika and Mohit in the ratio of 5 : 1.

2. 2 year's average profit $= \frac{3,60,000 + 3,20,000}{2} =$ ₹ 3,40,000

Rekha's share of profit $= 3,40,000 \times \frac{4}{10} \times \frac{3}{12} =$ ₹ 34,000

3. Interest on capital $= 4,50,000 \times \frac{10}{100} \times \frac{3}{12} =$ ₹ 11,250

16. Meera, Sarthak and Rohit were partners sharing profits in the ratio of 2 : 2 : 1. On 31st March, 2018 their balance sheet was as follows

Balance Sheet of Meera, Sarthak and Rohit
as at 31 March, 2018

Liabilities	Amt (₹)	Assets	Amt (₹)
Creditors	3,00,000	Fixed Assets	7,00,000
Contingency Reserve	1,00,000	Stock	2,00,000
Capital A/cs		Debtors	1,50,000
Meera	4,00,000	Cash at bank	3,50,000
Sarthak	3,50,000		
Rohit	2,50,000		
	14,00,000		14,00,000

Sarthak died on 15th June, 2018. According to the partnership deed, his executors were entitled to

(i) Balance in his capital account.

(ii) His share of goodwill will be calculated on the basis of thrice the average of the past 4 years' profits.

(iii) His share in profits upto the date of death on the basis of average profits of the last two years. The time period for which he survived in the year of death will be calculated in months.

(iv) Interest on capital @ 12% p.a. upto the date of his death.

The firm's profits for the last four years were 2014-15 : ₹ 1,20,000, 2015-16 : ₹ 2,00,000, 2016-17 : ₹ 2,60,000 and 2017-18 : ₹ 2,20,000.

Sarthak's executors were paid the amount due immediately. Prepare Sarthaks's capital account to be presented to his executors. **All India 2019**

Ans. Solve as Q. no. 15 on page 185-186.

Sarthak's share of goodwill = ₹ 2,40,000

Sarthak's share of profit = ₹ 20,000

Debit Sarthak's capital account with amount = ₹ 6,58,750

17. Ashok, Babu and Chetan were partners in a firm sharing profits in the ratio of 4 : 3 : 3. The firm closes its books on 31st March every year. On 31st December, 2016, Ashok died. The partnership deed provided that on the death of a partner, his executors will be entitled to the following

(i) Balance in his capital account. On 1st April, 2016, there was a balance of ₹ 90,000 in Ashok's capital account.

(ii) Interest on capital @ 12% per annum.

(iii) His share in the profits of the firm in the year of his death will be calculated on the basis of rate of net profit on sales of the previous year, which was 25%. The sales of the firm till 30th December, 2016 were ₹ 4,00,000.

(iv) His share in the goodwill of the firm. The goodwill of the firm on Ashok's death was valued at ₹ 4,50,000.

The partnership deed also provided for the following deductions from the amount payable to the executor of the deceased partner.

(*i*) His drawings in the year of his death. Ashok's drawings till 31st December, 2016 were ₹ 15,000.

(*ii*) Interest on drawing @ 12% per annum which was calculated as ₹ 1,500.

The accountant of the firm prepared Ashok's capital account to be presented to the executor of Ashok but in a hurry, he left it incomplete. Ashok's capital account as prepared by the firm's accountant is given below

Dr **Ashok's Capital Account** Cr

Date	Particulars	Amt (₹)	Date	Particulars	Amt (₹)
2016			2016		
Dec 31	....	15,000	Apr 1	....	90,000
Dec 31	....	...	Dec 31	....	8,100
Dec 31	....	...	Dec 31	....	40,000
			Dec 31	....	90,000
			Dec 31	....	90,000
		3,18,100			3,18,100

You are required to complete Ashok's capital account. **All India 2017**

Ans. Dr **Ashok's Capital Account** Cr

Date	Particulars	Amt (₹)	Date	Particulars	Amt (₹)
2016			2016		
Dec 31	To Drawings A/c	15,000	April 1	By Balance b/d	90,000
Dec 31	To Interest on Drawings A/c	1,500	Dec 31	By Interest on Capital A/c	8,100
Dec 31	To Ashok's Executor A/c	3,01,600	Dec 31	By Profit and Loss Suspense A/c	40,000
			Dec 31	By Babu's Capital A/c	90,000
			Dec 31	By Chetan's Capital A/c	90,000
		3,18,100			3,18,100

Working Notes

1. **Calculation of Interest on Capital**

$$=90,000 \times \frac{12}{100} \times \frac{9}{12} = ₹8,100$$

2. **Calculation of Profit**

$$= 4,00,000 \times \frac{25}{100} \times \frac{4}{10} = ₹\,40,000$$

3. **Calculation of Ashok's Share of Goodwill**

Ashok's share of goodwill $= 4,50,000 \times \frac{4}{10} =$ ₹1,80,000 to be contributed by Babu and Chetan in gaining ratio, *i.e.* 3 : 3 or 1 : 1.

18. Sandeep, Mandeep and Amandeep were partners in a firm sharing profits in the ratio of 2 : 2 : 1. The firm closes its books on 31st March every year. On 30th September, 2015 Mandeep died. The partnership deed provided that on the death of a partner, his executors will be entitled to the following

(*i*) Balance in his capital account and interest @ 12% per annum on capital. On 1st April, 2016 the balance in Mandeep's capital account was ₹ 1,00,000.

(*ii*) His share in the profits of the firm in the year of his death which will be calculated on the basis of rate of net profit on sales of the previous year which was 25%. The sales of the firm till 30th September, 2016 were ₹ 9,00,000.

(*iii*) His share in the goodwill of the firm. The goodwill of the firm on Mandeep's death was valued at ₹ 1,50,000.

The partnership deed also provided that the following deductions will be made from the amount payable to the executor of the deceased partner

(a) His drawing in the year of his death. Mandeep's drawings till 30th September, 2016 were ₹ 4,000.

(b) Interest on drawing @ 6% per annum which was calculated as ₹ 120.

The accountant of the firm prepared Mandeep's capital account to be presented to the executor of Mandeep but in a hurry, he left it incomplete.

Mandeep's capital account prepared by accountant of the firm is shown below

Dr **Mandeep's Capital Account** Cr

Date	Particulars	Amt (₹)	Date	Particulars	Amt (₹)
2016			2016		
Sep 30	....	4,000	April 1	....	1,00,000
Sep 30	....	...	Sep 30	....	6,000
Sep 30	....	...	Sep 30	....	90,000
			Sep 30	....	40,000
			Sep 30	....	20,000
		2,56,000			2,56,000

You are required to complete Mandeep's capital account. **Delhi 2017**

Ans. Solve as Q no. 17 on page 186 and 187.

Amount Transferred to Mandeep's Executor Account = ₹ 2,51,880.

19. Manav, Nath and Narayan were partners in a firm sharing profits in the ratio of 1 : 2 : 1. The firm closes its books on 31st March every year. On 30th September, 2015, Nath died. On that date, his capital account showed a debit balance of ₹ 5,000. There was a debit balance of ₹ 30,000 in the profit and loss account. The goodwill of the firm was valued at ₹ 3,80,000. Nath's share of profit in the year of his death was to be calculated on the basis of average profit of last 5 years, which was ₹ 90,000.
Pass necessary journal entries in the books of the firm on Nath's death. **All India 2016**

Ans. **JOURNAL**

Date	Particulars		LF	Amt (Dr)	Amt (Cr)
2015					
Sep 30	Manav's Capital A/c $(1,90,000 \times 1/2)$	Dr		95,000	
	Narayan's Capital A/c $(1,90,000 \times 1/2)$	Dr		95,000	
	To Nath's Capital A/c				1,90,000
	(Being Nath's share of goodwill adjusted in the capital accounts of gaining partners in gaining ratio)				
	Manav's Capital A/c $(30,000 \times 1/4)$	Dr		7,500	
	Nath's Capital A/c $(30,000 \times 2/4)$	Dr		15,000	
	Narayan's Capital A/c $(30,000 \times 1/4)$	Dr		7,500	
	To Profit and Loss A/c				30,000
	(Being the transfer of profit to old partners in old ratio)				
	Profit and Loss Suspense A/c $\left(90,000 \times \frac{2}{4} \times \frac{6}{12}\right)$	Dr		22,500	
	To Nath's Capital A/c				22,500
	(Being Nath's share of profit till the date of his death transferred to his capital account)				
	Nath's Capital A/c	Dr		1,92,500	
	To Nath's Executor A/c				1,92,500
	(Being the transfer of amount due to Nath's executor account)				

Working Notes

1. **Calculation of Nath's Share of Goodwill**

Firm's goodwill = ₹ 3,80,000; Nath's share of goodwill $= 3,80,000 \times \frac{2}{4} =$ ₹ 1,90,000

2. **Calculation of Amount Transferred to Nath's Executors Account**

Dr **Nath's Capital Account** Cr

Particulars	Amt (₹)	Particulars	Amt (₹)
To Balance b/d	5,000	By Manav's Capital A/c	95,000
To Profit and Loss A/c	15,000	By Narayan's Capital A/c	95,000
To Nath's Executor A/c	1,92,500	By Profit and Loss Suspense A/c	22,500
	2,12,500		2,12,500

20. Vikas, Vishal and Vaibhav were partners in a firm sharing profits in the ratio of 2:2:1. The firm closes its books on 31st March every year. On 31st December, 2015, Vaibhav died. On that date his capital account showed a credit balance of ₹ 3,80,000 and goodwill of the firm was valued at ₹ 1,20,000. There was a debit balance of ₹ 50,000 in the profit and loss account. Vaibhav's share of profit in the year of his death was to be calculated on the basis of the average profit of last five years. The average profit of last five years was ₹ 75,000.

Pass necessary journal entries in the books of the firm on Vaibhav's death. **Delhi 2016**

Ans. Solve as Q no. 19 on page 188 and 189.

Amount Transferred to Vaibhav's Executor Account = ₹ 4,05,250;

Vaibhav's Share of Goodwill = ₹ 24,000; Vaibhav's Share of Profit = ₹ 11,250.

21. Ram, Ghanshyam and Vrinda were partners in a firm sharing profits in the ratio of 4 : 3 : 1. The firm closes its books on 31st March every year. On 1st February, 2015, Ghanshyam died and it was decided that the new profit sharing ratio between Ram and Vrinda will be equal. The partnership deed provided for the following, on the death of a partner.

(a) His share of goodwill be calculated on the basis of the half of the profits credited to his account during the previous four completed years. The firm's profit for the last four years was: 2010-2011 ₹ 1,20,000, 2011-2012 ₹ 80,000, 2012-2013 ₹ 40,000 and 2013-2014 ₹ 80,000.

(b) His share of profit in the year of his death was to be computed on the basis of average profits of past two years.

Pass necessary journal entries relating to goodwill and profit to be transferred to Ghanshyam's capital account. Also show your workings clearly. **Delhi (C) 2016**

Ans. **JOURNAL**

Date	Particulars		LF	Amt (Dr)	Amt (Cr)
2015					
Feb 1	Vrinda's Capital A/c	Dr		60,000	
	To Ghanshyam's Capital A/c				60,000
	(Being the amount of goodwill adjusted)				
	Vrinda's Capital A/c	Dr		18,750	
	To Ghanshyam's Capital A/c				18,750
	(Being the share of profit adjusted)				

Working Notes

1. **Calculation of Gaining Ratio**

Gaining Ratio = New Share − Old Share

$$\text{Ram} = \frac{1}{2} - \frac{4}{8} = \frac{4-4}{8} = \text{Nil}; \quad \text{Vrinda} = \frac{1}{2} - \frac{1}{8} = \frac{4-1}{8} = \frac{3}{8}$$

Since Vrinda is the gaining partner, only she will contribute.

2. **Calculation of Share of Goodwill**

$$\text{Ghanshyam's share in goodwill} = (1{,}20{,}000 + 80{,}000 + 40{,}000 + 80{,}000) \times \frac{1}{2} \times \frac{3}{8} = ₹\,60{,}000$$

3. **Ghanshyam's Share in Profit** $= \left[\frac{40{,}000 + 80{,}000}{2}\right] \times \frac{3}{8} \times \frac{10}{12} = ₹\,18{,}750$

22. Monu, Nigam and Shreya were partners in a firm sharing profits and losses in the ratio of 4 : 3 : 1. The firm closes its books on 31st March every year. As per the terms of partnership deed on the death of any partner, the share of goodwill of the deceased partner will be calculated on the basis of 50% of the net profits credited to the partners' capital account during the last four completed years before death. Monu died on 1st July, 2015.
The profits for last four years were

Year	Profit (₹)
2011-12	97,000
2012-13	1,05,000
2013-14	30,000
2014-15	84,000

His share of profit in the year of his death was to be calculated on the basis of sales. Sales for the year ended 31st March, 2015 amounted to ₹ 21,00,000. From 1st April, 2015 to 30th June, 2015 the firm's sales were ₹ 2,00,000.

Pass necessary journal entries relating to the amount of goodwill and profit to be transferred to Monu's capital account. Also show your workings clearly. **All India (C) 2016**

Ans. **JOURNAL**

Date	Particulars		LF	Amt (Dr)	Amt (Cr)
2015					
Jul 1	Nigam's Capital A/c (79,000 × 3 / 4)	Dr		59,250	
	Shreya's Capital A/c (79,000 × 1 / 4)	Dr		19,750	
	To Monu's Capital A/c				79,000
	(Being amount of goodwill trasferred to Monu's capital account)				
	Profit and Loss Suspense A/c	Dr		4,000	
	To Monu's Capital A/c				4,000
	(Being share of profit transferred to deceased partner's capital account)				

Working Notes

1. **Calculation of Share of Goodwill**

$$\text{Monu's share in goodwill} = (97{,}000 + 1{,}05{,}000 + 30{,}000 + 84{,}000) \times \frac{50}{100} \times \frac{4}{8} = ₹\,79{,}000$$

2. **Calculation of Share in Profit**

$$\text{Monu's share in profit} = \frac{84{,}000}{21{,}00{,}000} \times 2{,}00{,}000 \times \frac{4}{8} = ₹\,4{,}000$$

23. Arun, Varun and Karan were partners in a firm sharing profits in the ratio of 4 : 3 : 3. On 31st March, 2014 their balance sheet was as follows

Balance Sheet
as at 31st March, 2014

Liabilities		Amt (₹)	Assets	Amt (₹)
Creditors		17,000	Cash	8,000
Bills Payable		12,000	Debtors	13,000
Karan's Loan		28,000	Bills Receivables	9,000
Capital A/cs			Furniture	27,000
Arun	70,000		Machinery	1,25,000
Varun	68,000	1,38,000	Karan's Capital	13,000
		1,95,000		1,95,000

On 30th September, 2014, Karan died. The partnership deed provided for the following to the executors of the deceased partner.

(*i*) His share in the goodwill of the firm calculated on the basis of three years purchase of the average profits of the last four years. The profits of the last four years were ₹ 1,90,000; ₹ 1,70,000; ₹ 1,80,000 and ₹ 1,60,000 respectively.

(*ii*) His share in the profits of the firm till the date of his death calculated on the basis of the average profits of the last four years.

(*iii*) Interest @ 8% per annum on the credit balance, if any, in his capital account.

(*iv*) Interest on his loan @ 12% per annum.

Prepare Karan's capital account to be presented to his executors, assuming that his loan and interest on loan were transferred to his capital account. **All India 2015**

Ans. Dr **Karan's Capital Account** Cr

Date	Particulars	Amt (₹)	Date	Particulars	Amt (₹)
2014			2014		
Apr 1	To Balance b/d	13,000	Sep 30	By Karan's Loan A/c	28,000
Sep 30	To Executor's A/c	2,00,430	Sep 30	By Arun's Capital A/c	90,000
			Sep 30	By Varun's Capital A/c	67,500
			Sep 30	By Profit and Loss Suspense A/c (Profit upto death)	26,250
			Sep 30	By Interest on Loan A/c $\left(28{,}000 \times \frac{12}{100} \times \frac{6}{12}\right)$	1,680
		2,13,430			2,13,430

Working Notes

1. **Calculation of Share of Goodwill**

$$\text{Average profit} = \frac{1{,}90{,}000 + 1{,}70{,}000 + 1{,}80{,}000 + 1{,}60{,}000}{4} = ₹\ 1{,}75{,}000$$

$$\text{Goodwill} = \text{Average Profit} \times \text{Number of Years' Purchase}$$
$$= 1{,}75{,}000 \times 3 = ₹\ 5{,}25{,}000$$

Karan's share = $5{,}25{,}000 \times \frac{3}{10}$ = ₹ 1,57,500, to be contributed by Arun and Varun in gaining ratio *i.e.* 4 : 3, Arun will contribute $= 1{,}57{,}500 \times \frac{4}{7} =$ ₹90,000; Varun will contribute $= 1{,}57{,}500 \times \frac{3}{7}$ = ₹67,500

2. **Calculation of Profit upto Death**

Average profit = ₹ 1,75,000

Karan's share of profit $= 1{,}75{,}000 \times \frac{3}{10} \times \frac{6}{12} =$ ₹ 26,250

NOTE As there is no credit balance in capital account of Karan, he will not get interest on capital.

24. Sunny, Honey and Rupesh were partners in a firm. On 31st March, 2014 their balance sheet was as follows

Balance Sheet
as at 31st March, 2014

Liabilities		Amt (₹)	Assets	Amt (₹)
Creditors		10,000	Plant and Machinery	40,000
General Reserve		30,000	Furniture	15,000
Capital A/cs			Investments	20,000
Sunny	30,000		Debtors	20,000
Honey	30,000		Stock	25,000
Rupesh	20,000	80,000		
		1,20,000		1,20,000

Honey died on 31st December, 2014. The partnership deed provides that the representatives of the deceased partner shall be entitled to

(*i*) Balance in the capital account of the deceased partner.

(*ii*) Interest on capital @ 6% per annum upto the date of his death.
(*iii*) His share in the undistributed profits or losses as per the balance sheet.
(*iv*) His share in the profits of the firm till the date of his death, calculated on the basis of rate of net profit on sales of the previous year. The rate of net profit on sale of previous year was 20%. Sales of the firm during the year till 31st December, 2014 was ₹ 6,00,000.

Prepare Honey's capital account to be presented to his executors. **Delhi 2015**

Ans. Dr **Honey's Capital Account** Cr

Date	Particulars	Amt (₹)	Date	Particulars	Amt (₹)
2014			2014		
Dec 31	To Honey's Executors A/c (Balance transfer)	81,350	Apr 1	By Balance b/d	30,000
			Dec 31	By General Reserve A/c $(30{,}000 \times 1/3)$	10,000
			Dec 31	By Interest on Capital A/c $\left(30{,}000 \times \frac{6}{100} \times \frac{9}{12}\right)$	1,350
			Dec 31	By Profit and Loss Suspense A/c $\left(6{,}00{,}000 \times \frac{20}{100} \times \frac{1}{3}\right)$	40,000
		81,350			81,350

25. Dev, Swati and Sanskar were partners in a firm sharing profits in the ratio of 2 : 2 : 1. On 31st March, 2014 their balance sheet was as follows

Balance Sheet
as at 31st March, 2014

Liabilities		Amt (₹)	Assets	Amt (₹)
Trade Payables		17,000	Building	1,04,000
Bank Loan		13,000	Inventory	16,000
Capital A/cs			Trade Receivables	23,000
Dev	77,000		Cash	40,000
Swati	87,000		Profit and Loss A/c	57,000
Sanskar	46,000	2,10,000		
		2,40,000		2,40,000

On 30th June, 2014 Dev died. According to partnership agreement, Dev was entitled to interest on capital at 12% per annum. His share of profit till the date of his death was to be calculated on the basis of the average profits of last four years.

The profits of the last four years were

Years	Profit (₹)
2010-2011	2,04,000
2011-2012	1,80,000
2012-2013	90,000
2013-2014 (Loss)	57,000

On 1st April, 2014, Dev withdrew ₹ 15,000 to pay for his medical bills.

Prepare Dev's account to be presented to his executors. **Delhi 2015**

Ans. Dr **Dev's Account** Cr

Date	Particulars	Amt (₹)	Date	Particulars	Amt (₹)
2014			2014		
Jun 30	To Profit and Loss A/c (57,000 × 2/5)	22,800	Apr 1	By Balance b/d	77,000
			Jun 30	By Interest on Capital	2,310
Jun 30	To Drawings A/c	15,000	Jun 30	By Profit and Loss Suspense A/c	10,425
Jun 30	To Executor's A/c (Balance transfer)	51,935			
		89,735			89,735

Working Notes

1. **Calculation of Interest on Capital**

$$= 77,000 \times \frac{12}{100} \times \frac{3}{12} = ₹ 2,310$$

2. **Calculation of Profit upto Date of Death**

$$\text{Average profit} = \frac{2,04,000 + 1,80,000 + 90,000 - 57,000}{4} = ₹\ 1,04,250$$

$$\text{Dev's share of profit} = 1,04,250 \times \frac{2}{5} \times \frac{3}{12} = ₹ 10,425$$

26. On 31st March, 2014, the balance sheet of Pooja, Qureshi and Ross, who were partners in a firm was as under

Balance Sheet
as on 31st March, 2014

Liabilities		Amt (₹)	Assets	Amt (₹)
Sundry Creditors		2,50,000	Building	2,60,000
Reserve Fund		2,00,000	Investment	1,10,000
Capital A/cs			Qureshi's Loan	1,00,000
Pooja	1,50,000		Debtors	1,50,000
Qureshi	1,00,000		Stock	1,20,000
Ross	1,00,000	3,50,000	Cash	60,000
		8,00,000		8,00,000

Qureshi died on 1st July, 2014. The profit sharing ratio of the partners was 2 : 1 : 1. On the death of the partner, the partnership deed provided for the following

(*i*) His share in the profits of the firm till the date of his death will be calculated on the basis of average profit of last three completed years.

(*ii*) Goodwill of the firm will be calculated on the basis of total profit of last two years.

(*iii*) Interest on loan given by the firm to a partner will be charged at the rate of 6% per annum or ₹ 4,000 whichever is more.

(*iv*) Profits for the last three years were ₹ 45,000, ₹ 48,000 and ₹ 33,000.

Prepare Qureshi's capital account to be rendered to his executors. **Delhi (C) 2015**

Ans. Dr **Qureshi's Capital Account** Cr

Particulars	Amt (₹)	Particulars	Amt (₹)
To Qureshi's Loan A/c	1,00,000	By Balance b/d	1,00,000
To Interest on Loan A/c	4,000	By Reserve Fund (2,00,000 × 1/4)	50,000
To Qureshi's Executor A/c	68,875	By Profit and Loss Suspense A/c	2,625
		By Pooja's Capital A/c	13,500
		By Ross's Capital A/c	6,750
	1,72,875		1,72,875

Working Notes

1. **Calculation of Qureshi's Share in Profit upto Death**

   Average profit $= \dfrac{45{,}000 + 48{,}000 + 33{,}000}{3} = ₹\ 42{,}000$; Qureshi's share $= 42{,}000 \times \dfrac{1}{4} \times \dfrac{3}{12} = ₹\ 2{,}625$

2. **Calculation of Share of Goodwill**

   Goodwill $= 48{,}000 + 33{,}000 = ₹\ 81{,}000$; Qureshi's share $= 81{,}000 \times \dfrac{1}{4} = ₹\ 20{,}250$

   Pooja will pay $= 20{,}250 \times \dfrac{2}{3} = ₹\ 13{,}500$; Ross will pay $= 20{,}250 \times \dfrac{1}{3} = ₹\ 6{,}750$

27. Monika, Sonika and Manisha were partners in a firm sharing profits in the ratio of 2 : 2 : 1 respectively. On 31st March, 2013 their balance sheet was as under

Balance Sheet
as at 31st March, 2013

Liabilities		Amt (₹)	Assets	Amt (₹)
Reserve Fund		1,50,000	Fixed Assets	3,60,000
Creditors		2,40,000	Stock	60,000
Capital A/cs			Debtors	1,20,000
Monika	1,80,000		Cash	2,70,000
Sonika	1,50,000			
Manisha	90,000	4,20,000		
		8,10,000		8,10,000

Sonika died on 30th June, 2013. It was agreed between her executors and the remaining partners that

(*i*) Goodwill of the firm be valued at 3 years' purchase of average profits for the last four years. The average profits were ₹ 2,00,000.

(*ii*) Interest on capital be provided at 12% per annum.

(*iii*) Her share in the profits upto the date of death will be calculated on the basis of average profits for the last 4 years.

Prepare Sonika's capital as on 30th June, 2013. **All India 2014**

Ans. Dr **Sonika's Capital Account** Cr

Date	Particulars	Amt (₹)	Date	Particulars	Amt (₹)
2013			2013		
June 30	To Sonika's Executor A/c	4,74,500	Apr 1	By Balance b/d	1,50,000
			June 30	By Reserve Fund A/c (1,50,000 × 2/5)	60,000
			June 30	By Interest on Capital A/c (1,50,000 × 12/100 × 3/12)	4,500
			June 30	By Profit and Loss Suspense A/c (Profit)	20,000
			June 30	By Monika's Capital A/c	1,60,000
			June 30	By Manisha's Capital A/c	80,000
		4,74,500			4,74,500

Working Notes

1. **Calculation of Sonika's Share of Goodwill**

Average profit of last 4 years = ₹ 2,00,000; Firm's goodwill = 2,00,000 × 3 = ₹ 6,00,000

$$\text{Sonika's share} = 6,00,000 \times \frac{2}{5} = ₹\ 2,40,000$$

Gaining ratio of Monika and Manisha = 2 : 1

Monika will contribute = $2,40,000 \times \frac{2}{3}$ = ₹ 1,60,000 ; Manisha will contribute = $2,40,000 \times \frac{1}{3}$ = ₹ 80,000

2. **Calculation of Sonika's Share of Profit**

$$\text{Sonika's share of profit} = 2,00,000 \times \frac{2}{5} \times \frac{3}{12} = ₹\ 20,000$$

28. Virad, Vishad and Roma were partners in a firm sharing profits in the ratio of 5 : 3 : 2 respectively. On 31st March, 2013 their balance sheet was as under

Balance Sheet
as on 31st March, 2013

Liabilities		Amt (₹)	Assets	Amt (₹)
Reserve Fund		60,000	Buildings	2,00,000
Creditors		1,10,000	Machinery	3,00,000
Capital A/cs			Patents	1,10,000
Virad	3,00,000		Stock	1,00,000
Vishad	2,50,000		Debtors	80,000
Roma	1,50,000	7,00,000	Cash	80,000
		8,70,000		8,70,000

Virad died on 1st October, 2013. It was agreed between his executors and the remaining partner's that

(*i*) Goodwill of the firm be valued at $2\frac{1}{2}$ years purchase of average profits for the last three years. The average profits were ₹ 1,50,000.

(*ii*) Interest on capital be provided at 10% per annum.

(*iii*) Profit for the year 2013-14 be taken as having accrued at the same rate as that of the previous year which was ₹ 1,50,000. Prepare Virad's capital account to be presented to his executors as on 1st October, 2013. **Delhi 2014**

Ans. Solve as Q no. 24 on page 192 and 193.

Amount Transferred to Virad's Executors Account = ₹ 5,70,000

6 Marks Questions

29. Girija, Yatin and Zubin were partners sharing profits in the ratio 5 : 3 : 2. Zubin died on 1st August, 2015. Amount due to Zubin's executor after all adjustments was ₹ 90,300. The executor was paid ₹ 10,300 in cash immediately and the balance in two equal annual instalments with interest @ 6% p.a. starting from 31st March, 2017. Account are closed on 31st March each year.

Prepare Zubin's executors account till he is finally paid. **Delhi 2019**

Ans.

Dr **Zubin's Executors Account** Cr

Date	Particulars	Amt (₹)	Date	Particulars	Amt (₹)
2015			2015		
Aug 1	To Cash	10,300	Aug 1	By Zubin's Capital A/c	90,300
Aug 1	To Zubin's Executors Loan A/c	80,000			
		90,300			90,300

Dr **Zubin's Executors Loan Account** Cr

Date	Particulars	Amt (₹)	Date	Particulars	Amt (₹)
2016			2015		
Mar 31	To Balance c/d	83,200	Aug 1	By Zubin's Executors A/c	80,000
			2016		
			Mar 31	By Interest A/c $(80{,}000 \times 6\% \times 8/12)$	3,200
		83,200			83,200
2017			2016		
Mar 31	To Cash A/c$(40{,}000 + 3{,}200 + 4{,}992)$	48,192	Apr 1	By Balance b/d	83,200
			2017		
			Mar 31	By Interest A/c $(83{,}200 \times 6\%)$	4,992
Mar 31	To Balance c/d	40,000			
		88,192			88,192
2018			2017		
Mar 31	To Cash A/c	42,400	Apr 1	By Balance b/d	40,000
			2018		
			Mar 31	By Interest A/c $(40{,}000 \times 6\%)$	2,400
		42,400			42,400

30. Pranav, Karan and Rahim were partners in a firm sharing profits and losses in the ratio of $2:2:1$. On 31st March, 2017 their balance sheet was as follows

Balance Sheet
as on 31st March, 2017

Liabilities		Amt (₹)	Assets	Amt (₹)
Creditors		3,00,000	Fixed Assets	4,50,000
General Reserve		1,50,000	Stock	1,50,000
Capitals A/cs			Debtors	2,00,000
Pranav	2,00,000		Bank	1,50,000
Karan	2,00,000			
Rahim	1,00,000	5,00,000		
		9,50,000		9,50,000

Karan died on 12th June, 2017 . According to the partnership deed, the legal representatives of the deceased partner were entitled to the following

(*i*) Balance in his capital account.

(*ii*) Interest on capital @ 12% per annum.

(*iii*) Share of goodwill. Goodwill of the firm on Karan's death was valued at ₹ 60,000.

(*iv*) Share in the profits of the firm till the date of his death, calculated on the basis of last year's profit. The profit of the firm for the year ended 31st March, 2017 was ₹ 5,00,000.

Prepare Karan's capital account to be presented to his representatives. **CBSE 2018**

Ans.

Dr **Karan's Capital Account** Cr

Date	Particulars	Amt (₹)	Date	Particulars	Amt (₹)
2017 June 12	To Karan's Executors A/c	3,28,800	2017 June 12	By Balance b/d	2,00,000
				By Interest on Capital A/c	4,800
				By Pranav's Capital A/c	16,000
				By Rahim's Capital A/c	8,000
				By General Reserve A/c	60,000
				By Profit and Loss Suspense A/c	40,000
		3,28,800			3,28,800

Working Notes

1. Interest on Capital $= 2,00,000 \times \frac{12}{100} \times \frac{73}{365} =$ ₹ 4,800
2. Share in Goodwill $= 60,000 \times \frac{2}{5} = 24,000$ to be borne by remaining partners in gaining ratio i.e. 2 : 1
3. Share in Profit $= 5,00,000 \times \frac{2}{5} \times \frac{73}{365} =$ ₹ 40,000
4. Share in General Reserve $= 1,50,000 \times \frac{2}{5} =$ ₹ 60,000

31. On 1st January, 2008, Uday and Kaushal entered into partnership with fixed capitals of ₹ 7,00,000 and ₹ 3,00,000 respectively. They were doing good business and were interested in its expansion but could not do the same because of lack of capital. Therefore, to have more capital, they admitted Govind as a new partner on 1st January, 2010. Govind brought ₹ 10,00,000 as capital and the new profit sharing ratio decided was 3 : 2 : 5. On 1st January, 2012, another new partner Hari was admitted with a capital of ₹ 8,00,000 for 1/10th share in the profits, which he acquired equally from Uday, Kaushal and Govind. On 1st April, 2014, Govind died and his share was taken over by Uday and Hari equally.

Calculate

(*i*) The sacrificing ratio of Uday and Kaushal on Govind's admission.

(*ii*) New profit sharing ratio of Uday, Kaushal, Govind and Hari on Hari's admission.

(*iii*) New profit sharing ratio of Uday, Kaushal and Hari on Govind's death. **All India 2015**

Ans. (*i*) **Sacrificing Ratio**

Sacrificing Ratio = Old Share – New Share

Uday $= \frac{1}{2} - \frac{3}{10} = \frac{5-3}{10} = \frac{2}{10}$; Kaushal $= \frac{1}{2} - \frac{2}{10} = \frac{5-2}{10} = \frac{3}{10}$

Sacrificing ratio = 2 : 3

(*ii*) **New Ratio**

Hari is admitted for $\frac{1}{10}$th share

Uday's sacrifice = $\frac{1}{3} \times \frac{1}{10} = \frac{1}{30}$; Kaushal's sacrifice = $\frac{1}{3} \times \frac{1}{10} = \frac{1}{30}$; Govind's sacrifice = $\frac{1}{3} \times \frac{1}{10} = \frac{1}{30}$

Uday's new share = $\frac{3}{10} - \frac{1}{30} = \frac{9-1}{30} = \frac{8}{30}$; Kaushal's new share = $\frac{2}{10} - \frac{1}{30} = \frac{6-1}{30} = \frac{5}{30}$

Govind's new share = $\frac{5}{10} - \frac{1}{30} = \frac{15-1}{30} = \frac{14}{30}$

New ratio = $\frac{8}{30} : \frac{5}{30} : \frac{14}{30} : \frac{1}{10}$ *Or* 8 : 5 : 14 : 3

(*iii*) **New Ratio**

Uday acquired from Govind = $\frac{14}{30} \times \frac{1}{2} = \frac{14}{60}$; Hari acquired from Govind = $\frac{14}{30} \times \frac{1}{2} = \frac{14}{60}$

Uday's new share = old share + Gaining share = $\frac{8}{30} + \frac{14}{60} = \frac{16+14}{60} = \frac{30}{60}$;

Hari's new share = $\frac{3}{30} + \frac{14}{60} = \frac{6+14}{60} = \frac{20}{60}$; Kaushal's new share = $\frac{5}{30} \times \frac{2}{2} = \frac{10}{60}$

New ratio = 30 : 10 : 20 *Or* 3 : 1 : 2

32. A, B and C are partners in a trading firm. The firm has a fixed total capital of ₹ 60,000 held equally by all the partners. Under the partnership deed, the partners were entitled for the following

(*i*) A and B to a salary of ₹ 1,800 and ₹ 1,600 per month respectively.

(*ii*) In the event of the death of a partner, goodwill was to be valued at 2 years' purchase of the average profit of the last 3 years.

(*iii*) Profit upto the date of death based on the profits of the previous year.

(*iv*) Partners were to be charged interest on drawings @ 5% per annum and allowed interest on capital @ 6% per annum.

A died on 1st January, 2011. His drawings to the date of death were ₹ 2,000 and the interest thereon was ₹ 60. The profits for the three years ending 31st March, 2008, 2009 and 2010 were ₹ 21,200, ₹ 3,200 (Dr) and ₹ 9,000 respectively.

Prepare capital account to calculate the amount to be paid to his executors. **All India (C) 2011**

Ans. Dr **A's Capital Account** Cr

Date	Particulars	Amt (₹)	Date	Particulars	Amt (₹)
2011			2010		
Jan 1	To Drawings A/c	2,000	Apr 1	By Balance b/d	20,000
Jan 1	To Interest on Drawings A/c	60	2011		
Jan 1	To A's Executor's A/c (Balancing figure)	43,290	Jan 1	By Salary A/c (1,800 × 9)	16,200
			Jan 1	By B's Capital A/c	3,000
			Jan 1	By C's Capital A/c	3,000
			Jan 1	By Profit and Loss Suspense A/c (Profit)	2,250
			Jan 1	By Interest on Capital A/c	900
		45,350			45,350

Working Notes

1. **Calculation of A's Share of Capital**

Total fixed capital of the firm = ₹ 60,000; A's share = $60,000 \times \frac{1}{3}$ = ₹ 20,000

2. **Calculation of A's Share of Goodwill**

Last 3 years' profit = 21,200 − 3,200 + 9,000 = ₹ 27,000; Average profit = $\frac{27,000}{3}$ = ₹ 9,000

Firm's Goodwill = Average Profit × Number of Years' Purchase
= 9,000 × 2 = ₹ 18,000

A's share of goodwill = $18,000 \times \frac{1}{3}$ = ₹ 6,000, to be contributed by B and C in their gaining ratio, *i.e.* 1 : 1. C will contribute = $6,000 \times \frac{1}{2}$ = ₹ 3,000; B will contribute = $6,000 \times \frac{1}{2}$ = ₹ 3,000

3. **Calculation of A's Share of Profit**

A's share of profit = $9,000 \times \frac{1}{3} \times \frac{9}{12}$ = ₹ 2,250

4. **Calculation of Interest on A's Capital**

Interest on A's capital = $20,000 \times \frac{6}{100} \times \frac{9}{12}$ = ₹ 900

8 Marks Questions

33. Khanna, Seth and Mehta were partners in a firm sharing profits in the ratio of 3 : 2 : 5. On 31st December, 2010 the balance sheet of Khanna, Seth and Mehta was as follows

Balance Sheet
as at 31st December, 2010

Liabilities		Amt (₹)	Assets	Amt (₹)
General Reserve		1,00,000	Goodwill	3,00,000
Loan from Seth		50,000	Land and Building	5,00,000
Creditors		75,000	Machinery	1,70,000
Capital A/cs			Stock	30,000
Khanna	3,00,000		Debtors	1,20,000
Seth	2,00,000		Cash	45,000
Mehta	5,00,000	10,00,000	Profit and Loss A/c	60,000
		12,25,000		12,25,000

On 14th March, 2011 Seth died. The partnership deed provided that on the death of a partner the executor of the deceased partner is entitled to

(*i*) Balance in capital account.
(*ii*) Share in profits upto the date of death on the basis of last year's profit.
(*iii*) His share in profit/loss on revaluation of assets and re-assessment of liabilities which were as follows
(a) Land and building was to be appreciated by ₹ 1,20,000.
(b) Machinery was to be depreciated to ₹ 1,35,000 and stock to ₹ 25,000.
(c) A provision of 2.5% for bad and doubtful debts was to be created on debtors.
(*iv*) The net amount payable to Seth's executors was transferred to his loan account which was to be paid later.

Prepare revaluation account, partners' capital account, Seth's executor's account and balance sheet of Khanna and Mehta who decided to continue the business keeping their capital balances in their new profit sharing ratio. Any surplus or deficit to be transferred to current accounts of the partners. **All India 2012**

Ans. Dr **Revaluation Account** Cr

Particulars		Amt (₹)	Particulars	Amt (₹)
To Machinery A/c		35,000	By Land and Building A/c	1,20,000
To Stock A/c		5,000		
To Provision for Doubtful Debts A/c		3,000		
To Profit Transferred to				
Khanna's Capital A/c	23,100			
Seth's Capital A/c	15,400			
Mehta's Capital A/c	38,500	77,000		
		1,20,000		1,20,000

Dr **Partners' Capital Account** Cr

Particulars	Khanna (₹)	Seth (₹)	Mehta (₹)	Particulars	Khanna (₹)	Seth (₹)	Mehta (₹)
To Goodwill A/c	90,000	60,000	1,50,000	By Balance b/d	3,00,000	2,00,000	5,00,000
To Profit and Loss A/c	18,000	12,000	30,000	By Revaluation A/c (Profit)	23,100	15,400	38,500
To Profit and Loss Suspense A/c (Loss)	—	2,400	—	By General Reserve A/c	30,000	20,000	50,000
To Seth's Executor's A/c	—	1,61,000	—				
To Balance c/d	2,45,100	—	4,08,500				
	3,53,100	2,35,400	5,88,500		3,53,100	2,35,400	5,88,500

Dr **Seth's Executor's Account** Cr

Particulars	Amt (₹)	Particulars	Amt (₹)
To Seth's Executor's Loan A/c	2,11,000	By Seth's Capital A/c	1,61,000
		By Seth's Loan A/c	50,000
	2,11,000		2,11,000

Balance Sheet
as at 14th March, 2011

Liabilities		Amt (₹)	Assets		Amt (₹)
Creditors		75,000	Land and Building		6,20,000
Seth's Executor's Loan A/c		2,11,000	Machinery		1,35,000
Profit and Loss Suspense A/c		2,400	Stock		25,000
Capital A/cs			Debtors	1,20,000	
Khanna	2,45,100		(–) Provision for Doubtful Debts	(3,000)	1,17,000
Mehta	4,08,500	6,53,600	Cash		45,000
		9,42,000			9,42,000

NOTE Profit and loss suspense account appeared on liabilities side of balance sheet as it is a loss.

Working Notes

1. **Calculation of Seth's Share of Profit**

   Number of days Seth worked for = Jan + Feb + March = 31 + 28 + 14 = 73 days

   $$\text{Share of Seth's profit} = 60{,}000 \times \frac{73}{365} \times \frac{2}{10} = ₹\ 2{,}400$$

2. **Calculation of Khanna's and Mehta's Capital**

   Khanna's capital after adjustment = 2,45,100

   Mehta's capital after adjustment = 4,08,500

   Total capital = ₹ 6,53,600

   $$\text{Khanna's capital} = 6{,}53{,}600 \times \frac{3}{8} = ₹\ 2{,}45{,}100\ ; \quad \text{Mehta's capital} = 6{,}53{,}600 \times \frac{5}{8} = ₹\ 4{,}08{,}500$$

   So, there is no deficit or surplus in Khanna's and Mehta's capital account which is to be adjusted through current accounts.

34. G, E and F were partners in a firm sharing profits in the ratio of 7 : 2 : 1. The balance sheet of the firm as on 31st March, 2011 was as follows

Balance Sheet

as at 31st March, 2011

Liabilities		Amt (₹)	Assets	Amt (₹)
General Reserve		20,000	Goodwill	40,000
Loan from E		30,000	Land and Building	60,000
Creditors		14,000	Machinery	40,000
Capital A/cs			Stock	7,000
G	70,000		Debtors	12,000
E	20,000		Cash	5,000
F	10,000	1,00,000		
		1,64,000		1,64,000

E died on 24th August, 2011. Partnership deed provides for the settlement of claims on the death of a partner in addition to his capital as under

(*i*) The share of profit of deceased partner to be computed upto the date of death on the basis of average profits of the past three years which was ₹ 80,000.

(*ii*) His share in profit/loss on revaluation of assets and re-assessment of liabilities which were as follows

Land and building were revalued at ₹ 94,000. Machinery at ₹ 38,000 and stock at ₹ 5,000. A provision of 2.5% was to be created on debtors for doubtful debts.

(*iii*) The net amount payable to E's executors was transferred to his loan account, to be paid later on.

Prepare revaluation account, partners' capital account, E's executor account and balance sheet of 'G' and 'F' who decided to continue the business keeping their capital balances in their new profit sharing ratio. Any surplus or deficit to be transferred to current account of the partners. **Delhi 2012**

Ans. Solve as Q no. 33 on page 200-202.

Profit on Revaluation = ₹ 29,700, Balance in Partners' Capital Account : G = ₹ 76,790, F = ₹ 10, 970; Total of Balance Sheet = ₹ 1,60,100; Amount Transferred to Executor's Loan Account = ₹ 58,340

35. M, N and O were partners in a firm sharing profits and losses equally. Their balance sheet on 31st December, 2009 was as follows

Balance Sheet
as at 31st December, 2009

Liabilities		Amt (₹)	Assets	Amt (₹)
General Reserve		30,000	Plant and Machinery	60,000
Creditors		20,000	Stock	30,000
Capital A/cs			Sundry Debtors	95,000
M	70,000		Cash at Bank	40,000
N	70,000		Cash in Hand	35,000
O	70,000	2,10,000		
		2,60,000		2,60,000

N died on 14th March, 2010. According to the partnership deed, executors of the deceased partner are entitled to

(*i*) Balance of partners' capital account.
(*ii*) Interest on capital @ 5% per annum.
(*iii*) Share of goodwill calculated on the basis of twice the average of past three years' profit.
(*iv*) Share of profits from the closure of the last accounting year till the date of death on the basis of twice the average of three completed years' profits before death.

Profits of 2007, 2008 and 2009 were ₹ 80,000, ₹ 90,000 and ₹ 1,00,000 respectively. Show the working for deceased partner's share of goodwill and profits till the date of his death. Pass the necessary journal entries and prepare N's capital account to be rendered to his executor.
Delhi 2011

Ans.

JOURNAL

Date	Particulars		LF	Amt (Dr)	Amt (Cr)
2010					
Mar 14	General Reserve A/c (30,000×1/3)	Dr		10,000	
	To N's Capital A/c				10,000
	(Being share of general reserve given to N)				
	Interest on Capital A/c	Dr		700	
	To N's Capital A/c				700
	(Being interest on capital given to N)				
	M's Capital A/c (60,000×1/2)	Dr		30,000	
	O's Capital A/c (60,000×1/2)	Dr		30,000	
	To N's Capital A/c				60,000
	(Being amount of goodwill adjusted in gaining ratio)				
	Profit and Loss Suspense A/c	Dr		12,000	
	To N's Capital A/c				12,000
	(Being N's share of profit transferred to his capital account)				
	N's Capital A/c	Dr		1,52,700	
	To N's Executor's A/c				1,52,700
	(Being amount due to N transferred to N's executor's account)				

Dr **N's Capital Account** Cr

Date	Particulars	Amt (₹)	Date	Particulars	Amt (₹)
2010			2010		
Mar 14	To N's Executor's Account A/c	1,52,700	Mar 14	By Balance b/d	70,000
			Mar 14	By General Reserve A/c	10,000
			Mar 14	By Interest on Capital A/c	700
			Mar 14	By M's Capital A/c	30,000
			Mar 14	By O's Capital A/c	30,000
			Mar 14	By Profit and Loss Suspense A/c (Profit)	12,000
		1,52,700			1,52,700

Working Notes

1. **Calculation of Interest on N's Capital**

$$\text{Interest on N's capital} = 70{,}000 \times \frac{5}{100} \times \frac{73}{365} = ₹\,700$$

2. **Calculation of Goodwill**

$$\text{3 years total profit} = 80{,}000 + 90{,}000 + 1{,}00{,}000 = ₹\,2{,}70{,}000$$

$$\text{Average profit} = \frac{2{,}70{,}000}{3} = ₹\,90{,}000$$

$$\text{Firm's Goodwill} = \text{Average Profit} \times \text{Number of Years' Purchase} = 90{,}000 \times 2 = ₹\,1{,}80{,}000$$

$$\text{N's share of goodwill} = 1{,}80{,}000 \times \frac{1}{3} = ₹\,60{,}000$$

3. **Calculation of N's Share of Profit**

$$\text{N's share of profit} = (90{,}000 \times 2) \times \frac{73}{365} \times \frac{1}{3} = ₹\,12{,}000$$

Multiple Choice Questions

For Complete Chapter (1 Mark)

1. Rajat, Mishi and Tanvi were partners in a firm sharing profits and losses in the ratio of 5 : 3 : 2. Tanvi died on 31st October, 2019. According to the partnership agreement, her share of profits from the closure of last accounting year till the date of her death was to be calculated on the basis of aggregate profits of two completed years before death. Profits of the firm for the years ending 31st March, 2018 and 31st March, 2019 were ₹ 57,000 and ₹ 63,000 respectively. The firm closes its books on 31st March every year. Tanvi's share of profits till the date of her death will be **CBSE 2020**

(a) ₹ 24,000
(b) ₹ 7,000
(c) ₹ 14,000
(d) ₹ 12,000

Hint: $(57{,}000 + 63{,}000) \times \frac{2}{10} \times \frac{7}{12} = ₹\,14{,}000$

2. Retirement of a partner is one of the modes of

(a) dissolution of partnership firm
(b) reconstitution of partnership firm
(c) dissolution of partnership
(d) Both (b) and (c)

Hint: Retirement of a partner is a mode of reconstitution of partnership firm as well as dissolution of partnership amongst the existing partners. Hence, on retirement of a partner, partnership firm is reconstructed or dissolved.

3. The provisions related to retirement of a partner are contained in .... of the Indian Partnership Act, 1932.
(a) Section 30 (2) (b) Section 31 (1) (c) Section 32 (1) (d) None of these

4. In case of death of a partner, the amount standing to the credit of his account is paid to
(a) his minor children (b) his wife
(c) his parents (d) his legal representative

5. Partner's executor's account is prepared
(a) at the time of retirement of partner (b) at the time of death of partner
(c) at the time of admission of partner (d) All of these

Hint: When a partner dies, legal heirs of the deceased partner are entitled to receive the amount due to the deceased partner. Amount due to them is determined by preparing deceased partner's capital account and his account is closed by transferring the balance to his executor's account.

6. In case of retirement/death of a partner, profit or loss on revaluation is distributed among .... in their .... profit sharing ratio.
(a) all partners ; new (b) all partners ; old
(c) remaining partners ; new (d) remaining partners ; old

7. Retirement of a partner leads to ...... of remaining partners.
(a) gain in profit sharing ratio (b) loss in profit sharing ratio
(c) no change in profit sharing ratio (d) None of these

Hint: When a partner retires, his share is taken up by the remaining partners. This results in gain in their profit sharing ratio.

8. At the time of retirement/death of a partner, the continuing partners compensate the retiring partner/deceased partner's executor in the form of
(a) share in general reserve (b) share in reserve fund
(c) share in estimated profits (d) share in goodwill

Hint: At the time of retirement or death of a partner, the combined share of continuing partners increase. So, the continuing partner compensate the retiring/deceased partner by paying him goodwill.

9. If at the time of death or retirement of a partner, goodwill appears in the balance sheet of the firm, then this goodwill is written-off in
(a) old ratio (b) gaining ratio (c) sacrificing ratio (d) new ratio

10. Journal entry for adjustment of goodwill, in case if any of the remaining partner has also sacrificed a part of his share in profits of the firm or retirement or death of a partner.
(a) Continuing Gaining Partners' Capital A/c Dr
To Retiring/Deceased Partner's Capital A/c
To Continuing Sacrificing Partners' Capital A/c
(b) Retiring/Deceased Partners' Capital A/c Dr
Continuing Sacrificing Partners' Capital A/c Dr
To Continuing Gaining Partners' Capital A/c
(c) Both (a) and (b)
(d) None of the above

Hint: Continuing sacrificing partners' capital account is also credited alongwith retiring or deceased partners' capital account with his proportion of sacrifice and the continuing gaining partners' capital accounts are debited.

11. As per Section 37 of the Indian Partnership Act, 1932, the executor would be entitled at their choice to the interest calculated from the date of death till the date of payment on the final amount due to the deceased partner at .... % per annum.

(a) 7 (b) 4 (c) 6 (d) 12

12. 'A', 'B' and 'C' are partners in a firm sharing profit in ratio of 2 : 2 : 1. The capital account of partners stood at ₹ 50,000, ₹ 50,000 and ₹ 25,000, respectively. 'B' retires from the firm. Balance in reserve account stood at ₹ 10,000. If goodwill is valued at ₹ 20,000 and profit on revaluation is ₹ 9,000, then what will be the amount of loan account of 'B'?

(a) ₹ 75,820 (b) ₹ 53,870
(c) ₹ 23,600 (d) ₹ 65,600

Hint: **Statement Showing the Amount Payable to B**

Particulars	Amt (₹)
Capital	50,000
(+) Share in Reserve $\left(10{,}000 \times \frac{2}{5}\right)$	4,000
(+) Share in Goodwill $\left(20{,}000 \times \frac{2}{5}\right)$	8,000
(+) Share in Profit on Revaluation $\left(9{,}000 \times \frac{2}{5}\right)$	3,600
Total	65,600

13. A and B were partners. They shared profits as under

$A = 1/2; \quad B = 1/3$

Carried to reserve $= 1/6$

B died. The balance of reserve on the date of death was ₹ 42,000. What should be B's share of reserve?

(a) ₹ 14,000 (b) ₹ 21,000
(c) ₹ 16,800 (d) ₹ 4,200

Hint: Profit sharing ratio between A and B is $\frac{1}{2}:\frac{1}{3}$, *i.e.* 3 : 2

$\therefore$ B's share of reserve $= 42{,}000 \times \frac{2}{5} =$ ₹16,800

ANSWERS

1. *(c)*	2. *(d)*	3. *(c)*	4. *(d)*	5. *(b)*	6. *(b)*	7. *(a)*	8. *(d)*	9. *(a)*	10. *(a)*
11. *(c)*	12. *(d)*	13. *(c)*							

CHAPTER 05

Dissolution of Partnership Firm

Meaning of Dissolution

Dissolution means breaking up or extinction, *i.e.* discontinuance of existing relationship among the partners. Under the Indian Partnership Act, 1932, dissolution may be either of partnership or of a firm.

Dissolution of Partnership It refers to the change in the existing relationship between the partners but the firm may continue its business as before.

Dissolution of Partnership Firm It refers to the dissolution of partnership among all the partners in the firm. In this case, business of the firm also comes to an end.

Modes of Dissolution of Partnership Firm

(*i*) Dissolution by mutual agreement
(*ii*) Compulsory dissolution
(*iii*) Dissolution on the happening of certain contingencies
(*iv*) Dissolution by notice
(*v*) Dissolution by court

Settlement of Accounts in Case of Dissolution of Firm

In settling the accounts of a firm after dissolution, the following rules subject to the agreement between the partners, shall be observed.

Treatment of Losses [Section 48 (a)] Losses including deficiencies shall be paid, first out of profits, then out of partners' capital and lastly, if necessary, by the partners individually in their profit sharing ratio.

Application of Assets [Section 48(b)] The assets of the firm, including any sum contributed by the partners to make up for deficiencies, shall be applied in the following manner

(*i*) First to pay firm's debts to third parties, *i.e.* outside parties.
(*ii*) Then to pay loans and advances from partners.
(*iii*) Then to pay capital of partners.
(*iv*) Lastly, the surplus (if any) shall be distributed among the partners in their profit sharing ratio.

Treatment of Firms Debt and Private Debts

Where both the debts of the firm and private debts of a partner co-exist, the following rules, as stated in Section 49 of the Act, shall apply

(*i*) Firm's property is applied first in payment of firm's debts and if there is any surplus, then the share of each partner is applied in the payment of his private debts or paid to him.

(*ii*) Partners' private property is applied first in payment of his private debts and the surplus (if any) in payment of firm's debts if the firms liabilities exceed the firm's assets.

Accounting Treatment on Dissolution of Firm

On dissolution, the books of the firm are closed. The process is completed by opening the following accounts

(*i*) Realisation account
(*ii*) Partners' capital account
(*iii*) Partners' loan account
(*iv*) Cash/bank account

Realisation Account

It is a nominal account prepared at the time of dissolution of partnership firm to show profit or loss on realisation of assets and payment of liabilities.

Journal Entries

For Transfer of Assets (Except cash and bank balance)	Realisation A/c Dr To Various Assets A/c (Individually)	At book value
For Transfer of Liabilities (Except partners' loan, capital and undistributed profits)	Liabilities A/c (Individually) Dr To Realisation A/c	At book value
For Cash Realised on Sale of Assets	Cash/Bank A/c Dr To Realisation A/c	At selling price
For an Assets Taken Over by Any Partner	Partners' Capital A/c Dr To Realisation A/c	At agreed value
For Sale of Unrecorded Assets	Cash/Bank A/c Dr To Realisation A/c	Amount received on sale
For Payment of Liabilities	Realisation A/c Dr To Cash/Bank A/c	Amount of payment
For Any Liability Taken Over by the Partner	Realisation A/c Dr To Partners' Capital A/c	At agreed value
For Payment of Unrecorded Liability	Realisation A/c Dr To Cash/Bank A/c	Amount of payment
For Payment of Realisation Expenses	Realisation A/c Dr To Cash/Bank A/c	Amount of payment
For Payment of Realisation Expenses by any Partner	Realisation A/c Dr To Partners' Capital A/c	Amount of payment
For Credit Balance of Realisation Account (Profit)	Realisation A/c Dr To Partners' Capital/Current A/c	In profit sharing ratio
For Debit Balance of Realisation Account (Loss)	Partners' Capital/Current A/c Dr To Realisation A/c	In profit sharing ratio

NOTE (*i*) Goodwill appearing in the balance sheet is treated as any other asset. In case, question is silent about the realisation of goodwill, it is assumed that goodwill does not have any value and no amount is realised for it.

(*ii*) When an asset is transferred to realisation account, its corresponding reserve or provision appearing on the liabilities side of balance sheet is also transferred to realisation account.

(*iii*) In the absence of any information regarding realisation of assets (tangible or intangible), tangible assets should be assumed that they are realised at book value while intangible assets should be considered as nil.

(*iv*) In the absence of any information regarding settlement of any outside liabilities, it should be assumed that an amount equal to the book value of such liability has been paid-off.

Format of Realisation Account

Dr **Realisation Account** Cr

Particulars	Amt (₹)	Particulars	Amt (₹)
To Sundry Assets A/c {Excluding cash, bank, fictitious asset, accumulated losses, debit balance of partners' capital/current account, loans to partner(s)}	...	By Sundry Liabilities A/c {Excluding partners' capital, loan from partner(s), reserve, accumulated profit, etc.}	...
To Provision on any Liability A/c	...	By Provision on any Assets A/c	...
To Bank/Cash A/c (Amount paid for discharging liabilities)	...	By Bank/Cash A/c (Amount received on realisation of assets)	...
To Bank/Cash A/c (Amount paid for unrecorded liabilities)	...	By Bank/Cash A/c (Amount received from unrecorded assets)	...
To Bank/Cash A/c (Expenses on realisation)	...	By Partners' Capital/Current/A/c (Asset taken over by a partner recorded or unrecorded)	...
To Partners' Capital/Current A/c (Liability taken over by a partner or remuneration /commission paid to him or any expenses beared by him)	...	By Partners' Capital/Current A/c (Loss on realisation)*	...
To Partners' Capital/Current A/c (Profit on realisation)*	...		
	...		...

*Any one of two amounts will appear.

Partners' Capital Account

Balances of partners' capital and current accounts are recorded in this account. Any asset of the firm taken over by the partner is recorded on the debit side and liability taken over is recorded on the credit side. Undistributed profits and reserves are recorded on the credit side and undistributed losses or fictitious assets are recorded on the debit side.

When capital accounts are maintained following fixed capital account method, partners have current accounts also. These current accounts may have credit or debit balance. Current accounts are closed by transferring them to concerned partners' fixed capital accounts.

The entries are as follows

(a) In case of debit balance in a current account of a partner	Concerned Partners' Capital A/c To Concerned Partners' Current A/c	Dr
(b) In case of credit balance in a current account of a partner	Concerned Partners' Current A/c To Concerned Partners' Capital A/c	Dr

Format of Partners' Capital Account

Dr **Partners' Capital Account** Cr

Particulars	X (₹)	Y (₹)	Particulars	X (₹)	Y (₹)
To Balance b/d (Debit balance)	...	...	By Balance b/d (Credit balance)	...	...
To Profit and Loss A/c	...	...	By General Reserve A/c	...	...
To Advertisement A/c	...	...	By Profit and Loss A/c	...	...
To Realisation A/c (Assets taken over)	...	...	By Workmen's Compensation Fund A/c	...	...
To Realisation A/c* (Loss on realisation)	...	...	By Investment Fluctuation fund A/c**	...	...
To Cash/Bank A/c (Excess cash paid)	...	...	By Realisation A/c (Liabilities taken over)	...	...
			By Realisation A/c* (Profit on realisation)	...	...
			By Cash/Bank A/c (Cash brought in)	...	...
	...	...		...	...

*Any one will appear. **If investment is not given in balance sheet.

Partners' Loan Account

If any loan is advanced by a partner to the firm, it will be paid-off only after all the outside liabilities are paid in full. Thus, partners' loan account is not transferred to realisation account and a separate account is prepared namely partners' loan account and is paid-off by passing the following entry

Partners' Loan A/c Dr

To Cash/Bank A/c

Bank or Cash Account

It is a real account. On debit side, opening balance, amount realised through sale of assets and any amount paid in by the partners are shown. On the credit side, all the payments for liabilities, realisation expenses and final settlement made to partners are shown. In case, both cash and bank balances appear in balance sheet, it is always better to open a single account.

Format of Cash/Bank Account

Dr **Cash/Bank Account** Cr

Particulars	Amt (₹)	Particulars	Amt (₹)
To Balance b/d (Cash in hand or cash at bank)	...	By Balance b/d (Bank overdraft)	...
To Realisation A/c (Assets realised)	...	By Realisation A/c (Liabilities paid)	...
To Partners' Capital A/c (Cash brought in by partner)	...	By Realisation A/c (Realisation expenses paid)	...
		By Partners' Loan A/c (Partners' loan paid)	...
		By Partners' Capital A/c (Excess cash paid to partner)	...
	...		...

Memorandum Balance Sheet

Memorandum balance sheet is prepared for calculating the missing figures of sundry assets. Sometimes, the total value of sundry assets is not given. However, the value realised from the assets is given. The partners' capital and other liabilities are also given. In that case, sundry assets have to be ascertained by preparing the old balance sheet. The amount of capital and other liabilities are added. The sum total is the total amount of assets.

Previous Years' Examination Questions

1 Mark Questions

1. Differentiate between 'Dissolution of partnership' and 'Dissolution of partnership firm' on the basis of 'Court's intervention'. **Delhi 2019; All India 2014**

Ans. Difference between dissolution of partnership firm and dissolution of partnership is

Basis	Dissolution of Partnership Firm	Dissolution of Partnership
Court's Intervention	It can be either voluntarily by the partners or compulsorily by the order of the court.	It is always voluntarily. There is no intervention of court.

2. Distinguish between 'Dissolution of partnership' and 'Dissolution of partnership firm' on the basis of 'Settlement of assets and liabilities'. **All India 2019; CBSE 2018**

Ans. Difference between dissolution of partnership and dissolution of partnership firm is

Basis	Dissolution of Partnership	Dissolution of Partnership Firm
Settlement of Assets and Liabilities	Assets and liabilities are revalued and the gain or loss on revaluation is distributed among all the partners in their old profit sharing ratio.	Assets of the firm are sold and liabilities are paid-off and the balance amount is distributed among all the partners.

3. State any two grounds on the basis of which court may order for the dissolution of partnership firm. **All India 2019**

Ans. Court may order for the dissolution of partnership firm when

(*i*) A partner becomes a person of unsound mind.

(*ii*) A partner is found guilty of misconduct.

4. State any two situations when a partnership firm may be compulsorily dissolved. **All India; Delhi 2019**

Or Identify a situation for compulsory dissolution of a partnership firm. **All India (c) 2014**

Ans. Situations when a partnership firm may be compulsorily dissolved are

(*i*) On insolvency of partners.

(*ii*) On business becoming illegal (unlawful).

5. State any two contingencies that may result into dissolution of a partnership firm. **Delhi 2019**

Ans. State any two contingencies that may result into dissolution of partnership firm

(*i*) on death of a partner. (*ii*) completion of work.

6. A, B and C were partners in a firm sharing profits and losses in the ratio of 2 : 2 : 1. On 31st March, 2018 their firm was dissolved. On that date, provision for bad debts showed a balance of ₹ 4,500.

Pass necessary journal entry for the treatment of provision for bad debts on the firm's dissolution. **All India 2019**

Ans. **JOURNAL**

Date	Particulars		LF	Amt (Dr)	Amt (Cr)
2018 Mar 31	Provision for Bad Debts A/c To Realisation A/c (Being provision for bad debts transferred to realisation account)	Dr		4,500	4,500

7. Pass the necessary journal entry for treatment of Partners' loan appearing on the asset side of the balance sheet in case of dissolution of a partnership firm. **All India 2019; Compartment 2018**

Ans.

Partners' Loan A/c To Cash/Bank A/c	Dr

8. B, C and D were partners in a firm sharing profits and losses in the ratio of 1 : 4 : 5. On 31st March, 2018 the firm was dissolved and on that date the balance sheet of the firm showed a loan of ₹ 10,000 given by C's brother F. C agreed to pay his brother's loan.

Pass necessary journal entry for the above on the firm's dissolution. **All India 2019**

Ans. **JOURNAL**

Date	Particulars		LF	Amt (Dr)	Amt (Cr)
2018 Mar 31	Realisation A/c To C's Capital A/c (Being C agreed to pay-off his brother F's loan)	Dr		10,000	10,000

9. Distinguish between 'Reconstitution of partnership' and 'Dissolution of partnership firm' on the basis of 'Closure of books.' **All India 2019**

Or Distinguish between 'Dissolution of partnership' and 'Dissolution of partnership firm' on the basis of 'Closure of books' **Delhi 2014**

Ans. Difference between dissolution of partnership and dissolution of partnership firm is

Basis	Dissolution of Partnership	Dissolution of Partnership Firm
Closure of Books	Books of accounts of the firm need not be closed.	Books of accounts of the firm are closed.

10. Distinguish between 'Dissolution of partnership' and 'Dissolution of partnership firm' on the basis of 'Economic relationship'. **Delhi; All India 2016**

Ans. Difference between dissolution of partnership and dissolution of partnership firm is

Basis	Dissolution of Partnership	Dissolution of Partnership Firm
Economic Relationship	Economic relationship between the partners continues though in a changed form.	Economic relationship between the partners comes to an end.

11. Identify a situation, under which court may order for dissolution of a partnership firm. **All India (C) 2014**

Ans. A court may order for dissolution of a partnership firm on insanity of a partner.

12. Name the asset that is not transferred to the debit side of realisation account, but brings certain amount of cash against its disposal at the time of dissolution of the firm. **Delhi (C) 2014**

Ans. Unrecorded asset

13. Name the liability which is not shown in the balance sheet, but paid at the time of dissolution of the firm. **Delhi (C) 2014**

Ans. Unrecorded liability

14. When an asset is taken over by a partner, why is his capital account debited? **Delhi (C) 2012**

Ans. When an asset is taken over by a partner, his capital account is debited because the Partners' claim over the firm is decreased by the amount of asset taken over by him, thus his capital account is decreased.

15. When a liability is to be discharged by a partner, why is his capital account credited? **All India (C) 2011**

Ans. When a liability is to be discharged by a partner, his capital account is credited because the Partners' claim is increased over the firm by the amount of liability discharged by him, thus his capital account is increased.

16. In case of dissolution of a firm, which liabilities are to be paid first? **Delhi (C) 2011**

Ans. According to Section 48 (b), the debts of the firm to the third parties are to be paid first.

17. In case of dissolution of a firm, which item on the liabilities side is to be paid last? **Delhi (C) 2011**

Ans. According to Section 48 (b), in case of dissolution of a firm, partners' capital is paid at last after all external liabilities are paid and all profits and losses are adjusted in capital account.

18. A and B are partners in a firm sharing profits in the ratio of 3 : 2. Mrs A has given a loan of ₹ 20,000 to the firm and the firm also obtained a loan of ₹ 10,000 from B. The firm was dissolved and its assets were realised for ₹ 25,000. State the order of payment of Mrs A's loan and B's loan with reason, if there were no creditor of the firm. **Delhi (C) 2010**

Ans. According to Section 48 of the Indian Partnership Act, 1932, first of all the payment of ₹ 20,000 will be made for Mrs A's loan as she is an outsider, then remaining ₹ 5,000 will be paid to B against his loan of ₹ 10,000.

4 Marks Questions

19. J, K and L were partners in a firm sharing profits in the ratio of 4 : 5 : 1. On 31st March, 2018 their firm was dissolved. On this date, the balance sheet showed a balance of ₹ 1,34,000 in debtors account and a balance of ₹ 14,000 in provision for bad debts account. Both the accounts were closed by transferring their balances to realisation account. ₹ 4,000 of the debtors became bad and nothing could be realised from them on dissolution. K agreed to look after the dissolution work for which he was allowed a remuneration of ₹ 16,000. K also agreed to bear dissolution expenses for which he was allowed a lumpsum payment of ₹ 4,000. Actual dissolution expenses were ₹ 6,500 and the same were paid from the firm's cash. Loss on dissolution amounted to ₹ 37,000.

Pass necessary journal entries for the above transactions in the books of the firm on its dissolution. **All India 2019**

Ans. **JOURNAL**

Date	Particulars		LF	Amt (Dr)	Amt (Cr)
	Cash A/c (1,34,000 – 4,000)	Dr		1,30,000	
	To Realisation A/c				1,30,000
	(Being debtors realised after bad debts adjustment)				
	Realisation A/c	Dr		16,000	
	To K's Capital A/c				16,000
	(Being remuneration paid for dissolution work)				
	Realisation A/c	Dr		4,000	
	To K's Capital A/c				4,000
	(Being dissolution expenses)				
	K's Capital A/c	Dr		6,500	
	To Cash A/c				6,500
	(Being realisation expenses paid which were to be borne by K)				
	J's Capital A/c	Dr		14,800	
	K's Capital A/c	Dr		18,500	
	L's Capital A/c	Dr		3,700	
	To Realisation A/c				37,000
	(Being loss on realisation transferred to partners' capital account)				

20. The firm of Manjeet, Sujeet and Jagjeet was dissolved on 31st March, 2018. It was agreed that Sujeet will take care of the dissolution related activities and will get 10% of the value of assets realised, Sujeet agreed to bear the realisation expenses. Assets realised ₹ 10,00,750 and realisation expenses were ₹ 90,000, which were paid from the firm's cash. ₹ 4,50,000 were paid to the creditors in full settlement of their claim.

Pass necessary journal entries for the above transactions in the books of the firm. **All India 2019**

Ans. **JOURNAL**

Date	Particulars		LF	Amt (Dr)	Amt (Cr)
	Realisation A/c	Dr		1,00,075	
	To Sujeet's Capital A/c				1,00,075
	(Being 10% of assets realised given to Sujeet for dissolution activities)				
	Bank A/c	Dr		10,00,750	
	To Realisation A/c				10,00,750
	(Being assets realised)				
	Realisation A/c	Dr		90,000	
	To Bank A/c				90,000
	(Being realisation expenses paid)				
	Realisation A/c	Dr		4,50,000	
	To Bank A/c				4,50,000
	(Being creditors paid)				

21. Jain, Sharma and Verma were partners in a firm sharing profits in the ratio of 1 : 2 : 1. On 31st March, 2018 their firm was dissolved. It was agreed that Sharma will look after the dissolution work and will be paid ₹ 15,000 as remuneration. The dissolution expenses were ₹ 5,000. ₹ 2,84,000 were paid to the creditors in full settlement of their claim of ₹ 3,00,000. Dissolution of the firm resulted into a loss of ₹ 18,000. Pass necessary journal entries for the above transactions. **All India 2019**

Ans.

JOURNAL

Date	Particulars		LF	Amt (Dr)	Amt (Cr)
2018					
Mar 31	Realisation A/c	Dr		15,000	
	To Sharma's Capital A/c				15,000
	(Being remuneration to partner credited to his capital account)				
	Realisation A/c	Dr		2,84,000	
	To Cash A/c				2,84,000
	(Being creditors paid)				
	Jain's Capital Ac	Dr		4,500	
	Sharma's Capital A/c	Dr		9,000	
	Verma's Capital A/c	Dr		4,500	
	To Realisation A/c				18,000
	(Being loss transferred to partners' captial account)				

22. Ravi, Shankar and Madhur were partners in a firm sharing profits in the ratio of 7 : 2 : 1. On 31st March, 2018, the firm was dissolved, after transferring sundry assets (other than cash in hand and cash at bank) and third party liabilities in the realisation accounts. The following transactions took place

(*i*) Debtors amounting to ₹ 1,40,000 were handed over to a debt collection agency which charged 5% commision. The remaining debtors were ₹ 47,000 out of which debtors of ₹ 17,000 could not be recovered because the same become insolvent.

(*ii*) Creditors amounting to ₹ 5,000 were paid ₹ 3,500 in full settlement of their claim and balance creditors were handed over stock of ₹ 90,000 in full settlement of their claim of ₹ 95,000.

(*iii*) A bills receivable ₹ 2,000 discounted with the bank was dishonoured by its acceptor and the same had to be met by the firm.

(*iv*) Profit on realisation amounted to ₹ 6,000.

Pass necessary journal entries for the above transactions in the books of Ravi, Shankar and Madhur. **Delhi 2019**

Ans.

JOURNAL

Date	Particulars		LF	Amt (Dr)	Amt (Cr)
(i)	Bank A/c (1,40,000 – 7,000)	Dr		1,33,000	
	To Realisation A/c				1,33,000
	(Being debtors realised and paid 5% commission)				
	Bank A/c	Dr		30,000	
	To Realisation A/c				30,000
	(Being remaining debtors realised)				
(ii)	Realisation A/c	Dr		3,500	
	To Bank A/c				3,500
	(Being creditors paid)				
	Note No entry will be passed for assets handed over to creditors in full settlement.				

Date	Particulars	LF	Amt (Dr)	Amt (Cr)
(iii)	Realisation A/c Dr To Bank A/c (Being bill dishonoured paid by firm)		2,000	2,000
(iv)	Realisation A/c Dr To Ravi's Capital A/c To Shankar's Capital A/c To Madhur's Capital A/c (Being profit on realisation distributed among partners)		6,000	4,200 1,200 600

23. Gaurav, Saurabh and Vaibhav were partners in a firm sharing profits and losses in the ratio of 2 : 2 : 1. They decided to dissolve the firm on 31st March, 2018. After transferring sundry assets (other than cash in hand and cash at bank) and third party liabilities to realisation account, the assets were realised and liabilities were paid-off as follows

(*i*) A machinery with a book value of ₹ 6,00,000 was taken over by Gaurav at 50% and stock worth ₹ 5,000 was taken over by a creditor of ₹ 9,000 in full settlement of his claim.

(*ii*) Land and building (book value ₹ 3,00,000) was sold for ₹ 4,00,000 through a broker who charged 2% commission.

(*iii*) The remaining creditors were paid ₹ 76,000 in full settlement of their claim and the remaining assets were taken over by Vaibhav for ₹ 17,000.

(*iv*) Bank loan of ₹ 3,00,000 was paid alongwith interest of ₹ 21,000.

Pass necessary journal entries for the above transactions in the books of the firm. **Delhi 2019**

Ans. **JOURNAL**

Date	Particulars	LF	Amt (Dr)	Amt (Cr)
(i)	Gaurav's Capital A/c (6,00,000 × 50%) Dr To Realisation A/c (Being machinery taken over at 50%) **Note** No entry will be passed for assets taken over by creditors in full settlement of claim.		3,00,000	3,00,000
(ii)	Bank A/c Dr To Realisation A/c (Being building sold)		4,00,000	4,00,000
	Realisation A/c Dr To Bank A/c (Being commission paid)		8,000	8,000
(iii)	Realisation A/c Dr To Bank A/c (Being remaining creditors paid)		76,000	76,000
	Vaibhav's Capital A/c Dr To Realisation A/c (Being assets taken over by Vaibhav)		17,000	17,000
(iv)	Realisation A/c Dr To Bank A/c (Being loan paid with interest)		3,21,000	3,21,000

24. Ankit, Bobby and Kartik were partners in a firm sharing profits in the ratio 4 : 3 : 3. The firm was dissolved on 31st March, 2018. Pass the necessary journal entries for the following transactions after various assets (other than cash and bank) and third party liabilities had been transferred to realisation account

(*i*) The firm had stock of ₹ 80,000. Ankit took over 50% of the stock at a discount of 20% while the remaining stock was sold off at a profit of 30% on cost.

(*ii*) A liability under a suit for damages included in creditors was settled at ₹ 32,000 as against only ₹ 13,000 provided in the books. Total creditors of the firm were ₹ 50,000.

(*iii*) Bobby's sister's loan of ₹ 20,000 was paid-off alongwith interest of ₹ 2,000.

(*iv*) Kartik's loan of ₹ 12,000 was settled at ₹ 12,500. **Delhi 2019**

Ans.

JOURNAL

Date	Particulars		LF	Amt (Dr)	Amt (Cr)
2018					
Mar 31 (i)	Ankit's Capital A/c (80,000 × 50% × 80%)	Dr		32,000	
	To Realisation A/c				32,000
	(Being 50% of the stock taken at 20% discount)				
Mar 31	Bank A/c (40,000 × 30% + 40,000)	Dr		52,000	
	To Realisation A/c				52,000
	(Being remaining 50% stock was sold at a profit of 30% on cost)				
Mar 31 (ii)	Realisation A/c	Dr		32,000	
	To Bank A/c				32,000
	(Being liability under a suit for damages was settled)				
Mar 31	Realisation A/c (50,000 – 13,000)	Dr		37,000	
	To Bank A/c				37,000
	(Being remaining creditors paid)				
Mar 31 (iii)	Realisation A/c	Dr		22,000	
	To Bank A/c				22,000
	(Being Bobby's sister's loan paid with interest)				
Mar 31 (iv)	Interest on Kartik's Loan A/c	Dr		500	
	To Kartik's Loan A/c				500
	(Being interest due)				
Mar 31	Kartik's Loan A/c	Dr		12,500	
	To Bank A/c				12,500
	(Being amount of loan paid with interest)				

Working Note

Total stock = ₹ 80,000

Ankit took = 80,000 × 50% = ₹ 40,000

(–) Discount (40,000 × 20%) = ₹ 8,000

₹ 32,000

Remaining Stock = ₹ 40,000

(+) Profit @ 30% = ₹ 12,000

₹ 52,000

5/6 Marks Questions

25. T, U and V were partners in a firm sharing profits and losses in the ratio of 2 : 1 : 2. Their firm was incurring huge losses thus it had to be closed. After transferring assets (other than cash in hand and bank) and third party liabilities to realisation account the following transactions took place

(*i*) T took away 50% of the stock at book value less 10% for ₹ 90,000 and the remaining stock was sold for ₹ 40,000.

(*ii*) Creditors of ₹ 78,000 took over machinery of ₹ 80,000 in full settlement of their claim.

(*iii*) ₹ 5,000 debtors previously written-off were recovered.

(*iv*) Mrs. V's loan of ₹ 72,000 was paid by the firm.

(*v*) Loss on dissolution was ₹ 80,000.

Pass necessary journal entries for the above transactions in the books of T, U and V.
CBSE Term II 2022

Ans. **JOURNAL**

Date	Particulars		LF	Amt (Dr)	Amt (Cr)
(i) (a)	T's Capital A/c	Dr		90,000	
	To Realisation A/c				90,000
	(Being 50% stock taken over by T)				
(b)	Cash A/c	Dr		40,000	
	To Realisation A/c				40,000
	(Being remaning stock sold for cash)				
(ii)	No entry				
(iii)	Cash A/c	Dr		5,000	
	To Realisation A/c				5,000
	(Being debtors previously written-off recovered)				
(iv)	Realisation A/c	Dr		72,000	
	To Cash A/c				72,000
	(Being Mrs. V's loan paid by the firm)				
(v)	T's Capital A/c	Dr		32,000	
	U's Capital A/c	Dr		16,000	
	V's Capital A/c	Dr		32,000	
	To Realisation A/c				80,000
	(Being loss on realisation transferred to partners' capital account)				

26. Vasudha and Dewan were partners in a firm sharing profits and losses in the ratio 2 : 3. The firm was dissolved on 31st March, 2019. After transfer of assets (other than cash) and external liabilities to Realisation Account, the following transactions took place

(*i*) Investments of the value of ₹ 60,000 were sold in the open market for ₹ 63,000 for which a commission of ₹ 700 was paid to the broker.

(*ii*) Creditors worth ₹ 65,000 were settled by handing over the entire stock to them along with a payment of ₹ 23,000 by cheque.

(*iii*) There was old furniture which had been completely written-off from the books of the firm. It was taken over by Vasudha at ₹ 2,000.

(*iv*) Dewan undertook to pay Mrs. Dewan's loan of ₹ 45,000.

(*v*) Dewan was appointed to look after the process of dissolution for which he was allowed a remuneration of ₹ 7,000. He agreed to bear the dissolution expenses. Actual expenses incurred by Dewan were ₹ 11,000, which were paid by the firm.

(*vi*) Loss on realisation amounted to ₹ 9,000

Pass the necessary journal entries to record the above transactions in the books of the firm. **CBSE 2020**

Ans.

JOURNAL

Date	Particulars		LF	Amt (Dr)	Amt (Cr)
(i)	Bank A/c	Dr		62,300	
	To Realisation A/c				62,300
	(Being investment sold)				
(ii)	Realisation A/c	Dr		23,000	
	To Bank A/c				23,000
	(Being creditors paid by cheque)				
(iii)	Vasudha's capital A/c	Dr		2,000	
	To Realisation A/c				2,000
	(Being furniture taken by her)				
(iv)	Realisation A/c	Dr		45,000	
	To Dewan's Capital A/c				45,000
	(Being Ms. Dewan's loan amount settled)				
(v)	Realisation A/c	Dr		7,000	
	Dewan's Capital A/c	Dr		4,000	
	To Bank A/c				11,000
	(Being dissolution expenses paid)				
(vi)	Vasudha's Capital A/c	Dr		3,600	
	Dewan's Capital A/c	Dr		5,400	
	To Realisation A/c				9,000
	(Being realisation loss transferred to capital account)				

27. A, B and C were partners sharing profits and losses in the ratio of 2 : 2 : 1. Their balance sheet as at 31st March, 2018 was as follows

Balance Sheet of A, B and C
as at 31st March, 2018

Liabilities		Amt (₹)	Assets		Amt (₹)
Capitals A/cs			Cash at Bank		3,00,000
			Sundry Debtors	1,95,000	
A	7,50,000		(–) Provision for Bad Debts	(5,000)	1,90,000
B	3,00,000				
C	2,50,000	13,00,000	Stock		3,00,000
Creditors		2,00,000	Fixed Assets		7,10,000
		15,00,000			15,00,000

On the above date, they dissolved the firm and following amounts were realised

Fixed Assets ₹ 6,75,000; Stock ₹ 3,39,000; Debtors ₹ 1,35,000; Creditors were paid ₹ 1,85,000 in full settlement of their claim. Expenses on realisation amounted to ₹ 19,000.

Pass the necessary journal entries on the dissolution of the firm. **All India 2019**

Ans.

JOURNAL

Date	Particulars		LF	Amt (Dr)	Amt (Cr)
	Realisation A/c	Dr		12,05,000	
	To Stock A/c				3,00,000
	To Debtors A/c				1,95,000
	To Fixed Assets A/c				7,10,000
	(Being assets transferred to realisation account)				
	Creditors A/c	Dr		2,00,000	
	Provision for Bad Debts	Dr		5,000	
	To Realisation A/c				2,05,000
	(Being liabilities transferred to realisation account)				
	Cash/Bank A/c	Dr		11,49,000	
	To Realisation A/c				11,49,000
	(Being assets realised)				
	Realisation A/c	Dr		1,85,000	
	To Cash/Bank A/c				1,85,000
	(Being creditors paid-off)				
	Realisation A/c	Dr		19,000	
	To Cash A/c				19,000
	(Being realisation expenses paid)				
	A's Capital A/c	Dr		22,000	
	B's Capital A/c	Dr		22,000	
	C's Capital A/c	Dr		11,000	
	To Realisation A/c				55,000
	(Being loss transferred to partners' capital account)				

28. Ashish and Kanav were partners in a firm sharing profits and losses in the ratio of 3 : 2. On 31st March, 2018 their balance sheet was as follows

Balance Sheet of Ashish and Kanav
as at 31st March, 2018

Liabilities		Amt (₹)	Assets	Amt (₹)
Trade Creditors		42,000	Bank	35,000
Employees' Provident Fund		60,000	Stock	24,000
Mrs Ashish's Loan		9,000	Debtors	19,000
Kanav's Loan		35,000	Furniture	40,000
Workmen's Compensation Fund		20,000	Plant	2,10,000
Investment Fluctuation Reserve		4,000	Investments	32,000
			Profit and Loss A/c	10,000
Capital A/cs				
Ashish	1,20,000			
Kanav	80,000	2,00,000		
		3,70,000		3,70,000

On the above date, they decided to dissolve the firm.

(*i*) Ashish agreed to take over furniture at ₹ 38,000 and pay-off Mrs Ashish's loan.

(*ii*) Debtors realised ₹ 18,500 and plant realised 10% more.

(*iii*) Kanav took over 40% of the stock at 20% less than the book value. Remaining stock was sold at a gain of 10%.

(*iv*) Trade creditors took over investments in full settlement.

(*v*) Kanav agreed to take over the responsibility of completing dissolution at an agreed remuneration of ₹ 12,000 and to bear realisation expenses. Actual expenses of realisation amounted to ₹ 8,000.

Prepare realisation account. **All India 2019**

Ans. Dr **Realisation Account** Cr

Particulars		Amt (₹)	Particulars		Amt (₹)
To Sundry Assets			By Sundry Liabilities		
Stock	24,000		Creditors	42,000	
Debtors	19,000		Employees' Provident fund	60,000	
Furniture	40,000		Mrs. Ashish's loan	9,000	
Plant	2,10,000		Investment Fluctuation Reserve	4,000	1,15,000
Investments	32,000	3,25,000	By Ashish's Capital (Furniture)		38,000
To Ashish's Capital (Mrs Ashish's loan)		9,000	By Kanav's Capital (40% stock)		7,680
To Bank Employees' Provident Fund		60,000	By Bank Debtors	18,500	
To Kanav's Capital (Realisation expenses)		12,000	Plant	2,31,000	
			60% Stock	15,840	2,65,340
To Profit Transferred to					
Ashish's Capital A/c	12,012				
Kanav's Capital A/c	8,008	20,020			
		4,26,020			4,26,020

Working Notes

1. 40% Stock = 24,000 × 40% = ₹ 9,600
   (−) 20% = ₹ (1,920)
   ₹ 7,680

2. 60% Stock = 24,000 × 60% = ₹ 14,400
   (+) 10% = ₹ 1,440
   ₹ 15,840

29. Girija and Ganesh were partners in a firm sharing profits and losses in the ratio of 2 : 3. On 31st March, 2018 their balance sheet was as follows

Balance Sheet of Girija and Ganesh
as at 31st March, 2018

Liabilities	Amt (₹)	Assets		Amt (₹)
Creditors	80,000	Cash at Bank		20,000
Bank Overdraft	50,000	Debtors	55,000	
Girija's Brother's Loan	77,000	(−) Provision for		
Ganesh's Loan	28,000	Doubtful Debts	(2,000)	53,000
Investment Fluctuation Fund	15,000	Stock		78,000

Liabilities		Amt (₹)	Assets	Amt (₹)
Capitals A/cs			Investments	89,000
Girija	1,50,000		Buildings	2,50,000
Ganesh	1,00,000	2,50,000	Profit and Loss A/c	10,000
		5,00,000		5,00,000

On the above date, the firm was dissolved. The assets were realised and the liabilities were paid-off as follows

(*i*) Debtors of ₹ 6,000 were proved bad.

(*ii*) Girija agreed to pay-off her brother's loan.

(*iii*) One of the creditors for ₹ 10,000 was paid only ₹ 3,000 in full settlement of his account.

(*iv*) Buildings were auctioned for ₹ 1,80,000 and the auctioneer's commission amounted to ₹ 8,000.

(*v*) Ganesh took over part of stock at ₹ 4,000 (being 20% less than the book value). Balance of the stock was handed over to the remaining creditors in full settlement of their account.

(*vi*) Investments realised ₹ 9,000 less.

(*vii*) Realisation expenses amounted to ₹ 17,000 and were paid by Ganesh.

Prepare realisation account, partners' capital accounts and bank account. **Compartment 2018**

Ans. Solve as Q. no. 48 on page 243 and 244.

Loss on Realisation-Girija = ₹ 36,000 ; Ganesh = ₹ 54,000

Partner's Capital A/c-Cash paid to Girija = ₹ 1,87,000 ; Cash paid to Ganesh = ₹ 53,000

Bank A/c = ₹ 3,21,000

30. Pass necessary journal entries on the dissolution of a partnership firm in the following cases

(*i*) Dissolution expenses were ₹ 800.

(*ii*) Dissolution expenses ₹ 800 were paid by Prabhu, a partner.

(*iii*) Geeta, a partner, was appointed to look after the dissolution work, for which she was allowed a remuneration of ₹10,000. Geeta agreed to bear the dissolution expenses. Actual dissolution expenses ₹ 9,500 were paid by Geeta.

(*iv*) Janki, a partner, agreed to look after the dissolution work for a commission of ₹ 5,000. Janki agreed to bear the dissolution expenses. Actual dissolution expenses ₹ 5,500 were paid by Mohan, another partner, on behalf of Janki.

(*v*) A partner, Kavita, agreed to look after the dissolution process for a commission of ₹ 9,000. She also agreed to bear the dissolution expenses. Kavita took over furniture of ₹ 9,000 for her commission. Furniture had already been transferred to realisation account.

(*vi*) A debtor, Ravinder, for ₹ 19,000 agreed to pay the dissolution expenses which were ₹ 18,000 in full settlement of his debt. **All India 2017**

Ans.

JOURNAL

Date	Particulars		LF	Amt (Dr)	Amt (Cr)
(i)	Realisation A/c	Dr		800	
	To Bank A/c				800
	(Being expenses on dissolution paid)				

Date	Particulars		LF	Amt (Dr)	Amt (Cr)
(ii)	Realisation A/c To Prabhu's Capital A/c (Being dissolution expenses paid by Prabhu credited to his capital account)	Dr		800	800
(iii)	Realisation A/c To Geeta's Capital A/c (Being the remuneration due to Geeta)	Dr		10,000	10,000
(iv)	Realisation A/c To Janki's Capital A/c (Being the remuneration due to Janki)	Dr		5,000	5,000
(v)	No Entry				
(vi)	No Entry				

31. Pass necessary journal entries on the dissolution of a partnership firm in the following cases

(*i*) L, a partner, was appointed to look after the dissolution process for which he was given a remuneration of ₹ 10,000.

(*ii*) Dissolution expenses ₹ 8,000 were paid by the partner M.

(*iii*) Dissolution expenses were ₹ 5,000.

(*iv*) P, a partner, was appointed to look after the process of dissolution for which he was allowed a remuneration of ₹ 7,000. P agreed to bear the dissolution expenses. Actual dissolution expenses ₹ 4,000 were paid by P.

(*v*) N, a partner, was appointed to look after the process of dissolution for which he was allowed a remuneration of ₹ 9,000. N agreed to bear the dissolution expenses. Actual dissolution expenses ₹ 4,000 were paid by the firm.

(*vi*) Q, a partner, was appointed to look after the process of dissolution for which he was allowed a remuneration of ₹ 18,000. Q agreed to take over stock worth ₹ 18,000 as his remuneration. The stock had already been transferred to realisation account.

Delhi 2017

Ans. For points (*ii*), (*iii*), (*iv*) and (*vi*). Solve as Q no. 30 on page 222 and 223.

JOURNAL

Date	Particulars		LF	Amt (Dr)	Amt (Cr)
(i)	Realisation A/c To L's Capital A/c (Being remuneration payable to L)	Dr		10,000	10,000
(v)	Realisation A/c To N's Capital A/c (Being remuneration payable to N)	Dr		9,000	9,000
	N's Capital A/c To Cash A/c (Being realisation expenses paid by firm on behalf of N)	Dr		4,000	4,000

32. Lal and Pal were partners in a firm sharing profits in the ratio of 3:7. On 1st April, 2015, their firm was dissolved. After transferring assets (other than cash) and outsider's liabilities to realisation account, you are given the following information

(*i*) A creditor of ₹ 3,60,000 accepted machinery valued at ₹ 5,00,000 and paid to the firm ₹ 1,40,000.

(*ii*) A second creditor for ₹ 50,000 accepted stock at ₹ 45,000 in full settlement of his claim.

(*iii*) A third creditor amounting to ₹ 90,000 accepted ₹ 45,000 in cash and investments worth ₹ 43,000 in full settlement of his claim.

(*iv*) Loss on dissolution was ₹ 15,000.

Pass necessary journal entries for the above transactions in the books of firm assuming that all payments were made by cheque. **All India 2016**

Ans.

JOURNAL

Date	Particulars		LF	Amt (Dr)	Amt (Cr)
2015 Apr 1					
(i)	Bank A/c	Dr		1,40,000	
	To Realisation A/c				1,40,000
	(Being payment received from creditors)				
(ii)	No Entry				
(iii)	Realisation A/c	Dr		45,000	
	To Bank A/c				45,000
	(Being partial payment made to creditors through cheque)				
(iv)	Lal's Capital A/c (15,000 × 3 / 10)	Dr		4,500	
	Pal's Capital A/c (15,000 × 7 / 10)	Dr		10,500	
	To Realisation A/c				15,000
	(Being loss on realisation transferred to partners' capital account in the ratio 3:7)				

33. L and M were partners in a firm sharing profits in the ratio of 2:3. On 28th February, 2016, the firm was dissolved. After transferring assets (other than cash) and outsiders' liabilities to realisation account you are given the following information

(*i*) A creditor for ₹ 1,40,000 accepted building valued at ₹ 1,80,000 and paid to the firm ₹ 40,000.

(*ii*) A second creditor for ₹ 30,000 accepted machinery valued at ₹ 28,000 in full settlement of his claim.

(*iii*) A third creditor amounting to ₹ 70,000 accepted ₹ 30,000 in cash and investments of the book value of ₹ 45,000 in full settlement of his claim.

(*iv*) Loss on dissolution was ₹ 4,000.

Pass necessary journal entries for the above transactions in the books of the firm assuming that all payments were made by cheque. **Delhi 2016**

Ans. Solve as Q no. 30 on page 222 and 223.

34. Mala, Neela and Kala were partners sharing profits in the ratio of 3 : 2 : 1. On 1st March, 2015, their firm was dissolved. The assets were realised and liabilities were paid-off. The accountant prepared realisation account, partners' capital account and cash account, but forgot to post few amounts in these accounts.

You are required to complete these below given accounts by posting correct amounts.

Dr **Realisation Account** Cr

Particulars		Amt (₹)	Particulars		Amt (₹)
To Sundry Assets A/c			By Provision for Doubtful Debts A/c		1,000
Machinery	10,000		By Sundry Creditors A/c		15,000
Stock	21,000		By Sheela's Loan A/c		13,000
Debtors	20,000		By Repairs and Renewals Reserve A/c		1,200
Prepaid Insurance	400		By Cash A/c (Assets sold)		
Investments	3,000	54,400	Machinery	8,000	
To Mala's Capital A/c (Sheela's loan)		13,000	Stock	14,000	
To Cash A/c (Creditors paid)		15,000	Debtors	16,000	38,000
To Cash A/c (Dishonoured bill paid)		5,000	By Mala's Capital A/c (Investments)		2,000
To Cash A/c (Expenses)		800	....		...
		88,200			88,200

Dr **Partners' Capital Account** Cr

Particulars	Mala (₹)	Neela (₹)	Kala (₹)	Particulars	Mala (₹)	Neela (₹)	Kala (₹)
....	...	—	—	....	...	...	...
....	...	...	...	....	...	—	—
To Cash A/c	12,000	9,000	—	By Cash A/c	—	—	1,000
	23,000	15,000	3,000		23,000	15,000	3,000

Dr **Cash Account** Cr

Particulars	Amt (₹)	Particulars	Amt (₹)
To Balance b/d	2,800	By Realisation A/c (Creditors paid)	15,000
To Realisation A/c (Sale of assets)	38,000	By Dishonoured Bill A/c	5,000
To Kala's Capital A/c	1,000	....	...
		By Mala's Capital A/c	12,000
		By Neela's Capital A/c	9,000
	41,800		41,800

All India 2015

Ans. Dr **Realisation Account** Cr

Particulars		Amt (₹)	Particulars		Amt (₹)
To Sundry Assets A/c			By Provision for Doubtful Debts A/c		1,000
Machinery	10,000		By Sundry Creditors A/c		15,000
Stock	21,000		By Sheela' Loan A/c		13,000
Debtors	20,000		By Repairs and Renewals Reserve A/c		1,200
Prepaid Insurance	400		By Cash A/c (Assets sold)		
Investments	3,000	54,400	Machinery	8,000	
To Mala's Capital A/c (Sheela's loan)		13,000	Stock	14,000	
To Cash A/c (Creditors paid)		15,000	Debtors	16,000	38,000
To Cash A/c (Dishonoured bill paid)		5,000	By Mala's Capital A/c (Investments)		2,000

Particulars		Amt (₹)	Particulars		Amt (₹)
To Cash A/c (Expenses)		800	By Loss Transferred to Capital A/cs		
			Mala	9,000	
			Neela	6,000	
			Kala	3,000	18,000
		88,200			88,200

Dr **Partners' Capital Account** Cr

Particulars	Mala (₹)	Neela (₹)	Kala (₹)	Particulars	Mala (₹)	Neela (₹)	Kala (₹)
To Realisation A/c (Investment)	2,000	—	—	By Balance b/d	10,000	15,000	2,000
To Realisation A/c (Loss)	9,000	6,000	3,000	By Realisation A/c (Sheela's loan)	13,000	—	—
To Cash A/c	12,000	9,000	—	By Cash A/c	—	—	1,000
	23,000	15,000	3,000		23,000	15,000	3,000

Dr **Cash Account** Cr

Particulars	Amt (₹)	Particulars	Amt (₹)
To Balance b/d	2,800	By Realisation A/c (Creditors paid)	15,000
To Realisation A/c (Sale of assets)	38,000	By Dishonoured Bill A/c	5,000
To Kala's Capital A/c	1,000	**By Realisation A/c (Expenses)**	**800**
		By Mala's Capital A/c	12,000
		By Neela' Capital A/c	9,000
	41,800		41,800

35. Bora, Singh and Ibrahim were partners in a firm sharing profits in the ratio 5 : 3 : 1. On 2nd March, 2015, their firm was dissolved. The assets were realised and the liabilities were paid-off. Given below are the realisation account, partners' capital accounts and bank account of the firm. The accountant of the firm left a few amounts unposted in these accounts. You are required to complete these accounts by posting the correct amounts.

Dr **Realisation Account** Cr

Particulars		Amt (₹)	Particulars		Amt (₹)
To Stock A/c		10,000	By Provision for Bad Debts A/c		5,000
To Debtors A/c		25,000	By Sundry Creditors A/c		16,600
To Plant and Machinery A/c		40,000	By Bills Payable A/c		3,400
To Bank A/c			By Mortgage Loan A/c		15,000
Sundry Creditors	16,000		By Bank A/c (Assets realised)		
Bills Payable	3,400		Stock	6,700	
Mortgage Loan	15,000	34,400	Debtors	12,500	
To Bank A/c (Outstanding repairs)		400	Plant and Machinery	36,000	55,200
To Bank A/c (Expenses)		620	By Bank A/c (Unrecorded assets realised)		6,220
			By		...
		1,10,420			1,10,420

Dr **Partners' Capital Account** Cr

Particulars	Bora (₹)	Singh (₹)	Ibrahim (₹)	Particulars	Bora (₹)	Singh (₹)	Ibrahim (₹)
....	...	...	...	By Balance b/d	22,000	18,000	10,000
....	...	...	...	By General Reserve A/c	2,500	1,500	500
	24,500	19,500	10,500		24,500	19,500	10,500

Dr **Bank Account** Cr

Particulars	Amt (₹)	Particulars	Amt (₹)
To Balance b/d	19,500	By Realisation A/c (Liabilities)	34,400
To Realisation A/c (Assets realised)	55,200	By Realisation A/c (Unrecorded liabilities)	400
....	...	By	...
		By	...
	80,920		80,920

Delhi 2015

Ans. Solve as Q no. 34 on page 224 to 226.
Loss on Realisation : Bora = ₹ 5,000, Singh = ₹ 3,000, Ibrahim = ₹ 1,000; Total of Bank Account = ₹ 80,920.

36. Bhuvan, Suraj and Ibrahim were partners in a firm sharing profits in the ratio of 3:2:1. On 30th June, 2014, they decided to dissolve the firm. Following was the balance sheet of the firm on that date.

Balance Sheet
as at 31st June, 2014

Liabilities		Amt (₹)	Assets	Amt (₹)
Creditors		50,400	Cash	13,700
Investment Fluctuation Fund		10,000	Stock	20,100
Reserve Fund		12,000	Debtors	62,600
Capitals A/c				
Bhuvan	30,000		Investments	16,000
Suraj	20,000		Furniture	20,000
Ibrahim	10,000	60,000		
		1,32,400		1,32,400

The assets were realised and the liabilities were paid-off as follows

(*i*) Investments were taken over by Bhuvan for ₹ 18,000.
(*ii*) Stock was taken over by Suraj for ₹ 17,500 and furniture was taken over by Ibrahim at book value.
(*iii*) ₹ 60,500 were realised from the debtors.
(*iv*) Creditors were settled in full and realisation expenses were ₹ 4,500.

Prepare realisation account, cash account and partners' capital accounts. **All India (C) 2015**

Ans. Dr **Realisation Account** Cr

Particulars		Amt (₹)	Particulars		Amt (₹)
To Sundry Assets A/c			By Sundry Liabilities A/c		
Stock	20,100		Creditors	50,400	
Debtors	62,600		Investment Fluctuation Fund	10,000	60,400
Furniture	20,000		By Bhuvan's Capital A/c (Investment)		18,000
Investments	16,000	1,18,700	By Suraj's Capital A/c (Stock)		17,500
To Cash A/c			By Ibrahim's Capital A/c (Furniture)		20,000
Creditors	50,400		By Cash A/c (Debtors)		60,500
Expenses	4,500	54,900			
To Profit Transferred to Capital A/c					
Bhuvan	1,400				
Suraj	933				
Ibrahim	467	2,800			
		1,76,400			1,76,400

Dr **Partners' Capital Account** Cr

Particulars	Bhuvan (₹)	Suraj (₹)	Ibrahim (₹)	Particulars	Bhuvan (₹)	Suraj (₹)	Ibrahim (₹)
To Realisation A/c (Assets taken over)	18,000	17,500	20,000	By Balance b/d	30,000	20,000	10,000
				By Reserve Fund A/c	6,000	4,000	2,000
To Cash A/c (Final payment)	19,400	7,433	—	By Realisation A/c (Profit)	1,400	933	467
				By Cash A/c (Cash brought in)	—	—	7,533
	37,400	24,933	20,000		37,400	24,933	20,000

Dr **Cash Account** Cr

Particulars	Amt (₹)	Particulars	Amt (₹)
To Balance b/d	13,700	By Realisation A/c (Creditors expenses paid)	54,900
To Realisation A/c (Asset realised)	60,500		
To Ibrahim's Capital A/c (Cash brought in)	7,533	By Bhuvan's Capital A/c (Final payment)	19,400
		By Suraj's Capital A/c (Final payment)	7,433
	81,733		81,733

37. Parth and Shivika were partners in a firm sharing profits in the ratio of 3:2. The balance sheet of the firm on 31st March, 2014, was as follows

Balance Sheet
as at 31st March, 2014

Liabilities		Amt (₹)	Assets	Amt (₹)
Sundry Creditors		80,000	Bank	1,72,000
Shivika's Sister's Loan		20,000	Debtors	27,000
Capitals A/cs			Stock	50,000
Parth	1,75,000		Furniture	2,20,000
Shivika	1,94,000	3,69,000		
		4,69,000		4,69,000

On the above date, the firm was dissolved. The assets were realised and the liabilities were paid-off as follows

(*i*) 50% of the furniture was taken over by Parth at 20% less than book value. The remaining furniture was sold for ₹ 1,05,000.
(*ii*) Debtors realised ₹ 26,000.
(*iii*) Stock was taken over by Shivika for ₹ 29,000.
(*iv*) Shivika's sister's loan was paid-off alongwith an interest of ₹ 2,000.
(*v*) Expenses on realisation amounted to ₹ 5,000.

Prepare realisation account, partners' capital accounts and bank account. **Delhi (C) 2015**

Ans. Dr **Realisation Account** Cr

Particulars		Amt (₹)	Particulars		Amt (₹)
To Sundry Assets A/c			By Sundry Liabilities A/c		
Debtors	27,000		Creditors	80,000	
Stock	50,000		Shivika's Sister's Loan	20,000	1,00,000
Furniture	2,20,000	2,97,000	By Parth's Capital A/c (50% furntiure)		88,000
To Bank A/c			By Bank A/c (Assets realised)		
Creditors	80,000		Furniture (50%)	1,05,000	
Shivika's Sisters's Loan with Interest (20,000 + 2,000)	22,000		Debtors	26,000	1,31,000
Expenses	5,000	1,07,000	By Shivika's Capital A/c (Stock)		29,000
			By Loss Transferred to Capital A/c		
			Parth	33,600	
			Shivika	22,400	56,000
		4,04,000			4,04,000

Dr **Partners' Capital Account** Cr

Particulars	Parth (₹)	Shivika (₹)	Particulars	Parth (₹)	Shivika (₹)
To Realisation A/c (Furniture)	88,000	—	By Balance c/d	1,75,000	1,94,000
To Realisation A/c (Stock)	—	29,000			
To Realisation A/c (Loss)	33,600	22,400			
To Bank A/c (Final payment)	53,400	1,42,600			
	1,75,000	1,94,000		1,75,000	1,94,000

Dr **Bank Account** Cr

Particulars		Amt (₹)	Particulars	Amt (₹)
To Balance b/d		1,72,000	By Realisation A/c (Creditors)	80,000
To Realisation A/c			By Realisation A/c (Shivika's sister's loan + interest)	22,000
Furniture	1,05,000			
Debtors	26,000	1,31,000	By Realisation A/c (Expenses)	5,000
			By Parth's Capital A/c (Final payment)	53,400
			By Shivika's Capital A/c (Final payment)	1,42,600
		3,03,000		3,03,000

38. Hanif and Jubed were partners in a firm sharing profits in the ratio of their capitals. On 31st March, 2013, their balance sheet was as follows

Balance Sheet
as at 31st March, 2013

Liabilities		Amt (₹)	Assets	Amt (₹)
Creditors		1,50,000	Bank	2,00,000
Workmen's Compensation Fund		3,00,000	Debtors	3,40,000
General Reserve		75,000	Stock	1,50,000
Hanif's Current A/c		25,000	Furniture	4,60,000
Capital A/cs			Machinery	8,20,000
Hanif	10,00,000		Jubed's Current A/c	80,000
Jubed	5,00,000	15,00,000		
		20,50,000		20,50,000

On the above date, the firm was dissolved

(*i*) Debtors were realised at a discount of 5%. 50% of the stock was taken over by Hanif at 10% less than the book value. Remaining stock was sold for ₹ 65,000.

(*ii*) Furniture was taken over by Jubed for ₹ 1,35,000. Machinery was sold as scrap for ₹ 74,000.

(*iii*) Creditors were paid in full.

(*iv*) Expenses on realisation ₹ 8,000 were paid by Hanif.

Prepare realisation account. **All India 2014**

Ans. Dr **Realisation Account** Cr

Particulars		Amt (₹)	Particulars		Amt (₹)
To Sundry Assets A/c			By Sundry Liabilities A/c		
Debtors	3,40,000		Creditors		1,50,000
Stock	1,50,000		By Bank A/c (Assets realised)		
Furniture	4,60,000		Debtors (3,40,000 – 5%)	3,23,000	
Machinery	8,20,000	17,70,000	Stock	65,000	
To Bank A/c (Creditors)		1,50,000	Machinery	74,000	4,62,000
To Hanif's Current A/c		8,000	By Hanif's Current A/c (Stock) (WN)		67,500
(Realisation expenses)			By Jubed's Current A/c (Furniture)		1,35,000
			By Loss Transferred to Current A/c		
			Hanif	7,42,333	
			Jubed	3,71,167	11,13,500
		19,28,000			19,28,000

Working Note

Stock taken over by Hanif = 50% of 15,000 = 75,000
(–) 10% = (7,500)
67,500

39. Shanti and Satya were partners in a firm sharing profits in the ratio of 4:1. On 31st March, 2013, their balance sheet was as follows

Balance Sheet
as at 31st March, 2013

Liabilities		Amt (₹)	Assets	Amt (₹)
Creditors		45,000	Bank	55,000
Workmen's Compensation Fund		40,000	Debtors	60,000
Satya's Current A/c		65,000	Stock	85,000
Capital A/cs			Furniture	1,00,000
Shanti	2,00,000		Machinery	1,30,000
Satya	1,00,000	3,00,000	Shanti's Current A/c	20,000
		4,50,000		4,50,000

On the above date, the firm was dissolved

(*i*) Shanti took over 40% of the stock at 10% less than its book value and the remaining stock was sold for ₹ 40,000. Furniture realised ₹ 80,000.

(*ii*) All unrecorded investment was sold for ₹ 20,000. Machinery was sold at a loss of ₹ 60,000.

(*iii*) Debtors realised ₹ 55,000.

(*iv*) There was an outstanding bill for repairs for which ₹ 19,000 were paid.

Prepare realisation account. **Delhi 2014**

Ans. Dr **Realisation Account** Cr

Particulars		Amt (₹)	Particulars		Amt (₹)
To Sundry Assets A/c			By Sundry Liabilities A/c		
Debtors	60,000		Creditors		45,000
Stock	85,000		By Bank A/c (Assets realised)		
Machinery	1,30,000		Machinery (1,30,000 − 60,000)	70,000	
Furniture	1,00,000	3,75,000	Stock	40,000	
To Bank A/c (Liabilities paid-off)			Furniture	80,000	
Creditors	45,000		Debtors	55,000	
Outstanding Repair Bill	19,000	64,000	Unrecorded Investment	20,000	2,65,000
			By Shanti's Current A/c (Stock) (WN)		30,600
			By Loss Transferred to Capital A/cs		
			Shanti	78,720	
			Satya	19,680	98,400
		4,39,000			4,39,000

Working Note

Stock taken over by Shanti = 40% of 85,000 = 34,000

(−) 10 % = (3,400)

30,600

40. Verma and Sharma were partners sharing profits in the ratio of 3 : 1. On 31st March, 2011, their balance sheet was as follows

Balance Sheet
as at 31st March, 2011

Liabilities		Amt (₹)	Assets	Amt (₹)
Creditors		70,000	Land and Building	70,000
Capital A/cs			Machinery	60,000
Verma	1,20,000		Debtors	80,000
Sharma	80,000	2,00,000	Bank	60,000
		2,70,000		2,70,000

The firm was dissolved on 1st April, 2011 and the assets and liabilities were settled as follows

(*i*) Creditors of ₹ 50,000 took over land and building in full settlement of their claim.
(*ii*) Remaining creditors were paid in cash.
(*iii*) Machinery was sold at a depreciation of 30%.
(*iv*) Debtors were collected at a cost of ₹ 500.
(*v*) Expenses on realisation were ₹ 1,700.

Pass necessary journal entries for dissolution of the firm. **Delhi 2012**

Ans.

JOURNAL

Date	Particulars		LF	Amt (Dr)	Amt (Cr)
2011 Apr 1	Realisation A/c	Dr		2,10,000	
	To Land and Building A/c				70,000
	To Machinery A/c				60,000
	To Debtors A/c				80,000
	(Being assets transferred to realisation account)				
	Creditors A/c	Dr		70,000	
	To Realisation A/c				70,000
	(Being creditors transferred to realisation account)				
	Realisation A/c	Dr		20,000	
	To Bank A/c (70,000 − 50,000)				20,000
	(Being remaining creditors paid-off)				
	Bank A/c (42,000 + 79,500)	Dr		1,21,500	
	To Realisation A/c				1,21,500
	(Being machinery of ₹ 42,000 and debtors at ₹ 79,500 realised)				
	Realisation A/c	Dr		1,700	
	To Bank A/c				1,700
	(Being realisation expenses paid)				
	Verma's Capital A/c (40,200 × 3/ 4)	Dr		30,150	
	Sharma's Capital A/c (40,200 × 1/ 4)	Dr		10,050	
	To Realisation A/c				40,200
	(Being realisation loss transferred to Partners' capital account)				
	Verma's Capital A/c	Dr		89,850	
	Sharma's Capital A/c	Dr		69,950	
	To Bank A/c				1,59,800
	(Being final payment made to partners)				

Working Notes

1. Dr **Realisation Account** Cr

Particulars		Amt (₹)	Particulars		Amt (₹)
To Sundry Assets A/c			By Creditors A/c		70,000
Land and Building	70,000		By Bank A/c		
Machinery	60,000		Machinery	42,000	
Debtors	80,000	2,10,000	Debtors	79,500	1,21,500
To Bank A/c (Creditors)		20,000	By Loss Transferred to		
To Bank A/c (Expenses)		1,700	Verma's Capital A/c	30,150	
			Sharma's Capital A/c	10,050	40,200
		2,31,700			2,31,700

2. Dr **Partners' Capital Account** Cr

Particulars	Verma (₹)	Sharma (₹)	Particulars	Verma (₹)	Sharma (₹)
To Realisation A/c (Loss)	30,150	10,050	By Balance b/d	1,20,000	80,000
To Bank A/c (Final payment)	89,850	69,950			
	1,20,000	80,000		1,20,000	80,000

3. No entry is required for adjustment (*i*), since creditors have accepted the asset (land and building) in full and final settlement.

41. A and B were partners in a firm sharing profits in the ratio of 3 : 2. On 31st March, 2011, the balance sheet of the firm was as follows

Balance Sheet
as at 31st March, 2011

Liabilities		Amt (₹)	Assets	Amt (₹)
Sundry Creditors		1,17,000	Building	2,40,000
Capital A/cs			Furniture	1,75,000
A	3,00,000		Debtors	80,000
B	2,00,000	5,00,000	Stock	75,000
			Cash	47,000
		6,17,000		6,17,000

The firm was dissolved on 1st April, 2011 and the assets and liabilities were settled as follows

(*i*) Building was taken over by creditors as their full and final payment.
(*ii*) Furniture was taken over by B for cash payment at 5% less than the book value.
(*iii*) Debtors were collected by a debt collection agency at a cost of ₹ 5,000.
(*iv*) Stock realised ₹ 70,500.
(*v*) B agreed to bear all realisation expenses. For this service, B is paid ₹ 500. Actual expense on realisation amounted to ₹ 1,000.

Pass necessary journal entries for dissolution of the firm. **Delhi 2012**

Ans.

JOURNAL

Date	Particulars		LF	Amt (Dr)	Amt (Cr)
2011 Apr 1	Realisation A/c	Dr		5,70,000	
	To Building A/c				2,40,000
	To Furniture A/c				1,75,000
	To Debtors A/c				80,000
	To Stock A/c				75,000
	(Being assets transferred to realisation account)				
	Creditors A/c	Dr		1,17,000	
	To Realisation A/c				1,17,000
	(Being creditors transferred to realisation account)				
	Cash A/c (75,000 + 70,500)	Dr		1,45,500	
	To Realisation A/c				1,45,500
	(Being cash realised from sundry assets)				
	Cash A/c (1,75,000 − 5% of 1,75,000)	Dr		1,66,250	
	To Realisation A/c				1,66,250
	(Being furniture taken over by B for cash payment)				
	Realisation A/c	Dr		500	
	To B's Capital A/c				500
	(Being B agreed to pay realisation expenses)				
	B's Capital A/c	Dr		1,000	
	To Cash A/c				1,000
	(Being realisation expenses paid by firm treated as B's drawings)				
	A's Capital A/c (1,41,750 × 3/5)	Dr		85,050	
	B's Capital A/c (1,41,750 × 2/5)	Dr		56,700	
	To Realisation A/c				1,41,750
	(Being realisation loss transferred to partners' capital account)				
	A's Capital A/c	Dr		2,14,950	
	B's Capital A/c	Dr		1,42,800	
	To Cash A/c				3,57,750
	(Being final payment made to partners)				

Working Notes

1. Dr **Realisation Account** Cr

Particulars		Amt (₹)	Particulars		Amt (₹)
To Sundry Assets A/c			By Creditors A/c		1,17,000
Building	2,40,000		By Cash A/c		
Furniture	1,75,000		Furniture	1,66,250	
Debtors	80,000		Debtors	75,000	
Stock	75,000	5,70,000	Stock	70,500	3,11,750
To B's Capital A/c (Expenses)		500	By Loss Transferred to		
			A's Capital A/c	85,050	
			B's Capital A/c	56,700	1,41,750
		5,70,500			5,70,500

2. Dr **Partners' Capital Account** Cr

Particulars	A (₹)	B (₹)	Particulars	A (₹)	B (₹)
To Realisation A/c (Loss)	85,050	56,700	By Balance b/d	3,00,000	2,00,000
To Cash A/c (Expenses on realisation)	–	1,000	By Realisation A/c (Expenses)	–	500
To Cash A/c	2,14,950	1,42,800			
	3,00,000	2,00,500		3,00,000	2,00,500

3. No entry is required for adjustment *(i)*, since creditors have accepted the asset (Building) in full and final settlement.

42. Sanjay and Sameer were partners in a firm sharing profits in the ratio of 2 : 3. On 31st March, 2011, the balance sheet of the firm was as follows

Balance Sheet
as at 31st March, 2011

Liabilities		Amt (₹)	Assets	Amt (₹)
Sundry Creditors		1,05,000	Land and Building	3,00,000
Workmen's Compensation Fund		1,00,000	Stock	1,00,000
Capital A/cs			Debtors	1,50,000
Sanjay	2,00,000		Bank	1,55,000
Sameer	3,00,000	5,00,000		
		7,05,000		7,05,000

The firm was dissolved on 1st April, 2011 and the assets and liabilities were settled as follows

(i) Sanjay agrees to take over land and building at ₹ 3,50,000 by paying cash.
(ii) Stock was sold for ₹ 90,000.
(iii) Creditors accepted debtors in full settlement of their claim.

Pass necessary journal entries for dissolution of the firm. **All India 2012**

Ans. **JOURNAL**

Date	Particulars		LF	Amt (Dr)	Amt (Cr)
2011 Apr 1	Realisation A/c	Dr		5,50,000	
	To Land and Building A/c				3,00,000
	To Stock A/c				1,00,000
	To Debtors A/c				1,50,000
	(Being assets transferred to realisation account)				
	Sundry Creditors A/c	Dr		1,05,000	
	To Realisation A/c				1,05,000
	(Being creditors transferred to realisation account)				
	Bank A/c	Dr		90,000	
	To Realisation A/c				90,000
	(Being assets realised)				
	Bank A/c	Dr		3,50,000	
	To Realisation A/c				3,50,000
	(Being land and building taken over by Sanjay for cash)				

Date	Particulars		LF	Amt (Dr)	Amt (Cr)
	Workmen's Compensation Fund A/c To Sanjay's Capital A/c (1,00,000 × 2/ 5) To Sameer's Capital A/c (1,00,000 × 3/ 5) (Being workmen's compensation fund distributed between the partners)	Dr		1,00,000	 40,000 60,000
	Sanjay's Capital A/c (5,000 × 2/ 5) Sameer's Capital A/c (5,000 × 3/ 5) To Realisation A/c (Being realisation loss transferred to partners' capital account)	Dr Dr		2,000 3,000	 5,000
	Sanjay's Capital A/c (5,95,000 × 2/ 5) Sameer's Capital A/c (5,95,000 × 3/ 5) To Bank A/c (Being final payment made to partners)	Dr Dr		2,38,000 3,57,000	 5,95,000

Working Notes

1. Dr **Realisation Account** Cr

Particulars		Amt (₹)	Particulars		Amt (₹)
To Sundry Assets A/c			By Creditors A/c		1,05,000
Land and Building	3,00,000		By Bank A/c (Stock)		90,000
Stock	1,00,000		By Bank A/c		3,50,000
Debtors	1,50,000	5,50,000	(Land and building taken over)		
			By Loss Transferred to		
			Sanjay's Capital A/c	2,000	
			Sameer's Capital A/c	3,000	5,000
		5,50,000			5,50,000

2. Dr **Partners' Capital Account** Cr

Particulars	Sanjay (₹)	Sameer (₹)	Particulars	Sanjay (₹)	Sameer (₹)
To Realisation A/c (Loss)	2,000	3,000	By Balance b/d	2,00,000	3,00,000
To Bank A/c	2,38,000	3,57,000	By Workmen's Compensation Fund A/c	40,000	60,000
	2,40,000	3,60,000		2,40,000	3,60,000

3. No entry is required for adjustment *(iii)*, since creditors have accepted debtors in full and final settlement.

43. Achal and Vichal were partners in a firm sharing profits in the ratio of 3 : 5. On 31st March, 2011, their balance sheet was as follows

Balance Sheet
as at 31st March, 2011

Liabilities		Amt (₹)	Assets	Amt (₹)
Creditors		1,79,000	Land and Building	4,00,000
Employees' Provident Fund		21,000	Machinery	3,00,000
Capital A/cs			Debtors	2,22,000
Achal	3,00,000		Cash at Bank	78,000
Vichal	5,00,000	8,00,000		
		10,00,000		10,00,000

The firm was dissolved on 1st April, 2011 and the assets and liabilities were settled as follows

(*i*) Land and building realised ₹ 4,30,000.

(*ii*) Debtors realised ₹ 2,25,000 (with interest) and ₹ 1,000 were recovered for bad debts written-off last year.

(*iii*) There was an unrecorded investment which was sold for ₹ 25,000.

(*iv*) Vichal took over machinery at ₹ 2,80,000 for cash.

(*v*) 50% of the creditors were paid ₹ 4,000 less in full settlement and the remaining creditors were paid full amount.

Pass necessary journal entries for dissolution of the firm. **All India 2012**

Ans.

JOURNAL

Date	Particulars		LF	Amt (Dr)	Amt (Cr)
2011					
Apr 1	Realisation A/c	Dr		9,22,000	
	To Land and Building A/c				4,00,000
	To Machinery A/c				3,00,000
	To Debtors A/c				2,22,000
	(Being assets transferred to realisation account)				
	Creditors A/c	Dr		1,79,000	
	Employees' Provident Fund A/c	Dr		21,000	
	To Realisation A/c				2,00,000
	(Being liabilities transferred to realisation account)				
	Bank A/c (2,25,000 + 1,000 + 25,000 + 4,30,000)	Dr		6,81,000	
	To Realisation A/c				6,81,000
	(Being cash realised from assets)				
	Bank A/c	Dr		2,80,000	
	To Realisation A/c				2,80,000
	(Being machinery took over by Vichal for cash)				
	Realisation A/c (85,500+ 89,500+ 21,000)	Dr		1,96,000	
	To Bank A/c				1,96,000
	(Being liabilities paid)				
	Realisation A/c	Dr		43,000	
	To Achal's Capital A/c (43,000 × 3/ 8)				16,125
	To Vichal's Capital A/c (43,000 × 5/ 8)				26,875
	(Being realisation profit transferred to partners' capital account)				
	Achal's Capital A/c	Dr		3,16,125	
	Vichal's Capital A/c	Dr		5,26,875	
	To Bank A/c				8,43,000
	(Being final payment made to partners)				

Working Notes

1. Dr **Realisation Account** Cr

Particulars		Amt (₹)	Particulars		Amt (₹)
To Sundry Assets A/c			By Sundry Liabilities A/c		
Land and Building	4,00,000		Creditors	1,79,000	
Machinery	3,00,000		Employees' Provident Fund	21,000	2,00,000
Debtors	2,22,000	9,22,000	By Bank A/c		
To Bank A/c			Land and Building	4,30,000	
Creditors	1,75,000		Debtors (With interest)	2,25,000	
Employees' Provident Fund	21,000	1,96,000	Bad Debts Recovered	1,000	
To Profit Transferred to			Investment	25,000	6,81,000
Achal's Capital A/c	16,125		By Bank A/c (Machinery taken over)		2,80,000
Vichal's Capital A/c	26,875	43,000			
		11,61,000			11,61,000

2. Dr **Partners' Capital Account** Cr

Particulars	Achal (₹)	Vichal (₹)	Particulars	Achal (₹)	Vichal (₹)
To Bank A/c (Final payment)	3,16,125	5,26,875	By Balance b/d	3,00,000	5,00,000
			By Realisation A/c (Profit)	16,125	26,875
	3,16,125	5,26,875		3,16,125	5,26,875

44. Pass the necessary journal entries for the following transactions on the dissolution of the firm of P and Q after the various assets (other than cash) and outside liabilities have been transferred to realisation account.

(*i*) Bank loan ₹ 12,000 was paid.

(*ii*) Stock worth ₹ 16,000 was taken over by a partner Q.

(*iii*) Partner P paid a creditor ₹ 4,000.

(*iv*) An asset not appearing in the books of accounts realised ₹ 1,200.

(*v*) Expenses of realisation ₹ 2,000 were paid by partner Q.

(*vi*) Profit on realisation ₹ 36,000 was distributed between P and Q in 5 : 4 ratio. **Delhi 2011**

Ans. **JOURNAL**

Date	Particulars		LF	Amt (Dr)	Amt (Cr)
(i)	Realisation A/c	Dr		12,000	
	To Bank A/c				12,000
	(Being bank loan paid)				
(ii)	Q's Capital A/c	Dr		16,000	
	To Realisation A/c				16,000
	(Being stock taken over by Q)				
(iii)	Realisation A/c	Dr		4,000	
	To P's Capital A/c				4,000
	(Being a creditor paid by P)				

Date	Particulars		LF	Amt (Dr)	Amt (Cr)
(iv)	Bank A/c To Realisation A/c (Being an unrecorded asset realised)	Dr		1,200	1,200
(v)	Realisation A/c To Q's Capital A/c (Being realisation expenses paid by Q)	Dr		2,000	2,000
(vi)	Realisation A/c To P's Capital A/c (36,000 × 5/9) To Q's Capital A/c (36,000 × 4/9) (Being realisation profit distributed among the partners in 5 : 4)	Dr		36,000	 20,000 16,000

45. Pass the necessary journal entries for the following transactions on the dissolution of the firm of James and Haider who were sharing profits and losses in the ratio of 2 : 1. The various assets (other than cash) and outside liabilities have been transferred to realisation account.

(*i*) James agreed to pay off his brother's loan ₹ 10,000.

(*ii*) Debtors realised ₹ 12,000.

(*iii*) Haider took over all investment at ₹ 12,000.

(*iv*) Sundry creditors ₹ 20,000 were paid at 5% discount.

(*v*) Realisation expenses amounted to ₹ 2,000.

(*vi*) Loss on realisation was ₹ 10,200. **All India 2011**

Ans. **JOURNAL**

Date	Particulars		LF	Amt (Dr)	Amt (Cr)
(i)	Realisation A/c To James' Capital A/c (Being James agreed to pay off his brother's loan)	Dr		10,000	10,000
(ii)	Bank A/c To Realisation A/c (Being debtors realised)	Dr		12,000	12,000
(iii)	Haider's Capital A/c To Realisation A/c (Being investment taken over by Haider)	Dr		12,000	12,000
(iv)	Realisation A/c To Bank A/c (20,000 − 5% of 20,000) (Being creditors paid)	Dr		19,000	19,000
(v)	Realisation A/c To Bank A/c (Being realisation expenses paid)	Dr		2,000	2,000
(vi)	James's Capital A/c (10,200 × 2/3) Haider's Capital A/c (10,200 × 1/3) To Realisation A/c (Being realisation loss transferred to partners' capital account)	Dr Dr		6,800 3,400	 10,200

8 Marks Questions

46. Srijan, Raman and Manan were partners in a firm sharing profits and losses in the ratio of 2:2:1. On 31st March, 2017 their balance sheet was as follows

Balance Sheet
as on 31st March, 2017

Liabilities		Amt (₹)	Assets	Amt (₹)
Capitals A/cs			Capital : Manan	10,000
Srijan	2,00,000		Plant	2,20,000
Raman	1,50,000	3,50,000	Investments	70,000
Creditors		75,000	Stock	50,000
Bills Payable		40,000	Debtors	60,000
Outstanding Salary		35,000	Bank	10,000
			Profit and Loss A/c	80,000
		5,00,000		5,00,000

On the above date, they decided to dissolve the firm.

(*i*) Srijan was appointed to realise the assets and discharge the liabilities. Srijan was to receive 5% commission on sale of assets (except cash) and was to bear all expenses of realisation.

(*ii*) Assets were realised as follows

	Amt (₹)
Plant	85,000
Stock	33,000
Debtors	47,000

(*iii*) Investments were realised at 95% of the book value.

(*iv*) The firm had to pay ₹ 7,500 for an outstanding repair bill not provided for earlier.

(*v*) A contingent liability in respect of bills receivable, discounted with the bank had also materialised and had to be discharged for ₹ 15,000.

(*vi*) Expenses of realisation amounting to ₹ 3,000 were paid by Srijan.

Prepare realisation account, partners' capital accounts and bank account. CBSE 2018

Ans. Dr **Realisation Account** Cr

Particulars		Amt (₹)	Particulars		Amt (₹)
To Sundry Assets A/c			By Sundry Liabilities A/c		
Plant	2,20,000		Creditors	75,000	
Investments	70,000		Bills Payable	40,000	
Stock	50,000		Outstanding Salary	35,000	1,50,000
Debtors	60,000	4,00,000	By Bank A/c		
To Bank A/c			Plant	85,000	
Creditors	75,000		Stock	33,000	
Bills Payable	40,000		Debtors	47,000	
Outstanding Salary	35,000	1,50,000	Investments (70,000 × 95%)	66,500	2,31,500

Particulars		Amt (₹)	Particulars		Amt (₹)
To Bank A/c			By Loss Transferred to Partners' Capital A/c		
Outstanding Bill for Repair	7,500		Srijan	81,030	
Dishonoured Bill	15,000	22,500	Raman	81,030	
To Srijan's Capital A/c (Commission)		11,575	Manan	40,515	2,02,575
		5,84,075			5,84,075

Dr **Partners' Capital Account** Cr

Particulars	Srijan (₹)	Raman (₹)	Manan (₹)	Particulars	Srijan (₹)	Raman (₹)	Manan (₹)
To Balance b/d	—	—	10,000	By Balance b/d	2,00,000	1,50,000	—
To Profit and Loss A/c	32,000	32,000	16,000	By Realisation A/c (Commission)	11,575	—	—
To Realisation A/c (Loss)	81,030	81,030	40,515				
To Bank A/c	98,545	36,970	—	By Bank A/c	—	—	66,515
	2,11,575	1,50,000	66,515		2,11,575	1,50,000	66,515

Dr **Bank Accounts** Cr

Particulars	Amt (₹)	Particulars	Amt (₹)
To Balance b/d	10,000	By Realisation A/c (Liabilities paid)	1,50,000
To Realisation A/c (Assets realised)	2,31,500	By Realisation A/c (Unrecorded liabilities paid)	22,500
To Manan's Capital A/c (Cash brought in)	66,515	By Srijan's Capital A/c (Final payment)	98,545
		By Raman's Capital A/c (Final payment)	36,970
	3,08,015		3,08,015

Working Note

$$\text{Commission payable to Srijan} = 2{,}31{,}500 \times \frac{5}{100} = ₹11{,}575$$

47. Arnab, Ragini and Dhrupad are partners sharing profits in the ratio of 3 : 1 : 1. On 31st March, 2015 they decided to dissolve their firm. On that date, their balance sheet was as under

Balance Sheet
as at 31st March, 2015

Liabilities		Amt (₹)	Assets		Amt (₹)
Creditors		60,000	Bank		50,000
Arnab's Brother's Loan		95,000	Debtors	1,70,000	
Dhrupad's Loan		1,00,000	(−) Provision for Bad Debts	(20,000)	1,50,000
Investment Fluctuation Fund		50,000	Stock		1,50,000
Capital A/cs			Investments		2,50,000
Arnab	2,75,000		Building		3,00,000
Ragini	2,00,000		Profit and Loss A/c		50,000
Dhrupad	1,70,000	6,45,000			
		9,50,000			9,50,000

The assets were realised and the liabilities were paid as under

(*i*) Arnab agreed to pay his brother's loan.

(*ii*) Investments realised 20% less.

(*iii*) Creditors were paid at 10% less.

(*iv*) Building was auctioned for ₹ 3,55,000. Commission on auction was ₹ 5,000.

(*v*) 50% of the stock was taken over by Ragini at market price which was 20% less than the book value and the remaining was sold at market price.

(*vi*) Dissolution expenses were ₹ 8,000. ₹ 3,000 were to be borne by the firm and the balance by Dhrupad. The expenses were paid by him.

Prepare realisation account, bank account and partners' capital accounts. **All India (C) 2016**

Ans. Dr **Realisation Account** Cr

Particulars		Amt (₹)	Particulars		Amt (₹)
To Sundry Assets A/c			By Sundry Liabilities A/c		
Debtors	1,70,000		Creditors	60,000	
Stock	1,50,000		Arnab's Brother's Loan	95,000	
Investments	2,50,000		Investment Fluctuation Fund	50,000	2,05,000
Building	3,00,000	8,70,000	By Provision for Doubtful Debts		20,000
To Arnab's Capital A/c (Brother's loan)		95,000	By Bank A/c (Assets realised)		
			Debtors	1,70,000	
To Bank A/c (Creditor) (60,000 − 10%)		54,000	Stock (75,000–20% of 75,000)	60,000	
To Dhrupad's Capital A/c (Expenses)		3,000			
To Profit on Realisation transferred to Partners' Capital A/c			Investment	2,00,000	
			Building (3,55,000–5,000)	3,50,000	7,80,000
Arnab	25,800		By Ragini's Capital A/c (Stock) 50% [75,000–15,000 (75,000×20%)]		60,000
Ragini	8,600				
Dhrupad	8,600	43,000			
		10,65,000			10,65,000

Dr **Partners' Capital Account** Cr

Particulars	Arnab (₹)	Ragini (₹)	Dhrupad (₹)	Particulars	Arnab (₹)	Ragini (₹)	Dhrupad (₹)
To Profit and Loss A/c	30,000	10,000	10,000	By Balance b/d	2,75,000	2,00,000	1,70,000
To Realisation A/c (Stock)	—	60,000	—	By Realisation A/c (Loan)	95,000	—	—
To Bank A/c (Final payment)	3,65,800	1,38,600	1,71,600	By Realisation A/c (Expenses)	—	—	3,000
				By Realisation A/c (Profit)	25,800	8,600	8,600
	3,95,800	2,08,600	1,81,600		3,95,000	2,08,600	1,81,600

Dr **Bank Account** Cr

Particulars	Amt (₹)	Particulars	Amt (₹)
To Balance b/d	50,000	By Dhrupad's Loan A/c	1,00,000
To Realisation A/c (Stock)	60,000	By Realisation A/c (Creditor)	54,000
To Realisation A/c (Investments)	2,00,000	By Arnab's Capital A/c (Final payment)	3,65,800
To Realisation A/c (Building)	3,50,000	By Ragini's Capital A/c (Final payment)	1,38,600
To Realisation A/c (Debtors)	1,70,000	By Dhrupad's Capital A/c (Final payment)	1,71,600
	8,30,000		8,30,000

48. Following is the balance sheet of Vinit and Yogesh as on 31st March, 2015.

Balance Sheet
as at 31st March, 2015

Liabilities		Amt (₹)	Assets		Amt (₹)
Creditors		3,60,000	Bank		80,000
Mrs Vinit's Loan		60,000	Stock		70,000
Yogesh's Loan		1,00,000	Investments		1,00,000
Investment Fluctuation Fund		30,000	Debtors	2,00,000	
Capital A/cs			(−) Provision for Bad Debts	(20,000)	1,80,000
Vinit	2,00,000		Fixed Assets		3,80,000
Yogesh	1,00,000	3,00,000	Profit and Loss A/c		40,000
		8,50,000			8,50,000

The firm was dissolved on 31st March, 2015. The assets were realised and the liabilities were paid as under

(*i*) Vinit promised to pay-off Mrs Vinit's loan and took away stock at 20% discount.

(*ii*) Yogesh took away 90% of the investments at 10% discount.

(*iii*) Sunil, a debtor of ₹ 50,000 had to pay the amount due 3 months after the date of dissolution. He was allowed a discount of 5% for making payment immediately. The remaining debtors were collected in full.

(*iv*) Creditors were paid ₹ 3,50,000 in full settlement of their claim.

(*v*) Fixed assets realised ₹ 2,82,000 and remaining investment realised ₹ 7,500.

(*vi*) There was an old furniture which had been written-off completely from the books. Yogesh took away the same for ₹ 4,000.

(*vii*) Realisation expenses ₹ 2,000 were paid by Vinit.

Prepare realisation account, bank account and partners' capital accounts. **Delhi (C) 2016**

Ans. Dr **Realisation Account** Cr

Particulars		Amt (₹)	Particulars		Amt (₹)
To Sundry Assets A/c			By Sundry Liabilities A/c		
Stock	70,000		Creditors	3,60,000	
Debtors	2,00,000		Mrs Vinit's Loan	60, 000	
Investments	1,00,000		Investment Fluctuation Fund	30,000	4,50,000
Fixed Assets	3,80,000	7,50,000	By Provision for Doubtful Debts		20,000

Particulars	Amt (₹)	Particulars		Amt (₹)
To Vinit's Capital A/c (Mrs Vinit's loan)	60,000	By Vinit's Capital A/c (Stock) (70,000 − 20% of 70,000)		56,000
To Bank A/c (Creditors)	3,50,000	By Yogesh's Capital A/c-Investment (90%) $\left[90{,}000-\left(90{,}000\times\frac{10}{100}\right)\right]$		81,000
To Vinit's Capital A/c (Expenses)	2,000	By Bank A/c (Assets realised)		
		Debtors [(50,000 − 5% of 50,000 + 1,50,000)]	1,97,500	
		Fixed Assets	2,82,000	
		Investments	7,500	4,87,000
		By Yogesh's Capital A/c (Old furniture)		4,000
		By Loss on Realisation Transferred to Capital A/c		
		Vinit	32,000	
		Yogesh	32,000	64,000
	11,62,000			11,62,000

Dr **Partners' Capital Account** Cr

Particulars	Vinit (₹)	Yogesh (₹)	Particulars	Vinit (₹)	Yogesh (₹)
To Profit and Loss A/c	20,000	20,000	By Balance b/d	2,00,000	1,00,000
To Realisation A/c (Stock)	56,000	—	By Realisation A/c (Loan)	60,000	—
To Realisation A/c (Investment)	—	81,000	By Realisation A/c (Expenses)	2,000	—
To Realisation A/c (Furniture)	—	4,000	By Bank A/c (Cash brought in)	—	37,000
To Realisation A/c (Loss)	32,000	32,000			
To Bank A/c (Final payment)	1,54,000	—			
	2,62,000	1,37,000		2,62,000	1,37,000

Dr **Bank Account** Cr

Particulars	Amt (₹)	Particulars	Amt (₹)
To Balance b/d	80,000	By Yogesh's Loan A/c	1,00,000
To Realisation A/c (Assets realised)	4,87,000	By Realisation A/c (Creditors)	3,50,000
To Yogesh's Capital A/c (Cash brought in)	37,000	By Vinit's Capital A/c (Final payment)	1,54,000
	6,04,000		6,04,000

49. Kumar, Shyam and Ratan were partners in a firm sharing profits in the ratio of 5 : 3 : 2 respectively. They decided to dissolve the firm with effect from 1st April, 2013. On that date, the balance sheet of the firm was as follows

Balance Sheet
as at 1st April, 2013

Liabilities		Amt (₹)	Assets	Amt (₹)
Creditors		1,20,000	Plant	80,000
Capital A/cs			Furniture	45,000
Kumar	68,000		Motor Van	25,000
Shyam	50,000		Stock	30,000
Ratan	27,000	1,45,000	Debtors	71,000
			Cash	14,000
		2,65,000		2,65,000

The dissolution resulted in the following

(*i*) Plant of ₹ 40,000 was taken over by Kumar at an agreed value of ₹ 45,000 and remaining plant realised ₹ 50,000.

(*ii*) Furniture realised ₹ 40,000.

(*iii*) Motor van was taken over by Shyam for ₹ 30,000.

(*iv*) Debtors realised ₹ 1,000 less.

(*v*) Creditors for ₹ 20,000 were untraceable and the remaining creditors were paid in full.

(*vi*) Realisation expenses amounted to ₹ 5,000.

Prepare the realisation account, capital accounts of partners and bank account of the firm.

All India (C) 2014

Ans. Dr **Realisation Account** Cr

Particulars		Amt (₹)	Particulars		Amt (₹)
To Sundry Assets A/c			By Sundry Liabilities A/c (Creditors)		1,20,000
Plant	80,000		By Kumar's Capital A/c (Plant taken over)		45,000
Furniture	45,000		By Shyam's Capital A/c (Motor van taken over)		30,000
Motor Van	25,000		By Cash A/c		
Stock	30,000		Stock	30,000	
Debtors	71,000	2,51,000	Plant	50,000	
To Cash A/c (Creditors)		1,00,000	Furniture	40,000	
To Cash A/c (Expenses)		5,000	Debtors (71,000 – 1,000)	70,000	1,90,000
To Profit on Realisation transferred to Partners' Capital A/c					
Kumar	14,500				
Shyam	8,700				
Ratan	5,800	29,000			
		3,85,000			3,85,000

Dr **Partners' Capital Account** Cr

Particulars	Kumar (₹)	Shyam (₹)	Ratan (₹)	Particulars	Kumar (₹)	Shyam (₹)	Ratan (₹)
To Realisation A/c (Assets taken over)	45,000	30,000	—	By Balance b/d	68,000	50,000	27,000
				By Realisation A/c (Profit)	14,500	8,700	5,800
To Cash A/c (Final payment)	37,500	28,700	32,800				
	82,500	58,700	32,800		82,500	58,700	32,800

Dr **Cash/Bank Account** Cr

Particulars	Amt (₹)	Particulars	Amt (₹)
To Balance b/d	14,000	By Realisation A/c (Creditors)	1,00,000
To Realisation A/c (Assets realised)	1,90,000	By Realisation A/c (Expenses)	5,000
		By Kumar's Capital A/c (Final payment)	37,500
		By Shyam's Capital A/c (Final payment)	28,700
		By Ratan's Capital A/c (Final payment)	32,800
	2,04,000		2,04,000

Multiple Choice Questions

(1 Mark)

1. .... refers to the change in the existing relationship between partners but the firm may continue its business as before.

(a) Dissolution of partnership (b) Dissolution of firm
(c) Either (a) or (b) (d) None of these

2. According to .... of the Indian Partnership Act, 1932, dissolution of the firm means dissolution of partnership among all the partners in the firm.

(a) Section 38 (b) Section 40
(c) Section 39 (d) Section 42

3. In case of dissolution of a firm, which item on the liabilities side is to be paid last?

(a) Creditors (b) Bank loan
(c) Partners' loan (d) Partners' capital

Hint: At the time of dissolution of firm, first the claims of outsiders are settled, followed by partners' loan and at last the partners' capital is repayed.

4. According to Section 49 of the Indian Partnership Act, 1932, "Firm's property is first applied for the .... and if surplus is left then it is utilised for the payment of partners' private debts."

(a) payment of firm's debt (b) personal expenses
(c) partners' share (d) None of these

5. Profit/Loss on realisation is transferred to the

(a) profit and loss adjustment account
(b) partners' capital account
(c) Both (a) and (b)
(d) None of the above

Hint: Reaslisation account shows either profit or loss. The profit/loss on realisation is transferred to the capital accounts of the partners in their profit sharing ratio.

6. Realisation account is a

(a) nominal account (b) real account
(c) personal account (d) None of these

Hint: Realisation account is a nominal account as it helps to ascertain the profit or loss on realisation.

7. In the books of XY firm, there was an unrecorded asset of ₹ 10,000. This asset realised for ₹ 12,000. In the realisation account

(a) cash account will be credited by ₹ 10,000
(b) cash account will be credited by ₹ 12,000
(c) cash account will be debited by ₹ 2,000
(d) None of the above

Hint: The journal entry for sale of asset, whether recorded or unrecorded is as follows

Cash A/c Dr
To Realisation A/c
(Being asset sold)

So, in realisation account cash account will be credited by ₹ 12,000, *i.e.* the sale proceeds.

8. Which account is prepared only once during the life of a partnership firm?

(a) Revaluation account
(b) Realisation account
(c) Partners' capital account
(d) Profit and loss appropriation account

9. 'E' and 'F' were partners sharing profits equally. They decided to dissolve the firm. The goodwill was taken over by 'E' at an agreed value of ₹ 54,000. The required journal entry will be

(a) Cash A/c Dr
To Realisation A/c
(b) 'E's' Capital A/c Dr
To Realisation A/c
(c) Realisation A/c Dr
To 'E's' Capital A/c
(d) None of the above

Hint: If goodwill of the firm is purchased by one of the partners' at the time of dissolution of firm, then the concerned partners' capital account is debited and realisation account is credited.

10. The amount of sundry assets transferred to realisation account was ₹ 80,000. 60% of them were sold at a profit of ₹ 2,000. 20% of the remaining were sold at a discount of 30% and remaining were taken over by 'Z' at book value. The amount realised from assets is

(a) ₹ 54,480 (b) ₹ 25,600
(c) ₹ 80,000 (d) ₹ 80,080

Hint: **Calculation of Amount Realised from Assets**

60% of ₹ 80,000	₹ 48,000	
(+) Profit	₹ 2,000	
		50,000
20% of 32,000 (80,000 – 48,000)	₹ 6,400	
(–) 30% Discount	(1,920)	
		4,480

Assets taken over by 'Z' = 80,000 – 48,000 – 6,400
= ₹ 25,600

Total amount realised = 50,000 + 4,480 + 25,600
= ₹ 80,080

11. Loan from partner is deemed to be an .... liability at the time of dissolution.

(a) external (b) internal
(c) not a liability (d) None of these

12. Rohit, a partner agreed to take over the responsibility of completing dissolution at an agreed remuneration of ₹ 4,000 and to bear all realisation expenses. Actual realisation expenses of ₹ 3,200 were paid by Rohit out of his private funds. In realisation account, Rohit's capital account will be

(a) debited with ₹ 4,000
(b) debited with ₹ 3,200
(c) credited with ₹ 4,000
(d) credited with ₹ 3,200

Hint: When a partner is paid a fixed amount for the purpose of bearing realisation expenses and actual expenses are borne by a partner, then in such a case the fixed amount payable to the partner is debited to realisation account and the actual expenses are not considered.

ANSWERS

1. *(a)*	2. *(c)*	3. *(d)*	4. *(a)*	5. *(b)*	6. *(a)*	7. *(b)*	8. *(b)*	9. *(b)*	10. *(d)*
11. *(b)*	12. *(a)*								

CHAPTER 06

Accounting for Share Capital

TOPIC 1

Introduction

Meaning & Definition of Company

A company is an incorporated association which is an artificial person, created by law, having separate legal entity distinct from its members, with a perpetual succession and a common seal.

According to Section 2 (20) of the Companies Act, 2013, "Company means a company incorporated under this act or any previous company law."

The **characteristics** or **features** of a company are

(*i*) Incorporated person
(*ii*) Voluntary association
(*iii*) Created by law
(*iv*) Transferability of shares
(*v*) Limited liability
(*vi*) Perpetual succession
(*vii*) Common seal
(*viii*) Separate legal entity from its members
(*ix*) May sue or be sued
(*x*) Management and ownership are separate

Types of Companies

Private Company

According to Section 2 (68) of the Companies Act, 2013, it is a company with minimum paid-up share capital as may be prescribed* and which by its Articles of Association

(*i*) Restricts the right to transfer its shares, if any.
(*ii*) Except in one person company, limits the number of its members excluding its present and past employee members to 200; (If any share is held jointly by two or more persons, they shall be treated as a single member.)
(*iii*) Prohibits any invitation to the public to subscribe for any securities of the company.

The minimum number of members required to form a private company is two. The name of a private company ends with the words, 'Private Limited'.

Public Company

As per Section 2 (71) of Companies Act, 2013, public company is a company which

(*i*) is not a private company.

(*ii*) has minimum capital of as may be prescribed*.

(*iii*) is a private company, which is a subsidiary of a public company.

Minimum requirement of a public company is seven persons. The name of the public company ends with the word 'Limited'.

One Person Company

Section 2(62) of the Companies Act, 2013 defines one person company as a company which has only one person as a member. It is a company incorporated as a private company which has only one member.

NOTE *Minimum paid-up capital is not prescribed. Private or public companies can have share capital as the promoters decide.

Share

According to Section 2 (84) of the Companies Act, 2013, share means a share in the share capital of a company and includes stock. The capital of company is divided into a number of equal units. Each unit is called a share. A company may divide its capital into share of ₹ 100, ₹ 10 or even ₹ 1 each.

Nature of Shares

As per Section 44 of the Companies Act, 2013, shares or debentures or other interest of any member in a company shall be movable property, transferable in the manner provided by the articles of the company.

According to Sale of Goods Act, 1930, "Goods mean any kind of movable property other than actionable claims and money, and includes stock and shares."

So, on the basis of above two definitions, it can be concluded that shares are basically goods which can be bought, sold or gifted.

Classes or Kinds of Shares

Preference Shares According to Section 43 (b) of the Companies Act, 2013, preference shares are the shares which carry the following two preferential rights

(*i*) Preferential right of dividend to be paid as fixed amount or an amount calculated at a fixed rate, which may either be free of or subject to income tax.

(*ii*) Return of capital on the winding up of the company before that of equity shares.

Holders of preference shares are called preference shareholders.

Equity Shares According to Section 43(a) of the Companies Act, 2013, equity share is that share which is not a preference share. Thus, this share does not carry any preferential right or in other words, equity share is one which is entitled to dividend and repayment of capital after the claim of preference shares is satisfied.

Share Capital

It is that part of the capital of a company, which is represented by the total nominal value of shares, which it has issued.

Kinds of Share Capital

Authorised Share Capital According to Section 2(8) of Companies Act, 2013, 'authorised capital' or 'nominal capital' means such capital as is authorised by the memorandum of a company to be the maximum amount of share capital of a company.

Issued Capital According to Section 2(50) of the Companies Act, 2013, issued capital means such capital as the company issues from time-to-time for subscription.

Subscribed Capital According to Section 2(86) of the Companies Act, 2013, 'subscribed capital' means such part of the capital which is for the time being subscribed by the members of a company.

(*i*) **Subscribed and Fully Paid-up** Shares are said to be 'subscribed and fully paid-up' when the entire nominal (face) value is called and also paid-up by the shareholders.

(*ii*) **Subscribed but not Fully Paid-up**
Shares are said to be 'subscribed but not fully paid-up' when
- The company has called-up the entire nominal (face) value of the share but has not received it.
- The company has not called-up the entire nominal (face) value of share.

A reference has been made to two terms
- **Called-up Capital** According to Section 2(15) of the Companies Act, 2013, 'called-up capital' means such part of the capital, which has been called for payment. Thus, it means the amount of nominal (face) value called-up by the company to be paid by the shareholders towards the share capital.
- **Paid-up Share Capital** According to Section 2(64) of the Companies Act, 2013, 'paid-up share capital' or 'share capital paid-up' means the amount that the shareholder has paid and the company has received against the amount 'called-up' against the shares towards share capital.

Reserve Capital

It is that portion of uncalled share capital which shall not be capable of being called up except in the event and for the purpose of the company being wound up.

Capital Reserve

'Capital reserve' is the reserve which is not free for distribution as dividend. It is mandatory to create capital reserve in case of capital profits earned by the company. Reserves which are created out of capital profits, are not readily available for distribution as dividend among the shareholders.

e.g. Premium on issue of shares or debentures, profits on re-issue of shares, profits prior to incorporation, etc.

Minimum Subscription

It is the amount stated in the prospectus as the minimum amount that must be subscribed.

Unless the sum payable on application for the sum so stated (minimum subscription) has been paid to and received by the company by cheque or other instrument, security cannot be allotted.

As per SEBI guidelines, a company must receive a minimum of 90% of the subscription against the entire issue before making any allotment of shares to the public.

Disclosure of Share Capital in Company's Balance Sheet

As per Schedule III of Companies Act, 2013, share capital is to be disclosed in company's balance sheet in the following manner

Balance Sheet
as at....

Particulars	Note No.	Current Year (₹)	Previous Year (₹)
I. EQUITY AND LIABILITIES			
1. Shareholders' Funds			
(a) Share Capital*	1	...	...

Notes to Accounts

Particulars		Amt (₹)
1. Share Capital		
Authorised Capital		
... Shares of ₹ ...each		...
Issued Capital		
... Shares of ₹ ...each		...
Subscribed Capital		
Subscribed and Fully Paid-up		
... Shares of ₹ ...each		...
Subscribed but not Fully Paid-up		
... Shares of ₹.. each ... Called-up ...		
(–) Calls-in-arrears (if any)	(...)	...
(+) Shares Forfeited A/c		...
		...

* As per Schedule III, disclosure requirements pertaining to share capital are to be provided in notes to accounts and note number be put against the item in the balance sheet.

Previous Years' Examination Questions

1 Mark Questions

1. That part of the subscribed capital which has not yet been called is known as .... **CBSE 2020**

Ans. reserve capital

2. What is meant by 'issued capital'? **Delhi 2019**

Ans. It means such capital as the company issues from time-to-time for subscription.

3. What is meant by 'reserve capital'? **All India 2019**

Ans. Part of capital of a company which is called-up only on winding up is called 'reserve capital'.

4. Is 'reserve capital' a part of 'unsubscribed capital' or 'uncalled capital'? **CBSE 2018**

Ans. Reserve capital is a part of uncalled capital.

5. Differentiate between issued share capital and subscribed share capital. **All India (C) 2016**

Ans. Difference between issued capital and subscribed share capital is

Basis	Issued Share Capital	Subscribed Share Capital
Meaning	It means such capital as the company issues from time-to-time for subscription.	It means such part of the capital which is for the time being subscribed by the members of a company.

6. What is the name given to the part of capital of a company which is called-up only on winding up? **Delhi (C) 2015; All India 2015, 2011 Modified**

Ans. Part of capital of a company which is called-up only on winding up is called 'reserve capital'.

7. D Ltd invited applications for issuing 10,00,000 equity shares of ₹ 10 each. The public applied for 8,55,000 shares. Can the company proceed for the allotment of shares? Give reason in support of your answer. **All India 2014**

Ans. No, the shares cannot be allotted because subscribed shares are less than 90%, *i.e.* as per SEBI guidelines, a company must receive a minimum of 90% of subscription.

8. What is meant by paid-up capital? **All India (C) 2014**

Ans. It is the amount that the shareholder has paid and the company has received against the amount called-up against the shares towards share capital.

9. What is meant by authorised capital of a company? **All India (C) 2014; Foreign 2011**

Ans. According to Section 2 (8) of the Companies Act, 2013, 'authorised capital' means such capital as is authorised by the memorandum of a company to be the maximum amount of share capital of a company.

10. Give the meaning of called-up capital. **All India 2011**

Ans. Called-up capital means such part of the capital, which has been called for payment. Thus, it means the amount of nominal (face) value called up by the company to be paid by the shareholders towards the share capital.

11. What are preliminary expenses? **Delhi 2010**

Ans. The expenses incurred in the promotion and formation of the company are known as preliminary expenses, such as registration fee paid to registrar of the companies, stamp duty, legal expenses, expenses regarding preparation and issue of prospectus, etc.

12. What is meant by 'capital reserve'? **All India 2010**

Ans. 'Capital reserve' is the reserve which is not free for distribution as dividend. It is mandatory to create capital reserve in case of capital profits earned by the company.

3 Marks Questions

13. What is meant by a 'share'? Give any two differences between 'preference shares' and 'equity shares'. **CBSE 2018**

Ans. According to Section 2(84) of the Companies Act, 2013, "Share means a share in the capital of a company and includes share". It is the unit into which the capital of a company is divided.

Difference between preference shares and equity shares is as follows

Basis	Preference Shares	Equity Shares
Dividend Rate	Preference shares are paid dividend at a fixed rate.	The rate of dividend may vary from year to year and on the availability of profits.
Redemption	They can be redeemed as provided by the articles and terms of issue.	They cannot be redeemed except under a scheme involving reduction of capital.

TOPIC 2
Issue of Shares

A company raises its capital by issue of shares. A company may issue shares

(*i*) **At Par** When shares are issued at their face value, the shares are said to have been issued at par, *i.e.* issue price and face value are same.

(*ii*) **At Premium** When shares are issued at a value that is higher than the face value of the shares, the shares are said to have been issued at premium, *i.e.* issue price is more than face value.

Utilisation of Securities Premium Reserve

Section 52 (2) of the Companies Act, 2013 restrict the use of the amount received as premium on securities for the following purposes

(*i*) In purchasing its own shares (buy back).
(*ii*) Issuing fully paid bonus shares to the members.
(*iii*) Writing-off preliminary expenses of the company.
(*iv*) Writing-off the expenses of, or the commission paid or discount allowed on any issue of securities or debentures of the company.
(*v*) Providing for the premium payable on the redemption of any redeemable preference shares or of any debentures of the company.

Issue of Shares for Cash

Accounting treatment for issue of shares can be discussed under two heads

I. Shares Payable in Lumpsum

Shares are said to have been issued against lumpsum payment when amount is payable in one instalment.

Journal entries will be as follows

For Receiving Share Application Money	Bank A/c To Share Application and Allotment A/c	Dr
For Allotment of Shares	**At Par** Share Application and Allotment A/c To Share Capital A/c	Dr
	At Premium Share Application and Allotment A/c To Share Capital A/c (With the face value of shares) To Securities Premium Reserve A/c (With the amount of premium)	Dr

II. Shares Payable in Instalments

The amount against the shares may be repaid in instalments. First instalment is called **application money** (it is paid alongwith the application).

Second instalment is called **allotment money** (it is collected by the company at the time of allotment).

The remaining part of share money, after allotment of shares, when called-up, is called **call money.** It may be collected in one or more instalments.

If only one call is made, then it is called first and final call in place of first call, otherwise the word final will be added to the last instalment.

(i) **On Receipt of Application Money**	Bank A/c To Share Application A/c	Dr	(With application money received) (Number of shares applied × Application money per share)
(ii) **On Acceptance of Applications**	Share Application A/c To Share Capital A/c	Dr	(With application money due on shares allotted) (Number of shares allotted × Application money per share)
(iii) **On Making Allotment Money Due**	(a) **At Par** Share Allotment A/c To Share Capital A/c	Dr	(With allotment money due) (Number of shares allotted × Allotment money per share)
	(b) **At Premium** Share Allotment A/c To Share Capital A/c To Securities Premium Reserve A/c	Dr	(With total) (With allotment money due) (With premium money due)
(iv) **On Receipt of Allotment Money**	Bank A/c To Share Allotment A/c	Dr	(With allotment money received)
(v) **On Making the First Call**	Share First Call A/c To Share Capital A/c	Dr	(With first call money due) (Number of shares allotted × First call money per share)
(vi) **On Receipt of the First Call**	Bank A/c To Share First Call A/c	Dr	(With first call money received)

Full Subscription of Shares

When the number of shares applied for, is equal to the number of shares offered for subscription, the shares are said to be fully subscribed.

Over Subscription of Shares

When the number of shares applied for, is more than the number of shares offered for subscription, the shares are said to be oversubscribed.

In case of oversubscription, following three alternatives are available

(*i*) Rejection of applications

(*ii*) Partial or pro-rata allotment

(*iii*) Combination of pro-rata allotment and rejection

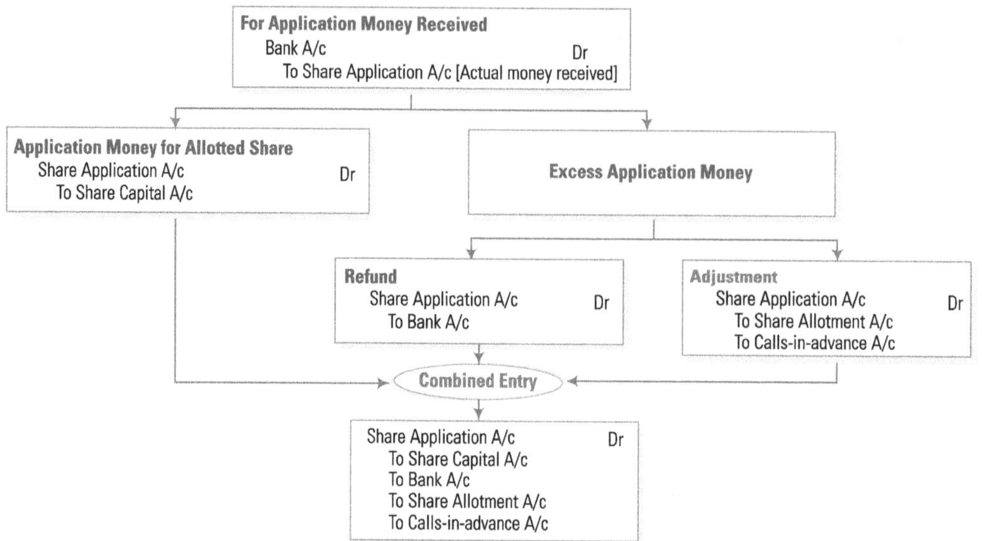

Accounting Entries in Case of Over Subscription

Under Subscription of Shares

When the number of shares applied for, is less than the number of shares offered to the public, the shares are said to be under subscribed.

Issue of Shares for Consideration other than Cash

I. Issue of Shares to Vendors

In this regard, the purchase of assets and issue of shares are to be treated as two separate transactions.

(i) (a) When Assets are Purchased	Assets A/c (Individually) To Vendor (Being assets purchased from ... vendor)	Dr	[With the amount of purchase price] [With the purchase consideration]
(b) When Business in Purchased	Sundry Assets A/c Goodwill A/c* To Sundry Liabilities A/c To Vendor To Capital Reserve A/c* (Being purchased from vendor for purchase consideration of ₹ ...)	Dr Dr	[With the agreed value of assets] [Balancing figure] [With agreed value of liabilities] [With purchase consideration] [Balancing figure]

NOTE 'Vendor' is credited with purchase consideration payable to him.
* Either goodwill or capital reserve will come.

(ii) On Issue of Shares	(a) **At Par** Vendor Dr To Share Capital A/c (Being ... shares of ₹ ... each issued to vendor)
	(b) **At Premium** Vendor Dr To Share Capital A/c To Securities Premium Reserve A/c (Being ... shares of ₹ ... each at a premium of ₹ .... issued to vendor)

II. Issue of Shares to Promoters

Formation Expenses/Incorporation Cost/Goodwill A/c To Share Capital A/c (Being ... shares of ₹ ... each issued to promoters of the company)	Dr

III. Issue of Shares to Underwriters

(i) **Making Underwriting Expenses Due**	Underwriting Expenses A/c Dr To Underwriters A/c (Being underwriting commission due)
(ii) **Issuing Shares to Underwriters**	Underwriters A/c Dr To Share Capital A/c (Being ... shares issued @ ₹ ... per share to underwriters)
(iii) **Transferring Underwriting Commission to Statement of Profit and Loss**	Statement of Profit and Loss Dr To Underwriting Commission A/c (Being underwriting commission transferred to statement of profit and loss)

Calls-in-arrears

When one or more shareholders fail to pay their dues at the time of allotment or call, it is technically called calls-in-arrears.

Table F of the Companies Act, 2013, provides for the payment of interest on calls-in-arrears at a rate not exceeding 10% per annum.

Calls-in-arrears are shown in notes to accounts as a deduction from subscribed but not fully paid-up capital.

Calls-in-advance

The part of the whole amount received from the shareholders before the call is made, is called calls-in-advance.

Table F of the Companies Act, 2013, provides for the payment of interest on calls-in-advance at a rate not exceeding 12% per annum.

Calls-in-advance is shown in the equity and liabilities part of the balance sheet under the head 'current liabilities' and sub-head other current liabilities.

Some Important Terms

1. Private Placement of Shares

It means issue and allotment of shares to a selected group of persons privately and not to public in general. It is generally made by private or unlisted companies. When a company issues shares through private placement route, a special resolution to this effect should be passed. All SEBI guidelines concerning preferential issue are applicable to private placement of shares as well.

2. Sweat Equity Shares

According to Section 2(88) of the Companies Act, 2013, the expression sweat equity shares means equity shares issued by a company to its employees or directors at a discount. A company may issue sweat equity shares of a class already issued by passing a special resolution. The resolution should specify the number of shares, their current market price, consideration and the class or classes of directors or employees to whom such shares are to be issued. A period of one year must have elapsed since the date of the company has commenced business. The company is also required to meet the regulations of SEBI.

3. Employees Stock Option Plan (ESOP)

It is a plan whereby an option is given by the company to its whole time directors, officers and employees to purchase or acquire at a future date, a specified number of shares at a pre-determined price, which is usually lower than the market price.

Shares allotted under this scheme shall be locked in for a minimum period of one year from the date of allotment.

A company may issue stock (shares) options fulfilling the following conditions

(*i*) These shares are of the same class of shares already issued.

(*ii*) It is authorised by a special resolution passed by the company.

(*iii*) The resolution specifies the number of shares, the current market price, consideration if any, and the class or classes of directors or employees to whom such equity shares are to be issued.

(*iv*) Not less than one year has, at the date of issue, elapsed since the date on which the company had commenced business.

(*v*) These shares are issued in accordance with SEBI regulations, if the shares are listed.

Previous Years' Examination Questions

1 Mark Questions

1. What is meant by private placement of shares? **All India 2019; Compartment 2018**

Ans. Private placement of shares means selling of shares to a relatively small number of selected investors. Private placement is the opposite of a public issue, in which securities are made available for sale in the open market.

2. What is meant by employee stock option plan? **Delhi 2019; All India (C) 2016**

Ans. Employees stock option plan is a plan whereby an option is given by the company to its whole time directors, officers and employees to purchase or acquire at a future date, a specified number of shares at a pre-determined price, which is usually lower than the market price.

3. On 28th February, 2016 the first call of ₹ 2 per share became due on 50,000 equity shares alloted by Kumar Ltd. Komal a holder of 1,000 shares did not pay the first call money. Kovil a holder of 750 shares paid the second and final call of ₹ 4 per share alongwith the first call. Pass the necessary journal entry for the amount received by opening calls-in-arrears and calls-in-advance account in the books of the company. **All India 2016**

Ans. **JOURNAL**

Date	Particulars		LF	Amt (Dr)	Amt (Cr)
2016					
Feb 28	Equity Share First Call A/c (50,000×2)	Dr		1,00,000	
	To Equity Share Capital A/c				1,00,000
	(Being the first call money due)				
	Bank A/c	Dr		1,01,000	
	Calls-in-arrears A/c (1,000×2)	Dr		2,000	
	To Equity Share First Call A/c				1,00,000
	To Calls-in-advance A/c (750×4)				3,000
	(Being the first call money received)				

Working Note

Amount Received on First Call

49,000 shares @ ₹ 2 each	98,000
750 shares @ ₹ 4 each	3,000
	₹ 1,01,000

4. On 1st January, 2016 the first call of ₹ 3 per share became due on 1,00,000 equity shares issued by Kamini Ltd. Karan, a holder of 500 shares did not pay the first call money. Arjun, a shareholder holding 1,000 shares paid the second and final call of ₹ 5 per share alongwith the first call.

Pass the necessary journal entry for the amount received by opening 'calls-in-arrears' and 'calls-in-advance' account in the books of the company. **Delhi 2016**

Ans. Solve as Q no. 3 on page 256 and 257.

Calls-in-arrears = ₹ 1,500; Calls-in-advance = ₹ 5,000

5. Nirman Ltd issued 50,000 equity shares of ₹ 10 each. The amount was payable as follows

On application : ₹ 3 per share
On allotment : ₹ 2 per share
On first and final call : Balance

Applications for 45,000 shares were received and shares were allotted to all the applicants, Pooja, to whom 500 shares were allotted, paid her entire share money at the time of allotment, whereas Kundan did not pay the first and final call on his 300 shares. What amount will be received at the time of making the first and final call? **All India 2015 Modified**

Ans. Calculation of amount received at the time of making first and final call.

Amount due at the time of first and final call

(45,000 − 500) × 5	=	2,22,500
(−) Calls-in-arrears (300 × 5)	=	(1,500)
		₹ 2,21,000

6. Joy Ltd issued 1,00,000 equity shares of ₹ 10 each. The amount was payable as follows

On application : ₹ 3 per share
On allotment : ₹ 4 per share
On first and final call : Balance

Applications for 95,000 shares were received and shares were allotted to all the applicants. Sonam, to whom 500 shares were allotted, failed to pay the allotment money and Gautam paid his entire amount due including the amount due on first and final call on the 750 shares allotted to him along with allotment. What amount will be received at the time of allotment? **Delhi 2015 Modified**

Ans. **Calculation of amount received at the time of allotment**

Amount due on allotment (95,000 × 4)	=	3,80,000
(−) Calls-in-arrears (500 × 4)	=	(2,000)
(+) Calls-in-advance (750 ×3)	=	2,250
		₹ 3,80,250

7. What is meant by over subscription? **All India (C) 2014**

Ans. When the number of shares applied for is more than the number of shares offered for subscription, the shares are said to be over subscribed.

8. What is meant by 'under subscription'? **All India (C) 2014**

Ans. Under subscription means that number of shares applied for is less than the number of shares issued.

9. Give any one purpose for which the amount received as 'securities premium reserve' may be utilised. **Delhi; All India (C) 2014**

Ans. Securities premium reserve can be utilised in writing-off preliminary expenses of the company.

10. What is meant by 'calls-in-arrears'? **All India 2013**

Ans. If shareholders make default in paying the money due on allotment or any call, the money not so paid is called calls-in-arrears.

11. What rate of interest the company pays on calls-in-advance, if it has not prepared its own Articles of Association? **Delhi 2013**

Ans. As per Table F of the Companies Act, interest on calls-in-advance is payable @ 12% per annum by the company.

12. What is meant by 'securities premium reserve'? **Delhi 2013**

Ans. A company can issue its shares at more than its face value. Excess of issue price of shares over its face value is termed as securities premium reserve.

13. What is meant by 'calls-in-advance'? **All India 2012**

Ans. Calls-in-advance means the amount paid by shareholders is in excess of the amount due from them. The company may receive calls-in-advance if the articles permit. It is shown as a current liability in the balance sheet.

14. State the steps other than rejecting applications that a company can take in case of over subscription. **Delhi (C) 2011**

Ans. The steps other than rejecting applications that a company can take in case of over subscription are

(*i*) All applicants are allotted shares on pro-rata basis.

(*ii*) Some applicants are allotted shares in full and some are allotted shares on pro-rata basis.

15. Can securities premium reserve be used as working capital? Give reason in support of your answer. **All India 2011**

Ans. Securities premium reserve cannot be used as working capital.

According to Section 52 (2) of the Companies Act, 2013, the securities premium reserve can be applied only for the following purposes

(*i*) Issuing fully paid bonus shares to the members.

(*ii*) Writing-off the preliminary expenses of the company.

(*iii*) Writing-off the expenses on issue of shares, commission paid on any issue of shares or debentures of the company and discount allowed on any issue of shares and debentures.

(*iv*) Providing for the premium payable on the redemption of redeemable preference shares or debentures of the company.

(*v*) In purchasing its own shares (buy back).

16. What is meant by pro-rata allotment of shares? **All India 2010**

Ans. In the case of over subscription, it is not possible to allot shares to all applicants. Applicants may be allotted less number of shares than they have applied for. This type of allotment of shares is known as pro-rata allotment of shares. e.g. If company allots 50,000 shares to applicants of 75,000 shares, it is pro-rata allotment in proportion of 2 : 3.

17. What is meant by issue of shares at par? **All India 2010**

Ans. When shares are issued at the face value, the shares are said to have been issued at par.

3 Marks Questions

18. What is meant by 'over subscription' of shares? With the help of an example, briefly explain the alternatives available for allotment of shares in case of over subscription. **All India 2019; Delhi 2017**

Ans. Refer to Q. no. 7 on page 258 and Q. no 26 on page 263.

19. 'WX Ltd' was registered with an authorised capital of 2,00,000 equity shares of ₹ 10 each. The company offered 1,50,000 shares to the public for subscription 1,45,000 shares were subscribed. All calls were made and were duly received except the final call of ₹ 3 on 5,000 shares.

Present the share capital of the company as per the provisions of Schedule III, Part I of the Companies Act, 2013. **All India 2019**

Ans.

Balance Sheet
as at ....

	Particulars	Note No.	Amt (₹)
I.	**EQUITY AND LIABILITIES**		
	1. **Shareholders' Funds**		
	(a) Share Capital	1	14,35,000
			14,35,000

Notes to Accounts

Note No.	Particulars		Amt (₹)
1.	**Share Capital**		
	Authorised capital		
	2,00,000 equity shares of ₹ 10 each		20,00,000
	Issued Capital		
	1,50,000 equity shares of ₹ 10 each		15,00,000
	Subscribed capital		
	Subscribed and fully paid-up		
	1,40,000 equity shares of ₹ 10 each		14,00,000
	Subscribed but not Fully Paid		
	5,000 equity shares of ₹ 10 each	50,000	
	(–) Calls-in-arrears (5,000 × 3)	(15,000)	35,000
			14,35,000

20. JN Ltd were registered with an authorised capital of 2,00,000 equity shares of ₹ 100 each. The company offered to the public for subscription 1,00,000 shares. Applications for 1,50,000 shares were received and allotment was made to all the applicants on pro-rata basis. All calls were made and were duly received except the second and final call of ₹ 4,000. The amount payable on second and final call was ₹ 20 per share.

Present the share capital in the balance sheet of the company as per Schedule III, Part I of the Companies Act, 2013. **All India 2019**

Ans.

Balance Sheet
as at 31st March, ...

	Particulars	Note No.	Amt (₹)
I.	**EQUITY AND LIABILITIES**		
	1. **Shareholders' Funds**		
	(a) Share Capital	1	99,96,000
			99,96,000

Notes to Accounts

Note No.	Particulars		Amt (₹)
1.	**Share Capital**		
	Authorised Capital		
	2,00,000 equity shares of ₹ 100 each		2,00,00,000
	Issued Capital		
	1,00,000 equity shares of ₹ 100 each		1,00,00,000
	Subscribed Capital		
	Subscribed and Fully Paid-up		
	99,800 equity shares of ₹ 100 each		99,80,000
	Subscribed but not Fully Paid		
	200 equity shares of ₹ 100 each	20,000	
	(–) Calls-in-arrears (200 × 20)	(4,000)	16,000
			99,96,000

21. Willow Ltd was registered with an authorised capital of ₹ 10,00,000 divided into 1,00,000 equity shares of ₹ 10 each. The company offered 80,000 shares for subscription to the public, out of which 75,000 shares were subscribed. All amounts were received except the final call of ₹ 2 per share on 3,000 shares. Fill in the missing figures in the balance sheet of Willow Ltd as per the provisions of Schedule III, Part I of the Companies Act, 2013.

Balance Sheet
as at 31st March, 2018 (An extract)

Particulars	Note No.	Amt (₹)
I. EQUITY AND LIABILITIES		
1. Shareholders' Funds		
(a) Share Capital	1	....
		....

Notes to Accounts

Note No.	Particulars		Amt (₹)
1.	**Share Capital**		
	Authorised Capital		
	....		....
	Issued Capital		
	....		....
	Subscribed Capital		
	Subscribed and Fully Paid-up		
	.... shares of ₹ 10 each		....
	Subscribed but not Fully Paid		
	.... shares of ₹ 10 each	....	
	(–)	(.........)	....
			....

All India 2019

Ans.

Balance Sheet
as at 31st March, 2018 (An Extract)

Particulars	Note No.	Amt (₹)
I. **EQUITY AND LIABILITIES**		
1. **Shareholders' Funds**		
(a) Share Capital	1	7,44,000
		7,44,000

Notes to Accounts

Note No.	Particulars		Amt (₹)
1.	**Share Capital**		
	Authorised Capital		
	1,00,000 equity shares of ₹ 10 each		10,00,000
	Issued Capital		
	80,000 equity shares of ₹ 10 each		8,00,000
	Subscribed Capital		
	Subscribed and Fully Paid-up		
	72,000 shares of ₹ 10 each		7,20,000
	Subscribed but not Fully Paid		
	3,000 shares of ₹ 10 each	30,000	
	(−) Calls-in-arrears (3,000 × 2)	(6,000)	24,000
			7,44,000

22. NK Ltd, a truck manufacturing company, is registered with an authorised capital of ₹ 1,00,00,000 divided into equity shares of ₹ 100 each. The subscribed and paid-up capital of the company is ₹ 50,00,000. To meet the capital expenditure requirements of the project, the company offered 20,000 shares to the public for subscription. The shares were fully subscribed and paid. Present the share capital in the balance sheet of the company as per the provisions of Schedule III of the Companies Act, 2013. **CBSE 2018 Modified**

Ans.

Balance Sheet
as at.........

	Particulars	Note No.	Current year (₹)
I.	**EQUITY AND LIABILITIES**		
	1. **Shareholders' Funds**		
	(a) Share Capital	1	70,00,000
			70,00,000

Notes to Accounts

Note No.	Particulars	Amt (₹)
1.	**Share Capital**	
	Authorised Capital	
	1,00,000 equity shares of ₹ 100 each	1,00,00,000
	Issued Capital	
	70,000 equity shares of ₹ 100 each	70,00,000
	Subscribed Capital	
	Subscribed and Fully Paid-up	
	70,000 equity shares of ₹ 100 each	70,00,000

23. Navnirman Ltd. issued 4,00,000 equity shares of ₹ 10 each at par. The amount per share was payable as follows ₹ 3 on application; ₹ 2 on allotment; ₹ 2 on first call and ₹ 3 on final call. The issue was fully subscribed and the shares were allotted fully to all the applicants. All calls were made. Mahi, a shareholder holding 6,000 shares paid the final call money alongwith the first call. Shrey holding 700 shares did not pay the first call on the due date. Shrey paid the first call alongwith the final call. The accountant of the company had correctly passed the entries till receipt of allotment money. After that the following entries were left incomplete by him. Complete these entries. **Compartment 2018**

JOURNAL of Navnirman Ltd

Date	Particulars		LF	Amt (Dr)	Amt (Cr)
	Equity Share First Call A/c	Dr		8,00,000	
	To				8,00,000
	(Being first call due on 4,00,000 shares @ ₹ 2 per share)				
	Bank A/c	Dr		....	
	....	Dr		....	
	To Equity Share First Call A/c				....
	To.........				....
	(.........)				
	Equity Share Second and Final Call A/c	Dr		....	
	To Equity Share Capital A/c				....
	(Being final call due on 4,00,000 shares @ ₹ 3 per share)				
	Bank A/c	Dr		....	
	....	Dr		....	
	To Equity Share Second and Final Call A/c				....
	To				....
	(.........)				

Ans.

JOURNAL of Navnirman Ltd

Date	Particulars		LF	Amt (Dr)	Amt (Cr)
	Equity Share First Call A/c	Dr		8,00,000	
	To Equity Share Capital A/c				8,00,000
	(Being first call due on 4,00,000 shares @ ₹ 2 per share)				
	Bank A/c	Dr		**8,16,600**	
	Calls-in-arrears A/c (700 ×2)	Dr		**1,400**	
	To Equity Share First Call A/c				**8,00,000**
	To Calls-in-advance A/c (6,000 ×3)				**18,000**
	(Being first call money received on 3,99,300 shares with advance on 6,000 shares)				
	Equity Share Second and Final Call A/c	Dr		**12,00,000**	
	To Equity Share Capital A/c (4,00,000 × 3)				**12,00,000**
	(Being final call due on 4,00,000 shares @ ₹ 3 per share)				
	Bank A/c	Dr		**11,83,400**	
	Calls-in-advance A/c	Dr		**18,000**	
	To Equity Share Second and Final Call A/c				**12,00,000**
	To **Calls-in-arrears A/c**				**1,400**
	(Being second and final call money received with arrear amount and advance received adjusted)				

24. K Ltd took over the assets of ₹ 15,00,000 and liabilities of ₹ 5,00,000 of P Ltd for a purchase consideration of ₹ 13,68,500. ₹ 25,500 were paid by issuing a promissory note in favour of P Ltd payable after two months and the balance was paid by issue of equity shares of ₹ 100 each at a premium of 25%. Pass necessary journal entries for the above transactions in the books of K Ltd. **All India 2016**

Ans. **JOURNAL**

Date	Particulars		LF	Amt (Dr)	Amt (Cr)
	Sundry Assets A/c	Dr		15,00,000	
	Goodwill A/c (Balancing figure)	Dr		3,68,500	
	To Sundry Liabilities A/c				5,00,000
	To P Ltd				13,68,500
	(Being the assets and liabilities taken over)				
	P Ltd	Dr		13,68,500	
	To Equity Share Capital A/c (10,744 × 100)				10,74,400
	To Securities Premium Reserve A/c (10,744 × 25)				2,68,600
	To Bills Payable A/c				25,500
	(Being payment made by issuing a promissory note and issuing 10,744 shares of ₹ 100 each at a premium of 25%)				

Working Note

$$\text{Number of Shares Issued} = \frac{13{,}43{,}000\ (13{,}68{,}500 - 25{,}500)}{125\ (100 + 25)} = 10{,}744 \text{ shares}$$

25. Sandesh Ltd took over the assets of ₹ 7,00,000 and liabilities of ₹ 2,00,000 from Sanchar Ltd for a purchase consideration of ₹ 4,59,500, ₹ 8,500 were paid by accepting a draft in favour of Sanchar Ltd payable after three months and the balance was paid by issue of equity shares of ₹ 10 each at a premium of 10% in favour of Sanchar Ltd. Pass necessary journal entries for the above transactions in the books of Sandesh Ltd. **Delhi 2016**

Ans. Solve as Q no. 24 on page 263.

Capital Reserve = ₹ 40,500

Number of equity shares issued = 41,000

26. Guru Ltd invited applications for issuing 5,00,000 equity shares of ₹ 10 each at a premium of ₹ 5 per share. Because of favourable market conditions the issue was over subscribed and applications for 15,00,000 shares were received.

Suggest the alternatives available to the Board of Directors for the allotment of shares. **All India 2015**

Ans. In case of over subscription of shares, the Board of Directors has the following alternatives

(*i*) Excess application fully rejected and money refunded.

(*ii*) Excess application fully adjusted towards allotment and calls.

(*iii*) Excess applications partly rejected and partly adjusted towards further calls.

27. State any three purposes other than 'issue of bonus shares' for which securities premium can be utilised. **All India; Delhi 2015**

Or State any three purposes other than 'buy-back of shares' for which securities premium can be utilised. **Foreign 2015**

Or Securities premium can also be utilised for three other purposes besides

(*i*) issuing fully paid bonus shares and

(*ii*) 'buy-back of shares'. State other purposes. **Delhi 2015**

Ans. According to Section 52 (2) of the Companies Act, 2013, the securities premium reserve may be applied for the following purposes

(*i*) To write off preliminary expenses of the company.

(*ii*) To write off the expenses of or the commission paid or discount allowed on any issue of shares or debentures of the company.

(*iii*) To provide for the premium payable on the redemption of any redeemable preference shares or of any debentures of the company.

28. 'Tractors India Ltd' is registered with an authorised capital of ₹ 10,00,000 divided into 1,00,000 equity shares of ₹ 10 each. The company issued 50,000 equity shares at a premium of ₹ 5 per share. ₹ 2 per share were payable with application, ₹ 8 per share including premium on allotment and the balance amount on first and final call. The issue was fully subscribed and all the amount due was received except the first and final call money on 500 shares allotted to Balaram.

Present the 'share capital' in the balance sheet of 'Tractors India Ltd' as per Schedule III, Part I of the Companies Act, 2013. Also prepare notes to accounts for the same. **Delhi 2015**

Ans.

Extract of Balance Sheet

as at...

Particulars	Note No.	Amt (₹)
I. EQUITY AND LIABILITIES		
1. Shareholders' Funds		
(a) Share Capital	1	4,97,500
(b) Reserves and Surplus	2	2,50,000

Notes to Accounts

Particulars		Amt (₹)
1. Share Capital		
Authorised Capital		
1,00,000 shares of ₹ 10 each		10,00,000
Issued Capital		
50,000 shares of ₹ 10 each		5,00,000
Subscribed Capital		
Subscribed but not Fully Paid-up		
50,000 shares of ₹ 10	5,00,000	
(–) Calls-in-arrears (500 shares of ₹ 5)	(2,500)	4,97,500
2. Reserves and Surplus		
Securities Premium Reserve (50,000 × 5)		2,50,000

29. Sundram Ltd purchased furniture for ₹ 3,00,000 from Ravindram Ltd, ₹ 1,00,000 were paid by drawing a promissory note in favour of Ravindram Ltd. The balance was paid by issue of equity shares of ₹ 10 each at a premium of 25%. Pass journal entries in the books of Sundram Ltd. **All India 2012**

Ans.

JOURNAL

Date	Particulars		LF	Amt (Dr)	Amt (Cr)
	Furniture A/c	Dr		3,00,000	
	To Ravindram Ltd				3,00,000
	(Being furniture purchased)				

Date	Particulars		LF	Amt (Dr)	Amt (Cr)
	Ravindram Ltd	Dr		3,00,000	
	To Bills Payable A/c				1,00,000
	To Equity Share Capital A/c (16,000 × 10)				1,60,000
	To Securities Premium Reserve A/c (16,000 × 2.5)				40,000
	(Being payment made by issuing of a promissory note of ₹ 1,00,000 and 16,000 equity shares @ ₹ 10 per share at a premium of 25%)				

Working Note

Number of Shares to be Issued to Ravindram Ltd = $\frac{2,00,000}{10 + 2.5}$ = 16,000 shares

30. Z Ltd purchased furniture costing ₹ 2,20,000 from CD Ltd. The payment was to be made by issuing of 9% preference share of ₹ 100 each at a premium of ₹ 10 per share. Pass necessary journal entries in the books of Z Ltd. **Delhi 2011**

Ans. **JOURNAL**

Date	Particulars		LF	Amt (Dr)	Amt (Cr)
	Furniture A/c	Dr		2,20,000	
	To CD Ltd				2,20,000
	(Being furniture purchased)				
	CD Ltd	Dr		2,20,000	
	To 9% Preference Share Capital A/c (2,000 × 100)				2,00,000
	To Securities Premium Reserve A/c (2,000 × 10)				20,000
	(Being payment made by issuing of 2,000 equity shares @ ₹ 100 per share at a premium of ₹ 10 per share)				

Working Note

Number of Shares to be Issued to CD Ltd = $\frac{2,20,000}{100 + 10}$ = 2,000 shares

31. DN Ltd issued 50,000 shares of ₹ 10 each payable as ₹ 2 per share on application, ₹ 3 per share on allotment and ₹ 5 on first and final call. Applications were received for 70,000 shares. It was decided that

(*i*) Refuse allotment to the applicants of 10,000 shares.

(*ii*) Allot 20,000 shares to Mohan who had applied for similar number.

(*iii*) Allot the remaining shares on pro-rata basis.

Mohan failed to pay the allotment money and Sohan who belonged to the category (*iii*) and was allotted 3,000 shares paid both the calls with allotment. Calculate the amount received on allotment. **All India; Delhi 2010 Modified**

Ans.

	Shares Applied	Shares Allotted	
(*i*)	10,000	Nil	
(*ii*)	20,000	20,000	
(*iii*)	40,000	30,000	(Pro-rata allotment)
	70,000	50,000	

Calculation of Amount Received on Allotment	Amt (₹)
Allotment money due (50,000 × 3)	1,50,000
(–) Excess received with application (40,000 – 30,000) × 2	(20,000)
	1,30,000
(–) Calls-in-arrears (Mohan) (20,000 × 3)	(60,000)
	70,000
(+) Calls-in-advance (Sohan) (3,000 × 5)	15,000
Amount received with allotment	₹ 85,000

4 Marks Questions

32. Pass necessary journal entries for the following transactions in the books of Gopal Ltd

(*i*) Purchased furniture for ₹ 2,50,000 from M/s Furniture Mart. The payment to M/s Furniture Mart was made by issuing equity shares of ₹ 10 each at a premium of 25%.

(*ii*) Purchased a running business from Aman Ltd for a sum of ₹ 15,00,000. The payment of ₹ 12,00,000 was made by issue of fully paid equity shares of ₹ 10 each and balance by a bank draft. The assets and liabilities consisted of the following: plant ₹ 3,50,000; stock ₹ 4,50,000; land and building ₹ 6,00,000; sundry creditors ₹ 1,00,000. **All India 2014**

Ans. (*i*)

JOURNAL

Date	Particulars		LF	Amt (Dr)	Amt (Cr)
	Furniture A/c	Dr		2,50,000	
	To M/s Furniture Mart				2,50,000
	(Being furniture purchased)				
	M/s Furniture Mart	Dr		2,50,000	
	To Equity Share Capital A/c (20,000 × 10)				2,00,000
	To Securities Premium Reserve A/c (20,000 × 2.5)				50,000
	(Being the issue of 20,000 shares of ₹ 10 each at a premium of 25%)				

Working Note

$$\text{Number of Shares to be Issued} = \frac{\text{Purchase Consideration}}{\text{Issue Price}} = \frac{2,50,000}{10 + 2.5} = 20,000 \text{ shares}$$

(*ii*)

JOURNAL

Date	Particulars		LF	Amt (Dr)	Amt (Cr)
	Plant A/c	Dr		3,50,000	
	Stock A/c	Dr		4,50,000	
	Land and Building A/c	Dr		6,00,000	
	Goodwill A/c (Balancing figure)	Dr		2,00,000	
	To Sundry Creditors A/c				1,00,000
	To Aman Ltd				15,00,000
	(Being the purchase of business)				
	Aman Ltd	Dr		15,00,000	
	To Equity Share Capital A/c (1,20,000 × 10)				12,00,000
	To Bank A/c				3,00,000
	(Being the payment made to Aman Ltd)				

Working Note

$$\text{Number of Shares to be Issued} = \frac{\text{Purchase Consideration}}{\text{Issue Price}} = \frac{12,00,000}{10} = 1,20,000 \text{ shares}$$

33. 1st April, 2012 Vivek Ltd was formed with an authorised capital of ₹ 1,00,00,000 divided into 2,00,000 equity shares of ₹ 50 each. The company issued prospectus inviting applications for 1,80,000 shares. The issue price was payable as under

On application : ₹ 15 ; On allotment : ₹ 20

On call : Balance amount

The issue was fully subscribed and the company allotted shares to all the applicants. The company did not make the call during the year.

Show the following

(*i*) Share capital in the balance sheet of the company as per Schedule III, Part I of the Companies Act, 2013.

(*ii*) Also prepare 'Notes to accounts' for the same. **Delhi 2014**

Ans.

Extract of Balance Sheet

as at .....

Particulars	Note No.	Amt (₹)
I. **EQUITY AND LIABILITIES**		
1. **Shareholders' Funds**		
(a) Share Capital	1	63,00,000

Notes to Accounts

Particulars	Amt (₹)
1. **Share Capital**	
Authorised Capital	
2,00,000 equity shares of ₹ 50 each	1,00,00,000
Issued Capital	
1,80,000 shares of ₹ 50 each	90,00,000
Subscribed Capital	
Subscribed but not Fully Paid-up	
1,80,000 shares of ₹ 50 each, ₹ 35 called-up	63,00,000

34. Rajan Ltd purchased a running business from Vikas Ltd for a sum of ₹ 2,50,000 payable as ₹ 2,20,000 in fully paid equity shares of ₹ 10 each and balance by a bank draft. The assets and liabilities consisted of the following

Plant and machinery ₹ 90,000; building ₹ 90,000; sundry debtors ₹ 30,000; stock ₹ 50,000; cash ₹ 20,000; sundry creditors ₹ 20,000. **Delhi 2014**

Ans.

JOURNAL

Date	Particulars		LF	Amt (Dr)	Amt (Cr)
	Plant and Machinery A/c	Dr		90,000	
	Building A/c	Dr		90,000	
	Sundry Debtors A/c	Dr		30,000	
	Stock A/c	Dr		50,000	
	Cash A/c	Dr		20,000	
	To Sundry Creditors A/c				20,000
	To Vikas Ltd				2,50,000
	To Capital Reserve A/c (Balancing figure)				10,000
	(Being running business purchased from Vikas Ltd and excess of assets and purchases consideration credited to capital reserve account)				

Date	Particulars		LF	Amt (Dr)	Amt (Cr)
	Vikas Ltd	Dr		2,50,000	
	To Equity Share Capital A/c (22,000 ×10)				2,20,000
	To Bank A/c				30,000
	(Being purchases consideration discharged)				

Working Note

$$\text{Number of Shares to be Issued} = \frac{\text{Purchase Consideration}}{\text{Issue Price}} = \frac{2,20,000}{10} = 22,000 \text{ shares}$$

35. Nikhil Ltd purchased a running business from Sonia Ltd for a sum of ₹ 22,00,000 by issuing 20,000 fully paid equity shares of ₹ 100 each at a premium of 10%. The assets and liabilities consisted of the following

Machinery ₹ 7,00,000; debtors ₹ 2,50,000; stock ₹ 5,00,000; building ₹ 11,50,000 and bills payable ₹ 2,50,000.

Pass necessary journal entries in the books of Nikhil Ltd for the above transactions. **All India 2013**

Ans. For journal entry relating to purchases of business, solve as Q no. 34 on page 267 and 268.

JOURNAL

Date	Particulars		LF	Amt (Dr)	Amt (Cr)
	Sonia Ltd A/c	Dr		22,00,000	
	To Equity Share Capital A/c (20,000 × 100)				20,00,000
	To Securities Premium Reserve A/c (20,000 × 10)				2,00,000
	(Being purchases consideration discharged by issue of 20,000 equity shares of ₹ 100 each at a premium of ₹ 10)				

Working Note

$$\text{Number of Equity Shares Issued} = \frac{22,00,000}{110} = 20,000 \text{ shares}$$

36. The authorised capital of Suhas Ltd is ₹ 50,00,000 divided into 25,000 shares of ₹ 200 each. Out of these, the company issued 12,000 shares of ₹ 200 each at a premium of 10%. The amount per share was payable as follows

₹ 60 on application

₹ 60 on allotment (including premium)

₹ 30 on first call and balance on final call.

Public applied for 11,000 shares. All the money was duly received.

Prepare an extract of balance sheet of Suhas Ltd as per Revised Schedule III, Part I of the Companies Act, 2013 disclosing the above information. Also prepare 'Notes to accounts' for the same. **All India 2013**

Ans.

Extract of Balance Sheet

as at...

Particulars	Note No.	Amt (₹)
I. EQUITY AND LIABILITIES		
1. Shareholders' Funds		
(a) Share Capital	1	22,00,000
(b) Reserves and Surplus (Securities premium reserve)		2,20,000
Total		24,20,000

Particulars	Note No.	Amt (₹)
II. ASSETS		
(i) Current Assets		
(a) Cash and Cash Equivalents (Cash at bank)		24,20,000
Total		24,20,000

Note to Accounts

Particulars	Amt (₹)
Share Capital	
Authorised Capital	
25,000 shares of ₹ 200 each	50,00,000
Issued Capital	
12,000 shares of ₹ 200 each	24,00,000
Subscribed Capital	
Subscribed and Fully Paid-up	
11,000 shares of ₹ 200	22,00,000

TOPIC 3

Forfeiture and Re-issue of Shares

Forfeiture of Shares

Forfeiture of shares means cancellation of shares and seizure of the amount already received from defaulting shareholders.

(*i*) Issued at Par

Share Capital A/c	Dr	[With called-up amount]
To Share Allotment A/c		[With amount due but not paid on allotment]
To Share Call A/c		[With amount due but not paid on call]
To Share Forfeiture A/c		[With amount already received]

(*ii*) Issued at Premium and Premium was Received

Share Capital A/c	Dr	[Amount called-up less premium]
To Share Allotment A/c		[Amount not received on allotment]
To Share Call A/c		[Amount not received on calls]
To Share Forfeiture A/c		[Amount received so far excluding securities premium reserve]

(*iii*) Issued at Premium and Premium was not Received

Share Capital A/c	Dr	[Amount called-up less premium]
Securities Premium Reserve A/c	Dr	[Premium amount called-up but not received]
To Share Allotment A/c		[Amount not received on allotment]
To Share Call A/c		[Amount not received on calls]
To Share Forfeiture A/c		[Amount received so far]

Re-issue of Forfeited Shares

The directors can either cancel or re-issue the forfeited shares. Shares forfeited can be re-issued at par, at premium or at a discount.

In case, they are re-issued at par, accounting entry will be

Bank A/c	Dr
To Share Capital A/c	

In case, shares are re-issued at a discount, the amount of discount allowed on the re-issue of forfeited shares must not exceed the amount forfeited on re-issued shares. The discount allowed on re-issue of forfeited shares should be debited to the 'share forfeiture account'.

The journal entry will be

Bank A/c	Dr	[With the amount received on re-issue]
*Share Forfeiture A/c	Dr	[With the discount allowed on re-issue]
To Share Capital A/c		[With the amount credited as paid-up]

**It is calculated as*

Number of Shares Re-issued × (Paid-up value – Re-issue price per share)

The amount of discount allowed on re-issue of forfeited shares should be less than or equal to the amount forfeited on those shares. If the forfeited shares are re-issued at a price higher than that paid-up, i.e. at a premium, the excess is credited to securities premium reserve account.

The journal entry will

Bank A/c	Dr
To Share Capital A/c	
To Securities Premium Reserve A/c	

Transfer of Balance in Forfeited Share Account after Re-issue

Forfeited Shares A/c	Dr
To Capital Reserve A/c	

Previous Years' Examination Questions

1 Mark Questions

1. Z Ltd forfeited 1,000 equity shares of ₹ 10 each for the non-payment of the first call of ₹ 2 per share. The final call of ₹ 3 per share was yet to be made. Calculate the maximum amount of discount at which these shares can be re-issued. **All India 2017**

Ans. The maximum amount of discount allowed on the re-issue of forfeited shares must not exceed the amount forfeited on re-issued shares. In this case, the maximum amount of discount at which shares can be re-issued is (1,000 × 5) = ₹ 5,000.

2. Y Ltd forfeited 100 equity shares of ₹ 10 each for the non-payment of first call of ₹ 2 per share. The final call of ₹ 2 per share was yet to be made. Calculate the maximum amount of discount at which these shares can be re-issued. **Delhi 2017**

Ans. Solve as Q no. 1 on page 270.

Maximum Discount at which shares can be re-issued (100 × 6) = ₹ 600

3. Give the meaning of forfeiture of shares. **All India 2014 (C), 2010; Foreign 2015**

Ans. Forfeiture of shares means cancellation of shares and seizure of the amount received from the defaulting shareholders, whose shares have been forfeited. Upon forfeiture, the name of original shareholder must be removed from the register of members. Forfeiture results in reduction of share capital.

4. A Ltd forfeited 100 equity shares of ₹ 10 each issued at premium of 20% for the non-payment of final call of ₹ 5 including premium. State the maximum amount of discount at which these shares can be re-issued. **All India 2014**

Ans. Maximum amount of discount that can be allowed at the time of re-issue is the amount forfeited on re-issued shares, *i.e.* $(100 \times 7) =$ ₹ 700.

5. What is the maximum amount of discount at which forfeited shares can be re-issued? **Delhi 2014 Modified**

Ans. When forfeited shares are re-issued at a discount, the discount cannot exceed the amount forfeited on re-issued shares.

3 Marks Questions

6. What is meant by 'forfeiture of shares'? When does 'gain on forfeited shares' arise and when is it transferred to capital reserve? **All India 2019**

Ans. 'Forfeiture of shares' refer to Q. no 3 on page 271.

When forfeited shares are re-issued at discount, gain on forfeited shares arises. The balance left in the share forfeited account after the re-issue is transferred to the capital reserve account.

7. Janta Ltd had an authorised capital of 2,00,000 equity shares of ₹ 10 each. The company offered to the public for subscription 1,00,000 shares. Applications were received for 97,000 shares. The amount was payable as follows on application was ₹ 2 per share, ₹ 4 was payable each on allotment and first and final call. A shareholder holding 600 shares failed to pay the allotment money. His shares were forfeited. The company did not make the first and final call.

Present the share capital in the balance sheet of the company as per Schedule III of the Companies Act, 2013. Also prepare notes to accounts. **Compartment 2018**

Ans.

Balance Sheet of Janta Ltd

as at ....

Particulars	Note No.	Amt (₹)
I. EQUITY AND LIABILITIES		
1. Shareholders' Funds		
(a) Share Capital	1	5,79,600

Notes to Accounts

Particulars		Amt (₹)
1. Share Capital		
Authorised Capital		
2,00,000 equity shares of ₹ 10 each		20,00,000
Issued Capital		
1,00,000 equity shares of ₹ 10 each		10,00,000
Subscribed Capital		
Subscribed and Fully Paid up		
96,400 Shares of ₹ 10 each, ₹ 6 called-up	5,78,400	
(+) Shares Forfeited Account	1,200	5,79,600

8. Sajag Ltd has an authorised capital of ₹ 30,00,000 divided into equity shares of ₹ 30 each. The compnay invited applications for issuing 70,000 shares. Applications for 68,000 shares were received.

All calls were made and were duly received except the final call of ₹ 10 per share on 5,000 shares. These shares were forfeited.

(*i*) Present the share capital in the balance sheet of the company as per Schedule III of the Companies Act, 2013.

(*ii*) Also prepare 'Notes to accounts' for the same. **All India (C) 2016**

Ans.

Extract of Balance Sheet

as at ....

Particulars	Note No.	Amt (₹)
I. **EQUITY AND LIABILITIES**		
Shareholders' Funds		
(a) Share Capital	1	19,90,000

Notes to Accounts

Particulars		Amt (₹)
1. **Share Capital**		
Authorised Capital		
1,00,000 equity shares of ₹ 30 each		30,00,000
Issued Capital		
70,000 equity shares of ₹ 30 each		21,00,000
Subscribed and Fully Paid-up		
63,000 shares of ₹ 30 each	18,90,000	
(+) Shares Forfeited Account (5,000 Shares @ ₹ 20)	1,00,000	19,90,000

9. Samprag Ltd has an authorised capital of ₹ 20,00,000 divided into equity shares of ₹ 10 each. The company invited applications for issuing 60,000 shares. Applications for 58,000 shares were received.

All calls were made and were duly received except the final call of ₹ 3 as share on 2,000 shares. These shares were forfeited.

(*i*) Present the share capital in the balance sheet of the company as per Schedule III of the Companies Act, 2013.

(*ii*) Also prepare 'Notes to accounts' for the same. **Delhi (C) 2016**

Ans. Solve as Q no. 8 on page 272. Share capital = ₹ 5,74,000

10. 'Suvidha Ltd' is registered with an authorised capital of ₹ 10,00,00,000 divided into 10,00,000 equity shares of ₹ 100 each. The company issued 1,00,000 shares for public subscription. A shareholder holding 100 shares, failed to pay the final call of ₹ 20 per share. His shares were forfeited. The forfeited shares were re-issued at ₹ 90 per share as fully paid-up.

Present the share capital in the balance sheet of the company as per Schedule III, Part I of the Companies Act, 2013. Also prepare notes to accounts. **All India 2015**

Ans.

Extract of Balance Sheet
as at ....

Particulars	Note No.	Amt (₹)
I. **EQUITY AND LIABILITIES**		
1. **Shareholders' Funds**		
(a) Share Capital	1	1,00,00,000
		1,00,00,000

Working Note

Particulars	Amt (₹)
1. **Share Capital**	
Authorised Capital	
10,00,000 equity shares of ₹ 100 each	10,00,00,000
Issued Capital	
1,00,000 equity shares of ₹ 100 each	1,00,00,000
Subscribed Capital	
Subscribed and Fully Paid-up	
1,00,000 shares of ₹ 100 each	1,00,00,000
	1,00,00,000

11. 'India Auto Ltd' is registered with an authorised capital of ₹ 7,00,00,000 divided into 7,00,000 shares of ₹ 100 each. The company issued 50,000 shares to the vendor for building purchased and 2,00,000 shares were issued to the public. The amount was payable as follows

On application and allotment	:	₹ 20 per share
On first call	:	₹ 50 per share
On second and final call	:	Balance

All calls were made and were duly received except on 100 shares held by Rajani, who failed to pay the second and final call. Her shares were forfeited.

Present the 'share capital' in the balance sheet of the company as per Schedule III, Part I of the Companies Act, 2013. Also prepare 'notes to accounts'. **All India 2015**

Ans.

Extract of Balance Sheet
as at...

Particulars	Note No.	Amt (₹)
I. **EQUITY AND LIABILITIES**		
1. **Shareholders' Funds**		
(a) Share Capital	1	2,49,97,000
		2,49,97,000

Notes to Accounts

Particulars	Amt (₹)
1. Share Capital	
Authorised Capital	
7,00,000 shares of ₹ 100 each	7,00,00,000
Issued Capital	
50,000 Shares of ₹ 100 each as fully paid for a consideration other than cash	50,00,000
2,00,000 Shares of ₹ 100 each	2,00,00,000
	2,50,00,000
Subscribed Capital	
Subscribed and Fully Paid-up	
50,000 shares of ₹ 100 each as purchase consideration	50,00,000
1,99,900 shares of ₹ 100 each	1,99,90,000
(+) Share Forfeited Account (100 × 70)	7,000
	2,49,97,000

12. SSS Ltd forfeited 1,000 equity shares of ₹ 100 each for the non-payment of first call ₹ 20 per share and second and final call of ₹ 25 per share. State

(*i*) Can these shares be re-issued?

(*ii*) If yes state the minimum amount at which these shares can be re-issued?

(*iii*) If these shares were re-issued at ₹ 50 per share fully paid up, what will be the amount of capital reserve? **Delhi 2010**

Ans. (*i*) Yes, forfeited shares can be re-issued.

(*ii*) Forfeited shares can re-issued at any rate of discount. The only condition is that the amount of discount allowed on the re-issue of forfeited shares must not exceed the amount forfeited on such shares. In this case, shares can be re-issued at a minimum price of ₹ 45 per share (*i.e.* 100 – 55).

(*iii*) **Calculation of Amount Transferred to Capital Reserve**

Amount forfeited (1,000 × 55)	=	55,000
(–) Discount on re-issue (1,000 × 50)	=	(50,000)
Gain on re-issue to be transferred to capital reserve	=	₹ 5,000

4 Marks Questions

13. On 1st April, 2012, Vishwas Ltd was formed with an authorised capital of ₹ 10,00,000 divided into 1,00,000 equity shares of ₹ 10 each. The company issued prospectus inviting applications for 90,000 equity shares. The company received applications for 85,000 equity shares. During the first year, ₹ 8 per share were called. Ram holding 1,000 shares and Shyam holding 2,000 shares did not pay the first call of ₹ 2 per share. Shyam's shares were forfeited after the first call and later on 1,500 of the forfeited shares were re-issued at ₹ 6 per share, ₹ 8 called-up.

Show the following

(*i*) Share capital in the balance sheet of the company as per Revised Schedule III Part I of the Companies Act, 2013.

(*ii*) Also prepare 'notes to accounts' for the same. **All India 2014**

Ans. (*i*)

Balance Sheet (Extract)
as at 1st April, 2012

Particulars	Note No.	Amt (₹)
I. **EQUITY AND LIABILITIES**		
1. **Shareholders' Funds**		
(a) Share Capital	1	6,77,000
(b) Reserves and Surplus	2	6,000
		6,83,000

(*ii*) ***Notes to Accounts***

Particulars		Amt (₹)
1. **Share Capital**		
Authorised Capital		
1,00,000 equity shares of ₹ 10 each		10,00,000
Issued Capital		
90,000 equity shares of ₹ 10 each		9,00,000
Subscribed Capital		
Subscribed but not Fully Paid-up		
84,500 equity shares of ₹ 10 each, ₹ 8 called up	6,76,000	
(–) Calls-in-arrears (1,000 × 2)	(2,000)	6,74,000
(+) Share Forfeited Account (500 × 6)		3,000
		6,77,000
2. **Reserves and Surplus**		
Capital Reserve		6,000

Working Note

Capital Reserve

(a) Amount forfeited on re-issued shares $= 12{,}000 \times \dfrac{1{,}500}{2{,}000} = ₹\,9{,}000$

(b) Amount utilised at the time of re-issue = ₹ 3,000 (1,500 × 2)

Capital reserve (a – b) = 9,000 – 3,000 = ₹ 6,000

NOTE Calls-in-arrears will be shown only of Ram's holding because Shyam's shares have been forfeited.

14. B Ltd was registered with an authorised capital of ₹ 20,00,000 divided into equity shares of ₹ 10 each.The company invited applications for the issue of 1,00,000 shares. Applications for 96,000 shares were received. All calls were made and were duly received except the final call of ₹ 2 per share on 2,000 shares. All these shares were forfeited and later on re-issued at ₹ 18,000 as fully paid.

(*i*) Show how 'share capital' will appear in the balance sheet of B Ltd as per Schedule III of the Companies Act, 2013.

(*ii*) Also prepare 'Notes to Accounts' for the same. **All India (C) 2014**

Ans. Solve as Q no. 10 on page 272 and 273.
Share Capital = ₹ 9,60,000

15. L Ltd forfeited 470 equity shares of ₹ 20 each issued at a premium of ₹ 3 per share for the non-payment of allotment money of ₹ 8 (including premium ₹ 3) and first call of ₹ 5 per share. Final call of ₹ 5 per share was not made. Out of these 235 shares were re-issued at ₹ 19 each fully paid. Pass necessary journal entries for the above transactions in the books of L Ltd. **Delhi (C) 2014**

Ans.

JOURNAL

Date	Particulars		LF	Amt (Dr)	Amt (Cr)
	Equity Share Capital A/c (470 × 15)	Dr		7,050	
	Securities Premium Reserve A/c (470 × 3)	Dr		1,410	
	To Equity Share Allotment A/c (470 × 8)				3,760
	To Equity Share First Call A/c (470 × 5)				2,350
	To Share Forfeiture A/c (470 × 5)				2,350
	(Being 470 shares forfeited for non-payment of allotment and first call)				
	Bank A/c (235×19)	Dr		4,465	
	Share Forfeiture A/c	Dr		235	
	To Equity Share Capital A/c (235×20)				4,700
	(Being 235 shares re-issued @ ₹ 19 per share)				
	Share Forfeiture A/c	Dr		940	
	To Capital Reserve A/c				940
	(Being the balance on re-issued shares transferred to capital reserve account)				

Working Note

Amount to be Transferred to Capital Reserve

Amount forfeited on re-issued shares $= \frac{2,350}{470} \times 235 = 1,175$

(–) Amount utilised at the time of re-issue = (235)

Capital reserve = ₹ 940

16. Give journal entries to record the following transaction of forfeiture and re-issue of shares and open share forfeiture account.

L Ltd forfeited 470 equity shares of ₹ 10 each issued at premium of ₹ 5 per share for non-payment of allotment money ₹ 8 per share (including share premium ₹ 5 per share) and the first and final call of ₹ 5 per share. Out of these, 60 equity shares were subsequently re-issued @ ₹ 14 per shares. **Delhi 2011**

Ans.

JOURNAL

Date	Particulars		LF	Amt (Dr)	Amt (Cr)
	Equity Share Capital A/c (470 × 10)	Dr		4,700	
	Securities Premium Reserve A/c (470× 5)	Dr		2,350	
	To Share Forfeiture A/c (470 × 2)				940
	To Equity Share Allotment A/c (470 × 8)				3,760
	To Equity Share First and Final Call A/c (470 × 5)				2,350
	(Being 470 shares forfeited for the non-payment of allotment and first and first call)				
	Bank A/c (60 × 14)	Dr		840	
	To Equity Share Capital A/c (60 × 10)				600
	To Securities Premium Reserve A/c (60 × 4)				240
	(Being re-issue of 60 shares @ ₹ 14 per share as fully paid-up)				
	Share Forfeiture A/c	Dr		120	
	To Capital Reserve A/c				120
	(Being balance of forfeited share account transferred to capital reserve account)				

Share Forfeiture Account

Dr Particulars	Amt (₹)	Particulars	Cr Amt (₹)
To Capital Reserve A/c	120	By Share Capital A/c	940
To Balance c/d (Balancing figure)	820		
	940		940

Working Note

Amount of 60 forfeited shares $= 940 \times \frac{60}{470} =$ ₹ 120 to be transferred to capital reserve account.

6 Marks Question

17. (*a*) Fill in the blank spaces in the journal entries given below **All India (C) 2015**

Date	Particulars		LF	Amt (Dr)	Amt (Cr)
(i)	Share Capital A/c	Dr		...	
	....	Dr		...	
	To Share Forfeited A/c				6,000
	To Share Allotment A/c				...
	To Share First Call A/c				...
	(Being 2,000 shares of ₹ 10 each ₹ 8 called-up issued at a premium of ₹ 2 per share forfeited for non-payment of allotment of ₹ 5 per share including premium and first call of ₹ 2 per share)				
(ii)	Bank A/c	Dr		19,600	
	To Share Capital A/c				...
	To				...
	(Being 1,400 shares re-issued for ₹ 19,600 as fully paid-up)				
(iii)	Share Forfeited A/c	Dr		...	
	To Capital Reserve A/c				...
	(Being profit on re-issue of forfeited shares transferred to capital reserve account)				

(*b*) Fill in the blank spaces in the journal entries given below

Date	Particulars		LF	Amt (Dr)	Amt (Cr)
(i)	Share Capital A/c	Dr		80,000	
	To Share Forfeited A/c				...
	To				...
	(Being 1,000 shares of ₹ 10 each ₹ 80 called up forfeited for non-payment of first call ₹ 60)				
(ii)	Bank A/c	Dr		56,000	
	Share Forfeited A/c	Dr		...	
	To Share Capital A/c				...
	(Being 800 shares re-issued @ ₹ 70 per share ₹ 80 paid-up)				
(iii)	Share Forfeited A/c	Dr		...	
	To Capital Reserve A/c				...
	(Being profit on re-issue of forfeited shares transferred to capital reserve account)				

Ans. (*a*)

JOURNAL

Date	Particulars		LF	Amt (Dr)	Amt (Cr)
(i)	Share Capital A/c	Dr		16,000	
	Securities Premium Reserve A/c	Dr		4,000	
	To Share Forfeited A/c				6,000
	To Share Allotment A/c				10,000
	To Share First Call A/c				4,000
	(Being 2,000 shares of ₹ 10 each ₹ 8 called-up issued at a premium of ₹ 2 per share forfeited for non-payment of allotment of ₹ 5 per share including premium and first call of ₹ 2 per share)				
(ii)	Bank A/c	Dr		19,600	
	To Share Capital A/c				14,000
	To Securities Premium Reserve A/c				5,600
	(Being 1,400 shares re-issued for ₹ 19,600 as fully paid-up)				
(iii)	Share Forfeited A/c	Dr		4,200	
	To Capital Reserve A/c				4,200
	(Being profit on re-issue of forfeited shares transferred to capital reserve account)				

(*b*)

JOURNAL

Date	Particulars		LF	Amt (Dr)	Amt (Cr)
(i)	Share Capital A/c	Dr		80,000	
	To Share Forfeited A/c				20,000
	To Share First Call A/c				60,000
	(Being 1,000 shares of ₹ 100 each ₹ 80 called up forfeited for non-payment of first call ₹ 60)				
(ii)	Bank A/c	Dr		56,000	
	Share Forfeited A/c	Dr		8,000	
	To Share Capital A/c				64,000
	(Being 800 shares re-issued @ ₹ 70 per share ₹ 80 paid-up)				
(iii)	Share Forfeited A/c	Dr		8,000	
	To Capital Reserve A/c				8,000
	(Being profit on re-issue of forfeited shares transferred to capital reserve account)				

8 Marks Questions

18. Rathi Ltd. invited applications for issuing 1,00,000 shares of ₹ 10 each at a premium of ₹ 2 per share. Amount per share was payable as follows
On Application — ₹ 4 (including premium ₹ 1); On Allotment — ₹ 4 (including premium ₹ 1)
On First and Final Call — Balance

Applications were received for 1,50,000 shares and allotment was made to the applicants as follows

(*i*) Applicants of 80,000 shares were allotted 60,000 shares.
(*ii*) Applicants of 50,000 shares were allotted 40,000 shares.
(*iii*) No shares were allotted to the remaining applicants and their application money was returned.

Yatin, who belonged to category (ii) and who had applied for 5,000 shares failed to pay the allotment and call money. His shares were forfeited. Later, half of Yatin's forfeited shares were reissued @ ₹ 18 per share as fully paid-up.

Pass the necessary journal entries to record the above transactions in the books of Rathi Ltd.
CBSE 2020

Ans.

JOURNAL

Date	Particulars		LF	Amt (Dr)	Amt (Cr)
	Bank A/c (1,50,000 × 4)	Dr		6,00,000	
	To Share Application A/c				6,00,000
	(Being application money received)				
	Share Application A/c	Dr		6,00,000	
	To Share Capital A/c (1,00,000 × 3)				3,00,000
	To Securities Premium Reserve A/c (1,00,000 × 1)				1,00,000
	To Shares Allotment A/c (30,000 × 4)				1,20,000
	To Bank A/c (20,000 × 4)				80,000
	(Being application money transferred to capital account)				
	Share Allotment A/c (1,00,000 × 4)	Dr		4,00,000	
	To Share Capital A/c (1,00,000 × 3)				3,00,000
	To Securities Premium Reserve A/c (1,00,000 × 1)				1,00,000
	(Being allotment money due)				
	Bank A/c	Dr		2,68,000	
	To Share Allotment A/c				2,68,000
	(Being allotment money received)				
	Share First and Final Call A/c (1,00,000 × 4)	Dr		4,00,000	
	To Share Capital A/c				4,00,000
	(Being first and final call money due)				
	Bank A/c	Dr		3,84,000	
	To Share First and Final Call A/c				3,84,000
	(Being final call money received)				
	Share Capital A/c (4,000 × 10)	Dr		40,000	
	Securities Premium Reserve A/c (4,000 × 1)	Dr		4,000	
	To Share Forfeited A/c				16,000
	To Share Allotment A/c				12,000
	To Share First and Final Call A/c				16,000
	(Being 4,000 shares forfeited)				
	Bank A/c (2,000 × 18)	Dr		36,000	
	To Share Capital A/c (2,000 × 10)				20,000
	To Securities Premium Reserve A/c (2,000 × 8)				16,000
	(Being 2,000 shares reissued)				
	Share Forfeiture A/c	Dr		8,000	
	To Capital Reserve A/c				8,000
	(Being balance of forfeiture transfer to capital reserve account)				

Working Note

No. of shares allotted to Yatin = $5{,}000 \times \frac{40{,}000}{50{,}000}$ = 4,000 shares

Application money received (5,000 × 4)	=	20,000
(−) Application money due (4,000 × 4)	=	(16,000)
Excess money received	=	4,000
Allotment excess money received	=	16,000
Calls-in-arrear amount	=	12,000

19. Denspar Ltd invited applications for issuing 2,00,000 equity shares of ₹ 10 each at a premium of ₹ 20 per share. The amount was payable as follows

On application : ₹ 2 per share

On allotment : ₹ 13 per share (including ₹ 10 premium)

On first call : ₹ 7 per share (including ₹ 5 premium)

On final call : ₹ 8 per share (including ₹ 5 premium)

Applications for 1,80,000 shares were received. Shares were allotted to all the applicatns. Yogesh, a shareholder holding 5,000 shares paid his entire share money alongwith the allotment money. Vishesh, a holder of 7,000 shares, failed to pay the allotment money. Afterwards the first call was made. Vishesh paid the allotment money alongwith the first call money. Samyesh, holding 2,000 shares did not pay the final call. Samyesh's shares were forfeited immediately after the final call. Out of the forfeited shares, 1,500 shares were re-issued at ₹ 8 per share fully paid-up.

Pass the necessary journal entries for the above transactions in the books of Denspar Ltd.
All India 2019

Ans.

JOURNAL

In the Books of Denspar Ltd

Date	Particulars		LF	Amt (Dr)	Amt (Cr)
	Bank A/c (1,80,000 × 2)	Dr		3,60,000	
	To Equity Share Application A/c				3,60,000
	(Being application money received)				
	Equity Share Application A/c	Dr		3,60,000	
	To Equity Share Capital A/c				3,60,000
	(Being application money transferred to capital account)				
	Equity Share Allotment A/c (1,80,000 × 13)	Dr		23,40,000	
	To Equity Share Capital A/c (1,80,000 × 3)				5,40,000
	To Security Premium A/c (1,80,000 × 10)				18,00,000
	(Being allotment money due)				
	Bank A/c	Dr		23,24,000	
	To Equity Share Allotment A/c				22,49,000
	To Calls-in-Advance A/c (5,000 × 15)				75,000
	(Being allotment received)				
	Equity Share First Call A/c (1,80,000 × 7)	Dr		12,60,000	
	To Equity Share Capital A/c (1,80,000 × 2)				3,60,000
	To Security Premium A/c (1,80,000 × 5)				9,00,000
	(Being first call money due)				

Date	Particulars		LF	Amt (Dr)	Amt (Cr)
	Bank A/c	Dr		13,16,000	
	Calls-in-Advance A/c (5,000 × 7)	Dr		35,000	
	To Equity Share First Call A/c				12,60,000
	To Equity Share Allotment A/c				91,000
	(Being first call money received with allotment arrear)				
	Equity Share Final Call A/c (1,80,000 × 8)	Dr		14,40,000	
	To Equity Share Capital A/c (1,80,000 × 3)				5,40,000
	To Security Premium A/c (1,80,000 × 5)				9,00,000
	(Being final call money due)				
	Bank A/c	Dr		13,84,000	
	Calls-in-Advance A/c (5,000 × 8)	Dr		40,000	
	To Equity Share Final Call A/c				14,24,000
	(Being final call money received)				
	Equity Share Capital A/c (2,000 × 10)	Dr		20,000	
	Security Premium A/c (2,000 × 5)	Dr		10,000	
	To Share Forfeited A/c (2,000 × 7)				14,000
	To Equity Share Final Call A/c (2,000 × 8)				16,000
	(Being 2,000 shares forfeited for non-payment of final call)				
	Bank A/c (1,500 × 8)	Dr		12,000	
	Shared Forfeiture A/c (1,500 × 2)	Dr		3,000	
	To Equity Share Capital A/c (1,500 × 10)				15,000
	(Being 1,500 shares re-issued @ ₹ 8 per each)				
	Share Forfeiture A/c			7,500	
	To Capital Reserve A/c				7,500
	(Being profit on re-issue of shares transferred to capital reserve account)				

Working Notes

	Amt (₹)
1. Amount due at allotment	= 23,40,000
(−) Calls in Arrears (7,000 × 13)	= (91,000)
	= 22,49,000
(+) Calls in advance (5,000 × 15)	= 75,000
Amount received at allotment	= 23,24,000
2. Amount of share forfeiture for 1,500 shares (1,500 × 7)	= 10,500
(−) On re-issue (1,500 × 2)	= (3,000)
Transferred to capital reserve	= 7,500

20. KLN Ltd invited applications for issuing 1,00,000 shares of ₹ 10 each at a premium of ₹ 2 per share. The amount was payable as follows

On Application	₹ 3 per share (including premium ₹ 1)
On Allotment	₹ 4 per share (including premium ₹ 1)
On First call	₹ 3 per share
On Second and Final Call	Balance amount

Application for 1,90,000 shares were received. Allotment was made to the applicants as follows

Category	No. of Shares Applied	No. of Shares Allotted
I	50,000	40,000
II	1,00,000	60,000

Remaining applications were rejected.

Rajat, a shareholder belonging to Category I who had applied for 2,500 shares, failed to pay the amount due on allotment and first call. His shares were immediately forfeited.

Reema, a shareholder belonging to Category II who was holding 3,000 shares failed to pay the first call and second call money. Her shares were also forfeited. Afterwards 4,000 shares were re-issued @ ₹ 8 per share fully paid-up. These included all the forfeited shares of Reema.

Pass necessary journal entries for the above transactions in the books of KLN Ltd.
All India 2019

Ans.

JOURNAL
In the Books of KLN Ltd

Date	Particulars		LF	Amt (Dr)	Amt (Cr)
	Bank A/c (1,90,000 × 3)	Dr		5,70,000	
	To Share Application A/c				5,70,000
	(Being application money received)				
	Share Application A/c	Dr		5,70,000	
	To Share Capital A/c (1,00,000 × 2)				2,00,000
	To Securities Premium A/c (1,00,000 × 1)				1,00,000
	To Share Allotment A/c (50,000 × 3)				1,50,000
	To Bank A/c (40,000 × 3)				1,20,000
	(Being application money transferred to capital account and excess money adjusted towards allotment and refund)				
	Share Allotment A/c (1,00,000 × 4)	Dr		4,00,000	
	To Share Capital A/c (1,00,000 × 3)				3,00,000
	To Securities Premium A/c (1,00,000 × 1)				1,00,000
	(Being allotment money due)				
	Bank A/c (4,00,000 – 1,50,000 – 6,500)	Dr		2,43,500	
	To Share Allotment A/c				2,43,500
	(Being allotment money received)				
	Share First Call A/c (1,00,000 × 3)	Dr		3,00,000	
	To Share Capital A/c				3,00,000
	(Being first call money due)				
	Bank A/c (3,00,000 – 6,000 – 9,000)	Dr		2,85,000	
	To Share First Call A/c				2,85,000
	(Being first call money received)				

Date	Particulars		LF	Amt (Dr)	Amt (Cr)
	Share Capital A/c (2,000 × 8)	Dr		16,000	
	Securities Premium A/c (2,000 × 1)	Dr		2,000	
	To Share Forfeiture A/c				5,500
	To Share Allotment A/c				6,500
	To Share First Call A/c				6,000
	(Being 2,000 shares of Rajat forfeited)				
	Shares Second and Final Call A/c (98,000 × 2)	Dr		1,96,000	
	To Share Capital A/c				1,96,000
	(Being second and final call money due)				
	Bank A/c (1,96,000–6,000)	Dr		1,90,000	
	To Share Second and Final Call A/c				1,90,000
	(Being second and final call money received)				
	Share Capital A/c (3,000 × 10)	Dr		30,000	
	To Share Forfeiture A/c (3,000 × 15)				15,000
	To Share First Call (3,000 × 3)				9,000
	To Share Second and Final Call (3,000 × 2)				6,000
	(Being 3,000 shares of Reema forfeited)				
	Bank A/c	Dr		32,000	
	Shared Forfeiture A/c	Dr		8,000	
	To Share Capital A/c				40,000
	(Being 4,000 shares re-issued)				
	Shared Forfeiture A/c	Dr		9,750	
	To Capital Reserve A/c				9,750
	(Being share forfeiture amount transferred to capital reserve account)				

Working Notes

1. Number of shares allotted to Rajat $\left(2{,}500 \times \frac{40{,}000}{50{,}000}\right) = 2{,}000$ shares

		Amt (₹)
Amount received on application	(2,500 × 3) =	7,500
(–) Amount due on application	(2,000 × 3) =	(6,000)
Excess		1,500
Amount due on allotment	(2,000 × 4) =	8,000
Calls-in-arrears at allotment		6,500

2. Amount forfeited on Rajat's 1,000 shares $\left(\frac{5{,}500}{2{,}000} \times 1000\right) = 2{,}750$

Amount forfeited on Reema's 3,000 shares	= 15,000
	17,750
(–) Loss on shares re-issued	(8,000)
Transferred to capital reserve	9,750

21. S Ltd invited applications for issuing 1,00,000 equity shares of ₹ 10 each. The shares were issued at a premium of ₹ 5 per share. The amount was payable as follows

On application and allotment – ₹ 8 per share (including premium ₹ 8)

On the first and final call – Balance including premium

Applications for 1,50,000 shares were received. Applications for 10,000 shares were rejected and pro-rata allotment was made to the remaining applicants on the following basis

(*i*) Applicants for 80,000 shares were allotted 60,000 shares.

(*ii*) Applicants for 60,000 shares were allotted 40,000 shares.

Excess amount received on application and allotment was to be adjusted against sums due on call. X, who belonged to the first category and was allotted 300 shares, failed to pay the first and final call money. Y, who belonged to the second category and was allotted 200 shares, also failed to pay the first and final call money. Their shares were forfeited. The forfeited shares were re-issued @ ₹ 12 per share as fully paid-up.

Pass necessary cash book and journal entries for the above transactions in the books of the company. **All India 2019**

Ans.

JOURNAL

Date	Particulars		LF	Amt (Dr)	Amt (Cr)
	Bank A/c (1,50,000 × 8)	Dr		12,00,000	
	To Share Application and Allotment A/c				12,00,000
	(Being application and allotment money received)				
	Share Application and Allotment A/c	Dr		12,00,000	
	To Share Capital A/c (1,00,000 × 5)				5,00,000
	To Securities Premium A/c (1,00,000 × 3)				3,00,000
	To Calls-in-Advance (40,000 × 8)				3,20,000
	To Bank A/c (10,000 × 8)				80,000
	(Being 1,00,000 shares allotted excess money refunded)				
	Share First and Final Call A/c (1,00,000 × 7)	Dr		7,00,000	
	To Share Capital A/c (1,00,000 × 5)				5,00,000
	To Securities Premium A/c (1,00,000 × 2)				2,00,000
	(Being first and final call money due)				
	Bank A/c	Dr		3,78,100	
	Calls-in-Advance A/c	Dr		3,20,000	
	To Share First and Final Call A/c				6,98,100
	(Being first and final call money received)				
	Share Capital A/c (500 × 10)	Dr		5,000	
	Securities Premium A/c (500 × 2)	Dr		1,000	
	To Share Forfeiture A/c				4,100
	To Share First and Final Call A/c				1,900
	(Being 500 shares forfeited)				
	Bank A/c (500 × 12)	Dr		6,000	
	To Share Capital A/c (500 × 10)				5,000
	To Securities Premium A/c (500 × 2)				1,000
	(Being 500 shares forfeited re-issued @ ₹ 12 each fully paid-up)				
	Share Forfeiture A/c	Dr		4,100	
	To Capital Reserve A/c				4,100
	(Being profit on re-issue of shares transferred to capital reserve account)				

Working Notes

1. Number of shares applied by X = $300 \times \frac{8}{6}$ = 400 shares

		Amt (₹)
Application and allotment money received	(400 × 8) =	3,200
(–) Application and allotment due	(300 × 8) =	(2,400)
Excess	=	800
First and final call money due	(300 × 7) =	2,100
Calls-in-arrears	=	1,300

2. Shares applied by Y = $200 \times \frac{6}{4}$ = 300 shares

Application and allotment money received	(300 × 8) =	2,400
(–) Application and allotment money due	(200 × 8) =	(1,600)
Excess	=	800
First and final call money due	(200 × 7) =	1,400
Calls-in-arrears	=	600

22. Jain Ltd invited applications for issuing 1,12,000 equity shares of ₹ 10 each at par. The amount per share was payable as follows

On application – ₹ 1 On allotment – ₹ 2

On first call – ₹ 3 On second and final call – ₹ 4

Applications for 1,00,000 shares were received. Shares were fully allotted to all the applicants. Ramesh failed to pay his allotment money which was ₹ 2,000. His shares were forfeited immediately. Suresh did not pay the first call on 500 shares applied by him. His shares were forfeited after the first call. The forfeited shares of Ramesh and Suresh were re-issued at ₹ 9 per share fully paid-up. Afterwards the second and final call was made and was duly received.

Pass necessary journal entries for the above transactions in the books of Jain. **All India 2019**

Ans.

JOURNAL

Date	Particulars		LF	Amt (Dr)	Amt (Cr)
	Bank A/c (1,00,000 × 1)	Dr		1,00,000	
	To Equity Share Application A/c				1,00,000
	(Being application money received)				
	Equity Share Application A/c	Dr		1,00,000	
	To Equity Share Capital A/c	Dr			1,00,000
	(Being application money transferred to capital account)				
	Equity Share Allotment A/c (1,00,000 × 2)	Dr		2,00,000	
	To Equity Share Capital A/c				2,00,000
	(Being allotment money due)				
	Bank A/c	Dr		1,98,000	
	To Equity Share Allotment A/c				1,98,000
	(Being allotment money received)				

Date	Particulars		LF	Amt (Dr)	Amt (Cr)
	Equity Share Capital A/c (1,000 × 3)	Dr		3,000	
	To Share Forfeiture A/c (1,000 × 1)				1,000
	To Equity Share Allotment A/c (1,000 × 2)				2,000
	(Being 1,000 shares forfeited for non-payment of allotment money)				
	Equity Share First Call A/c (99,000 × 3)	Dr		2,97,000	
	To Equity Share Capital A/c				2,97,000
	(Being first call money due)				
	Bank A/c	Dr		2,95,500	
	To Equity Share First Call A/c				2,95,500
	(Being first call money received)				
	Equity Share Capital A/c (500 × 6)	Dr		3,000	
	To Share Forfeiture A/c (500 × 3)				1,500
	To Equity Share First Call A/c (500 × 3)				1,500
	(Being 500 share forfeited for non-payment of first call)				
	Bank A/c (1,500 × 9)	Dr		13,500	
	Share Forfeiture A/c (1,500 × 1)	Dr		1,500	
	To Equity Share Capital A/c (1,500 × 10)				15,000
	(Being 1,500 share re-issued @ ₹ 9 per share fully paid-up)				
	Share Forfeiture A/c	Dr		1,000	
	To Capital Reserve A/c				1,000
	(Being profit on re-issue transferred to capital reserve account)				
	Equity Share Second and Final Call A/c (98,500 × 4)	Dr		3,94,000	
	To Equity Share Capital A/c				3,94,000
	(Being second and final call money due on 98,500 shares)				
	Bank A/c	Dr		3,94,000	
	To Equity Share Second and Final Call A/c				3,94,000
	(Being second and final call money received)				

Working Note

$$\text{Number of share allotted to Ramesh} = \frac{2,000}{2} = 1,000 \text{ shares}$$

23. DF Ltd invited applications for issuing 50,000 shares of ₹ 10 each at a premium of ₹ 2 per share. The amount was payable as follows

On application - ₹ 3 per share (including premium ₹ 1)

On allotment - ₹ 3 per share (including premium ₹ 1)

On first call - ₹ 3 per share

On second and final call - Balance amount

Application for 70,000 shares were received. Allotment was made on the following basis

Application for 5,000 shares-full ; Applications for 50,000 shares - 90%

Balance of the applications were rejected. ₹ 1,11,000 were received on account of allotment. The amount of allotment due from the shareholders to whom shares were allotted on pro-rata basis was fully received. A few shareholders to whom shares were allotted in full, failed to pay the allotment money ₹ 1,20,000 were received on first call. Directors decided to forfeit those shares on which allotment and call money was due. Half of the forfeited shares were re-issued @ ₹ 8 per share fully paid-up. Final call was not made.

Pass the necessary journal entries for the above transactions in the book of DF Ltd. **Delhi 2019**

Ans.

JOURNAL

In the Books of DF Ltd

Date	Particulars		LF	Amt (Dr)	Amt (Cr)
	Bank A/c (70,000 × 3)	Dr		2,10,000	
	To Share Application A/c				2,10,000
	(Being application money received)				
	Share Application A/c	Dr		2,10,000	
	To Share Capital A/c (50,000 × 2)				1,00,000
	To Securities Premium Reserve A/c (50,000 × 1)				50,000
	To Share Allotment A/c (5,000 × 3)				15,000
	To Bank A/c (15,000 × 3)				45,000
	(Being money received on application transferred to capital account and excess money adjusted at allotment and refunded)				
	Share Allotment A/c (50,000 × 3)	Dr		1,50,000	
	To Share Capital A/c (50,000 × 2)				1,00,000
	To Securities Premium Reserve A/c (50,000 × 1)				50,000
	(Being allotment money due)				
	Bank A/c	Dr		1,11,000	
	To Share Allotment A/c				1,11,000
	(Being allotment money received)				
	Share First Call A/c (50,000 × 3)	Dr		1,50,000	
	To Share Capital A/c				1,50,000
	(Being first call money due)				
	Bank A/c	Dr		1,20,000	
	To Share First Call A/c				1,20,000
	(Being first call money received)				
	Share Capital A/c (8,000 × 7)	Dr		56,000	
	Securities Premium Reserve A/c (8,000 × 1)	Dr		8,000	
	To Share Forfeiture A/c				16,000
	To Share Allotment A/c				24,000
	To Share First call A/c				24,000
	(Being shares forfeited)				
	Bank A/c (4,000 × 8)	Dr		32,000	
	Shares Forfeiture A/c (4,000 × 2)	Dr		8,000	
	To Share Capital A/c (5,000 × 10)				40,000
	(Being shares re-issued)				
	Shares Forfeiture A/c (W.N.3)	Dr		2,000	
	To Capital Reserve A/c				2,000
	(Being profit on re-issue transferred to capital reserve account)				

Working Notes

1.

Particulars	Amt (₹)
Amount due on allotment	1,50,000
(–) Received with application	(15,000)
	1,35,000
(–) Actual amount received	(1,11,000)
Call-in-arrears at allotment	24,000

Number of shares who didn't pay allotment $= \frac{24,000}{3} = 8,000$ shares

2.

Particulars	Amt (₹)
Amount due on first call	1,50,000
(–) Actual amount received	(1,20,000)
Calls-in-arrears of first call	30,000

No. of shares who didn't pay first call $= \frac{30,000}{3} = 10,000$ shares

(–) Shares who didn't pay allotment = 8,000

Shares who didn't pay only first call 2,000

3.

Amount of forfeiture on 8,000 shares = 56,000

Amount of forfeiture on 5,000 shares $\left(\frac{16,000}{8,000} \times 5,000\right)$ = 10,000

(–) Forfeiture on re-issue = (8,000)

Transfer to capital reserve = 2,000

24. EF Ltd invited applications for issuing 80,000 equity shares of ₹ 50 each at a premium of 20%. The amount was payable as follows

On application – ₹ 20 per share (including premium ₹ 5)

On allotment – ₹ 15 per share (including premium ₹ 5)

On first call – ₹ 15 per share

On second and final call – Balance amount

Applications for 1,20,000 shares were received. Applications for 20,000 shares were rejected and pro-rata allotment was made to the remaining applications.

Seema, holding 4,000 shares failed to pay the allotment money. Afterwards the first call was made. Seema paid allotment money alongwith the first call. Sahaj, who had applied for 2,500 shares failed to pay the first call money. Sahaj's shares were forfeited and subsequently re-issued to Geeta for ₹ 60 per share, ₹ 50 per share paid-up. Final call was not made.

Pass necessary journal entries for the above transactions in the books of EF Ltd by opening calls-in-arrears account. **Delhi 2019**

Ans. **JOURNAL**

Date	Particulars		LF	Amt (Dr)	Amt (Cr)
	Bank A/c (1,20,000 × 20)	Dr		24,00,000	
	To Equity Share Application A/c				24,00,000
	(Being application money received)				
	Equity Share Application A/c	Dr		24,00,000	
	To Equity Share Capital A/c (80,000 × 15)				12,00,000
	To Securities Premium Reserve A/c (80,000 × 5)				4,00,000
	To Equity Share Allotment A/c (20,000 × 20)				4,00,000
	To Bank A/c (20,000 × 20)				4,00,000
	(Being application money transferred to capital account and excess money refunded and adjusted)				
	Equity Share Allotment A/c (80,000 × 15)	Dr		12,00,000	
	To Equity Share Capital A/c (80,000 × 10)				8,00,000
	To Securities Premium Reserve A/c (80,000 × 5)				4,00,000
	(Being allotment money due)				
	Bank A/c	Dr		7,60,000	
	Calls-in-Arrears A/c (W.N.1)	Dr		40,000	
	To Equity Share Allotment A/c				8,00,000
	(Being allotment money received)				
	Equity Share First Call A/c (80,000 × 15)	Dr		12,00,000	
	To Equity Share Capital A/c				12,00,000
	(Being first call money due)				
	Bank A/c	Dr		12,10,000	
	Call-in-Arrears A/c (Sahaj) (2,000 × 15)	Dr		30,000	
	To Equity Share First Call A/c				12,00,000
	To Calls-in-Arrears A/c (Seema)				40,000
	(Being first call money received)				
	Equity Share Capital A/c (2,000 × 40)	Dr		80,000	
	To Shares Forfeiture A/c (2,000 × 25)				50,000
	To Calls-in-Arrears A/c (2,000 × 15)				30,000
	(Being 2,000 shares forfeited)				
	Bank A/c (2,000 × 60)	Dr		1,20,000	
	To Equity Share Capital A/c (2,000 × 50)				1,00,000
	To Securities Premium Reserve A/c (3,000 × 10)				20,000
	(Being 2,000 shares re-issued)				
	Shares Forfeiture A/c	Dr		50,000	
	To Capital Reserve A/c				50,000
	(Being amount of share forfeiture transferred to capital reserve account)				

Working Note

Number of shares applied by Seema $= 4,000 \times \dfrac{1,00,000}{80,000} = 5,000$ shares

Application money received $(5,000 \times 20)$	$= 1,00,000$
$(-)$ Application money due $(4,000 \times 20)$	$= (80,000)$
Excess	20,000
Allotment money due $(4,000 \times 15)$	$= 60,000$
Arrear at allotment	40,000

25. X Ltd invited applications for issuing 50,000 equity shares of ₹ 10 each. The amount was payable as follows

On application	₹ 2 per share
On allotment	₹ 2 per share
On first call	₹ 3 per share
On second and final call	Balance amount

Applications for 70,000 shares were received. Applications for 10,000 shares were rejected and the application money was refunded.

Shares were allotted to the remaining applicants on a pro-rata basis and excess money received with applications was transferred towards sums due on allotment and calls, if any.

Gopal, who applied for 600 shares, paid his entire share money with application. Ghosh, who had applied for 6,000 shares, failed to pay the allotment money and his shares were immediately forfeited. These forfeited shares were re-issued to Sultan for ₹ 20,000; ₹ 4 per share paid-up. The first call money and the second and final call money was called and duly received. Pass necessary journal entries for the above transactions in the books of X Ltd. Open calls-in-advance account and calls-in-arrears account wherever necessary. **CBSE 2018**

Ans.

JOURNAL

Date	Particulars		LF	Amt (Dr)	Amt (Cr)
	Bank A/c	Dr		1,44,800	
	To Equity Share Application A/c				1,44,800
	(Being application money received)				
	Equity Share Application A/c	Dr		1,44,800	
	To Equity Share Capital A/c				1,00,000
	To Equity Share Allotment A/c				20,800
	To Bank A/c				21,000
	To Calls-in-Advance A/c				3,000
	(Being application money due)				
	Equity Share Allotment A/c	Dr		1,00,000	
	To Equity Share Capital A/c				1,00,000
	(Being allotment money due)				
	Bank A/c	Dr		71,200	
	Calls-in-arrears A/c	Dr		8,000	
	To Equity Share Allotment A/c				79,200
	(Being allotment money received)				

Date	Particulars		LF	Amt (Dr)	Amt (Cr)
	Equity Share Capital A/c	Dr		20,000	
	To Calls-in-Arrears A/c				8,000
	To Share Forfeiture A/c				12,000
	(Being share forfeited)				
	Bank A/c	Dr		20,000	
	To Equity Share Capital A/c				20,000
	(Being shares issued to Sultan)				
	Share Forfeiture A/c	Dr		12,000	
	To Capital Reserve A/c				12,000
	(Being amount transferred to capital reserve account)				
	Equity Share First Call A/c	Dr		1,50,000	
	To Equity Share Capital A/c				1,50,000
	(Being first call money due)				
	Bank A/c	Dr		1,48,500	
	Calls-in-Advance A/c	Dr		1,500	
	To Equity Share First Call A/c				1,50,000
	(Being first call money received)				
	Equity Share Second and Final Call A/c	Dr		1,50,000	
	To Equity Share Capital A/c				1,50,000
	(Being second call money due)				
	Bank A/c	Dr		1,48,500	
	Calls-in-Advance A/c	Dr		1,500	
	To Equity Share Second and Final Call A/c				1,50,000
	(Being second and final call money received)				

Analysis Table

	Shares applied	Shares allotted	Money received on application @ ₹ 2	Money transferred to share capital @ ₹ 2	Excess	Allotment @ ₹ 2	Calls-in-Advance @ ₹ 6	Money Refund
I	10,000	—	20,000	—	20,000	—	—	20,000
II	59,400	49,500	1,18,800	99,000	19,800	19,800	—	—
III	600	500	6,000	1,000	5,000	1,000	3,000	1,000
	70,000	50,000	1,44,800	1,00,000	44,800	20,800	3,000	21,000

26. A Ltd invited applications for issuing 1,00,000 shares of ₹ 10 each at a premium of ₹ 1 per share. The amount was payable as follows

On application	₹ 3 per share
On allotment	₹ 3 per share (including premium)
On first call	₹ 3 per share
On second and final call	Balance amount

Applications for 1,60,000 shares were received. Allotment was made on the following basis

(*i*) To applicants for 90,000 shares 40,000 shares
(*ii*) To applicants for 50,000 shares 40,000 shares
(*iii*) To applicants for 20,000 shares Full shares

Excess money paid on application is to be adjusted against the amount due on allotment and calls.

Rishabh, a shareholder, who applied for 1,500 shares and belonged to Category (*ii*), did not pay allotment, first and second and final call money. Another shareholder, Sudha, who applied for 1,800 shares and belonged to Category (*i*), did not pay the first and second and final call money.

All the shares of Rishabh and Sudha were forfeited and were subsequently re-issued at ₹ 7 per share fully paid.

Pass the necessary journal entries in the books of A Ltd. Open calls-in-arrears account and calls-in-advance account wherever required. **CBSE 2018**

Ans.

JOURNAL

Date	Particulars		LF	Amt (Dr)	Amt (Cr)
	Bank A/c (1,60,000 × 3)	Dr		4,80,000	
	To Equity Share Application A/c				4,80,000
	(Being application money received)				
	Equity Share Application A/c	Dr		4,80,000	
	To Equity Share Capital A/c				3,00,000
	To Equity Share Allotment A/c				1,50,000
	To Calls-in-Advance A/c				30,000
	(Being application money transferred to share capital account)				
	Equity Share Allotment A/c	Dr		3,00,000	
	To Equity Share Capital A/c				2,00,000
	To Securities Premium Reserve A/c				1,00,000
	(Being allotment money due)				
	Bank A/c	Dr		1,47,300	
	Calls-in-Arrears A/c	Dr		2,700	
	To Equity Share Allotment A/c				1,50,000
	(Being allotment money received except on 1,200 shares)				
	Equity Share First Call A/c	Dr		3,00,000	
	To Equity Share Capital A/c				3,00,000
	(Being first call money due)				
	Bank A/c	Dr		2,64,000	
	Calls-in-Advance A/c	Dr		30,000	
	Calls-in-Arrears A/c	Dr		5,400	
	To Equity Share First Call A/c				3,00,000
	(Being first call money received)				

Date	Particulars		LF	Amt (Dr)	Amt (Cr)
	Equity Share Second and Final Call A/c	Dr		2,00,000	
	To Equity Share Capital A/c				2,00,000
	(Being second and final call money due)				
	Bank A/c	Dr		1,96,000	
	Calls-in-Arrears A/c	Dr		4,000	
	To Equity Share Second and Final Call A/c				2,00,000
	(Being second and final call money received)				
	Share Capital A/c	Dr		20,000	
	Securities Premium Reserve A/c	Dr		1,200	
	To Calls-in-Arrears A/c				12,100
	To Share Forfeiture A/c				9,100
	(Being shares forfeited)				
	Bank A/c	Dr		14,000	
	Share Forfeited A/c	Dr		6,000	
	To Share Capital A/c				20,000
	(Being forfeited share re-issued)				
	Share Forfeited A/c	Dr		3,100	
	To Capital Reserve A/c				3,100
	(Being forfeited amount transfer to capital reserve account)				

Working Note

Shares applied	Shares allotted	Money received on application @ ₹ 3	Money transferred to share capital	Excess money adjusted in allotment
90,000	40,000	2,70,000	1,20,000	1,20,000
50,000	40,000	1,50,000	1,20,000	30,000
20,000	20,000	60,000	60,000	—
1,60,000	1,00,000	4,80,000	3,00,000	1,50,000

1. **Calculation of Calls-in-Arrears on Rishabh's Shares**

	Amt (₹)
Allotment due $(1{,}200 \times 3) =$	3,600
(–) Excess on application $(1{,}500 - 1{,}200) \times 3 =$	(900)
	2,700

2. **Calculation of Calls-in-Arrears on First Call**

Amount due $(2{,}000 \times 3) =$	6,000
(–) Excess on application	
Adjusted on allotment $(1{,}800 - 800) \times 3 - 2{,}400 =$	(600)
	5,400

3. **Calculation of Amount Forfeited**

Rishabh $(1{,}500 \times 3)$		4,500
Sudha $(1{,}800 \times 3)$	5,400	
(–) Excess adjusted	(800)	4,600
Total amount forfeited		9,100

27. X Ltd invited applications for issuing 5,00,000 equity shares of ₹ 10 each at par. The amount per share was payable as follows

On application - ₹ 1 per share; On allotment - ₹ 2 per share; On first call - ₹ 3 per share; On second and final call - Balance amount

Applications for 8,00,000 shares were received. Applications for 1,00,000 shares were rejected and pro-rata allotment was made to the remaining applicants. Excess money received with applications was adjusted towards sums due on allotment. All calls were made. Ashok, a shareholder, holding 5,000 shares failed to pay the allotment and the call money. Mohan, a shareholder who had applied for 7,000 shares, failed to pay the first and second and final call. Shares of Ashok and Mohan were forfeited after the second and final call. Of the forfeited shares, 8,000 shares were re-issued at ₹ 12 per share fully paid-up. The re-issued shares included all the forfeited shares of Ashok.

Pass necessary journal entries for the above transactions in the books of X. Ltd.
Compartment 2018

Ans.

JOURNAL

Date	Particulars	LF	Amt (Dr)	Amt (Cr)
	Bank A/c (8,00,000×1) Dr		8,00,000	
	To Equity Share Application A/c			8,00,000
	(Being application money received)			
	Equity Share Application A/c Dr		8,00,000	
	To Equity Share Capital A/c (5,00,000×1)			5,00,000
	To Equity Share Allotment A/c (2,00,000×1)			2,00,000
	To Bank A/c (1,00,000 × 1)			1,00,000
	(Being application money transferred to share capital account and excess money adjusted towards allotment and returned)			
	Equity Share Allotment A/c (5,00,000×2) Dr		10,00,000	
	To Equity Share Capital A/c			10,00,000
	(Being allotment money due)			
	Bank A/c (W.N.2) Dr		7,92,000	
	To Equity Share Allotment A/c			7,92,000
	(Being allotment money received)			
	Equity Share First Call A/c (5,00,000×3) Dr		15,00,000	
	To Equity Share Capital A/c			15,00,000
	(Being first call money due)			
	Bank A/c (15,00,000−15,000−15,000) Dr		14,70,000	
	To Equity Share First Call A/c			14,70,000
	(Being first call money received)			
	Equity Share Second and Final Call A/c (5,00,000×4) Dr		20,00,000	
	To Equity Share Capital A/c			20,00,000
	(Being second and final call money due)			
	Bank A/c Dr		19,60,000	
	To Equity Share Second and Final Call A/c			19,60,000
	(Being second and final call money received)			
	Equity Share Capital A/c (10,000 × 10) Dr		1,00,000	
	To Forfeited Shares A/c			22,000
	To Equity Share Allotment A/c			8,000
	To Equity Share First Call A/c			30,000
	To Equity Share Second and Final Call A/c			40,000
	(Being shares of Ashok and Mohan for non-payment of money)			

Date	Particulars	LF	Amt (Dr)	Amt (Cr)
	Bank A/c (8,000×12) Dr To Equity Share Capital A/c (8,000×10) To Securities Premium Reserve A/c (8,000×2) (Being 8,000 shares re-issued @ ₹ 12 per share fully paid)		96,000	 80,000 16,000
	Forfeited Shares A/c (W. No. 4) Dr To Capital Reserve A/c (Being amount of share forfeiture transferred to capital reserve account)		16,000	 16,000

Working Notes

1. Number of shares applied by Ashok $= 5{,}000 \times \frac{7}{5} = 7{,}000$ shares

   Application money received $(7{,}000 \times 1) = 7{,}000$

   Application money due excess $(5{,}000 \times 1) = \underline{5{,}000}$ $2{,}000$

   (Allotment money due) (Arrears at allotment) $5{,}000 \times 2 = \underline{10{,}000}$ $\underline{8{,}000}$

2. Allotment due = 10,00,000
   (–) Received with application = (2,00,000)
   8,00,000
   (–) Calls-is-arrears at allotment = (8,000)
   Allotment money received 7,92,000

3. Number of shares allotted to Mohan $= 7{,}000 \times \frac{5}{7} = 5{,}000$ shares

4. Forfeited shares Ashok = 7,000

   Mohan $= \left(\frac{15{,}000}{5{,}000} \times 3{,}000\right) = \underline{9{,}000}$ $\underline{16{,}000}$ transferred to capital reserve

28. VXN Ltd invited applications for issuing 50,000 equity shares of ₹ 10 each at a premium of ₹ 8 per share. The amount was payable as follows

On application	:	₹ 4 per share (including ₹ 2 premium)
On allotment	:	₹ 6 per share (including ₹ 3 premium)
On first call	:	₹ 5 per share (including ₹ 1 premium)
On second and final call	:	Balance amount

The issue was fully subscribed. Gopal, a shareholder holding 200 shares, did not pay the allotment money and Madhav, a holder of 400 shares, paid his entire share money along with the allotment money. Gopal's shares were immediately forfeited after allotment. Afterwards, the first call was made. Krishna, a holder of 100 shares, failed to pay the first call money and Girdhar, a holder of 300 shares, paid the second call money also along with the first call. Krishna's shares were forfeited immediately after the first call. Second and final call was made afterwards and was duly received. All the forfeited shares were re-issued at ₹ 9 per share fully paid-up.

Pass necessary journal entries for the above transactions in the books of the company.

All India 2017

Ans.

JOURNAL

Date	Particulars		LF	Amt (Dr)	Amt (Cr)
	Bank A/c (50,000 × 4)	Dr		2,00,000	
	To Equity Share Application A/c				2,00,000
	(Being application money received on 50,000 shares)				
	Equity Share Application A/c	Dr		2,00,000	
	To Equity Share Capital A/c (50,000 × 2)				1,00,000
	To Securities Premium Reserve A/c (50,000 × 2)				1,00,000
	(Being application money transferred to share capital account)				
	Equity Share Allotment A/c (50,000 × 6)	Dr		3,00,000	
	To Equity Share Capital A/c (50,000 × 3)				1,50,000
	To Securities Premium Reserve A/c (50,000 × 3)				1,50,000
	(Being allotment money due)				
	Bank A/c (49,800 × 6) + (400 × 8)	Dr		3,02,000	
	Calls-in-Arrears A/c	Dr		1,200	
	To Equity Share Allotment A/c				3,00,000
	To Calls-in-Advance A/c				3,200
	(Being allotment money received)				
	Equity Share Capital A/c (200 × 5)	Dr		1,000	
	Securities Premium Reserve A/c (200 × 3)	Dr		600	
	To Calls-in-Arrears (200 × 6)				1,200
	To Equity Share Forfeiture A/c (200 × 2)				400
	(Being Gopal's shares forfeited for non-payment of allotment money)				
	Equity Share First Call A/c (49,800 × 5)	Dr		2,49,000	
	To Equity Share Capital A/c (49,800 × 4)				1,99,200
	To Securities Premium Reserve A/c (49,800 × 1)				49,800
	(Being first call money due)				
	Bank A/c (49,700 × 5) − (400 × 5) + (300 × 3)	Dr		2,47,400	
	Calls-in-Arrears A/c	Dr		500	
	Calls-in-Advance A/c (400 × 5)	Dr		2,000	
	To Calls-in-Advance A/c (300 × 3)				900
	To Equity Share First Call A/c				2,49,000
	(Being first call money received)				
	Equity Share Capital A/c (100 × 9)	Dr		900	
	Securities Premium Reserve A/c (100 × 1)	Dr		100	
	To Calls-in-Arrears A/c (100 × 5)				500
	To Equity Share Forfeiture A/c (100 × 5)				500
	(Being Krishna's shares forfeited for non-payment of first call)				
	Equity Share Second and Final Call A/c (49,700 × 3)	Dr		1,49,100	
	To Equity Share Capital A/c (49,700 × 1)				49,700
	To Securities Premium Reserve A/c (49,700 × 2)				99,400
	(Being second and final call due)				

Date	Particulars		LF	Amt (Dr)	Amt (Cr)
	Bank A/c	Dr		1,47,000	
	Calls-in-Advance A/c (400 × 3) + (300 × 3)	Dr		2,100	
	To Equity Share Second and Final Call A/c				1,49,100
	(Being second and final call money received account)				
	Bank A/c (300 × 9)	Dr		2,700	
	Equity Share Forfeiture A/c	Dr		300	
	To Equity Share Capital A/c (300 × 10)				3,000
	(Being 300 shares re-issued @ ₹ 9 per share fully paid-up)				
	Equity Share Forfeiture A/c (400 + 500 − 300)	Dr		600	
	To Capital Reserve A/c				600
	(Being profit on re-issue transferred to capital reserve account)				

29. JJK Ltd invited applications for issuing 50,000 equity shares of ₹ 10 each at par. The amount was payable as follows

On application — ₹ 2 per share

On allotment — ₹ 4 per share

On first and final call — Balance amount

The issue was over-subscribed three times. Applications for 30% shares were rejected and money refunded. Allotment was made to the remaining applicants as follows

Category	Number of shares applied	Number of shares allotted
I	80,000	40,000
II	25,000	10,000

Excess money paid by the applicants who were allotted shares was adjusted towards the sums due on allotment.

Deepak, a shareholder belonging to Category I, who had applied for 1,000 shares, failed to pay the allotment money. Raju, a shareholder holding 100 shares, also failed to pay the allotment money. Raju belonged to Category II. Shares of both Deepak and Raju were forfeited immediately after allotment. Afterwards, first and final call was made and was duly received. The forfeited shares of Deepak and Raju were re-issued at ₹ 11 per share fully paid up.

Pass necessary journal entries for the above transactions in the books of the company.

All India 2017

Ans.

JOURNAL

Date	Particulars		LF	Amt (Dr)	Amt (Cr)
	Bank A/c (1,50,000 × 2)	Dr		3,00,000	
	To Equity Share Application A/c				3,00,000
	(Being application money received)				
	Equity Share Application A/c	Dr		3,00,000	
	To Equity Share Capital A/c				1,00,000
	To Equity Share Allotment A/c				1,10,000
	To Bank A/c				90,000
	(Being application money transferred to share capital account and excess adjusted)				

Date	Particulars		LF	Amt (Dr)	Amt (Cr)
	Equity Share Allotment A/c (50,000 × 4) To Equity Share Capital A/c (Being allotment money due)	Dr		2,00,000	 2,00,000
	Bank A/c Calls-in-Arrears A/c To Equity Share Allotment A/c (Being allotment money received)	Dr Dr		88,900 1,100	 90,000
	Equity Share Capital A/c (600×6) To Calls-in-Arrears A/c (1,000+100) To Equity Share Forfeiture A/c (Being shares forfeited for non-payment of allotment money)	Dr		3,600	 1,100 2,500
	Equity Share First and Final Call A/c To Equity Share Capital A/c (49,400×4) (Being first call money due)	Dr		1,97,600	 1,97,600
	Bank A/c To Equity Share First and Final Call A/c (Being first and final call money received)	Dr		1,97,600	 1,97,600
	Bank A/c (600 × 11) To Equity Share Capital A/c (600×10) To Securities Premium Reserve A/c (600×1) (Being 600 shares re-issued @ ₹ 11 per share)	Dr		6,600	 6,000 600
	Share Forfeiture A/c To Capital Reserve A/c (Being profit on re-issue transferred to capital reserve account)	Dr		2,500	 2,500

Analysis Table

	Shares applied I	Shares allotted II	Application money received @ ₹ 2 per share III	Application money transferred to share capital IV	Excess application money V = III – IV	Share allotment money due @ ₹ 4	Excess application money adjusted on allotment	Money refunded
I	80,000	40,000	1,60,000 (80,000 × 2)	80,000 (40,000 × 2)	80,000	1,60,000 (40,000 × 4)	80,000	—
II	25,000	10,000	50,000 (25,000 × 2)	20,000 (10,000 × 2)	30,000	40,000 (10,000 × 4)	30,000	—
III	45,000	—	90,000 (45,000 × 2)	—	—	—	—	90,000
	1,50,000	50,000	3,00,000	1,00,000	1,10,000	2,00,000	1,10,000	90,000

Working Notes

1. **Calls-in-arrears of Deepak**

Share allotted to Deepak $\frac{40,000}{80,000} \times 1,000 = 500$

			Amt (₹)
Application money received	(1,000 × 2)	=	2,000
(−) Amount adjusted on application	(500 × 2)	=	(1,000)
Excess application money adjusted on allotment			1,000
Money due on allotment	(500 × 4)	=	2,000
(−) Excess application money adjusted on allotment		=	(1,000)
Calls-in-arrears			1,000

2. **Calls-in-arrears by Raju**

Share applied by Raju $= \frac{25,000}{10,000} \times 100 = 250$

Application money received	(250 × 2) =	500
(−) Amount adjusted onapplication	(100 × 2) =	(200)
Excess application money adjusted on allotment		300
Money due on allotment	(100 × 4) =	400
(−) Excess application money adjusted on allotment =		(300)
Calls-in-arrears		100

3. **Money Received on Allotment**	**Amt (₹)**
Total amount due on allotment	2,00,000
(−) Excess application money adjusted	(1,10,000)
Allotment money to be received	90,000
(−) Calls-in-arrears by Deepak	(1,000)
(−) Calls-in-arrears by Raju	(100)
Allotment money received	88,900

30. XL Ltd invited applications for issuing 1,00,000 equity shares of ₹ 10 each at par. The amount was payable as follows

On application — ₹ 3 per share

On allotment — ₹ 4 per share

On first and final call — ₹ 3 per share

The issue was over-subscribed by three times. Applications for 20% shares were rejected and the money refunded. Allotment was made to the remaining applications as follows

Category	Number of shares applied	Number of shares allotted
I	1,60,000	80,000
II	80,000	20,000

Excess money received with applications was adjusted towards sums due on allotment and first and final call. All calls were made and were duly received except the final call by a shareholder belonging to Category I who has applied for 320 shares. His shares were forfeited. The forfeited shares were re-issued at ₹ 15 per share fully paid-up.

Pass necessary journal entries for the above transactions in the book of XL Ltd. Open calls in-arrears and calls-in-advance account whenever required. **Delhi 2017**

Ans. Solve as Q. no. 29 on page 297-299.
Capital Reserve = ₹ 1,120

31. AXN Ltd invited applications for issuing 1,00,000 equity shares of ₹ 10 each at a premium of ₹ 6 per share. The amount was payable as follows

On application — ₹ 4 per share (including ₹ 2 premium)
On allotment — ₹ 5 per share (including ₹ 2 premium).
On first call — ₹ 4 per share (including ₹ 2 premium).
On second and final call — Balance amount

The issue was fully subscribed.

Kumar, the holder of 400 shares did not pay the allotment money and Ravi, the holder of 1,000 shares paid his entire share money alongwith allotment money.

Kumar's shares were forfeited immediately after allotment. Afterwards first call was made. Gupta, a holder of 300 shares failed to pay the first call money and Gopal, a holder of 600 shares paid the second call money also alongwith first call. Gupta's shares were forfeited immediately after the first call. Second and final call was made afterwards. The whole amount due on second call was received.

All the forfeited shares were re-issued at ₹ 9 per share fully paid-up.

Pass necessary journal entries for the above transactions in the books of the company.
Delhi 2017

Ans. Solve as Q. No. 28 on page 295-297.
Capital Reserve = ₹ 1,600

32. SK Ltd invited applications for issuing 3,20,000 equity shares of ₹ 10 each at a premium of ₹ 5 per share. The amount was payable as follows

On application — ₹ 3 per share (including premium ₹ 1 per share)
On allotment — ₹ 5 per share (including premium ₹ 2 per share)
On first and final call — Balance amount

Applications for 4,00,000 shares were received. Applications for 40,000 shares were rejected and application money refunded. Shares were alloted on pro-rata basis to the remaining applicants. Excess money received with applications was adjusted towards sums due on allotment. Jeevan holding 800 shares failed to pay the allotment money and his shares were immediately forfeited.

Afterwards final call was made, Ganesh, who had applied for 2,700 shares failed to pay the final call. His shares were also forfeited. Out of the forfeited shares 1,500 shares were re-issued at ₹ 8 per share fully paid up. The re-issued shares included all the forfeited shares of Jeevan.

Pass necessary journal entries for the above transactions in the books of the company.
All India 2016

Ans.

JOURNAL

Date	Particulars		LF	Amt (Dr)	Amt (Cr)
	Bank A/c (4,00,000 × 3)	Dr		12,00,000	
	To Equity Share Application A/c				12,00,000
	(Being application money received on 4,00,000 shares)				
	Equity Share Application A/c	Dr		12,00,000	
	To Equity Share Capital A/c (3,20,000 × 2)				6,40,000
	To Securities Premium Reserve A/c (3,20,000 × 1)				3,20,000
	To Equity Share Allotment A/c				1,20,000
	To Bank A/c (40,000 × 3)				1,20,000
	(Being amount of application money transferred to share capital account and excess money is adjusted towards allotment)				
	Equity Share Allotment A/c (3,20,000 × 5)	Dr		16,00,000	
	To Equity Share Capital A/c (3,20,000 × 3)				9,60,000
	To Securities Premium Reserve A/c (3,20,000 × 2)				6,40,000
	(Being amount due on allotment)				
	Bank A/c (16,00,000 – 1,20,000 – 3,700)	Dr		14,76,300	
	To Equity Share Allotment A/c				14,76,300
	(Being amount received on allotment)				
	Equity Share Capital A/c (800 × 5)	Dr		4,000	
	Securities Premium Reserve A/c (800 × 2)	Dr		1,600	
	To Share Forfeiture A/c				1,900
	To Share Allotment A/c				3,700
	(Being 800 shares of Jeevan forfeited due to non-payment of allotment money)				
	Equity Share First and Final Call A/c (3,19,200 × 7)	Dr		22,34,400	
	To Equity Share Capital A/c (3,19,200 × 5)				15,96,000
	To Securities Premium Reserve A/c (3,19,200 × 2)				6,38,400
	(Being amount due on first and final call on 3,19,200 shares)				
	Bank A/c (22,34,400 – 16,800)	Dr		22,17,600	
	To Equity Share First and Final Call A/c				22,17,600
	(Being amount received on first and final call account)				
	Equity Share Capital A/c (2,400 × 10)	Dr		24,000	
	Securities Premium Reserve A/c (2,400 × 2)	Dr		4,800	
	To Equity Share Forfeiture A/c				12,000
	To Equity Share First and Final Call A/c (2,400 × 7)				16,800
	(Being Ganesh's shares forfeited)				
	Bank A/c (1,500 × 8)	Dr		12,000	
	Share Forfeiture A/c (1,500 × 2)	Dr		3,000	
	To Equity Share Capital A/c (1,500 × 10)				15,000
	(Being forfeited shares re-issued @ ₹ 8 per share fully paid-up)				
	Equity Share Forfeiture A/c	Dr		2,400	
	To Capital Reserve A/c				2,400
	(Being excess amount on forfeiture transferred to capital reserve account)				

Working Notes

Computation Table

Categories	Shares applied	Shares allotted	Money received on application @ ₹ 3 each	Money transferred to share capital @ ₹ 2 each	Money transferred to securities premium @ ₹ 1 each	Excess application money	Aamount adjusted on allotment	Money refunded
I	40,000	—	1,20,000	—	—	1,20,000	—	1,20,000
II	3,60,000	3,20,000	10,80,000	6,40,000	3,20,000	1,20,000	1,20,000	—
	4,00,000	3,20,000	12,00,000	6,40,000	3,20,000	2,40,000	1,20,000	1,20,000

1. **Calculation of Amount Unpaid on Allotment**

$$\text{Shares applied by Jeevan} = \frac{3,60,000}{3,20,000} \times 800 = 900 \text{ shares}$$

	Amt (₹)
Excess money received from Jeevan	(100 × 3) = 300
Amount due on allotment	(800 × 3) = 2,400
(−) Excess application money	= (300)
Amount unpaid on allotment	= 2,100
(+) Amount unpaid on securities premium reserve =	1,600 (800 × 2)
Total amount unpaid on allotment	= ₹ 3,700

2. **Calculation of Amount Received from Jeevan**

Amount received on application = 1,600 (800 × 2) excluding premium
(+) Excess application money = 300
₹ 1,900

3. **Unpaid Amount of First and Final Call**

$$\text{Shares allotted to Ganesh} = \frac{3,20,000}{3,60,000} \times 2,700 = 2,400 \text{ shares}$$

Unpaid amount on first and final call = ₹ 16,800 (2,400 × 7)

4. **Calculation of Amount Received from Gupta**

Amount received on application = 4,800 (2,400 × 2) excluding premium
(+) Amount received on allotment = 7,200 (2,400 × 3)
₹ 12,000

Calculation of Capital Reserve

(*i*) 800 shares of Jeevan

Share forfeiture (Cr) = 1,900
(−) Share forfeiture (Dr) = (1,600) (800 × 2)
Capital reserve 300

(*ii*) 200 shares of Ganesh

$$\text{Share forfeiture (Cr)} = 3{,}500 \left(\frac{12{,}000}{2{,}400} \times 700\right)$$

$$(-)\ \text{Share forfeiture (Dr)} = (1{,}400)\ \ (700 \times 2)$$

$$\text{Capital reserve} = 2{,}100$$

Total capital reserve = ₹ 2,400 (2,100 + 300)

33. BBG Ltd had issued 1,00,000 equity shares of ₹ 10 each at a premium of ₹ 3 per share payable with application money. While passing journal entries related to the issue, some blanks are left, you are required to complete these blanks. **All India 2016**

JOURNAL

Date	Particulars		LF	Amt (Dr)	Amt (Cr)
2015 Jan 5	....	Dr		...	
	To				...
	(Being application money received for 1,40,000 shares @ ₹ 6 per share including premium)				
Jan 17	Equity Share Application A/c	Dr		...	
	To				...
	To				...
	To				...
	To				...
	(Being application money transferred to share capital account, securities premium account refunded for 20,000 shares for rejected applications and balance adjusted towards money due on allotment as shares were alloted on pro-rata basis)				
Jan 17	....	Dr		...	
	To				...
	(Being allotment money due @ ₹ 4 per share)				
Feb 20	....	Dr		...	
	To				...
	(Being balance allotment amount received)				
Apr 1	....	Dr		...	
	To				...
	(Being first and final call money due)				
Apr 20	....	Dr		...	
	Calls-in-Arrears A/c	Dr		3,000	
	To				...
	(Being first and final call money received)				

Date	Particulars		LF	Amt (Dr)	Amt (Cr)
May 20	....	Dr		...	
	To				...
	To				...
	(Being the shares forfeited on which first and final call was not received)				
Jun 15	....	Dr		...	
	....	Dr		3,000	
	To				...
	(Being forfeited shares re-issued)				
......	....	Dr		...	
	To				...
	(..)				

Ans.

JOURNAL

Date	Particulars		LF	Amt (Dr)	Amt (Cr)
2015					
Jan 5	**Bank A/c** (1,40,000 × 6)	Dr		8,40,000	
	To **Equity Share Application A/c**				8,40,000
	(Being application money received for 1,40,000 shares @ ₹ 6 per share including premium)				
Jan 17	Equity Share Application A/c	Dr		8,40,000	
	To **Equity Share Capital A/c** (1,00,000 × 3)				3,00,000
	To **Securities Premium Reserve A/c** (1,00,000 × 3)				3,00,000
	To **Equity Share Allotment A/c**				1,20,000
	To **Bank A/c** (20,000 × 6)				1,20,000
	(Being application money transferred to share capital account, securities premium account, refunded for 20,000 shares for rejected applications and balance adjusted towards money due on allotment as shares were alloted on pro-rata basis)				
Jan 17	**Equity Share Allotment A/c**	Dr		4,00,000	
	To **Equity Share Capital A/c** (1,00,000 × 4)				4,00,000
	(Being allotment money due @ ₹ 4 per share)				
Feb 20	**Bank A/c** (4,00,000 – 1,20,000)	Dr		2,80,000	
	To **Equity Share Allotment A/c**				2,80,000
	(Being balance allotment amount received)				
Apr 1	**Equity Share First and Final Call A/c**	Dr		3,00,000	
	To **Equity Share Capital A/c** (1,00,000 × 3)				3,00,000
	(Being first and final call money due)				

Date	Particulars		LF	Amt (Dr)	Amt (Cr)
Apr 20	Bank A/c	Dr		2,97,000	
	Calls-in-Arrears A/c	Dr		3,000	
	To Equity Share First and Final Call A/c				3,00,000
	(Being first and final call money received)				
May 20	Equity Share Capital A/c (1,000 × 10)	Dr		10,000	
	To Equity Share Forfeiture A/c				7,000
	To Calls-in-Arrears A/c (1,000 × 3)				3,000
	(Being forfeited the shares on which first and final call was not received)				
Jun 15	Bank A/c (1,000 × 7)	Dr		7,000	
	Equity Share Forfeiture A/c	Dr		3,000	
	To Equity Share Capital A/c (1,000 × 10)				10,000
	(Being forfeited shares re-issued)				
Jun 15	Equity Share Forfeiture A/c	Dr		4,000	
	To Capital Reserve A/c				4,000
	(Being excess amount on forfeiture transferred to capital reserve account)				

34. KS Ltd invited applications for issuing 1,60,000 equity shares of ₹ 10 each at a premium of ₹ 6 per share. The amount was payable as follows

On application — ₹ 4 per share (including premium ₹ 1 per share)
On allotment — ₹ 6 per share (including premium ₹ 3 per share)
On first and final call — Balance amount

Applications for 3,20,000 shares were received. Applications for 80,000 shares were rejected and application money refunded. Shares were allotted on pro-rata basis to the remaining applicants. Excess money received with applications was adjusted towards sum due on allotment. Jain holding 800 shares failed to pay the allotment money. His shares were forfeited immediately after allotment. Afterwards the final call was made. Gupta who had applied for 1,200 shares failed to pay the final call. These shares were also forfeited. Out of the forfeited shares 1,000 shares were re-issued at ₹ 8 per share fully paid-up. The re-issued shares included all the forfeited shares of Jain.

Pass necessary journal entries for the above transactions in the books of KS Ltd. **Delhi 2016**

Ans. Solve as Q no. 32 on page 300-303.

Capital Reserve = ₹ 3,200

35. GG Ltd had issued 50,000 equity shares of ₹ 10 each at a premium of ₹ 2 per share payable with application money. The incomplete journal entries related to the issue are given below. You are required to complete these blanks.

JOURNAL

Date	Particulars		LF	Amt (Dr)	Amt (Cr)
2015 Jan 10	....	Dr		...	
	To				...
	(Being amount received on application for 70,000 shares @ ₹ 5 per share including premium)				

Date	Particulars		LF	Amt (Dr)	Amt (Cr)
Jan 16	Equity Share Application A/c	Dr		...	
	To				...
	To				...
	To				...
	To				...
	(Being transfer of application money to share capital, securities premium account money refunded for 8,000 shares for rejected applications and balance adjusted towards amount due on allotment as shares were allotted on pro-rata basis)				
Jan 31	....	Dr		...	
	To				...
	(Being amount due on allotment @ ₹ 4 per share)				
Feb 20	....	Dr		...	
	To....................				...
	(Being balance amount received on allotment)				
Apr 1	....	Dr		...	
	To				...
	(Being first and final call money due)				
Apr 20	....	Dr		...	
	Calls - in- arrears A/c	Dr		1,500	
	To....................				...
	(Being money received on first and final call)				
Aug 27	....	Dr		...	
	To				...
	To				...
	(Being the shares forfeited on which call money was not received)				
Oct 3	....	Dr		...	
	....	Dr		...	
	To				...
	(Being the forfeited shares re-issued @ ₹ 8 per share fully paid-up)				
....	....	Dr		...	
	To				...
	(..)				

Delhi 2016

Ans. Solve as Q no. 33 on page 303-305.

Capital Reserve = ₹ 2,500

36. Radha Mohan Ltd invited applications for issuing 4,00,000 equity shares of ₹ 50 each. The amount was payable as follows

On application	—	₹ 15 per share
On allotment	—	₹ 25 per share
On first and final call	—	₹ 10 per share

Applications for 6,00,000 shares were received and pro-rata allotment was made to all the applicants on following basis

Applicants for 4,00,000 shares were allotted 3,00,000 shares.

Applicants for 2,00,000 shares were alloted 1,00,000 shares.

It was decided that excess amount received on applications will be adjusted towards sums due on allotment and surplus if any, will be refunded. Vibhuti, who was alloted 6,000 shares out of the group applying for 4,00,000 shares did not pay the allotment money and his shares were forfeited immediately. Afterwards, these forfeited shares were re-issued at ₹ 30 per share fully paid-up. Later on, first and final call was made. Shahid, who had applied for 2,000 shares out of the group applying for 2,00,000 shares failed to pay first and final call and his shares were also forfeited. These shares were afterwards re-issued at ₹ 60 per share fully paid-up.

Pass necessary journal entries in the books of Radha Mohan Ltd for the above transactions.
All India (C) 2016

Ans. **JOURNAL**

Date	Particulars		LF	Amt (Dr)	Amt (Cr)
	Bank A/c (6,00,000×15)	Dr		90,00,000	
	To Equity Share Application A/c				90,00,000
	(Being application money received on 6,00,000 equity shares @ ₹ 15 each)				
	Equity Share Application A/c (6,00,000×15)	Dr		90,00,000	
	To Equity Share Capital A/c (4,00,000 × 15)				60,00,000
	To Equity Share Allotment A/c (2,00,000 × 15)				30,00,000
	(Being application money transferred to share capital account)				
	Equity Share Allotment A/c (4,00,000 × 25)	Dr		1,00,00,000	
	To Equity Share Capital A/c				1,00,00,000
	(Being share allotment made due)				
	Bank A/c (4,00,000×25) – (30,00,000) – (1,20,000)	Dr		68,80,000	
	To Equity Share Allotment A/c				68,80,000
	(Being allotment money received on 3,94,000 shares)				
	Equity Share Capital A/c (6,000 × 40)	Dr		2,40,000	
	To Equity Share Allotment A/c				1,20,000
	To Share Forfeiture A/c				1,20,000
	(Being 6,000 shares forfeited for non-payment of allotment money)				
	Bank A/c (6,000× 30)	Dr		1,80,000	
	Share Forfeiture A/c	Dr		1,20,000	
	To Equity Share Capital A/c (6,000× 50)				3,00,000
	(Being forfeited shares re-issued @ ₹ 30 each as fully paid-up)				
	Equity Share First and Final Call A/c (3,94,000×10)	Dr		39,40,000	
	To Equity Share Capital A/c				39,40,000
	(Being first and final call money due)				
	Bank A/c (3,93,000×10)	Dr		39,30,000	
	To Equity Share First and Final Call A/c				39,30,000
	(Being first and final call money received on 3,93,000 shares)				

Date	Particulars		LF	Amt (Dr)	Amt (Cr)
	Equity Share Capital A/c (1,000 × 50)	Dr		50,000	
	To Share Forfeiture A/c (1,000 × 40)				40,000
	To Equity Share First and Final Call A/c (1,000 × 10)				10,000
	(Being 1,000 shares forfeiture for non-payment of first and final call)				
	Bank A/c (1,000 × 60)	Dr		60,000	
	To Equity Share Capital A/c (1,000 × 50)				50,000
	To Securities Premium Reserve A/c (1,000 × 10)				10,000
	(Being forfeited shares re-issued @ ₹ 60 each as fully paid-up)				
	Shares Forfeited A/c	Dr		40,000	
	To Capital Reserve A/c				40,000
	(Being gain on re-issue transferred to capital reserve account)				

Working Notes

1. **Capital Reserve**

Number of shares applied by Vibhuti $= 6{,}000 \times \frac{4{,}00{,}000}{3{,}00{,}000} = 8{,}000$ shares

		Amt (₹)
Money paid by Vibhuti on application (8,000 × 15)	=	1,20,000
(−) Amount adjusted with application (6,000 × 15)	=	(90,000)
Excess application money adjusted on allotment	=	₹ 30,000
Money due on allotment (6,000 × 25)	=	1,50,000
(−) Excess application money adjusted	=	(30,000)
Money not paid by Vibhuti on allotment	=	₹ 1,20,000

2. **Money Received on Allotment**

Amount due on allotment (4,00,000 × 25)	=	1,00,00,000
(−) Excess application money adjusted	=	(30,00,000)
	=	70,00,000
(−) Money not received from Vibhuti on allotment	=	(1,20,000)
	=	₹ 68,80,000

3. **Number of Shares Alloted to Shahid** $= 2{,}000 \times \frac{1{,}00{,}000}{2{,}00{,}000} = 1{,}000$ shares

37. Sukanya Ltd invited applications for issuing 1,00,000 equity shares of ₹ 10 each. The shares were issued at a premium of ₹ 20 per share. The amount was payable as follows

On application and allotment — ₹ 14 per share (including premium of ₹ 10)
On first call — ₹ 8 per share (including premium of ₹ 5)
On final call — ₹ 8 per share (including premium of ₹ 5)

Applications for 96,000 shares were received. Rohit a shareholder holding 7,000 shares failed to pay both the calls and Namit, a holder of 5,000 shares did not pay the final call. Shares of Rohit and Namit were forfeited. Of the forfeited shares 8,000 shares including all the shares of Rohit were re-issued to Reena at ₹ 8 per share fully paid-up. Pass necessary journal entries for the above transactions in the books of Sukanya Ltd. **All India (C) 2016**

Ans.

JOURNAL

Date	Particulars		LF	Amt (Dr)	Amt (Cr)
	Bank A/c (96,000×14)	Dr		13,44,000	
	To Equity Share Application and Allotment A/c				13,44,000
	(Being amount received on application and allotment)				
	Equity Share Application and Allotment A/c	Dr		13,44,000	
	To Equity Share Capital A/c (96,000 × 4)				3,84,000
	To Securities Premium Reserve A/c (96,000 × 10)				9,60,000
	(Being application money transferred to share capital account)				
	Equity Share first call A/c (96,000×8)	Dr		7,68,000	
	To Equity Share Capital A/c (96,000 × 3)				2,88,000
	To Securities Premium Reserve A/c (96,000 × 5)				4,80,000
	(Being first call money due)				
	Bank A/c (89,000 × 8)	Dr		7,12,000	
	To Equity Share First Call A/c				7,12,000
	(Being money received on first call)				
	Equity Share Final Call A/c	Dr		7,68,000	
	To Equity Share Capital A/c (96,000× 3)				2,88,000
	To Securities Premium Reserve A/c (96,000 × 5)				4,80,000
	(Being final call money due)				
	Bank A/c (84,000× 8)	Dr		6,72,000	
	To Equity Share Final Call A/c				6,72,000
	(Being money received on final call)				
	Equity Share Capital A/c (12,000×10)	Dr		1,20,000	
	Securities Premium Reserve A/c (7,000×10) + (5,000× 5)	Dr		95,000	
	To Equity Share First Call A/c (7,000× 8)				56,000
	To Equity Share Final Call A/c (7,000× 4) + (5,000× 7)				96,000
	To Shares Forfeiture A/c				63,000
	(Being shares forfeited)				
	Bank A/c (8,000× 8)	Dr		64,000	
	Shares Forfeited A/c (8,000×2)	Dr		16,000	
	To Equity Share Capital A/c (8,000×10)				80,000
	(Being forfeited shares re-issued @ ₹ 8 each as fully paid-up)				
	Shares Forfeited A/c	Dr		19,000	
	To Capital Reserve A/c				19,000
	(Being gain on re-issue of transferred to capital reserve account)				

Working Note

Calculation of Gain on Re-issue	**Amt (₹)**
Amount forfeited on 7,000 shares of Rohit (7,000 × 4)	28,000
(+) Amount forfeited on 1,000 shares of Namit $(35{,}000 \times \frac{1{,}000}{5{,}000})$	7,000
	35,000
(−) Discount on re-issue (8,000 × 2)	(16,000)
	19,000

38. RK Ltd invited applications for issuing 80,000 equity shares of ₹ 10 each at a premium of ₹ 35 per share. The amount was payable as follows

On application — ₹ 8 (including ₹ 5 premium) per share

On allotment — ₹ 12 (including ₹ 10 premium) per share

On first and final call — Balance amount

Applications for 75,000 shares were received and allotment was made to all the applicants. Rahim, a shareholder, who was allotted 3,000 shares failed to pay allotment money and his shares were immediately forfeited.

Afterwards, the first and final call was made. Suhani who held 3,000 shares failed to pay the final call. Her shares were also forfeited. All the forfeited shares were re-issued for a sum of ₹ 62,000 as fully paid-up. Pass necessary journal entries for the above transactions in the books of RK Ltd. **Delhi (C) 2016**

Ans.

JOURNAL

Date	Particulars		LF	Amt (Dr)	Amt (Cr)
	Bank A/c (75,000 × 8)	Dr		6,00,000	
	To Equity Share Application A/c				6,00,000
	(Being application money received on 75,000 shares)				
	Equity Share Application A/c	Dr		6,00,000	
	To Equity Share Capital A/c (75,000 × 3)				2,25,000
	To Securities Premium Reserves A/c (75,000 × 5)				3,75,000
	(Being application money transferred to share capital account)				
	Equity Share allotment A/c	Dr		9,00,000	
	To Equity Share Capital A/c (75,000 × 2)				1,50,000
	To Securities Premium Reserve A/c (75,000 × 10)				7,50,000
	(Being share allotment money due)				
	Bank A/c (72,000 × 12)	Dr		8,64,000	
	To Equity Share Allotment A/c				8,64,000
	(Being allotment money received)				
	Equity Share Capital A/c (3,000 × 5)	Dr		15,000	
	Securities Premium Reserve A/c (3,000 × 10)	Dr		30,000	
	To Equity Share Allotment A/c (3,000 × 12)				36,000
	To Shares Forfeiture A/c (3,000 × 3)				9,000
	(Being 3,000 shares forfeited on non-payment of allotment money)				
	Equity Share First and Final Call A/c (72,000 × 25)	Dr		18,00,000	
	To Equity Share Capital A/c (72,000 × 5)				3,60,000
	To Securities Premium Reserve A/c (72,000 × 20)				14,40,000
	(Being first and final call money due)				
	Bank A/c (69,000 × 25)	Dr		17,25,000	
	To Equity Share First and Final Call A/c				17,25,000
	(Being first and final call money received)				
	Equity Share Capital A/c (3,000 × 10)	Dr		30,000	
	Securities Premium Reserve A/c (3,000 × 20)	Dr		60,000	
	To Equity Share First and Final Call A/c (3,000 × 25)				75,000
	To Shares Forfeiture A/c (3,000 × 5)				15,000
	(Being shares forfeiture for non-payment of call money)				

Date	Particulars		LF	Amt (Dr)	Amt (Cr)
	Bank A/c	Dr		62,000	
	To Equity Share Capital A/c (6,000×10)				60,000
	To Securities Premium Reserve A/c				2,000
	(Being forfeited shares received for ₹ 62,000 as fully paid-up)				
	Shares Forfeiture A/c	Dr		24,000	
	To Capital Reserve A/c				24,000
	(Being gain on re-issue transferred to capital reserve account)				

39. Sargam Ltd invited applications for issuing 80,000 equity shares of ₹ 100 each at a premium. The amount was payable as follows

On application — ₹ 20 per share

On allotment — ₹ 60 (including premium) per share

On first and final call — ₹ 40 per share

Applications for 1,20,000 shares were received. Allotment was made on pro-rata basis to all the applicants. Excess money received on applications was adjusted on sums due to allotment. Sitaram, who had applied for 6,000 shares failed to pay the allotment money and Harnam did not pay first and final call on 800 shares allotted to him. The shares of Sitaram and Harnam were forfeited. 4,200 of these shares were re-issued for ₹ 100 per share as fully paid-up. The re-issued shares included all the forfeited shares of Harnam.

Pass necessary journal entries for the above transactions in the books of Sargam Ltd.

Delhi (C) 2016

Ans.

JOURNAL

Date	Particulars		LF	Amt (Dr)	Amt (Cr)
	Bank A/c (1,20,000×20)	Dr		24,00,000	
	To Equity Share Application A/c				24,00,000
	(Being application money received)				
	Equity Share Application A/c (1,20,000×20)	Dr		24,00,000	
	To Equity Share Capital A/c (80,000×20)				16,00,000
	To Equity Share Allotment A/c (40,000×20)				8,00,000
	(Being application money transferred to share capital account)				
	Equity Share Allotment A/c (80,000×60)	Dr		48,00,000	
	To Equity Share Capital A/c (80,000× 40)				32,00,000
	To Securities Premium Reserve A/c (80,000×20)				16,00,000
	(Being allotment money due)				
	Bank A/c (48,00,000 – 8,00,000 – 2,00,000)	Dr		38,00,000	
	To Equity Share Allotment A/c				38,00,000
	(Being allotment money received)				
	Equity Share First and Final Call A/c	Dr		32,00,000	
	To Equity Share Capital A/c (80,000× 40)				32,00,000
	(Being first and final call money due)				
	Bank A/c [80,000 – 4,000 – 800) × 40]	Dr		30,08,000	
	To Equity Share First and Final Call A/c				30,08,000
	(Being first and final call money received)				

Date	Particulars		LF	Amt (Dr)	Amt (Cr)
	Equity Share Capital A/c (4,800×100)	Dr		4,80,000	
	Securities Premium Reserve A/c (4,000×20)	Dr		80,000	
	To Equity Share Allotment A/c				2,00,000
	To Equity Share First and Final Call A/c (4,800× 40)				1,92,000
	To Share Forfeiture A/c (6,000×20)+ (800×60)				1,68,000
	(Being shares forfeited for non-payment)				
	Bank A/c (4,200×100)	Dr		4,20,000	
	To Equity Share Capital A/c				4,20,000
	(Being shares re-issued @ ₹ 100 per shares)				
	Shares Forfeiture A/c	Dr		1,50,000	
	To Capital Reserve A/c				1,50,000
	(Being gain on re-issue transferred to capital reserve account)				

Working Notes

1. **Calculation of allotment money not paid by Sitaram**

   Number of shares allotted to Sitaram $= \frac{80,000}{1,20,000} \times 6,000 = 4,000$ shares

2. **Money not paid on allotment**

	Amt (₹)
Money paid on application (6,000 × 20)	1,20,000
(−) Amount adjusted on allotment (4,000 × 20)	(80,000)
Excess application money adjusted on allotment	40,000
Money due on allotment (4,000 × 60)	2,40,000
(−) Excess application money adjusted	(40,000)
Money not paid on allotment by Sitaram	2,00,000

3. **Money received on allotment**

Total amount due on allotment (80,000 × 60)	48,00,000
(−) Excess application money adjusted	(8,00,000)
	40,00,000
(−) Money not received from Sitaram on allotment	(2,00,000)
	38,00,000
Amount forfeited on Sitaram 3,400 shares $= 1,20,000 \times \frac{3,400}{4,000}$	1,02,000
Amount forfeited on Harnam's 800 shares	48,000
	1,50,000

40. 'BMY Ltd' invited applications for issuing 1,00,000 equity shares of ₹ 10 each at a premium of ₹ 10 per share. The amount was payable as follows

On application — ₹ 10 per share (including ₹ 5 premium)

On allotment — The balance

The issue was fully subscribed. A shareholder holding 300 shares paid the full share money with application. Another shareholder holding 200 shares failed to pay the allotment money. His shares were forfeited. Later on, these shares were re-issued for ₹ 4,000 as fully paid-up. Pass necessary journal entries for the above transactions in the books of BMY Ltd.

All India 2015

Ans. **JOURNAL**

Date	Particulars		LF	Amt (Dr)	Amt (Cr)
	Bank A/c (1,00,000×10+300×10)	Dr		10,03,000	
	To Equity Share Application A/c				10,03,000
	(Being application money received on 1,00,000 besides call-in-advance)				
	Equity Share Application A/c	Dr		10,03,000	
	To Equity Share Capital A/c (1,00,000×5)				5,00,000
	To Securities Premium Reserve A/c (1,00,000×5)				5,00,000
	To Calls-in-Advance A/c (300×10)				3,000
	(Being transfer of allotment money to share capital)				
	Equity Share Allotment A/c	Dr		10,00,000	
	To Equity Share Capital A/c (1,00,000×5)				5,00,000
	To Securities Premium Reserve A/c (1,00,000×5)				5,00,000
	(Being share allotment money due)				
	Bank A/c	Dr		9,95,000	
	Calls-in-Arrears A/c (200×10)	Dr		2,000	
	Calls-in-Advance A/c (300×10)	Dr		3,000	
	To Equity Share Allotment A/c				10,00,000
	(Being allotment money received)				
	Equity Share Capital A/c (200×10)	Dr		2,000	
	Securities Premium Reserve A/c (200×5)	Dr		1,000	
	To Share Forfeiture A/c (200×5)				1,000
	To Calls-in-Arrears A/c (200×10)				2,000
	(Being 200 shares forfeited due to non-payment of allotment)				
	Bank A/c	Dr		4,000	
	To Equity Share Capital A/c				2,000
	To Securities Premium Reserve A/c				2,000
	(Being forfeited shares re-issued as fully paid-up)				
	Share Forfeiture A/c	Dr		1,000	
	To Capital Reserve A/c				1,000
	(Being profit on forfeiture transferred to capital reserve account)				

41. 'Blue Star Ltd' was registered with an authorised capital of ₹ 2,00,000 divided into 20,000 shares of ₹ 10 each. 6,000 of these shares were issued to the vendor for building purchased. 8,000 shares were issued to the public and ₹ 5 per share were called-up as follows

On application — ₹ 2 per share
On allotment — ₹ 1 per share
On first call — Balance of the calledup amount

The amounts received on these shares were as follows

On 6,000 shares — Full amount called
On 1,250 shares — ₹ 3 per share
On 750 shares — ₹ 2 per share

The directors forfeited 750 shares on which ₹ 2 per share were received. Pass necessary journal entries for the above transactions in the book of Blue Star Ltd. **All India 2015**

Ans.

JOURNAL

Date	Particulars		LF	Amt (Dr)	Amt (Cr)
	Building A/c	Dr		60,000	
	To Vendor A/c				60,000
	(Being building purchased for ₹ 6,00,000)				
	Vendor A/c	Dr		60,000	
	To Equity Share Capital A/c				60,000
	(Being issue of 6,000 shares towards purchase consideration)				
	Bank A/c (8,000 × 2)	Dr		16,000	
	To Equity Share Application A/c				16,000
	(Being application money received on 8,000 shares @ ₹ 2 per share)				
	Equity Share Application A/c	Dr		16,000	
	To Equity Share Capital A/c				16,000
	(Being transfer of application money)				
	Equity Share Allotment A/c	Dr		8,000	
	To Equity Share Capital A/c (8,000 × 1)				8,000
	(Being allotment money due on 8,000 shares)				
	Bank A/c	Dr		7,250	
	Calls-in-Arrears A/c	Dr		750	
	To Equity Share Allotment A/c				8,000
	(Being allotment money received on 7,250 shares)				
	Equity Share First Call A/c	Dr		16,000	
	To Equity Share Capital A/c (8,000 × 2)				16,000
	(Being first call money due on 8,000 shares)				
	Bank A/c	Dr		12,000	
	Calls-in-Arrears A/c (2,500 + 1,500)	Dr		4,000	
	To Equity Share First Call A/c				16,000
	(Being first call money received on 6,000 shares)				
	Equity Share Capital A/c (750 × 5)	Dr		3,750	
	To Share Forfeited A/c (750 × 2)				1,500
	To Calls-in-Arrears A/c (750 × 3)				2,250
	(Being 750 shares forfeited due to non-payment of allotment and call)				

42. 'Y Ltd' invited applications for issuing 15,000 equity shares of ₹ 10 each on which ₹ 6 per share were called-up, which were payable as follows

On application — ₹ 2 per share
On allotment — ₹ 1 per share
On first call — ₹ 3 per share

The issue was fully subscribed and the amount was received as follows

On 10,000 shares — ₹ 6 per share
On 3,000 shares — ₹ 3 per share
On 2,000 shares — ₹ 2 per share

The directors forfeited those shares on which less than ₹ 6 per share were received. The forfeited shares were re-issued at ₹ 9 per share, as ₹ 6 per share paid-up.

Pass necessary journal entries for the above transactions in the books of the company.
All India 2015

Ans. **JOURNAL**

Date	Particulars		LF	Amt (Dr)	Amt (Cr)
	Bank A/c (15,000×2)	Dr		30,000	
	To Equity Share Application A/c				30,000
	(Being application money received on 15,000 equity shares at ₹ 2 per share)				
	Equity Share Application A/c	Dr		30,000	
	To Share Capital A/c				30,000
	(Being application money transferred to share capital account)				
	Share Allotment A/c	Dr		15,000	
	To Equity Share Capital A/c (15,000×1)				15,000
	(Being allotment money transferred to share capital account)				
	Bank A/c	Dr		13,000	
	Calls-in-Arrears A/c	Dr		2,000	
	To Share Allotment A/c				15,000
	(Being allotment money received on 13,000 shares @ ₹ 1 each)				
	Equity Share First Call A/c	Dr		45,000	
	To Equity Share Capital A/c (15,000 × 3)				45,000
	(Being first call money due on 15,000 shares @ ₹ 3 per share)				
	Bank A/c	Dr		30,000	
	Calls-in-arrears A/c	Dr		15,000	
	To Equity Share First Call A/c				45,000
	(Being first call money received on 10,000 shares ₹ 3 per share)				
	Equity Share Capital A/c (5,000 × 6)	Dr		30,000	
	To Share Forfeiture A/c				13,000
	To Calls-in-Arrears A/c				17,000
	(Being 5,000 shares forfeited due to non-payment of allotment and first call money)				
	Bank A/c (5,000 × 9)	Dr		45,000	
	To Equity Share Capital A/c (5,000 × 6)				30,000
	To Securities Premium Reserve A/c (5,000 × 3)				15,000
	(Being forfeited shares were re-issued at ₹ 9 per share ₹ 6 paid-up)				
	Share Forfeiture A/c	Dr		13,000	
	To Capital Reserve A/c				13,000
	(Being profit on forfeiture transferred to capital reserve account)				

43. Alfa Ltd invited applications for issuing 75,000 equity shares of ₹ 10 each. The amount was payable as follows

On application and allotment	—	₹ 4 per share
On first call	—	₹ 3 per share
On second and final call	—	Balance amount

Applications for 1,00,000 shares were received. Shares were allotted to all the applicants on pro-rata basis and excess money received with applications was transferred towards sums due on first call. Vibha who was allotted 750 shares failed to pay the first call. Her shares were immediately forfeited. Afterwards the second call was made.

The amount due on second call was also received except on 1,000 shares, applied by Monika. Her shares were also forfeited. All the forfeited shares were re-issued to Mohit for ₹ 9,000 as fully paid-up.

Pass necessary journal entries in the books of Alfa Ltd for the above transactions. **Delhi 2015**

Ans. **JOURNAL**

Date	Particulars		LF	Amt (Dr)	Amt (Cr)
	Bank A/c (1,00,000 × 4)	Dr		4,00,000	
	To Equity Share Application and Allotment A/c				4,00,000
	(Being application and allotment money on 1,00,000 shares received @ ₹ 4 per share)				
	Equity Share Application and Allotment A/c	Dr		4,00,000	
	To Equity Share Capital A/c (75,000 × 4)				3,00,000
	To Equity Share First Call A/c				1,00,000
	(Being transfer of application money)				
	Equity Share First Call A/c	Dr		2,25,000	
	To Equity Share Capital A/c (75,000 × 3)				2,25,000
	(Being transfer of first call money on 75,000 shares @ ₹ 3 per share)				
	Bank A/c	Dr		1,23,750	
	Calls-in-Arrears A/c	Dr		1,250	
	To Equity Share First Call A/c				1,25,000
	(Being first call money received)				
	Equity Share Capital A/c (750 × 7)	Dr		5,250	
	To Share Forfeiture A/c				4,000
	To Calls-in-Arrears A/c				1,250
	(Being 750 shares of Vibha forfeited due to non-payment of first call)				
	Equity Share Second and Final Call A/c (74,250 × 3)	Dr		2,22,750	
	To Equity Share Capital A/c				2,22,750
	(Being second and final call money transfer on 74,250 shares @ ₹ 3)				
	Bank A/c	Dr		2,20,500	
	Calls-in-Arrears A/c	Dr		2,250	
	To Equity Share Second and Final Call A/c				2,22,750
	(Being second and final call money received on 73,500 shares at ₹ 3 per share)				
	Equity Share Capital A/c (750 × 10)	Dr		7,500	
	To Share Forfeiture A/c (750 × 7)				5,250
	To Calls-in-Arrears A/c (750 × 3)				2,250
	(Being 750 shares of Monika forfeited due to non-payment of second and final call)				
	Bank A/c	Dr		9,000	
	Share Forfeiture A/c	Dr		6,000	
	To Equity Share Capital A/c (1,500 × 10)				15,000
	(Being 1,500 forfeited shares were re-issued)				
	Share Forfeiture A/c	Dr		3,250	
	To Capital Reserve A/c (4,000 + 5,250 − 6,000)				3,250
	(Being profit on forfeiture of shares transferred to capital reserve account)				

Working Notes

1. **Calculation of amount not received from Vibha**

   (*i*) Applied share computation $= \frac{1,00,000}{75,000} \times 750 = 1,000$ shares

   (*ii*) Amount not received on first call by Vibha

		Amt (₹)
Application money already received	= 1,000 × 4 =	4,000
(–) She should pay on application	= 750 × 4 =	3,000
Excess money		= ₹ 1,000

She should pay on first call = 750 × 3 =	2,250
(–) Excess money =	(1,000)
Amount not received	₹ 1,250

2. **Calculation of shares allotted to Monika**

   Allotted shares $= \frac{75,000}{1,00,000} \times 1,000 = 750$ shares

44. Jeevan Dhara Ltd invited applications for issuing 1,20,000 equity shares of ₹ 10 each at a premium of ₹ 2 per share. The amount was payable as follows

On application	— ₹ 2 per share
On allotment	— ₹ 5 per share (including premium)
On first and final call	— Balance amount

Applications for 1,50,000 shares were received. Shares were allotted to all the applicants on pro-rata basis. Excess money received on applications was adjusted towards sums due on allotment. All calls were made. Manu who had applied for 3,000 shares failed to pay the amount due on allotment and first and final call. Madhur who was allotted 2,400 shares failed to pay the first and final call. Shares of both Manu and Madhur were forfeited. The forfeited shares were re-issued at ₹ 9 per share as fully paid-up.

Pass necessary journal entries for the above transactions in the books of Jeevan Dhara Ltd.
Delhi 2015

Ans. Solve as Q no. 39 on page 311 and 312.

Capital Reserve = ₹ 13,200

45. 'Guru Ltd' invited applications for issuing 80,000 equity shares of ₹ 10 each at a premium of ₹ 10 per share. The amount was payable as follows

On application and allotment	— ₹ 10 (including ₹ 5 premium)
On first and final call	— ₹ 10 (including ₹ 5 premium)

Applications for 1,00,000 share were received. Applications for 10,000 shares were rejected and application money was refunded. Shares were allotted on pro-rata basis to the remaining applicants.

Excess application money received from applicants to whom shares were allotted on pro-rata basis was adjusted towards sums due on first and final call. All calls were made and were duly received except the first and final call money from Kumar who had applied for 1,800 shares. His shares were forfeited. The forfeited shares were re-issued at ₹ 9 per share as fully paid-up.

Pass necessary journal entries for the above transactions in the books of 'Guru Ltd'.
Foreign 2015

Ans.

JOURNAL

Date	Particulars		LF	Amt (Dr)	Amt (Cr)
	Bank A/c (1,00,000 × 10)	Dr		10,00,000	
	To Equity Share Application and Allotment A/c				10,00,000
	(Being application money received on 1,00,000 shares)				
	Equity Share Application and Allotment A/c	Dr		10,00,000	
	To Equity Share Capital A/c (80,000 × 5)				4,00,000
	To Securities Premium Reserve A/c (80,000 × 5)				4,00,000
	To Equity Share First and Final Call A/c				1,00,000
	To Bank A/c (10,000 × 10)				1,00,000
	(Being application money transferred to share capital account and excess money is adjusted in final call account)				
	Equity Share First and Final Call A/c	Dr		8,00,000	
	To Equity Share Capital A/c (80,000 × 5)				4,00,000
	To Securities Premium Reserve A/c (80,000 × 5)				4,00,000
	(Being amount due on first and final call)				
	Bank A/c	Dr		6,86,000	
	To Equity Share First and Final Call A/c				6,86,000
	(Being amount received on first and final call)				
	Equity Share Capital A/c (1,600 × 10)	Dr		16,000	
	Securities Premium Reserve A/c (1,600 × 5)	Dr		8,000	
	To Equity Share Forfeiture A/c				10,000
	To Equity Share First and Final Call A/c				14,000
	(Being Kumar's share forfeited)				
	Bank A/c (1,600 × 9)	Dr		14,400	
	Equity Share Forfeiture A/c	Dr		1,600	
	To Equity Share Capital A/c (1,600 × 10)				16,000
	(Being forfeited shares re-issued for ₹ 9 as fully paid-up)				
	Equity Share Forfeiture A/c	Dr		8,400	
	To Capital Reserve A/c				8,400
	(Being excess amount on forfeiture transferred to capital reserve account)				

Working Notes

Computation Table

Categories	Shares applied	Shares allotted	Money received on application @ ₹ 10 each	Money transferred to share capital @ ₹ 5 each	Money transferred to securities premium reserve	Excess application money
I	10,000	—	1,00,000	—	—	—
II	90,000	80,000	9,00,000	4,00,000	4,00,000	1,00,000
	1,00,000	80,000	10,00,000	4,00,000	4,00,000	1,00,000

1. **Calculation of Amount not Received on First and Final Call**

Shares allotted to Kumar $= \frac{80,000}{90,000} \times 1,800 = 1,600$ shares

Amount received on 1,800 shares @ ₹ 10 each = ₹ 18,000

Amount transferred to share capital account $(1,600 \times 5)$ = ₹ 8,000

Amount transferred to securities premium account (1,600 × 5) = ₹ 8,000

Excess money received on application = ₹ 2,000

Amount due on first and final call for 1,600 shares of Kumar @ ₹ 10 each = ₹ 16,000 (8,000 + 8,000)

Amount not received on securities premium = ₹ 8,000

Amount not received on first and final call = ₹ 6,000 (8,000 – 2,000)

2. **Calculation of Amount Credited in Share Forfeiture Account**

		Amt (₹)
Amount received on application and allotment	=	18,000 (1,800 × 10)
(–) Amount received for securities premium	=	8,000 (1,600 × 5)
Amount to be credited in share forfeiture account		₹ 10,000

46. Kayafab Ltd issued 1,00,000 equity shares of ₹ 10 each payable as ₹ 2 on application; ₹ 4 on allotment and ₹ 2 each on first and final call. Applications were received for 1,50,000 shares. Applicants of 50,000 shares were sent letters of regret and application money was refunded Madhur, a holder of 3,000 shares failed to pay allotment money which he paid alongwith the first call. Rohan, a shareholder holding 700 shares paid both the calls alongwith allotment. Sohan, a holder of 1,000 shares did not pay the first call and the final call. His shares were forfeited. The forfeited shares were re-issued at ₹ 11 per share as fully paid-up.

Pass necessary journal entries for the above transactions in the books of the company.
All India (C) 2015

Ans.

JOURNAL

Date	Particulars		LF	Amt (Dr)	Amt (Cr)
	Bank A/c (1,50,000 × 2)	Dr		3,00,000	
	To Equity Share Application A/c				3,00,000
	(Being application money received)				
	Equity Share Application A/c	Dr		3,00,000	
	To Share Capital A/c (1,00,000 × 2)				2,00,000
	To Bank A/c (50,000 × 2)				1,00,000
	(Being application money transferred to share capital account)				
	Equity Share Allotment A/c (1,00,000 × 4)	Dr		4,00,000	
	To Share Capital A/c				4,00,000
	(Being allotment money due)				
	Bank A/c	Dr		3,90,800	
	To Equity Share Allotment A/c (97,000 × 4)				3,88,000
	To Calls-in-Advance A/c (700 × 2) + (700 × 2)				2,800
	(Being allotment money received)				
	Equity Share First Call A/c (1,00,000 × 2)	Dr		2,00,000	
	To Share Capital A/c				2,00,000
	(Being first call money due)				
	Bank A/c	Dr		2,08,600	
	Calls-in-Advance A/c (700 × 2)	Dr		1,400	
	To Equity Share First Call A/c (99,000 × 2)				1,98,000
	To Equity Share Allotment A/c (3,000 × 4)				12,000
	(Being first call money received)				
	Equity Share Second and Final Call A/c (1,00,000 × 2)	Dr		2,00,000	
	To Share Capital A/c				2,00,000
	(Being final call money due)				

Date	Particulars		LF	Amt (Dr)	Amt (Cr)
	Bank A/c (98,300×2)	Dr		1,96,600	
	Call-in-Advance A/c (700×2)	Dr		1,400	
	To Share Second and Final Call A/c				1,98,000
	(Being amount received on second and final call)				
	Equity Share Capital A/c (1,000×10)	Dr		10,000	
	To Share Forfeiture A/c (1,000×6)				6,000
	To Equity Share First Call A/c (1,000×2)				2,000
	To Equity Share Second Call A/c (1,000×2)				2,000
	(Being shares forfeited)				
	Bank A/c (1,000×11)	Dr		11,000	
	To Share Capital A/c (1,000×10)				10,000
	To Securities Premium Reserve (1,000 × 1)				1,000
	(Being shares re-issued @ ₹ 11 per share fully paid-up)				
	Share Forfeiture A/c	Dr		6,000	
	To Capital Reserve A/c				6,000
	(Being gain on re-issue transferred to capital reserve account)				

47. X Ltd invited applications for issuing 75,000 equity shares of ₹ 10 each at a premium of ₹ 5 per share. The amount was payable as follows

On application and allotment — ₹ 9 per share (including premium)

On first and final call — Balance amount

Applications for 3,00,000 shares were received. Applications for 2,00,000 shares were rejected and money refunded. Shares were allotted on pro-rata basis to the remaining applicants. The first and final call was made. The amount was duly received except on 1,500 shares applied by Ravi. His shares were forfeited. The forfeited shares were re-issued at a discount of ₹ 4 per share. Pass necessary journal entries for the above transactions in the books of X Ltd. **All India 2014**

Ans.

JOURNAL

Date	Particulars		LF	Amt (Dr)	Amt (Cr)
	Bank A/c (3,00,000 × 9)	Dr		27,00,000	
	To Share Application and Allotment A/c				27,00,000
	(Being share application and allotment received on 3,00,000 of ₹ 9 each including premium of ₹ 5 each)				
	Share Application and Allotment A/c	Dr		27,00,000	
	To Share Capital A/c (75,000 × 4)				3,00,000
	To Securities Premium Reserve A/c (75,000 × 5)				3,75,000
	To Bank A/c (2,00,000 × 9)				18,00,000
	To Share First and Final Call A/c				2,25,000
	(Being share application of 75,000 shares transferred to share capital account share application and allotment on 2,00,000 shares refunded and rest is adjusted on share first and final call)				
	Share First and Final Call A/c (75,000×6)	Dr		4,50,000	
	To Share Capital A/c				4,50,000
	(Being share first and final call due on 75,000 shares of ₹ 6 each)				
	Bank A/c	Dr		2,21,625	
	To Share First and Final Call A/c				2,21,625
	(Being share first and final call received)				

Date	Particulars		LF	Amt (Dr)	Amt (Cr)
	Share Capital A/c (1,125 × 10)	Dr		11,250	
	To Share Forfeiture A/c				7,875
	To Share First and Final Call A/c				3,375
	(Being 1,125 shares were forfeited for non-payment of share first and final call of ₹ 6 each)				
	Bank A/c (1,125 × 6)	Dr		6,750	
	Shares Forfeiture A/c	Dr		4,500	
	To Share Capital A/c (1,125 × 10)				11,250
	(Being 1,125 forfeited shares were re-issued at a discount of ₹ 4 per share)				
	Share Forfeiture A/c	Dr		3,375	
	To Capital Reserve A/c				3,375
	(Being share forfeiture transferred to capital reserve)				

Analysis Table

Shares applied	Shares allotted	Money received on application and allotment @ ₹ 9 each	Money transferred to share capital @ ₹ 4 each	Money transferred to securities premium @ ₹ 5 each	Excess application and allotment money	Share first and final call @ ₹ 6 each	Amount adjusted on share first and final call after	Money refunded
2,00,000	—	18,00,000	—	—	—	—	—	18,00,000
1,00,000	75,000	9,00,000	3,00,000 (75,000 × 4)	3,75,000 (75,000 × 5)	2,25,00	4,50,000	2,25,0000	—
3,00,000	75,000	27,00,000	3,00,000	3,75,000	2,25,000	4,50,000	2,25,000	18,00,000

Working Notes

Those who applied for 1,00,000 shares were allotted = 75,000 shares

Ravi who applied for 1,500 shares was allotted $= 75{,}000 \times \frac{1{,}500}{1{,}00{,}000} = 1{,}125$ shares

Share Application and Allotment received on 1,500 shares of ₹ 9 each (including premium of ₹ 5 each)	= 13,500
Shares allotted (1,125 × 9)	= (10,125)
Excess application and allotment money received	= 3,375
Share first and final call due to 1,125 shares of ₹ 6 each	= 6,750
Share first and final call not received	= ₹ 3,375 (6,750 – 3,375)
Therefore, share first and final call received	= ₹ 2,21,625 (2,25,000 – 3,375)

48. Bhagwati Ltd invited applications for issuing 2,00,000 equity shares of ₹ 10 each. The amounts were payable as follows

On application	—	₹ 3 per share
On allotment	—	₹ 5 per share
On first and final call	—	₹ 2 per share

Applications were received for 3,00,000 shares and pro-rata allotment was made to all the applicants. Money overpaid on application was adjusted towards allotment. B, who was allotted 3,000 shares, failed to pay the first and final call money. His shares were forfeited. Out of the forfeited shares, 2,500 shares were re-issued as fully paid-up @ ₹ 8 per share.

Pass necessary journal entries to record the above transactions in the books of Bhagwati Ltd. **All India (C) 2014**

Ans. **JOURNAL**

Date	Particulars		LF	Amt (Dr)	Amt (Cr)
	Bank A/c (3,00,000 × 3)	Dr		9,00,000	
	To Equity Share Application A/c				9,00,000
	(Being application money received for 3,00,000 shares)				
	Equity Share Application A/c	Dr		9,00,000	
	To Equity Share Capital A/c				6,00,000
	To Equity Share Allotment A/c				3,00,000
	(Being application money transferred to share capital account and excess adjusted in allotment)				
	Equity Share Allotment A/c	Dr		10,00,000	
	To Equity Share Capital A/c (2,00,000 × 5)				10,00,000
	(Being allotment made due on 2,00,000 shares)				
	Bank A/c	Dr		7,00,000	
	To Equity Share Allotment A/c				7,00,000
	(Being the balance of allotment money received)				
	Equity Share First and Final Call A/c	Dr		4,00,000	
	To Equity Share Capital A/c (2,00,000 × 2)				4,00,000
	(Being first and final call made due)				
	Bank A/c (1,97,000 × 2)	Dr		3,94,000	
	To Equity Share First and Final Call A/c				3,94,000
	(Being final call received on 1,97,000 Shares)				
	Equity Share Capital A/c (3,000 × 10)	Dr		30,000	
	To Share First and Final Call A/c (3,000 × 2)				6,000
	To Share Forfeiture A/c				24,000
	(Being 3,000 shares forfeited for non-payment of final call)				
	Bank A/c (2,500 × 8)	Dr		20,000	
	Share Forfeiture A/c	Dr		5,000	
	To Equity Share Capital A/c (2,500 × 10)				25,000
	(Being 2,500 shares re-issued @ ₹ 8 per share)				
	Share Forfeiture A/c	Dr		15,000	
	To Capital Reserve A/c				15,000
	(Being the balance on re-issued shares transferred to capital reserve account)				

Working Notes

1. **Amount Received at the Time of Allotment**

Amount due on allotment	=	10,00,000
(–) Excess received at the time of application	=	(3,00,000)
		₹ 7,00,000

2. Amount forfeited on re-issued shares $= \frac{24,000}{3,000} \times 2,500 = 20,000$

(–) Amount utilised at the time of re-issue = (5,000)

Amount transferred to capital reserve ₹ 15,000

49. Record the journal entries for forfeiture and re-issue in the following cases

(*i*) X Ltd forfeited 200 shares of ₹ 100 each, ₹ 70 called-up, on which the shareholders had paid application and allotment money of ₹ 50 per share. Out of these,150 shares were re-issued to Naresh as ₹ 70 paid-up for ₹ 80 per share.

(*ii*) Y Ltd forfeited 180 shares of ₹ 10 each, ₹ 8 called-up, issued at a premium of ₹ 2 per share to R for non-payment of allotment money of ₹ 5 per share (including premium). Out of these, 160 shares were re-issued to Sanjay as ₹ 8 called-up for ₹ 10 per share fully paid-up. **All India 2013**

Ans.

JOURNAL

Date	Particulars		LF	Amt (Dr)	Amt (Cr)
(i) (a)	Share Capital A/c (200 × 70)	Dr		14,000	
	To Calls-in-Arrears A/c (200 × 20)				4,000
	To Share Forfeiture A/c (200 × 50)				10,000
	(Being 200 shares on which ₹ 70 is called-up, forfeited for non-payment of ₹ 20 per share)				
(b)	Bank A/c (150 × 80)	Dr		12,000	
	To Share Capital A/c (150 × 70)				10,500
	To Securities Premium Reserve A/c (150 × 10)				1,500
	(Being 150 forfeited shares re-issued for ₹ 80 per share, ₹ 70 being paid-up)				
(c)	Share Forfeiture A/c	Dr		7,500	
	To Capital Reserve A/c				7,500
	(Being share forfeited amount on 150 shares transferred to capital reserve account)				
(ii) (a)	Share Capital A/c (180 × 8)	Dr		1,440	
	Securities Premium Reserve A/c (180 × 2)	Dr		360	
	To Share Allotment A/c (180 × 5)				900
	To Share Forfeiture A/c (180 × 5)				900
	(Being 180 shares forfeited on which ₹ 8 is called-up, for non-payment of allotment money including premium)				
(b)	Bank A/c (160 × 8)	Dr		1,280	
	Share Forfeiture A/c	Dr		320	
	To Share Capital A/c (160 × 10)				1,600
	(Being 160 forfeited shares re-issued for ₹ 10 per share, ₹ 8 being called-up)				
(c)	Share Forfeiture A/c	Dr		480	
	To Capital Reserve A/c				480
	(Being share forfeited amount on 160 shares transferred to capital reserve account)				

Working Notes

1. **Amount to be Transferred to Capital Reserve Account**

Forfeited amount of 200 shares $= 10{,}000$ of 150 shares $= \frac{10{,}000}{200} \times 150 = 7{,}500$

(–) Amount utilised on re-issue = Nil

₹ 7,500

2. **Amount to be Transferred to Capital Reserve Account**

Forfeited amount of 160 shares $= \frac{900}{180} \times 160 = 800$

(–) Amount utilised in re-issue = (320)

₹ 480

50. Record the journal entries for forfeiture and re-issue of shares in the following cases

(*i*) X Ltd forfeited 20 shares of ₹ 10 each,₹ 7 called-up on which the shareholder had paid application and allotment money of ₹ 5 per share. Out of these, 15 shares were re-issued to Naresh as ₹ 7 per share paid-up for ₹ 8 per share.

(*ii*) Y Ltd forfeited 90 shares of ₹ 10 each, ₹ 8 called up issued at a premium of ₹ 2 per share to 'R' for non-payment of allotment money of ₹ 5 per share (including premium). Out of these, 80 shares were re-issued to Sanjay as ₹ 8 called-up for ₹ 10 per share. **Delhi 2013**

Ans. Solve as Q. no. 49 on page 323 and 324.

(i) Capital Reserve = ₹ 75 (ii) Capital Reserve = ₹ 400

51. RK Ltd invited applications for issuing 70,000 equity shares of ₹ 10 each at a premium of ₹ 35 per share. The amount was payable as follows

On application	—	₹ 15 per share (including ₹ 12 premium)
On allotment	—	₹ 10 per share (including ₹ 8 premium)
On first and final call	—	Balance amount

Applications for 65,000 shares were received and allotment was made to all applicants. A shareholder Ram, who was allotted 2,000 shares, failed to pay the allotment money. His shares were forfeited immediately after allotment. Afterwards the first and final call was made. Sohan, who had 3,000 shares, failed to pay the first and final call. His shares were also forfeited. Out of the forfeited shares 4,000 shares were re-issued @ ₹ 50 per share fully paid-up. The re-issued shares included all the shares of Ram.

Pass necessary journal entries for the above transactions in the books of RK Ltd. **All India 2012**

Ans.

JOURNAL

Date	Particulars		LF	Amt (Dr)	Amt (Cr)
	Bank A/c (65,000 × 15)	Dr		9,75,000	
	To Equity Share Application A/c				9,75,000
	(Being share application money received on 65,000 equity shares @ ₹ 15 per share including premium)				
	Equity Share Application A/c	Dr		9,75,000	
	To Equity Share Capital A/c (65,000 × 3)				1,95,000
	To Securities Premium Reserve A/c (65,000 × 12)				7,80,000
	(Being share application money transferred)				

Date	Particulars		LF	Amt (Dr)	Amt (Cr)
	Equity Share Allotment A/c	Dr		6,50,000	
	To Equity Share Capital A/c (65,000 × 2)				1,30,000
	To Securities Premium Reserve A/c (65,000 × 8)				5,20,000
	(Being allotment money due on 65,000 equity shares @ ₹ 10 per shares including premium of ₹ 8 each)				
	Bank A/c	Dr		6,30,000	
	To Equity Share Allotment A/c				6,30,000
	(Being share allotment money received on 63,000 equity shares @ ₹ 10 per shares including premium)				
	Equity Share Capital A/c (2,000 × 5)	Dr		10,000	
	Securities Premium Reserve A/c (2,000 × 8)	Dr		16,000	
	To Share Forfeiture A/c (2,000 × 3)				6,000
	To Equity Share Allotment A/c (2,000 × 10)				20,000
	(Being 2,000 shares forfeited for the non-payment of allotment of ₹ 10 per share including premium)				
	Equity Share First and Final Call A/c (63,000 × 20)	Dr		12,60,000	
	To Equity Share Capital A/c (63,000 × 5)				3,15,000
	To Securities Premium Reserve A/c (63,000 × 15)				9,45,000
	(Being share first and final call due on 63,000 equity shares @ ₹ 20 per share including premium of ₹ 15 each)				
	Bank A/c	Dr		12,00,000	
	To Equity Share First and Final Call A/c (60,000 × 20)				12,00,000
	(Being share first and final call money received on 60,000 equity shares @ ₹ 20 per share including premium)				
	Equity Share Capital A/c (3,000 × 10)	Dr		30,000	
	Securities Premium Reserve A/c (3,000 × 15)	Dr		45,000	
	To Share Forfeiture A/c (3,000 × 5)				15,000
	To Equity Share First and Final Call A/c (3,000 × 20)				60,000
	(Being 3,000 shares forfeited for the non-payment of first and final call of ₹ 20 per shares including premium)				
	Bank A/c (4,000 × 50)	Dr		2,00,000	
	To Equity Share Capital A/c (4,000 × 10)				40,000
	To Securities Premium Reserve A/c (4,000 × 40)				1,60,000
	(Being re-issue of 4,000 forfeited shares @ ₹ 50 per share as fully paid-up)				
	Share Forfeiture A/c	Dr		16,000	
	To Capital Reserve A/c (WN)				16,000
	(Being balance of forfeited shares account transferred to capital reserve account)				

Working Note

	Amt (₹)
Amount of Ram's 2,000 forfeited shares	= 6,000
Amount of Sohan's 2,000 forfeited share $\left(15{,}000 \times \frac{2{,}000}{3{,}000}\right)$	= 10,000
Amount to be transferred to capital reserve	₹ 16,000

52. Shyam Ltd invited applications for issuing 80,000 equity shares of ₹ 10 each at a premium of ₹ 40 per share. The amount was payable as follows

On application	—	₹ 35 per share (including ₹ 30 premium)
On allotment	—	₹ 8 per share (including ₹ 4 premium)
On first and final call	—	Balance amount

Applications for 77,000 shares were received. Shares were allotted to all the applicants. Sundram to whom 7,000 shares were allotted failed to pay the allotment money. His shares were forfeited immediately after allotment.

Afterwards the first and final call was made. Satyam, the holder of 500 shares failed to pay the first and final call. His shares were also forfeited. Out of the forfeited shares 1,000 shares were re-issued at ₹ 50 per share fully paid-up. The re-issued shares included all the shares of Satyam. Pass necessary journal entries for the above transactions in the books of Shyam Ltd. **Delhi 2012**

Ans. Solve as Q no. 51 on page 324 and 325.

Capital Reserve = ₹ 7,000

Multiple Choice Questions

For Complete Chapter (1 Mark)

1. A Ltd. forfeited a share of ₹ 100 issued at a premium of 20% for non-payment of first call of ₹ 30 per share and final call of ₹ 10 per share. The minimum price at which this share can be reissued is .... **CBSE Term I 2021**

(a) ₹ 40 per share (b) ₹ 60 per share
(c) ₹ 100 per share (d) ₹ 80 per share

Hint: A company can reissue forfeited shares at a minimum price which should not be less than the price not received on shares earlier.

2. Lata Ltd. forfeited Maya's shares. Maya who had applied for 600 shares of ₹ 10 each and was allotted 400 shares failed to pay allotment money of ₹ 4 per share including premium of ₹ 2. She had paid only the application money of ₹ 2 per share. 'The first and final call was not yet called. The Journal entry for forfeiture of shares by opening calls in arrears account will be **CBSE Term I 2021**

(a)	Share Capital A/c	Dr	1,600	
	To Share Forfeited A/c			800
	To Calls-in-arrears A/c			800
(b)	Share Capital A/c	Dr	1,600	
	Securities Premium Reserve A/c	Dr	800	
	To Share Forfeited A/c			1,200
	To Calls-in-arrears A/c			1,200
(c)	Share Capital A/c	Dr	1,600	
	Securities Premium Reserve A/c	Dr	800	
	To Share Forfeited A/c			1,600
	To Calls-in-arrears A/c			800
(d)	Share Capital A/c	Dr	2,000	
	To Share Forfeited A/c			1,200
	To Calls-in-arrears A/c			800

3. Versha Ltd. purchased the running business of Vikram Ltd. consisting of total assets of ₹ 10,00,000 and liabilities of ₹ 2,00,000. Versha Ltd. paid ₹ 2,00,000 immediately in cash and balance by issuing 7,000 shares of ₹ 100 each at a premium of ₹ 20 per share. The goodwill account will be debited by .... **CBSE Term I 2021**

(a) ₹ 2,40,000 (b) ₹ 2,00,000
(c) ₹ 8,00,000 (d) Nil

Hint: Amount of goodwill
$= [2,00,000 + 8,40,000\ (7,000 \times 120)]$
$- (10,00,000 - 2,00,000) =$ ₹ 2,40,000

4. Jupiter Ltd. invited applications for issuing 25,000 equity shares of ₹ 10 each and received applications for 30,000 shares along with the application money of ₹ 2 per share. Which of the following alternative, can be followed for the allotment of shares? CBSE Term I 2021

(i) Refund the excess application money and allot full shares to rest of the applicants.

(ii) Not to allot any share to some applications, allot full to some applicants and allot remaining on pro-rata basis.

(iii) Not to allot any share and refund the total application money to the applications.

(a) Only (i) (b) Only (ii)
(c) Only (iii) (d) Any one of (i) and (ii)

5. Nominal share capital is CBSE Term I 2021

(a) that part of authorised capital which is issued by the company.
(b) the amount of capital which is actually applied for by the prospective shareholders.
(c) the maximum amount of share capital which a company is authorised to issue.
(d) the amount actually paid by the shareholders.

6. Vandana Ltd, issued 6,000 equity shares ₹ 10 each at 10% premium. The issue was fully subscribed. Amount per share was payable as follows
On application ₹ 3, On allotment ₹ 3 (including premium), On first call ₹ 3 and on final call ₹ 2. A, a holder of 200 shares paid the entire money along with allotment. The amount received on allotment will be .... CBSE Term I 2021

(a) ₹ 18,000 (b) ₹ 19,000
(c) ₹ 25,000 (d) ₹ 21,000

Hint: Amount received on allotment
= Amount due on allotment + Calls-in-advance
$= 18,000 + 1,000\ (200 \times 5)$
= ₹ 19,000

7. The company has to get minimum subscription within .... from the date of issue of the prospectus. When minimum subscription has been received, the directors of the company proceed to make .... which implies a valid contract between the company and the applicants who now become the allottees and assume the status of shareholders or members. CBSE Term I 2021

(a) 120 days, allotment of shares
(b) 130 days, application of shares
(c) 14 days, allotment of shares
(d) 15 days, allotment of shares

8. Money received in advance from shareholders before it is actually called up by the directors is CBSE Term I 2021, 2020

(a) debited to calls-in-advance account.
(b) credited to calls-in-advance account.
(c) debited to calls account.
(d) credited to calls account.

9. **Assertion** (A) Maximum amount of discount allowed at the time of reissue of forfeited shares should not exceed the forfeited amount.

Reason (R) The excess amount of forfeited shares account is transferred to capital reserve account. CBSE Term I 2021

Alternatives

(a) Assertion (A) is correct, but Reason (R) wrong
(b) Both Assertion (A) and Reason (R) are correct
(c) Assertion (A) is wrong, but Reason (R) is correct
(d) Both Assertion (A) and Reason (R) are wrong

10. Vista Ltd. forfeited 200 shares held by Ravi for non-payment of allotment money of ₹ 40 per share (including premium of ₹ 10 per share).

The first and final call of ₹ 20 per share was not yet called. In the forfeiture entry share capital account will be
CBSE Term I 2021

(a) Debited by ₹ 20,000
(b) Debited by ₹ 18,000
(c) Debited by ₹ 16,000
(d) Credited by ₹ 16,000

11. If the purchase consideration is less than the amount of net assets taken over, which account will be credited for the difference amount? **CBSE Term I 2021**

(a) Goodwill Account

(b) Vendor's Account

(c) Capital Reserve Account

(d) Asset Accounts

12. Uncalled capital is that portion of the .... which has not yet been called up and the portion of such uncalled capital to be called only in the event of winding up of the company is called .... **CBSE Term I 2021**

(a) subscribed capital; reserve capital

(b) issued capital; reserve capital

(c) authorised capital; capital reserve

(d) registered capital; capital reserve

Direction *Question no. 13 and 14 are based on the hypothetical situation given below*

Vinod Ltd. having authorised capital ₹ 1,00,00,000 divided into equity shares of ₹ 100 each, invited applications for issuing 25,000 equity shares at par. The amount per share was payable as follows: On application ₹ 20 per share, on allotment ₹ 30 per share, on first call ₹ 25 per share and on second and final call ₹ 25 per share. Applications were received for 24,000 shares and the shares were allotted to all the applicants. All calls were made and were received as follows

On 18,000 shares — Full amount;

On 2,000 shares — ₹ 75 per share

On 2,500 shares — ₹ 50 per share;

On 1,500 shares — ₹ 20 per share

The company forfeited those shares on which less than ₹ 75 per share were received. The forfeited shares were reissued at ₹ 95 per share fully paid up. **CBSE Term I 2021**

13. How much amount was received on allotment?

(a) ₹ 6,75,000 (b) ₹7,20,000

(c) ₹ 6,00,000 (d) ₹4,80,000

Hint: Amount received on allotment

$= (18{,}000 + 2{,}000 + 2{,}500) \times 30$

$= 22{,}500 \times 30 = ₹\ 6{,}75{,}000$

14. How much total amount was credited to share forfeiture account on forfeiture of shares?

(a) ₹ 3,80,000 (b) ₹1,35,000

(c) ₹ 1,55,000 (d) ₹2,45,000

Hint: Amount credited to share forfeiture account

$= (2{,}500 \times 50) + (1{,}500 \times 20)$

$= 1{,}25{,}000 + 30{,}000 = ₹\ 1{,}55{,}000$

15. Subscribed capital is **2020**

(a) that part of authorised capital which is issued to the public for subscription.

(b) that part of issued capital which has been actually subscribed by the public

(c) that part of subscribed capital which has been called-up on the shares

(d) that part of subscribed capital which has not yet been called-up on the shares

16. A Ltd forfeited 300 shares of 10 each, fully called-up, held by B for non-payment of allotment money of ₹ 3 per equity share and final call money of ₹ 4 per share. Out of these, 250 shares were re-issued to C for a total payment of ₹ 1,800. Calculate the amount to be transferred to capital reserve account?

(a) ₹ 750 (b) ₹ 50

(c) ₹ 700 (d) ₹ 900

Hint: Total amount forfeited on 300 shares @ ₹ 3 per share = 900

∴ Amount forfeited on 250 shares @ ₹ 3 per share = 750

(–) Discount allowed on re-issue of 250 forfeited shares $(250 \times 10 - 1{,}800)$ = (700)

Profit on re-issue of forfeited shares transferred to capital reserve = ₹ 50

Direction *Read the following hypothetical text and answer the questions 17 to 20.*

Nidiya Limited was incorporated on 1st April, 2017 with registered office in Mumbai. The capital clause of Memorandum of Association reflected a registered capital of 8,00,000 equity shares of ₹ 10 each and 1,00,000 preference shares of ₹ 50 each.

Since some large investments were required for building and machinery the company in consultation with vendors, Ms.VPS Enterprises, issued 1,00,000 equity shares and 20,000 preference shares at par to them in full consideration of assets acquired. Besides this the company issued 2,00,000 equity shares for cash at par payable as ₹ 3 on application, 2 on allotment, 3 on first call and 2 on second call.

Till date second call has not yet been made and all the shareholders have paid except Mr. Ajay who did not pay allotment and calls on his 300 shares and Mr. Vipul who did not pay first call on his 200 shares. Shares of Mr. Ajay were then forfeited and out of them 100 shares were reissued at ₹ 12 per share. Based on above information you are required to answer the following questions. **CBSE QB**

17. Shares issue to vendors of building and machinery, Ms.VPS Enterprises, would be classified as

(a) Preferential Allotment

(b) Employee Stock Option Plan

(c) Issue for consideration other than cash

(d) Right Issue of Shares

18. How many equity shares of the company have been subscribed?

(a) 3,00,000 (b) 2,99,500

(c) 2,99,800 (d) None of these

Hint:

	Amt (₹)
Shares subscribed	= 1,00,000
	2,00,000
	3,00,000
	(200)
	2,99,800
(−) Calls in arrears (200 × 3)	(600)
(+) Share forfeited account (200 × 3)	600
	2,99,800

19. What is the amount of security premium reflected in the balance sheet at the end of the year?

(a) ₹ 200 (b) ₹ 600

(c) ₹ 400 (d) ₹ 1,000

Hint: Security premium reflected in the Balance Sheet at the end of year would be ₹ 400 (100 × 4).

20. What amount of share forfeiture would be reflected in the balance sheet?

(a) ₹ 600 (b) ₹ 900

(c) ₹ 200 (d) ₹ 300

Hint: Share forfeiture reflected in balance would be ₹ 600 (200 × 3).

ANSWERS

1. *(a)*	2. *(b)*	3. *(a)*	4. *(d)*	5. *(c)*	6. *(b)*	7. *(a)*	8. *(b)*	9. *(b)*	10. *(c)*
11. *(c)*	12. *(a)*	13. *(a)*	14. *(c)*	15. *(b)*	16. *(b)*	17. *(c)*	18. *(c)*	19. *(c)*	20. *(a)*

CHAPTER 07

Accounting for Debentures

TOPIC 1

Introduction and Issue of Debentures

Meaning and Definition of Debentures

Debenture means a document of companies indebtedness issued under the seal of the company and containing a contract for the repayment of the principal sum at a specified date with interest at a fixed rate.

According to Section 2(30) of the Companies Act, 2013, "Debenture includes debenture stock, bonds and any other instrument of the company evidencing a debt, whether constituting a charge on the assets of the company or not."

NOTE Bond is also an instrument of acknowledgement of debt. Bond is similar to debenture in terms of contents and texture. However, bonds can be issued without pre-determined rate of interest.

Types of Debentures

A company may issue different kinds of debentures which can be classified as

(*i*) Secured or mortgage debentures
(*ii*) Unsecured or naked debentures
(*iii*) Redeemable debentures
(*iv*) Irredeemable/perpetual debentures
(*v*) Registered debentures
(*vi*) Bearer debentures
(*vii*) Convertible debentures
(*viii*) Non-convertible debentures

Issue of Debentures for Cash

The procedure of issue of debentures is same as in case of issue of shares, the difference lies only is the title or name of accounts. The amount of debentures can be collected in lumpsum or in instalments, i.e, on application, on allotment and on calls.

Debentures, whether issued for cash or otherwise, may be issued

(*i*) at par (*ii*) at premium (*iii*) at discount

Journal entries required to be passed in these two instances are discussed below

When Debenture Amount is Received in Lumpsum

(If the full amount is payable alongwith application)

Transaction	Entry	Amount
(i) **On Receipt of Application Money**	Bank A/c Dr To Debenture Application and Allotment A/c	[With the application money received]
(ii) **On Acceptance of Application Money**	(a) **When debentures are issued at par** Debenture Application and Allotment A/c Dr To X% Debentures A/c	[With the money adjusted on allotted debentures]
	(b) **When debentures are issued at premium** Debenture Application and Allotment A/c Dr To X% Debentures A/c To Securities Premium Reserve A/c	
	(c) **When debentures are issued at discount** Debenture Application and Allotment A/c Dr Discount on Issue of Debentures A/c Dr To X% Debentures A/c	
(iii) **On Refund of Excess Application Money**	Debenture Application and Allotment A/c Dr To Bank A/c	[With the application money refunded]

When Debenture Amount is Received in Instalments

(i) **On Receipt of Applications**	Bank A/c Dr To Debenture Application A/c	[With the application money received]
(ii) **On Acceptance of Applications**	Debenture Application A/c Dr To X% Debentures A/c	[With the amount of application money on the allotted debentures]
(iii) **When Allotment Money is Due**	**At Par** Debenture Allotment A/c Dr To X% Debentures A/c	[With the amount due on allotment of the debentures]
	At Premium Debenture Allotment A/c Dr To X% Debentures A/c To Securities Premium Reserve A/c	[With the money due on allotment] [With the nominal value of debentures due at the time of allotment] [With the premium money received]
	At Discount Debenture Allotment A/c Dr Discount on Issue of Debentures A/c Dr To X% Debentures A/c	[With the amount due on allotment] [With the amount of discount] [With the face value]
(iv) **On Adjustment of Excess Debenture Application Money**	Debenture Application A/c Dr To Debenture Allotment A/c	[With the surplus application money on partially accepted applications]
(v) **On Refund of Excess Debenture Application Money**	Debenture Application A/c Dr To Bank A/c	[With the application money on rejected applications]

(vi) **On Receipt of Allotment Money**	Bank A/c To Debenture Allotment A/c	Dr	[With the amount actually received on allotment]
(vii) **On Making Calls**	Debenture Call A/c To X% Debentures A/c	Dr	[With the money due on a particular call]
(viii) **On Receipt of Call Money**	Bank A/c To Debenture Call A/c	Dr	[With the amount received on particular call]

Accounting Treatment of Discount on Debentures

Discount on issue of debentures is a capital loss and the amount of discount is debited to a separate account titled 'discount on issue of debentures account'.

Discount on Issue of Debentures and Loss on Issue of Debentures Former is a loss for the company, incurred at the time of issue of debentures. While latter is a wider term and includes both the discount on issue of debentures and premium payable on debentures.

Writing off Discount/Loss on Issue of Debentures According to the revised guidelines of CBSE, 'Discount/Loss on Issue of Debentures' is to be written-off from the company books by utilising 'Securities Premium Reserve' or surplus, i.e. balance in statement of profit and loss, under the head 'Reserves and Surplus'.

It will be written-off in same year (at the end) in which this discount/loss occured.

Accounting Treatment

Securities Premium Reserve A/c	Dr	...	
Statement of Profit and Loss	Dr	...	
To Discount/Loss on Issues of Debentures A/c			...
(Being discount/loss on debentures are completely written-off)			

Note If 'SPR' not exists in the question, then loss/discount is completely written-off by debiting statement of profit and loss account.

If 'SPR' exists in the companies books, then only balance amount is charged from statement of profit and loss account.

Oversubscription of Debentures

When the number of debentures applied for is more than those offered for subscription, it is known as **oversubscription**. A company cannot allot more debentures than it has offered for subscription. In such a situation, the company may make allotment as is made in the case of shares that is

First alternative — Rejecting excess application

Second alternative — Partial or pro-rata allotment

Third alternative — A combination of the above two alternatives

Issue of Debentures for Consideration other than Cash

When debentures are issued to vendors against purchase of assets or against purchase of business, it is termed as issue of debentures for consideration other than cash. In this case, consideration for issue of debentures is not cash but the assets or business. Debentures in this instance, can also be issued at par, premium or discount.

Following journal entries will be passed in this case

(*i*) **On Purchase of Assets or Business**

(a) **When Assets are Purchased**	Sundry Assets A/c To Vendor's A/c	Dr	[With the value of assets]
(b) **When Business is Purchased**	Sundry Assets A/c Goodwill A/c* To Sundry Liabilities A/c To Vendor's A/c To Capital Reserve A/c*	Dr Dr	[With the value of assets] [Balancing figure] [With sundry liabilities] [With purchase consideration] [Balancing figure]

(ii) **On Issue of Debentures**

(a) **When Debentures are Issued at Par**	Vendor's A/c To X% Debentures A/c	Dr	[With purchase consideration] [With the nominal value of debentures]
(b) **When Debentures are Issued at Premium**	Vendor's A/c To X% Debentures A/c To Securities Premium Reserve A/c	Dr	[With purchase consideration] [With nominal value of debentures] [With premium]
(c) **When Debentures are Issued at Discount**	Vendor's A/c Discount on Issue of Debentures A/c To X% Debentures A/c	Dr Dr	[With purchase consideration] [With discount] [With nominal value of debentures]

NOTE (*i*) Purchase consideration is the amount paid by the purchasing company for purchasing of assets/business from another enterprise.

(*ii*) *Either of the two, *i.e.* capital reserve or goodwill will come.

(*iii*) If the purchase consideration is greater than the value of the net assets acquired, the difference is debited to goodwill account.

(*iv*) If the amount of purchase consideration is lower than the value of net assets acquired, the difference is credited to capital reserve account.

(*v*) Number of Debentures to be Issued = $\frac{\text{Purchase Consideration}}{\text{Issue Price of Debentures}}$

Issue of Debentures as Collateral Security

When a company takes a loan, it may provide primary security on its assets. However, the lending institution may insist on some more assets as secondary or collateral security. In such a situation, the company may issue debentures to the lender as secondary or collateral security, such an issue of debentures is known as 'debentures issued as collateral security'.

Debentures issued as collateral security can be dealt in two ways

(*i*) **First Method** (Without Passing Journal Entry) In this method, no journal entry is passed in the books for issue of debentures as collateral security.

However, the fact of debentures issued as collateral security is disclosed by way of information below debentures, which are shown as long-term borrowings under non-current liabilities or as short-term borrowings under current liabilities.

(*ii*) **Second Method** (With Journal Entry) Debentures issued as collateral security may be recorded in the books of accounts by passing a journal entry.

Following journal entry will be passed for issue of debentures as collateral security

Debenture Suspense A/c	Dr	[This appears on assets side]
To X% Debentures A/c		[This appears on liabilities side]

When the loan is paid the above entry is cancelled by passing its reverse entry. In balance sheet, debentures issued as collateral security must be shown separately from other debentures.

Disclosure of Debentures Issued as Collateral Security in the Balance Sheet
As debenture issued as collateral security is related to the loan of the company, therefore, it is shown in the note in which the loan secured by debenture is shown.

Balance Sheet
as at ...

Particulars	Note No.	Amt (₹)
I. **EQUITY AND LIABILITIES**		
Non-current Liabilities		
Long-term Borrowings	1	

Note to Accounts

Particulars		Amt (₹)
1. Long-term Borrowings		
Term Loan from Bank		...
(Secured by issue of X% Debentures of ₹ .... each as Collateral Security)	...	
(−) Debenture Suspense	(...)	...
		...

Interest on Debentures

Interest on debentures is calculated at a fixed rate on its face value and is usually payable half yearly. Debenture interest is a charge on profit and it is not an appropriation of profit. Hence, interest on debentures is payable even if the company suffers a loss, *i.e.* does not earn profit.

According to Income Tax Act, 1961, "A company paying interest on debentures is required to deduct income tax at the prescribed rate from the gross amount of debenture interest before any payment is made to debentureholders", it is called Tax Deducted at Source (TDS).

Entries for interest on debentures are as follows

(i) When Interest is Due and Tax is Deducted at Source	Debenture Interest A/c To Debentureholders' A/c To TDS/Income Tax Payable A/c	Dr	[With gross interest] [With net interest] [With income tax deducted]
(ii) When Interest is Paid	Debentureholders' A/c To Bank or Cash A/c	Dr	[With net interest]
(iii) When TDS is Deposited in the Government Account	TDS/Income Tax Payable A/c To Bank A/c	Dr	[With the amount of income tax deducted at source]
(iv) On Transfer of Interest on Debentures to Profit and Loss Account	Statement of Profit and Loss To Debenture Interest A/c	Dr	[With the amount of gross interest]

Previous Years' Examination Questions

1 Mark Questions

1. Vashya Ltd. issued 30,000, 10% Debentures of ₹ 100 each as collateral security for a loan of ₹ 25,00,000 taken from Bank of India. Fill in the blanks for the journal entry for issue of debentures as a collateral security **CBSE 2020**

Vashya Ltd.
JOURNAL

Date	Particulars	LF	Amt (Dr)	Amt (Cr)
	……… A/c Dr To ……… A/c (Being ₹ 30,00,000; 10% debentures issued as collateral security for a loan of ₹ 25,00,000)		…	…

Ans. **JOURNAL**

Date	Particulars	LF	Amt (Dr)	Amt (Cr)
	Debenture Suspense A/c Dr		30,00,000	
	To 10% Debentures A/c			30,00,000
	(Being ₹ 30,00,000; 10% debentures issued as a collateral security for a loan of ₹ 25,00,000)			

2. What is meant by 'Issue of Debentures as Collateral Security'? **All India 2019; CBSE 2018**

Ans. When a company issues debentures to the lender as secondary or collateral security, such an issue of debenture is known as debenture issued as collateral security.

3. X Ltd invited applications for issuing 500, 12% debentures of ₹ 100 each at a discount of 5%. These debentures were redeemable after three years at par. Applications for 600 debentures were received. Pro-rata allotment was made to all the applicants. Pass necessary journal entries for the issue of debentures assuming that the whole amount was payable with application. **All India 2017**

Ans. **JOURNAL**

Date	Particulars	LF	Amt (Dr)	Amt (Cr)
	Bank A/c (600 × 95) Dr		57,000	
	To Debenture Application and Allotment A/c			57,000
	(Being the application money received)			
	Debenture Application and Allotment A/c Dr		57,000	
	Discount on Issue of Debenture A/c (500 × 5) Dr		2,500	
	To 12% Debentures A/c (500 × 100)			50,000
	To Bank A/c			9,500
	(Being the application money transferred to debentures account and excess refunded)			

4. X Ltd invited applications for issuing 1,000, 9% debentures of ₹ 100 each at a discount of 6%. Applications for 1,200 debentures were received. Pro-rata allotment was made to all the applicants.

Pass necessary journal entries for the issue of debentures assuming that the whole amount was payable with application. **Delhi 2017**

Ans. Solve as Q no. 3 on page 335.

Discount on Issue of Debentures = ₹ 6,000; Amount Refunded = ₹ 18,800

5. Give the meaning of 'debenture'. **Delhi 2014**

Or What is meant by debenture? **Delhi (C) 2014**

Ans. It means a document showing a company's indebtedness, issued under the seal of the company and containing a contract for the repayment of the principal sum at a specified date with interest at a fixed rate.

6. Give the meaning of a bond. **All India (C) 2014**

Ans. Bond is an instrument of acknowledgement of debt, but it does not carry a pre-determined rate of interest.

7. What is meant by issue of debentures as a collateral security? **All India 2014, 2013(C)**

Or Give the meaning of issue of debentures as collateral security. **All India 2011**

Ans. When a company issues its own debentures to the lenders as a secondary security in addition to some other asset already pledged or mortgaged, it is called issue of debentures as collateral security.

8. Pass the necessary journal entry when 10,000 debentures of ₹ 100 each are issued as collateral security against a bank loan of ₹ 8,00,000. **Delhi (C) 2011**

Ans.

JOURNAL

Date	Particulars		LF	Amt (Dr)	Amt (Cr)
	Debenture Suspense A/c	Dr		10,00,000	
	To X% Debentures A/c				10,00,000
	(Being 10,000 debentures of ₹ 100 each issued as collateral security)				

9. Beta Ltd issued 5,000, 9% debentures of ₹ 500 each. Pass the necessary journal entries for the issue of debentures in the books of the company in the following case. When debentures are issued at a premium of 25% to the vendors for machinery purchased for ₹ 6,25,000. **Delhi (C) 2011**

Ans.

JOURNAL

Date	Particulars		LF	Amt (Dr)	Amt (Cr)
	Machinery A/c	Dr		6,25,000	
	To Vendor's A/c				6,25,000
	(Being machinery purchased)				
	Vendor's A/c	Dr		6,25,000	
	To 9% Debentures A/c (1,000 × 500)				5,00,000
	To Securities Premium Reserve A/c (1,000 × 125)				1,25,000
	(Being debentures issued to vendor)				

Working Note

$$\text{Number of Debentures Issued} = \frac{\text{Amount Due to Vendor}}{\text{Issue Price Per Debenture}} = \frac{6{,}25{,}000}{625\,(500+125)} = 1{,}000 \text{ debentures}$$

3 Marks Questions

10. X Ltd. purchased assets of ₹ 18,00,000 and took over liabilities of ₹ 6,00,000 of Y Ltd. for a purchase consideration of ₹ 10,00,000. The payment to Y Ltd, was made by issue of 9% debentures of ₹ 100 each at ₹ 125. Calculate the number of 9% debentures issued in favour of Y Ltd. and pass the necessary journal entries for the above transactions in the books of X Ltd. **CBSE Term II 2022**

Ans. **JOURNAL**

Date	Particulars		LF	Amt (Dr)	Amt (Cr)
	Sundry Assets A/c	Dr		18,00,000	
	To Sundry Liabilities A/c				6,00,000
	To Y Ltd. (Given)				10,00,000
	To Capital Reserve A/c				2,00,000
	(Being assets and liabilities of Y Ltd. taken over by X Ltd.)				
	Y Ltd.	Dr		10,00,000	
	To 9% Debentures A/c				8,00,000
	To Securities Premium Reserve A/c				2,00,000
	(Being 8,000, 9% debentures issued @ ₹ 125 to Y Ltd.)				

Working Note

$$\text{Number of Debentures Issued} = \frac{10,00,000}{125} = 8,000 \text{ debentures}$$

11. Pass necessary journal entries in the books of Z Ltd. for the following transactions.

(*i*) Z Ltd. invited applications for issuing 10,000, 9% debentures of ₹ 100 each at a premium of ₹ 10 per debenture. The full amount was payable on application. Applications were received for 15,000 debentures. Applications for 3,000 debentures were rejected and the applications money was refunded. Debentures were allotted to the remaining applicants on a pro-rata basis.

(*ii*) The company has a balance of ₹ 60,000 in securities premium reserve account. Loss on issue of debentures ₹ 1,00,000 was written-off as per the provisions of the Companies Act, 2013. **CBSE Term II 2022**

Ans. (*i*) **JOURNAL**

Date	Particulars		LF	Amt (Dr)	Amt (Cr)
	Bank A/c	Dr		16,50,000	
	To Debenture Application and Allotment A/c				16,50,000
	(Being application money for 15,000 debentures received)				
	Debenture Application and Allotment A/c	Dr		16,50,000	
	To 9% Debentures A/c				10,00,000
	To Securities Premium Reserve A/c				1,00,000
	To Bank A/c				5,50,000
	(Being application money transferred to debenture account and excess money refunded)				

(*ii*) **JOURNAL**

Date	Particulars		LF	Amt (Dr)	Amt (Cr)
	Securities Premium Reserve A/c	Dr		60,000	
	Statement of Profit and Loss	Dr		40,000	
	To Loss on Issue of Debentures A/c				1,00,000
	(Being loss on debentures written-off)				

12. Garvit Ltd invited applications for issuing 3,000, 11% Debentures of ₹ 100 each at a discount of 6%. The full amount was payable on application. Applications were received for 3,600 debentures. Applications for 600 debentures were rejected and the application money was refunded. Debentures were allotted to the remaining applicants. Pass the necessary journal entries for the above transactions in the books of Garvit Ltd. **Delhi 2019**

Ans.

JOURNAL

Date	Particulars		LF	Amt (Dr)	Amt (Cr)
	Bank A/c (3,600 × 94)	Dr		3,38,400	
	To Debenture Application and Allotment A/c				3,38,400
	(Being application money received on 3,600 debentures of ₹ 100 each at 6% discount)				
	Debenture Application and Allotment A/c	Dr		3,38,400	
	Discount on Issue of Debenture A/c (3,000 × 6)	Dr		18,000	
	To 11% Debenture A/c (3,000 × 100)				3,00,000
	To Bank A/c (600 × 94)				56,400
	(Being application money transferred to debenture account and excess money refunded)				

13. On 1st April, 2015, P Ltd issues 6,000, 12% Debentures of ₹ 100 each at par redeemable at a premium of 7%. The debentures were to be redeemed at the end of third year. Prepare loss on issue of 12% Debentures Account. **Delhi 2019**

Ans. Dr **Loss on Issue of 12% Debentures Account** Cr

Date	Particulars	Amt (₹)	Date	Particulars	Amt (₹)
2015			2016		
Apr 1	To 12% Debentures A/c (6,00,000 × 7%)	42,000	Mar 31	By Statement of Profit and Loss	42,000
		42,000			42,000

14. UZ Ltd purchased plant and machinery from Elk Machine Ltd for ₹ 6,90,000. Elk Ltd was paid by accepting a draft of ₹ 90,000 payable after three months and the balance by issue of 6% debentures of ₹ 100 each at a discount of 20%. Pass necessary journal entries for the above transactions in the books of UZ Ltd. **All India 2019**

Ans.

JOURNAL

In the Books of UZ Ltd

Date	Particulars		LF	Amt (Dr)	Amt (Cr)
	Plant and Machinery A/c	Dr		6,90,000	
	To Elk Machine Ltd				6,90,000
	(Being assets purchased)				
	Elk Machines Ltd	Dr		6,90,000	
	Discount on issue of shares A/c (7,500 × 20)	Dr		1,50,000	
	To 6% Debentures (7,500 × 100)				7,50,000
	To Bills Payable A/c				90,000
	(Being purchase consideration discharged by issue of 6% debentures and bills payable)				

Working Note

$$\text{Number of Debentures Issued} = \frac{6,00,000}{100-20} = 7,500 \text{ debentures}$$

15. Disha Ltd purchased machinery from Nisha Ltd and paid to Nisha Ltd as follows

(*i*) By issuing 10,000, equity shares of ₹ 10 each at a premium of 10%.

(*ii*) By issuing 200, 9% debentures of ₹ 100 each at a discount of 10%.

(*iii*) Balance by accepting a bill of exchange of ₹ 50,000 payable after one month.

Pass necessary journal entries in the books of Disha Ltd. For the purchase of machinery and making payment to Nisha Ltd. **All India 2017**

Ans. **JOURNAL**

Date	Particulars		LF	Amt (Dr)	Amt (Cr)
	Machinery A/c	Dr		1,78,000	
	To Nisha Ltd				1,78,000
	(Being machinery purchased from Nisha Ltd)				
	Nisha Ltd	Dr		1,78,000	
	Discount on Issue of Debentures A/c (200 × 10)	Dr		2,000	
	To Equity Share Capital A/c (10,000 × 10)				1,00,000
	To Securities Premium Reserve A/c (10,000 × 1)				10,000
	To 9% Debentures A/c (200 × 100)				20,000
	To Bills Payable A/c				50,000
	(Being purchase consideration discharged by issue of equity shares, debentures and bills payable)				

Working Note

Purchase Price $=(10{,}000 \times 11)+(200 \times 90)+50{,}000=1{,}10{,}000+18{,}000+50{,}000=$ ₹1,78,000

16. Fill in the blanks in the following case. **All India (C) 2016**

JOURNAL

Date	Particulars		LF	Amt (Dr)	Amt (Cr)
	Sundry Assets A/c	Dr		18,00,000	
	....	Dr		...	
	To Sundry Creditors A/c				2,00,000
	To				...
	(Being business of Rohit & Co. purchased for a consideration of ₹ 20,00,000)				
	....	Dr		20,00,000	
	....	Dr		...	
	To 8% Debentures A/c				...
	(Being paid to Rohit & Co. by issue of ....., 8% debentures of ₹ 150 each at a discount of ₹ 50 per debenture)				

Ans. **JOURNAL**

Date	Particulars		LF	Amt (Dr)	Amt (Cr)
	Sundry Assets A/c	Dr		18,00,000	
	Goodwill A/c	Dr		**4,00,000**	
	To Sundry Creditors A/c				2,00,000
	To Rohit & Co				**20,00,000**
	(Being business of Rohit & Co. purchased for a consideration of ₹ 20,00,000)				

Date	Particulars		LF	Amt (Dr)	Amt (Cr)
	Rohit & Co	Dr		20,00,000	
	Discount on Issue of Debentures A/c $(20,000 \times 50)$	Dr		10,00,000	
	To 8% Debentures A/c $(20,000 \times 150)$				30,00,000
	(Being paid to Rohit & Co. by issue of 20,000, 8% debentures of ₹ 150 each at a discount of ₹ 50 per debenture)				

Working Note

$$\text{Number of Debentures Issued} = \frac{20,00,000}{(150-50)} = 20,000$$

17. Tata Ltd issued 5,000, 10% debentures of ₹ 100 each on 1st April, 2012. The issue was fully subscribed. According to the terms of issue, interest on debentures is payable half yearly on 30th September and 31st March and tax deducted at source is 10%.

Pass the necessary entries related to the debenture interest for the half yearly ending on 31st March, 2013 and transfer of interest on debentures to statement of profit and loss.
All India 2014

Ans.

JOURNAL

Date	Particulars		LF	Amt (Dr)	Amt (Cr)
2012 Sep 30	Debenture Interest A/c $\left(5,00,000 \times \frac{10}{100} \times \frac{6}{12}\right)$	Dr		25,000	
	To Income Tax Payable A/c $(25,000 \times 10\%)$				2,500
	To Debentureholders' A/c				22,500
	(Being interest made due for half yearly ending 30th September)				
Sep 30	Debentureholders' A/c	Dr		22,500	
	To Bank A/c				22,500
	(Being interest paid to debentureholders)				
Sep 30	Income Tax Payable A/c	Dr		2,500	
	To Bank A/c				2,500
	(Being payments of tax on interest on debentures)				
2013 Mar 31	Debenture Interest A/c $\left(5,00,000 \times \frac{10}{100} \times \frac{6}{12}\right)$	Dr		25,000	
	To Income Tax Payable A/c $(25,000 \times 10\%)$				2,500
	To Debentureholders' A/c				22,500
	(Being interest made due for half yearly ending 31st March)				
Mar 31	Debentureholders' A/c	Dr		22,500	
	To Bank A/c				22,500
	(Being interest paid to debentureholders)				
Mar 31	Income Tax Payable A/c	Dr		2,500	
	To Bank A/c				2,500
	(Being payment of tax or interest on debentures)				
Mar 31	Statement of Profit and Loss	Dr		50,000	
	To Interest on Debentures A/c				50,000
	(Being interest on debentures transferred to statement of profit and loss)				

18. BG Ltd issued 2,000, 12% debentures of ₹ 100 each on 1st April, 2012. The issue was fully subscribed. According to the terms of issue, interest on the debentures is payable half yearly on 30th September and 31st March and the tax deducted at source is 10%. Pass necessary journal entries related to the debenture interest for the half-yearly ending 31st March, 2013 and transfer of interest on debentures of the year to the statement of profit and loss. **Delhi 2014**

Ans. Solve as Q no. 17 on page 340.

Interest on Debenture Transferred to Statement of Profit and Loss = ₹ 24,000

19. Sargam Ltd issued ₹ 1,00,000, 6% debentures of ₹ 10 each at a premium of ₹ 2 per debenture on 1st April, 2012. The issue was fully subscribed. Interest will be paid at the end of each financial year. Pass necessary journal entries for the year 2012-13. **All India (C) 2014**

Ans. **JOURNAL**

Date	Particulars		LF	Amt (Dr)	Amt (Cr)
2012 Apr 1	Bank A/c (10,000×12)	Dr		1,20,000	
	To Debenture Application and Allotment A/c				1,20,000
	(Being lumpsum of ₹ 12 received at the time of issue of debenture)				
Apr 1	Debenture Application and Allotment A/c	Dr		1,20,000	
	To 6% Debentures A/c (10,000×10)				1,00,000
	To Securities Premium Reserve A/c (10,000×2)				20,000
	(Being application and allotment money transferred to debentures and securities premium account)				
2013 Mar 31	Debenture Interest A/c (1,00,000 × 6%)	Dr		6,000	
	To Debentureholders' A/c				6,000
	(Being annual interest made due @ 6%)				
Mar 31	Debentureholders' A/c	Dr		6,000	
	To Bank A/c				6,000
	(Being interest paid to debentureholders)				
Mar 31	Statement of Profit and Loss	Dr		6,000	
	To Debenture Interest A/c				6,000
	(Being debenture interest charged to statement of profit and loss)				

NOTE In the absence of any information, TDS has not been deducted on debenture interest.

20. Nav Lakshmi Ltd invited applications for issuing 3,000, 12% debentures of ₹ 100 each at a premium of ₹ 50 per debenture. The full amount was payable on application. Applications were received for 4,000 debentures. Applications for 1,000 debentures were rejected and application money was refunded. Debentures were allotted to the remaining applicants.

Pass necessary journal entries for the above transactions in the books of Nav Lakshmi Ltd. **All India 2012**

Ans. **JOURNAL**

Date	Particulars		LF	Amt (Dr)	Amt (Cr)
	Bank A/c (4,000×150)	Dr		6,00,000	
	To Debenture Application and Allotment A/c				6,00,000
	(Being application money received on 4,000 debentures)				
	Debenture Application and Allotment A/c	Dr		6,00,000	
	To 12% Debentures A/c (3,000 × 100)				3,00,000
	To Securities Premium Reserve A/c (3,000 × 50)				1,50,000
	To Bank A/c (1,000 × 150)				1,50,000
	(Being application money transferred to 12% debentures account and excess refunded)				

21. Narain Laxmi Ltd invited applications for issuing 7,500, 12% debentures of ₹ 100 each at a premium of ₹ 35 per debenture. The full amount was payable on application.

Applications were received for 10,000 debentures. Applications for 2,500 debentures were rejected and the application money was refunded. Debentures were allotted to the remaining applicants.
Pass necessary journal entries for the above transactions in the books of Narain Laxmi Ltd.
Delhi 2012

Ans. Solve as Q no. 20 on page 341 and 342.

4 Marks Question

22. Venus Ltd is a real estate company. To discharge its corporate social responsibility, it decided to construct a night shelter for the homeless. The company took over assets of ₹ 10,00,000 and liabilities of ₹ 1,80,000 of Cayns Ltd for ₹ 7,60,000. Venus Ltd issued 9% debentures of ₹ 100 each at a discount of 5% in full satisfaction of the purchase consideration in favour of Cayns Ltd.

Pass necessary journal entries in the books of Venus Ltd. for the above transactions.
Compartment 2018 Modified

Ans. **JOURNAL**

Date	Particulars		LF	Amt (Dr)	Amt (Cr)
	Assets A/c	Dr		10,00,000	
	To Liabilities A/c				1,80,000
	To Cayns Ltd				7,60,000
	To Capital Reserve A/c				60,000
	(Being business purchased of Cayns Ltd.)				
	Cayns Ltd	Dr		7,60,000	
	Discount on Issue of Debentures A/c (8,000 × 5)	Dr		40,000	
	To, 9% Debentures A/c (8,000 × 100)				8,00,000
	(Being 9% debentures issued at 5% discount to Cayns Ltd)				

Working Note

$$\text{Number of Debentures Issued} = \frac{7,60,000}{100-5} = 8,000,\ 9\%\ \text{Debentures}$$

6 Marks Questions

23. (*i*) On 1st April, 2019, Bright Ltd. issued, 4,00,000, 6% Debentures of ₹ 100 each at a discount of 5%, redeemable after three years. The amount per debenture was payable as follows

On Application — ₹ 80 per debenture; On Allotment — Balance

The debentures were fully subscribed and all money was duly received.

Pass necessary journal entries for issues of debentures.

(*ii*) Disha Ltd. took assets of ₹ 8,00,000 and liabilities of ₹ 3,00,000 from Kriti Ltd. for a purchase consideration of ₹ 6,00,000. The payment was made by issue of 9% Debentures of ₹ 100 each at 20% premium.

Pass the necessary journal entries for the above transactions in the books of Disha Ltd.

CBSE 2020

Ans. (*i*) **In the Books of Bright Ltd.**

JOURNAL

Date	Particulars		LF	Amt (Dr)	Amt (Cr)
	Bank A/c (4,00,000 × 80)	Dr		3,20,00,000	
	To Debenture Application A/c				3,20,00,000
	(Being application money received)				
	Debenture Application A/c	Dr		3,20,00,000	
	To 6% Debentures A/c				3,20,00,000
	(Being application money transferred to 6% debentures account)				
	Debentures Allotment A/c	Dr		60,00,000	
	Discount on Issue of Debentures A/c	Dr		20,00,000	
	To 6% Debentures A/c (4,00,000 × 20)				80,00,000
	(Being allotment money due)				
	Bank A/c	Dr		60,00,000	
	To Debentures Allotment A/c				60,00,000
	(Being allotment money received)				

(*ii*) **In the Books of Disha Ltd.**

JOURNAL

Date	Particulars		LF	Amt (Dr)	Amt (Cr)
	Assets A/c	Dr		8,00,000	
	Goodwill A/c	Dr		1,00,000	
	To Liabilities A/c				3,00,000
	To Kriti Ltd				6,00,000
	(Being business purchased)				
	Kriti Ltd	Dr		6,00,000	
	To 9% Debentures A/c				5,00,000
	To Securities Premium Reserve A/c				1,00,000
	(Being debentures issued in purchase consideration)				

Working Note

$$\text{Number of Debentures Issued} = \frac{6,00,000}{120} = 5,000 \text{ Debentures}$$

24. SSS Ltd issued 25,000, 10% debentures of ₹ 100 each. Give journal entries and the balance sheet in each of the following cases when

(*i*) The debentures were issued at a premium of 20%.

(*ii*) The debentures were issued as a collateral security to bank against a loan of ₹ 20,00,000.

(*iii*) The debentures were issued to a supplier of machinery costing ₹ 28,00,000 as his full and final payment. **Delhi (C) 2011**

Ans. (*i*)

JOURNAL

Date	Particulars		LF	Amt (Dr)	Amt (Cr)
	Bank A/c (25,000 × 120)	Dr		30,00,000	
	To Debenture Application and Allotment A/c				30,00,000
	(Being application money received)				
	Debenture Application and Allotment A/c	Dr		30,00,000	
	To 10% Debentures A/c (25,000 × 100)				25,00,000
	To Securities Premium Reserve A/c (25,000 × 20)				5,00,000
	(Being application money transferred to 10% debentures account)				

Balance Sheet

as at ...

Particulars	Note No.	Amt (₹)
I. EQUITY AND LIABILITIES		
1. Shareholders' Funds		
Reserves and Surplus	1	5,00,000
2. Non-current Liabilities		
Long-term Borrowings	2	25,00,000
Total		30,00,000
II. ASSETS		
1. Current Assets		
Cash and Cash Equivalents	3	30,00,000
Total		30,00,000

Notes to Accounts

Particulars	Amt (₹)
1. Reserves and Surplus	
Securities Premium Reserve	5,00,000
2. Non-current Liabilities	
10% Debentures	25,00,000
3. Cash and Cash Equivalents	
Cash at Bank	30,00,000

(*ii*)

JOURNAL

Date	Particulars		LF	Amt (Dr)	Amt (Cr)
(a)	Bank A/c	Dr		20,00,000	
	To Bank loan A/c				
	(Being bank loan taken)				20,00,000
(b)	Debenture Suspense A/c	Dr		25,00,000	
	To 10% Debentures A/c				25,00,000
	(Being 25,000, 10% debentures of ₹ 100 each issued as collateral security)				

Balance Sheet
as at ......

Particulars	Note No.	Amt (₹)
I. **EQUITY AND LIABILITIES**		
Non-current Liabilities		
Long-term Borrowings	1	20,00,000

Notes to Accounts

Particulars		Amt (₹)
1. **Long-term Borrowings**		
Loan from Bank		20,00,000
25,000, 10% Debentures at Par Value of ₹ 100 each Issued as Collateral Security	25,00,000	
(–) Debenture Suspenses	(25,00,000)	—
		20,00,000

(*iii*)

JOURNAL

Date	Particulars		LF	Amt (Dr)	Amt (Cr)
(a)	Machinery A/c	Dr		28,00,000	
	To Vendor's A/c				28,00,000
	(Being machinery purchased)				
(b)	Vendor's A/c	Dr		28,00,000	
	To 10% Debentures A/c (25,000 × 100)				25,00,000
	To Securities Premium Reseve A/c				3,00,000
	(Being 25,000, 10% debentures issued to the supplier of machinery at premium)				

Balance Sheet
as at .....

Particulars	Note No.	Amt (₹)
I. **EQUITY AND LIABILITIES**		
1. **Shareholders' Funds**		
Reserves and Surplus	1	3,00,000
2. **Non-current Liabilities**		
Long-term Borrowings	2	25,00,000
Total		28,00,000

Particulars	Note No.	Amt (₹)
II. ASSETS		
1. Non-current Assets		
(a) Fixed Assets		
Tangible Assets	3	28,00,000
Total		28,00,000

Notes to Accounts

Particulars	Amt (₹)
1. **Reserves and Surplus**	
Securities Premium Reserve	3,00,000
2. **Long-term Borrowings**	
10% Debentures (25,000 debentures @ ₹ 100)	25,00,000
3. **Tangible Fixed Assets**	
Machinery	28,00,000

TOPIC 2

Various Cases from the Point of View of Redemption

When a company issues debentures, it usually mentions the terms on which they will be redeemed at their maturity. Redemption means paying back the amount to debentureholders. The issue of debentures can be made at par, at premium or at discount, however, the redemption of debentures can be made at par or at premium. Combining various conditions/ terms of issue and redemption of debentures, there may be the following possibilities

Case	Journal Entry		Narration
(i) When Debentures are Issued at Par and Redeemable at Par	(a) Bank A/c To Debenture Application and Allotment A/c	Dr	[With the application money]
	(b) Debenture Application and Allotment To X% Debentures A/c	Dr	[With the application money] [With the nominal value]
(ii) When Debentures are Issued at Par and Redeemable at Premium	(a) Bank A/c To Debenture Application and Allotment A/c	Dr	[With the application money]
	(b) Debenture Application and Allotment A/c Loss on Issue of Debentures A/c To X% Debentures A/c To Premium on Redemption of Debentures A/c	Dr Dr	[With the application money] [With premium on redemption] [With the nominal value] [With premium payable on redemption]

NOTE When debentures are redeemable at premium, loss on issue of debenture account is debited as it shows provision made on account of premium on redemption. Also premium on redemption of debenture account is credited as it is the liability of company to pay in future.

Case	Journal Entry		Narration
(iii) When Debentures are Issued at Premium and Redeemable at Par	(a) Bank A/c To Debenture Application and Allotment A/c	Dr	[With the application money]
	(b) Debenture Application and Allotment A/c To X% Debentures A/c To Securities Premium Reserve A/c	Dr	[With the application money] [With the nominal value] [With the amount of premium]

(iv) **When Debentures are Issued at Premium and Redeemable at Premium**	(a) Bank A/c To Debenture Application and Allotment A/c	Dr	 [With the application money]

	(b) Debenture Application and Allotment A/c
	Loss on Issue of Debentures A/c
	  To X% Debentures A/c
	  To Securities Premium Reserve A/c
	  To Premium on Redemption of Debentures A/c
		Dr
		Dr
			[With the application money]
			[With premium on redemption]
			[With the nominal value]
			[With premium on issue]
			[With premium payable on redemption]

(v) **When Debentures are Issued at Discount and Redeemable at Par**	(a) Bank A/c To Debenture Application and Allotment A/c	Dr	 [With the application money]
	(b) Debenture Application and Allotment A/c Discount on Issue of Debentures A/c To X% Debentures A/c	Dr Dr	[With the application money] [With the amount of discount] [With the nominal value]
(vi) **When Debentures are Issued at Discount and Redeemable at Premium**	(a) Bank A/c To Debenture Application and Allotment A/c	Dr	 [With the application money]

	(b) Debenture Application and Allotment A/c
	Loss on Issue of Debentures A/c
	  To X% Debentures A/c
	  To Premium on Redemption of Debentures A/c
		Dr
		Dr
			[With the application money]
			[With discount + premium on redemption]
			[With the nominal value]
			[With premium payable on redemption]

NOTE When debentures are issued at a discount and are redeemable at a premium, the amount of discount on issue is also debited to 'loss on issue of debentures' and when debentures are issued at a discount and are redeemable at par, the amount is debited to discount on issue of debentures account as usual.

Redemption of Debentures

Redemption of debentures means repaying or returning the amount of debentures to the debentureholders after the period for which they were issued. It refers to extinguishing or discharging the liability on account of debentures in accordance with the terms of issue.

The debentures may be redeemed

(i) Out of capital.
(ii) Out of profits.
(iii) By converting them into shares or new debentures.
(iv) Redemption from the proceeds of fresh issue of shares and debentures.
(v) Redemption out of profit and capital.

Previous Years'
Examination Questions

3 Marks Questions

1. Pass necessary journal entries and prepare 9% debentures account for the issue of 7,500, 9% debentures of ₹ 50 each at a discount of 6%, redeemable at a premium of 10%. **All India 2019**

Ans. **JOURNAL**

Date	Particulars		LF	Amt (Dr)	Amt (Cr)
	Bank A/c (7,500 × 47)	Dr		3,52,500	
	To Debentures Application and Allotment A/c				3,52,500
	(Being application money received on debentures issued at 6%)				
	Debentures Application and Allotment A/c	Dr		3,52,500	
	Loss on Issue of Debentures A/c (7,500 × 8)	Dr		60,000	
	To 9% Debentures A/c (7,500 × 50)				3,75,000
	To Premium on Redemption of Debentures A/c (7,500 × 5)				37,500
	(Being application money transferred to 9% debentures account)				

Dr **9% Debentures Account** Cr

Particulars	Amt (₹)	Particulars	Amt (₹)
To Balance c/d	3,75,000	By Debentures application and allotment A/c	3,52,500
		By Loss on Issue of Debentures A/c	22,500
	3,75,000		3,75,000

2. X Ltd issued 1,000, 9% Debentures of ₹ 100 each at a discount of 6%. These debentures were redeemable at a premium of 10% after five years.Pass necessary journal entries for issue of debentures and prepare 9% Debentures Account. **All India 2019**

Ans. Solve as Q. no. 1 on page 348. Loss on Issue of Debentures = ₹ 16,000

9% Debentures Account Balance = ₹ 1,00,000

3. On 1st April, 2018, RJ Ltd issued ₹ 10,00,000, 9% debentures of ₹ 100 each at a discount of 10%. These debentures were redeemable at a premium of 5% after four years. Pass necessary journal entries for the issue of debentures and prepare 9% debentures loan account. **All India 2019**

Ans. Solve as Q. no. 1 on page 348. Loss on Issue of Debentures = ₹ 1,50,000

9% Debentures Account Balance = ₹10,00,000

4. ZK Ltd issued ₹ 4,00,000, 9% debentures of ₹ 100 each at a discount of 5% redeemable at a premium of 10%. Pass necessary journal entries for the above transactions in the books of ZK Ltd. **All India 2019**

Ans.

In the Books of ZK Ltd.

JOURNAL

Date	Particulars		LF	Amt (Dr)	Amt (Cr)
	Bank A/c (4,000 × 95)	Dr		3,80,000	
	To Debenture Application and Allotment A/c				3,80,000
	(Being application money received on 4,000, 9% debentures of ₹ 95 each)				
	Debenture Application and Allotment A/c	Dr		3,80,000	
	Loss on Issue of Debentures A/c (4,000 × 15)	Dr		60,000	
	To 9% Debentures A/c (4,000 × 100)				4,00,000
	To Premium on Redemption of Debentures A/c (4,000 × 10)				40,000
	(Being issue of 4,000, 9% debentures at 5% discount and redeemable at 10% premium)				

5. On 2nd March, 2016 L and B Ltd issued 635, 9% debentures of ₹ 500 each. Pass necessary journal entries for the issue of debentures in the following situations

(*i*) When debentures were issued at 5% discount, redeemable at 10% premium.

(*ii*) When debentures were issued at 12% premium, redeemable at 6% premium. **All India 2016**

Ans.

JOURNAL

Date	Particulars		LF	Amt (Dr)	Amt (Cr)
(i)	Bank A/c (635 × 475)	Dr		3,01,625	
	To Debenture Application and Allotment A/c				3,01,625
	(Being application money received on 635 debentures of ₹ 475 each)				
	Debenture Application and Allotment A/c	Dr		3,01,625	
	Loss on Issue of Debentures A/c (31,750 + 15,875)	Dr		47,625	
	To 9% Debentures A/c (635 × 500)				3,17,500
	To Premium on Redemption A/c (635 × 50)				31,750
	(Being the issue of 635 debentures at 5% discount, redeemable at 10% premium)				
(ii)	Bank A/c (635 × 560)	Dr		3,55,600	
	To Debenture Application and Allotment A/c				3,55,600
	(Being application money received on 635 debentures of ₹ 560 each)				
	Debenture Application and Allotment A/c	Dr		3,55,600	
	Loss on Issue of Debentures A/c (635 × 30)	Dr		19,050	
	To 9% Debentures A/c (635 × 500)				3,17,500
	To Securities Premium Reserve A/c (635 × 60)				38,100
	To Premium on Redemption A/c (635 × 30)				19,050
	(Being the issue of 635 debentures at 12% premium and redeemable at 6% premium)				

6. KTR Ltd issued 365, 9% debentures of ₹ 1,000 each on 4th March, 2016. Pass necessary journal entries for the issue of debentures in the following situations

(*i*) When debentures were issued at par redeemable at a premium of 10%.

(*ii*) When debentures were issued at 6% discount redeemable at 5% premium. **Delhi 2016**

Ans. (*i*)

JOURNAL

Date	Particulars		LF	Amt (Dr)	Amt (Cr)
	Bank A/c (365 × 1,000)	Dr		3,65,000	
	To Debenture Application and Allotment A/c				3,65,000
	(Being application money received)				
	Debenture Application and Allotment A/c	Dr		3,65,000	
	Loss on Issue of Debentures A/c (365 × 100)	Dr		36,500	
	To 9% Debentures A/c (365 × 1,000)				3,65,000
	To Premium on Redemption of Debentures A/c (365 × 100)				36,500
	(Being debentures issued at par, redeemable at premium)				

(*ii*) Solve as Q no. 5 (*i*) on page 349.

7. Fill in the blanks in the following case

JOURNAL

Date	Particulars		LF	Amt (Dr)	Amt (Cr)
	....	Dr		...	
	To				...
	(Being application money received on 2,000, 12% debentures of ₹ 100 each issued at a premium of 10% and redeemable at a premium of 10%)				
	....	Dr		...	
	....	Dr		...	
	To				...
	To				...
	To				...
	(....................................)				

All India (C) 2016

Ans.

JOURNAL

Date	Particulars		LF	Amt (Dr)	Amt (Cr)
	Bank A/c (2,000 × 110)	Dr		2,20,000	
	To Debenture Application and Allotment A/c				2,20,000
	(Being application money received on 2,000, 12% debentures of ₹ 100 each issued at a premium of 10% and redeemable at a premium of 10%)				
	Debenture Application and Allotment A/c	Dr		2,20,000	
	Loss on Issue of Debentures A/c (2,000 × 10)	Dr		20,000	
	To 12% Debentures A/c (2,000 × 100)				2,00,000
	To Securities Premium Reserve A/c (2,000 × 10)				20,000
	To Premium on Redemption of Debentures A/c (2,000 × 10)				20,000
	(Being amount received on issue of 12% debentures adjusted)				

8. Fill in the blanks in the following case

JOURNAL

Date	Particulars		LF	Amt (Dr)	Amt (Cr)
	....	Dr		...	
	To				...
	(Being application and allotment money received on 2,000, 12% debentures of ₹ 100 each issued at a premium of 5% and redeemable at a premium of 10%)				
	....	Dr		...	
	....	Dr		...	
	To				...
	To				...
	To				...
	(.................................)				

Delhi (C) 2016

Ans. Solve as Q no. 7 on page 350.

9. Alok Ltd issued 7,000, 10% debentues of ₹ 500 each at a premium of ₹ 50 per debenture redeemable at a premium of 10% after 5 years. According to the terms of issue, 200 was payable on application and balance on allotment. Record necessary journal entries at the time of issue of 10% debentures. **All India (C) 2015**

Ans. JOURNAL

Date	Particulars		LF	Amt (Dr)	Amt (Cr)
	Bank A/c (7,000×200)	Dr		14,00,000	
	To Debenture Application A/c				14,00,000
	(Being the debenture application money received on 7,000 debentures)				
	Debenture Application A/c	Dr		14,00,000	
	To 10% Debentures A/c				14,00,000
	(Being the application money transferred to debentures account)				
	Debenture Allotment A/c (7,000× 350)	Dr		24,50,000	
	Loss on Issue of Debentures A/c (7,000× 50)	Dr		3,50,000	
	To 10% Debentures A/c (7,000× 300)				21,00,000
	To Securities Premium Reserve A/c (7,000× 50)				3,50,000
	To Premium on Redemption of Debentures A/c (7,000× 50)				3,50,000
	(Being the amount due on 7,000 debentures)				
	Bank A/c	Dr		24,50,000	
	To Debenture Allotment A/c				24,50,000
	(Being the amount received against allotment)				

10. Pass the necessary journal entries for issue of 1,000, 7% debentures of ₹ 100 each in the following cases

(*i*) Issued at 5% premium, redeemable at a premium of 10%.

(*ii*) Issued at a discount of 5%, redeemable at par. **Delhi 2013**

Ans. (*i*) Solve as Q no. 5 (*ii*) on page 349.

(*ii*) **JOURNAL**

Date	Particulars		LF	Amt (Dr)	Amt (Cr)
(a)	Bank A/c (1000 × 95)	Dr		95,000	
	To Debenture Application and Allotment A/c				95,000
	(Being application money received on 1,000 debentures @ ₹ 95)				
(b)	Debenture Application and Allotment A/c	Dr		95,000	
	Discount on Issue of Debentures A/c (1,000 × 5)	Dr		5,000	
	To 7% Debentures A/c (1,000 × 100)				1,00,000
	(Being application money transferred to debentures account)				

11. Pass the necessary journal entries for the issue of debentures in the following cases

(*i*) ₹ 40,000, 12% debentures of ₹ 100 each issued at a premium of 5% redeemable at par.

(*ii*) ₹ 70,000, 12% debentures of ₹ 100 each issued at a premium of 5% redeemable at ₹ 110.

Delhi 2013

Ans. **JOURNAL**

Date	Particulars		LF	Amt (Dr)	Amt (Cr)
(i) (a)	Bank A/c (400 × 105)	Dr		42,000	
	To Debenture Application and Allotment A/c				42,000
	(Being application money received on 400 debentures of ₹ 100 each, including premium of ₹ 5)				
(b)	Debenture Application and Allotment A/c	Dr		42,000	
	To 12% Debentures A/c (400 × 100)				40,000
	To Securities Premium Reserve A/c (400 × 5)				2,000
	(Being debenture application money transferred to 12% debentures and securities premium account)				

(*ii*) Solve as Q no. 5 (*ii*) on page 349.

12. Pass the necessary journal entries for the issue of 7% debentures in the following cases

(*i*) 200 debentures of ₹ 150 each issued at 10% premium redeemable at ₹ 200 each.

(*ii*) 200 debentures of ₹ 200 each issued at a discount of 10% redeemable at par. **All India 2013**

Ans. **JOURNAL**

Date	Particulars		LF	Amt (Dr)	Amt (Cr)
(i) (a)	Bank A/c (200 × 165)	Dr		33,000	
	To Debenture Application and Allotment A/c				33,000
	(Being application money received on 200, 7% debentures along with premium of ₹ 15 each)				
(b)	Debenture Application and Allotment A/c	Dr		33,000	
	Loss on Issue of Debentures A/c (200 × 50)	Dr		10,000	
	To 7% Debentures A/c (200 × 150)				30,000
	To Securities Premium Reserve A/c (200 × 15)				3,000
	To Premium on Redemption of Debentures A/c (200 × 50)				10,000
	(Being debenture application money transferred to debentures account and securities premium reserve account and premium on redemption recorded)				

(*ii*) Solve as Q no. 10 (*ii*) on page 351 and 352.

5/6 Marks Questions

13. Pass necessary journal entries for the issue of debentures in the following cases

(*i*) Issued 50,000, 9% debentures of ₹ 100 each at par redeemable at par.

(*ii*) Issued 10,000, 8% debentures of ₹ 100 each at 7% premium redeemable at par.

(*iii*) Issued 750, 8% debentures of ₹ 100 each at 10% discount redeemable at par.

(*iv*) Issued 1,000 9% debentures of ₹ 100 each at 5% premium redeemable at 8% premium.

(*v*) Issued 500, 9% debentures of ₹ 100 each at 10% discount redeemable at 10% premium.

CBSE Term II 2022

Ans. **JOURNAL**

Date	Particulars		LF	Amt (Dr)	Amt (Cr)
(i) (a)	Bank A/c	Dr		50,00,000	
	To Debenture Application and Allotment A/c				50,00,000
	(Being the application money received on 50,000 9% debenture @ ₹ 100 each)				
	Debenture Application and Allotment A/c	Dr		50,00,000	
	To 9% Debentures A/c				50,00,000
	(Being the application money transferred to debentures account)				

(*ii*) Solve as Q. 11 (*i*) on Page 352.

(*iii*) Solve as Q. 10 (*ii*) on Page 351 and 352.

(*ii*) Solve as Q. 5 (*ii*) on Page 349.

(*ii*) Solve as Q. 5 (*i*) on Page 349.

14. Pass the necessary journal entries for the issue of debentures for the following transactions

(*i*) Anand Ltd. issued 800, 9% Debentures of ₹ 500 each at a premium of 20%, to the vendors for machinery purchased from them costing ₹ 4,80,000.

(*ii*) Dawar Ltd. issued 5,000, 7% Debentures of ₹ 200 each at a premium of 5%, redeemable at a premium of 10%.

(*iii*) Novelty Ltd. issued 1,000, 8% Debentures of ₹ 100 each at a discount of 5%, redeemable at a premium of 10%. **CBSE 2020**

Ans. (*i*) Solve as Q. no. 9 on Page no. 351.

(*ii*) Solve as Q. no. 5 (*ii*) on Page no. 349.

(*iii*) Solve as Q. no. 5 (*i*) on Page no. 349.

15. On 1st April, 2015, JK Ltd issued 8,000, 9% debentures of ₹ 1,000 each at a discount of 6%, redeemable at a premium of 5% after 3 years. The company closes its book on 31st March every year. Interest on 9% debentures is payable on 30th September and 31st March every year. The rate of tax deducted at source is 10%. Pass necessary journal entries for the issue of 9% debentures and debenture interest for the year ended 31st March, 2016. **All India 2017**

Ans.

JOURNAL

Date	Particulars		LF	Amt (Dr)	Amt (Cr)
2015 Apr 1	Bank A/c (8,000 × 940)	Dr		75,20,000	
	To Debenture Application and Allotment A/c				75,20,000
	(Being debenture application money received)				
Apr 1	Debenture Application and Allotment A/c	Dr		75,20,000	
	Loss on Issue of Debentures A/c [8,000 × (50 + 60)]	Dr		8,80,000	
	To 9% Debentures A/c (8,000 × 1,000)				80,00,000
	To Premium on Redemption of Debentures A/c (8,000 × 50)				4,00,000
	(Being debenture application money transferred to debentures account)				
Sep 30	Debenture Interest A/c	Dr		3,60,000	
	To Debentureholders' A/c				3,24,000
	To TDS Payable A/c				36,000
	(Being amount of interest due and tax deducted at source)				
Sep 30	Debentureholders' A/c	Dr		3,24,000	
	TDS Payable A/c	Dr		36,000	
	To Bank A/c				3,60,000
	(Being interest paid to debentureholders and TDS deposited with government)				
2016 Mar 31	Debenture Interest A/c	Dr		3,60,000	
	To Debentureholders' A/c				3,24,000
	To TDS Payable A/c				36,000
	(Being amount of interest due and tax deducted at source)				
Mar 31	Debentureholders' A/c	Dr		3,24,000	
	TDS Payable A/c	Dr		36,000	
	To Bank A/c				3,60,000
	(Being interest paid to debentureholders and TDS deposited with government)				
Mar 31	Statement of Profit and Loss	Dr		7,20,000	
	To Debenture Interest A/c (3,60,000 + 3,60,000)				7,20,000
	(Being annual debenture interest transferred to statement of profit and loss)				

Working Notes

1. **Loss on Issue of Debentures** — **Amt (₹)**

Discount on issue = 8,000 × 60	= 4,80,000
(+) Premium on redemption = 8,000 × 50	= 4,00,000
	₹ 8,80,000

2. **Debenture Interest for Six Months**

$$80,00,000 \times \frac{9}{100} \times \frac{6}{12} = ₹\,3,60,000$$

3. **Tax Deducted at Source**

$$3,60,000 \times \frac{10}{100} = ₹\,36,000$$

16. On 1st April, 2015 KK Ltd issued 500, 9% debentures of ₹ 500 each at a discount of 4%, redeemable at a premium of 5% after three years. Pass necessary journal entries for the issue of debentures and debenture interest for the year ended 31st March, 2016 assuming that interest is payable on 30th September and 31st March and the rate of tax deducted at source is 10%. The company closes its books on 31st March every year. **Delhi 2017**

Ans. Solve as Q no. 15 on page 353 and 354.

Debenture Interest Transferred to Statement of Profit and Loss = ₹ 22,500 (11,250 + 11,250)

Multiple Choice Questions

For Complete Chapter **(1 Mark)**

1 Mark Questions

1. Debentures which are transferable by mere delivery are

(a) registered debentures
(b) first debentures
(c) bearer debentures
(d) secured debentures

2. A company AB Ltd issued ₹ 10,00,000 12% debentures of ₹ 100 each to public. In the terms of issue, these debentures are redeemable after 10 months ending on 31st January, 2018. Interest is payable on monthly basis. These debentures will be shown in balance sheet as on 31st March, 2017 under the heading

(a) long-term liability
(b) current liability
(c) fixed assets (d) current assets

Hint: Whenever debentures are issued for less than 12 months or debentures are redeemable within 12 months, then these are shown under 'current liability'.

3. Discount on issue of debentures is

(a) capital loss (b) capital income
(c) revenue loss (d) revenue income

Hint: Company can issue debentures at discount and this discount is a capital loss in nature. It is written-off either through security premium account or statement of profit and loss.

4. When debentures are issued at lumpsum, journalise the acceptance of application of debentures from public.

(a) Bank A/c Dr
To Debenture Application A/c
(b) Debenture Application A/c Dr
To X% Debentures A/c
(c) Debenture App. and Allot. A/c Dr
To X% Debentures A/c
(d) None of the above

Hint: When the whole amount of debentures is received on application, then debenture application and allotment account will be opened rather than debenture application and at the time of accepting those applications, debenture application and allotment account will be debited and X% debentures account will be credited.

5. Journalise the writing-off discount on issue of debentures, when company has all reserves and profits required to cover this loss.

(a) General Reserve A/c Dr
To Statement of Profit and Loss
To Discount on Issue of Debentures A/c
(b) Discount on Issue of Debentures A/c Dr
To General Reserve A/c
To Statement of Profit and Loss
(c) Loss on Issue of Debentures A/c Dr
To Statement of Profit and Loss
(d) None of the above

Hint: To write-off discount or loss on issue of debentures, first of all security premium reserve account is debited and if that is not able to cover all losses, then statement of profit and loss account is utilised. Since, discount/loss is to be written-off, so this account is credited and reserve account is debited. Accordingly, the journal entry will be

Security Premium A/c Dr
Statement of Profit and Loss Dr
To Discount on Issue of Debentures A/c

6. A Ltd issued 5,000, 10% debentures @ 100 each at a discount of ₹ 10. Amount was payable as follows application ₹50, balance on allotment. All amount due were received on time except a holder of 1,000 debentures who did not pay allotment. Journalise the entry for receipt of allotment.

(a) Bank A/c Dr 2,50,000
To Debenture Allotment A/c 2,50,000

(b) Bank A/c Dr 1,60,000
To Debenture Allotment A/c 1,60,000

(c) Bank A/c Dr 2,00,000
To Debenture Allotment A/c 1,60,000
To Discount on Issue of Debentures A/c 40,000

(d) None of the above

Hint: Since, debentures are issued at discount, so allotment amount is net of application and discount, *i.e.* ₹ 40 (100 – 50 – 10).

Thus, amount payable on 5,000 debentures was (5,000×40) ₹ 2,00,000 but a holder of 1,000 debentures did not pay allotment. Therefore, amount received net of arrear is
= 2,00,000 – 40,000 = ₹ 1,60,000.

7. Holder of debentures as a collateral security is entitled to

(a) interest on debentures
(b) dividend
(c) commission (d) None of these

Hint: When debentures are issued as collateral security, then it is not a real issue. So, the lenders who holds debentures is not entitled for any consideration against these debentures.

8. A company ABC Ltd has purchased an asset costing ₹11,00,000. Vendor issued 9% debentures of ₹ 100 each at 10% premium as consideration against asset purchased. Calculate number of debentures to be issued?

(a) 10,000 (b) 11,000
(c) 12,000 (d) 13,000

Hint: Number of Debentures to be Issued

$$= \frac{\text{Purchase Consideration}}{\text{Issue Price (Face Value + Premium Per Debenture)}}$$

$$= \frac{11,00,000}{110\ (100+10)} = 10,000 \text{ debentures}$$

9. A company has taken a loan of ₹ 20,00,000. The lender took 8% debentures as collateral. The director of the company wants to journalise this collateral. Accountant does not know the exact entry and has passed the following entries. Advise him as to which entry is correct?

(a) Lender Dr 20,00,000
To 8% Debentures A/c 20,00,000

(b) Bank Loan A/c Dr 20,00,000
To 8% Debentures A/c 20,00,000

(c) Debenture Suspense A/c Dr 20,00,000
To 8% Debentures A/c 20,00,000

(d) None of the above

Hint: When a company issues debentures as collateral security and it has to journalise it, then debenture suspense account is opened and an entry is passed in which debenture suspense account is debited and debenture account is credited.

10. S Ltd bought business of R Ltd and purchase consideration is to be decided by net asset value method. Total assets and liabilities which were taken over were ₹ 11,20,000 and ₹ 2,00,000 respectively. ₹ 2,00,000 was paid in cash and for the balance amount, 6% debentures of ₹ 100 each were issued at a premium of 20%. Pass journal entry of issue of debentures in the books of S Ltd.

(a) R Ltd Dr 7,20,000
To 6% Debentures A/c 6,00,000
To Securities Premium Reserve A/c 1,20,000

(b) R Ltd Dr 7,20,000
To 6% Debentures A/c 7,20,000

(c) R Ltd Dr 9,20,000
To Cash A/c 2,00,000
To 6% Debentures A/c 7,20,000

(d) None of the above

Hint: Purchase Consideration = Net Assets
= Total Assets – Total Liabilities
= 11,20,000 – 2,00,000 = ₹ 9,20,000

₹ 2,00,000 has been paid in cash and the balance of ₹ 7,20,000 by issue of debentures at premium.

∴ Number of debentures to be issued

$$= \frac{9,20,000 - 2,00,000}{120(100+20)}$$

$$= \frac{7,20,000}{120} = 6,000 \text{ debentures}$$

ANSWERS

1. (c)	2. (b)	3. (a)	4. (c)	5. (d)	6. (b)	7. (d)	8. (a)	9. (c)	10. (a)

PART B

Financial Statement Analysis

CHAPTER 01

Financial Statements of a Company

Meaning of Financial Statements

The statements which are prepared to ascertain the profit earned or loss suffered and position of assets and liabilities at a particular date are known as financial statements. These are the final product of accounting process. A set of financial statements as per Section 2(40) of the Companies Act, 2013 include

(*i*) Balance sheet, *i.e.* position statement.

(*ii*) Statement of profit and loss, *i.e.* income statement.

(*iii*) Cash flow statement.

(*iv*) Statement of changes in equity.

(*v*) Notes to accounts.

Section 129 of the Companies Act, 2013 requires the company to prepare its financial statements every year in prescribed form, *i.e.* Schedule III of the Companies Act, 2013.

Characteristics of Financial Statements

(*i*) Financial statements relate to a specific past period and thus are historical in nature.

(*ii*) Financial statements are expressed in monetary terms.

(*iii*) Financial statements show profitability through statement of profit and loss and financial position through balance sheet.

Nature of Financial Statements

(*i*) These are prepared on the basis of factor recorded in accounting books.

(*ii*) Certain accounting conventions are required to be followed while preparing financial statements.

(*iii*) These are prepared on certain basic assumptions known as postulates or concepts.

(*iv*) Personal opinion, judgements and estimates also effect the financial statements.

Objectives of Financial Statements

(*i*) To provide information about the earning capacity of the business.
(*ii*) To provide the information about the economic resources and obligation of an enterprise.
(*iii*) To provide information about the cash flows.
(*iv*) To disclose various accounting policies.
(*v*) To help judge the effectiveness of management.

Uses and Importance of Financial Statements

(*i*) Report on stewardship function
(*ii*) Basis for fiscal policies
(*iii*) Basis of granting of credit
(*iv*) Basis for prospective investors
(*v*) Guide to the value of the investment already made
(*vi*) Aids trade associations in helping their members

Limitations of Financial Statements

(*i*) Accounting concepts and conventions involve personal judgement, so these statements are not free from bias.
(*ii*) Qualitative aspects of financial statements are ignored.
(*iii*) The present value of assets and liabilities and price-level changes are ignored.
(*iv*) Financial statements are historical in nature and relate to past period only.
(*v*) Financial statements can be prepared on the basis of different accounting practices. *e.g.* Profit/Loss is different under different practices/assumptions.

Users of Financial Statements

The various users of financial statements are as follows

(*i*) Internal users
(a) Owners (b) Management (c) Employees
(*ii*) External users
(a) Banks and financial institutions
(b) Present and future investors
(c) Creditors or suppliers
(d) Government and its authorities
(e) Securities and Exchange Board of India
(f) Consumers or customers

Statement of Profit and Loss

Statement of profit and loss shows the net result of business operations, *i.e.* financial performance during an accounting period. The vertical form for preparing statement of profit and loss is prescribed in Schedule III, Part II of the Companies Act, 2013.

Format of Statement of Profit and Loss

Statement of Profit and Loss
for the year ending .... (₹ in ......)

Particulars	Note No.	Figures For the Current Reporting Period	Figures For the Previous Reporting Period
I. Revenue from Operations		...	...
II. Other Income		...	...
III. Total Revenue (I + II)		...	...
IV. Expenses			
Cost of Materials Consumed			...
Purchases of Stock-in-trade		...	...
Changes in Inventories of Finished Goods		...	...
Work-in-progress and Stock-in-trade		...	...
Employees Benefits Expenses		...	...
Finance Costs		...	...
Depreciation and Amortisation Expenses		...	...
Other Expenses		...	...
Total Expenses		...	...
V. Profit before Tax (III – IV)		...	...
VI. (–) Tax		(...)	(...)
VII. Profit (Loss) for the Period (V – VI)		...	...

Balance Sheet

It may be defined as a statement of assets and liabilities of the company, at a particular date. It must exhibit a true and fair view of the financial position at the close of the year. It is prepared and presented in the form prescribed in Schedule III, Part I of the Companies Act, 2013, and is broadly divided into two parts (*i*) equity and liabilities and (*ii*) assets.

Format of Balance Sheet

Name of the Company
Balance Sheet
as at ...... (₹ in .....)

Particulars	Note No.	Figures as at the End of Current Reporting Period	Figures as at the End of Previous Reporting Period
I. **EQUITY AND LIABILITIES**			
1. **Shareholders' Funds**			
(a) Share Capital		...	...
(b) Reserves and Surplus		...	...
*(c) Money Received Against Share Warrants		...	...
*2. **Share Application Money Pending Allotment**		...	...

Particulars	Note No.	Figures as at the End of Current Reporting Period	Figures as at the End of Previous Reporting Period
3. **Non-current Liabilities**			
(a) Long-term Borrowings		...	...
*(b) Deferred Tax Liabilities (Net)		...	...
*(c) Other Long-term Liabilities		...	...
(d) Long-term Provisions		...	...
4. **Current Liabilities**			
(a) Short-term Borrowings		...	...
(b) Trade Payables		...	...
(c) Other Current Liabilities		...	...
(d) Short-term Provisions		...	...
Total		...	...
II. **ASSETS**			
1. **Non-current Assets**			
(a) Fixed Assets			
(i) Tangible Assets		...	...
(ii) Intangible Assets		...	...
*(iii) Capital Work-in-Progress		...	...
*(iv) Intangible Assets Under Development		...	...
(b) Non-current Investments		...	...
*(c) Deferred Tax Assets (Net)		...	...
(d) Long-term Loans and Advances		...	...
*(e) Other Non-current Assets		...	...
2. **Current Assets**			
(a) Current Investments		...	...
(b) Inventories		...	...
(c) Trade Receivables		...	...
(d) Cash and Cash Equivalents		...	...
(e) Short-term Loans and Advances		...	...
(f) Other Current Assets		...	...
Total		...	...

* As per CBSE syllabus, the accounting treatment of star marked items will not be evaluated.

Previous Years' Examination Questions

1 Mark Question

1. 'Income received in advance' appears in the balance sheet of a company under the sub-head .... **CBSE 2020**

Ans. other-current liabilities

2 Marks Questions

2. List any four items of 'reserves' that are shown under the heading 'reserves and surplus' in the balance sheet of a company as per Schedule III of the Companies Act, 2013. **All India 2016**

Ans. The four items shown under the heading 'reserves and surplus' are

(*i*) Capital reserve
(*ii*) Securities premium reserve
(*iii*) Capital redemption reserve
(*iv*) Debenture redemption reserve

3. Name any two items that are shown under the head 'other current liabilities' and any two items that are shown under the head 'other current assets' in the balance sheet of a company as per Schedule III of the Companies Act, 2013. **Delhi 2016**

Ans. The two items shown under the head 'other current liabilities' are

(*i*) Unpaid dividends
(*ii*) Income received in advance

The two items shown under the head 'other current assets' are

(*i*) Prepaid expenses
(*ii*) Advance taxes

4. Identify the major heads under which the following items will be shown in the balance sheet of a company as per Schedule III of Companies Act, 2013. **All India 2016**

(*i*) Provision for tax
(*ii*) Loans payable on demand
(*iii*) Computer and related equipment
(*iv*) Goods acquired for trading

Ans.

S. No.	Items	Major Heads
(i)	Provision for Tax	Current Liabilities
(ii)	Loans Payable on Demand	Current Liabilities
(iii)	Computer and Related Equipment	Non-current Assets
(iv)	Goods Acquired for Trading	Current Assets

5. Name the major heads under which the following items will be presented in the balance sheet of a company as per Schedule III of the Companies Act, 2013. **Delhi (C) 2016**

(*i*) Loose tools
(*ii*) Copyrights and Patents
(*iii*) Unpaid dividend
(*iv*) Land and Building

Ans.

S. No.	Items	Major Heads
(i)	Loose Tools	Current Assets
(ii)	Copyrights and Patents	Non-current Assets
(iii)	Unpaid Dividend	Current Liabilities
(iv)	Land and Building	Non-current Assets

3 Marks Questions

6. Under which sub-headings, the following items will be placed in the balance sheet of a company as per Schedule III, Part I of the Companies Act, 2013.

(*i*) Accrued incomes
(*ii*) Loose tools
(*iii*) Provision for employees benefits
(*iv*) Unpaid dividend
(*v*) Short-term loans
(*vi*) Long-term loans
(*vii*) Calls-in-advance **Compartment 2018; Delhi 2014 Modified**

Ans.

S.No.	Items	Major Headings
(i)	Accrued Incomes	Other Current Assets
(ii)	Loose Tools	Inventories
(iii)	Provision for Employees Benefits	Short-term Provision
(iv)	Unpaid Dividend	Other Current Liabilities
(v)	Short-term Loans	Short-term Borrowings
(vi)	Long-term Loans	Long-term Borrowings
(vii)	Calls-in-advance	Current Liabilities

7. Under which sub-headings will the following items be placed in the balance sheet of a company as per Schedule III, Part I of the Companies Act, 2013.

(*i*) Capital reserves
(*ii*) Bonds
(*iii*) Loans repayable on demand
(*iv*) Vehicles
(*v*) Goodwill
(*vi*) Loose tools **All India 2014**

Ans.

S.No.	Items	Major Headings
(i)	Capital Reserves	Reserves and Surplus
(ii)	Bonds	Long-term Borrowings
(iii)	Loans Repayable on Demand	Short-term Borrowings
(iv)	Vehicles	Fixed (Tangible) Assets
(v)	Goodwill	Fixed (Intangible) Assets
(vi)	Loose Tools	Inventories

8. State under which major headings the following items will be presented in the balance sheet of a company as per Schedule III, Part I of the Companies Act, 2013.

(*i*) Long-term borrowings
(*ii*) Trade payables
(*iii*) Provision for tax
(*iv*) Securities premium reserve
(*v*) Patents
(*vi*) Accrued incomes
(*vii*) Current investment **Delhi (C) 2014 Modified**

Ans.

S.No.	Items	Major Headings
(i)	Long-term Borrowings	Non-current Liabilities
(ii)	Trade Payables	Current Liabilities
(iii)	Provision for Tax	Current Liabilities
(iv)	Securities Premium Reserve	Shareholders' Funds
(v)	Patents	Non-current Assets
(vi)	Accrued Incomes	Current Assets
(vii)	Current Investment	Current Assets

9. Under what heads and sub-heads, will the following items appear in the balance sheet of a company as per Schedule III, Part I of the Companies Act, 2013.

(*i*) Stores and spares (*ii*) Proposed dividend

(*iii*) Computer software **All India 2013**

Ans.

S.No.	Items	Major Headings	Sub-headings
(i)	Stores and Spares	Current Assets	Inventories
(ii)	Proposed Dividend	Current Liabilities	Short-term Provisions
(iii)	Computer Software	Non-current Assets	Fixed Assets (Intangible assets)

10. Under what heads and sub-heads, will the following items appear in the balance sheet of a company as per Schedule III, Part I of the Companies Act, 2013.

(*i*) Debentures (*ii*) Loose tools

(*iii*) Calls-in-advance **All India 2013**

Ans.

S.No.	Items	Major Headings	Sub-headings
(i)	Debentures	Non-current Liabilities	Long-term Borrowings
(ii)	Loose Tools	Current Assets	Inventories
(iii)	Calls-in-advance	Current Liabilities	Other Current Liabilities

11. Under what heads and sub-heads, will the following items appear in the balance sheet of a company as per Schedule III, Part I of the Companies Act, 2013.

(*i*) Mining rights

(*ii*) Encashment of employees earned leave payable on retirement

(*iii*) Vehicles **Delhi 2013**

Ans.

S.No.	Items	Major Headings	Sub-headings
(i)	Mining Rights	Non-current Assets	Fixed Assets (Intangible assets)
(ii)	Encashment of Employees Earned Leave Payable on Retirement	Non-current Liabilities	Long-term Provisions
(iii)	Vehicles	Non-current Assets	Fixed Assets (Tangible assets)

12. Under what heads and sub-heads, the following items will appear in the balance sheet of a company as per Schedule III, Part I of the Companies Act, 2013.

(*i*) Tax reserve

(*ii*) Interest on calls-in-advance

(*iii*) Stores and spares **Delhi 2013**

Ans.

S.No.	Items	Major Headings	Sub-headings
(i)	Tax Reserve	Current Liabilities	Short-term Provisions
(ii)	Interest on Calls-in-advance	Current Liabilities	Other Current Liabilities
(iii)	Stores and Spares	Current Assets	Inventories

13. Under what heads and sub-heads, the following items will appear in the balance sheet of a company as per Schedule III, Part I of the Companies Act, 2013.

(*i*) Premium on redemption of debentures

(*ii*) Loose tools

(*iii*) Balances with banks **Delhi 2013**

Ans.

S.No.	Items	Major Headings	Sub-headings
(i)	Premium on Redemption of Debentures	Non-current Liabilities	Other Long-term Liabilities
(ii)	Loose Tools	Current Assets	Inventories
(iii)	Balances with Banks	Current Assets	Cash and Cash Equivalents

14. Under what heads and sub-heads, will the following items appear in the balance sheet of a company as per Schedule III, Part I of the Companies Act, 2013.

(*i*) Subsidy reserve

(*ii*) Mining rights

(*iii*) Provision for doubtful debts **All India 2013**

Ans.

S.No.	Items	Major Headings	Sub-headings
(i)	Subsidy Reserve	Shareholders' Funds	Reserves and Surplus
(ii)	Mining Rights	Non-current Assets	Fixed Assets (Intangible assets)
(iii)	Provision for Doubtful Debts	Current Liabilities	Short-term Provisions

15. State the major headings under which the following items will be put as per Schedule III, Part I of the Companies Act, 2013.

(*i*) Long-term investments

(*ii*) Trade receivables

(*iii*) Motor car

(*iv*) Discount on issue of shares

(*v*) Securities premium reserve

(*vi*) Unclaimed dividend **All India 2011**

Ans.

S.No.	Items	Major Headings
(i)	Long-term Investments	Non-current Assets
(ii)	Trade Receivables	Current Assets
(iii)	Motor Car	Non-current Assets
(iv)	Discount on Issue of Shares	Adjusted through Share Forfeiture Account*
(v)	Securities Premium Reserve	Shareholders' Funds
(vi)	Unclaimed Dividend	Current Liabilities

NOTE *Discount is allowed on reissue of forfeited shares only.

16. Give the major headings under which the following items will be shown in a company's balance sheet as per Schedule III, Part I of the Companies Act, 2013.

(*i*) Trade payables (Sundry creditors)
(*ii*) Provision for tax
(*iii*) Preliminary expenses
(*iv*) Loose tools
(*v*) Interest accrued on investments
(*vi*) Goodwill **All India 2011**

Ans.

S.No.	Items	Major Headings
(i)	Trade Payables (Sundry creditors)	Current Liabilities
(ii)	Provision for Tax	Current Liabilities
(iii)	Preliminary Expenses	Deducted from Securities Premium Reserve
(iv)	Loose Tools	Current Assets
(v)	Interest Accrued on Investments	Current Assets
(vi)	Goodwill	Non-current Assets

17. How will you disclose the following items while preparing the balance sheet of a company, as per Schedule III of the Companies Act, 2013?

(*i*) Bank overdraft
(*ii*) Share issue expenses
(*iii*) Matured debentures
(*iv*) Building under construction. **Delhi 2011 Modified**

Ans.

S.No.	Items	Major Headings	Sub-headings
(i)	Bank Overdraft	Current Liabilities	Short-term Borrowings
(ii)	Share Issue Expenses	Non-current Assets	Other Non-current Assets
(iii)	Matured Debentures	Current Liabilities	Other Current Liabilities
(iv)	Building under Construction	Non-current Assets	Fixed Assets (Capital work-in-progress)

18. List the items which are shown under the heading 'current assets' in the balance sheet of a company as per Schedule III, Part I of the Companies Act, 2013. **Delhi 2011; Modified**

Ans. Current Assets

(*i*) Current investments
(*ii*) Inventories
(*iii*) Trade receivables
(*iv*) Cash and cash equivalents
(*v*) Short-term loans and advances
(*vi*) Other current assets

19. List the items which are shown under the heading 'current liabilities' as per Schedule III, Part I of the Companies Act, 2013. **Delhi 2011**

Ans. Current Liabilities

(*i*) Short-term borrowings
(*ii*) Trade payables
(*iii*) Other current liabilities
(*iv*) Short-term provisions

4 Marks Questions

20. State under which major headings and sub-headings will the following items be presented in the Balance Sheet of a company as per Schedule-III, Part-I of the Companies Act, 2013.

(i) Prepaid Insurance
(ii) Investment in Debentures
(iii) Calls-in-arrears
(iv) Unpaid Dividend
(v) Capital Reserve
(vi) Loose Tools
(vii) Capital Work-in-progress
(viii) Patents being developed by the company. **Delhi 2019**

Ans.

S. No.	Major Headings	Sub-headings
(i)	Current Assets	Other Current Assets
(ii)	Non-current Assets	Non-current Investments
(iii)	Shareholder's Funds	Share Capital (Notes to accounts)
(iv)	Current Liabilities	Other Current Liabilities
(v)	Shareholder's Funds	Reserves and Surplus
(vi)	Current Assets	Inventories
(vii)	Non-current Assets	Fixed Assets
(viii)	Non-current Assets	Intangible Assets under Development

21. Under which major heads and sub-heads will the following items be placed in the Balance Sheet of the company as per Schedule III, Part I of the Companies Act, 2013?

(i) Cheques and bank drafts in hand
(ii) Loose tools
(iii) Securities premium reserve
(iv) Long-term investments with maturity period less than six months
(v) Work-in-progress
(vi) Mining rights
(vii) Publishing titles
(viii) Debtors **All India 2019**

Ans.

S. No.	Major Head	Sub-head
(i)	Current Assets	Cash & Cash Equivalents
(ii)	Current Assets	Inventories
(iii)	Shareholder's Fund	Reserves and Surplus
(iv)	Current Assets	Current Investments
(v)	Current Assets	Inventories
(vi)	Non-current Assets	Intangible Assets
(vii)	Non-current Assets	Intangible Assets
(viii)	Current Assets	Trade Receivables

22. Under which major headings and sub-headings will the following items be presented in theBalance Sheet of a company as per Schedule III, Part I of the Companies Act, 2013?

(i) Interest accrued and due on debentures
(ii) Loose tools
(iii) Accrued interest on calls-in-advance
(iv) Interest due on calls-in-arrears
(v) Trademarks
(vi) Premium on redemption of debentures
(vii) Plant and Machinery
(viii) Patents **All India 2019**

Ans.

S. No.	Major Headings	Sub-headings
(i)	Current Liabilities	Other Current Liabilities
(ii)	Current Assets	Inventories
(iii)	Current Liabilities	Other Current Liabilities
(iv)	Current Assets	Other Current Assets
(v)	Non-current Assets	Fixed Assets–Intangible Assets
(vi)	Non-current Liabilities	Other Non-current Liabilities
(vii)	Non-current Assets	Fixed Assets–Tangible Assets
(viii)	Non-current Assets	Fixed Assets–Intangible Assets

23. JW Ltd was a company manufacturing geysers. As a part of its long-term goal for expansion, the company decided to identify the opportunity in rural areas. Initial plan was rolled out for Bhiwani village in Haryana. Since the village did not have regular supply of electricity, the company decided to manufacture solar geysers. The core team consisting of the Regional Manager, Accountant and the Marketing Manager was taken from the Head Office and the remaining employees were selected from the village and neighbourhood areas.

At the time of preparation of financial statements, the accountant of the company fell sick and the company deputed a junior accountant temporarily from the village for two months.

The balance sheet prepared by the junior accountant showed the following items against the major heads and sub-heads mentioned which were not as per Schedule III of the Companies Act, 2013.

Item	Major Head/Sub-Head
Loose Tools	Trade Receivables
Cheques in Hand	Current Investments
Term Loan from Bank	Other Long-term Liabilities
Computer Software	Tangible Fixed Assets

Present the above items under the correct major heads and sub-heads as per Schedule III of the Companies Act, 2013. **CBSE 2018 Modified**

Ans.

Items	Major Heads	Sub-Heads
Loose Tools	Current Assets	Inventories
Cheques-in-hand	Current Assets	Cash and Cash Equivalents
Term Loan from Bank	Non-current Liabilities	Long-term Borrowings
Computer Software	Non-current Assets	Fixed Assets (Intangible)

24. (*i*) Give the meaning of 'long-term provisions'.

(*ii*) List any four items other than 'stock-in-trade' that are presented under the sub-head 'inventories' as per Schedule III of the Companies Act, 2013. **All India 2016**

Ans. (*i*) Long-term provisions are the provisions against which liability will arise after 12 months of the date of balance sheet or after the period of operating cycle. e.g. Provision made for retirement benefits payable to employees who will retire after 12 months from the date of balance sheet, provision for warranty claims that relates to the period after 12 months of the date of balance sheet.

(*ii*) The items other than 'stock-in-trade' that are presented under the sub-head inventories are

(a) Raw material
(b) Work-in-progress
(c) Finished goods
(d) Stores and spares

25. Under which major headings and sub-headings will the following items be shown in the balance sheet of a company as per Schedule III Part I of the Companies Act, 2013?

(*i*) Net loss as shown by statement of profit and loss
(*ii*) Capital redemption reserve
(*iii*) Bonds
(*iv*) Loans repayable on demand
(*v*) Unpaid dividend
(*vi*) Buildings
(*vii*) Trademarks
(*viii*) Raw materials **All India 2015**

Ans.

S.No.	Items	Major Headings	Sub-headings
(i)	Net Loss as shown by Statement of Profit and Loss	Shareholders' Funds	Shown by way of deduction under Reserves and Surplus
(ii)	Capital Redemption Reserve	Shareholders' Funds	Reserves and Surplus
(iii)	Bonds	Non-current Liabilities	Long-term Borrowings
(iv)	Loans Repayable on Demand	Current Liabilities	Short-term Borrowings
(v)	Unpaid Dividend	Current Liabilities	Other Current Liabilities
(vi)	Buildings	Non-current Assets	Tangible Fixed Assets
(vii)	Trademarks	Non-current Assets	Intangible Fixed Assets
(viii)	Raw Materials	Current Assets	Inventories

26. Under which heads and sub-heads the following items will be placed in the balance sheet of a company as per Schedule III, Part I of the Companies Act, 2013?

(*i*) Cash in hand
(*ii*) Mining rights
(*iii*) Short-term deposits
(*iv*) Debenture redemption reserve
(*v*) Income received in advance
(*vi*) Balance of the statement of profit and loss
(*vii*) Office equipments
(*viii*) Work-in-progress. **Delhi 2015**

Ans.

S.No.	Items	Major Headings	Sub-headings
(i)	Cash in Hand	Current Assets	Cash and Cash Equivalents
(ii)	Mining Rights	Non-current Assets	Intangible Fixed Assets
(iii)	Short-term Deposits	Current Assets	Cash and Cash Equivalents
(iv)	Debenture Redemption Reserve	Shareholders' Funds	Reserves and Surplus
(v)	Income Received in Advance	Current Liabilities	Other Current Liabilities
(vi)	Balance of the Statement of Profit and Loss	Shareholders' Funds	Reserves and Surplus
(vii)	Office Equipments	Non-current Assets	Tangible Fixed Assets
(viii)	Work-in-progress	Current Assets	Inventories

27. Under which major headings and sub-headings will the following items be shown in the balance sheet of a company as per Schedule III, Part I of the Companies Act, 2013?

(*i*) Balance of the statement of profit and loss
(*ii*) Loan of ₹ 1,00,000 payable after three years
(*iii*) Short-term deposits payable on demand
(*iv*) Loose tools
(*v*) Trademark
(*vi*) Land
(*vii*) Cash at bank
(*viii*) Trade payables **All India 2015**

Ans.

S.No.	Items	Major Headings	Sub-headings
(i)	Balance of the Statement of Profit and Loss	Shareholders' Funds	Reserves and Surplus
(ii)	Loan of ₹ 1,00,000 Payable after Three Years	Non-current Liabilities	Long-term Borrowings
(iii)	Short-term Deposits Payable on Demand	Current Assets	Short-term Loans and Advances
(iv)	Loose Tools	Current Assets	Inventories
(v)	Trademark	Non-current Assets	Intangible Fixed Assets
(vi)	Land	Non-current Assets	Tangible Fixed Assets
(vii)	Cash at Bank	Current Assets	Cash and Cash Equivalents
(viii)	Trade Payables	Current Liabilities	Trade Payables

28. Under which major headings, the following items will be presented in the balance sheet of a company as per Schedule III, Part I of the Companies Act, 2013?

(*i*) Loans provided repayable on demand
(*ii*) Goodwill (*iii*) Copyrights
(*iv*) Loose tools (*v*) Cheques
(*vi*) General reserve (*vii*) Stock of finished goods
(*viii*) 9% debentures repayable after three years **Delhi 2015**

Ans.

S.No.	Items	Major Headings
(i)	Loans Provided Repayable on Demand	Current Assets
(ii)	Goodwill	Non-current Assets
(iii)	Copyrights	Non-current Assets
(iv)	Loose Tools	Current Assets
(v)	Cheques	Current Assets
(vi)	General Reserve	Shareholders' Funds
(vii)	Stock of Finished Goods	Current Assets
(viii)	9% Debentures Repayable after Three Years	Non-current Liabilities

29. Under which major heads and sub-heads will the following items be placed in the balance sheet of a company as per Schedule III, Part I of the Companies Act, 2013?

(*i*) Bank overdraft
(*ii*) Cash and cash equivalents
(*iii*) Securities premium reserve
(*iv*) Negative balance of the statement of profit and loss
(*v*) Goodwill
(*vi*) Trademark
(*vii*) 5 years loan obtained from SBI
(*viii*) Investments **Foreign 2015**

Ans.

S.No.	Items	Major Headings	Sub-headings
(i)	Bank Overdraft	Current Liabilities	Short-term Borrowings
(ii)	Cash and Cash Equivalents	Current Assets	Cash and Cash Equivalents
(iii)	Securities Premium Reserve	Shareholders' Funds	Reserves and Surplus
(iv)	Negative Balance of the Statement of Profit and Loss	Shareholders' Funds	Shown by Way of Deduction from Reserves and Surplus
(v)	Goodwill	Non-current Assets	Intangible Fixed Assets
(vi)	Trademark	Non-current Assets	Intangible Fixed Assets
(vii)	5 Years Loan Obtained from SBI	Non-current Liabilities	Long-term Borrowings
(viii)	Investments	Non-current Assets	Non-current Investments

Multiple Choice Questions

(1 Mark)

1. Ajanta Ltd. issued 10% Debentures of ₹ 8,00,000 on 1st April, 2019 which are redeemable in five equal yearly instalments starting from 1st April, 2022.

How would this information be presented in the balance sheet as at 31st March, 2021?

CBSE Term I 2021

(a) ₹ 8,00,000 as long-term borrowings
(b) ₹ 8,00,000 as other non-current liability
(c) ₹ 8,00,000 as current liability
(d) ₹ 1,60,000 as other current liability, and ₹ 6,40,000 as long-term borrowing

2. Match the items given in Column I with the correct heading/sub-heading given in Column II.

CBSE Term I 2021

Column I	Column II
A. 9% Debenture redeemable during the current year	(i) Intangible assets
B. Loose tools	(ii) Current liabilities
C. Copyright	(iii) Cash and cash equivalents
D. Cash at bank	(iv) Inventories

Codes

	A	B	C	D
(a)	(i)	(ii)	(iii)	(iv)
(b)	(iii)	(ii)	(iv)	(i)
(c)	(iv)	(iii)	(ii)	(i)
(d)	(ii)	(iv)	(i)	(iii)

3. 'Public Deposits' appear in the company's balance sheet under the head/sub-head

CBSE 2020

(a) Intangible Assets
(b) Current Liabilities
(c) Shareholders' Funds
(d) Non-current Liabilities

4. Financial statements are presented by directors to shareholders at every
(a) board meeting
(b) special (extraordinary) general meeting
(c) annual general meeting
(d) None of the above

5. A company should disclose all the information in
(a) statement (b) annual report
(c) accounts book (d) None of these

Hint: As per law, the annual report of a company should disclose the prescribed information to enable the users to make informed judgements and decisions. The information is disclosed in the financial statements, director's report and by separate statements being part of the annual report.

6. Financial statements include balance sheet, statement of profit and loss, cash flow statement etc. Besides these statements, a special statement is also included in financial statements if applicable on company. You are required to find that statement.
(a) Statement of cash inflow and outflow
(b) Statement of changes in equity
(c) Statement of incomes and expenses
(d) Statement of assets and liabilities

7. Statement of profit and loss shows
(a) financial position
(b) financial performance
(c) assets and liabilities
(d) None of the above

Hint: Statement of profit and loss shows the net results of business operations during an accounting period.

8. Format of profit and loss is prepared as specified in
(a) Part II, Schedule III (b) Income Tax Act
(c) SEBI Act (d) None of these

9. Which of the following is included under 'other income' head?
(a) Purchase of stock (b) Sales of stock
(c) Interest received (d) None of these

Hint: Other income head include revenues which is not 'revenue from operation' like interest received, dividend received. So, interest received is included under 'other income' head.

10. A company took a loan of ₹ 1,00,000 and paid interest of ₹ 10,000 for this year @ 10% on loan amount. This interest will be shown under .... head.

(a) finance cost
(b) employee benefit expense
(c) revenue from operation
(d) None of the above

Hint: Those expenses which are paid for financing the company are included in finance cost. Interest on loan is one of them.

11. Calculate revenue from operations from following.

Sales = ₹ 1,04,00,000
Sales return = ₹ 4,00,000
Sales of scrap = ₹ 50,000
Dividend received = ₹ 20,000
Interest on fixed deposit = ₹ 60,000

(a) ₹ 1,00,00,000 (b) ₹ 1,01,30,000
(c) ₹ 1,00,80,000 (d) ₹ 1,00,50,000

Hint: **Revenue from Operations**

Sales	=	1,04,00,000
(–) Sales Return	=	(4,00,000)
		1,00,00,000
(+) Sale of scrap	=	50,000
		₹ 1,00,50,000

12. Compute cost of material consumed from following.

Opening inventory = ₹ 5,00,000
Materials purchased = ₹ 40,00,000
Closing inventory = ₹ 6,00,000

(a) ₹ 40,00,000
(b) ₹ 39,00,000
(c) ₹ 38,00,000
(d) ₹ 41,00,000

Hint: **Cost of Material Consumed**

Opening Inventory	=	5,00,000
(+) Purchase	=	40,00,000
		45,00,000
(–) Closing Inventory	=	(6,00,000)
		₹ 39,00,000

13. Which of the following is included on assets side?

(a) Share capital (b) Inventories
(c) Bills payable (d) None of these

Hint: Inventory is an asset which is included under heading 'Current assets'. It can be converted into liquid, *i.e.* cash within 12 months.

14. Find out which of the following is a reserve for distributing dividend?

(a) General reserve
(b) Capital reserve
(c) Revaluation reserve
(d) None of the above

Hint: All reserves are made from profits. Free reserves are allowed for distribution of dividend and general reserve is a free reserve like credit balance of profit and loss account.

15. Find which of the following is shown in notes to accounts only.

(a) Inventories
(b) Current investments
(c) Contingent liability
(d) Building

Hint: Contingent liabilities are not recorded in the books of accounts and are disclosed in notes to accounts of balance sheet. These liabilities are those liabilities which can be occurred in future or not, there is always a doubtful situation. So, these are not included in books because exact figure is also not definite.

ANSWERS

1. *(d)*	2. *(d)*	3. *(d)*	4. *(c)*	5. *(b)*	6. *(b)*	7. *(b)*	8. *(a)*	9. *(c)*	10. *(a)*
11. *(d)*	12. *(b)*	13. *(b)*	14. *(a)*	15. *(c)*					

CHAPTER 02

Financial Statement Analysis

Introduction to Financial Statement Analysis

The process of critical evaluation of the financial information contained in the financial statements, in order to understand and make decisions regarding the operations of the firm, is called financial statement analysis.

According to **Myer**, "Financial statement analysis is largely a study of relationships among the various financial factors in a business, as disclosed by a single set of statements and a study of trends of these factors, as shown in a series of statements."

Objectives and Significance of Financial Statement Analysis

The objectives of financial statement analysis are

(*i*) To measure the operating efficiency and profitability of the business.
(*ii*) To measure the short-term and long-term financial position.
(*iii*) To indicate the trend of achievements.
(*iv*) To assess the growth potential of the business.
(*v*) To compare intra-firm position, inter-firm position and pattern position within the industry.
(*vi*) To judge the financial stability of an enterprise.

Types of Financial Statement Analysis

The types of financial statement analysis are

(*i*) External analysis
(*ii*) Internal analysis
(*iii*) Horizontal analysis
(*iv*) Vertical analysis
(*v*) Long-term analysis
(*vi*) Short-term analysis

Uses or Advantages of Financial Statement Analysis

The advantages of financial statement analysis are

(*i*) Security analysis
(*ii*) Credit analysis
(*iii*) Debt analysis
(*iv*) Dividend decision
(*v*) General business analysis

Limitations of Financial Statement Analysis

The limitations of financial statement analysis are

(*i*) Financial statement analysis ignore qualitative aspects like quality of management, labour force and public relations.

(*ii*) Suffering from the limitations of financial statements, which are as follows

- (a) Financial statements are historical in nature.
- (b) Financial statements do not show price level changes hence, affect the analysis also.
- (c) The results obtained by analysis of financial statements may be misleading due to window dressing.
- (d) Financial statements are affected by the personal ability and bias of the analyst.

Parties Interested in Financial Statement Analysis

The parties interested in financial statement analysis are as follows

(*i*) Finance manager (*ii*) Investors (*iii*) Customers (*iv*) Management
(*v*) Labour unions (*vi*) Tax authorities (*vii*) Trade creditors (*viii*) Government
(*ix*) Researchers (*x*) Bankers and lenders (*xi*) Regulatory authorities (*xii*) Other parties

Tools or Techniques of Financial Statement Analysis

Financial statements of companies are basically summarised financial reports. The figures given in these reports are to be analysed in relation to other figures over a period of time. It is done to identify the strength and weakness of business. Also, meaningful conclusions can be drawn based on such analysis. There are number of techniques (tools) available for this purpose.

The most commonly used techniques of financial statement analysis are as follows

(*i*) **Comparative Statements** Statements used to compare the items of income statement, i.e. statement of profit and loss and balance sheet for ascertaining the trend of the performance and profitability of an enterprise are known as comparative financial statements.

(*ii*) **Common Size Statements** The statement wherein figures reported are converted into percentage to some common base is known as common size statement. Each percentage shows the relation of the individual item to its respective total.

(*iii*) **Ratio Analysis** It is a technique which involves analysing the financial statements by calculating various ratios.

(*iv*) **Cash Flow Statement** It is a statement showing inflows (receipts) and outflows (payments) of cash and cash equivalents of the business during a particular period. It is a statement showing the changes in the financial position of a business concern during different intervals of time.

Note Comparative statements and common size statements are out of the scope of syllabus. Ratio analysis and cash flow statement are discussed in subsequent chapters.

Previous Years' Examination Questions

1 Mark Questions

1. State any two limitations of financial statement analysis.
Compartment 2018; Delhi (C) 2015

Or State any one limitation of financial statement analysis.
Delhi 2014, 2013, 2010; Delhi (C) 2014, All India 2014, 2014 (C), 2013, 2010

Ans. Limitations of financial statement analysis are

(*i*) Financial statement analysis ignore qualitative aspects like quality of management, labour force and public relations.

(*ii*) The results obtained by analysis of financial statements may be misleading due to window dressing.

2. What is meant by analysis of financial statements? Delhi (C) 2015; All India 2011

Ans. The process of critical evaluation of the financial information contained in the financial statements, in order to understand and make decisions regarding the operations of the firm, is called financial statement analysis.

3. State any two objectives of financial statement analysis. All India; Delhi (C) 2015

Or State any one objective of financial statement analysis.
All India 2014, 2013; Delhi 2013, 2010 Delhi (C) 2014

Ans. Objectives of financial statement analysis are

(*i*) To judge the operating efficiency and profitability of the business.

(*ii*) To measure the short-term and long-term financial position of the enterprise.

4. Name any two tools of analysis of financial statements. All India (C) 2014

Ans. Two tools of analysis of financial statements are

(*i*) Comparative financial statements

(*ii*) Common size statements

5. State one advantage of financial statement analysis. Delhi 2013

Ans. Financial statement analysis helps the management to judge the overall as well as segmentwise operational efficiency of the business.

6. Explain how financial statement analysis ignores qualitative elements? All India 2013

Or State how qualitative aspects are ignored in financial statement analysis? Delhi (C) 2011

Ans. Financial statement analysis ignore qualitative elements as it is confined to the monetary matters only because quality cannot be measured in monetary terms.

7. State the significance of analysis of financial statements to 'top management'.
All India 2012

Ans. Financial statement analysis enables the 'top management' to evaluate the overall efficiency of the business. It provides adequate information for planning , budgeting and controlling the affairs of the business in future.

8. State the significance of analysis of financial statements to 'lenders'. Delhi 2012

Ans. Lenders can judge the long-term and short-term solvency of the business or its ability to repay debts and interest through analysis of financial statements which will help them to decide whether they should lend or not.

9. How is the financial statement analysis useful to finance manager? All India 2011

Ans. Financial statement analysis is useful to finance manager for taking financial decisions for the business. It provides adequate information for financial planning.

10. State the interest of tax authorities in the analysis of financial statements.
All India 2011

Ans. Tax authorities are interested to analyse the financial statements to know about the revenue of business firm and to ensure proper assessment of liabilities of the business as per the laws in force, from time to time.

11. State the interest of investors in the analysis of financial statements. **All India 2011**

Ans. Investors are interested in knowing the earning capacity of the business and its prospects for future growth and returns through analysis of financial statements, so that they can decide whether they should invest or not.

12. What is meant by a common size statements? **Delhi 2011**

Ans. The statement wherein figures reported are converted into percentage to some common base are known are common size statements. Each percentage shows the relation of the individual item to its respective total. In common size income statement, revenue from operations (net sales) figure is assumed to be 100 and all other figures of expenses and other incomes are expressed as a percentage of sales. In common size balance sheet, the total of assets or liabilities is assumed to be 100 and figures are expressed as a percentage of the total.

13. How the earning capacity of a business is assessed by financial statement analysis? **Delhi 2010**

Ans. The earning capacity of a business is assessed by financial statement analysis through profitability ratios.

14. How the solvency of a business is assessed by financial statement analysis? **Delhi 2010**

Ans. The solvency of a business is assessed by financial statement analysis through long-term and short-term solvency ratios.

15. How does subjectivity become a limitation of financial statement analysis? **Delhi 2010**

Ans. Subjectivity becomes a limitation of financial statement analysis because an analyst has to exercise his own judgement and bias in the process of drawing conclusions.

16. How is 'window dressing' a limitation of financial statement analysis? **All India 2010**

Ans. 'Window dressing' refers to displaying the rosy picture of an enterprise through financial statements. Sometimes, material information is concealed in financial statements due to 'window dressing'.

2 Marks Question

17. One of the objectives of 'financial statement analysis' is to identify the reasons for change in the financial position of the enterprise. State two more objectives of this analysis. **Delhi; All India 2016**

Or One of the objectives of 'financial statement analysis' is to judge the ability of the firm to repay its debt and assessing the short-term as well as the long-term liquidity position of the firm. State two more objectives of this analysis. **Delhi; All India 2016**

Or One of the objectives of 'financial statement analysis' is to ascertain the relative importance of the different components of the financial position of the firm. State two more objectives of this analysis. **Delhi; All India 2016**

Ans. The two more objectives of this analysis are

(*i*) To compare the intra-firm position, inter-firm position and pattern position within the industry.

(*ii*) To measure the operating efficiency and profitability of the enterprise.

4 Marks Questions

18. Explain briefly any four objectives of 'Analysis of financial statements'. **Delhi 2019**

Or State the objectives of 'analysis of financial statements'. **Delhi; All India 2017**

Ans. The objectives of analysis of financial statements are as follows

(*i*) To judge the financial stability of an enterprise.

(*ii*) To measure the short-term and long-term solvency of enterprise.

(*iii*) To measure the operating efficiency and profitability of an enterprise.

(*iv*) To compare the intra-firm position, inter-firm position and pattern position within the industry.

19. Explain the importance of financial analysis of (*i*) labour unions and (*ii*) creditors. **All India 2019**

Ans. (*i*) **Labour unions** They analyse the financial statement to assess whether the business concern is earning a fair rate of return on capital employed and whether they should demand for increased wages or not. So, financial statement analysis helps the labour unions in settling wage agreements.

(*ii*) **Creditors** A creditor, through an analysis of financial statements, judges not only the present ability of the company to meet its obligations, but also the probability of its continued ability to meet all its financial obligations. Trade creditors are particularly interested in the firm's ability to meet their claims over a short period of time.

20. Explain briefly any four limitations of 'analysis of financial statements'. **All India 2019, 2017; Delhi 2017**

Ans. The limitations of analysis of financial statements are as follows

(*i*) It ignores price level changes.
(*ii*) It is not free from bias.
(*iii*) It suffers from limitations of financial statements.
(*iv*) It ignores qualitative aspects.

21. What is meant by 'analysis of financial statements'? State any two objectives of such an analysis. **All India 2017**

Ans. The process of critical evaluation of the financial information contained in the financial statements, in order to understand and make decisions regarding the operations of the firm is called financial statement analysis .

The objectives of such analysis are as follows

(*i*) To judge the financial stability of an enterprise.
(*ii*) To measure the short-term and long-term solvency of the enterprise.

Multiple Choice Questions

(1 Mark)

1. Financial statement analysis includes .... and .... of financial statements. **CBSE Term I 2021**

(a) analysis, preparation
(b) preparation, interpretation
(c) preparation, analysis
(d) analysis, interpretation

2. Which of the following is not a limitation of 'financial statements analysis'? **CBSE 2020**

(a) It is affected by personal bias.
(b) Inter-firm comparative study possible.
(c) Lack of qualitative analysis.
(d) Ignores price level changes.

3. The analysis of financial statements is important for

(a) management (b) trade unions
(c) creditors (d) All of these

Hint: Analysis helps the management to exercise control over the business. It helps the creditors to judge the ability of the company to meet its liabilities. It helps trade union to settle wage disputes.

4. Which of the following statements are false?

(*i*) When all the comparative figures in a balance sheet are stated as percentage of the total, it is termed as horizontal analysis.
(*ii*) When financial statements of several years are analysed, it is termed as vertical analysis.
(*iii*) Vertical analysis is also termed as time series analysis.

Codes

(a) Both (i) and (ii) (b) Both (i) and (iii)
(c) Both (ii) and (iii) (d) All three (i), (ii), (iii)

Hint: (*i*) When all the comparative figures in a balance sheet are stated as percentage of total, it is termed as vertical analysis.
(*ii*) When financial statements of several years are analysed, it is termed as horizontal analysis.
(*iii*) Vertical analysis is also termed as static analysis. Horizontal analysis is also termed as dynamic analysis or time series analysis.

5. The process of critical evaluation of the financial information contained in the financial statements in order to understand and make decisions regarding the operations of the firm is called ....

(a) Financial Statement Analysis
(b) Cash Flow Analysis
(c) Cost Analysis
(d) None of the above

6. Sumatra limited wants to assess the future profit earning capacity of its business. It will conduct

(a) external analysis

(b) short-term analysis

(c) long-term analysis

(d) None of the above

Hint: Long-term analysis of financial statements is done to examine the long-term financial stability and long-term solvency as well as future profit earning capacity of a company.

7. Tools of analysis and interpretation of financial statement are

(a) comparative balance sheet and income statement

(b) common size trial balance

(c) trend ratio

(d) ratios, comparative balance sheet and common size statements

8. Comparative statement is a .... analysis.

(a) horizontal

(b) vertical

(c) diagonal

(d) None of the above

ANSWERS

1. *(d)*	2. *(b)*	3. *(d)*	4. *(d)*	5. *(a)*	6. *(c)*	7. *(d)*	8. *(a)*

CHAPTER 03

Accounting Ratios

TOPIC 1

Introduction to Ratios

Meaning of Ratios and Accounting Ratios

Ratio It is an arithmetical expression of relationship between two related or interdependent items. It is the numerical or quantitative relationship between two items/variables.

Accounting Ratios When ratios are calculated on the basis of accounting information, they are called accounting ratios. It is a mathematical expression that shows the relationship between two items or groups of items shown in financial statements. Accounting ratios can be expressed as a pure ratio, percentage, in times or fraction.

Ratio Analysis

It is a technique which involves analysing the financial statements by calculating various ratios. It is the most important and powerful tool for measuring performance of a business enterprise.

Objectives of Ratio Analysis

The objectives of ratio analysis are

(*i*) To know the areas of an enterprise which need more attention.
(*ii*) To know about the potential areas, which can be improved on.
(*iii*) To make inter as well as intra firm comparisons.
(*iv*) To provide analysis of the liquidity, solvency, activity and profitability of an enterprise.
(*v*) To provide information useful for making estimates and preparing the plans for future.

Advantages of Ratio Analysis

The advantages of ratio analysis are

(*i*) It is useful in analysis of financial statements.
(*ii*) Helps in simplifying accounting figures.
(*iii*) Useful in judging the operating efficiency of business.
(*iv*) Helps in identification of problem areas.
(*v*) Helpful in comparative analysis.

Limitations of Ratio Analysis

The limitations of ratio analysis are

(*i*) Accounting ratios ignore qualitative factors.
(*ii*) Ratios are affected by window-dressing.
(*iii*) Effects of inherent limitations of accounting.
(*iv*) Ignores price levael changes.
(*v*) Affected by personal bias and ability of the analyst.

Previous Years' Examination Questions

1 Mark Questions

1. State how personal bias can get reflected in ratio analysis. **All India (C) 2011**

Ans. In many situations, the accountant has to make the choice out of various alternatives available, e.g. choice in the method of depreciation (straight line or written down), choice in the method of inventory valuation (LIFO, FIFO or HIFO). Since the subjectivity is inherent in personal judgement, the financial statements are therefore not free from personal bias. As a result, ratio analysis cannot be said to be free from bias.

2. State any two limitations of ratio analysis. **All India (C) 2010**

Ans. The two limitations of ratio analysis are

(*i*) Accounting ratios ignore qualitative factors.
(*ii*) Affected by personal bias and ability of the analyst.

3. What is meant by accounting ratios? **Delhi (C) 2010**

Ans. An accounting ratio is a mathematical expression of the relationship between two items or group of items shown in the financial statements.

TOPIC 2

Classification of Accounting Ratios

In view of the requirements of various users, the accounting ratios may be classified as under

1. Liquidity (Short-term Solvency) Ratios

These ratios measure the firm's ability to fulfil its short-term financial obligations.

(i) Current Ratio/Working Capital Ratio

This ratio establishes relationship between current assets and current liabilities and is used to assess the short-term financial position of the business concern. Current ratio of 2 :1 is considered to be ideal.

$$\left[\text{Current Ratio/ Working Capital Ratio} = \frac{\text{Current Assets}}{\text{Current Liabilities}}\right]$$

- **Items Included in Current Assets**
  (a) Current investments
  (b) Inventories (Excluding loose tools, stores and spares)
  (c) Trade receivables (Bills receivable and sundry debtors less provision for doubtful debts)
  (d) Cash and cash equivalents (Cash in hand, cash at bank, cheques/drafts in hand)
  (e) Short-term loans and advances
  (f) Other current assets (Prepaid expenses, interest receivable etc.)
- **Items Included in Current Liabilities**
  (a) Short-term borrowings
  (b) Trade payables (Bills payable and sundry creditors)
  (c) Other current liabilities (Current maturities of long-term debts, interest accrued but not due on borrowings, interest accrued and due on borrowings, outstanding expenses, unclaimed dividend, calls-in-advance etc)
  (d) Short-term provisions

NOTE As per CBSE circular, 'other current assets' except prepaid expenses, accrued income and advance tax are not to be evaluated.

(ii) Liquid Ratio/Quick Ratio/Acid Test Ratio

This ratio establishes relationship between liquid assets and current liabilities and is used to measure the firm's ability to pay the claims of creditors immediately. This ratio is a better indicator of liquidity and 1 : 1 is considered to be ideal.

$$\left[\text{Liquid Ratio/ Quick Ratio/ Acid Test Ratio} = \frac{\text{Liquid Assets or Quick Assets}}{\text{Current Liabilities}}\right]$$

- **Items Included in Liquid/Quick Assets**
  (a) Current investments
  (b) Trade receivables (Bill receivables, debtors less provisions for doubtful debts)
  (c) Cash and cash equivalents
  (d) Short-term loans and advances
  (e) Other current assets except prepaid expenses

  Items excluded in liquid assets are inventories, prepaid expenses.
- **Items Included in Current Liabilities**
  (a) Short-term borrowings
  (b) Trade payables (Bills payable and sundry creditors)
  (c) Other short-term liabilities
  (d) Short-term provisions

NOTE As per CBSE circular, accounting treatment of 'other current assets' is restricted to prepaid expenses, advance tax and accrued income only.

2. Solvency (Long-term Solvency) Ratios

Solvency ratios judge the long-term financial position of an enterprise, *i.e.* whether business is able to pay its long-term liabilities or not.

(i) Debt to Equity Ratio

It establishes the relationship between long-term debt (external equities) and the equity (internal equities), *i.e.* shareholders' funds. It is computed to ascertain soundness of the long-term financial position of the firm. Generally, the ratio of 2 : 1 is considered as an ideal.

$$\left[\text{Debt to Equity Ratio} = \frac{\text{Debt (Long-term external equities)}}{\text{Equity (Shareholders' funds)}}\right]$$

- **Items Included in Long-term Debts** It includes long-term borrowings and long-term provisions.
- **Items Included in Equity or Shareholders' Funds**

  Equity or Shareholders' Funds = Equity Share Capital + Preference Share Capital + Reserves and Surplus

Or *Non-current Asset (Tangible assets + Intangible assets + Non-current trade investments + Long-term loans and advances) + Working Capital** – Non-current Liabilities (Long-term borrowings + Long-term provisions)

**Working Capital = Current Assets – Current Liabilities

NOTE *As per CBSE circular, accounting treatment of 'other non-current assets' and 'other long-term liabilities' is not to be evaluated.

(ii) Debt to Capital Employed Ratio

This ratio expresses the relation between long-term debt and capital employed/net assets (total of external and internal funds). Low ratio provides security to lenders and high ratio helps management in trading on equity.

$$\left[\text{Debt to Capital Employed Ratio} = \frac{\text{Long-term Debt}}{\text{Capital Employed (or Net Assets)}}\right]$$

- **Items Included in Long-term Debt**

  (a) Long-term borrowings (b) Long-term provision

- **Items Included in Capital Employed**

  (a) Long-term debt (b) Shareholders' funds

(iii) Total Assets to Debt Ratio

It establishes relationship between total assets and total long-term debts.

$$\left[\text{Total Assets to Debt Ratio} = \frac{\text{Total Assets}}{\text{Long-term Debts}}\right]$$

- **Items Included in Total Assets**

  (a) *Non-current Assets [Fixed assets (Tangible and intangible assets) + Non-current Investments + Long-term Loans and Advances]

(b) Current Assets [Current investments + Inventories (including spare parts and loose tools) + Trade Receivables + Cash and Cash Equivalents + Short-term Loans and Advances + Other Current Assets]

- **Items Included in Long-term Debts**

(a) Long-term borrowings (b) Long-term provisions

NOTE *As per CBSE circular, accounting treatment of 'other non-current assets', 'other long-term liabilities' and 'deferred tax assets (net)' is not to be evaluated.

(iv) Proprietary Ratio

It establishes the relationship between proprietors' funds and total assets. This ratio shows the portion of shareholders' funds in the total assets of the business.

$$\left[\text{Proprietary Ratio} = \frac{\text{Proprietors' Funds or Shareholders' Funds}}{\text{Total Assets}}\right]$$

- **Proprietors' Funds or Shareholders' Funds**

Liabilities Approach Share Capital + Reserves and Surplus

Or **Assets Approach**

*Non-current Assets (Tangible assets + Intangible assets + Non-current trade investments + Long-term loans and advances) + Working Capital – Non-current Liabilities (Long-term borrowings + Long-term provisions)

- **Total Assets** It includes

(a) Non-current Assets [Fixed assets (Tangible and intangible assets) + Non-current Investments + Long-term Loans and Advances]

(b) Current Assets [Current investments + Inventories (including spare parts and loose tools) + Trade Receivables + Cash and Cash Equivalents + Short-term Loans and Advances + Other Current Assets]

NOTE *As per CBSE circular, money received against share warrants, share application money pending allotment, deferred tax liabilities (net), deferred tax assets (net), other long-term liabilities, other non-current assets and other current assets (unamortised expenses) are not to be evaluated.

(v) Interest Coverage Ratio or Debt Service Ratio

This ratio expresses the relationship between net profit before interest and tax and interest payable on long-term debts. The ideal interest coverage ratio is 6 to 7 times.

$$\left[\text{Interest Coverage Ratio} = \frac{\text{Net Profit before Interest and Tax}}{\text{Interest on Long-term Debts}}\right]$$

3. Turnover or Performance or Activity Ratios

These ratios measure how efficiently a company is using its assets to generate sales. These ratios are expressed in times.

(i) Inventory (Stock) Turnover Ratio

This ratio shows the relationship between the cost of revenue from operations during a given period and the average amount of inventory carried during that period. It indicates the number of times the stock is turned into sales during the accounting period, *i.e.* it measures how fast the stock is moving through the firm and generating sales.

$$\left[\text{Inventory Turnover Ratio} = \frac{\text{Cost of Revenue from Operations, } i.e. \text{ Cost of Goods Sold}}{\text{Average Inventory}}\right]$$

- **Cost of Revenue from Operations, *i.e.* Cost of Goods Sold**

= Cost of Materials Consumed + Purchases of Stock-in-trade + Changes in Inventories of Finished Goods, Work-in-progress and Stock-in-trade + Direct Expenses

Or = Opening Inventory + Purchases + Direct Expenses – Closing Inventory

Or = Revenue from Operations (Sales) – Gross Profit

- **Average Inventory** $= \frac{\text{Opening Inventory + Closing Inventory}}{2}$

(ii) Trade Receivables or Debtors Turnover Ratio

This ratio depicts the relationship between credit revenue from operations and average trade receivables of the year. It indicates economy and efficiency in the collection of amount due from debtors.

$$\left[\text{Debtors / Trade Receivables Turnover Ratio} = \frac{\text{Credit Revenue from Operations, } i.e. \text{ Net Credit Sales}}{\text{Average Trade Receivables}}\right]$$

- **Credit Revenue from Operations** = Credit Revenue from Operations – Sales Return

Or = Revenue from Operations – Cash Revenue from Operations

- **Average Trade Receivables** = Opening Receivables (Debtors + Bills Receivable) $+ \frac{\text{Closing Receivables (Debtors + Bills receivable)}}{2}$

If information about opening balances of debtors and bills receivable is missing then, only closing debtors and bills receivable will be considered.

Also, if credit sales are not specified, then total sales will be deemed to be as credit sales.

$$\text{Average Collection Period} = \frac{\text{Number of Days / Weeks / Months in a Year}}{\text{Trade Receivables or Debtors Turnover Ratio}}$$

(iii) Trade Payables or Creditors Turnover Ratio

This ratio shows the relationship between net credit purchases and total payables or average payables. It indicates the speed with which the amount is being paid to creditors. The higher the ratio, the better it is.

$$\left[\text{Creditors / Trade Payables Turnover Ratio} = \frac{\text{Net Credit Purchases}}{\text{Average Trade Payables}}\right]$$

- **Net Credit Purchases** = Net Purchases – Cash Purchases

- **Average Trade Payables**

$$= \frac{\text{Opening Payables (Creditors + Bills payable) + Closing Payables (Creditors + Bills payable)}}{2}$$

In the absence of opening creditors and bills payable, closing creditors and bills payable can be used in the above formula.

Also, if credit purchases are not given, then all purchases are deemed to be on credit.

$$\text{Average Payment Period} = \frac{\text{Number of Days / Weeks / Months in a Year}}{\text{Trade Payables or Creditors Turnover Ratio}}$$

(iv) Working Capital Turnover Ratio

This ratio shows the relationship between working capital and revenue from operations. It shows the number of times the working capital has been rotated in generating sales.

$$\left[\text{Working Capital Turnover Ratio} = \frac{\text{Cost of Revenue from Operations or Revenue from Operations, } i.e. \text{ Net Sales}}{\text{Working Capital}}\right]$$

- **Working Capital** = Current Assets – Current Liabilities

(v) Net Asset/Capital Employed Turnover Ratio

This ratio expresses the relationship between revenue from operations and net assets in the business

$$\left[\text{Net Asset/ Capital Employed Turnover Ratio} = \frac{\text{Revenue from Operations}}{\text{Capital Employed}}\right]$$

- **Items Included in Capital Employed**

  (a) Long-term debt (b) Shareholders' funds

(vi) Fixed Asset Turnover Ratio

This ratio expresses relationship between net revenue from operations and net fixed assets.
A higher ratio implies that management is using its fixed assets more effectively.

$$\left[\text{Fixed Asset Turnover Ratio} = \frac{\text{Net Revenue from Operations}}{\text{Net Fixed Assets}}\right]$$

4. Profitability Ratios

These ratios measure the profitability of a business and helps in assessing the overall efficiency of the business. These ratios are expressed in percentage form.

(i) Gross Profit Ratio

This ratio shows the relationship between the gross profit and revenue from operations (net sales)

$$\left[\text{Gross Profit Ratio} = \frac{\text{Gross Profit}}{\text{Revenue from Operations, } i.e. \text{ Net Sales}} \times 100\right]$$

- **Gross Profit** = Net Revenue from Operations, *i.e.* Sales – *Cost of Revenue from Operations, *i.e.* Cost of Goods Sold

- ***Cost of Revenue from Operations** = Opening Inventory (excluding spare parts and loose tools) + Purchases + Direct Expenses – Closing Inventory (excluding spare parts and loose tools)

Or In case, statement of profit and loss is given, cost of revenue from operations *i.e.* cost of goods sold is computed by adding cost of materials consumed, purchases of stock-in-trade, changes in inventories of finished goods, work-in-progress and stock-in-trade and direct expenses.

Or Revenue from Operations – Gross Profit

(ii) Operating Ratio (Operating cost ratio)

This ratio establishes the relationship between operating cost and revenue from operations i.e. net sales.

$$\left[\text{Operating Ratio} = \frac{\text{Operating Cost}}{\text{Revenue from Operations (Net sales)}} \times 100 \right.$$

Or

$$\left. = \frac{\text{Cost of Revenue from Operations} + \text{Operating Expenses}}{\text{Revenue from Operations, } i.e. \text{ Net Sales}} \times 100 \right]$$

- **Operating Cost** These are the cost which are associated with the operating activities of the business, *e.g.* employees benefit expenses and other expenses.

Non-operating incomes and expenses (*i.e.* those incomes and expenses which are not incurred for the operating activities of the business) are excluded.

Alternatively operating cost may be calculated as follows

Operating Cost = Cost of Materials Consumed + Purchases of Stock-in-trade + Change in Inventories of Finished Goods, Work-in-progress and Stock-in-trade + Employees Benefits Expenses + Other Expenses (Other than non-operating expenses)

- **Cost of Revenue from Operations** = Cost of Materials Consumed + Purchases of Stock-in-trade + Change in Inventories of Finished Goods, Work-in-progress and Stock in-trade + Direct Expenses

Or Revenue from Operations – Gross Profit

Or Operating Inventory (excluding spare parts and loose tools) + Net Purchase + Direct Expenses – Closing Inventory (excluding spare parts and loose tools)

- **Operating Expenses** = Employees Benefits Expenses + Other Expenses (Other than non-operating expenses) + Depreciation and Amortisation expenses

Or Office expenses, administrative expenses, selling and distribution expenses, employees benefit expenses, depreciation and amortisation expenses.

(iii) Operating Profit Ratio

This ratio establishes the relationship between the operating profit and revenue from operations, *i.e.* net sales. Operating profit ratio is an indicator of operational efficiency of the business.

$$\left[\text{Operating Profit Ratio} = \frac{\text{Operating Profit}}{\text{Revenue from Operations, } i.e. \text{ Net Sales}} \times 100\right]$$

- **Operating Profit** = Net Profit (Before tax) + Non–operating Expenses/Losses – Non-operating Income

Or

Gross Profit + Other Operating Income – Other Operating Expenses

Or

Revenue from Operations – Operating Cost

(iv) Net Profit Ratio

Net profit ratio shows the relationship between net profit and revenue from operations, *i.e.* net sales. Net profit ratio is an indicator of overall operational efficiency of the business.

$$\left[\text{Net Profit Ratio} = \frac{\text{Net Profit after Tax}}{\text{Revenue from Operations, } i.e. \text{ Net Sales}} \times 100\right]$$

- **Net Profit** = Revenue from Operations – Cost of Revenue from Operations – Operating Expenses – Non-operating Expenses + Non-operating Income – Tax

(v) Return on Investment/Capital Employed

It establishes the relationship between net profit before interest, tax and preference dividend and capital employed (equity + debts).

$$\left[\text{Return on Investment} = \frac{\text{Net Profit before Interest, Tax and Preference Dividend}}{\text{Capital Employed}} \times 100\right]$$

- **Capital employed** can be calculated from liabilities side approach and assets side approach as follows

  When Liabilities Approach is Followed It is computed by adding
  (a) Shareholders' funds (*i.e.* share capital, reserves and surplus).
  (b) Non-current liabilities (*i.e.* long-term borrowings and long-term provisions).

  When Assets Approach is Followed It is computed by adding
  (*i*) Non-current assets, *i.e.*
    (a) Fixed assets (tangible fixed assets, intangible fixed assets).
    (b) Non-current trade investments. (It is assumed that all non-current investments are trade investments).
    (c) Long-term loans and advances.
  (*ii*) Working Capital, *i.e.* Current Assets – Current Liabilities

  NOTE Since, non-operating assets are excluded while determining capital employed, income from non-operating assets should also be excluded from profit.

Previous Years' Examination Questions

1 Mark Questions

1. 'Purchase of goods ₹ 35,000 for cash will increase the operating ratio'. Is the statement correct? Give reasons. **CBSE 2020**

Ans. No. Since, it will increase purchases as well as closing stock also.

2. State with reason whether repayment of long-term loan will result in increase, decrease or no change of debt equity ratio. **All India 2012**

Ans. Debt-equity ratio will decrease as repayment of long-term loan will reduce the long- term debt but the shareholders' funds will remain same.

2 Marks Questions

3. A company had current assets ₹ 3,00,000 and current liabilities ₹ 1,40,000. Afterwards, it purchased goods worth ₹ 20,000 on credit. Calculate the current ratio after the purchase of goods.
All India 2019

Ans. New current assets = 3,00,000 + 20,000

= ₹ 3,20,000

New current liabilities = 1,40,000 + 20,000

= ₹ 1,60,000

$$\text{Current Ratio} = \frac{\text{Current Assets}}{\text{Current Liabilities}}$$

$$= \frac{3,20,000}{1,60,000} = 2:1$$

4. From the following information calculate interest coverage ratio. Net profit after interest and tax ₹ 1,20,000; Rate of income tax 40% ; 15% debentures ₹ 1,00,000; 12% mortgage loan ₹ 10,000.
All India 2019

Ans. Rate of tax 40%

Profit after tax = 100 − 40 = 60%

and according to question profit after tax is ₹ 1,20,000.

So, profit before tax = $\frac{1,20,000}{60\%}$ = 2,00,000

(+)	Interest on debentures	=	15,000
	Interest on mortgage loan	=	12,000
	Net profit before interest and tax		2,27,000

Interest Coverage Ratio

$$= \frac{\text{Net Profit before Interest and Tax}}{\text{Interest on Long-term Debt}}$$

$$= \frac{2,27,000}{27,000} = 8.407 \text{ times}$$

5. What is meant by 'profitability ratios'?
All India 2016

Ans. Profitability ratios measure the profitability of a business. Profitability ratios help in assessing the overall efficiency of the business. These ratios are calculated to analyse the earning capacity of the business which is the outcome of utilisation of resources employed in the business. Various profitability ratios commonly used to analyse the earning capacity of the business are gross profit ratio, net profit ratio, operating ratio, return on investment, operating profit ratio.

6. The current ratio of Y Ltd is 2 : 1. State with reason, which of the following transactions would (a) increase, (b) decrease or (c) not change the ratio

(*i*) Trade receivables included debtors of ₹ 40,000 which were received.

(*ii*) Company purchased furniture of ₹ 45,000. The vendor was paid by issue of equity shares of ₹ 10 each at par.
Delhi 2014

Ans. (*i*) **Not change the ratio** Simultaneous increase and decrease by same amount in current assets will not effect the value of current assets or current liabilities, therefore, there is no effect on the current ratio.

(*ii*) **Not change the ratio** Issue of shares for furniture purchased do not effect either current assets or current liabilities. Therefore, current ratio will not be effected.

7. The quick ratio of Z Ltd is 1:1. State with reason which of the following transactions would (a) increase, (b) decrease or (c) not change the ratio

(*i*) Included in the trade payables was a bills payable of ₹ 3,000 which was met on maturity.

(*ii*) Debentures of ₹ 50,000 were converted into equity shares. **Delhi 2014**

Ans. (*i*) **Not change the ratio** Simultaneous decrease in both current assets and current liabilities will not effect the quick ratio.

(*ii*) **Not change the ratio** Debentures converted into shares do not effect either quick assets or current liabilities. Therefore, quick ratio will not be effected.

3 Marks Questions

8. Calculate the Current Ratio and Debt-equity Ratio from the following information **CBSE 2020**

	Amt (₹)
Non-current Assets	16,00,000
Current Assets	4,00,000
Working Capital	2,00,000
Non-current Liabilities	12,00,000

Ans. (i) Current Liabilities = Current Assets – Working Capital = 4,00,000 – 2,00,000 = ₹ 2,00,000

$$\text{Current Ratio} = \frac{\text{Current Assets}}{\text{Current Liabilities}} = \frac{4,00,000}{2,00,000} = 2:1$$

(ii) Equity = Total Assets – Liabilities
= 20,00,000 – 14,00,000 = ₹ 6,00,000

$$\text{Debt-equity Ratio} = \frac{\text{Debt}}{\text{Equity}} = \frac{12,00,000}{6,00,000} = 2:1$$

9. From the following information, determine the opening inventory and the closing inventory

Inventory Turnover Ratio = 5 times
Revenue from Operations = ₹ 8,00,000
Gross Profit Ratio = 25%
Closing inventory was ₹ 20,000 more than the opening inventory. **CBSE 2020**

Ans. Revenue from Operations = ₹ 8,00,000
Gross Profit = Revenue from Operations × Gross Profit Ratio

$$= 8,00,000 \times \frac{25}{100} = ₹\ 2,00,000$$

Cost of Revenue from Operations
= 8,00,000 – 2,00,000 = ₹ 6,00,000

Average Inventory

$$= \frac{\text{Cost of Revenue from Operations}}{\text{Inventory Turnover Ratio}}$$

$$= \frac{6,00,000}{5} = ₹\ 1,20,000$$

Let opening inventory be ₹ x
∴ Closing inventory will be ₹ x + 20,000

$$\text{Hence, average inventory} = \frac{x + x + 20,000}{2}$$

$$\frac{2x + 20,000}{2} = 1,20,000$$

$$2x + 20,000 = 1,20,000 \times 2$$

$$2x = 2,40,000 - 20,000$$

$$x = \frac{2,20,000}{2};\ x = ₹\ 1,10,000$$

Opening inventory = ₹ 1,10,000
∴ Closing inventory = x + 20,000 = 1,10,000 + 20,000 = ₹ 1,30,000

10. X Ltd has a current ratio of 3 : 1 and quick ratio of 2 :1. If the excess of current assets over quick assets as represented by inventory is ₹ 40,000, calculate current assets and current liabilities. **All India 2012**

Ans. Let the current liabilities = x

$$\text{Current Ratio} = 3:1, \text{ i.e. } \frac{\text{Current Assets}}{\text{Current Liabilities}} = \frac{3}{1}$$

Therefore, Current assets = $3x$

$$\text{Quick Ratio} = 2:1, \textit{ i.e. } \frac{\text{Liquid Assets}}{\text{Current Liabilities}} = \frac{2}{1}$$

Therefore, quick or liquid assets = $2x$

Liquid Assets = Current Assets – Inventory

$$2x = 3x - 40,000$$
$$2x - 3x = -40,000$$
$$-x = -40,000$$
$$x = 40,000$$

Current Liabilities = ₹ 40,000
Current Assets = 3 × ₹ 40,000 = ₹ 1,20,000

11. OM Ltd has a current ratio of 3.5 : 1 and quick ratio of 2 : 1. If the excess of current assets over quick assets as represented by inventory is ₹ 1,50,000, calculate current assets and current liabilities. **Delhi 2012**

Ans. Solve as Q. no. 10 on page 391.
Current Liabilities = ₹ 1,00,000;
Current Assets = ₹ 3,50,000

12. On basis of the following information, calculate

(*i*) Debt equity ratio
(*ii*) Working capital turnover ratio **Dehli 2011**

Information	Amt (₹)
Revenue from operations	60,00,000
Cost of revenue operations	45,00,000
Other current assets	11,00,000
Current liabilities	4,00,000
Paid-up share capital	6,00,000
6% debentures	3,00,000
9% loan	1,00,000
Debenture redemption reserve	2,00,000
Closing inventory	1,00,000

Ans. (*i*) Debt Equity Ratio

$$= \frac{\text{Debt}}{\text{Equity}} = \frac{\text{Long-term Debts or Loans*}}{\text{Shareholders' Funds**}}$$

$$= \frac{4,00,000}{8,00,000} = 1:2$$

*Long-term Debts = 6% Debentures + 9% Loan
= 3,00,000 + 1,00,000 = ₹ 4,00,000

**Shareholders' Funds = Paid-up Share Capital + Debenture Redemption Reserve
= 6,00,000 + 2,00,000 = ₹ 8,00,000

(*ii*) Working Capital Turnover Ratio

$$= \frac{\text{Revenue from Operations}}{\text{Working Capital*}}$$

$$= \frac{60,00,000}{8,00,000} = 7.5 \text{ times}$$

*Working Capital = Current Assets** – Current Liabilities***
= 12,00,000 – 4,00,000
= ₹ 8,00,000

**Current Assets = Other Current Assets + Closing Inventory
= 11,00,000 + 1,00,000
= ₹ 12,00,000

***Current Liabilities = ₹ 4,00,000

13. The quick ratio of a company is 2 : 1. State giving reasons, (for any four) which of the following would improve, reduce or not change the ratio

(*i*) Purchase of machinery for cash
(*ii*) Purchase of goods on credit
(*iii*) Sale of furniture at cost
(*iv*) Sale of goods at a profit
(*v*) Cash received from debtors

Delhi (C) 2011

Ans. (*i*) **Purchase of Machinery for Cash**

Effect Reduce

Reason Purchase of machinery for cash will decrease the quick assets, but the current liabilities will remain unchanged.

(*ii*) **Purchase of Goods on Credit**

Effect Reduce

Reason Purchase of goods on credit will increase the current liabilities, but the quick assets will remain unchanged.

(*iii*) **Sale of Furniture at Cost**

Effect Improve

Reason Sale of furniture at cost will increase the quick assets, but the current liabilities will remain unchanged.

(*iv*) **Sale of Goods at a Profit**

Effect Improve

Reason Sale of goods at a profit will increase the quick assets, but the current liabilities will remain unchanged.

(*v*) **Cash Received from Debtors**

Effect No change

Reason Cash received from debtors will not change the quick assets because the quick assets are increased and decreased with the same amount, and the current liabilities remain unchanged.

14. The debt equity ratio of a company is 1:1 state giving reasons, (any four) which of the following would improve, reduce or not change the ratio

(*i*) Purchase of machinery for cash
(*ii*) Purchase of goods on credit
(*iii*) Sale of furniture at cost
(*iv*) Sale of goods at a profit
(*v*) Redemption of debentures at a premium **All India (C) 2011**

Ans. (*i*) **Purchase of Machinery for Cash**

Effect No change

Reason Neither the long-term debt nor the shareholders' funds are affected by purchase of machinery for cash.

(*ii*) **Purchase of Goods on Credit**

Effect No change

Reason Neither the long-term debt nor the shareholders' funds are affected by purchase of goods on credit.

(*iii*) **Sale of Furniture at Cost**

Effect No change

Reason Neither the long-term debt nor the shareholders' funds are affected by sell of furniture at cost.

(*iv*) **Sale of Goods at a Profit**

Effect Reduce

Reason Shareholders' funds are increased by the amount of profit on sale of goods, but the long-term debts remain unchanged.

(*v*) **Redemption of Debentures at a Premium**

Effect Reduce

Reason Redemption of debentures will reduce the long-term debts, but shareholders' funds remain unchanged. Here,it is assumed that premium payable on redemption of debenture is written-off through existing securities premium reserve.

15. Assuming that the debt equity ratio is 2 : 1. State giving reasons whether this ratio would increase, decrease or remain unchanged in the following cases. (Any four)

(*i*) Purchase of fixed assets on a credit of two months
(*ii*) Purchase of fixed assets on long-term deferred payment basis
(*iii*) Issue of new shares for cash
(*iv*) Issue of bonus shares
(*v*) Sale of fixed assets at a loss of ₹ 3,000.

Delhi; All India 2010

Ans. (*i*) **Purchase of Fixed Assets on a Credit of Two Months**

Effect No change

Reason Neither the long-term debt nor the shareholders' funds are affected by purchase of fixed assets on a credit of two months.

(*ii*) **Purchase of Fixed Assets on a Long-term Deferred Payment Basis**

Effect Increase

Reason The long-term debts are increased by the purchase of fixed assets on a long-term deferred payment basis, but the shareholders' fund remains unchanged.

(*iii*) **Issue of New Shares for Cash**

Effect Decrease

Reason Shareholders' funds are increased by the issue of new shares for cash, but the long-term debts remain unchanged.

(*iv*) **Issue of Bonus Shares**

Effect No change

Reason Shareholders' funds increase and decrease by the same amount.

(*v*) **Sale of Fixed Assets at a Loss of ₹ 3,000**

Effect Increase

Reason The shareholders' funds will reduce by the amount of loss of 3,000, but the long-term debt remain unchanged.

16. From the following information, calculate any two of the following ratios

(*i*) Current ratio
(*ii*) Debt equity ratio
(*iii*) Inventory turnover ratio

Information

Revenue from operations (Net sales) ₹ 5,00,000 , opening inventory ₹ 7,000, closing inventory ₹ 4,000 more than the opening inventory, net purchase ₹ 1,00,000 less than revenue from operations, operating expenses ₹ 30,000, liquid assets ₹ 75,000, prepaid expenses ₹ 2,000, current liabilities ₹ 60,000, 9% debentures ₹ 3,00,000, long-term loan from bank ₹ 1,00,000, equity share capital ₹ 10,00,000 and 8% preference share capital ₹ 2,00,000. **Delhi (C) 2010**

Ans. (*i*) $\text{Current Ratio} = \frac{\text{Current Assets *}}{\text{Current Liabilities}}$

$= \frac{88,000}{60,000} = 1.47 : 1$

*Current Assets = Liquid Assets + Closing Inventory** + Prepaid Expenses

= 75,000 + 11,000 + 2,000

= ₹ 88,000

**Closing Inventory = Opening Inventory + 4,000

= 7,000 + 4,000 = ₹ 11,000

(*ii*) Debt Equity Ratio

$= \frac{\text{Debt}}{\text{Equity}}$ *Or* $\frac{\text{Long-term Debts or Loans *}}{\text{Shareholders' Funds **}}$

$= \frac{4,00,000}{12,00,000} = 0.33 : 1$

*Long-term Debts = 9% Debentures + Long-term Loan from Bank

= 3,00,000 + 1,00,000 = ₹ 4,00,000

**Shareholders' Funds = Equity Share Capital + Preference Share Capital

= 10,00,000 + 2,00,000 = ₹ 12,00,000

(*iii*) Inventory Turnover Ratio

$= \frac{\text{Cost of Revenue from Operations (Cost of goods sold) *}}{\text{Average Inventory **}}$

$= \frac{3,96,000}{9,000} = 44 \text{ times}$

*Cost of Revenue from Operations

= Opening Inventory + Net Purchases − Closing Inventory

= 7,000 + (5,00,000 − 1,00,000) − 11,000

= ₹ 3,96,000

$$**\text{Average Inventory} = \frac{\text{Opening Inventory} + \text{Closing Inventory}}{2}$$

$$= \frac{7,000 + 11,000}{2} = ₹\ 9,000$$

17. From the following information, calculate any two of the following ratios

(i) Liquid ratio (ii) Gross profit ratio (iii) Debt equity ratio

Information

Revenue from operations (Net sales) ₹ 4,00,000, opening inventory ₹ 10,000, closing inventory ₹ 3,000 less than the opening inventory, net purchase 80% of revenue from operations, direct expenses ₹ 20,000, current assets ₹ 1,00,000, prepaid expenses ₹ 3,000, current liabilities ₹ 60,000, 9% debentures ₹ 4,00,000, long-term loan from bank ₹ 1,50,000, equity share capital ₹ 8,00,000 and 8% preference share capital ₹ 3,00,000. **All India (C) 2010**

Ans. (i) $\text{Liquid Ratio} = \frac{\text{Current Assets} - \text{Inventory} - \text{Prepaid Expenses}}{\text{Current Liabilities}} = \frac{1,00,000 - 7,000 - 3,000}{60,000} = \frac{90,000}{60,000} = 1.5:1$

Closing Inventory = Opening Inventory − 3,000 = 10,000 − 3,000 = ₹ 7,000

(ii) $\text{Gross Profit Ratio} = \frac{\text{Gross Profit}^*}{\text{Revenue from Operations (Net sales)}} \times 100 = \frac{57,000}{4,00,000} \times 100 = 14.25\%$

Net Purchases = 80% of Revenue from Operations = $4,00,000 \times \frac{80}{100}$ = ₹ 3,20,000

Cost of Revenue from Operations = Opening Inventory + Net Purchases + Direct Expenses − Closing Inventory

= 10,000 + 3,20,000 + 20,000 − 7,000 = ₹ 3,43,000

*Gross Profit = Revenue from Operations − Cost of Revenue from Operations

= 4,00,000 − 3,43,000 = ₹ 57,000

(iii) $\text{Debt Equity Ratio} = \frac{\text{Debt}}{\text{Equity}}$ *Or* $\frac{\text{Long-term Debts}^*}{\text{Shareholders' Funds}^{**}} = \frac{5,50,000}{11,00,000} = 0.5:1$

*Long-term Debts = 9% Debentures + Long-term Loan from Bank

= 4,00,000 + 1,50,000 = ₹ 5,50,000

**Shareholders' Funds = Equity Share Capital + 8% Preference Share Capital

= 8,00,000 + 3,00,000 = ₹ 11,00,000

4 Marks Questions

18. Quick ratio of a company is 1 : 1. State, with reason, whether the following transactions will increase, decrease or not change the ratio

(i) Paid insurance premium in advance ₹ 10,000.

(ii) Purchased goods on credit ₹ 8,000.

(iii) Issued fully paid equity shares of ₹ 1,00,000.

(iv) Issued 9% debentures of ₹ 5,00,000 to the vendor for machinery purchased. **All India 2019**

Ans. (i) Decrease

As payment of insurance premium will decrease the quick assets.

(ii) Decrease

As purchase of goods on credit will increase the current liabilities.

(iii) Increase

As issue of equity shares will increase quick assets.

(iv) No change

As issue of debentures to vendor of machinery would have no impact on quick assets and current liabilities.

19. From the following information of Shiva Ltd, calculate total assets to debt ratio

Information	Amt (₹)
Equity Share Capital	5,00,000
9% Preference Share Capital	4,00,000
Fixed Assets	12,00,000
Non-current Investments	1,50,000
Reserves and Surplus	2,40,000
Current Assets	1,90,000
Current Liabilities	1,00,000

All India 2019

Ans. Total Assets = Fixed Assets + Non-current Investments + Current Assets

= 12,00,000 + 1,50,000 + 1,90,000 = ₹ 15,40,000

Now, Total Liabilities = Total Assets

Equity Share Capital + 9% Preference Share Capital + Reserve and Surplus

+ Non-current Liabilities (Debt) + Current Liabilities = ₹ 15,40,000

5,00,000 + 4,00,000 + 2,40,000 + 1,00,000 + Non-current Liabilities = ₹15,40,000

Non-current Liabilities (Debt) = 15,40,000 − 12,40,000 = ₹ 3,00,000

Now, Total Assets to Debt Ratio $= \frac{\text{Total Assets}}{\text{Debt}} = \frac{15,40,000}{3,00,000} = 5.133 : 1$

20. (*i*) Calculate revenue from operations of BN Ltd. From the following information

Current assets	₹ 8,00,000
Quick ratio is	1.5 : 1
Current ratio is	2 : 1
Inventory turnover ratio is	6 times

(*ii*) The operating ratio of a company is 60%. State whether 'Purchase of goods costing ₹ 20,000' will increase, decrease or not change the operating ratio. **Delhi 2019**

Ans. (*i*) Current assets = ₹ 8,00,000

Current ratio = 2:1 $\Rightarrow \frac{\text{Current Assets}}{\text{Current Liabilities}} = \frac{2}{1}$

$\frac{8,00,000}{\text{Current Liabilities}} = \frac{2}{1}$; Current Liabilities = ₹ 4,00,000 ...(1)

Quick Ratio $= \frac{\text{Quick Assets}}{\text{Current Liablities}}$

$\frac{1.5}{1} = \frac{\text{Quick Assets}}{4,00,000}$

Quick Assets = ₹ 6,00,000 ...(2)

Inventory = Current Assets − Quick Assets

= 8,00,000 − 6,00,000 = ₹ 2,00,000 ...(3)

Inventory Turnover Ratio $= \frac{\text{Cost of Revenue from Operations}}{\text{Average Inventory}}$

$6 = \frac{\text{Cost of Revenue from Operations}}{2,00,000}$

Cost of Revenue from Operations = ₹ 12,00,000 ...(4)

Profit = 25% on cost = 12,00,000 × 25% = ₹ 3,00,000 ...(5)

Revenue from Operations = 12,00,000 + 3,00,000 = ₹ 15,00,000

(*ii*) No Change

Purchase of goods will increase operating cost as well as cost of goods sold.

21. (*i*) Calculate 'Total assets to debt ratio' from the following information

Information	Amt (₹)
Equity Share Capital	4,00,000
Long-term Borrowings	1,80,000
Surplus, i.e. Balance in Statement of Profit and Loss	1,00,000
General Reserve	70,000
Current Liabilities	30,000
Long-term Provisions	1,20,000

(*ii*) The debt equity ratio of a company is 1 : 2. State whether 'Issue of bonus shares' will increase, decrease or not change the debt equity ratio. **Delhi 2019**

Ans. (*i*) Total Liabilities = Equity Share Capital + Long-term Borrowings + Surplus + General Reserve + Current Liabilities + Long-term Provisions

= 4,00,000 + 1,80,000 + 1,00,000 + 70,000 + 30,000 + 1,20,000 = ₹ 9,00,000

Total Assets = Total Liabilities = ₹ 9,00,000

Long-term Debt = Long-term Borrowings + Long-term Provisions

= 1,80,000 + 1,20,000 = ₹ 3,00,000

$$\text{Total Assets to Debt Ratio} = \frac{\text{Total Assets}}{\text{Long-term Debt}} = \frac{9,00,000}{3,00,000} = 3:1$$

(*ii*) Decrease

As issue of bonus shares will increase the shareholders funds/equity.

22. The operating ratio of a company is 80%. State whether the following transactions will increase, decrease or not change the ratio

(*i*) Purchased goods on credit ₹ 20,000

(*ii*) Paid wages ₹ 5,000

(*iii*) Redeemed ₹ 8,000, 9% debentures

(*iv*) Sold goods ₹ 50,000 for cash. **All India 2019**

Ans. (*i*) Purchased goods on credit ₹ 20,000

⇒ No change

As both purchase and closing stock will increase, so there will be no effect on cost of goods sold.

(*ii*) Paid wages ₹ 5,000

⇒ Increase

As wages paid will increase the operating cost.

(*iii*) Redeemed ₹ 8,000, 9% Debentures

⇒ No change

As redemption of debentures is a non-operating activity.

(*iv*) Sold goods ₹ 50,000 for cash

⇒ Decrease

As goods sold will increase the net sales.

23. From the following information obtained from the books of Kundan Ltd, calculate the inventory turnover ratio for the years 2015-16 and 2016-17.

	2015-16 (₹)	2016-17 (₹)
Inventory on 31st March	7,00,000	17,00,000
Revenue from Operations	50,00,000	75,00,000

(Gross profit is 25% on cost of revenue from operations)

In the year 2015-16, inventory increased by ₹ 2,00,000. **CBSE 2018**

Ans. **For 2015-16**

$$\text{Inventory Turnover Ratio} = \frac{\text{Cost of Revenue from Operations}^*}{\text{Average Inventory}^{**}} = \frac{40,00,000}{6,00,000} = 6.67 \text{ times}$$

$$^*\text{Cost of Revenue from Operations} = \text{Revenue from Operations} - \text{Gross Profit}$$

$$= 50,00,000 - 10,00,000\left(50,00,000 \times \frac{25}{125}\right) = ₹\ 40,00,000$$

$$^{**}\text{Average Inventory} = \frac{\text{Operating Inventory} + \text{Closing Inventory}}{2} = \frac{5,00,000 + 7,00,000}{2} = ₹\ 6,00,000$$

For 2016-17

$$\text{Inventory Turnover Ratio} = \frac{\text{Cost of Revenue from Operations}^*}{\text{Average Inventory}^{**}} = \frac{60,00,000}{12,00,000} = 5 \text{ times}$$

$$^*\text{Cost of Revenue from Operations} = \text{Revenue from Operations} - \text{Gross Profit}$$

$$= 75,00,000 - 15,00,000\left(75,00,000 \times \frac{25}{125}\right) = ₹\ 60,00,000$$

$$^{**}\text{ Average Inventory} = \frac{\text{Operating Inventory} + \text{Closing Inventory}}{2} = \frac{7,00,000 + 17,00,000}{2} = ₹\ 12,00,000$$

24. Y Ltd's profits after insterest and tax was ₹ 1,00,000. Its current assets were ₹ 4,00,000 current liabilities ₹ 2,00,000; fixed assets ₹ 6,00,000 and 10% long-term debt ₹ 4,00,000. The rate of tax was 20%. Calculate 'Return on Investment' of Y Ltd. **Compartment 2018**

Ans. Net profit after interest and tax = ₹ 1,00,000

$(+)$ Tax $1,00,000 \times \frac{20}{80}$ = ₹ 25,000

$(+)$ Interest $4,00,000 \times 10\%$ = ₹ 40,000

Net profit before interest and tax ₹ 1,65,000

Working Capital = Current Assets − Current Liabilities

= 4,00,000 − 2,00,000 = ₹ 2,00,000

Capital Employed = Fixed Assets + Working Capital

= 6,00,000 + 2,00,000 = ₹ 8,00,000

Return on Investment

$$= \frac{\text{Net Profit before Interest and Tax}}{\text{Capital Employed}} \times 100 = \frac{1,65,000}{8,00,000} \times 100 = 20.625\%$$

25. A company earn gross profit 25% on cost. For the year ended 31st March, 2017 its gross profit was ₹ 5,00,000; equity share capital of the company was ₹ 10,00,000; reserves and surplus ₹ 2,00,000; long-term loan ₹ 3,00,000 and non-current assets were ₹ 10,00,000.

Compute the 'working capital turnover ratio' of the company. **Compartment 2018**

Ans. Gross Profit = 25% on cost

Gross profit ₹ 5,00,000

$\therefore$ Revenue from Operation $= \frac{125}{25} \times 5,00,000$

$= ₹\ 25,00,000$

Working Capital = Equity Share Capital + Reserve and Surplus + Long-term Loan − Non-current Assets

= 10,00,000 + 2,00,000 + 3,00,000 − 10,00,000

= ₹ 5,00,000

Working Capital Turnover Ratio

$= \frac{\text{Revenue from Operation}}{\text{Working Capital}}$

$= \frac{25,00,000}{5,00,000} = 5 \text{ times}$

26. The proprietary ratio of M Ltd is 0.80 : 1. State with reasons whether the following transactions will increase, decrease or not change the proprietary ratio

(*i*) Obtained a loan from bank ₹ 2,00,000 payable after five years.

(*ii*) Purchased machinery for cash ₹ 75,000

(*iii*) Redeemed 5% redeemable preference shares ₹ 1,00,000.

(*iv*) Issued equity shares to the vendors of machinery purchased for ₹ 4,00,000. **All India 2017**

Ans. (*i*) **Decrease** Loan obtained from bank will increase the total assets but the shareholders' funds will remain the same, so proprietary ratio will decrease.

(*ii*) **No change** Machinery purchased for cash will increase and simultaneously decrease the total assets therefore proprietary ratio will remain unchanged.

(*iii*) **Decrease** Redemption of preference shares will decrease total assets and shareholders' funds simultaneously, so proprietary ratio will decrease.

(*iv*) **Increase** Machinery purchased by issue of equity shares will increase total assets and shareholders' funds simultaneously, so proprietary ratio will increase.

27. The quick ratio of a company is 0.8 : 1. State with reason whether the following transactions will increase, decrease or not change the quick ratio

(*i*) Purchase of loose tools ₹ 2,000.

(*ii*) Insurance premium paid in advance ₹ 500.

(*iii*) Sale of goods on credit ₹ 3,000.

(*iv*) Honoured a bills payable ₹ 5,000 on maturity. **Delhi 2017**

Ans. (*i*) **Decrease** Purchasing loose tools will decrease the current assets but the current liabilities will remain unaffected, so quick ratio will decrease.

(*ii*) **Decrease** Insurance premium paid in advance will decrease the current assets but the current liabilities will remain unaffected, so quick ratio will decrease.

(*iii*) **Increase** Goods sold on credit will increase the quick ratio as current liabilities will remain unchanged and quick assets will increase, so quick ratio will increase.

(*iv*) **Decrease** Bills payable honoured on maturity will decrease the quick assets and current liabilities simultaneously, so quick ratio will decrease.

28. (*i*) What is meant by 'activity ratios'?

(*ii*) From the following information calculate inventory turnover ratio, revenue from operations ₹ 16,00,000, average inventory ₹ 2,20,000, gross loss ratio 5%. **All India 2016**

Ans. (*i*) Activity ratios show how efficiently a company is using its assets to generate sales. These ratios express the number of times assets employed or for that matter, any constituents of assets, is turned into sales during an accounting period. These ratios are also known as turnover ratios or performance ratios. These ratios are calculated on the basis of sales or cost of sales. The various activity ratios are inventory turnover ratios, trade receivables or debtors turnover ratio, trade payables or creditors turnover ratio, working capital turnover ratio.

(*ii*) Inventory Turnover Ratio

$= \frac{\text{Cost of Revenue from Operations *}}{\text{Average Inventory}}$

$= \frac{16,80,000}{2,20,000} = 7.64 \text{ times}$

$\text{Gross Loss Ratio} = \frac{\text{Gross Loss}}{\text{Revenue from Operations}}$

$5\% = \frac{\text{Gross loss}}{16,00,000}$

$\Rightarrow$ Gross Loss = 5% of 16,00,000 = ₹ 80,000

* Cost of Revenue from Operations = Revenue from Operations + Gross Loss

$= 16,00,000 + 80,000 = ₹ 16,80,000$

29. (*i*) What is meant by 'solvency of business'?

(*ii*) From the following details obtained from the financial statements of Jeev Ltd, calculate interest coverage ratio

Net profit after tax ₹ 1,20,000

12% long-term debt ₹ 20,00,000

Tax rate 40% **Delhi 2016**

Ans. (*i*) Solvency of a business means the ability of business to pay off its long-term liabilities. Solvency ratios such as debt equity ratio, total assets to debt ratio, interest coverage ratio etc are some of the important solvency ratios that help the investors to know about the credibility of business and accordingly take rational investment decisions. Better the solvency position of the business, the better the market standing of such firms.

(*ii*) Interest Coverage Ratio

$$= \frac{\text{Profit before Interest and Tax}}{\text{Interest on Long-term Debt}}$$

$$= \frac{4,40,000}{2,40,000} = 1.83 \text{ times}$$

Calculation of net profit before interest and tax

Net profit after tax = 1,20,000 ; Tax = 40%

If profit after tax is 60, profit before tax is 100 and if profit after tax is ₹ 1,20,000

Profit before tax would be

$$= \frac{100}{60} \times 1,20,000 = ₹ 2,00,000$$

Interest on long-term debt

$= 20,00,000 \times 12\% = ₹ 2,40,000$

Therefore, Profit before interest and tax

$= 2,00,000 + 2,40,000 = ₹ 4,40,000$

30. (*i*) What is meant by 'profitability of business'?

(*ii*) From the following information, calculate operating profit ratio.

Opening stock ₹ 10,000, purchases ₹ 1,20,000, revenue from operations ₹ 4,00,000, purchase returns ₹ 5,000, returns from revenue from operations ₹ 15,000, selling expenses ₹ 70,000, administrative expenses ₹ 40,000, closing stock ₹ 60,000. **Delhi 2016**

Ans. (*i*) Profitability is the basic objective of every business. Profitability is the measure of efficiency and success of the business. It is related to the income of the business, *i.e.* how much a concern is earning in relation to the capital invested by it. The various ratios which helps to measure the profitability of a business are gross profit ratio, net profit ratio, operating ratio etc. All these ratios are used to assess a business ability to generate earnings as compared to its expenses and other relevant cost during a specific period of time.

(*ii*) Operating Profit Ratio

$$= \frac{\text{Operating Profit *}}{\text{Revenue from Operations **}} \times 100$$

$$= \frac{2,10,000}{3,85,000} \times 100 = 54.55$$

*Operating Profit = Revenue from Operations** – Cost of Revenue from Operations (Opening stock + Purchases – Closing stock) – Selling Expenses – Administrative Expenses

$= 3,85,000 - [10,000 + 1,15,000$

$(1,20,000 - 5,000) - 60,000] - 70,000 - 40,000$

$= 3,85,000 - 65,000 - 70,000 - 40,000$

$= ₹ 2,10,000$

**Revenue from Operations = Revenue from Operations – Returns from Revenue from Operations

$= 4,00,000 - 15,000 = ₹ 3,85,000$

31. (*i*) What is meant by 'liquidity of business'?

(*ii*) From the following information calculate operating ratio

Revenue from operations ₹ 6,80,000, rate of gross profit on cost 25%, selling expenses ₹ 1,44,000, administrative expenses ₹ 73,000. **Delhi 2016**

Ans. (*i*) Liquidity of business refers to the ability of the firm to meet its short-term obligations. Its the ability of an organisation to meet its current financial obligations. Liquidity ratios measure the ability of a company to meet its short-term debt obligations. The various liquidity ratios used for this purpose are current ratio and acid test ratio/quick ratio.

(*ii*) Operating Ratio

$$= \frac{\text{Operating Cost}}{\text{Net Sales}} \times 100 = \frac{7,61,000}{6,80,000} \times 100$$

$= 111.91\%$

Operating Cost = Cost of Goods Sold + Operating Expenses

$= 5{,}44{,}000 + 1{,}44{,}000 + 73{,}000 = ₹\ 7{,}61{,}000$

Gross profit $= \frac{1}{4}$ on cost *Or* $\frac{1}{5}$ on sales $= \frac{1}{5} \times 6{,}80{,}000 = ₹\ 1{,}36{,}000$

Let cost of goods sold be $= x \Rightarrow 1{,}36{,}000 = \frac{1}{4} \times x \Rightarrow x = ₹\ 5{,}44{,}000$

NOTE Operating expenses include selling and administrative expenses

32. (*i*) From the following, calculate 'Trade receivables turnover ratio'.

Total revenue from operations for the year	₹ 8,40,000
Cash revenue from operations	40% of credit revenue from operations
Closing trade receivables	₹ 2,00,000
Excess of closing trade receivables over opening trade receivables	₹ 80,000

(*ii*) From the following information calculate 'Interest coverage ratio'

Profit after interest and tax	₹ 4,97,000
Rate of income tax	30%
12% debentures	₹ 6,00,000

All India (C) 2016

Ans. (*i*) Trade Receivables Turnover Ratio $= \frac{\text{Credit Revenue from Operations *}}{\text{Average Trade Receivables **}} = \frac{6{,}00{,}000}{1{,}60{,}000} = 3.75$ times

Let, credit revenue from operations be x

Cash revenue from operations be $x \times 40\% = 0.4x$

Total Revenue from Operations = Cash Revenue from Operations + Credit Revenue from Operations

$8{,}40{,}000 = 0.4x + x$

$8{,}40{,}000 = 1.4x$

*Credit revenue from operations $\Rightarrow x \Rightarrow 6{,}00{,}000$

**Average Trade Receivables

$= \frac{\text{Opening Trade Receivables} + \text{Closing Trade Receivables}}{2}$

$= \frac{1{,}20{,}000 + 2{,}00{,}000}{2} = ₹\ 1{,}60{,}000$

Opening trade receivables $= 2{,}00{,}000 - 80{,}000 = ₹1{,}20{,}000$

(*ii*) Interest Coverage Ratio $= \frac{\text{Net Profit before Interest and Tax}}{\text{Interest on Long-term Borrowings}} = \frac{7{,}82{,}000}{72{,}000} = 10.86$ times

Net profit after interest and tax	= 4,97,000
(+) Tax (4,97,000 × 30 / 70)	= 2,13,000
(+) Interest on debentures (6,00,000 × 12%)	= 72,000
Net profit before interest and tax	₹ 7,82,000

33. From the given information calculate the following

(*i*) Cost of revenue from operations (*ii*) Opening and closing inventory

(*iii*) Quick assets (*iv*) Current assets

Information Inventory turnover ratio 6 times, inventory at the end is ₹ 6,000 more than the inventory in the beginning, revenue from operations (all credits) ₹ 2,40,000, Gross profit 25% on cost, current liabilities ₹ 80,000, quick ratio 0.80 : 1. **Delhi (C) 2016**

Ans. (*i*) Let cost be 100

Gross profit be = 25

Revenue from operations = 100 + 25 = 125

Revenue from operations (all credits) = 2,40,000

$\therefore$ Cost of revenue from operations = $2{,}40{,}000 \times \frac{100}{125}$

Cost of revenue from operations = ₹1,92,000

(*ii*) Let opening inventory be = x

Closing inventory be = $x + 6{,}000$

$$\text{Average Inventory} = \frac{x + x + 6{,}000}{2} = \frac{2x + 6{,}000}{2} = x + 3{,}000$$

$$\text{Inventory Turnover Ratio} = \frac{\text{Cost of Revenue from Operations}}{\text{Average Inventory}}$$

$$6 = \frac{1{,}92{,}000}{x + 3{,}000}$$

$$6x + 18{,}000 = 1{,}92{,}000$$

$$6x = 1{,}92{,}000 - 18{,}000$$

$$x = \frac{1{,}74{,}000}{6} = 29{,}000$$

Opening inventory $\Rightarrow x \Rightarrow 29{,}000 = x + 6{,}000$

Closing inventory = 29,000 + 6,000 = ₹35,000

(*iii*) $\text{Quick Ratio} = \frac{\text{Quick Assets}}{\text{Current Liabilities}}$

$$0.80 = \frac{\text{Quick Assets}}{80{,}000}$$

Quick Assets = ₹ 64,000

(*iv*) Current Assets = Quick Assets + Inventory = 64,000 + 35,000

Current Assets = ₹99,000

34. The current ratio of a company is 2.1 : 1.2. State with reasons which of the following transactions will increase, decrease or not change the ratio

(*i*) Redeemed 9% debentures of ₹ 1,00,000 at a premium of 10%.

(*ii*) Received from debtors ₹ 17,000.

(*iii*) Issued ₹ 2,00,000 equity shares to the vendors of machinery.

(*iv*) Accepted bills of exchange drawn by the creditors ₹ 7,000. **All India 2015**

Ans. (*i*) **Decrease** Current assets will decrease because of outflow of cash but current liabilities will remain unchanged therefore current ratio will decrease.

(*ii*) **Not change the ratio** Simultaneous increase and decrease in the value of current assets i.e. cash and debtors by the same amount will not effect the ratio.

(*iii*) **Not change the ratio** Issue of shares for purchase of machinery do not effect either current assets or current liabilities, therefore current ratio will not be effected.

(*iv*) **Not change the ratio** In this case one current liability (*i.e.* creditors) is getting converted into another current liability (*i.e.* bills payable), therefore current ratio will not be effected.

35. From the following information related to Naveen Ltd, calculate (*i*) Return on investment (*ii*) Total assets to debt ratio.

Information Fixed assets ₹ 75,00,000; current assets ₹ 40,00,000; current liabilities ₹ 27,00,000; 12% debentures ₹ 80,00,000 and net profit before interest, tax and dividend ₹ 14,50,000. **Delhi 2015**

Ans. (*i*) $\text{Return on Investment} = \frac{\text{Net Profit before Interest, Tax and Preference Dividend}}{\text{Capital Employed*}} \times 100$

$$= \frac{14{,}50{,}000}{88{,}00{,}000} \times 100 = 16.48\%$$

*Capital Employed = Fixed Assets + Currents Assets – Current Liabilities
= 75,00,000 + 40,00,000 – 27,00,000 = ₹ 88,00,000

(*ii*) Total Assets to Debt Ratio = $\frac{\text{Total Assets*}}{\text{Debt}} = \frac{1,15,00,000}{80,00,000} = 1.44:1$

*Total Assets = Fixed Assets + Current Assets = 75,00,000 + 40,00,000 = ₹ 1,15,00,000

36. The current ratio of a company is 2.5 : 1.5. State with reasons which of the following transactions will increase, decrease or not change the ratio

(*i*) Discounted a bills receivable of ₹ 10,000 from bank. Bank charged discount of ₹ 200.

(*ii*) A bill receivable ₹ 8,000 discounted with bank was dishonoured.

(*iii*) Cash deposited into bank 7,000.

(*iv*) Paid cash ₹ 5,000 to the creditors. **Foreign 2015**

Ans.

Effect	Explanation
(i) Decrease	Discounting a bills receivable from bank reduces asset by ₹ 10,000 (bills receivable) and increases asset by ₹ 9,800 (bank balance).
(ii) No change	Dishonour of discounted bills receivable results in increase in asset (debtors) and decrease in asset (bank) with the same amount.
(iii) No change	Increase in one current asset (bank) with a simultaneous decrease in other current asset (cash) with the same amount leaves current ratio unaffected.
(iv) Increase	Payment of current liabilities (creditors) will improve the current ratio from 1.67 (2.5 : 1.5) to 2 (2:1).

37. From the following information, calculate total assets to debt ratio

Information	Amt (₹)
Capital Employed	25,00,000
Investments	2,10,000
Land	8,50,000
Trade Receivables	2,75,000
Cash and Cash Equivalents	1,50,000
Equity Share Capital	14,30,000
8% Debentures	4,00,000
Capital Reserve	2,75,000
Surplus, i.e. Balance in Statement of Profit and Loss	1,50,000

All India (C) 2015

Ans. Total Assets to Debt Ratio = $\frac{\text{Total Assets}}{\text{Debt}} = \frac{14,85,000}{6,45,000} = 2.30:1$

Total Assets = Investments + Land + Trade Receivables + Cash and Cash Equivalent
= 2,10,000 + 8,50,000 + 2,75,000 + 1,50,000 = ₹14,85,000

Debt = Capital Employed – (Equity share capital + Reserves + Surplus)
= 25,00,000 – 18,55,000 (14,30,000 + 2,75,000 + 1,50,000) = ₹ 6,45,000

38. With the help of the following information, calculate return on investment. Net profit after interest and tax ₹ 6,00,000; 10% debentures ₹ 10,00,000; tax @ 40%; capital employed ₹ 80,00,000. **Delhi (C) 2015**

Ans. $$\text{Return on Investment} = \frac{\text{Net Profit before Interest, Tax and Dividend}}{\text{Capital Employed}} \times 100$$

$$= \frac{11,00,000}{80,00,000} \times 100 = 13.75\%$$

$$\begin{aligned} \text{Net profit after interest and tax} &= 6,00,000 \\ (+)\ \text{Tax}\ (6,00,000 \times 40/60) &= 4,00,000 \\ (+)\ \text{Interest}\ (10,00,000 \times 10\%) &= 1,00,000 \\ &\text{₹}\ \underline{11,00,000} \end{aligned}$$

39. From the following calculate the 'gross profit ratio' and 'working capital turnover ratio' **Delhi (C) 2014**

Information	Amt (₹)
Revenue from Operations	30,00,000
Cost of Revenue from Operations	20,00,000
Current Assets	6,00,000
Current Liabilities	2,00,000
Paid-up Share Capital	5,00,000

Ans. (*i*) $$\text{Gross Profit Ratio} = \frac{\text{Gross Profit}^*}{\text{Revenue from Operations (Net sales)}} \times 100 = \frac{10,00,000}{30,00,000} \times 100 = 33.33\%$$

$$\begin{aligned} ^*\text{Gross Profit} &= \text{Revenue from Operations} - \text{Cost of Revenue from Operations} \\ &= 30,00,000 - 20,00,000 = \text{₹}10,00,000 \end{aligned}$$

(*ii*) $$\text{Working Capital Turnover Ratio} = \frac{\text{Revenue from Operations (Net sales)}}{\text{Working Capital}^*} = \frac{30,00,000}{4,00,000} = 7.5:1$$

$$\begin{aligned} ^*\text{Working Capital} &= \text{Current Assets} - \text{Current Liabilities} \\ &= 6,00,000 - 2,00,000 \\ &= \text{₹}4,00,000 \end{aligned}$$

40. (*i*) From the following information, compute 'debt equity ratio'

Items	Amt (₹)
Long-term Borrowings	2,00,000
Long-term Provisions	1,00,000
Current Liabilities	50,000
Non-current Assets	3,60,000
Current Assets	90,000

(*ii*) The current ratio of X Ltd is 2 : 1. State with reason which of the following transaction would increase, decrease or not change the ratio

(a) Included in the trade payables was a bills payable of ₹ 9,000 which was met on maturity.

(b) Company issued 1,00,000 equity shares of ₹ 10 each to the vendors of machinery purchased. **Delhi 2014**

Ans. (*i*) $$\text{Debt Equity Ratio} = \frac{\text{Long - term Debt}^*}{\text{Equity (Shareholders funds)}^{**}} = \frac{3,00,000}{1,00,000} = 3:1$$

*Long-term Debt = Long-term Borrowings + Long-term Provisions

= 2,00,000 + 1,00,000 = ₹ 3,00,000

**Shareholders' Funds = Total Assets – Total Liabilities

= 4,50,000 – 3,50,000 = ₹ 1,00,000

Total Assets = Non-current Assets + Current Assets

= 3,60,000 + 90,000 = ₹4,50,000

Total Liabilities = Long-term Borrowings + Long-term Provisions + Current Liabilities

= 2,00,000 + 1,00,000 + 50,000 = ₹3,50,000

(*ii*) (a) **Increase in the ratio** Simultaneous decrease in both current assets and current liabilities, *i.e.* cash and trade payable will increase the current ratio.

(b) **No change in the ratio** Issue of shares for machinery purchased do not affect either current assets or current liabilities, therefore, the current ratio will not be affected.

41. (*i*) The quick ratio of a company is 1.5 : 1. State with reason which of the following transactions would increase, decrease or not change the ratio

(a) Paid rent ₹ 3,000 in advance.

(b) Trade receivables included a debtor Shri Ashok who paid his entire amount due ₹ 9,700.

(*ii*) From the following information compute 'proprietary ratio' **All India 2014**

Information	Amt (₹)
Long-term Borrowings	2,00,000
Long-term Pprovisions	1,00,000
Current Lliabilities	50,000
Non-current Assets	3,60,000
Current Assets	90,000

Ans. (*i*) (a) Not change the ratio

Reason As there is a simultaneous increase and decrease in current assets by the same amount, *i.e.* prepaid expenses and cash, therefore it will not affect the value of current assets.

(b) Not change the ratio

Reason As there is a simultaneous increase and decrease in current assets by the same amount, *i.e.* cash and trade receivables, therefore it will not affect the value of current assets.

(*ii*) Proprietary Ratio

$$= \frac{\text{Proprietor's Funds or Shareholders' Funds*}}{\text{Total Assets}}$$

$$= \frac{1,00,000}{4,50,000} = 0.22 : 1$$

***Calculation of Shareholders' Funds**

By Assets Approach	Amt (₹)
Non-current Assets	3,60,000
Current Assets	90,000
Total Assets	4,50,000
(–) Current Liabilities	(50,000)
(–) Long-term Borrowings	(2,00,000)
(–) Long-term Provisions	(1,00,000)
Shareholders' Funds	₹ 1,00,000

42. From the following calculate

(*i*) Operating profit ratio

(*ii*) Working capital turnover ratio.

All India (C) 2014

Information	Amt (₹)
Revenue from Operations	2,00,000
Gross Profit	75,000
Office Expenses	15,000
Selling Expenses	26,000
Interest on Debentures	5,000
Accidental Losses	12,000
Income from Rent	2,500
Commission Received	2,000
Current Assets	60,000
Current Liabilities	10,000

Ans. (*i*) Operating Profit Ratio

$$= \frac{\text{Operating Profit *}}{\text{Revenue from Operations (Net sales)}} \times 100$$

$$= \frac{36,000}{2,00,000} \times 100 = 18\%$$

*Operating Profit = Gross Profit – Other Operating Expenses + Other Operating Incomes

= 75,000 – 41,000 + 2,000 = ₹ 36,000

Other Operating Expenses = Office Expenses + Selling Expenses
= 15,000 + 26,000
= ₹41,000

Other Operating Incomes = Commission Received
= ₹2,000

(*ii*) Working Capital Turnover Ratio

$$= \frac{\text{Revenue from Operations}}{\text{Working Capital *}}$$

$$= \frac{2,00,000}{50,000} = 4 \text{ times}$$

*Working Capital = Current Assets – Current Liabilities
= 60,000 – 10,000
= ₹50,000

43. From the following, calculate
(*i*) Current ratio; and
(*ii*) Working capital turnover ratio

	Particulars	Amt (₹)
(i)	Revenue from Operations	1,50,000
(ii)	Total Assets	1,00,000
(iii)	Shareholders' Funds	60,000
(iv)	Non-current Liabilities	20,000
(v)	Non-current Assets	50,000

All India (C) 2014

Ans. (*i*) Current Ratio $= \frac{\text{Current Assets *}}{\text{Current Liabilities **}}$

$$= \frac{50,000}{20,000} = 2.5:1$$

Total Assets = Current Assets + Non-current Assets

1,00,000 = Current Assets + 50,000

*Current Assets= 1,00,000 – 50,000 = ₹ 50,000

**Current Liabilities = Total Assets – Shareholders' Funds – Non-current Liabilities
= 1,00,000 – 60,000 – 20,000
= ₹ 20,000

(*ii*) Working Capital Turnover Ratio

$$= \frac{\text{Revenue from Operations}}{\text{Working Capital}}$$

$$= \frac{1,50,000}{30,000} = 5 \text{ times}$$

Working Capital = Current Assets – Current Liabilities = 50,000 – 20,000 = ₹30,000

44. (*i*) Compute 'debtors turnover ratio' from the following information
Revenue from operations (Total sales) ₹ 5,20,000, cash revenue from operations 60% of the credit revenue from operations, closing debtors ₹ 80,000, opening debtors are 3/4th of closing debtors.

(*ii*) Current liabilities of a company are ₹ 1,60,000. Its liquid ratio is 1.5 : 1 and current ratio is 2.5 : 1. Calculate quick assets and current assets. **All India 2013**

Ans. (*i*) Debtors Turnover Ratio

$$= \frac{\text{Credit Revenue from Operations}}{\text{Average Debtors *}} = \frac{3,25,000}{70,000}$$

= 4.64 times

Let Credit revenue from operations be y

Cash revenue from operations = 60% of credit revenue from operations

Revenue from Operations = Cash Revenue from Operations + Credit Revenue from Operations

5,20,000 = 60% of y + y
5,20,000 = 0.6y + y

$$\frac{5,20,000}{1.6} = y$$

y = ₹ 3,25,000

*Average Debtors

$$= \frac{\text{Opening Debtors ** + Closing Debtors}}{2}$$

$$= \frac{60,000 + 80,000}{2} = ₹70,000$$

**Opening Debtors $= \frac{3}{4} \times$ Closing Debtors

$$= \frac{3}{4} \times 80,000 = ₹ 60,000$$

(*ii*) Liquid Ratio $= \frac{\text{Liquid Assets or Quick Assets *}}{\text{Current Liabilities}}$

$$= \frac{1.5}{1} = \frac{\text{Quick assets}}{1,60,000}$$

*Quick Assets = 1.5 × 1,60,000 = 2,40,000

Current Ratio $= \frac{\text{Current Assets}}{\text{Current Liabilities}} = \frac{2.5}{1}$

$$= \frac{\text{Current assets}}{1,60,000}$$

Current Assets = 1,60,000 × 2.5 = ₹ 4,00,000

45. (*i*) Compute 'working capital turnover ratio' from the following information
Cash revenue from operations ₹ 1,30,000, credit revenue from operations ₹ 3,80,000, returns from revenue from operations ₹ 10,000, liquid assets ₹ 1,40,000, current liabilities ₹ 1,05,000 and inventory ₹ 90,000.

(*ii*) Calculate 'debt equity ratio' from the following information
Total assets ₹ 3,50,000, total debt ₹ 2,50,000 and current liabilities ₹ 80,000. **Delhi 2013**

Ans. (*i*) Working Capital Turnover Ratio $= \frac{\text{Revenue form Operations *}}{\text{Working Capital **}} = \frac{5,00,000}{1,25,000} = 4$ times

*Revenue from Operations = Cash Revenue from Operations + Credit Revenue from Operations – Returns from Revenue from Operations
= 1,30,000 + 3,80,000 – 10,000
= ₹ 5,00,000

Current Assets = Liquid Assets + Inventory = 1,40,000 + 90,000 = ₹ 2,30,000
**Working Capital = Current Assets – Current Liabilities = 2,30,000 – 1,05,000 = ₹ 1,25,000

(*ii*) Debt Equity Ratio $= \frac{\text{Long - term Debt *}}{\text{Equity **}} = \frac{1,70,000}{1,00,000} = 1.7 : 1$

*Long-term Debt = Total Debts – Current Liabilities
= 2,50,000 – 80,000 = ₹ 1,70,000

**Equity or Shareholders' Funds = Total Assets – Total Debt
= 3,50,000 – 2,50,000 = ₹ 1,00,000

46. From the following information, calculate any two of the following ratios
(*i*) Debt equity ratio (*ii*) Working capital turnover ratio
(*iii*) Return on investment

Information Equity share capital ₹ 10,00,000, general reserve ₹ 1,00,000, balance of statement of profit and loss after interest and tax ₹ 3,00,000, 12% debentures ₹ 4,00,000, creditors ₹ 3,00,000, land and buildings ₹ 13,00,000, furniture ₹ 3,00,000, debtors ₹ 2,90,000, cash ₹ 1,10,000.
Revenue from operations, *i.e.* sales for the year ended 31st March, 2011 was ₹ 30,00,000. Tax paid is 50%. **All India 2012; Modified**

Ans. (*i*) Debt Equity Ratio $= \frac{\text{Debt}}{\text{Equity}} = \frac{\text{Long - term Debts or Loans *}}{\text{Shareholders' Funds **}} = \frac{4,00,000}{14,00,000} = 0.286 : 1$

*Long-term debts = 12% debentures = 4,00,000

**Shareholders' Funds = Equity Share Capital + General Reserve + Balance of Statement of Profit and Loss
= 10,00,000 + 1,00,000 + 3,00,000 = ₹ 14,00,000

(*ii*) Working Capital Turnover Ratio $= \frac{\text{Revenue from Operations (Net sales)}}{\text{Working Capital *}} = \frac{30,00,000}{1,00,000} = 30$ times

*Working Capital = Current Assets – Current Liabilities = 4,00,000 – 3,00,000 = ₹ 1,00,000
Current Assets = Cash + Debtors = 1,10,000 + 2,90,000 = ₹ 4,00,000
Current Liabilities = Creditors = ₹ 3,00,000

(*iii*) Return on Investment $= \frac{\text{Profit before Interest and Tax}^*}{\text{Capital Employed}^{**}} \times 100 = \frac{6,48,000}{18,00,000} \times 100 = 36\%$

Profit before Tax $= \frac{\text{Profit after Tax}}{100 - \text{Tax Rate}} \times 100 = \frac{3,00,000}{100-50} \times 100 =$ ₹ 6,00,000

*Profit before Interest and Tax = 6,00,000 + 48,000 (Interest on debentures) = ₹6,48,000

**Capital Employed = Equity Share Capital + General Reserve + Balance in Statement of Profit and Loss + 12% Debentures

= 10,00,000 + 1,00,000 + 3,00,000 + 4,00,000

= ₹18,00,000

47. From the following information, calculate any two of the following ratios

(*i*) Debt equity ratio (*ii*) Working capital turnover ratio

(*iii*) Return on investment

Information Equity share capital ₹ 50,000 ; general reserve ₹ 5,000; statement of profit and loss after tax and interest ₹ 15,000; 9% debenture ₹ 20,000; creditors ₹ 15,000; land and building ₹ 65,000; equipments ₹ 15,000; debtors ₹ 14,500 and cash ₹ 5,500; revenue from operations for the year ended 31st March, 2011 was ₹ 50,000. Tax rate 50%. **Delhi 2012 (Modified)**

Ans. Solve as Q no. 46 as page 406 and 407.

Debt Equity Ratio = 0.286 : 1; Working Capital Turnover Ratio = 30 times; Return on Investment = 35.33%

Multiple Choice Questions

For Complete Chapter (1 Mark)

1. .... ratios indicate the speed at which activities of the business are being performed. **CBSE Term I 2021**

(a) Profitability (b) Turnover
(c) Solvency (d) Liquidity

2. From the following information, calculate inventory turnover ratio.
Revenue from operations = ₹ 2,00,000;
Average inventory = ₹ 20,000; Gross profit ratio = 10% **CBSE Term I 2021**

(a) 9 times (b) 10 times
(c) 12 times (d) 20 times

Hint: Gross Profit Ratio $= \frac{\text{Gross Profit}}{\text{Revenue from Operations}} \times 100$

$10 = \frac{x}{2,00,000} \times 100$

$\therefore \quad x =$ ₹ 20,000

Inventory Turnover Ratio

$= \frac{\text{Cost of Revenue from Operations}}{\text{Average Inventory}}$

$= \frac{2,00,000 - 20,000}{20,000} = 9$ times

3. If operating ratio is 65%, operating profit ratio will be ....**CBSE Term I 2021**

(a) 20% (b) 25% (c) 35% (d) 30%

Hint: Operating Ratio + Operating Profit Ratio = 100

4. What will be the impact of issuing ₹ 5,00,000 equity share to vendor for building purchased on the debt and equity of X Ltd.? **CBSE Term I 2021**

(a) Debt will increase and equity will decrease.
(b) Debt will remain same and equity will increase.
(c) Debt will decrease and equity will increase.
(d) Debt will remain same and equity will decrease.

5. From the following information, calculate interest coverage ratio
CBSE Term I 2021

Net profit after tax	₹ 6,00,000
10% Debentures	₹ 50,00,000
Tax Rate	40%

(a) 1.2 times (b) 3 times
(c) 2 times (d) 5 times

Hint: Net profit after tax = 6,00,000
(+) Tax (6,00,000 × 40/60) = 4,00,000
(+) Interest on debentures = 5,00,000
Net profit before interest and tax = 15,00,000

Interest Coverage Ratio = $\frac{15,00,000}{5,00,000}$

6. **Assertion** (A) A high debt-equity ratio is risky.
Reason (R) It may put the firm into difficulty to pay long-term debts. **CBSE Term I 2021**

Alternatives
(a) Assertion (A) is correct, but Reason (R) is wrong
(b) Both Assertion (A) and Reason (R) are correct
(c) Assertion (A) is wrong, but Reason (R) is correct
(d) Both Assertion (A) and Reason (R) are wrong

7. **Assertion** (A) Current ratio establishes relationship between current assets and current liabilities.

Reason (R) The objective of this ratio is to measure the ability of the firm to meet its short-term obligations as and when due without relying upon the realisation of inventories. **CBSE Term I 2021**

Alternatives
(a) Assertion (A) is true, but Reason (R) is false
(b) Both Assertion (A) and Reason (R) are true, and Reason (R) is a correct explanation of Assertion (A)
(c) Both Assertion (A)and Reason (R) are false
(d) Assertion (A) is false, but Reason (R) is true

8. **Assertion** (A) Return on investment explains the overall utilisation funds by a business enterprise.

Reason (R) It measures return (Net Profit before interest and tax) on total funds (Capital employed). **CBSE Term I 2021**

Alternatives
(a) Both Assertion (A) and Reason (R) are true, but Reason (R) is not the correct explanation of Assertion (A)
(b) Both Assertion (A) and Reason (R) are true and Reason (R) is correct explanation of Assertion (A)
(c) Both Assertion (A) and Reason (R) are false
(d) Assertion (A) is false, but Reason (R) is true

9. Cross-sectional analysis is related
(a) to take a correct action
(b) to compare firm's present ratio with past
(c) to compare of a firm ratio with other
(d) None of the above

Hint: In this type of analysis, a firm is compared with some firms or industry at a same point of time. It is done to improve the efficiency of the business.

10. Current ratio is
(a) $\frac{\text{Current Assets}}{\text{Quick Liabilities}}$
(b) $\frac{\text{Current Assets}}{\text{Current Liabilities}}$
(c) $\frac{\text{Quick Assets}}{\text{Current Liabilities}}$
(d) $\frac{\text{Liquid Assets}}{\text{Liquid Liabilities}}$

11. Working capital is the
(a) difference between current assets and current liabilities
(b) difference between current assets and quick liabilities
(c) capital and liabilities difference
(d) cash and bank difference

Hint: Working capital refers to excess of current assets over current liabilities.

12. From the following, calculate current assets?

Cash balance	₹ 5,000
Trade payable	₹ 40,000
Inventory	₹ 50,000
Trade receivable	₹ 65,000
Prepaid expenses	₹ 10,000
Creditors	₹ 30,000

(a) ₹ 1,25,000 (b) ₹ 1,30,000
(c) ₹ 1,60,000 (d) ₹ 1,20,000

Hint: Current Assets = Cash + Inventory + Trade Receivable + Prepaid Expenses
= 5,000 + 50,000 + 65,000 + 10,000 = ₹1,30,000

13. If inventory is ₹ 1,00,000, current assets ₹ 8,00,000 and current liabilities ₹ 4,00,000, then what will be the liquid ratio?

(a) 1.75 : 1 (b) 2 : 1
(c) 2 : 3 (d) 3 : 1

Hint: $\text{Liquid Ratio} = \frac{\text{Current Asset} - \text{Inventory}}{\text{Current Liabilities}}$

$= \frac{8,00,000 - 1,00,000}{4,00,000} = 1.75 : 1$

14. Which of the following transaction will improve the quick ratio?

(a) Purchase of inventory for cash
(b) Cash collected from debtors
(c) Sale of goods (costing 10,000 for ₹ 50,000)
(d) None of the above

Hint: Sale of goods for cash will increase the total of the quick assets therefore, the quick ratio will be improved.

15. A firm has current ratio of 4 : 1 and quick ratio of 2.5 : 1. Assuming inventories are ₹15,000, find out total current assets?

(a) ₹ 10,000 (b) ₹ 25,000
(c) ₹ 40,000 (d) ₹ 15,000

Hint: $\text{Current Ratio} = \frac{\text{Current Assets}}{\text{Current Liabilities}} \Rightarrow \frac{4}{1} = \frac{CA}{CL}$

$\therefore \quad CA = 4CL \quad \ldots(i)$

$\text{Quick Ratio} = \frac{\text{Quick Assets}}{\text{Current Liabilities}} \Rightarrow \frac{25}{1} = \frac{QA}{CL}$

$QA = 25CL \quad \ldots(ii)$

$\text{Inventories} = CA - QA$

$15,000 = 4CL - 25CL$

$15,000 = 1.5CL$

$\therefore \quad CL = \frac{15,000}{1.5} \Rightarrow ₹10,000$

$CA = 4CL = 4 \times 10,000 = ₹40,000$

16. Assuming that debt to equity ratio is 2 : 1, then which of the following transaction will have no effect on it?

(a) Purchase of a fixed assets by taking loan
(b) Sale of fixed assets (book value ₹ 40,000) at loss of 15,000
(c) Issue of bonus share
(d) Declaration of final dividend

Hint: Issue of bonus shares is a conversion of accumulated profit into share capital, total long-term debt and shareholder's funds are not affected. So, the ratio will not change.

17. Calculate interest coverage ratio. If profit after interest and tax ₹ 2,10,000, Rate of tax 40%, 15% debenture ₹ 3,00,000.

(a) 6 times (b) 8.8 times
(c) 11 times (d) 4 times

Hint: $\text{Profit before interest and tax} = \frac{2,10,000 \times 100}{60}$

$= ₹ 3,50,000$

15% debenture interest = ₹ 45,000

Profit before interest and tax

$= 3,50,000 + 45,000 = ₹ 3,95,000$

Interest Coverage Ratio

$= \frac{\text{Profit before Interest and Tax}}{\text{Fixed Interest Charge}}$

$= \frac{3,95,000}{45,000} = 8.8 \text{ times}$

18. From the following information, calculate operating profit ratio.

Opening stock ₹ 10,000; purchases ₹ 1,20,000; revenue from operations ₹ 4,00,000; purchase returns ₹ 5,000; returns from revenue from operations ₹ 15,000; selling expenses ₹ 70,000; administrative expenses ₹ 40,000; closing stock ₹ 60,000.

(a) 54.5% (b) 62.8%
(c) 90.2% (d) None of these

Hint: Net revenue from operations = 4,00,000 – 15,000
= ₹ 3,85,000

Cost of Revenue from Operations = Opening Stock + Purchases – Purchases Returns – Closing Stock
= 10,000 + 1,20,000 – 5,000 – 60,000 = ₹ 65,000

Operating Profit = Net Revenue from Operations – Cost of Revenue from Operations – Selling Expenses – Administrative Expenses
= 3,85,000 – 65,000 – 70,000 – 40,000
= 3,85,000 – 1,75,000 = ₹ 2,10,000

Operating Profit Ratio

$= \frac{\text{Operating Profit}}{\text{Net Revenue from Operations}} \times 100$

$= \frac{2,10,000}{3,85,000} \times 100 = 54.5\%$

Direction *Question no. 19 to 22 are based on the hypothetical situation of Rehan Limited.* **CBSE QB**

Year Amount	2020 (in ₹)	2019 (in ₹)	2018 (in ₹)
Outstanding Expenses	50,000	40,000	25,000
Prepaid Expenses	3,00,000	2,50,000	3,50,000
Trade Payables	18,00,000	16,00,000	14,00,000
Inventory	11,00,000	10,00,000	11,00,000
Trade Receivables	12,00,000	8,00,000	10,00,000
Cash in Hand	17,00,000	12,00,000	15,00,000
Revenue from Operations	24,00,000	18,00,000	20,00,000
Gross Profit Ratio	12%	15%	18%

19. Current Ratio for the year 2020 will be .... (Choose the correct alternative)

(a) 2:1 (b) 1.8:1
(c) 2.32:1 (d) 2.4:1

Hint: Current Ratio $= \frac{\text{Current Assets}}{\text{Current Liabilities}}$

$= \frac{43,00,000}{18,50,000} = 2.32 : 1$

Current Assets = Prepaid Expenses + Inventory + Trade Receivables + Cash in Hand

= 3,00,000 + 12,00,000 + 11,00,000 + 17,00,000

= ₹ 43,00,000

Current Liabilities = Outstanding Expenses + Trade Payables

= 50,000 + 18,00,000

= ₹ 18,50,000

20. Quick Ratio for the year 2018 will be .... (Choose the correct alternative)

(a) 1.75:1 (b) 1.8:1
(c) 0.94:1 (d) 1.25:1

Hint: Quick Ratio $= \frac{\text{Liquid Assets}}{\text{Current Liabilities}} = \frac{25,00,000}{14,25,000}$

$= 1.75 : 1$

Liquid Assets = Trade Receivables + Cash in Hand

= 10,00,000 + 15,00,000

= ₹ 25,00,000

Current Liabilities = Outstanding Expenses + Trade Payables

= 25,000 + 14,00,000

= ₹ 14,25,000

21. Inventory turnover ratio for the year 2020 will be .... . (Choose the correct alternative)

(a) 1.62 times (b) 1.82 times
(c) 1.55 times (d) 1.92 times

Hint: Inventory Turnover Ratio (2020)

$= \frac{\text{Cost of Revenue from Operations}}{\text{Average Inventory}}$

$= \frac{21,12,000}{11,00,000} = 1.92$ times

Average Inventory

$= \frac{\text{Opening Inventory} + \text{Closing Inventory}}{2}$

$= \frac{10,00,000 + 12,00,000}{2} =$ ₹ 11,00,000

22. Cost of Revenue from Operations for the year 2020 would be .... (Choose the correct alternative)

(a) ₹ 21,12,000 (b) ₹ 21,13,000
(c) ₹ 21,15,000 (d) ₹ 21,17,000

Hint: Cost of Revenue from Operations (2020)

	Amt (₹)
Revenue from Operation	24,00,000
(–) Gross Profit $\left(24,00,000 \times \frac{12}{100}\right)$	(2,88,000)
	21,12,000

ANSWERS

1. (b)	2. (a)	3. (c)	4. (b)	5. (b)	6. (b)	7. (a)	8. (b)	9. (c)	10. (b)
11. (a)	12. (b)	13. (a)	14. (c)	15. (c)	16. (c)	17. (b)	18. (a)	19. (c)	20. (a)
21. (d)	22. (a)								

CHAPTER 04

Cash Flow Statement

Meaning of Cash Flow Statement

It is a statement showing the changes in financial position of a business concern during different intervals of time in terms of cash and cash equivalents.

Objectives of Cash Flow Statement

The objectives of cash flow statement are

(*i*) To provide information about the cash inflows and cash outflows from operating activities.

(*ii*) To show the impact of the operating, financing and investing activities on cash resources.

(*iii*) To help the management in cash planning and control so that there is no shortage or surplus of cash at any point of time.

(*iv*) To explain the causes for changes in cash balance.

Benefits of Cash Flow Statement

The benefits of cash flow statement are

(*i*) Useful in short-term financial planning.

(*ii*) Useful in efficient cash management.

(*iii*) Helpful in formulation of business policies.

(*iv*) Assists in preparation of cash budget.

(*v*) Used for assessment of cash flow from various activities, viz operating, investing and financing activities.

Limitations of Cash Flow Statement

The limitations of cash flow statement are

(*i*) Based on historical cost principle.

(*ii*) Based on secondary data.

(*iii*) Ignores non-cash transactions.

(*iv*) Ignores basic accounting principles.

(*v*) Cash flow statement is not a substitute for income statement.

(*vi*) Provides misleading results if based on wrong data.

Important Terms related to Cash Flow Statement

(*i*) **Cash Flows** Cash flows are inflows and outflows of cash and cash equivalents which imply movement of cash in and out from non-cash items.

Receipt of cash from a non-cash item is termed as **cash inflow**, while cash payment in respect of such items is termed as **cash outflow**.

(*ii*) **Cash and Cash Equivalents** As per AS-3, **cash** comprises cash in hand and demand deposits with banks, and **cash equivalents** means short-term highly liquid investments that are readily convertible into known amounts of cash and which are subject to an insignificant risk of changes in value.

e.g. Short-term marketable securities, which can be readily converted into cash, are treated as cash equivalents.

(*iii*) **Non-cash Transactions** Those transactions in which flow (inflow or outflow) of cash and cash equivalents does not take place are called non-cash transactions. e.g.

(a) Issue of equity shares or debentures against purchase of an asset.
(b) Issue of equity shares on conversion of convertible debentures.
(c) Charging of depreciation on a fixed tangible asset.
(d) Amortisation of a fixed intangible asset.
(e) Writing-off of a old fixed tangible asset.
(f) Declaration of final dividend on shares.

Classification of Business Activities for Preparing Cash Flow Statement

Accounting Standard-3 (Revised) requires that the changes resulting in inflows and outflows of cash and cash equivalents should be classified into following three activities for the purpose of preparing cash flow statement.

(*i*) Cash flow from operating activities
(*ii*) Cash flow from investing activities
(*iii*) Cash flow from financing activities

Cash Flow from Operating Activities

Operating activities are the principal revenue producing activities of the enterprise and other activities that are not investing or financing activities.

Separate disclosure of cash from operating activities is important because the amount of cash flow arising from operating activities is a key indicator of the extent to which the business operations of the enterprise have generated cash, *i.e.* whether cash generation is adequate to maintain operational capability of the enterprise, pay dividends, repay loans and make new investments.

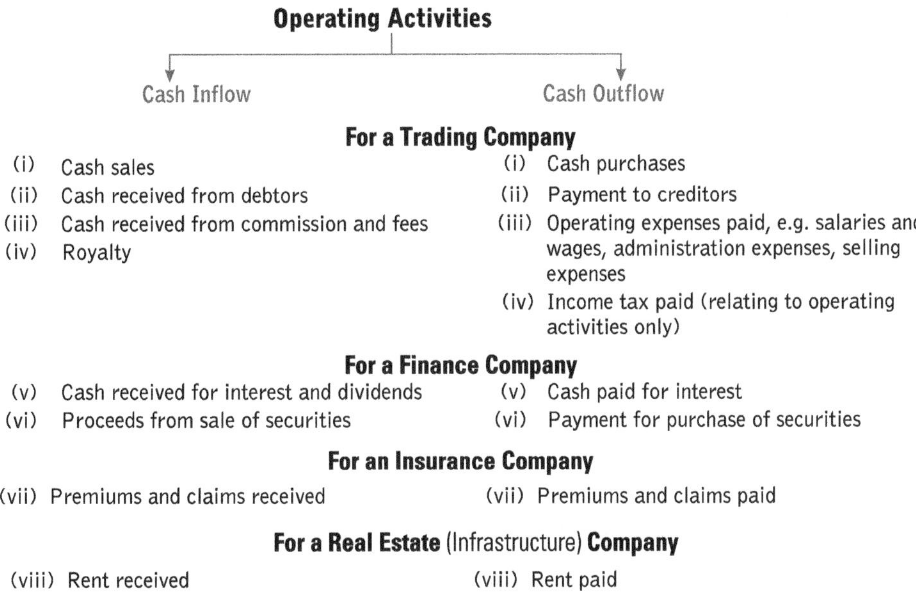

Cash Flow from Investing Activities

Investing activities are the activities related to acquisition and disposal of the long-term assets and other investments, not included in cash equivalents.

Separate disclosure of cash flows from investing activities is important because it shows the extent to which investments have been made for resources intended to generate future income and cash flows.

Cash flow from investing activities are exhibited as follows

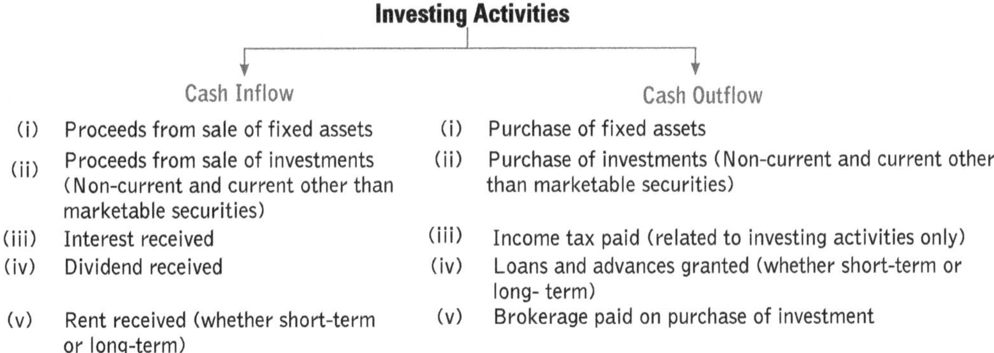

Cash Flow from Financing Activities

Financing activities are the activities which result in change in the size and composition of the owner's capital (including preference share capital) and borrowings (including debentures) of the enterprise from other sources.

Separate disclosure of cash flows arising from financing activities is important because it is useful in predicting claims on future cash flows by providers of funds (both capital and borrowings) to the enterprise.

Cash flow arising from financing activities are exhibited as follows

Financing Activities

Cash Inflow

(i) Proceeds from issue of shares for cash
(ii) Proceeds from issue of debentures for cash
(iii) Proceeds from long-term borrowings
(iv) Securities premium reserve received
(v) Increase in balance of bank overdraft or cash credit account

Cash Outflow

(i) Payment of loans
(ii) Redemption of preference shares, debentures for cash
(iii) Buy-back of equity shares
(iv) Payment of dividend
(v) Payment of interest on loans and debentures
(vi) Premium paid on redemption of preference shares, debentures
(vii) Income tax paid (related to financing activities only)
(viii) Loans repaid
(ix) Brokerage and underwriting commission paid on issue of shares and debentures
(x) Decrease in balance of bank overdraft or cash credit account

Format of Cash Flow Statement

Indirect Method [As per Accounting Standard-3 (Revised)]
for the year ended...

Particulars		Amt (₹)
I. **Cash Flow from Operating Activities**		
Net Profit before Taxation and Extraordinary Items (W.N.)		...
Adjustment for Non-cash and Non-operating Items		
(+) Items to be Added		
Depreciation	...	
Goodwill, Patents and Trademarks Amortised	...	
Interest on Borrowings and Debentures	...	
Loss on Sale of Fixed Assets	...	
Increase in Provision for Doubtful Debts	...	...
(–) Items to be Deducted		
Interest Income	(...)	
Dividend Income	(...)	
Rental Income	(...)	
Profit (Gain) on Sale of Fixed Assets	(...)	(...)
Operating Profit before Working Capital Changes		...
(+) Decrease in Current Assets and Increase in Current Liabilities		...
(–) Increase in Current Assets and Decrease in Current Liabilities		(...)
Cash Generated from Operations		...
(–) Income Tax Paid (Net of tax refund received)		(...)
Net Cash from (or used in) Operating Activities		...
II. **Cash Flow from Investing Activities**		
Proceeds from Sale of Tangible Fixed Assets	...	
Proceeds from Sale of Investments (Other than marketable securities)	...	
Proceeds from Sale of Intangible Fixed Assets	...	
Interest and Dividend Received (For non-financial companies only)	...	
Rent Received	...	

Particulars		Amt (₹)
Purchase of Tangible Fixed Assets	(...)	
Purchase of Investments (Other than marketable securities)	(...)	
Purchase of Intangible Fixed Assets like Goodwill	(...)	
Net Cash from (or used in) Investing Activities		...
III. **Cash Flow from Financing Activities**		
Proceeds from Issue of Shares and Debentures	...	
Proceeds from Other Long-term Borrowings	...	
Increase in Bank Overdraft and Cash Credit	...	
Decrease in Bank Overdraft and Cash Credit	(...)	
Final Dividend Paid	(...)	
Interim Dividend Paid	(...)	
Interest on Debentures and Loans Paid	(...)	
Repayment of Loans	(...)	
Redemption of Debentures/Preference Shares	(...)	
Net Cash from (or used in) Financing Activities		...
IV. **Net Increase/Decrease in Cash and Cash Equivalents** (I + II + III)		...
V. (+) **Cash and Cash Equivalents in the Beginning of the Year**		
Cash in Hand	...	
Cash at Bank	...	
Short-term Deposits	...	
Marketable Securities	...	...
		...
VI. **Cash and Cash Equivalents at the End of the Year**		
Cash in Hand	...	
Cash at Bank	...	
Short-term Deposits	...	
Marketable Securities	...	...
		...

Working Note

Calculation of Net Profit before Tax and Extraordinary Items

Net Profit as per Statement of Profit and Loss (Difference between closing balance and opening balance of statement of profit and loss)	...
(+) Transfer to Reserves	...
Proposed Dividend of Previous Year	...
Interim Dividend Paid During the Year	...
Provision for Tax Made During the Current Year	...
(–) Refund of Tax Credited to the Statement of Profit and Loss	(...)
Net Profit before Tax and Extraordinary Items	...

Previous Years' Examination Questions

1/2 Mark Questions

1. What is meant by 'cash flow statement'? **Term II 2022; Delhi 2017; All India 2014, 2011**

Ans. Cash flow statement is a statement showing the changes in financial position of a business concern during different intervals of time in terms of cash and cash equivalents.

2. For a company manufacturing garments, procurement of raw material, incurrence of manufacturing expenses, sale of garments are classified .... activities. **CBSE 2020**

Ans. operating

3. While preparing cash flow statement, if net cash flow from operating, investing and financing activities is negative the same is .... to opening cash balance to obtain .... cash balance. **CBSE 2020**

Ans. deducted, closing

4. 'Payment of dividend and interest' will be classified as which type of activity while preparing cash flow statement? **All India 2019, 2011**

Or While preparing cash flow statement, 'receipt of interest and dividend' will be classified under which type of activity in case of a non-financial enterprise? **All India 2019**

Or 'Payment and receipt of interest and dividend' is classified as which type of activity while preparing cash flow statement? **Delhi 2017**

Ans. Payment and receipt of interest and dividend is classified as financing activity while preparing cash flow statement of a non-financial company.

5. What is meant by 'cash flow'? **All India 2019, 2014; Delhi 2019, 2014, 2011 (C)**

Or State the meaning of 'cash flow' while preparing cash flow statement. **All India 2014**

Ans. 'Cash flow' implies inflow and outflow of cash and cash equivalents. Receipt of cash from an item other than cash and cash equivalents is termed as 'cash inflow' while cash payment in respect of such item is termed as 'cash outflow'.

6. When can 'receipt of dividend' be classified as an operating activity? State. Also give reason in support of your answer. **All India 2019**

Ans. When dividend is received by a finance company, then it can be considered as an operating activity. It is so, because investing is a primary business of finance company.

7. Mevo Ltd a financial enterprise had advanced a loan of ₹ 3,00,000, invested ₹ 6,00,000 in shares of the other companies and purchased machinery for ₹ 9,00,000. It received dividend of ₹ 70,000 on investment in shares. The company sold an old machine of the book value of ₹ 79,000 at a loss of ₹ 10,000.

Compute cash flows investing activities. **Dehli 2019**

Ans. **Calculation of Cash Flow from Investing Activities**

Particulars	Amt (₹)
Purchase of Machinery	(9,00,000)
Sale of Machinery	69,000
Purchase of Investments	(6,00,000)
Cash used in Investing Activities	14,31,000

8. Are 'assets acquired by issue of shares' disclosed in the cash flow statement? Give reason in support of your answer. **All India 2019**

Ans. No, 'assets acquired by issue of shares' are not disclosed in the cash flow statement due to non-cash nature of the transction.

9. K Ltd a manufacturing company obtained a loan of ₹ 6,00,000, advanced a loan of ₹ 1,00,000 and purchased machinery for ₹ 5,00,000. Calculate the amount of cash flow from financing and investing activities. **Delhi 2019**

Ans. **Cash Flow from Investing Activities**

Particulars	Amt (₹)
Loan Given	(1,00,000)
Purchase of Machinery	(5,00,000)
Cash used in Investing Activity	(6,00,000)

Cash Flow from Financing Activities

Particulars	Amt (₹)
Loan Taken	6,00,000
Cash Flow from Financing Activity	6,00,000

10. Under which type of activity will you classify cash advances and loans made to third party while preparing cash flow statement? **All India 2019; Compartment 2018**

Ans. Investing activities

11. State the primary objective of preparing a cash flow statement.
All India 2019, 2017; CBSE 2018; Compartment 2018

Ans. The primary objective of preparing cash flow statement is to provide useful information about the cash flows of an enterprise during a particular period under various heads, *i.e.* operating, investing and financing activities.

12. What is meant by 'cash and cash equivalents'? **All India 2019**

Or Give the meaning of 'cash equivalents' for the purpose of preparing cash flow statement. **Delhi 2016**

Or What is meant by 'cash equivalents'?
All India 2014, 2011; Delhi (C) 2014

Ans. **Cash** comprises cash in hand and demand deposits with banks and **Cash equivalents** are short-term highly liquid investments that can be easily convertible into known amount of cash and which are subject to an insignificant risk of change in value. e.g. Short-term marketable securities, which can be readily converted into cash, are treated as cash equivalents.

13. What is meant by 'inflow of cash'?
All India 2019

Ans. 'Inflow of cash' means funds received by a company due to operating, investing or financing activities.

14. How is goodwill written-off treated while calculating cash flow from operating activities? **All India 2019**

Ans. Goodwill written-off is added to profit before tax and extraordinary items to calculate operating profit before working capital changes while calculating cash flow from operating activities.

15. When does an investment qualify as cash equivalent? **All India 2019**

Ans. When the maturity period of investment is not more than three months.

16. 'Interest received and paid' is considered as which type of activity by a finance company while preparing a cash flow statement? **CBSE 2018**

Ans. Interest received by a finance company is an operating activity. Interest paid by a finance company is also an operating activity.

17. Normally, what should be the maturity period for a short-term investment from the date of its acquisition to be qualified as cash equivalents? **All India 2017**

Ans. The maturity period for a short-term investment from the date of acquisition to be qualified as cash equivalents should not be more than three months.

18. Will 'net decrease in working capital' other than cash and cash equivalents, increase, decrease or not change cash flow from operating activities? Give reason in support of your answer.
Delhi; All India 2017

Ans. Net decrease in working capital implies increase in cash flow from operating activities due to inflow of cash.

19. State whether the following will increase, decrease or have no effect on cash flow from operating activities while preparing 'cash flow statement'.

(*i*) Decrease in outstanding employees benefits expenses by ₹ 3,000.

(*ii*) Increase in prepaid insurance by ₹ 2,000. **All India 2017**

Ans. (*i*) Outstanding employee benefits expenses is a current liability. So, decrease in current liability will decrease cash flow from operating activities.

(*ii*) Prepaid insurance is a current asset. Increase in current asset will decrease cash flow from operating activities.

20. Short-term investments are not considered while preparing cash flow statement. Why? **Delhi 2017**

Ans. Short-term investments are a part of cash and cash equivalents therefore, they are not considered under operating, investing or financing activities.

21. Net increase in working capital other than cash and cash equivalents will increase, decrease or not change cash flow from operating activities. Give reason in support of your answer. **Delhi 2017**

Ans. Net increase in working capital implies decrease in current assets and increase in current liabilities is more than the increase in current assets and decrease in current liabilities. So, it will increase the cash flow from operating activities.

22. Cheques and drafts in hand are not considered while preparing cash flow statement. Why? **Delhi 2017**

Ans. Cheques and drafts are a part of cash equivalents and therefore not considered under operating, investing or financing activities.

23. State any two advantages of preparing cash flow statements. **Delhi 2017**

Ans. The advantages of cash flow statement are as follows

(*i*) It helps in knowing the liquidity/actual cash position of the company.

(*ii*) Any discrepancy in the financial reporting can be gauged through the cash flow statement by comparing the cash position of both.

24. State any two objectives of preparing 'cash flow statement'. **All India 2016**

Ans. The objectives of preparing cash flow statement are

(*i*) To ascertain the sources and applications (receipts and payments) of cash and cash equivalents under operating, investing and financing activities of the enterprise.

(*ii*) To ascertain net change in cash and cash equivalents being the difference between sources (receipts) and applications (payments) under the three activities between the dates of two balance sheets.

25. "An enterprise may hold securities and loans for dealing or trading purpose in which case they are similar to inventory acquired specifically for resale." Is the statement correct? Cash flows from such activities will be classified under which type of activity while preparing cash flow statement? **Delhi; All India 2016**

Ans. Yes, this statement is correct. This statement refers to finance companies. Cash flows from such activities for these companies is classified under operating activity.

26. Does movement between items that constitute cash or cash equivalents result into cash flow? Give reason in support of your answer. **All India 2016**

Ans. No, the movement of items that constitute cash or cash equivalents does not result into cash flow. This is because such movements indicate a mere change in the form of available cash balance rather than actual cash outflows or inflows.

27. Why is separate disclosure of cash flows from investing activities important? State. **All India 2016**

Ans. Separate disclosure of cash flows from investing activities is important because it shows the extent to which the investment have been made for resources intended to generate future income and cash flows.

28. Deepu Ltd a non-financing company received dividend on shares. How will it be presented while preparing a 'cash flow statement'? **All India (C) 2016**

Ans. Dividend received by a non-financing company is a investing activity.

29. Why is depreciation added back to net profit while preparing 'cash flow statement'? **Al India (C) 2016**

Ans. Depreciation is added back to net profit while preparing cash flow statement as it is a non-cash expense and does not involve any outflow of cash but results in decrease in profits.

30. Hider Ltd a mutual fund company invested ₹ 5,00,000 in shares of Prayag Ltd. It received dividend of ₹ 45,000 during the year. How will it be depicted in the cash flow statement? **Delhi (C) 2016**

Ans. Dividend of ₹ 45,000 received by the mutual fund company will be depicted as a operating activity while preparing cash flow statement.

31. Nazma Ltd received interest on an item and the accountant classified it under investing activity while preparing cash flow statement. Name another item for which such a treatment is possible. **Delhi (C) 2016**

Ans. The another item for which such a treatment is possible is dividend received.

32. While preparing cash flow statement, the accountant of a financing company showed 'dividend received ₹ 50,000 on investments' as an investing activity. Was he correct in doing so? Give reason. **All India 2015**

Or While preparing the 'Cash Flow Statement' the accountant of Gulfam Ltd, a financing company showed 'dividend received on investment' as 'investing activity'. Was he correct in doing so? Give reason. **Delhi 2015**

Ans. No, the accountant was not correct in doing so. In case of a financing company, 'dividend received on investments' should be classified under the head 'operating activity'.

33. The accountant of Manav Ltd while preparing cash flow statement added depreciation provided on fixed assets to net profit for calculating cash flow from operating activities. Was he correct in doing so? Give reason. **All India; Delhi 2015**

Or While preparing cash flow statement of Sharda Ltd. 'Depreciation provided on fixed assets' was added to net profit to calculate cash flow from operating activities. Was the accountant correct in doing so? Give reason. **Delhi 2015**

Ans. Yes, the accountant is correct, because depreciation is a non-cash expense and it must be added to net profit to calculate cash flow from operating activities.

34. While preparing the cash flow statement of Alka Ltd, 'dividend paid' was shown as an operating activity by the accountant of the company. Was he correct in doing so ? Give reason. **Delhi 2015**

Ans. The treatment of the accountant is incorrect. The treatment of dividend paid while preparing the cash flow statement would be to show it under the head financing activity as 'minus items'.

35. The accountant of 'Nav Jeevan Ltd' while preparing cash flow statement added the proposed dividend of the current year to net profit while calculating cash flow from operating activities. Was he correct in doing so? Give reason. **Foreign 2015**

Ans. No, the accountant was not correct in doing so. As per AS-4, proposed dividend of current year will be accounted for in the next year after it is declared by the shareholders.

36. Payment of bonus to the employees by an insurance company is classified under which activity while preparing cash flow statement. **All India 2015 Modified**

Ans. It is classified as operating activity.

37. Kaveri Ltd a financing company obtained loans and advances of ₹ 5,00,000 during the year @ 12% per annum. In which activity will it be included while preparing cash flow statement? **Delhi (C) 2015 Modified**

Ans. It will be included in operating activity.

38. G Ltd is carrying on a paper manufacturing business. In the current year, it purchased machinery for ₹ 30,00,000; it paid salaries of ₹ 60,000 to its employees, it required funds for expansion and therefore, issued shares of ₹ 20,00,000.

It earned a profit of ₹ 9,00,000 for the current year. Find out cash flows from operating activities. **Delhi 2015**

Ans. ₹ 9,00,000 profit earned during the year will be the cash flow from operating activities.

39. 'Koval Ltd' is a financing company. Under which activity will the amount of interest to be paid on a loan settled in the current year be shown, while preparing cash flow statement? **All India (C) 2015 Modified**

Ans. It will be classified under operating activity.

40. 'Shri Ltd' was carrying on a business of packaging in Delhi and earned good profits in the past years. The company wanted to expand its business and required additional funds.

To meet its requirements the company issued equity shares of ₹ 30,00,000. It purchased a computerised machine for ₹ 20,00,000. It also purchased raw material amounting to ₹ 2,00,000.

During the current year, the net profit of the company was ₹ 15,00,000. Find out cash flow from operating activities from the above transactions. **All India (C) 2015**

Ans. Net profit earned during the current year, *i.e.* ₹ 15,00,000 will be the cash flow from operating activities.

41. Why is specific disclosure of cash flow from financing activities important while preparing cash flow statement? **All India 2014**

Ans. Separate disclosure of cash flows arising from financing activities is important because it is useful in predicting claims on future cash flows by providers of funds (both capital and borrowings) to the enterprise.

42. Why is separate disclosure of cash flow from investing activities important while preparing cash flow statement? **All India 2014**

Ans. Separate disclosure of cash flows from investing activities is important because they represent to which investment have been made for resources, intended to generate future income and cash flows.

43. Dividend paid by a financial company is classified under which type of activity, while preparing cash flow statement? **All India (C) 2014**

Ans. It is classified under 'financing activity'.

44. What is meant by outflow of cash while preparing cash flow statement? **Delhi (C) 2014**

Ans. Cash outflow arises when the net effect of transactions is a decrease in the amount of cash and cash equivalents.

45. State the objective of preparing a cash flow statement. **Delhi 2014, 2012, 2011 (C); All India 2014, 2014 (C)**

Or Why is a cash flow statement prepared? **All India 2014; Delhi (C) 2010**

Ans. A cash flow statement provides information about the historical changes in cash and cash equivalents of an enterprise by classifying cash flows into operating, investing and financing activities between the dates of two balance sheets.

46. State with reason whether the issue of 9% debentures to the vendors for the purchase of machinery of ₹ 50,000 will result into inflow, outflow or no flow of cash. **All India (C) 2014**

Ans. There is no flow of cash by the issue of 9% debentures to the vendors for the purchase of machinery of ₹ 50,000 because this transaction will not change the balance of cash and cash equivalents.

47. What is meant by 'cash from operating activities'? **Delhi 2013**

Ans. 'Cash from operating activities' are the principal revenue producing activities of the enterprise and other activities, that are not investing or financing activities.

48. Under which type of activity will you classify 'dividend received by a finance company' while preparing cash flow statement? **Delhi 2013**

Ans. Dividend received by a finance company is an operating activity.

49. State with reason whether 'purchase of fixed asset on long-term deferred payment' would result in inflow, outflow or no flow of cash. **Delhi 2013**

Ans. No flow of cash because no cash is involved in this transaction.

50. Under which type of activity will you classify 'refund of income tax received' while preparing the cash flow statement? **Delhi 2013**

Ans. Operating activity

51. When does the flow of cash take place? **Delhi 2013**

Ans. Cash flow arises when the net effect of a transaction either increases or decreases the amount of cash or cash equivalent.

52. State with reason whether 'discount received on making payment to suppliers' would result into inflow, outflow or no flow of cash. **All India 2013**

Ans. Discount received on making payment to suppliers will result in no flow of cash because discount received is a non-cash transaction and does not result in actual payment of cash.

53. Under which type of activity will you classify 'interest paid on long-term borrowings' while preparing cash flow statement? **All India 2013**

Ans. Interest paid on long-term borrowings is a financing activity.

54. State with reason whether 'old furniture written-off' would result into inflow/ outflow or no flow of cash. **All India 2013**

Ans. Old furniture written-off will result in no flow of cash because it does not affect cash as it is a non-cash transaction.

55. Under which type of activity will you classify 'proceeds from sale of investment' while preparing cash flow statement? **Delhi 2013**

Ans. Proceeds from sale of investments is an investing activity.

56. Under which type of activity will you classify 'proceeds from sale of patents' while preparing cash flow statement? **All India 2013**

Ans. Proceeds from sale of patents is an investing activity.

57. Give an example of the activity which remains financing activity for every enterprise. **All India 2013**

Ans. Dividend paid

58. Under which type of activity will you classify 'commission and royalty received' while preparing cash flow statement? **All India 2013**

Ans. Commission and royalty received is an operating activity.

59. While preparing cash flow statement which type of activity is, 'payment of cash to acquire debentures by an investment company'? **Delhi 2012**

Ans. Operating activity

60. While preparing cash flow statement which type of activity is, 'payment of cash to acquire shares of another company by a trading company'? **All India 2012**

Ans. Investing activity

61. State with reason whether 'deposit of cash into bank' will result into inflow, outflow or no flow of cash. **Delhi 2011**

Ans. 'Deposit of cash into bank' does not result in cash flow. It is simply a movement between two components of cash and cash equivalents.

62. List any two investing activities which result into outflow of cash. **All India 2011; Delhi (C) 2011**

Ans. Two investing activities which result into outflow of cash are

(*i*) Building purchased

(*ii*) Investments purchased

63. List any two financing activities that will result into outflow of cash. **All India 2011; Delhi (C) 2011**

Ans. Two financing activities that result into outflow of cash are

(*i*) Redemption of debentures

(*ii*) Interest paid on debentures

64. Name any two financing activities that result into inflow of cash. **All India (C) 2011**

Ans. The two financing activities that result into inflow of cash are

(*i*) Cash proceeds from issue of shares

(*ii*) Cash proceeds from issue of debentures

65. Name any two investing activities that result into inflow of cash. **All India (C) 2011**

Ans. Two investing activities that result into inflow of cash are

(*i*) Cash proceeds from sale of building

(*ii*) Cash proceeds from sale of investments

66. State with reason whether 'withdrawal of cash from bank' will result into, inflow, outflow or no flow of cash. **Foreign 2011**

Ans. 'Withdrawal of cash from bank' does not result in cash flow. It is simply a movement between two components of cash and cash equivalents.

67. What is meant by cash flow from financing activities? **Delhi 2011**

Ans. Financing activities are the activities which result in change in the size and composition of the owner's capital (including preference share capital) and borrowings (including debentures) of the enterprise from other sources. It includes proceeds from issue of shares or other similar instruments, issue of debentures, loans, bonds, other short term or long term borrowings and repayment of amount borrowed.

68. State with reason whether 'cash paid to a creditor' will result into inflow, outflow or no flow of cash. **Delhi 2011**

Or State with reason whether payment of cash to creditors will result into inflow, outflow or no flow of cash. **All India 2011**

Ans. Cash paid to a creditor will result in outflow of cash.

69. Under which type of activity will you classify 'proceeds from sale of buildings' while preparing cash flow statement? **All India 2010**

Ans. It will be classified as an investing activity.

70. Redemption of debentures would result in inflow, outflow or no flow of cash? Give your answer with reason. **All India 2010**

Ans. Redemption of debentures will result in outflow of cash as payment is made to the debentureholders.

71. Under which type of activity will you classify 'issue of equity shares at premium' while preparing cash flow statement? **All India 2010**

Ans. It will be classified as a financing activity.

72. Purchase of patents would result in inflow, outflow or no flow of cash? Give your answer with reason? **All India 2010**

Ans. Purchase of patents would result in outflow of cash, because it involves payment of cash for acquisition of an asset.

73. Under which type of activity will you classify 'issuing 9% debentures' while preparing cash flow statement? **Delhi 2010**

Ans. Financing activity

74. Declaration of final dividend would result into inflow, outflow or no flow of cash? Give your answer with reason. **Delhi 2010**

Ans. No flow of cash as final dividend is only declared, not yet paid.

75. Under which type of activity will you classify 'proceeds from sale of machinery' while preparing cash flow statement? **Delhi 2010**

Ans. Investing activity

76. Interest received on debentures would result into inflow, outflow or no flow of cash? Give reason. **All India 2010**

Ans. Cash inflow, because cash comes in due to interest received on debentures.

77. Give one difference between an operating activity and a financing activity. **Delhi (C) 2010**

Ans. Operating activity is the principal revenue producing activity of an enterprise whereas, financing activity are those activities which change the size and composition of owner's equity and borrowings of an enterprise.

78. Give any two transactions which result into 'inflow of cash'. **All India (C) 2010**

Ans. The two transacting which result into 'inflow of cash' are

(*i*) Cash proceeds from sale of investments.

(*ii*) Cash proceeds from issue of debentures.

79. Give one difference between an operating activity and an investing activity. **All India (C) 2010**

Ans. Operating activity is the principal revenue producing activity of an enterprise whereas, investing activity includes the acquisition and disposal of fixed assets.

80. Give one transaction which may result into outflow of cash and one which may result into no flow of cash. **All India (C) 2010**

Ans. **Outflow of cash** Purchase of investments.

No flow of cash Cash deposited into the bank.

81. Under which type of activity will you classify 'furniture purchased for cash' while preparing cash flow statement? **Delhi 2010**

Ans. It will be classified under investing activity.

82. Sale of marketable securities at par would result in inflow, outflow or no flow of cash. Give your answer with reason. **All India 2010**

Ans. No flow of cash as marketable securities are cash equivalents.

83. Under which type of activity will you classify 'cash received from debtors' while preparing cash flow statement. **Delhi 2010**

Ans. Cash received from debtors will be classified under operating activity.

84. Interest paid on debentures would result in inflow, outflow or no flow of cash. Give your answer with reason. **Delhi 2010**

Ans. Interest paid on debentures would result in outflow of cash because it involves payment of cash to debentureholders.

5/6 Marks Questions

85. From the following Balance Sheet of Jay Ltd. as at 31st March, 2022, calculate Cash Flows from Operating Activities. **CBSE Term II 2022**

Jay Ltd.
Balance Sheet
as at 31st March, 2022

	Particulars	Note No.	31st March, 2022 (₹)	31st March, 2021 (₹)
I.	**EQUITY AND LIABILITIES**			
	1. **Shareholders' Funds**			
	(a) Share Capital	1	50,00,000	30,00,000
	(b) Reserve and Surplus	2	10,00,000	6,00,000
	2. **Non-Current Liabilities**			
	Long-term Borrowing	3	8,00,000	4,00,000
	3. **Current Liabilities**			
	(a) Trade Payables		2,00,000	3,00,000
	(b) Other Current Liabilities	4	3,00,000	1,00,000
	(c) Short-term Provisions	5	1,50,000	1,00,000
	Total		74,50,000	45,00,000
II.	**ASSETS**			
	1. **Non-current Assets**			
	Fixed Assets			
	(i) Tangible Assets	6	60,00,000	40,00,000
	(ii) Intangible Assets	7	4,00,000	4,00,000
	2. **Current Assets**			
	(a) Inventories		7,00,000	40,000
	(b) Cash and Cash Equivalents		3,50,000	60,000
	Total		74,50,000	45,00,000

Notes of Accounts

Note No.	Particulars	31st March, 2022 (₹)	31st March, 2021 (₹)
1.	**Share Capital** Equity Share Capital	50,00,000	30,00,000
2.	**Reserve and Surplus** Surplus balance in the statement of profit and loss	10,00,000	6,00,000
3.	**Long-term Borrowing** 10% debentures	8,00,000	4,00,000
4.	**Other Current Liabilities** Outstanding rent	3,00,000	1,00,000
5.	**Short-term Provisions** Provision for tax	1,50,000	1,00,000
6.	**Tangible Assets** Land	60,00,000	40,00,000
7.	**Intangible Assets** Patents	4,00,000	4,00,000

Additional Information

₹4,00,000, 10% Debentures were issued on 31st March, 2022.

Ans.

Cash Flow from Operating Activities
for the year ended 31st March, 2022

Particulars		Amt (₹)
Cash Flow from Operating Activities		
Net Profit before Tax and Extraordinary Items (WN1)		5,50,000
Adjustments for		
(+) Interest on Debentures		40,000
Operating Profit before Working Capital Change		5,90,000
(+) Decrease in Current Assets and Increase in Current Liabilities : Outstanding Rent	2,00,000	
(−) Increase in Current Assets and Decrease in Current Liabilities : Trade Payables	(1,00,000)	
Inventories	(6,60,000)	(5,60,000)
Cash Generated from Operations		30,000
(−) Income Tax Paid		(1,00,000)
Net Cash used in Operating Activities		(70,000)

Working Note

1. **Net Profit before Tax and Extraordinary Items**

Net Profit for the year (10,00,000 – 6,00,000) = 4,00,000
(+) Provision for tax = 1,50,000
₹ 5,50,000

86. From the following balance sheet of DCX Ltd and the additional information as at 31st March, 2018. Prepare a cash flow statement.

Balance Sheet of DCX Ltd
as at 31st March, 2018

	Particulars	Note No.	31.3.2018 (₹)	31.3.2017 (₹)
I.	**EQUITY AND LIABILITIES**			
	1. **Shareholders' Funds**			
	(a) Share Capital		30,00,000	21,00,000
	(b) Reserves and Surplus	1	4,00,000	5,00,000
	2. **Non-current Liabilities**			
	Long-term Borrowings	2	8,00,000	5,00,000
	3. **Current Liabilities**			
	(a) Trade Payables		1,50,000	1,00,000
	(b) Short-term Provisions	3	76,000	56,000
	Total		44,26,000	32,56,000
II.	**ASSETS**			
	1. **Non-current Assets**			
	Fixed Assets			
	(a) Tangible Assets	4	27,00,000	20,00,000
	(b) Intangible Assets		8,00,000	7,00,000
	2. **Current Assets**			
	(a) Current Investments		89,000	78,000
	(b) Inventories		8,00,000	4,00,000
	(c) Cash and Cash Equivalents		37,000	78,000
	Total		44,26,000	32,56,000

Notes to Accounts

Note No.	Particulars	31.3.2018 (₹)	31.3.2017 (₹)
1.	**Reserves and Surplus**		
	(Surplus, i.e. Balance in the Statement of Profit and Loss)	4,00,000	5,00,000
		4,00,000	5,00,000
2.	**Long-term Borrowings**		
	8% Debentures	8,00,000	5,00,000
		8,00,000	5,00,000
3.	**Short-term Provisions**		
	Provision for Tax	76,000	56,000
		76,000	56,000
4.	**Tangible Assets**		
	Machinery	33,00,000	25,00,000
	(−) Accumulated Depreciation	(6,00,000)	(5,00,000)
		27,00,000	20,00,000

Additional Information

(*i*) During the year a machinery costing ₹ 8,00,000 on which accumulated depreciation was ₹ 3,20,000 was sold for ₹ 6,40,000.

(*ii*) Debentures were issued on 1st April, 2017. **All India 2019**

Ans.

Cash Flow Statement
for the Year ended 31st March, 2018

	Particulars		Amt (₹)
A.	**Cash Flow From Operating Activities**		
	Net Profit before Tax and Extraordinary Items (W.N.1)		(24,000)
	(+) Depreciation on Machinery	4,20,000	
	Interest on Debentures	64,000	
	(−) Profit on Sale of Machinery	(1,60,000)	3,24,000
	Net Operating Profit before Working Capital Changes		3,00,000
	(+) Increase in Current Liabilities and Decrease in Current Assets Trade Payables	50,000	
	(−) Increase in Current Assets and Decrease in Current Liabilities: Inventories	(4,00,000)	(3,50,000)
	Cash Generated from Operations		(50,000)
	(−) Tax Paid		(56,000)
	Net Cash Used in Operating Activities		(1,06,000)
B.	**Cash Flow from Investing Activities**		
	Sale of Machinery	6,40,000	
	Purchase of Machinery	(16,00,000)	
	Purchase of Intangible Assets	(1,00,000)	
	Net Cash Used in Investing Activities		(10,60,000)

	Particulars		Amt (₹)
C.	**Cash Flow from Financing Activities**		
	Issue of Equity Shares	9,00,000	
	Issue of Debentures	3,00,000	
	Interest on Debentures Paid	(64,000)	
	Net cash From Financing Activities		11,36,000
D.	**Net Decrease in Cash and Cash Equivalent (A + B + C)**		(30,000)
	(+) Opening Cash and Cash Equivalent	78,000	
	Opening Current Investments	78,000	1,56,000
	Cash and Cash Equivalent as on 31st March, 2018		1,26,000

Working Notes

1. Surplus as per Statement of Profit and Loss (4,00,000 – 5,00,000) = (1,00,000)

   (+) Provision for Tax = 76,000

   Net Profit beforeTax and Extraordinary Items = (24,000)

2. Dr **Machinery Account** Cr

Particulars	Amt (₹)	Particulars	Amt (₹)
To Balance b/d	25,00,000	By Bank A/c (Sale)	6,40,000
To Statement of Profit and Loss	1,60,000	By Accumulated Depreciation	3,20,000
To Bank A/c (Purchase) (Balancing figure)	16,00,000	By Balance c/d	33,00,000
	42,60,000		42,60,000

3. Dr **Accumulated Depreciation Account** Cr

Particulars	Amt (₹)	Particulars	Amt (₹)
To Machinery A/c	3,20,000	By Balance b/d	5,00,000
To Balance c/d	6,00,000	By Statement of Profit and Loss (Balancing figure)	4,20,000
	9,20,000		9,20,000

87. The following is the balance sheet of R M Ltd as at 31st March, 2017. Prepare a cash flow statement.

Balance Sheet of R M Ltd
as at 31st March, 2017

Particulars	Note No.	31.3.2017 (₹)	31.3.2016 (₹)
I. **EQUITY AND LIABILITIES**			
1. **Shareholders' Funds**			
(a) Share Capital		15,00,000	10,00,000
(b) Reserves and Surplus (Balance in Statement of Profit and Loss)		7,50,000	6,00,000
2. **Non-current Liabilities**			
Long-term Borrowings	1	1,00,000	2,00,000
3. **Current Liabilities**			
(a) Trade Payables		1,00,000	1,10,000
(b) Short-term Provisions	2	95,000	80,000
Total		25,45,000	19,90,000
II. **ASSETS**			
1. **Non-Current Assets**			
(a) Fixed Assets			
(i) Tangible Assets	3	10,10,000	9,00,000
(ii) Intangible Assets	4	2,80,000	2,00,000
(b) Non-current Investments		5,00,000	—
2. **Current Assets**			
(a) Inventories		1,80,000	1,00,000
(b) Trade Receivables		2,00,000	1,50,000
(c) Cash and Cash Equivalents	5	3,75,000	6,40,000
Total		25,45,000	19,90,000

Notes to Accounts

Note No.	Particulars	31.3.2017 (₹)	31.3.2016 (₹)
1.	**Long-term Borrowings**		
	9% Debentures	1,00,000	2,00,000
		1,00,000	2,00,000
2.	**Short-term Provisions**		
	Provision for Tax	95,000	80,000
		95,000	80,000
3.	**Tangible Assets**		
	Plant and Machinery	12,10,000	11,40,000
	Accumulated Depreciation	(2,00,000)	(2,40,000)
		10,10,000	9,00,000
4.	**Intangible Assets**		
	Goodwill	2,80,000	2,00,000
		2,80,000	2,00,000
5.	**Cash and Cash Equivalents**		
	(i) Cash in Hand	70,000	3,50,000
	(ii) Bank Balance	3,05,000	2,90,000
		3,75,000	6,40,000

Additional Information

(*i*) During the year, a machine costing ₹ 80,000 on which accumulated depreciation was ₹ 50,000 was sold for ₹ 30,000.

(*ii*) 9% Debentures were released on 31st March, 2017. **All India 2019**

Ans.

Cash Flow Statement

for the year ended 31st March, 2016 and 2017

Particulars		Amt (₹)
A. **Cash Flow from Operating Activities**		
Net Profit before Tax and Extraordinary Items (W N 3)		2,45,000
(+) Depreciation Charged During the Year	10,000	
Interest on 9% Debentures (2,00,000 × 9%)	18,000	28,000
Operating Profit Before Working Capital Changes		2,73,000
(+) Increase in Current Liabilities and Decrease in Current Assets		
(−) Increase in Current Assets and Decrease in Current Liabilities		
Trade Payables	(10,000)	
Inventories	(80,000)	
Trade Receivables	(50,000)	(,140,000)
Cash generated from Operations		1,33,000
(−) Tax Paid		(80,000)
Net Cash flow from Operating Activities		53,000
B. Cash Flow from Investing Activities		
Purchase of Plant and Machinery (W N 1)	(1,50,000)	
Purchase of Goodwill	(80,000)	
Sale of Machinery	30,000	
Purchase of Non-current Investments	(5,00,000)	
Net Cash Used in Investment Activities		(7,00,000)
C. Cash Flow from Financing Activities		
Redemption of Debentures	(1,00,000)	
Interest Paid on Debentures	(18,000)	
Proceeds from Issue of Shares	5,00,000	
Net Cash from Financing Activities		3,82,000
Net Decrease in Cash and Cash Equivalent (A + B + C)		(2,65,000)
(+) Cash and Cash Equivalent in the Beginning		
Cash in Hand	3,50,000	
Cash at Bank	2,90,000	6,40,000
Cash and Cash Equivalent in the End		3,75,000
Cash in Hand	70,000	
Cash in Bank	3,05,000	3,75,000

Working Notes

1. Dr **Plant and Machinery Account** Cr

Particulars	Amt (₹)	Particulars	Amt (₹)
To Balance b/d	11,40,000	By Bank	30,000
To Bank (Purchase)	1,50,000	By Accumulated Depreciation A/c	50,000
(Balancing figure)		By Balance c/d	12,10,000
	12,90,000		12,90,000

2. Dr **Accumulated Depreciation Account** Cr

Particulars	Amt (₹)	Particulars	Amt (₹)
To Plant and Machinery A/c	50,000	By Balance b/d	2,40,000
To Balance c/d	2,00,000	By Statement of Profit & Loss A/c	10,000
		(Balancing figure)	
	2,50,000		2,50,000

3. Net Profit as per Statement of Profit and loss (7,50,000 – 6,00,000) = ₹ 1,50,0000
(+) Provision for tax = ₹ 95,000
Net profit before tax and extraordinary items = ₹ 2,45,000

88. From the following balance sheet of Kiero Ltd and the additional information as on 31st March, 2018, prepare a cash flow statement. **All India 2019**

Balance Sheet of Kiero Ltd
as at 31st March, 2018

	Particulars	Note No.	31-3-18 (₹)	31-3-17 (₹)
I.	**EQUITY AND LIABILITIES**			
	1. **Shareholders' Funds**			
	(a) Share Capital		7,90,000	5,80,000
	(b) Reserves and Surplus	1	4,60,000	1,20,000
	2. **Non-current Liabilities**			
	Long-term Borrowings	2	5,00,000	3,00,000
	3. Current Liabilities			
	(a) Short-term Borrowings	3	1,15,000	42,000
	(b) Short-term Provisions	4	1,18,000	46,000
	Total		19,83,000	10,88,000
II.	**ASSETS**			
	1. Non-current Assets			
	Fixed Assets			
	(i) Tangible Assets	5	9,80,000	6,35,000
	(ii) Intangible Assets	6	2,68,000	1,70,000
	2. **Current Assets**			
	(a) Current Investments		1,40,000	70,000
	(b) Trade Receivables		4,40,000	1,50,000
	(c) Cash and Cash Equivalents		1,55,000	63,000
	Total		19,83,000	10,88,000

Notes to Accounts

Note No.	Particulars	31st March 2018 (₹)	31st March 2017 (₹)
1.	Reserves and Surplus		
	Surplus(Balance in Statement of Profit and Loss)	3,20,000	60,000
	General Reserve	1,40,000	60,000
		4,60,000	1,20,000
2.	**Long-term Borrowings**		
	12% Debentures	5,00,000	3,00,000
		5,00,000	3,00,000
3.	**Short-term Borrowings**		
	Bank Overdraft	1,15,000	42,000
		1,15,000	42,000
4.	**Short-term Provisions**		
	Provision for Tax	1,18,000	46,000
		1,18,000	46,000
5.	**Tangible Assets**		
	Plant and Machinery	11,00,000	7,50,000
	(–) Accumulated Depreciation	(1,20,000)	(1,15,000)
		9,80,000	6,35,000
6.	**Intangible Assets**		
	Goodwill	2,68,000	1,70,000
		2,68,000	1,70,000

Additional Information

12% debentures were issued on 1st September, 2017. **Delhi 2019**

Ans.

Cash Flow Statement

For the year ended 31st March, 2018

	Particulars		Amt (₹)
A.	**Cash Flow from Operating Activities**		
	Net Profit before Tax and Extraordinary Items (W N 2)		4,58,000
	(+) Depreciation on Machinery	5,000	
	Interest on Debentures	50,000	55,000
	Net Operating Profit before Working Capital Changes		5,13,000
	(+) Increase in Current Liabilities and Decrease in Current Assets	–	
	(–) Increase in Current Assets and Decrease in Current Liabilities		
	Trade Receivables	(2,90,000)	(2,90,000)
	Cash Generated from Operations		2,23,000
	(–) Tax Paid		(46,000)
	Net Cash from Operating Activities		1,77,000
B.	**Cash Flow from Investing Activities**		
	Purchase of Plant and Machinery	(3,50,000)	
	Purchase of Goodwill	(98,000)	
	Net Cash Used in Investing Activities		(4,48,000)

	Particulars		Amt (₹)
C.	**Cash Flow from Financing Activities**		
	Proceeds from Issue of Share Capital	2,10,000	
	Proceeds from issue of 12% Debentures	2,00,000	
	Increase in Bank Overdraft	73,000	
	Interest on Debentures Paid	(50,000)	
	Net Cash from Financing Activities		4,33,000
D.	**Net increase in Cash and Cash Equivalent** (A + B + C)		1,62,000
	(+) **Cash and Cash Equivalent in the Beginning**		
	Cash and Bank	63,000	
	Current Investments	70,000	1,33,000
E.	**Cash and Cash Equivalent in the End**		2,95,000
	Cash and Bank	1,55,000	
	Current Investments	1,40,000	2,95,000

Working Notes

1. Interest on debentures **Amt (₹)**

$$3{,}00{,}000 \times 12\% = ₹\,36{,}000$$

$$2{,}00{,}000 \times 12\% \times \frac{7}{12} = ₹\,14{,}000$$

$$₹\,50{,}000$$

2. Net Profit as per statement of profit and loss = ₹ 2,60,000
   (+) Transfer to general reserve = ₹ 80,000
   (–) Provision for tax = ₹ 1,18,000
   Net Profit before Tax and Extraordinary Items = ₹ 4,58,000

89. From the following balance sheet of JY Ltd as at 31st March, 2017 , prepare a cash flow statement.

Balance Sheet of JY Ltd
as at 31st March, 2017

Particulars	Note No.	31st March, 2017 (₹)	31st March, 2016 (₹)
I EQUITY AND LIABILITIES			
1. **Shareholders' Funds**			
(a) Share Capital		5,00,000	5,00,000
(b) Reserves and Surplus	1	1,00,000	(25,000)
2. **Non-current Liabilities**			
Long-term Borrowings	2	2,50,000	1,50,000
3. **Current Liabilities**			
(a) Short-term Borrowings	3	1,50,000	1,00,000
(b) Short-term Provisions	4	1,25,000	75,000
Total		11,25,000	8,00,000

Particulars	Note No.	31st March, 2017 (₹)	31st March, 2016 (₹)
II ASSETS			
1. Non-current Assets			
(a) Fixed Assets			
(i) Tangible	5	6,00,000	4,50,000
2. Current Assets			
(a) Trade Receivables		2,75,000	2,25,000
(b) Cash and Cash Equivalents		50,000	25,000
(c) Short-term Loans and Advances		2,00,000	1,00,000
Total		11,25,000	8,00,000

Notes to Accounts

Note No.	Particulars	31st March, 2017 (₹)	31st March, 2016 (₹)
1.	**Reserves and Surplus**		
	(Surplus, i.e. Balance in the Statement of Profit and Loss)	1,00,000	(25,000)
		1,00,000	(25,000)
2.	**Long-term Borrowings**		
	10% Debentures	2,50,000	1,50,000
		2,50,000	1,50,000
3.	**Short-term Borrowings**		
	Bank Overdraft	1,50,000	1,00,000
		1,50,000	1,00,000
4.	**Short-term Provisions**		
	Provision for Tax	1,25,000	75,000
		1,25,000	75,000
5.	**Tangible Assets**		
	Machinery	7,37,500	5,25,000
	Accumulated Depreciation	(1,37,500)	(75,000)
		6,00,000	4,50,000

Additional Information

(i) Proposed divident : 2016 – ₹ 50,000, 2017– ₹ 75,000

(ii) ₹ 1,00,000, 10% debentures were issued on 31st March, 2017. **CBSE 2018 (M)**

Ans.

Cash Flow Statement

for the year ended 31st March, 2017

Particulars		Amt (₹)
A. Cash Flow from Operating Activities		
Net Profit before Tax and Extraordinary Items		3,00,000
Adjustments for		
(+) Depreciation	62,500	
(+) Interest on Debentures (1,50,000 × 10%)	15,000	77,500
Operating Profit before Working Capital Changes		3,77,500
(+) Decrease in Current Assets and Increase in Current Liabilities		—

Particulars		Amt (₹)
(−) Increase in Current Assets and Decrease in Current Liabilities		
Trade Receivables	(50,000)	
Short-term Loan and Advances	(1,00,000)	(1,50,000)
Cash Generated from Operations		2,27,500
(−) Income Tax Paid		(75,000)
Net Cash from Operating Activities		1,52,500
B. Cash Flow from Investing Activities		
Purchase of Machinery	(2,12,500)	
Cash Used in Investing Activities		(2,12,500)
C. Cash Flow from Financing Activities		
Proceeds from Issue of Debentures	1,00,000	
Increase in Bank Overdraft	50,000	
Dividend Paid	(50,000)	
Interest on Debentures	(15,000)	
Cash Flow from Financing Activities		85,000
D. **Net Increase in Cash and Cash Equivalents** (A + B + C)		25,000
(+) Opening Cash and Cash Equivalents		25,000
Closing Cash and Cash Equivalents		50,000

Working Note

1. **Calculation of Net Profit before Tax and Extraordinary Items**

Particulars		Amt (₹)
Surplus, i.e. Balance in Statement of Profit and Loss (Closing)	1,00,000	
(−) Surplus, i.e. Balance in Statement of Profit and Loss (Opening)	(25,000)	1,25,000
(+) Proposed Dividend	50,000	
Provision for Tax	1,25,000	1,75,000
Net Profit before Tax and Extraordinary Items		3,00,000

90. Following is the balance sheet of Mevanca Ltd as at 31st March, 2017.

Balance Sheet of Mevanca Ltd
as at 31st March, 2017

Particulars	Note No.	31st March, 2017 (₹)	31st March, 2016 (₹)
I **EQUITY AND LIABILITIES**			
1. **Shareholders' Funds**			
(a) Share Capital		3,00,000	1,00,000
(b) Reserves and Surplus	1	25,000	1,20,000
2. **Non-current Liabilities**			
Long-term Borrowings	2	80,000	60,000
3. **Current Liabilities**			
(a) Trade Payables		6,000	20,000
(b) Short-term Provision	3	68,000	70,000
Total		4,79,000	3,70,000

Particulars	Note No.	31st March, 2017 (₹)	31st March, 2016 (₹)
II. ASSETS			
1. Non-current Assets Fixed Assets	4	3,36,000	1,92,000
2. Current Assets			
(a) Invetories		67,000	60,000
(b) Trade Receivables		51,000	65,000
(c) Cash and Cash Equivalents		25,000	49,000
(d) Other Current Assets		-	4,000
Total		4,79,000	3,70,000

Note to Accounts

Particulars	31st March, 2017 (₹)	31st March, 2016 (₹)
1. Reserves and Surplus		
Surplus i.e, Balance in Statement of Profit and Loss	25,000	1,20,000
	25,000	1,20,000
2. Long-term Borrowings 10% Long-term Loan	80,000	60,000
	80,000	60,000
3. Short-term Provisions Provision for Tax	68,000	70,000
	68,000	70,000
4. Fixed Assets		
Machinery Accumulated Depreciation	3,48,000 (48,000)	2,15,000 (23,000)
	3,36,000	1,92,000

Additional Information

(*i*) Additional loan was taken on 1st July, 2016.

(*ii*) Tax of ₹ 53,000 was paid during the year.

Prepare cash flow statement. **Compartment 2018**

Ans. **Cash Flow Statement for the year ending 31st March, 2017**

	Particulars		Amt (₹)
A.	Cash Flow from Operating Activities		
	Net Profit before Tax and Extraordinary Items (W N 1)		44,000
	(+) Depreciation on Machinery	25,000	
	Interest on Loan	7,500	32,500
			(11,500)
	Operating Profit before Working Capital Changes		
	(+) Decrease in Current Assets and Increase in Current Liabilities		
	Trade Receivables	14,000	
	Other Current Assets	4,000	18,000
	(−) Increase in Current Assets and Decrease in Current Liabilities		
	Trade Payables	(14,000)	
	Inventories	(7,000)	(21,000)
			(14,500)

	Particulars		Amt (₹)
	Cash Generated from Operations		
	(–) Tax Paid		(53,000)
	Net Cash used in Operating Activities		(67,500)
B.	**Cash Flow from Investing Activities**		
	Purchase of Machinery	(1,69,000)	(1,69,000)
	Net Cash used in Investing Activities		
C.	**Cash Flow from Financing Activities**		
	Issue of share	2,00,000	
	Long-term Loan Taken	20,000	
	Interest on Loan	(7,500)	2,12,500
	Net Cash from Financing Activities		
D.	**Net Decrease in Cash and Cash Equivalents** (A+B+C)		(24,000)
	(+) **Cash and Cash Equivalent at the beginning of Period**		49,000
E.	**Cash and Cash Equivalent at the End of Period**		25,000

Working Notes

1. Net Profit as per Statement of Profit and Loss (95,000)
   (+) Provision for Tax 51,000
   Net Profit before Tax and Extraordinary Items (44,000)

2. Dr **Provision for Tax Account** Cr

Particulars	Amt (₹)	Particulars	Amt (₹)
To Cash	53,000	By Balance b/d	70,000
To Balance c/d	68,000	By Statement of Profit and Loss A/c	51,000
	1,21,000		1,21,000

91. Following is the balance sheet of MM Ltd as on 31st March, 2015.

Balance Sheet
as at 31st March, 2015

Particulars	Note No.	31st March, 2015 (₹)	31st March, 2014 (₹)
I. **EQUITY AND LIABILITIES**			
1. **Shareholders' Funds**			
(a) Share Capital		5,00,000	4,00,000
(b) Reserves and Surplus	1	2,00,000	(50,000)
2. **Non-current Liabilities**			
Long-term Borrowings	2	4,50,000	5,00,000
3. **Current Liabilities**			
(a) Short-term Borrowings	3	1,50,000	50,000
(b) Short-term Provisions	4	70,000	90,000
Total		13,70,000	9,90,000

Particulars	Note No.	31st March, 2015 (₹)	31st March, 2014 (₹)
II. ASSETS			
1. Non-current Assets			
(a) Fixed Assets			
(i) Tangible	5	10,03,000	7,20,000
(ii) Intangible	6	20,000	30,000
(b) Non-current Investments		1,00,000	75,000
2. Current Assets			
(a) Current Investments		50,000	60,000
(b) Inventories	7	1,07,000	45,000
(c) Cash and Cash Equivalents		90,000	60,000
Total		13,70,000	9,90,000

Notes to Accounts

Particulars	31st March, 2015 (₹)	31st March, 2014 (₹)
1. **Reserves and Surplus**		
Surplus i.e. Balance in Statement of Profit and Loss	2,00,000	(50,000)
2. **Long-term Borrowings**		
12% Debentures	4,50,000	5,00,000
3. **Short-term Borrowings**		
Bank Overdraft	1,50,000	50,000
4. **Short-term Provisions**		
Provision for Tax	70,000	90,000
5. **Tangible Assets**		
Machinery	12,03,000	8,21,000
(–) Accumulated Depreciation	(2,00,000)	(1,01,000)
	10,03,000	7,20,000
6. **Intangible Assets**		
Goodwill	20,000	30,000
7. **Inventories**		
Stock-in-trade	1,07,000	45,000

Additional Information

(*i*) 12% debentures were redeemed on 31st March, 2015.
(*ii*) Tax ₹ 70,000 was paid during the year.
Prepare cash flow statement. **All India 2016**

Ans.

Cash Flow Statement
for the year ended 31st March, 2015

Particulars		Amt (₹)
A. Cash Flow from Operating Activities		
Net Profit before Tax and Extraordinary Items (WN)		3,00,000
Adjustments for		
(+) Depreciation	99,000	
(+) Intangible Assets Written off	10,000	
(+) Interest on Debentures (5,00,000 × 12%)	60,000	1,69,000
Operating Profit before Working Capital Changes		4,69,000
(–) Increase in Current Assets and Decrease in Current Liabilities		
Inventories	(62,000)	(62,000)
Cash Generated from Operations		4,07,000
(–) Tax Paid		(70,000)
Net Cash Flow from Operating Activities		3,37,000
B. **Cash Flow from Investing Activities**		
Purchase of Fixed Assets	(3,82,000)	
Purchase of Non-current Investments	(25,000)	
Net Cash Used in Investing Activities		(4,07,000)
C. **Cash Flow from Financing Activities**		
Proceeds from Issue of Share Capital	1,00,000	
Redemption of Debentures	(50,000)	
Interest Paid on Debentures	(60,000)	
Increase in Bank Overdraft	1,00,000	
Net Cash Flow from Financing Activities		90,000
D. Net Increase in Cash and Cash Equivalents (A + B + C)		20,000
(+) Opening Cash and Cash Equivalents, i.e. Cash + Current Investments (60,000 + 60,000)		1,20,000
E. Closing Cash and Cash Equivalents, i.e. Cash + Current Investments (90,000 + 50,000)		1,40,000

Working Notes

1. **Calculation of Net Profit before Tax and Extraordinary Items**

Net Profit for the Year [2,00,000 – (–50,000)]	2,50,000
(+) Provision for Tax	50,000
	₹ 3,00,000

2. Dr **Provision for Tax Account** Cr

Particulars	Amt (₹)	Particulars	Amt (₹)
To Bank A/c	70,000	By Balance b/d	90,000
To Balance c/d	70,000	By Statement of Profit and Loss A/c	50,000
	1,40,000		1,40,000

92. Calculate 'Cash flows from operating activities' from the following information

Particulars	31st March, 2015 (₹)	31st March, 2014 (₹)
Surplus (i.e., Balance in the Statement of Profit and Loss)	80,000	1,00,000
Trade Receivables	2,50,000	2,40,000
Goodwill	15,000	20,000
Outstanding Expenses	8,000	—
General Reserve	80,000	50,000
Provision for Depreciation on Plant	1,00,000	82,000
Prepaid Expenses	—	6,000
Trade Payables	84,000	60,000

Additional Information

(*i*) Plant costing ₹ 60,000 having book value of ₹ 36,000 was sold for ₹ 40,000 during the year

(*ii*) Income tax paid during the year was ₹ 30,000

(*iii*) Dividend paid during the year was ₹ 18,000 **All India (C) 2016**

Ans.

Cash Flow from Operating Activities
for the year ended 31st March, 2015

Particulars		Amt (₹)
Cash Flow from Operating Activities		
Net Profit before Tax and Extraordinary items		58,000
Adjustments for		
(+) Goodwill Written-off	5,000	
(+) Depreciation	42,000	
(−) Profit on Sale of Plant	(4,000)	43,000
Operating Profit before Working Capital Changes		1,01,000
(+) Decrease in Current Assets and Increase in Current Liabilities		
Outstanding Expenses	8,000	
Prepaid Expenses	6,000	
Trade Payables	24,000	
(−) Increase in Current Assets and Decrease in Current Liabilities		
Trade Receivables	(10,000)	28,000
Cash Generated from Operations		1,29,000
(−) Income Tax Paid		(30,000)
Net Cash Flow from Operating Activities		99,000

Working Notes

1. **Calculation of Net Profit before Tax and Extraordinary Items**

Net Profit for the year (80,000 − 1,00,000)	=		(20,000)
(+) Transfer to General Reserve	=	30,000	
(+) Dividend Paid	=	18,000	
(+) Tax Paid	=	30,000	78,000
	=		58,000

2. Dr **Provision for Depreciation Account** Cr

Particulars	Amt (₹)	Particulars	Amt (₹)
To Machinery A/c (Transfer)	24,000	By Balance b/d	82,000
To Balance c/d	1,00,000	By Depreciation A/c (Balancing figure)	42,000
	1,24,000		1,24,000

93. From the following information, calculate cash flow from operating activities

Particulars	31st March, 2015 Amt (₹)	31st March, 2014 Amt (₹)
Surplus (i.e., Balance in the Statement of Profit and Loss)	71,000	89,000
Inventory	12,000	4,000
Trade Receivables	58,000	45,000
Outstanding Expenses	14,600	10,000
Goodwill	57,000	27,000
Cash in Hand	9,000	12,000
Machinery	82,000	56,000

Additional Information

(*i*) A piece of machinery costing ₹ 50,000 on which depreciation of ₹ 20,000 had been charged was sold for ₹ 10,000. Depreciation charged during the year was ₹ 18,000

(*ii*) Income tax ₹ 23,000 was paid during the year

(*iii*) Dividend paid during the year was ₹ 36,000. **Delhi (C) 2016**

Ans. **Cash Flow from Operating Activities**
for the year ended 31st March, 2015

Particulars		Amt (₹)
Cash Flow from Operating Activities		
Net Profit before Tax and Extraordinary Items		41,000
Adjustments for		
(+) Depreciation	18,000	
(+) Loss on Sale of Machinery	20,000	38,000
Operating Profit before Working Capital Changes		79,000
(+) Decrease in Current Assets and Increase in Current Liabilities		
Outstanding Expenses	4,600	
(−) Increase in Current Assets and Decrease in Current Liabilities		
Inventories	(8,000)	
Trade Receivables	(13,000)	(16,400)
Cash Generated from Operations		62,600
(−) Tax Paid		(23,000)
Net Cash flow from Operating Activities		39,600

Working Notes

1. **Calculation of Net Profit before Tax and Extraordinary Items**

Net Profit before Tax (71,000 − 89,000)		(18,000)
(+) Dividend paid	36,000	
Tax Paid	23,000	59,000
		41,000

2. **Calculation of Loss on Sale of Machinery**

Cost of machine	= 50,000
(–) Depreciation	= (20,000)
Book value of machine	= 30,000
(–) Sales value	= (10,000)
Loss on sale	₹ 20,000

94. Following is the balance sheet of Solar Power Ltd as at 31st March, 2014.

Balance Sheet
as at 31st March, 2014

Particulars	Note No.	31st March, 2014 Amt (₹)	31st March, 2013 Amt (₹)
I. EQUITY AND LIABILITIES			
1. Shareholders' Funds			
(a) Share Capital		24,00,000	22,00,000
(b) Reserves and Surplus	1	6,00,000	4,00,000
2. Non-current Liabilities			
Long-term Borrowings		4,80,000	3,40,000
3. Current Liabilities			
(a) Trade Payables		3,58,000	4,08,000
(b) Short-term Provisions		1,00,000	1,54,000
Total		39,38,000	35,02,000
II. ASSETS			
1. Non-current Assets			
(a) Tangible	2	21,40,000	17,00,000
(b) Intangible	3	80,000	2,24,000
2. Current Assets			
(a) Current Investments		4,80,000	3,00,000
(b) Inventories		2,58,000	2,42,000
(c) Trade Receivables		3,40,000	2,86,000
(d) Cash and Cash Equivalents		6,40,000	7,50,000
Total		39,38,000	35,02,000

Notes to Accounts

Particulars	31st March, 2014 Amt (₹)	31st March 2013 Amt (₹)
1. Reserves and Surplus		
Surplus (Balance in Statement of Profit and Loss)	6,00,000	4,00,000
2. Tangible Assets		
Machinery	25,40,000	20,00,000
(–) Accumulated Depreciation	(4,00,000)	(3,00,000)
	21,40,000	17,00,000
3. Intangible Assets		
Goodwill	80,000	2,24,000

Additional Information

During the year a piece of machinery costing ₹ 48,000 on which accumulated depreciation was ₹ 32,000 was sold for ₹ 12,000. Prepare cash flow statement. **All India 2015**

Ans.

Cash Flow Statement
for the year ending 31st March, 2014

Particulars		Amt (₹)
A. **Cash Flow from Operating Activities**		
Net Profit before Taxation and Extraordinary Items [Surplus of statement of profit and loss]		2,00,000
Adjustments for		
(+) Depreciation [WN (2)]	1,32,000	
(+) Loss on Sale of Machinery	4,000	
(+) Goodwill Written-off	1,44,000	2,80,000
Operating Profit before Working Capital Changes		4,80,000
(–) Increase in Current Assets and Decrease in Current Liabilities		
Trade Payables	(50,000)	
Short-term Provisions	(54,000)	
Inventories	(16,000)	
Trade Receivables	(54,000)	(1,74,000)
Net Cash Flow from Operating Activities		3,06,000
B. **Cash Flow from Investing Activities**		
Purchase of Machinery [WN (I)]	(5,88,000)	
Sale of Machinery	12,000	
Net Cash Flow used in Investing Activities		(5,76,000)
C. **Cash Flow from Financing Activities**		
Issue of Shares	2,00,000	
Loan Raised	1,40,000	
Net Cash Flow from Financing Activities		3,40,000
D. **Net Increase in Cash and Cash Equivalents** (A + B + C)		70,000
(+) Opening Cash and Cash Equivalents (Cash 7,50,000 + Current Investments 3,00,000)		10,50,000
E. Closing Cash and Cash Equivalents (Cash 6,40,000 + Current Investments 4,80,000)		11,20,000

Working Notes

1. Dr **Machinery Account** Cr

Particulars	Amt (₹)	Particulars	Amt (₹)
To Balance b/d	20,00,000	By Accumulated Depreciation A/c	32,000
To Cash A/c (Purchase)	5,88,000	By Cash A/c (Sale)	12,000
		By Depreciation A/c (Statement of Profit and Loss) (Loss on sale)	4,000
		By Balance c/d	25,40,000
	25,88,000		25,88,000

2. Dr **Accumulated Depreciation Account** Cr

Particulars	Amt (₹)	Particulars	Amt (₹)
To Machinery A/c	32,000	By Balance b/d	3,00,000
To Balance c/d	4,00,000	By Depreciation A/c(Statement of Profit and Loss) (Balancing figure)	1,32,000
	4,32,000		4,32,000

95. Following is the balance sheet of Thermal Power Ltd as at 31st March, 2014.

Balance Sheet
as at 31st March, 2014

Particulars	Note No.	2013-14 Amt (₹)	2012-13 Amt (₹)
I. **EQUITY AND LIABILITIES**			
1. **Shareholders' Funds**			
(a) Share Capital		12,00,000	11,00,000
(b) Reserves and Surplus	1	3,00,000	2,00,000
2. **Non-current Liabilities**			
Long-term Borrowings		2,40,000	1,70,000
3. **Current Liabilities**			
(a) Trade Payables		1,79,000	2,04,000
(b) Short-term Provisions		50,000	77,000
Total		19,69,000	17,51,000
II. **ASSETS**			
1. **Non-current Assets**			
(a) Fixed Assets			
(i) Tangible	2	10,70,000	8,50,000
(ii) Intangible	3	40,000	1,12,000
2. **Current Assets**			
(a) Current Investments		2,40,000	1,50,000
(b) Inventories		1,29,000	1,21,000
(c) Trade Receivables		1,70,000	1,43,000
(d) Cash and Cash Equivalents		3,20,000	3,75,000
Total		19,69,000	17,51,000

Notes to Accounts

Particulars	2013-14 Amt (₹)	2012-13 Amt (₹)
1. **Reserves and Surplus**		
Surplus (Balance in Statement of Profit and Loss)	3,00,000	2,00,000
2. **Tangible Assets**		
Machinery	12,70,000	10,00,000
(–) Accumulated Depreciation	(2,00,000)	(1,50,000)
	10,70,000	8,50,000
3. **Intangible Assets**		
Goodwill	40,000	1,12,000

Additional Information

During the year a piece of machinery, costing ₹ 24,000 on which accumulated depreciation was ₹ 16,000, was sold for ₹ 6,000.

Prepare cash flow statement. **Delhi 2015**

Ans. Solve as Q. no. 94 on page 440-442.
Cash Flow from Operating Activity = ₹ 1,53,000; Cash Used in Investing Activity = ₹ (2,88,000);
Cash Flow from Financing Activity = ₹ 1,70,000

96. Prepare a cash flow statement on the basis of the information given in the balance sheet of Simco Ltd as at 31st March, 2013 and 2012.

Particulars	Note No.	31st March, 2013 (₹)	31st March, 2012 (₹)
I. **EQUITY AND LIABILITIES**			
1. **Shareholders' Funds**			
(a) Share Capital		2,00,000	1,50,000
(b) Reserves and Surplus	1	90,000	75,000
2. **Non-current Liabilities**			
Long-term Borrowings		87,500	87,500
3. **Current Liabilities**			
Trade Payables		10,000	76,000
Total		3,87,500	3,88,500
II. **ASSETS**			
1. **Non-current Assets**			
(a) Fixed Assets			
Tangible Assets		1,87,500	1,40,000
(b) Non-current Investments		1,05,500	1,02,500
2. **Current Assets**			
(a) Current Investment (Marketable)		12,500	33,500
(b) Inventories		4,000	5,500
(c) Trade Receivables		9,500	23,000
(d) Cash and Cash Equivalents		68,500	84,000
Total		3,87,500	3,88,500

Notes to Accounts

Particulars	2013 (₹)	2012 (₹)
1. **Reserve and Surplus**		
Surplus, i.e. Balance in Statement of Profit and Loss	90,000	75,000

All India 2014

Ans.

Cash Flow Statement
for the year ended 31st March, 2013

Particulars		Amt (₹)
I. **Cash Flow from Operating Activities**		
Net Profit before Tax and Extraordinary Items (90,000 − 75,000)		15,000
(+) Decrease in Current Asset and Increase in Current Liabilities		
Trade Receivables	13,500	
Inventories	1,500	
(−) Decrease in Current Liabilities and Increase in Current Assets		
Trade Payables	(66,000)	(51,000)
Net Cash Used in Operating Activities		(36,000)
II. **Cash Flow from Investing Activities**		
Purchase of Tangible Assets	(47,500)	
Purchase of Non-current Investment	(3,000)	
Net Cash Used in Investing Activities		(50,500)
III. **Cash Flow from Financing Activities**		
Issue of Share Capital	50,000	
Net Cash Flow from Financing Activities		50,000
IV. **Net Decrease in Cash and Cash Equivalents** (I + II + III)		(36,500)
(+) Cash and Cash Equivalents in the Beginning (Cash 84,000 + Current Investment 33,500)		1,17,500
V. **Cash and Cash Equivalents at the End** (Cash 68,500 + Current Investment 12,500)		81,000

97. Prepare a cash flow statement on the basis of the information given in the balance sheets of Liva Ltd as at 31st March, 2013 and 2012.

Balance Sheet
as at 31st March, 2013

Particulars	Note No.	31st March, 2013 Amt (₹)	31st March 2012 Amt (₹)
I. **EQUITY AND LIABILITIES**			
1. **Shareholders' Funds**			
(a) Share Capital		2,10,000	1,80,000
(b) Reserves and Surplus	1	1,32,000	24,000
2. **Non-current Liabilities**			
Long-term Borrowings		1,50,000	1,50,000
3. **Current Liabilities**			
Trade Payables		75,000	27,000
Total		5,67,000	3,81,000

Particulars	Note No.	31st March, 2013 Amt (₹)	31st March 2012 Amt (₹)
II. ASSETS			
1. **Non-current Assets**			
(a) Fixed Assets			
Tangible Assets		2,94,000	2,52,000
(b) Non-current Investments		48,000	18,000
2. **Current Assets**			
(a) Current Investments (Marketable)		54,000	60,000
(b) Inventories		1,07,000	24,000
(c) Trade Receivables		40,000	17,500
(d) Cash and Cash Equivalents		24,000	9,500
Total		5,67,000	3,81,000

Notes to Accounts

Particulars	2013 (₹)	2012 (₹)
1. **Reserves and Surplus**		
Surplus (Balance in Statement of Profit and Loss)	1,32,000	24,000

Delhi 2014

Ans. Solve as Q. No. 96 on page 443 and 444.

Cash Flow from Operating Activities = ₹ 50,500

Cash Used in Investing Activities = ₹ (72,000)

Cash Flow from Financing Activities = ₹ 30,000

98. Following is the balance sheet of Wisben Ltd as on 31st March, 2012.

Balance Sheet

as at 31st March, 2012

Particulars	Note No.	2012 Amt (₹)	2011 Amt (₹)
I. **EQUITY AND LIABILITIES**			
1. **Shareholders' Funds**			
(a) Share Capital		7,00,000	6,00,000
(b) Reserves and Surplus (Balance in statement of profit and loss)		2,00,000	1,10,000
2. **Non-current Liabilities**			
Long-term Borrowings		3,00,000	2,00,000
3. **Current Liabilities**			
Trade Payables		30,000	25,000
Total		12,30,000	9,35,000
II. **ASSETS**			
1. **Non-current Assets**			
Fixed Assets			
Tangible Assets		11,00,000	8,00,000

Particulars	Note No.	2012 Amt (₹)	2011 Amt (₹)
2. **Current Assets**			
(a) Inventories		70,000	60,000
(b) Trade Receivables		32,000	40,000
(c) Cash and Cash Equivalents		28,000	35,000
Total		12,30,000	9,35,000

Additional Information

During the year, a piece of machinery of the book value of ₹ 80,000 was sold for ₹ 65,000. Depreciation provided on tangible assets during the year amounted to ₹ 2,00,000.

Prepare a cash flow statement. **Delhi 2013**

Ans.

Cash Flow Statement

for the year ended 31st March, 2012

Particulars		Amt (₹)
I. **Cash Flow from Operating Activities**		
Net Profit before Tax and Extraordinary Items (2,00,000 – 1,10,000)		90,000
Adjustments for		
(+) Loss on Sale of Machinery	15,000	
(+) Depreciation	2,00,000	2,15,000
Operating Profit before Working Capital Changes		3,05,000
(+) Decrease in Current Assets and Increase in Current Liabilities		
Trade Receivables	8,000	
Trade Payables	5,000	
(–) Increase in Current Assets and Decrease in Current Liabilities		
Inventories	(10,000)	3,000
Net Cash Flow from Operating Activities		3,08,000
II. **Cash Flow from Investing Activities**		
Proceeds from Sale of Machinery	65,000	
Payment for Purchases of Tangible Assets (WN)	(5,80,000)	
Net Cash Used in Investing Activities		(5,15,000)
III. **Cash Flow from Financing Activities**		
Proceeds from Issue of Share Capital	1,00,000	
Proceeds from Long-term Borrowings	1,00,000	
Net Cash Flow from Financing Activities		2,00,000
IV. **Net Decrease in Cash and Cash Equivalents** (I + II + III)		(7,000)
(+) Cash and Cash Equivalents in the Beginning of the Year		35,000
V. **Cash and Cash Equivalents at the End of the Year**		28,000

Working Note

Dr **Tangible Assets Account** Cr

Particulars	Amt (₹)	Particulars	Amt (₹)
To Balance b/d	8,00,000	By Bank A/c (Sale)	65,000
To Bank A/c (Purchases) (Balancing figure)	5,80,000	By Depreciation A/c	2,00,000
		By Statement of Profit and Loss (Loss on sale)	15,000
		By Balance c/d	11,00,000
	13,80,000		13,80,000

99. Following is the balance sheet of Krishtec Ltd for the year ended 31st March, 2011 and 2012.

Balance Sheet
as at 31st March, 2011-12

Particulars	2011-12 Amt (₹)	2010-11 Amt (₹)
I. **EQUITY AND LIABILITIES**		
1. **Shareholders' Funds**		
(a) Share Capital	12,00,000	8,00,000
(b) Reserves and Surplus (Balance in statement of profit and loss)	3,50,000	4,00,000
2. **Non-current Liabilities**		
Long-term Borrowings	4,40,000	3,50,000
3. **Current Liabilities**		
Trade Payables	60,000	50,000
Total	20,50,000	16,00,000
II. **ASSETS**		
1. **Non-current Assets**		
Fixed Assets		
Tangible Assets	12,00,000	9,00,000
2. **Current Assets**		
(a) Inventories	2,00,000	1,00,000
(b) Trade Receivables	3,10,000	2,30,000
(c) Cash and Cash Equivalents	3,40,000	3,70,000
Total	20,50,000	16,00,000

Prepare a cash flow statement after taking into account the following adjustments

(*i*) The company paid interest ₹ 36,000 on its long-term borrowings.

(*ii*) Depreciation charged on tangible fixed assets was ₹ 1,20,000. **All India 2013**

Ans.

Cash Flow Statement
for the year ended 31st March, 2012

Particulars		Amt (₹)
I. **Cash Flow from Operating Activities**		
Net Profit before Tax and Extraordinary Items (3,50,000 – 4,00,000)		(50,000)
Adjustments for		
(+) Depreciation	1,20,000	
(+) Interest Paid	36,000	1,56,000

Particulars		Amt (₹)
Net Profit before Working Capital Changes		1,06,000
(+) *Decrease in Current Assets and Increase in Current Liabilities*		
Trade Payables	10,000	
(–) *Increase in Current Assets and Decrease in Current Liabilities*		
Inventories	(1,00,000)	
Trade Receivable	(80,000)	(1,70,000)
Net Cash Used in Operating Activities		(64,000)
II. **Cash Flow from Investing Activities**		
Purchase of Tangible Assets (WN)	(4,20,000)	
Net Cash Used in Investing Activities		(4,20,000)
III. **Cash Flow from Financing Activities**		
Interest Paid on Long-term Borrowings	(36,000)	
Proceeds from Issue of Share Capital	4,00,000	
Proceeds from Long-term Borrowings	90,000	
Net Cash Flow from Financing Activity		4,54,000
IV. **Net Decrease in Cash and Cash Equivalents** (I + II + III)		(30,000)
(+) Cash and Cash Equivalents in the Beginning of the Year		3,70,000
V. **Cash and Cash Equivalents at the End of the Year**		3,40,000

Working Note

Dr **Fixed Assets Account** Cr

Particulars	Amt (₹)	Particulars	Amt (₹)
To Balance b/d	9,00,000	By Depreciation A/c	1,20,000
To Bank A/c (Purchase) (Balancing figure)	4,20,000	By Balance c/d	12,00,000
	13,20,000		13,20,000

100. From the following balance sheet of BCR Ltd as at 31st March, 2010 and 2011. Prepare a cash flow statement.

Balance Sheet
as at 31st March, 2010

Particulars	Note No.	31st March, 2011 Amt (₹)	31st March, 2010 Amt (₹)
I. **EQUITY AND LIABILITIES**			
1. **Shareholders' Funds**			
(a) Equity Share Capital		7,00,000	5,00,000
(b) Reserves and Surplus (Balance in statement of profit and loss)		3,50,000	2,00,000
2. **Current Liabilities**			
(a) Short-term Borrowings (Bank loan)		50,000	1,00,000
(b) Trade Payables (Creditors)		52,000	55,000
(c) Short-term Provisions	1	50,000	30,000
Total		12,02,000	8,85,000

Particulars	Note No.	31st March, 2011 Amt (₹)	31st March, 2010 Amt (₹)
II. **ASSETS**			
1. **Non-current Assets**			
(a) Fixed Assets	2	5,95,000	6,00,000
(b) Non-current Investment		1,00,000	–
2. **Current Assets**			
(a) Trade Receivables (Debtors)		1,47,000	80,000
(b) Inventories (Stock)		1,30,000	55,000
(c) Cash and Cash Equivalents (Bank)		2,30,000	1,50,000
Total		12,02,000	8,85,000

Notes to Accounts

Particulars	31st March, 2011 Amt (₹)	31st March, 2010 Amt (₹)
1. **Short-term Provisions**		
Provision for Tax	50,000	30,000
	50,000	30,000
2. **Fixed Assets**		
Tangible (Equipment)	5,00,000	5,00,000
Intangible (Patents)	95,000	1,00,000
	5,95,000	6,00,000

Additional Information

Proposed dividend – 2010 – ₹ 50,000, 2011 – ₹ 70,000

During the year, equipment costing ₹ 1,00,000 was purchased. Loss on sale of equipment amounted to ₹ 12,000. ₹ 18,000 depreciation was charged on equipment. **All India 2012, Modified**

Ans.

Cash Flow Statement
for the year ended 31st March, 2011

Particulars		Amt (₹)
I. **Cash Flow from Operating Activities**		
Net Profit before Tax and Extraordinary Items [WN (i)]		2,50,000
Adjustments for		
(+) Depreciation on Equipments	18,000	
(+) Patents Written-off	5,000	
(+) Loss on Sale of Equipments	12,000	35,000
Operating Profit before Working Capital Changes		2,85,000
(–) *Increase in Current Assets and Decrease in Current Liabilities*		
Debtors	(67,000)	
Stock	(75,000)	
Creditors	(3,000)	(1,45,000)
Cash Generated from Operations		1,40,000
(–) Income Tax Paid		(30,000)
Net Cash Flow from Operating Activities		1,10,000

Particulars		Amt (₹)
II. **Cash Flow from Investing Activities**		
Proceeds from Sale of Equipments [WN (ii)]	70,000	
Purchase of Equipments	(1,00,000)	
Purchase of Investment	(1,00,000)	
Net Cash Used in Investing Activities		(1,30,000)
III. **Cash Flow from Financing Activities**		
Proceeds from Issue of Shares	2,00,000	
Repayment of Bank Loan	(50,000)	
Dividend Paid	(50,000)	
Net Cash Flow from Financing Activities		1,00,000
IV. **Net Increase in Cash and Cash Equivalents** (I + II + III)		80,000
(+) Cash and Cash Equivalents at the Beginning of Period		1,50,000
V. **Cash and Cash Equivalents at the End of Period**		2,30,000

Working Notes

1. **Calculation of Net Profit before Tax and Extraordinary Items**

Net Profit for the Year (3,50,000 – 2,00,000)	1,50,000
(+) Proposed Dividend	50,000
Provision for Tax	50,000
	₹ 2,50,000

2. Dr **Equipments Account** Cr

Particulars	Amt (₹)	Particulars	Amt (₹)
To Balance b/d	5,00,000	By Depreciation A/c	18,000
To Bank A/c (Purchase)	1,00,000	By Statement of Profit and Loss (Loss on sale of building)	12,000
		By Bank A/c (Balancing figure)	70,000
		By Balance c/d	5,00,000
	6,00,000		6,00,000

101. From the following balance sheet of Vikas Ltd as at 31st March, 2009 and 2010. Prepare the cash flow statement.

Balance Sheet
as at 31st March, 2009

Particulars	Note No.	31st March, 2010 (₹)	31st March, 2009 (₹)
I. **EQUITY AND LIABILITIES**			
1. **Shareholders' Funds**			
(a) Share Capital		1,30,000	90,000
(b) Reserves and Surplus		84,000	48,000
2. **Current Liablities**			
Trade Payables		22,000	17,400
Total		2,36,000	1,55,400

Particulars	Note No.	31st March, 2010 (₹)	31st March, 2009 (₹)
II. **ASSETS**			
1. **Non-current Assets**			
Fixed Assets		1,66,000	93,400
2. **Current Assets**			
(a) Inventories (Stock)		26,000	22,000
(b) Trade Receivables (Debtors)		39,000	36,000
(c) Cash		5,000	4,000
Total		2,36,000	1,55,400

Notes to Accounts

Particulars	31st March, 2010 (₹)	31st March, 2009 (₹)
1. **Reserves and Surplus**		
General Reserve	54,000	28,000
Surplus, i.e. Balance in Statement of Profit and Loss	30,000	20,000
	84,000	48,000

Additional Information

(*i*) Depreciation charged on fixed assets for the year 2009-2010 was ₹ 20,000.

(*ii*) Income tax ₹ 5,000 has been paid in advance during the year. **All India 2011**

Ans.

Cash Flow Statement
for the year ended 31st March, 2010

Particulars		Amt (₹)
I. **Cash Flow from Operating Activities**		
Net Profit before Tax and Extraordinary Items [WN 1]		41,000
Adjustments for		
(+) Depreciation on Fixed Assets	20,000	20,000
Operating Profit before Working Capital Changes		61,000
(+) Decrease in Current Assets and Increase in Current Liabilities		
Creditors	4,600	
(–) Increase in Current Assets and Decrease in Current Liabilities		
Debtors	(3,000)	
Stock	(4,000)	(2,400)
Cash Generated from Operations		58,600
(–) Income Tax Paid		(5,000)
Net Cash Flow from Operating Activities		53,600
II. **Cash Flow from Investing Activities**		
Purchase of Fixed Assets [WN 2]	(92,600)	
Net Cash Used in Investing Activities		(92,600)
III. **Cash Flow from Financing Activities**		
Proceeds from Issue of Shares	40,000	
Net Cash Flow from Financing Activities		40,000
IV. **Net Increase in Cash and Cash Equivalents** (I + II + III)		1,000
(+) Cash and Cash Equivalents at the Beginning of Period		4,000
V. **Cash and Cash Equivalents at the End of Period**		5,000

Working Note

1. **Calculation of Net Profit before Tax and Extraordinary Items**

Net profit for the year (30,000 – 20,000)	10,000
(+) Transfer to general reserve	26,000
(+) Provision for tax	5,000
	₹ 41,000

2. Dr **Fixed Assets Account** Cr

Particulars	Amt (₹)	Particulars	Amt (₹)
To Balance b/d	93,400	By Depreciation A/c	20,000
To Bank A/c (Balancing figure)	92,600	By Balance c/d	1,66,000
	1,86,000		1,86,000

Multiple Choice Questions

(1 Mark)

1. Paid ₹ 4,00,000 to acquire shares in RV Ltd and received a dividend of ₹ 40,000 after acquisition. These transactions will result in **CBSE 2020**

(a) cash used in investing activities ₹ 4,00,000.

(b) cash generated from financing activities ₹ 4,40,000.

(c) cash used in investing activities ₹ 3,60,000.

(d) cash generated from financing activities ₹ 3,60,000.

2. 'Sale of marketable securities at par' would result into

(a) cash outflow (b) cash inflow (c) no flow (d) None of these

Hint: No flow of cash will take place on sale of marketable securities as it is cash equivalent. Because it will only create assets which can be converted into cash in future at the time of requirement.

3. 'Interest received by other than financial enterprise' is shown in cash flow statement under

(a) operating activities (b) investing activities

(c) financing activities (d) No adjustment is made

4. While calculating cash flow from operating activity, payment and receipts shown in profit and loss account are converted into payment and receipt in cash by eliminating

(a) non-cash expenses from expenses incurred

(b) non-cash revenue from revenue earned

(c) non-cash expenses from profit

(d) Both (a) and (b)

Hint: Cash flow from operating activity is calculated by profit and loss account conversion into cash except non-cash expenses incurred and non-cash revenue earned. It means only cash items will be calculated and considered while calculating cash flow from operating activity.

5. Profit before tax of a company was ₹ 2,74,000. Calculate profit before working capital changes from the following information.

I. Depreciation on fixed asset ₹ 20,000
II. Transfer to general reserve ₹ 44,000
III. Loss on sale of furniture ₹ 1,000
IV. Profit on sale of machinery ₹ 6,000

Codes

(a) ₹ 2,89,000
(b) ₹ 3,01,000
(c) ₹ 2,95,000
(d) ₹ 2,99,000

Hint:

Profit before tax	=	2,74,000
(+) Depreciation	=	20,000
(+) Loss on sale of furniture	=	1,000
(−) Profit on sale of machine	=	(6,000)
Operating profit before working capital changes	=	2,89,000

6. Rent received will be classified under

(a) financing activity
(b) operating activity
(c) investing activity
(d) All of these

Hint: Rent received, whether short-term or long-term will be the part of investing activity. Only in case of real estate company, it will be classified under operating activity.

7. ABC Ltd has the investment @ 10%, opening balance of the investment was ₹ 5,00,000 and closing balance was ₹ 10,00,000. Half of the investment held in the beginning of the year was sold at 10% profit. Calculate purchase value of investment.

(a) ₹ (12,50,000)
(b) ₹ (12,75,000)
(c) ₹ (7,50,000)
(d) ₹ (8,75,000)

Hint:

Opening balance of investment	5,00,000
(−) Sale of investment (50% of 5,00,000 + 10% of ₹ 2,50,000)	(2,75,000)
(−) Closing balance of investment	(10,00,000)
(+) Profit on sale (Half investment of 2,50,000 @ 10%)	25,000
Purchase value of investment	(7,50,000)

8. Opening balance and closing balance of machinery (at cost) was ₹ 8,00,000 and ₹ 8,40,000 respectively and depreciation opening and closing balance was ₹ 2,00,000 and ₹ 2,20,000. During the year, a machine costing ₹ 80,000 with its accumulated depreciation of ₹ 48,000 was sold for ₹ 40,000. Calculate purchase value of machinery.

(a) ₹ 1,20,000
(b) ₹ 1,30,000
(c) ₹ 50,000
(d) ₹ 1,25,000

Hint:

Opening balance of machine	8,00,000
(−) Sale of machine	(40,000)
(−) Accumulated depreciation	(48,000)
(−) Closing balance of machine	(8,40,000)
(+) Profit on sale of machine (80,000 − 48,000 = 32,000) (40,000 − 32,000 = 8,000)	8,000
Purchase value of machinery	(1,20,000)

9. Dividend paid by a company is classified under finance activity, whether it is non-finance or finance company because

(a) dividend is associated with share capital
(b) dividend is part of profit and loss account
(c) dividend is part of balance sheet
(d) None of the above

Hint: If any company is paying dividend, then it will be a financing activity because dividend is paid on share capital and it is associated with share capital.

10. ABC Ltd had opening and closing balance of equity shares of ₹ 20,00,000 and ₹ 30,00,000. Company issued bonus shares in the ratio of 2 : 1 by capitalising reserve. What will be net cash flow from this transaction?

(a) ₹ 10,00,000
(b) ₹ 20,00,000
(c) ₹ 30,00,000
(d) No cash flow

Hint: Whenever a company provides any shares against money, then the amount received is financing activity and shares issued on bonus will be treated as no cash activity because bonus shares are issued for free without any consideration.

11. Ram Ltd is a financial company whose equity share capital in the year 2010 was ₹ 28,00,000 which got increased to ₹ 35,00,000 in the year 2011. Calculate the amount of issue of equity share capital.

(a) ₹ (7,00,000)
(b) ₹ 35,00,000
(c) ₹ 28,00,000
(d) None of these

Hint:

Opening balance of equity share capital	= 28,00,000
(–) Closing balance of equity share capital	= (35,00,000)
Amount of issue of equity share capital	= (7,00,000)

Direction *Read the following hypothetical text and answer the question no. 12 to15*

Krishika an alumni of IIM Ahemdabad initiated her startup Krishika Ltd. in 2018. The profits of Krishika Ltd. in the year 2019-20 after all appropriations was ₹ 31,25,000. This profit was arrived after taking into consideration the following items

S. No.	Particulars	Amt in (₹)
1.	Gain on sale of fixed tangible assets	12,50,000
2.	Goodwill written-off	7,80,000
3.	Transfer to General Reserve	8,75,000
4.	Provision for taxation	4,37,500

Additional Information

Particulars	31.03.2020 (in ₹)	31.03.2019 (in ₹)
Prepaid Expenses	7,50,000	5,00,000
Inventory	10,50,000	8,20,000
Trade Payables	4,50,000	3,50,000
Trade Receivables	6,20,000	5,90,000

CBSE QB

12. Net Profit before Tax will be .... (Choose the correct alternative)

(a) ₹ 22,50,000
(b) ₹ 35,62,500
(c) ₹ 39,67,500
(d) ₹ 44,37,500

Hint:

	Amt (₹)
Net profit after tax	31,25,000
(+) Transfer to reserves	8,75,000
(+) Provision for tax	4,37,500
Net profit before Tax	44,37,500

13. Operating profit before working capital changes will be .... (Choose the correct alternative)

(a) ₹ 52,17,500 (b) ₹ 64,67,500
(c) ₹ 39,67,500 (d) ₹ 39,69,500

Hint:

	Amt (₹)
Net profit before tax	44,37,500
(+) Goodwill written-off	7,80,000
(–) Gain on sale of fixed tangible asset	(12,50,000)
Operating profit before working capital changes	39,67,500

14. Cash from operating activities before tax will be .... (Choose the correct alternative)

(a) ₹ 35,57,500 (b) ₹ 40,67,500
(c) ₹ 37,87,500 (d) ₹ 35,67,300

Hint: **Cash Flow from Operating Activities before Tax**

Particulars		Amt (₹)
Operating profit before working capital changes		39,67,500
(+) Decrease in current assets and increase in current liabilities		
Trade payable		1,00,000
(–) Increase in current assets and decrease in current liabilities		
Prepaid Expenses	(2,50,000)	
Inventory	(2,30,000)	
Trade Receivables	(30,000)	(5,10,000)
		35,57,500

15. Cash flow from Operating Activities will be .... (Choose the correct alternative)

(a) ₹ 39,95,000 (b) ₹ 31,20,000
(c) ₹ 40,67,500 (d) ₹ 31,00,000

Hint:

	Amt (₹)
Cash flow from operating activities before tax	35,57,500
(–) Tax	(4,37,500)
Cash flow from operating activities after tax	31,20,000

ANSWERS

1. *(c)*	2. *(c)*	3. *(b)*	4. *(d)*	5. *(a)*	6. *(c)*	7. *(c)*	8. *(a)*	9. *(a)*	10. *(d)*
11. *(a)*	12. *(d)*	13. *(c)*	14. *(a)*	15. *(b)*					

Sample Question Papers (1-3)

Sample Paper 1

Accountancy (Unsolved)

(A Highly Simulated Practice Question Paper for CBSE Class XII Examination)

General Instructions

1 This question paper contains two parts A and B.
2 Part A is compulsory for all.
3 Part B has two options-Analysis of Financial Statements and Computerised Accounting*. Attempt only one option of Part B.
4 Question nos. 1 to 13 and 23 to 29 are objective type questions carrying 1 mark each.
5 Question nos. 14 and 30 are short answer type-1 questions carrying 3 marks each.
6 Question nos. 15 to 18 and 31 are short answer type-II questions carrying 4 marks each.
7 Question nos. 19, 20 and 32 are long answer type-I questions carrying 6 marks each.
8 Question nos. 21 and 22 are long answer type-II questions carrying 8 marks each.
* Computerised Accounting has not been covered.

Time : 3 hours | Max. Marks : 80

Part : A

(Accounting for Partnership Firms and Companies)

1. A partnership firm earned net profits for last 3 years as ₹ 1,90,000, ₹ 2,20,000, ₹ 2,50,000 respectively. The capital employed in firm is ₹ 40,00,000. 15% is considered to be a fair return on capital. Remuneration to partners is to be ₹ 1,00,000 per annum. Calculate super profit. **(1)**

(a) ₹ 1,20,000 (b) ₹ 1,60,000
(c) ₹ 1,00,000 (d) ₹ 60,000

2. Which amongst the following is/are mode(s) of issuing shares for cash to public? **(1)**

(a) Public issue of shares (b) Private placement of shares
(c) General issue of preference shares (d) Both (a) and (b)

3. TDS refers to .... relating to debenture interest. **(1)**

(a) Tax Deducted at Source (b) Debenture Security
(c) Debentured Secured (d) None of these

4. If partners' capitals are fixed, drawing will be recorded in **(1)**

(a) Partners' capital account (b) Partners' current accout
(c) Profit and loss appropriation (d) None of these

5. Revaluation account is prepared at the time of (1)

(a) Admission of a partner
(b) Retirement of a partner
(c) Dissolution of firm
(d) Both (a) and (b)

6. Interest on drawings is charged @ 6% on total drawings of each partner and Z a partner withdrew ₹ 50,000 during a year. Interest on drawings will be (1)

(a) ₹ 500 (b) ₹ 3,000 (c) ₹ 250 (d) ₹ 1,500

7. If debit side of realisation account exceeds the credit side it is (1)

(a) Profit
(b) Loss
(c) Neither profit nor loss
(d) None of these

8. A company issued 25,000 shares and received applications for 35,000 shares. Company wants to allot shares to everyone who has applied. What will be the ratio for allotment? (1)

(a) 6 :7 (b) 7:5 (c) 5 :7 (d) 7:6

9. P and Q are partners sharing profits in 2 : 1 ratio. R, a new partner admitted for 1/4 th share. At the time of admission, loss from revaluation is ₹ 4,500. Pass a necessary journal entry for the distribution of loss between the partners. (1)

(a) A's Capital A/c	Dr	3,000	
B's Capital A/c	Dr	1,500	
To Revaluation A/c			4,500
(b) A's Capital A/c	Dr	4,500	
To B's Capital A/c			4,500
(c) Revaluation A/c	Dr	4,500	
To A's Capital A/c			3,000
To B's Capital A/c			1,500
(d) B's Capital A/c	Dr	4,500	
To A's Capital A/c			4,500

10. Asset which is not transferred to debit side of realisation account but brings certain amount of cash against its disposal at the time of dissolution of the firm is ...... (1)

11. A and B are partners sharing profits in 5 : 3 : 2 ratio. They have admitted C into partnership for 1/6 th share. (1)

Extract of Balance Sheet

Liabilities	Amt (₹)	Assets	Amt (₹)
Investment Fluctuation Fund	54,000	Investment (Cost)	6,00,000

If market value of investment is ₹ 5,80,000, then the investment fluctuation fund will be shown in the balance sheet of the firm at

(a) ₹ 54,000 (b) ₹ 40,000 (c) ₹ 20,000 (d) ₹ 26,000

12. X, Y and Z are partners in a firm. If A is admitted as a new partner (1)
 (a) Old firm is dissolved
 (b) Old firm and old partnership is reconstituted
 (c) Old partnership is reconstituted
 (d) None of the above

13. Partners may dissolve a firm by mutual agreement. This is specified in section .... of the Act. (1)
 (a) 39 (b) 40 (c) 41 (d) 42

14. Priyanka Ltd has a registered capital of ₹ 25,00,000 lakh divided into 1,00,000 equity shares of ₹ 10 each and 15,000, 8% preference shares of ₹ 100 each. The company issued 5,000 preference shares on which the amount was payable as follows

 ₹ 30 on application

 ₹ 25 on allotment

 ₹ 25 on first call and the balance of ₹ 20 on final call

 The issue was fully subscribed. Pass necessary journal entries, when it was the policy of the company to maintain only one account for application and allotment. (3)

Or Niharika Ltd purchased a running business from Sunehari Ltd for a sum of ₹ 30,00,000 by issuing 25,000 fully paid equity shares of ₹ 100 each at a premium of 20%. The assets and liabilities consisted of the following

 Machinery ₹ 9,00,000, debtors ₹ 12,50,000, stock ₹ 8,00,000, building ₹ 10,00,000 and bills payable ₹ 7,50,000.

 Pass necessary journal entries in the books of Niharika Ltd for the above transactions.

15. Kartik and Aroha are partners in a firm sharing profits in the ratio of 2 : 3. The balance sheet of the firm as at 31st March, 2018 is given below

Balance Sheet
as at 31st March, 2018

Liabilities		Amt (₹)	Assets	Amt (₹)
Creditors		6,200	Bills Receivable	3,600
Bills Payable		1,800	Stock	16,000
Capital A/cs			Machinery	18,400
Kartik	16,000		Land and Building	10,000
Aroha	24,000	40,000		
		48,000		48,000

The partners decided to share profits in equal ratio with effect from 1st April, 2018. The following adjustments were agreed upon.

(*i*) Land and building was valued at ₹ 16,000 and machinery at ₹ 16,400 and were to appear at revalued amounts in the balance sheet.

(*ii*) The goodwill of the firm was valued at ₹ 800 but it was not to appear in books.

Pass the necessary journal entries to give effect to the above and also prepare revaluation accounts. **(4)**

Or

Hari, Mohan and Sohan were partners in a firm sharing profits in 2 : 2 : 1 ratio. The firm closes its books on 31st March every year. Mohan died on 24th August, 2019. On Mohan's death, the goodwill of the firm was valued at ₹ 75,000. The partnership deed provided that on the death of a partner, his share in the profit of the firm in the year of his death will be calculated on the basis of last year's profit. The profit of the firm for the year ended 31st March, 2019 was ₹ 2,00,000.

Calculate Mohan's share of profit till the time of his death and pass the necessary journal entries for the treatment of goodwill and his share of profit.

16. P, Q and R are partners in a firm. They contributed ₹ 50,000 each as capital three years ago. At that time, R agreed to look after the business as P and Q were busy. The profits for the past three years were ₹ 15,000, ₹ 15,000 and ₹ 60,000 respectively. While going through the books of accounts, P noticed that the profit had been distributed in the ratio of 1 : 1 : 2. When she enquired from R about this, R answered that since she looked after the business, she should get more profit. P disagreed and it was decided to distribute profit equally retrospectively for the last three years.

You are required to make necessary correction in the books of accounts of P, Q and R by passing an adjustment entry. **(4)**

17. A and B decided to start a partnership firm to manufacture jute bags. They contributed capitals of ₹ 1,00,000 and ₹ 50,000 on 1st April, 2013 for this. A expressed his willingness to admit C as a partner without capital, B agreed to this. The terms of partnership were as follows

(a) A, B and C will share profits in the ratio of 2 : 2 : 1.

(b) Interest on capital will be provided @ 6% per annum.

Due to shortage of capital, A contributed ₹ 25,000 on 30th September, 2014 and B contributed ₹ 10,000 on 1st January, 2015 as additional capital. The profit of the firm for the year ended 31st March, 2015 was ₹ 1,68,900.
Prepare profit and loss appropriation account for the year ending 31st March, 2015. **(4)**

18. Complete the following journal entries. **(4)**

JOURNAL

Date	Particulars		LF	Amt (Dr)	Amt (Cr)
	Share Capital A/c (300 × 8)	Dr		2,400	
	To Share First Call A/c (300 × 3)				900
	To				....
	(Being 300 shares forfeited)				
	....	Dr		....	
	....	Dr		....	
	To				....
	(Being 100 shares re-issued at ₹ 7, ₹ 8 called-up)				
	....	Dr		....	
	To				....
	(Being balance transferred to capital reserve)				

19. (a) XYZ Ltd took over the assets amounting to ₹ 1,72,000 and liabilities of ₹ 44,400 of PQR Ltd at an agreed value of ₹ 1,27,600. The purchase price was discharged by issuing 8% debentures of ₹ 100 each at a premium of 10%. Give journal entries in the books of XYZ Ltd.

(b) ABC Ltd issued 1,000, 12% debentures of ₹ 10 each to the public at a premium of 10%. These debentures are redeemable after 5 years at a premium of 20%. Journalise only for issue of debentures. **(6)**

20. P, Q and R were partners sharing profit and loss in the ratio of 2 : 2 : 1. Q decides to retire on 31st March, 2014. On the date of his retirement, some of the assets and liabilities appeared in the books as follows

Creditors ₹ 70,000; Building ₹ 1,00,000; Plant and machinery ₹ 40,000; Stock of raw materials ₹ 20,000; Stock of finished goods ₹ 30,000 and debtors ₹ 20,000.

The following was agreed among the partners on Q's retirement

(*i*) Building to be appreciated by 20%.

(*ii*) Plant and machinery to be depreciated by 10%.

(*iii*) A provision of 5% on debtors to be created for doubtful debts.

(*iv*) Stock of raw materials to be valued at ₹ 18,000 and finished goods at ₹ 35,000.

(*v*) An old computer previously written-off was sold for ₹ 2,000 as scrap.

Prepare revaluation account. **(6)**

Or Give journal entries for the following transactions.

(*i*) To record the realisation of various assets and liabilities.

(*ii*) A firm has a stock of ₹ 1,60,000. Aziz, a partner took over 50% of the stock at a discount of 20%.

(*iii*) Remaining stock was sold at a profit of 30% on cost.

(*iv*) Land and building (book value ₹ 1,60,000) sold for ₹ 3,00,000 through a broker who charged 2% commission on the deal.

(v) Plant and machinery (book value ₹ 60,000) was handed over to a creditor at an agreed valuation of 10% less than the book value.

(vi) Investment whose face value was ₹ 4,000 was realised at 50%.

21. Sun Moon Ltd invited applications for 11,000 shares of ₹ 100 each to be issued at a premium of 10% payable as follows

On application	₹ 25
On allotment	₹ 40
On first and final call	₹ 35

Applications were received for 10,000 shares and all of these were accepted. All the money due was received except the first and final call on 100 shares which were forfeited. 60 of these forfeited shares were re-issued @ ₹ 90 per share credited as fully paid.

You are required to

(i) Pass the necessary journal entries.

(ii) Prepare the balance sheet of the company. (8)

Or Capricon Ltd was registered with an authorised capital of ₹ 20,00,000 divided into equity shares of ₹ 10 each. It invited applications for issuing 1,00,000 equity shares at a premium of ₹ 2 per share. The amount was payable as follows

On application	₹ 4 per share (Including premium)
On allotment	₹ 3 per share
Balance on first and final call	

Applications were received for 1,30,000 shares. Applications for 10,000 shares were rejected and the application money received on them was refunded. Pro-rata allotment was made to the remaining applications. Amount overpaid on these applications was adjusted towards the amount due on allotment.

S, who had applied for 1,200 shares, failed to pay the allotment and call money. The company forfeited his shares, out of which, 800 shares were re-issued to R at ₹ 9 per share fully paid-up.

You are required to

(i) Pass the journal entries in the books of the company through calls-in-arrears account.

(ii) Prepare the share allotment account.

22. Prince, Queen and Raja commenced business on 1st January, 2019 with capitals of ₹ 2,00,000, ₹ 2,00,000 and ₹ 1,00,000 respectively. Profits are shared in the ratio of 4 : 3 : 3. Capital carried interest @ 5% per annum. During the year 2019, the firm suffered a loss of ₹ 1,50,000 before allowing interest on capital. Drawings of each partner during the year were ₹ 20,000.

On 31st December, 2019, the partners agreed to dissolve the firm as it was no longer profitable. The creditors on that date were ₹ 40,000. The assets realised a net value of ₹ 3,20,000 and the expenses of realisation were ₹ 7,000.

Prepare the realisation account, partners' capital account and cash account alongwith necessary working to close the books of the firm. (8)

Or Aman, Naman and Raman were in partnership sharing profits in proportion to their capitals. Their balance sheet on 31st March, 2019 was as follows

Balance Sheet
as at 31st March, 2019

Liabilities		Amt (₹)	Assets		Amt (₹)
Creditors		15,600	Cash		16,000
Reserve		6,000	Debtors	20,000	
Capital A/cs			(–) Provision for Doubtful Debts	(400)	19,600
Aman	90,000		Stock		18,000
Naman	60,000		Machinery		48,000
Raman	30,000	1,80,000	Buildings		1,00,000
		2,01,600			2,01,600

On the above date, Naman retired from the firm owing to ill health and the following adjustments were agreed upon

(*i*) Buildings be appreciated by 10%.
(*ii*) Provision for doubtful debts be increased to 5% on debtors.
(*iii*) Machinery be depreciated by 15%.
(*iv*) Goodwill of the firm be valued at ₹ 36,000 and be adjusted into the capital accounts of Aman and Raman who will share profits in the future in the ratio of 3 : 1.
(*v*) A provision is to be made for outstanding repairs bill of ₹ 3,000.
(*vi*) Included in the value of creditors ₹ 1,800 for an outstanding legal claim, which is not likely to arise.
(*vii*) Out of the insurance premium paid, ₹ 2,000 is for the next year. The amount was debited to profit and loss account.
(*viii*) The partners decide to fix the capital of the new firm at ₹ 1,20,000 in the profit sharing ratio.
(*ix*) Naman to be paid ₹ 9,000 in cash and balance to be transferred to his loan account.

Prepare the revaluation account, partners' capital account and the balance sheet of the new firm after Naman's retirement.

Part : B

(Analysis of Financial Statements)

23. Debentures are included in (1)

(a) Current liability (b) Fixed assets (c) Current assets (d) None of these

24. The .... measures the activity of a firm's inventory. (1)

25. Ideal current ratio for a better financial position of company is (1)

(a) 2 : 1 (b) 1 : 1 (c) 3 : 1 (d) 4 : 1

26. Which of the following item(s) can be shown on the assets side of Balance Sheet? (1)

(a) Sundry Debtors (b) Public Deposits
(c) Livestock (d) Both (a) and (c)

27. Calculate current liabilities, when working capital is ₹ 2,00,000 and current assets are ₹ 4,00,000. **(1)**

(a) ₹ 1,00,000 (b) ₹ 75,000

(c) ₹ 2,00,000 (d) ₹ 6,00,000

28. 'Brokerage paid on purchase of non-current investment' is what kind of activity? **(1)**

(a) Cash outflow from operating activity

(b) Cash outflow from investing activity

(c) Cash inflow from financing activity

(d) None of the above

29. While preparing cash flow statement, Varun Ltd, a company engaged in the business of financing has shown interest earned under investing activity. Is the treatment correct? **(1)**

30. (*i*) From the following information, calculate inventory turnover ratio.

Revenue from operations ₹ 8,00,000, average inventory ₹ 1,10,000, gross loss on revenue from operations is 10%.

(*ii*) Calculate total assets to debt ratio from the given information.

Shareholders' funds ₹ 14,00,000, total debts ₹ 18,00,000, current liabilities ₹ 2,00,000. **(3)**

Or Calculate Return on Investment (RoI) and debt to equity ratio from the following information

Net profit after interest and tax	₹ 3,00,000
10% Debentures	₹ 5,00,000
Tax rate	40%
Capital employed	₹ 40,00,000

31. What is meant by analysis of financial statements? State any two objectives of such an analysis. **(4)**

Or State any four limitations of analysis of financial statements.

32. From the following balance sheets of Dhan Laxmi Ltd as at 31st March, 2019 and 2020, prepare the cash flow statement.

Particulars	Note No.	31st March, 2020 (₹)	31st March, 2019 (₹)
I. **EQUITY AND LIABILITIES**			
1. **Shareholders' Funds**			
(a) Share Capital	1	85,000	46,000
(b) Reserves and Surplus	2	17,000	24,000
2. **Non-current Liabilities**			
Long-term Borrowings (10% Debentures)		18,000	20,000
Total		1,20,000	90,000

Particulars	Note No.	31st March, 2020 (₹)	31st March, 2019 (₹)
II. **ASSETS**			
1. **Non-current Assets**			
Fixed Assets		70,000	50,000
2. **Current Assets**			
(a) Inventories		25,000	21,000
(b) Trade Receivables		19,000	14,000
(c) Cash and Cash Equivalents		6,000	5,000
Total		1,20,000	90,000

Notes to Accounts

Particulars	31st March, 2020 (₹)	31st March, 2019 (₹)
1. **Share Capital**		
Equity Share Capital	75,000	40,000
8% Preference Share Capital	10,000	6,000
	85,000	46,000
2. **Reserves and Surplus**		
Balance in Statement of Profit and Loss	12,000	17,000
General Reserve	5,000	7,000
	17,000	24,000

Additional Information

(*i*) During the year, machine costing ₹ 8,000 was sold for ₹ 5,000.

(*ii*) Dividend paid ₹ 8,000. **(6)**

Answers

1. (d) ₹ 60,000
2. (d) Both (a) and (b)
3. (a) Tax Deducted at Source
4. (b) Partners' current account
5. (d) Both (a) and (b)
6. (d) ₹ 1,500

   Hint: $50,000 \times \frac{6}{100} \times \frac{6}{12} = ₹1,500$
7. (b) Loss
8. (c) 5 : 7

   Hint: 25,000 : 35,000
9. (a)

A's Capital A/c	Dr	3,000	
B's Capital A/c	Dr	1,500	
To Revaluation A/c			4,500

10. unrecorded asset

11. (c) ₹ 20,000

Hint: ₹ 20,000 (6,00,000 – 5,80,000)

12. (c) Old partnership is reconstituted

13. (b) 40

14. *Or* Capital reserve = ₹ 2,00,000

15. Revaluation profit: Kartik = ₹ 1,600, Aroha = ₹ 2,400; Kartik gains 1/10th share and Aroha sacrifices 1/10th share

Or Mohan's share of profit = ₹ 32,000 ; Mohan's share of goodwill = ₹ 30,000

16. Debit R with ₹ 15,000 and Credit P and Q with ₹ 7,500 each

17. Profit transferred to capital accounts = ₹ 1,59,000

20. Profit on revaluation = ₹ 20,000

21. Capital reserve = ₹ 3,300

Or Capital reserve = ₹ 1,440

22. Loss on realisation = ₹ 17,000; Total of cash account = ₹ 3,20,000

Or Profit on revaluation = ₹ 3,000; Balance sheet total = ₹ 2,02,800

23. (d) None of these

24. inventory turnover

25. (a) 2 : 1

26. (d) Both (a) and (c)

27. (d) ₹ 6,00,000

Hint: Current liabilities = Working capital + Current assets

= 2,00,000 + 4,00,000

= ₹ 6,00,000

28. (b) Cash outflow from investing activity

30. (*i*) 8 times (*ii*) 2 : 1

Or RoI = 13.75%

Debt to equity ratio = 1 : 7

32. Cash used in operating activities = ₹ (3,000) ; Cash used in investing activities = ₹ (23,000)

Cash from financing activities = ₹ 27,000

Sample Paper 2

Accountancy (Unsolved)

(A Highly Simulated Practice Question Paper for CBSE Class XII Examination)

General Instructions

1 This question paper contains two parts A and B.
2 Part A is compulsory for all.
3 Part B has two options-Analysis of Financial Statements and Computerised Accounting*. Attempt only one option of Part B.
4 Question nos. 1 to 13 and 23 to 29 are objective type questions carrying 1 mark each.
5 Question nos. 14 and 30 are short answer type-1 questions carrying 3 marks each.
6 Question nos. 15 to 18 and 31 are short answer type-II questions carrying 4 marks each.
7 Question nos. 19, 20 and 32 are long answer type-I questions carrying 6 marks each.
8 Question nos. 21 and 22 are long answer type-II questions carrying 8 marks each.
* Computerised Accounting has not been covered.

Time : 3 hours Max. Marks : 80

Part : A

(Accounting for Partnership Firms and Companies)

1. In the profit and loss appropriation account, net profit is always taken after **(1)**
(a) Interest on Partner's Loan (b) Manager's Commission
(c) Both (a) and (b) (d) None of these

2. Retiring partner's share of goodwill is debited to remaining partner's capital account in their **(1)**
(a) Sacrificing ratio (b) Gaining ratio
(c) New ratio (d) Old ratio

3. 'X', 'Y' and 'Z' are sharing profits in the ratio of 2 : 2 : 1. 'Y' died on 30th June, 2019. Accounts are closed on 31st March. Sales for the year ended 31st March, 2019 amounted to ₹ 6,00,000. Sales of ₹ 2,00,000 amounted for the period between 1st April, 2019 to 30th June, 2019. The profits for the year ended 31st March, 2019 amounted to ₹ 60,000. 'Y's share in profits will be **(1)**
(a) ₹ 15,000 (b) ₹ 20,000
(c) ₹ 8,000 (d) ₹ 12,000

4. While passing an entry for forfeiture where shares were issued at par, forfeiture account will be **(1)**

(a) debited with the amount received
(b) credited with the amount already received
(c) debited with called-up amount
(d) credited with called-up amount

5. The part of capital of a company which is called-up only on winding-up is called **(1)**

(a) Reserve Capital
(b) Authorised Capital
(c) Subscribed Capital
(d) Capital Reserve

6. In case of gurantee, any deficiency in the share of profit of guaranteed partner is met by remaining partners in their .... **(1)**

7. At the time of dissolution, creditors were worth ₹ 8,000. They accepted machinery valued at ₹ 9,000 in settlement of their claim. In this case the journal entry would be **(1)**

(a) Realisation A/c Dr
To Cash A/c

(b) No Entry

(c) Cash A/c Dr
To Realisation A/c

(d) Creditors A/c Dr
To Realisation A/c

8. A and B are partners in a firm sharing profits in 5 : 1 ratio. **(1)**

Extract of Balance Sheet

Liabilities	Amt (₹)	Assets	Amt (₹)
		Machinery	20,000

If the value of machinery in the balance sheet is under valued by 20%, then at what value will machinery be shown in the new balance sheet.

(a) ₹ 18,000 (b) ₹ 25,000 (c) ₹ 23,000 (d) ₹ 16,000

9. Interest allowed by the company on the amount of calls in advance is **(1)**

(a) 12% (b) 8% (c) 6% (d) 15%

10. Which of the following item is dealt through profit and loss account? **(1)**

(a) Interest on Partner's Loan
(b) Partner's Salary
(c) Partner's Commission
(d) Interest on Partner's Capital

11. A, B and C are partners sharing profits in the ratio of 4 : 3 : 2. B retires and the goodwill of the firm is valued at ₹ 9,000. B's share of goodwill will be **(1)**

(a) ₹ 900 (b) ₹ 4,000 (c) ₹ 5,000 (d) ₹ 3,000

12. X and Y are partners sharing profits in 5 : 1 ratio. Z is admitted and the new profit sharing ratio is now 5 : 3 : 1. At the date of admission, general reserve appears in books at ₹ 24,000. Y's share in reserve will be **(1)**

(a) ₹ 4,000 (b) ₹ 20,000 (c) ₹ 7,200 (d) None of these

13. The share of premium for goodwill brought in by new partner is divided in which ratio **(1)**

(a) New ratio (b) Old ratio (c) Sacrificing ratio (d) None of these

14. PQR Ltd issued 24,000, 8% debentures of ₹ 100 each at a discount of 5% payable 25% on application, 20% on allotment and balance after three months. Pass necessary journal entries in the books of the company, assuming that the amounts were received as they became due. **(3)**

Or XYZ Ltd issued 2,000, 9% debentures of ₹ 100 each on the following terms.

₹ 20 on application, ₹ 20 on allotment, ₹ 30 on first call, ₹ 30 on final call.

The public applied for 2,400 debentures. Applications for 1,800 debentures were accepted in full. Applications for 400 debentures were allotted 200 debentures and applications for 200 debentures were rejected. Pass necessary journal entries.

15. V, W and X were partners in a firm sharing profits and losses in the ratio of 5 : 3 : 2. On 31st March, 2020, their balance sheet was as follows

Balance Sheet
as at 31st March, 2020

Liabilities		Amt (₹)	Assets	Amt (₹)
Capital A/cs			Land and Building	1,00,000
V	1,50,000		Patents	30,000
W	1,25,000		Plant and Machinery	1,50,000
X	75,000	3,50,000	Stock	75,000
Sundry Creditors		85,000	Debtors	40,000
			Cash at Bank	40,000
		4,35,000		4,35,000

X died on 31st July, 2020. It was agreed that

(*i*) Goodwill be valued at $2\frac{1}{2}$ years' purchase of the average profits of the last four years, which were as follows

Year	Profit (₹)
2015 – 2016	65,000
2016 – 2017	60,000
2017 – 2018	80,000
2018 – 2019	75,000

(*ii*) Machinery be valued at ₹ 1,40,000, patents at ₹ 40,000 and building at ₹ 1,25,000.

(*iii*) For the purpose of calculating X's share of profits in the year of his death, the profits in 2020-2021 should be taken to have been accrued on the same scale as in 2019-2020.

(*iv*) A sum of ₹ 35,000 was paid immediately to the executors of X and the balance was paid in four half-yearly instalments together with interest at 12% per annum starting from 31st July, 2020.

Give necessary journal entries to record the above transactions. **(4)**

Or A and B are partners sharing profits in the ratio of 3 : 2. They admit C into the firm for 3/10 th profit, which he takes 2/10 th from A and 1/10 th from B and brings a part of his share of premium for goodwill in cash. Fill in the missing information in the following journal entries and compute the new ratio of A,B and C.

JOURNAL

Date	Particulars		LF	Amt (Dr)	Amt (Cr)
	Bank A/c	Dr		....	
	To Premium for Goodwill A/c				....
	(................................)				
	Premium for Goodwill A/c	Dr		60,000	
	C's Current A/c	Dr		1,65,000	
	To				....
	To				....
	(...........................)				

16. The authorised capital of Gemini Ltd is ₹ 45,00,000 divided into 30,000 shares of ₹ 150 each. Out of these, company issued 15,000 shares of ₹ 150 each at a premium of ₹ 10 per share. The amount was payable as follows

₹ 50 per share on application, ₹ 40 per share on allotment (including premium), ₹ 30 per share on first call and balance on final call. Public applied for 14,000 shares. All the money was duly received.

Prepare an extract of balance sheet of Gemini Ltd as per Schedule III, Part I of the Companies Act, 2013 disclosing the above information. Also, prepare 'notes to accounts' for the same. **(4)**

17. Richa asked her colleague Akanksha to form a partnership. Akanksha agreed to the proposal on the following terms

(*i*) Profits will be shared equally.

(*ii*) Richa will be allowed a salary of ₹ 400 per month.

(*iii*) Akanksha who will manage the sales department will be allowed a commission equal to 10% of the net profits, after allowing Richa's salary.

(*iv*) 7% interest will be allowed on partner's fixed capital.

(*v*) 5% interest will be charged on partner's annual drawings.

(*vi*) The fixed capitals of Richa and Akanksha are ₹ 1,00,000 and ₹ 80,000 respectively. Their annual drawings were ₹ 16,000 and ₹ 14,000 respectively. The net profit for the year ending 31st March, 2012 amounted to ₹ 40,000.

You are required to prepare firm's profit and loss appropriation account. **(4)**

18. A and B are partners in a firm. Their capitals are: A ₹ 15,000 and B ₹ 10,000. During the year ended 31st March, 2020, the firm earned a profit of ₹ 7,500. Assuming that the normal rate of return is 20%, calculate the value of goodwill of the firm of A and B.

(*i*) By capitalisation method; and

(*ii*) By super profit method, if the goodwill is valued at 4 years' purchase of super profit. **(4)**

19. (a) Pass the necessary journal entries for issue of 100, 10% debentures of ₹ 10 each in the following cases

(*i*) Issued at 5% premium, redeemable at a premium of 10%.

(*ii*) Issued at a discount of 5%, redeemable at par.

(b) ABC Ltd purchased machinery from XYZ Ltd for ₹ 5,00,000 to start a business of manufacturing low cost school dresses for children belonging to low income group. It made the payment as follows

₹ 1,00,000 by cheque; 2,500, 10% preference shares of ₹ 100 each at par, and 1,500, 10% debentures of ₹100 each at par.

You are required to pass the journal entries for the transactions. **(6)**

20. Archie, Betty and Veronica are partners sharing profits in the ratio of 3 : 2 : 1. With effect from 1st April, 2018, they decide to share profits in the ratio of 2 : 2 : 1. Their balance sheet as at 31st March, 2018 is given below

Balance Sheet

as at 31st March, 2018

Liabilities		Amt (₹)	Assets	Amt (₹)
Creditors		1,00,000	Cash	62,000
Outstanding Expenses		12,000	Debtors	50,000
Capital A/cs			Stock	75,000
Archie	3,75,000		Plant and Machinery	3,25,000
Betty	2,25,000		Land and Building	4,00,000
Veronica	2,00,000	8,00,000		
		9,12,000		9,12,000

For the above purpose, it was agreed that

(*i*) Plant and machinery should be written down by ₹ 25,000.

(*ii*) Stock is found overvalued by 10%. It was decided to reduce its value accordingly.

(*iii*) Land and building has to be appreciated by 25%.

(*iv*) Creditors amounting to ₹ 5,500 are not likely to claim their amount.

(*v*) Goodwill at the time of reconstitution, is to be valued at 3 years' purchase of average profits of last five years, which were ₹ 22,500.

You are required to give effect to the above adjustments by opening revaluation account. **(6)**

Or Pass the necessary journal entries for the following transactions on the dissolution of the firm of Sudha and Shiva after the various assets (other than cash) and outside liabilities have been transferred to realisation account.

(*i*) Sudha agreed to pay off her husband's loan ₹ 19,000.

(*ii*) A debtor whose debt of ₹ 9,000 was written-off in the books, paid ₹ 7,500 in full settlement.

(*iii*) Shiva took over all investments at ₹ 13,300.

(*iv*) Sundry creditors ₹ 10,000 were paid at 9% discount.

(*v*) Realisation expenses ₹ 3,400 were paid by Sudha for which she was allowed ₹ 3,000.

(*vi*) Loss on realisation ₹ 9,400 was divided between Sudha and Shiva in 3 : 2 ratio.

21. Nitin, Nitish and Mayank are partners sharing profits and losses in the ratio of 2 : 3 : 5. On 31st March, 2022, their balance sheet was as under

Balance Sheet
as at 31st March, 2022

Liabilities		Amt (₹)	Assets	Amt (₹)
Capital A/cs			Cash	1,80,000
Nitin	3,60,000		Bills Receivable	1,40,000
Nitish	4,40,000		Stock	4,40,000
Mayank	5,20,000	13,20,000	Debtors	4,20,000
Creditors		6,40,000	Machinery	9,40,000
Bills Payable		2,20,000	Goodwill	2,00,000
General Reserve		1,40,000		
		23,20,000		23,20,000

They decided to admit Amit into the partnership on the following terms

(*i*) Machinery is to be depreciated by 15%.

(*ii*) Stock is to be revalued at ₹ 4,80,000.

(*iii*) It is found that the creditors included a sum of ₹ 1,20,000 which was not to be paid.

(*iv*) Outstanding rent is ₹ 19,000.

(*v*) Amit is to bring in ₹ 60,000 as goodwill and sufficient capital for 2/5th share.

(*vi*) The partners decided to use 10% of the profits every year in providing drinking water in schools, where required.

Prepare revaluation account, partners' capital accounts, cash account and the balance sheet of the new firm. **(8)**

Or Pass the necessary journal entries for the following transactions on the dissolution of the firm of Ram and Shyam (who were sharing profits in the ratio of 3 : 1) after the transfer of all assets (other than cash) and external liabilities to realisation account.

(*i*) An unrecorded furniture of ₹ 1,00,000 is taken over by Ram at a discount of 60%.

(*ii*) An unrecorded liability of ₹ 60,000 is settled and paid by Shyam at a discount of 40%.

(*iii*) A machine having a book value of ₹ 60,000 is given away to Kartik, a firm's creditor of ₹ 88,000 at an agreed valuation of 80% towards full and final payment of his dues.

(*iv*) A furniture having a book value of ₹ 60,000 is given away to Kartik, a firm's creditor of ₹ 88,000 at a discount of 20% towards partial payment of his dues.

(*v*) Amit, a creditor to whom ₹ 40,000 were due, took over patents having a book value of ₹ 60,000 at 80%. Balance was paid by him in cash.

(*vi*) Ram pays the realisation expenses of ₹ 40,000 on behalf of the firm.

(*vii*) Firm pays actual realisation expenses of ₹ 36,000 on behalf of Shyam, a partner who has to bear the expenses.

(*viii*) Loan from Ram, a partner of ₹ 44,000 appears on the liabilities side of the balance sheet of the firm and the Ram's capital account has a debit balance of ₹ 4,000.

22. Zee Ltd invited applications for issuing 60,000 equity shares of ₹ 100 each at a premium of ₹ 50 per share. The amount was payable as follows

On application — ₹ 75 per share (including ₹ 25 premium)

On allotment — ₹ 50 per share (including ₹ 25 premium)

On first and final call — Balance amount

Applications for 55,000 shares were received. Allotment was made to all the applicants and the company received all money due on allotment except from P who was allotted 500 shares and his shares were immediately forfeited. Afterwards, the first and final call was made. Q to whom 300 shares were allotted, failed to pay the first and final call. His shares were also forfeited. 300 shares of P and 200 shares of Q were re-issued for ₹ 75,000 fully paid-up.

Pass necessary journal entries in the books of Zee Ltd for the above transactions. **(8)**

Or Give journal entries to record the following transactions of forfeiture and re-issue of shares and open share forfeiture account in the books of the respective companies.

(*i*) X Ltd forfeited 200 shares of ₹ 100 each, ₹ 70 called-up, on which the shareholders had paid application and allotment money of ₹ 50 per share. Out of these, 150 shares were re-issued to Naresh as ₹ 70 paid-up for ₹ 80 per share.

(*ii*) Rihu Ltd forfeited 940 equity shares of ₹ 10 each, issued at a premium of ₹ 5 per share for non-payment of allotment money of ₹ 8 per share (including share premium of ₹ 5 per share) and the first and final call of ₹ 5 per share. Out of these, 60 equity shares were subsequently re-issued at ₹ 14 per share.

Part : B

(Analysis of Financial Statements)

23. What type of an activity is dividend paid by a finance company? **(1)**

(a) Financing Activity Inflow
(b) Financing Activity Outflow
(c) Operating Activity Inflow
(d) Operating Activity Outflow

24. External users of financial statements are **(1)**

(a) Banks
(b) Suppliers
(c) Both (a) and (b)
(d) Director of Company

25. The .... is useful in evaluating credit and collection policies. **(1)**

26. What does a low trade receivables turnover ratio indicate? **(1)**

27. What will be the value of shareholder's fund, if 12% debentures are ₹ 2,50,000 and debt equity ratio is 2.5 : 1? **(1)**

(a) ₹ 2,50,000
(b) ₹ 1,00,000
(c) ₹ 2,00,000
(d) ₹ 1,50,000

28. Short-term investments are also known as **(1)**

(a) Cash and Cash Equivalents
(b) Marketable Securities
(c) Both (a) and (b)
(d) None of these

29. What will be the amount of source or use of cash when a fixed asset (having book value ₹ 60,000) is sold at a loss of ₹ 20,000 in terms of cash flow? **(1)**

(a) ₹ 60,000
(b) ₹ 20,000
(c) ₹ 40,000
(d) ₹ 80,000

30. Calculate debtors in the beginning and at the end of the year.

Net Credit Sales 1,00,000

Debtors Turnover Ratio 8 times

Debtors at the end are ₹ 3,500 more than at the beginning. **(3)**

Or Assuming that debt to equity ratio is 2 : 1, state giving reasons, whether this ratio will increase, decrease or will have no change is each of the following cases.

(*i*) Issue of bonus shares

(*ii*) Issue of new shares for cash

(*iii*) Declaration of final dividend

31. Mention about any four parties which are interested in financial statement analysis. **(4)**

Or Prepare balance sheet of XYZ Ltd as at 31st March, 2018 from the following information.

Particulars	Amt (₹)	Particulars	Amt (₹)
Equity Share Capital	40,00,000	Surplus i.e. Balance in Statement of Profit and Loss (Cr)	6,00,000
12% Preference Share Capital	20,00,000	Stock	12,00,000
Fixed Assets (At cost)	93,20,000	Sundry Debtors	16,00,000
Depreciation Written-off till Date	33,20,000	Cash	3,00,000
Investments	8,00,000	Loans and Advances	1,00,000
Current Liabilities	16,00,000	Provision for Taxation	4,00,000
12% Debentures	12,00,000	Workmen Compensation Reserve	2,00,000

32. From the following balance sheets of Javed Ltd as at 31st March, 2019 and 2020, prepare a cash flow statement.

Balance Sheet
as at 31st March, 2019 and 2020

Particulars	Note No.	31st March, 2020 (₹)	31st March, 2019 (₹)
I. EQUITY AND LIABILITIES			
1. **Shareholders' Funds**			
(a) Equity Share Capital		14,00,000	10,00,000
(b) Reserves and Surplus (Balance in statement of profit and loss)		7,00,000	4,00,000
2. **Current Liabilities**			
(a) Short-term Borrowings (Bank loan)		2,04,000	3,10,000
(b) Short-term Provisions	1	1,00,000	60,000
Total		24,04,000	17,70,000
II. ASSETS			
1. **Non-current Assets**			
(a) Fixed Assets	2	11,90,000	12,00,000
(b) Non-current Investments		2,00,000	—
2. **Current Assets**			
(a) Trade Receivables (Debtors)		2,94,000	1,60,000
(b) Inventories (Stock)		2,60,000	1,10,000
(c) Cash and Cash Equivalents (Bank)		4,60,000	3,00,000
Total		24,04,000	17,70,000

Notes to Accounts

Particulars	2020 (₹)	2019 (₹)
1. **Short-term Provisions**		
Provision for Tax	1,00,000	60,000
	1,00,000	60,000
2. **Fixed Assets**		
Tangible (Equipment)	10,00,000	10,00,000
Intangible (Patents)	1,90,000	2,00,000
	11,90,000	12,00,000

Additional Information

(*i*) Propsed dividend for 2020 ₹ 1,40,000 and for 2019 ₹ 1,00,000.

(*ii*) During the year, equipment costing ₹ 2,00,000 was purchased. Loss on sale of equipment amounted to ₹ 24,000, ₹ 36,000 depreciation was charged on equipment.

(6)

Answers

1. (c) Both (a) and (b)
2. (b) Gaining ratio
3. (c) ₹ 8,000
4. (b) credited with the amount already received
5. (a) Reserve Capital
6. agreed ratio
7. (b) No Entry
8. (b) ₹ 25,000

   Hint $20{,}000 \times \frac{100}{80} = ₹25{,}000$
9. (a) 12%
10. (a) Interest on Partner's Loan
11. (d) ₹ 3000

    Hint $9{,}000 \times \frac{3}{9} = ₹3{,}000$
12. (a) ₹ 4,000

    Hint $24{,}000 \times \frac{2}{12} = ₹4{,}000$
13. (c) Sacrificing ratio
16. Share Capital = ₹ 21,00,000

    Reserve and Surplus = ₹ 1,40,000
17. Profit transferred to Richa's and Akanksha's capital accounts = ₹ 10,290 each
18. (i) ₹ 12,500 (ii) ₹ 10,000
20. Profit on revaluation = ₹ 73,000
21. Neither profit nor loss on revaluation; Capitals: Nitin = ₹ 3,60,000, Nitish = ₹ 4,40,000, Mayank = ₹ 5,20,000, Amit = ₹ 8,80,000; Cash balance = ₹ 11,20,000; Balance sheet total = ₹ 29,59,000
22. Capital reserve = ₹ 30,000

    Or (i) Capital reserve = ₹ 7,500 (ii) Capital reserve = ₹ 240
23. (b) Financing Activity Outflow
24. (c) Both (a) and (b)
25. average collection period
27. (b) ₹ 1,00,000

    Hint Debt Equity Ratio $= \frac{\text{Debt}}{\text{Equity}} = \frac{2.5}{1} = \frac{2{,}50{,}000}{\text{Equity}} = ₹\,1{,}00{,}000$
28. (b) Marketable Securities
29. (c) ₹ 40,000

    Hint Source of cash = 60,000 – 20,000 = ₹ 40,000
30. Opening debtors = ₹ 10,750; Closing debtors = ₹ 14,250
31. *Or* Balance sheet total = ₹ 1,00,000
32. Cash from operating activities = ₹ 1,20,000

    Cash used in investing activities = ₹ (2,20,000); Cash from financing activities = ₹ 2,60,000

Sample Paper 3

Accountancy (Unsolved)

(A Highly Simulated Practice Question Paper for CBSE Class XII Examination)

General Instructions

1 This question paper contains two parts A and B.
2 Part A is compulsory for all.
3 Part B has two options-Analysis of Financial Statements and Computerised Accounting*. Attempt only one option of Part B.
4 Question nos. 1 to 13 and 23 to 29 are objective type questions carrying 1 mark each.
5 Question nos. 14 and 30 are short answer type-1 questions carrying 3 marks each.
6 Question nos. 15 to 18 and 31 are short answer type-II questions carrying 4 marks each.
7 Question nos. 19, 20 and 32 are long answer type-I questions carrying 6 marks each.
8 Question nos. 21 and 22 are long answer type-II questions carrying 8 marks each.

* Computerised Accounting has not been covered.

Time : 3 hours   Max. Marks : 80

Part : A

(Accounting for Partnership Firms and Companies)

1. 'A', 'B' and 'C' are partners sharing profits in the ratio of 2 : 1 : 1. 'C' retires and assets and liabilities are revalued; resulting in a profit of ₹ 12,000. 'C's' share will be **(1)**

(a) ₹ 6,000   (b) ₹ 3,000   (c) ₹ 2,000   (d) ₹ 12,000

2. Kumar Ltd purchased an asset of ₹ 6,30,000 from Bhanu Ltd. Kumar Ltd paid this amount by issuing equity shares of ₹ 100 each fully paid-up. What will be the correct entry for issue of equity shares? **(1)**

(a) Bhanu Ltd	Dr	6,30,000	
To Equity Share Capital A/c			6,30,000
(b) Equity Share Capital A/c	Dr	6,30,000	
To Bhanu Ltd			6,30,000
(c) Bhanu Ltd	Dr	6,30,000	
To Assets A/c			6,30,000
(d) Assets A/c	Dr	6,30,000	
To Bhanu Ltd			6,30,000

3. X, Y and Z are partners with capitals of ₹ 50,000, ₹ 37,500 and ₹ 25,000 respectively. On Z's retirement, his share is acquired by X and Y in ratio of 5 : 3. Gaining ratio will be **(1)**

(a) 3 : 2   (b) 2 : 2   (c) 5 : 3   (d) None of these

4. The maximum number of members in a private company can be (1)

(a) 200 (b) 50 (c) 100 (d) 10

5. Vrijesh Ltd's registered capital is ₹ 50,00,000 in shares of ₹ 10 each. The company issued 2,00,000 of such shares, payable @ ₹ 3 per share on allotment. What will be the amount due on allotment, if shareholder holding 20,000 shares paid all call money at the time of allotment only? (1)

(a) ₹ 20,00,000 (b) ₹ 6,00,000 (c) ₹ 2,00,000 (d) ₹ 50,00,000

6. When an asset is taken over by a partner, his capital account is (1)

(a) debited (b) credited

(c) no entry will be passed (d) None of these

7. A, B & C are partner in a firm with profit sharing ratio 3 : 2 : 1 respectively. (1)

Extract of Balance Sheet

Liabilities	Amt (₹)	Assets	Amt (₹)
Workmen Compensation Reserve	24,000		

At the time of retirement of C, if liability for workmen compensation to the extent of ₹ 12,000 is to be created, then at what amount will workmen compensation reserve be shown in new Balance Sheet?

(a) ₹ 24,000 (b) ₹ 36,000

(c) ₹ 12,000 (d) Not to be shown in Balance Sheet

8. Partner's current account is maintained under (1)

(a) fixed capital method (b) fluctuating capital method

(c) Both (a) and (b) (d) None of these

9. A firm having the assets of ₹ 2,00,000 and liabilities of ₹ 84,000 earns the annual profit of ₹ 18,000. The rate of normal profit being 12%, the amount of goodwill by capitalisation of super profit method will be (1)

(a) ₹ 35,000 (b) ₹ 34,000 (c) ₹ 36,000 (d) ₹ 33,000

10. Change in the existing agreement of partners is known as (1)

(a) Reconstitution of partnership firm (b) Revaluation of partnership firm

(c) Dissolution of partnership firm (d) Realisation of partnership firm

11. Realisation account is prepared at the time of (1)

(a) Admission of partner (b) Change in profit sharing ratio

(c) Dissolution of a firm (d) Retirement of a partner

12. Final amount of a deceased partner's capital is payable to his .... (1)

13. Share of retiring partner after all adjustments is ₹ 25,000. He is paid ₹ 37,500. His share of goodwill is (1)

(a) ₹ 25,000 (b) ₹ 37,500 (c) ₹ 12,500 (d) None of these

14. Vishal Ltd forfeited 2,000 equity shares of ₹ 10 each, issued at a premium of ₹ 5 per share, held by R for non-payment of the final call of ₹ 3 per share. Out of these, 100 shares were re-issued to V at a discount of ₹ 4 per share. Pass necessary journal entries. (3)

Or A Ltd. forfeited 200 shares of ₹ 10 each, ₹ 7 called-up on which M had paid application and allotment money of ₹ 5 per share. Of these, 150 shares were re-issued to N as fully paid-up for ₹ 6 per share. Pass necessary journal entries.

15. Monika, Aarti and Isha were partners sharing profit in the ratio of 2:2:1 respectively. Following was their balance sheet as at 31st March, 2020.

Balance Sheet
as at 31st March, 2020

Liabilities		Amt (₹)	Assets	Amt (₹)
Capital A/cs			Cash	82,000
Monika	2,40,000		Stock	1,20,000
Aarti	1,60,000		Debtors	88,000
Isha	2,00,000	6,00,000	Building	4,00,000
Creditors		1,20,000	Plant	1,60,000
Bills Payable		80,000		
Profit and Loss A/c		50,000		
		8,50,000		8,50,000

On the above date, Monika retired and following were agreed

(*i*) Stock was valued at ₹ 1,18,000, debtors ₹ 80,000, building ₹ 4,20,000 plant ₹ 1,40,000 and creditors ₹ 1,00,000.

(*ii*) Amount due to Monika will be paid immediately.

Pass necessary journal entries to record above transactions and prepare revaluation account. **(4)**

Or D, L and F were partners in a firm sharing profits and losses equally. Their balance sheet as at 31st December, 2018 was as follows

Balance Sheet
as at 31st December, 2018

Liabilities		Amt (₹)	Assets	Amt (₹)
Capital A/cs			Machinery	30,000
D	35,000		Stock	15,000
L	35,000		Debtors	47,500
F	35,000	1,05,000	Cash at Bank	20,000
Reserve		15,000	Cash in Hand	17,500
Sundry Creditors		10,000		
		1,30,000		1,30,000

L died on 14th March, 2019. According to the partnership deed, executors of the deceased partner are entitled to

(*i*) Balance of partners' capital account. (*ii*) Interest on capital @ 5% per annum.

(*iii*) Share of goodwill calculated on the basis of twice the average of past three years' profits.

(*iv*) Share of profits from the closure of the last accounting year till the date of death on the basis of twice the average of three completed years' profits before death.

Profits for 2016, 2017 and 2018 were ₹ 40,000, ₹ 45,000 and ₹ 50,000 respectively. Show the working for deceased partner's share of goodwill and profits till the date of his death. Pass the necessary journal entries to record the above said transactions.

16. Raj, Arman and Sharman are partners in a firm. On 1st April, 2018, their capitals stood at ₹ 1,00,000, ₹ 50,000 and ₹ 50,000 respectively. The business is looked after by Sharman. As per the provisions of the partnership deed

(*i*) Sharman was entitled for a salary of ₹ 2,000 per month to which both Raj and Arman agreed.

(*ii*) Partners were entitled to interest on capital @ 5% per annum.

(*iii*) Profits were to be shared in the ratio of capitals.

The net profit for the year ended 31st March, 2019 of ₹ 66,000 was divided equally without providing for the above terms. Pass an adjustment entry to rectify the above error. **(4)**

17. A partnership firm earned net profits during the last three years as follows

Year	Net profit (₹)
2016-2017	1,90,000
2017-2018	2,20,000
2018-2019	2,50,000

The capital employed in the firm throughout the above mentioned period has been ₹ 4,00,000. Having regard to the risk involved, 15% is considered to be a fair return on the capital. The remuneration of all the partners during this period is estimated to be ₹ 1,00,000 per annum.

Calculate the value of goodwill on the basis of two years' purchase of super profits earned on average basis during the above mentioned three years. **(4)**

18. Complete the following journal entries. **(4)**

JOURNAL

Date	Particulars		LF	Amt (Dr)	Amt (Cr)
	Sundry Assets A/c	Dr		10,00,000	
	....	Dr			
	To Sundry Liabilities A/c				1,50,000
	To Vendor's A/c				8,80,000
	(Being the purchase consideration for acquiring the business)				
	....	Dr		....	
	To Equity Share Capital A/c (5,000 × 100)				5,00,000
	To				....
	To				....
	To				....
	(Being the purchase consideration settled by issue of 5,000 equity shares of ₹ 100 each at a premium of 10%, 3,000 equity shares of ₹ 100 each and ₹ 30,000 in cash)				

19. (i) W Ltd purchased a running business from Z Ltd for a sum of ₹ 30,00,000, payable ₹ 1,00,000 by cheque and for the balance issued 10% debentures of ₹ 100 each at par. The assets and liabilities consisted of the following

Furniture ₹ 8,00,000, Machinery ₹ 12,00,000, Stock ₹ 10,00,000,
Debtors ₹ 6,00,000 and Creditors ₹ 4,00,000

Record necessary journal entries in the books of Z Ltd.

(ii) Sewa Ltd invited applications for issuing 3,000, 12% debentures of ₹ 100 each at a premium of ₹ 50 per debenture. The full amount was payable on application. Applications were received for 4,000 debentures. Applications for 1,000 debentures were rejected and application money was refunded. Debentures were allotted to the remaining applicants. Pass necessary journal entries for the above transactions in the books of Sewa Ltd. **(3 × 2 = 6)**

20. A, B and C are in partnership with capital of ₹ 2,40,000 (Credit), ₹ 2,00,000 (Credit) and ₹ 16,000 (Debit) respectively on 1st April, 2017. Their partnership deed provides for the following

(i) 7.5% of net profit to be transferred to general reserve.

(ii) Partners are to be only allowed interest on capital @ 5% per annum and are to be charged interest on drawings @ 6% per annum.

(iii) C is entitled to a salary of ₹ 14,000.

(iv) A is entitled to a remuneration of 10% of the net profit before making any appropriation.

(v) B is also entitled to a commission of 8% of the net profit before charging interest on drawings but after making all appropriations.

During the year, A withdrew ₹ 2,000 at the beginning of every month, B ₹ 2,000 during the middle of the month and C ₹ 2,000 at the end of every month. On 1st October, 2017, C granted a loan of ₹ 12,00,000.

The manager is entitled to a salary of ₹ 2,000 per month and a commission of 10% of net profits after charging his salary and commission.

The net profit of the firm for the year ended on 31st March, 2017 before providing for any of the above adjustments was ₹ 3,24,000.

Prepare profit and loss appropriation account for the year ended on 31st March, 2018. **(6)**

Or Parul, Payal and Priyanka are partners. They decided to dissolve the firm. Pass the necessary journal entries for the following after the various assets (other than cash and bank) and outside liabilities have been transferred to realisation account.

(i) There were total debtors of ₹ 76,000. A provision for bad and doubtful debts also stood in the books at ₹ 6,000. ₹ 12,000 debtors proved bad and rest paid the amount due.

(ii) Parul agreed to pay off her husband's loan of ₹ 7,000 at a discount of 5%.

(iii) A machine which is not recorded in the books was taken over by Payal at ₹ 3,000 whereas its expected value was ₹ 5,000.

(iv) Priyanka paid realisation expenses of ₹ 15,000 out of her pocket and she was to get remuneration of ₹ 18,000 for completing the dissolution process.

(v) A contingent liability (not provided for) of ₹ 4,000 was also discharged.

(vi) The firm had a debit balance of ₹ 27,000 in the profit and loss account on the date of dissolution.

21. R,O and N shared profits in the ratio of 2 : 2 : 1. On 31st December, 2019, their balance sheet was as follows

Balance Sheet
as at 31st December, 2019

Liabilities		Amt (₹)	Assets	Amt (₹)
Sundry Creditors		1,00,000	Cash	60,000
Bills Payable		60,000	Sundry Debtors	1,00,000
Provident Fund		40,000	Stock	72,000
Investment Fluctuation Fund		16,000	Investments	40,000
Commission Received in Advance		24,000	Plant and Machinery	1,80,000
Capital A/cs			Profit and Loss A/c	68,000
R	1,00,000			
O	1,20,000			
N	60,000	2,80,000		
		5,20,000		5,20,000

On this date, the firm was dissolved. R was appointed to realise the assets. R was to receive 5% commission on the sale of assets (except cash) and was to bear all expenses of realisation. R realised the assets as follows

Stock ₹ 72,000, debtors ₹ 90,000, investments 80% of the book value, plant ₹ 1,31,000. Expenses of realisation amounted to ₹ 11,000. Commission received in advance was returned to the customers after deducting ₹ 8,000. Firm had to pay ₹ 16,000 for outstanding wages. This liability was not provided for in the above balance sheet. ₹ 40,000 had to be paid for provident fund.

Prepare realisation account, partners' capital accounts and cash account. **(8)**

Or Radha and Meera were partners sharing profits equally. Their balance sheet as at 31st March, 2019 was as under

Balance Sheet
as at 31st March, 2019

Liabilities		Amt (₹)	Assets		Amt (₹)
Creditors		1,00,000	Cash in Hand		24,000
Bills Payable		30,000	Cash at Bank		30,000
Outstanding Expenses		6,000	Sundry Debtors	40,000	
Capital A/cs			(–) Provision for Doubtful Debts	(1,000)	39,000
Radha	1,20,000		Stock		40,000
Meera	80,000	2,00,000	Furniture		20,000
			Plant and Machinery		36,000
			Building		1,47,000
		3,36,000			3,36,000

Menu is admitted as a partner from 1st April, 2019 on the following terms

(i) Menu will get 1/5th share in profits and she will bring in ₹ 40,000 as his capital and ₹ 10,000 as his share of goodwill.

(ii) Goodwill brought in by Menu will be withdrawn by Radha and Meera.

(iii) The provision for doubtful debts should be brought up to 5% on debtors.

(iv) Machinery be depreciated by ₹ 4,000 and furniture by 12.5%.

(v) Stock be valued at ₹ 46,000.

(vi) Land and building be appreciated by 20%.

(vii) Investments of ₹ 4,000 which did not appear in books should be duly recorded.

Record the necessary journal entries and prepare the balance sheet of the new firm.

22. ABC Ltd issued 5,00,000 shares of ₹ 10 each at a premium of ₹ 4 per share payable as follows ₹ 4 on application , ₹ 6 on allotment , ₹ 4 on call. Applications were received for 7,00,000 shares and pro-rata allotment was made as follows

To the applicants of 5,00,000 shares, 4,00,000 shares were issued and for the rest, 1,00,000 shares were issued.

All money due were received except the allotment and call money from P who had applied for 7,500 shares (out of the group of 5,00,000 shares). All his shares were forfeited 3,750 of the forfeited shares were re-issued for ₹ 8 per share fully paid-up. Pass necessary journal entries for the above transactions. **(8)**

Or XYZ Ltd invited applications for 50,000 equity shares of ₹ 10 each. The shares were issued at a premium of ₹ 5 per share. The amount was payable as follows On application and allotment ₹ 8 per share (including premium ₹ 3).

The balance including premium on the first and final call.
Applications for 75,000 shares were received. Applications for 5,000 shares were rejected and pro-rata allotment was made to the remaining applicants on the following basis

(i) Applicants for 40,000 shares were allotted 30,000 shares.

(ii) Applicants for 30,000 shares were allotted 20,000 shares.

A , who belonged to the first category and was allotted 150 shares, failed to pay the first call money. B, who belonged to the second category and was allotted 100 shares, also failed to pay the first call money. Their shares were forfeited. The forfeited shares were re-issued @ ₹ 12 per share fully paid-up. Pass necessary journal entries and prepare Cash Book.

Part : B

(Analysis of Financial Statements)

23. Prepaid rent is a ...... **(1)**

24. Which ratios provide information critical to the long-run operation of the firm? **(1)**

(a) Liquidity (b) Activity (c) Solvency (d) Profitability

25. Calculate quick assets, if current assets are ₹ 20,000, inventory ₹ 3,000, prepaid expenses ₹ 4,500, outstanding rent ₹ 2,500. (1)

(a) ₹ 12,500 (b) ₹ 14,500 (c) ₹ 10,500 (d) ₹ 20,000

26. A company's revenue from operations is ₹ 10,00,000, cost of revenue from operations is ₹ 7,00,000 and indirect expenses are ₹ 1,00,000, then what is the amount of gross profit? (1)

(a) ₹ 1,50,000 (b) ₹ 2,50,000 (c) ₹ 3,00,000 (d) ₹ 8,00,000

27. Principle revenue producing activities for an insurance company are (1)

(a) Receipt of premium (b) Payment of claims
(c) Both (a) and (b) (d) None of these

28. What type of an activity is purchase of fixed assets? (1)

(a) Operating Activity Inflow (b) Operating Activity Outflow
(c) Investing Activity Inflow (d) Investing Activity Outflow

29. Give one transaction which may result into outflow of cash and one which may result into no flow of cash. (1)

30. Calculate current assets of a company from the following information
Stock turnover ratio = 4 times. Stock at the end is ₹ 10,000 more than the stock in the beginning. Sales ₹ 1,50,000 and gross profit ratio is 20% of sales.
Current liabilities = ₹ 20,000, Quick ratio = 0.75. (3)

Or X Ltd has a current ratio of 3 : 1 and quick ratio of 2 :1. If the excess of current assets over quick assets as represented by inventory is ₹ 40,000, calculate current assets and current liabilities.

31. Prepare the balance sheet for Rishant Ltd as at 31st March, 2012 from the following information as per provisions of Schedule III, Part I of the Companies Act, 2013.

Particulars	Amt (₹)
General Reserve	3,00,000
8% Debentures	3,00,000
Balance of Statement of Profit and Loss (Credit)	1,20,000
Depreciation of Fixed Assets	70,000
Tangible Fixed Assets (Cost)	9,00,000
Trade Payables	2,50,000
Preference Share Capital	5,00,000
Inventories	64,000
Trade Receivables	2,56,000
Cash and Cash Equivalents	3,20,000

(4)

Or List the items which are shown under the heading 'current liabilities' as per schedule III, Part I of the Companies Act, 2013.

32. From the following balance sheet of Vansh Ltd as on 31st March, 2019 and 2020, prepare the cash flow statement.

Particulars	Note No.	31st March, 2020 (₹)	31st March, 2019 (₹)
I. **EQUITY AND LIABILITIES**			
1. **Shareholders' Funds**			
(a) Share Capital		9,00,000	9,00,000
(b) Reserves and Surplus	1	7,56,000	7,12,000
2. **Non-current Liabilities**			
Long-term Borrowings (Mortgage loan)		5,40,000	—
3. **Current Liabilities**			
(a) Trade Payables (Creditors)		2,68,000	3,36,000
(b) Short-term Provisions (Provision for taxation)		20,000	1,50,000
Total		24,84,000	20,98,000
II. **ASSETS**			
1. **Non-current Assets**			
(a) Fixed Assets		6,40,000	8,00,000
(b) Non-current Investments		1,20,000	1,00,000
2. **Current Assets**			
(a) Inventories (Stock)		4,20,000	4,80,000
(b) Trade Receivables (Debtors)		9,10,000	4,20,000
(c) Cash and Cash Equivalents		3,94,000	2,98,000
Total		24,84,000	20,98,000

Notes to Accounts

Particulars	2020 (₹)	2019 (₹)
1. **Reserves and Surplus**		
Reserves	6,20,000	6,00,000
Balance in Statement of Profit and Loss	1,36,000	1,12,000
	7,56,000	7,12,000

Additional Information

(*i*) Investments costing ₹ 16,000 were sold during the year 2019-20 for ₹ 17,000.

(*ii*) Provision for taxation made during the year was ₹ 18,000.

(*iii*) During the year, part of the fixed assets costing ₹ 20,000 was sold for ₹ 24,000 and the profit was included in the statement of profit and loss.

(*iv*) Dividend paid during the year amounted to ₹ 80,000. **(6)**

Answers

1. (b) ₹ 3,000

   Hint: $12{,}000 \times \frac{1}{4} = ₹3{,}000$

2. (a) Bhanu Ltd Dr 6,30,000

   To Equity Share Capital A/c 6,30,000

3. (c) 5 : 3
4. (a) 200
5. (b) ₹ 6,00,000
6. (a) debited
7. (c) ₹ 12,000
8. (a) fixed capital method
9. (b) ₹ 34,000

   Hint: Normal Profit = $(2{,}00{,}000 - 84{,}000) \times 12 / 100 = ₹ 13{,}920$

   Super Profit = $18{,}000 - 13{,}920 = ₹ 4{,}080$; Goodwill = $\frac{4{,}080}{12} \times 100 = ₹ 34{,}000$

10. (a) Reconstitution of partnership firm
11. (c) Dissolution of a firm
12. executors
13. (c) ₹ 12,500

    Hint: $37{,}500 - 25{,}000 = ₹ 12{,}500$

14. Capital reserve = ₹ 300 *Or* Capital reserve = ₹ 150
16. Raj (Debit) = ₹ 1,000; Arman (Debit) = ₹ 11,500; Sharman (Credit) = ₹ 12,500
17. Goodwill = ₹ 1,20,000
20. Profit transferred to A's Capital A/c - ₹ 50,720, B's Capital A/c - ₹ 50,720, C's Capital A/c - ₹ 50,720
21. Loss on realisation = ₹ 75,250 ; Total of cash account = ₹ 3,85,000

    Or Balance sheet total = ₹ 4,07,900

22. ₹ 11,250 *Or* ₹ 2,050
23. Current asset
24. (c) Solvency
25. (a) ₹ 12,500

    Hint: Quick Assets = $20{,}000 - 3{,}000 - 4{,}500 = ₹ 12{,}500$

26. (c) 3,00,000 *Hint* Gross Profit = $10{,}00{,}000 - 7{,}00{,}000 = ₹ 3{,}00{,}000$
27. (c) Both (a) and (b)
28. (d) Investing Activity Outflow
30. ₹ 50,000

    Or Current Liabilities = ₹ 40,000; Current Assets = $3 \times 40{,}000 = ₹ 1{,}20{,}000$

31. Balance sheet total = ₹ 14,70,000
32. Cash used in operating activities = ₹ (3,69,000)

    Cash from investing activities = ₹ 5,000

    Cash from financing activities = ₹ 4,60,000

Lightning Source UK Ltd.
Milton Keynes UK
UKHW031807131022
410417UK00009B/460

9 789326 198615